Dictionary of Race, Ethnicity and Culture

Dictionary of Race, Ethnicity and Culture

edited by:

Guido Bolaffi, Raffaele Bracalenti,
Peter Braham and Sandro Gindro

SAGE Publications
London • Thousand Oaks • New Delhi

SAGE Publications Ltd
6 Bonhill Street
London EC2A 4PU

SAGE Publications Inc.
2455 Teller Road
Thousand Oaks, California 91320

SAGE Publications India Pvt. Ltd
32, M-Block Market
Greater Kailash – I
New Delhi 110 048

British Library Cataloguing in Publication data
A catalogue record for this book is available from the British
Library

ISBN 0-7619-6899-7
     0-7619-6900-4 (pbk)

Library of Congress control number available

Contents

Acknowledgements

The editors would like to record their profound debt to the many colleagues and collaborators whose work has contributed so much to this dictionary. It is impossible to thank all of them, but we would like to express particular gratitude to Patrizia Santoro of IPRS for her invaluable organisational and secretarial skills, Sally Titcomb and Francesca Pegazzano, whose contribution went far beyond their translating expertise, Kiren Shoman, Keith von Tersch and Ian Antcliff of SAGE for their patience and professionalism in solving the problems that arose and for encouraging us in this long project, and finally, Sarita Malik, for her critical reading of the first manuscript.

For Sandro Gindro, without whose love of life and humankind
this book would have never been born, but who died shortly
before its publication.

Foreword

All science worth its name seeks to analyse and explain familiar phenomena by exploring their deeper connections, and expresses its findings in a precise and clearly defined language. Unlike the natural sciences, social sciences do not have a language of their own. While on rare occasions they invent new terms, for the most part they take over the familiar words of ordinary discourse, invest them with new and reasonably precise meanings, and transform them into concepts and terms. Since the activities they study concern us deeply, their conceptual vocabulary does not remain confined to academic discourse. It is taken over by journalists, politicians and ordinary men and women and used as part of a popular discourse. In the process it loses its preciseness, gets misinterpreted or oversimplified, and is invested with dubious and ideologically charged meanings.

This has several consequences. Since academic and popular speech use the same terms in quite different and even opposite senses, they become mutually unintelligible. In a recent report on *The Future of Multi-Ethnic Britain*, we used the term 'post-nation state' in its academic sense, and found to our horror that most journalists, politicians and ordinary readers took it to mean disintegration of the state into loose clusters of communities! Furthermore, those ordinary men and women who are seriously interested in knowing what social sciences have to say about different areas of social life have no means of doing so except by wading through the enormous and sometimes incomprehensible academic tomes which they have neither the competence nor the time to understand. Both the integrity of the academic and popular debates and their fruitful interaction require that academics should find ways of rendering their concepts and theories accessible to a wider audience.

It is in this context that we can best understand the emergence of the new genre of literature that is best called the professional dictionary. Neither like the ordinary dictionaries that are inescapably brief, insufficiently informative and largely concerned with the ordinary usage of words, nor like the bulky and diffuse encyclopaedias, these dictionaries provide concise and authoritative academic statements of the available body of theoretical knowledge within a manageable volume. They are either discipline-based (as in the case of such titles as the dictionary of sociology, politics, philosophy or economics) or subject-based. The latter genre is particularly relevant to areas that fall under several disciplines and can only be studied in an interdisciplinary manner. Professional dictionaries have to satisfy both experts and non-experts, render difficult ideas accessible without distorting them or appearing patronizing, and both assuage and arouse intellectual curiosity, and this is not at all easy. The difficulty is acute in the case of subject-based dictionaries, which should neither be dominated by a single discipline nor marred by a soggy interdisciplinary mishmash and which should alert their readers to national differences without losing the theoretical focus.

The *Dictionary of Race, Ethnicity and Culture* is a fine example of a subject-based professional dictionary. As its very title indicates, it recognizes that the often unrelated areas of race, ethnicity and culture are historically and theoretically inseparable. They feed off each other, and their study involves common conceptual and theoretical tools and forms a coherent area of investigation. The 200 entries cover nearly all the important concepts, and include terms borrowed from ordinary discourse and transformed into technical concepts as well as those specifically coined by social scientists. The entries are succinct but not oversimplified, are clearly written, long enough to be informative yet short enough for a quick reference, and are composed by distinguished and carefully selected contributors drawn from a range of countries and disciplines. Since concepts develop over time and are often differently understood in different countries, the *Dictionary* wisely deals with the entries in a historical and comparative manner. Many of its entries also bring to bear on various topics the complementary perspectives of psychology, psychoanalysis, sociology and social anthropology, and offer unusually rich and illuminating accounts of the relevant subject matter.

On many occasions I have had students desperately seeking reliable accounts of crucial concepts while writing essays on race, ethnicity and culture, and have also had journalists and political colleagues asking for intelligible explanations of terms they have encountered in academic writings. I can now confidently direct them to this excellent guide.

Bikhu Parekh

Introduction

'Race' and ethnicity have long been central concepts for social scientific inquiry. Their meaning and import have, however, changed dramatically from one era to another. Much of the work of the late nineteenth century, for example, focused on issues like competition between 'different races', on ways to improve the health of 'the race' (one's own), on the problem of miscegenation, and on the impact of immigration on the 'racial make-up' and cultural identity of national populations. Nowadays, only the last of these continues to spark serious discussion.

Nonetheless, 'race' and ethnicity continue to play a fundamental part in the way people perceive the world, and so these concepts force themselves into the study of modern society. And how could it be otherwise in a world that is ever more cosmopolitan and multi-ethnic, a world in which migration is a phenomenon that affects every metropolitan country, as all of them – at one time or another in the period since the Second World War – have required more labour than their internal resources could generate, and in a world where *knowledge* about conflict between different 'racial' and ethnic groups looms large and is more quickly available than it was even in the relatively recent past?

Although 'race' and ethnicity may be central to our view of the world, the concept of 'race' defies scientific definition. Social scientists therefore confront a *social construct*, but a construct that is replete with misinformation and distorted by what is *believed* to be self-evident about 'racial' and ethnic differences. It follows that part of our task in compiling this *Dictionary* is to challenge what is too readily accepted as true about 'race' and to complicate the seemingly uncomplicated.

We decided to include terms and concepts that are commonly encountered in relation to 'race' and ethnicity in everyday life, in politics, in the media, and in academia, but which nonetheless in our opinion require explanation, contextualization, illumination; often these are terms and concepts that need to be challenged as well. We believe that by taking everyday and familiar language as a starting-point, this *Dictionary* offers an innovative and user-friendly approach to a complex subject. Moreover, we think that this approach is not only accessible to the general reader with an interest in the subject, but also offers a comprehensive reference tool for scholars, professional workers and students engaged in the field of 'race' and ethnicity.

Underpinning a belief in 'race' are ideas not only about the importance of phenotypal differences, but also, increasingly, about the importance of cultural differences. Our subject matter then is not confined to beliefs about the importance of skin colour and physiognomy, but extends equally to beliefs about the significance of differences in social customs and religious beliefs. However, in our view it is not enough to eschew a biological approach that demarcates supposedly different 'races' and replace it with an anthropological approach that explores different cultures or religions. Our decision to link 'race' and 'ethnicity' with '*culture*' is specifically intended to illuminate the complexity and multifaceted nature of the interactions of individuals and groups and to do so by taking account not only of the social, political and economic dimensions, but also of the psychological dimension. This is one reason why this *Dictionary* is multidisciplinary, rather than being discipline-based.

In this regard what we have attempted to produce is not simply a dictionary in the conventional sense, but a dictionary that serves as a guide to debates about 'race', ethnicity and culture. And it is precisely because such debates are so contentious and so often founded on flawed assumptions that there is a pressing need for this dictionary.

Clearly much more than a media issue – as encapsulated in news headlines – the extent to which 'race' and racism can be seen to 'make news' is inescapable and so must be addressed here. 'Race' is widely regarded as an explosive electoral issue, as evidenced in Britain by accusations of politicians 'playing the "race card"'. Yet reports that dominate the headlines for a day or two may soon mean little or be forgotten altogether. Why then recall stories that seem so time-specific? Studies of the way the media treat 'race' and ethnicity sometimes survey hundreds, even thousands, of individual reports and, inevitably, most of these reports are rooted in a particular moment; but their impact is cumulative as well as transitory, contributing to what is generally taken for granted about the subject. For instance, from the 1950s until relatively recent times, despite the fact that there was substantial *white* immigration into the UK, the word 'immigrant' in a British newspaper headline was used to refer almost exclusively to *black* immigrants and this would have been readily appreciated by newspaper readers and journalists alike. In the news pages, as well as in the editorial columns, not only was immigration racialized, but 'race' became routinely associated with violence, threat, conflict and tension and in headlines the word 'Race' was often coupled with words like 'Hate', 'Clash' and 'Riot'. By contrast, little attention was devoted to patterns of discrimination and disadvantage or to the competition for scarce resources that, arguably, caused the tension and conflict that *was* so widely reported.

Apologists for media coverage often claim that the media present news 'as it is', not 'as we would like it to be'. This is disingenuous because it underplays the extent to which certain events are illuminated and others neglected or ignored, and it glosses over the way the reporting of issues and events is in many respects preconceived. By habitually portraying ethnic and racial minorities negatively and stereotypically, the mass media contribute to the complex processes of reproduction on which the ideological and structural dimensions of racism depend (Van Djik, 1991: ix). Indeed, from one point of view racism is perceived as a function of the *scale of immigration*, whereas from another it may appear to be one of the *minority presence itself*. Racism in Europe is therefore closely linked to the issue of immigration, both past and present, and this general context helps to shape the way specific events are reported and comprehended.

It is this connection between the particular and the general that was at the heart of the Macpherson Inquiry into matters arising from the murder in south London in 1993 of the black student, Stephen Lawrence. The publication of its findings dominated British news bulletins and newspapers for many days. The

Macpherson Inquiry raised a number of critical questions for British society ranging from the way the police dealt with racial incidents, to 'institutional racism' and to wider – though contested – societal goals. For example, should everyone be treated equally irrespective of skin colour, religion or creed? Or, if society is composed of distinct groups, how far should such diversity be recognized in public policy? Although much of this debate was conducted in a positive spirit, whether Macpherson will turn out to be a watershed in the history of race relations in the UK is far from certain.

These issues take us quickly into the political realm, another area into which this *Dictionary* must delve. As a general rule, we need to take note of the extent to which discussion about 'race' and ethnicity, and about racial and ethnic injustice and the means to overcome it, continues to be influenced by the negative way that successive governments in various European countries have depicted immigration. For example, in the UK, official response to post-war immigration has been marked by references to 'floods' of immigrants and has been influenced by the belief (revealed in exchanges between ministers that were made public only much later) that would-be-immigrants were different, inferior and could not be assimilated by a society that was otherwise homogeneous. Accordingly, in recent decades governments of both Right and Left have attempted to control the arrival of more immigrants by a range of restrictive measures. Perhaps as a consequence of the social and political tensions underlying such control, immigration was largely divorced from its economic genesis. The role immigrant workers have played in supplying vital labour has therefore been overshadowed by the arousal of hostility and social tension that accompanied immigration – especially in relation to its perceived effect on certain localities, the exacerbation of housing problems within these areas and the potential electoral consequences of these developments.

These past perceptions have significant present-day consequences, in that current attempts to create social justice for minorities have to be constructed in the face of the assumption that their original presence was undesirable, an assumption that is replicated in the way that the issue of asylum seekers has generally been debated in recent times. In turn, the debate about asylum seekers reinvigorates negative perceptions of the pre-existing ethnic minority presence. For instance, the assertion that many asylum seekers are in reality 'economic migrants' suggests that many of them arrive under false pretences, taking full advantage of feelings of sympathy for the oppressed, and that in so doing they constitute a large and unjustified drain on public resources.

There is a second reason for being cautious about the impact that the Macpherson agenda might have. This is that there exists a substantial body of opinion which does not merely reject charges of institutional racism, but which actively resents criticism or questioning of British society that emanates from the perspectives of racial equality or multiculturalism. From this point of view particular exception is taken to the idea that concepts of Britishness, social cohesion or the way the national story is 'imagined' should either be reassessed to take account of the presence of ethnic minorities or be made somehow 'inclusive' of their aspirations and experiences.

The force of this opinion was especially evident in the furore that greeted the publication of the report of the Commission inquiring into *The Future of Multi-*

Ethnic Britain (Parekh, 2000b). This reaction was perceptively described by Shah as providing 'vivid testimony to the continuing power of race to unsettle the nation' (Shah, 2000). This phenomenon is visible in various countries and we can discern just such an 'unsettling effect' in *l'affaire du foulard* which began in France in 1989 and which, according to Parekh, has haunted French society ever since. This involved the right of Muslim girls attending school to wear the *hijab* or headscarf. The Conseil d'Etat delivered an opinion (*avis*) that the wearing of the *hijab* did not violate the *laïcité* of French state schools provided that this did not constitute an act of 'pressure, provocation, proselytism or propaganda', though this was to be decided by the appropriate local education authority on a case-by-case basis. The ambiguity of this opinion led to confusion and was soon followed by a ruling by the French Education Minister that whereas discreet religious symbols (such as the cross) could be worn, the *hijab* was ostentatious and embodied elements of proselytism and discrimination and was therefore unacceptable. Parekh concludes that the debate over the *hijab* 'went to the heart of French conceptions of citizenship and national identity and divided the country'. The minority view was that it represented difference and celebrated plurality, but

> For a large body of Frenchmen, France was a single and indivisible nation based on a single culture (and) The school was the central tool of assimilation into French culture and could not tolerate ethnic self-expression. (Parekh, 2000b: 250)

This conception of an ethnic or immigrant presence in an otherwise homogeneous nation can have profound implications for multiculturalism. For example, in the 1970s immigration policy in Sweden was designed to bolster the position of immigrant groups not through assimilation, but by promoting cultural diversity. However, since then there has been a marked rise in racist actions, discrimination, segregation and unemployment. Not only has the foreign-born population been particularly hard hit by this, but there is a growing feeling among the Swedish-born population that immigration and integration policies have been too lenient (Westin, 1998: 57). In part, this can be explained by the gap between myth and reality:

> One of the nationalist myths is that Sweden used to be an ethnically homogeneous nation – one people, one race, one language, one church, one historically given territory, one common culture, and one recognised centre of power. Even those who refute nationalistic views usually accept this description. For nationalists, multiculturalism is the result of uncontrolled and encouraged immigration of 'racially inferior' and culturally alien elements. (Westin, 1998: 59)

Recent decades have also witnessed a huge outpouring of empirical and analytical studies of 'race' and ethnicity, especially in the UK, in other Western European countries and in North America. Given this abundance can a *Dictionary of Race, Ethnicity and Culture* make a useful contribution? Obviously we think so, for abundant as this material is, it is open to criticism insofar as scholars in this area have too often limited their vision to their own country and, perhaps, one other 'parallel' country. In addition, 'there is an absence or inadequacy of research data in significant areas of public policy . . . [related to] race and diversity issues' (Parekh, 2000a: xi). We hope to offer some corrections in that regard.

Our first objective has been to provide informative, up-to-date, well-referenced and user-friendly entries about issues that are often extremely contentious. Our second objective is to refrain from privileging our own specific perspectives and to avoid the presentation of particular positions as 'unchallengeable'. This is not to claim that this *Dictionary* is or can be completely value-free or neutral. Obviously, choices had to be made to include or exclude certain topics and to devote more space to some topics than to others. Instead we have tried to provide evidence of the debates – including the scientific debates – and the controversies that surround many 'race'-related and ethnic-related issues and of the ways in which these debates have evolved.

Our next objective has been not only to draw on the contributions and perspectives that different disciplines offer, but also to encompass different cultural traditions and outlooks. We can learn a lesson in this regard from the now classic work *Immigrant Workers and the Class Structure in Western Europe* (Castles and Kosack, 1973). Writing in the early 1970s, Castles and Kosack identified *immigration* as one of the most fiercely debated issues in Britain. To support their claim they cited the extent of media coverage, various political campaigns, the establishment of government commissions and the enactment of immigration control measures. In the UK, they noted, this debate proceeded on the assumption that immigration was a matter of 'colour', and so white immigration to Britain, whether from the Irish Republic, the 'Old Commonwealth' or elsewhere, even though substantial, was generally ignored. Castles and Kosack perceived this approach as owing much to an over-reliance on parallels between events in Britain and the USA, largely in terms of 'race relations'. Consequently, they chose instead to compare the situation of immigrants to Britain with that of immigrants in three other Western European countries – France, the Federal Republic of Germany (as it then was) and Switzerland. Their focus was on the way that immigrant workers obtained the worst jobs in whichever Western European country they entered, jobs largely abandoned by indigenous workers.

The relevance of Castles and Kosack's approach lies not in their specific agenda – which was to reveal what they saw as the 'function' of immigrant workers in the socio-economic structure of the various receiving societies – but in the general guidance that it offers for analysis of 'race', ethnicity and culture. First, it is not satisfactory to present examples only from countries that are widely assumed to be parallel cases – such as the UK and the USA. Instead we need empirical examples from a range of countries – not just from countries where immigration has been long established and where 'race relations' have been much studied, but also from countries where immigration is more recent.

Several issues that have arisen since Castles and Kosack's book appeared are relevant in this context. One is that the pattern of international migration evident in Western Europe in the 1960s and 1970s has changed in significant ways. Temporary migrants have become permanent settlers and a 'second generation' (or even a third) of those of immigrant origin – born or brought up in Western Europe – has appeared, characterized by different experiences and expectations from those of the first generation. This generational development has raised a profusion of issues concerning not only racism and discrimination, but also equal opportunity, citizenship and family reunification. Moreover, these subjects have become recognized as pivotal rather than tangential matters for society in various ways, for as well as affecting the identity of minority groups themselves, they also have a number of important implications for the identity of the society in which immigrants live. In these circumstances it is not surprising that the analysis of 'race' and ethnicity has come to occupy a more central role within the social sciences.

Another issue that confronts us is that since the passing of the era of mass labour recruitment of the 1960s and 1970s, new types and patterns of migration have arisen. First, countries that once exported labour have become significant receivers of migrants in their own right. It is worth noting that at the time of Castles and Kosack's study, Italy exported migrant labour to Germany, Switzerland and elsewhere and, although there was considerable internal migration from south to north within Italy, it was not itself a country of immigration. But at the beginning of the twenty-first century, Italy has a growing immigrant population – both legal and illegal, notably from North Africa and ex-Yugoslavia, and immigration has become a significant issue in Italian politics. This transformation raises a number of questions. Will the situation in Italy replicate to a greater or lesser degree the pattern in countries where immigration is longer established? Will debates about immigration control, assimilation, multiculturalism, discrimination and racism in Italy develop in a way that seems familiar to those who have explored these issues in the UK or in other countries where immigration and 'race' have been studied over a long period? In addition to this change in the European migration dynamic, the number of asylum seekers and refugees has grown significantly as a result of ethnic, political and military conflicts – a phenomenon facilitated by the speed and sophistication of modern-day communications. Controversies about the rights of entry and conditions of residence for these groups and about the reception they receive have also grown.

These developments are neither self-explanatory nor straightforward. They require careful study and discussion. Not only must the experience of one country be compared and contrasted with that of others, but the perception of what is at issue may vary not merely between analysts within a country, but also from country to country. In particular, assumptions about key issues of 'race' and ethnicity are not always the same. 'Race relations', for example, may be defined more or less narrowly, and while in some instances differentiating groups on the basis of ethnicity in order to assess inequalities is seen as necessary and unexceptional, in others it is regarded as highly problematic and undesirable. Moreover, different social science disciplines approach 'race' and ethnicity from very different perspectives.

In order to encompass these and other differences in the approach to 'race' and ethnicity, the editors were keen to secure the collaboration of contributors from a number of disciplines – sociology, social anthropology, social psychology and history – and from different countries, including the UK, the USA, Canada, Italy, Sweden, Germany and Morocco. Thus the entries reflect different academic backgrounds and approaches to the study of 'race', ethnicity and culture – a range which is too often lacking in the literature in this area. It is the editors' hope and belief that the *Dictionary*'s multidisciplinary approach will prove useful to the modern reader, who is now facing issues which extend well beyond both disciplinary boundaries and national boundaries.

What we have sought then is a breadth and diversity intended to produce a reference tool which is useful and relevant in different countries and fields. This is important not least because the discussion and conceptualization of 'race' varies from one country to another. For instance, in France there has been considerable resistance to using colour or ethnicity as a measure of inequalities in access or opportunity, and certain academics have been fiercely criticized for attempting to do so. Or to take another example, the often negative reaction in Britain to the arrival of immigrants and the growing ethnic minority presence, whereby 'immigration' and its aftermath is invariably thought of as a problem and hardly ever as an opportunity, is neither inevitable nor universal. Thus a report in *The Times* on 'white flight' in US cities concludes: 'In the past, "white flight" was considered uniformly negative. It was seen as a sign of cities declining. But unlike Europeans, many Americans see their country as a land of opportunity and welcome immigrants as a sign of economic strength' (*The Times*, 1 May 2001).

This is not to suggest that we can claim to encompass every opinion and position on the plethora of issues connected to 'race' and ethnicity in each of many national contexts referred to in this *Dictionary*. What we do offer is an overview of the way that these issues are perceived and the different meanings given to key terms in various countries. We also seek to encompass the historical and cultural issues that have shaped these varying perceptions. In this context, one of the most significant 'divides' concerns what is denoted by the term 'race' itself. In the USA and the UK the word 'race' is often qualified by putting it in quotation marks, as we do here. This serves to suggest that while it has no basis in scientific research, it is nonetheless a powerful social construct with significant practical consequences. More particularly, 'race' is used interchangeably with 'colour' both as a discriminator and as a measure of unequal distribution of life chances.

Members of minority groups in the UK (and elsewhere) are no doubt well aware that racism comes in different forms: on the one hand, it may be subtle and hidden, while on the other, it may be overt – as indicated in a Policy Studies Institute investigation in the mid-1990s which found that approximately one in eight of those of Caribbean, Bangladeshi, Indian, Pakistani and Chinese origin surveyed had encountered racist abuse in the previous 12 months (Modood et al., 1997). But categorization based on colour is not universally recognized, nor is 'colour racism' the only form of racism that manifests itself. In Western Europe generally – the UK excepted – the assumption that race can be equated with colour is contested on various grounds: by pointing to the Nazi era and so bracketing racism with anti-Semitism; and by highlighting the existence of 'Orientalism' and, more recently, of 'Islamophobia' – antipathies which are in large measure culturally based. To reflect these differences, the term 'racisms', in the plural, is often and increasingly preferred to the singular 'racism'. To speak of 'racisms' suggests that the idea of 'race' to denote 'otherness', 'difference', 'inferiority' and so on, may be based on cultural or religious factors just as much as on the idea of some biological difference or skin colour.

The identification of 'otherness' is not some objective process, whereby an obvious and unequivocal difference is noted and then acted upon. On the contrary, it is highly subjective insofar as it ascribes great significance to certain perceived differences, while ascribing little or no significance to others. The concept of 'otherness' has become increasingly prominent in the social sciences largely because of the transformation of the fundamental concept of identity brought about by Marxism, feminism and psychoanalysis – among other influences. These theoretical shifts have undermined the concept of the 'other' as a distinct reality that can be easily assigned to specific categories. In particular, the contribution of psychoanalysis to understanding the impact of the unconscious in the formulation of value judgements has shown the impossibility of assuming a neutral position of observing the 'other', be it an individual or a group. As Hall has argued:

> Something we have learnt from the whole discussion of identification, in feminism and psychoanalysis, is the degree to which that structure is always constructed through ambivalence. Always constructed through splitting. Splitting between that which one is, and that which is the other. The attempt to expel the other to the other side of the universe is always compounded by love and desire. This is a different language from the language of, as it were, the Others who are completely different from oneself.
> This is the Other that belongs inside me. This is the Other that one can only know from the place from which one stands. This is the self as it is inscribed in the gaze of the Other. (Hall, 1997: 47–48)

This passage offers a vivid example of the way in which concepts usually associated with psychology and psychoanalysis are highly relevant to the other social sciences. In view of this, the *Dictionary* contains a number of entries, such as 'Identity' and (the) 'Unconscious', where insights provided by psychology and psychoanalysis can serve to illuminate our understanding of significant aspects of 'race', racism, migration, hostility, discrimination, and so on. We refer here in particular to aspects of these phenomena that sometimes seem to fall outside rational explanation. Psychological and psychoanalytic approaches are especially helpful in explaining migrants and travellers as being in some way 'strange', as the archetypal 'other', as not subscribing to or as rejecting the range of norms that 'insiders' recognize without needing to be told. Even today, the outward justification provided for the frequent instinctive rejection of 'strangers' is that they are different, alien, even threatening because they deviate from the supposed norms – in terms of their language, dress, customs, demeanour, beliefs, etc. – a perception that in reality stems from the unconscious. That this perception is deep-rooted is evident, for example, in the etymological origin of the word 'stranger', which stems from the same Latin root *extraneus* as 'strange' and 'extraordinary'.

This *Dictionary* has been profoundly influenced by the enlightening work, produced towards the end of the twentieth century, regarding the ways in which societies have persistently described and constructed different 'others' and different types of 'stranger'. These descriptions and constructions have frequently been produced with the aim of controlling these 'outgroups' or keeping them in a condition of inferiority or marginalization. Scientific claims have often supported the exercise of this control, which has often found expression in biological racism or sociobiology. No social science can be totally blameless in this respect – and all have been instrumental in the maintenance of the established order by reinforcing inequality and discrimination. However, in the second half of the twentieth century the misuse of psychology and psychiatry is especially noteworthy. This matter has been explored by Foucault and Szasz among others, and the ensuing debate has done much to sensitize researchers – including psychologists and psychoanalysts – to the issues and risks underlying any study that constructs people as 'others', whether they are ethnic or 'racial' minorities, women or marginalized persons. As Szasz put it:

'Schizophrenia' is a strategic label as 'Jew' was in Nazi Germany. If you want to exclude people from the social order, you must justify this to others, but especially to yourself. So you invent a justificatory rhetoric. That's what the really nasty psychiatric words are all about: they are justificatory rhetoric, labelling a package 'garbage', it means 'take it away! 'Get it out of my sight!' etc. That's what the word 'Jew' meant in Nazi Germany: it did not mean a person with a certain kind of religious belief. It meant 'vermin!', 'gas him!' I am afraid that 'schizophrenia' and 'sociopathic personality' and many other psychiatric diagnostic terms mean exactly the same thing; they mean 'human garbage', 'take him away!', get him out of my sight.' (Szasz, 1997: 453–61)

We find this passage striking, not because we share Szasz' mistrust of medicine and psychiatry, but rather because it offers a clear example of how certain scientific paradigms can find useful application in other disciplines, and how exploitation, rejection and marginalization occur beyond the fields of politics and sociology.

Raffaele Bracalenti and Peter Braham, Rome and London, July 2002

REFERENCES

Castles, S. and Kosack, G. (1973) *Immigrant Workers and the Class Structure in Western Europe*, Oxford, Oxford University Press.

Foucault, M. (1972, 1999) *Histoire de la folie à L'âge classique*, Paris, Gallimard.

Hall, S. (1997) 'Old and new identities', in King, A. (ed.) *Culture, Globalization and the World-System*, University of Minnesota Press, Minneapolis.

Modood, T., et al. (1997) *Ethnic Minorities in Britain: Diversity and Disadvantage*, London, Policy Studies Institute.

Parekh, B. (2000a) *Rethinking Multiculturalism: Cultural Diversity and Political Theory*, Basingstoke, Macmillan.

Parekh, B. (2000b) *The Future of Multi-Ethnic Britain* (The Parekh Report), London, Profile Books.

Shah, S. (2000) 'Get your facts right first, please,' *The Guardian*, 20 October.

Szasz, T. (1997) Interview, *New Physician*, 18(June): 453–461.

Van Djik, T. (1991) *Racism and the Press*, London, Routledge.

Westin, C. (1998) 'Temporal and spatial aspects of multiculturality: reflections on the meaning of time and space in relation to the blurred boundaries of multicultural societies', in Bauböck, R. and Rundell, J. (eds), *Blurred Boundaries: Migration, Ethnicity, Citizenship*, Aldershot, Ashgate.

A

ABORIGINE: see NATIVE

ACCULTURATION (It. *acculturazione*; Fr. *acculturation*;
Ger. *Akkulturation*) Deriving from the word 'culture', the term 'acculturation' indicates the processes of transformation and ADAPTATION which take place within cultures when two or more groups – each of which has specific cultural and behavioural models – enter into relations with one another.

An established part of the lexicon of cultural anthropology for more than 60 years, the term 'acculturation' was first defined by a subcommittee of the United States Social Science Research Council – composed of three anthropologists, R. Linton, M. J. Herskovits and R. Redfield – appointed to decide upon the meaning of the term and, thus, provide a point of reference for later discussions. According to the *Memorandum* that they produced, acculturation includes all phenomena in which groups of individuals – each group having a different cultural background – interact in a continuous and first-hand manner and thus implement further transformations in the original cultural model of one or both cultural groups. Prior to this definition, in 1880, J. W. Powell, Director of the American Bureau of Ethnology (Powell, 1880), had already written that the force of acculturation was changing the linguistic traditions of American Indians through the loan of sounds and words and the crushing presence of millions of *civilized people* (our emphasis) (CIVILIZATION). Today the term 'acculturation' essentially refers to the phenomena of adaptation and transformation which derive from situations of conflict between different cultures, the settling of various cultural groups in a common territory as a result of the so-called 'great migration' (to the USA in the nineteenth century) and the increased exchange of communications which has led to the creation of the 'global village' (GLOBALIZATION). Acculturation was compared with ENCULTURATION by M. J. Herskovits (1948) and M. Titiev (1954).

The phenomenon of acculturation refers to both the acquisition of a new CULTURE – 'other' than the culture of origin – by an individual, e.g. a MIGRANT, and, more generally, to the acquisition by a social group of the cultural traits of another society. Thus, the term refers not only to the 'process of cultural change', but also to the resulting condition. Further distinction should also be made between 'reciprocal acculturation' and 'asymmetric acculturation'. 'Reciprocal acculturation' refers to processes of bi-directional cultural transfer and was thoroughly examined in a seminar organized by the Social Science Research Council in 1954 entitled 'Acculturation: An Exploratory Formulation'. 'Reciprocal acculturation' can be considered 'transformation through a network' as it takes place in a complex scenario of reciprocity in which a culture can only export its cultural models on a continuous basis if it is also open to return stimuli which modify its models. 'Asymmetric acculturation' refers to a particular intercultural relationship established between a 'superior' and an 'inferior' culture when the latter has no choice but to accept the traits of the dominant culture. A classic example of asymmetric acculturation is the Westernization of the world resulting from European acculturation during the colonial period and, more recently, during the neo-colonial period. T. Tentori (1990) observes that the leaders of cultural transformation processes are not necessarily the economically, politically and culturally stronger, older and richer populations. From a historical point of view, by means of example, Tentori proves this to be true ever since ancient times, referring to the fact that the wealthy city of Carthage was conquered by the strength of the Roman army, that Greek culture had an important influence on the Roman conquerors (*Graecia capta ferum victorem cepit*) and that many ancient European centres of culture and tradition were transformed or overwhelmed by Barbarian invasions. [G. H.]

Herskovits, M. J. (1948) *A Man and his Works*, Knopf, New York.
Linton, R., Herskovits, M. J., Redfield, R. (1936) Memorandum for the study of acculturation, in *American Anthropologist*, Washington, Vol. 38, pp. 149–152.
Powell, J. W. (1880) *Introduction to the Study of Indian Languages*, Government Printing Office, Washington.
Redfield, R., Linton, R., Herskovits, M. J. (1936) 'Outline for the Study of Acculturation', *American Anthropologist*, New Series, 38.
Tentori, T. (1990) *Antropologia culturale*, Studium, Rome.
Titiev, M. (1954) *The Science of Man*, Holt Rinehart & Winston, New York.

ACCULTURATION GROUP (It. *gruppo di acculturazione*; Fr. *groupe d'acculturation*; Ger. *Akkulturationsgruppe*) Part of the concept of

ACCULTURATION, the term 'acculturation group' is used in the analysis of internal migrations (MIGRATION) to identify the groups which performed a mediatory function between the MIGRANTS and the autochthons. Acculturation groups may be created directly by local authorities, or they may be organizations formed by voluntary services, trade unions or other societies; they are often informal groups composed of fellow-countrymen, friends who come together to perform the function of cultural mediators (CROSS-CULTURAL MEDIATION). The use of the term is mainly confined to Italy. In the last few years, the use of the term 'cultural mediator' has become more widespread; however, the profile of this figure is not yet accurately defined, especially in the legal sense, although several education authorities accept their participation in schools, and daily necessity has led to their help being requested both in the health and social sectors and in the labour market. [M. V.]

Clark, W. A. V. (1985) *Human Migrations*, Sage, Beverly Hills.
Davis, K. (1974) 'The migrations of human populations', *Scientific American*, 231.

ADAPTATION (It. *adattamento*; Fr. *adaptation*; Ger. *Anpassung*) Deriving from the Latin term *adaptus* – meaning 'suitable' or 'adapted' – composed of *ad* plus *aptu* (apt), the term 'adaptation' – together with the term 'adjustment' deriving from the old French *adjuster* composed of *ad* (to) and *juste* (right) – describes two features of peoples and groups: plasticity and the ability to learn and to change. Thus the process of adaptation

or adjustment refers to the ability of societies to adapt to their environments.

More precisely, in the case of MIGRATION, the term refers to the changes brought about in the newcomer and the host country in order to reduce conflict and increase psychological and social well-being. The concept of adaptation has both sociological and psychological dimensions, and raises significant psychological issues. Although the term 'adaptation' seems to have assumed negative connotations, implying the renunciation of the original values of the newcomer in order to be accepted into the host society (ASSIMILATION), the term 'adjustment' seems to focus more on the psychological process of mourning implicit in any migration process and therefore does not refer to 'compulsory' renunciation of the newcomers' values. The adjustment process constitutes a positive psychological response which is started by the emotional and social changes resulting from the migration process. The focus of this approach lies on the recognition and treatment of the pain experienced by the individual in such a way that this person can be helped.

Besides the positive meaning of adjustment, many authors have shown a suspicious attitude in interpreting the reaction of newcomers to the host society in terms of psychological skills and well-being. Indeed, there is a clear relationship between adjustment and CONFORMISM and adjustment and social control. On the other hand, there is an obvious risk of interpreting culturally differentiated behaviour as psychopathological symptoms (Fernando, 1991). Furthermore, much concern has been raised about the risk of a 'political' use of psychological treatment and psychiatric diagnosis as a result of studies by scholars such as Foucault (1991) and Szasz (1994) which stress the importance of psychiatry and psychology in ensuring social control over marginalized minorities (MARGINALIZATION).

While adjustment focuses on individual psychological response, adaptation is more bound to the world of sociology. Despite modern awareness that any relationship between groups and cultures must be bi-directional, and therefore produce changes in both sides, the concern that the adaptation process is merely a strong form of assimilation still pervades the term in its negative connotation. It is worth mentioning that even in the field of genetic evolution from which the term was borrowed, the term adaptation has acquired this bi-directional meaning of changes produced both in the environment and in the organism by the interaction. Continuous adaptation to the physical and sociocultural environments presented is a feature common to all cultures and thus analysis of cultural and educational mechanisms can be used to produce patterns and models of adaptation (DIVERSITY–SIMILARITY). For example, it has been shown that most rituals – although differing greatly from society to society – can be considered collective habits, accepted and sanctioned by tradition and necessary in order to allow adaptation to different social situations. Generally speaking, the mechanism used by a group or society to adapt to a new situation tends to be codified in terms of norms and social habits and often assumes the form of ritual or RITE. Even though many anthropologists have striven to recognize a structure common to all rites, closer analysis of the interaction of individuals and groups has led to recognition of a far wider range of types of behaviour differing both in the adaptation strategies employed and the time required. In other words, the process of adaptation is neither universal nor biologically determined. In the modern world, in which interdependent relationships and global connections have been established at various levels, it is no longer possible to sustain the existence of isolated, yet internally homogeneous, societies (or groups within them). All societies are involved in a constant process of adaptation and so, in relation to migrants, adaptation is always trans-actional rather than unidirectional – the host society also has to adapt to the arrival and settling of foreigners or migrants, or groups of foreigners or migrants (FOREIGNER, MIGRANT). Adaptation is a complex process involving tension, resistance, rejection and even isolation by one or both sides. Furthermore, while the adaptation process may result in conformism, the acquisition of the culture of the host country by migrants, or a change in values of the autochthon population, other outcomes include the forming of gangs, violence, self-marginalization, forms of psychological unease and even suicide. [M. C. G.]

Bateson, G., Bateson, M. C. (2000) *Steps to an Ecology of Mind: Collected Essays in Anthropology, Psychiatry, Evolution, and Epistemology*, University of Chicago Press, Chicago.

Fernando, S. (1991) *Mental Health, Race and Culture*, Macmillan, London.

Foucault, M. (1991) *Discipline and Punish*, Penguin Books, London.

Szasz, T. (1994) *Cruel Compassion: Psychiatric Control of Society's Unwanted*, John Wiley & Sons, New York.

ADJUSTMENT: see ADAPTATION

AFFIRMATIVE ACTION (It. *azione positiva*; Fr. *discrimination positive*; Ger. *positive Diskriminierung*)

The term 'affirmative action' was developed in the United States to describe government programmes implemented to support socially discriminated against and disadvantaged groups by introducing some form of preferential treatment to reverse historic inequalities. Affirmative action programmes have also been adopted in other countries to support immigrant minorities (ETHNIC MINORITY) and other socially disadvantaged groups. Such programmes are not so much the effect of political doctrine as a set of executive committee decisions, administrative circulars and legal rulings adopted over a long period of time. Affirmative actions are generally intended to be temporary government programmes and, as such, to be interrupted as soon as initial discrimination is reduced or eliminated. From a more specifically racial point of view, this kind of intervention acknowledges the existence of both racially discriminated groups and racial discrimination (RACE, RACE AND INEQUALITY).

The term 'affirmative action' first emerged in the United States in the 1960s, when the Black civil rights movement developed what Malcolm X called the 'debt doctrine' which demanded of the authorities that – if they were sincere in their intention to bridge the gap between blacks and whites – they would have to go beyond simple impartiality and introduce measures to compensate for the cumulative effects of privation and discrimination that black people had experienced in the past.

Historically speaking, affirmative action initiatives were introduced in 1941 (when President Roosevelt signed Executive Order 8802 allowing the integration of blacks into factory work-forces producing war materials). The term was used in an official capacity for the first time by John F. Kennedy, who in 1961 signed Executive Order 10925, which not only led to the founding of the Committee on Equal Employment Opportunity, but also invited federal entrepreneurs to adopt affirmative action in order to eliminate discrimina-tion in the workplace. Sanctions – including the cancellation of govern-ment contracts – were to be applied to any company that did not conform to this decree. Subsequently the policy was enforced through the approval of the Civil Rights Act in 1964, which explicitly forbade any discrimination in the work-place on the basis of race, religion, sex or ethnic origin. President Lyndon B. Johnson strongly supported affirmative action in a famous speech at Harvard University, acknowledging that over previous decades, conditions had dras-tically worsened for blacks (or at least failed to improve with the same speed as they had for whites), especially with regard to unemployment – particularly among young people – poverty and infant mortality. It was not until Johnson drew up Executive Order 11246 in 1965 that a national affirmative action pro-gramme was implemented with the aim of offering equal employment oppor-tunities regardless of race, religion or country of origin (women did not receive protection against discrimination on grounds of gender until some three years later).

The legal basis for affirmative action has tended to ebb and flow. Early pro-motion of affirmative action in several landmark legal judgments – especially during the 1970s with reference to Title VII – was followed by several judgments which served to restrict the impact of these earlier judgments (e.g. the case of *Bakke* v. *The University of California*).

Between 1969 and 1977, Presidents Nixon and Ford enhanced affirmative action programmes by implementing a federal plan to counter discrimination in the construction industry (Philadelphia Plan, in 1969) and supporting business enterprises run by blacks and Hispanics. In addition, the Nixon administration even outlined specific objectives and deadlines in order to better define programmes and assess their results. Things changed with the Reagan and Bush Administrations, though Bush did sign the Civil Rights Act of 1991, under pressure from Congress. The Clinton administration, despite President Clin-ton having appointed to his first cabinet three women, four African-Americans and two Hispanics, was nonetheless criticized for its policies on equal opportunities, and its policy on affirma-tive action did not really differ from the approach of the two administrations which preceded it.

Affirmative action programmes have attracted criticism for several contrasting reasons. On one hand they have been depicted as a violation of the US Constitution insofar as they treat social problems on the basis of ethnic demarca-tions and quotas. In addition, critics of affirmative action have pointed out that under Title VII of the Civil Rights Act of 1964, preferential treatment on grounds of race, skin colour, gender or country of origin is expressly forbidden (EQUAL-ITY). Indeed, it has been suggested, for example by the US sociologist Nathan Glazer, that affirmative action pro-grammes constitute unjust preferential treatment, because they produce reverse discrimination – an outcome which he terms *affirmative discrimination* (1975). On the other hand, some commentators have argued that affirmative action programmes are undesirable because they may harm the interests of African-Americans in that the quality which justifies their preferential treatment is predicated on an implied inferiority (Steele, 1994: 41). Of course, affirmative action programmes do not merely apply to African-Americans. Thus, following the Mount Pleasant riots in 1992 affirmative action programmes have also been intensified with regard to Hispanics and citizens of Latin American origin, while Asian-Americans – who were traditionally considered to belong to the occupational elite of their countries of origin but now include a large proportion of unskilled and uneducated workers among their numbers – have also seen the implementation of affirmative action initiatives in their favour in order to help reduce 'Downtown Chinese' crime figures (Ezorsky, 1991: 59). [M. V.]

Bergman, B. R. (1996) *In Defense of Affirmative Action*, Basic Books, New York.

Curry, G. E. (1996) *The Affirmative Action Debate*, Addison-Wesley, Reading, MA.

Ezorsky, G. (1991) *Racism and Justice*, Cornell University Press, Ithaca, NY.

Glazer, N. (1975) *Affirmative Discrimination: Ethnic Inequality and Public Policy*, Basic Books, New York.

International Convention on the Elimination of All Forms of Racial Discrimination, New York, source: www.hri.org

Lynch, F. R. (1989) *Invisible Victims: White Males and the Crisis of Affirmative Actions*, Greenwood Press, New York.

Steele, S. (1994) 'A negative vote on affirmative action', in Mills, N., *Debating Affirmative Action*, Delta, New York.

West, C. (1993) *Race Matters*, Beacon Press, Boston, MA.

Wilson, W. J. (1978) *The Declining Significance of Race: Blacks and Changing American Institutions*, University of Chicago Press, Chicago.

AFROCENTRISM
(It. *afrocentrismo*; Fr. *afrocentrisme*; Ger. *Afrozentrismus*) This term is composed of Afro, from the Latin term *afer*, meaning African, and centre, and indicates the development and centring of African history and culture. Afrocentrism became popular in many African movements in the 1970s and, above all, the 1980s, and was promoted among the 'African DIASPORA' – the descendants of slaves, currently living in countries where the black community is a minority ethnic group (United States, Canada, Great Britain, etc.). Afrocentrism has become a subject of cultural interest (with magazines entitled *Afrocentric Scholar* and the *Afrocentric Review*, for example) as well as the starting-point for black nationalist movements (BLACK POWER). The Afrocentrism approach counters EUROCENTRISM and white-centrism (WHITENESS) and covers subjects previously developed throughout a wide range of nationalist movements based on specific black traditions and promoting African history and culture (NEGRITUDE). It may also be considered as a sign of the failure of policies which began in the 1960s and aimed at the integration of minorities.

Modern-day supporters of Afrocentrism, such as Molefi Kete Asante from the United States, still talk of the need for blacks to escape from the universality of Eurocentrics and to defend every moment of their daily lives from HOMOLOGATION by models aimed at denigrating African peoples and cultures. An almost prophetic connotation of this concept joins this defensive quality: 'Afrocentricity is the belief in the centrality of Africans in post-modern history' (Asante, 1995: 6). Different demands came to light through Afrocentrism in the 1990s, mostly in the United States. Here, for example, following the introduction of politically correct terms, many intellectuals proposed changing the books and programmes used in state schools in such a way as to move away from pluralist multiculturalism and to focus on one specific point of view, thereby denying the existence of a single distinct American culture (MULTICUL-TURALISM). According to these intellectuals, African-Americans can only have higher *self-esteem* and be more integrated if they are aware of their history and culture of origin (Africa). For this purpose, some educational districts in which black people constitute the majority of the school population (for instance in Atlanta, Detroit and Washington, DC) adopted Afrocentric curricula, in other words curricula which make Africa the centre of their cultural universe. The use of African names to replace 'slave' names has also become very popular. There is even an attempt at reinterpreting Eurocentric concepts of culture from an Afrocentric viewpoint (for example, affirming the existence of African classical MUSIC). Moderate Afrocentrism can be considered as a preliminary phase to the development of a form of pluralism where different cultural expressions are given the same importance. On the other hand, extremist Afrocentrism can only lead to the creation of a separatist multiracial society where each race or culture with a specific ETHNICITY lives separately.

Over the last few years, debates on Afrocentrism in the States have also had to take into account the difficult relations between Afro-Americans and African immigrants. Africans who immigrated to the States in the 1970s were usually students or scholars who supported the aims and struggles of black nationalist movements and made a great contribution towards making Africa and Africanism prestigious. However, over the last ten years many immigrants and refugees from Africa – often from French-speaking countries – have entered into financial competition with the Afro-Americans in addition to having different cultural and political backgrounds.

Similar problems occur in relations between African-Americans and the African population in Africa, where not only are the African-Americans disturbed by the cultural and psychological diversity (DIVERSITY–SIMILARITY) of those who are supposedly their descendants, but they often keep their distance, considering Afro-Americans essentially as Americans. [M. V.]

Asante, M. K. (1987) *The Afrocentric Idea*, Temple University Press, Philadelphia.
Asante, M. K. (1995) *Afrocentricity*, Africa World Press, Trenton, NJ.
Asante, M. K. (1996) *Afrocentricity and Knowledge*, Temple University Press, Philadelphia.
West, C. (1994) *Race Matters*, Vintage Books, New York.

AGGRESSION

(It. *aggressività*; Fr. *agressivité*; Ger. *Aggressivität*) The term 'aggression', from the Latin *aggredi* from *ad-gradi*, meaning 'advance towards', is used to describe a generally hostile type of behaviour which is directed either at the self or at others. The term is closely connected and often confused with the concept of destructiveness. While the latter term has purely negative connotations, aggression can also be seen to be positive, expressing competitiveness, assertiveness and the capacity to make an impact on the world and to fight. Nevertheless, the two concepts cannot be completely separated, as an individual's desire for assertion can sometimes degenerate into self-destructiveness or destructiveness towards others.

At the beginning of the twentieth century experiments on animals led neurophysiologists to believe that they had identified the area of the brain where anger was generated in the *locus niger*, at the base of the encephalon. Further research and experiments on the central nervous system identified different areas and neuronal connections each time. Cannon (1929) and Massermann (1943) proved the neurological character of aggressive behaviour by demonstrating that such behaviour is stimulated by the amygdale and hippocampus nucleuses (Murphy, 1951); however they also recognized the fundamental role played by the individual's environment and culture. The hypothesis of the environmental origin of aggression was put forward by Konrad Lorenz, who considered it to be a defence mechanism of the individual and of the species, and, in the natural world, a drive towards territorial possession. In his treatise *On Aggression* (1966) Lorenz theorized that aggression, which he defined as the 'so-called evil', was a positive and useful component from an evolutionary point of view, both for animals and, by analogy, for humans. Appropriately channelled aggression helps initiate a positive struggle and guarantees survival through the procurement of food and the practice of sexuality. Other scholars argue that aggression is the result of social and environmental repression, which hinders the full satisfaction of individual desires. Thus, in order to reduce hostile or destructive tendencies or behaviour, it would be necessary to remove the sources of restriction and repression. Mainly favoured by behavioural psychologists, this theory ascribes a sort of liberating significance to aggression. According to this viewpoint, each act of aggression is followed by a cathartic effect, thanks to which the probability of new violent explosions is reduced. This conclusion little considers the resoundingly obvious fact that aggression often generates new aggression, eventually leading to forms of gratuitous violence, with a progressively strengthening and catalytic effect.

Among the psychoanalytic theories on aggression, the Freudian contribution and understanding of the phenomenon is extremely important in that it stresses the interconnection of human drives and thus successfully conveys the reality and complexity of human behaviour. As regards the origin of aggression, Freud wavers between considering it to be an expression of the sex drive (1915) and of the death instinct (1924). Alfred Adler describes a situation in which the individual compensates his/her frustration and non-gratification with a 'will for power' which leads him/her to become aggressive towards society (1912). Socioanalytical scholars have approached the issue of aggression through the analysis of the phenomenon of war, i.e. the utmost institutional expression of destructive tendencies on the part of one group towards another. Franco Fornari (1975), for instance, sees war as an expression of the human need to project and expel aggressive fantasies from the group, simultaneously negating any responsibility for them. According to socio-analytical theory, aggression among groups, which is institutionalized in war, represents a social mechanism whereby individuals are liberated from their profound persecutory and depressive tensions. It is quite common for psychological literature to trivialize aggression, viewing it as a typical characteristic of males as opposed to the typically weak and passive nature of females. Although it is true that social roles in various contexts often impose behaviour which is orientated in one direction or another to a greater or lesser extent, the aggression impulse is actually independent from the cultural codes normally used to direct it, and actions which in many situations are considered to be aggressive and violent, may not be seen to be so in other cultural contexts. This cultural dimension of aggression has led experts to consider the nature of aggressive feelings, i.e. whether they are inborn and primary or stem from social conditioning and education. Theories which focus on the ethological and instinctual nature of aggression have often been used to justify violent and aggressive behaviour. This is why many scholars prefer not to consider aggression to be an inborn drive, but see it as the outcome of an individual's relationship with the environment, and consider the drive towards love to be the only true essence of human beings (Gindro, 1993). [S. G.]

Adler, A. (1912) *The Neurotic Constitution: Outlines of a Comparative Individualistic Psychology* (1930), Dodd, Mead, New York. [First published 1912 in German; first issued in English translation in 1916.]

Cannon, W. B. (1929) *Bodily Changes in Pain, Anger, Fear and Rage*, Appleton, New York.

Fornari, F. (1975) *The Psychoanalysis of War* (1965), Indiana University Press, Bloomington, IN.

Freud, S. (1915) *Instincts and their Vicissitudes*, in Strachey, J. (ed.), *The Standard Edition of the Complete Psychological Works of Sigmund Freud* [SE] Hogarth Press, London, XIV: 109–140.

Freud, S. (1924) *The Economic Problem of Masochism*, SE, XIX: 159–170.

Gindro, S. (1993) *L'oro della psicoanalisi*, Alfredo Guida Editore, Napoli.

Lorenz, K. (1966) *On Aggression*, Methuen & Co., London.

Massermann, J. (1943) *Behavior and Neurosis*, University of Chicago Press, Chicago.

Murphy, G. (1951) *An Historical Introduction to Modern Psychology*, Routledge, London.

ALIEN: see FOREIGNER

ALIENATION

(It. *alienazione*; Fr. *aliénation*; Ger. *Entfremdung*) The term 'alienation', which comes from the Latin *alienus* (other, estranged, hostile), is widely used to describe people who experience separation or estrangement within modern society and is instilled with both sociological and psychological meaning. Indeed, the term is used to describe the feelings of modern human beings who are unable to influence the social mechanisms and functioning of a capitalistic society and is thus connected with any condition of deprivation of power – especially in the sociological sense – and the related psychological feelings and emotions.

Any attempt to reconstruct the history of the use of the term in Western culture must consider the juridical, religious and philosophical connotations of the term and the religious debate which preoccupied German philosophers of the nineteenth century. Since this period, the term 'alienation' has been used to describe a special condition of powerlessness. The nineteenth-century use of the word offers a clear explanation of why the term is so often used to describe the social and psychological conditions of migrants and marginalized people (MARGINALIZATION) today and to identify the reason for such phenomena. Yet economists and sociologists have failed to explain why some people migrate and others do not, given equality of economic and social conditions, and the fact that MIGRATION is not just a matter of poverty or demographic pressure but also includes an individual dimension (PUSH FACTORS – PULL FACTORS). This dimension can be described as a condition of detachment (or alienation) from the migrant's original world. In the English language, the connection between the condition of alienation and the condition of being a migrant is evident in the use of the term 'alien' to indicate a foreigner or migrant.

EVOLUTION OF THE CONCEPT: FROM JURIDICAL AND RELIGIOUS ORIGINS TO PHILOSOPHICAL AND POLITICAL SIGNIFICANCE

The term 'alienation' has its origins in the field of jurisprudence, where it signifies the giving up of an object, either in exchange for compensation or gratuitously, or the cession of a person considered to be an object, if the laws so permit and SLAVERY is legal. The modern meaning of the word also has theological antecedents. According to St Augustine, the greatest pain of eternal punishment was precisely the fact of being alienated from God. According to Calvin, man's alienation from God was the most serious consequence of original sin. With Rousseau the term takes on a more philosophical sense. In *The Social Contract*, Rousseau used the term to define the yielding of individual rights to the community as part of the constitutive process of a society (Camporesi, 1974). Contrary to this, the proponents of natural law theorized about the existence of 'inalienable' rights, that is to say, rights which human beings cannot yield. Later some of these were solemnly proclaimed in the declarations of rights issued during the French Revolution, and most recently in the United Nations' *Universal Declaration of Human Rights*.

In classical German philosophy, *Entfremdung* denotes the process of exteriorization of the Spirit from nature and, generally speaking, exteriorization of the Other from the self. This use, which is already present in Fichte, was later taken up and extended by Hegel,

though not without being influenced by the philosophy of ancient idealism (Plato had already represented matter, nature and life as being other from the pure Idea) as well as the Protestant pessimistic theology and the contractualism of Rousseau. In Hegel's philosophy the term indicates the process through which the Spirit initially posits precisely what, for it, appears to be other or strange. Feuerbach uses the word in a quite the contrary, materialistic sense. He no longer makes reference to Humankind. In his view, divinity is only a human creation which alienates its own qualities in God, emancipating them . . . estranged from humankind and dominates it. In 1844 Marx (1963) applied a rigorous critical analysis to Hegel's conception starting from Feuerbach's materialistic positions. According to Marx, 'in the conditions described by political economy' (namely, in capitalist society) the object which is produced by labour appears to the worker as an 'extraneous entity', like a 'power independent from the producer'. Labour becomes attached to an object and the accomplishment of labour, its objectification (*Vergegenständlichung*) takes on the character of a loss or enslavement to the object; its appropriation by the capitalist as estrangement (*Entfremdung*) or alienation (*Entäusserung*). Marx stresses the difference between objectification and alienation. Objectification, or human work and its results, is only alienation in the conditions described by political economy, within capitalist society, and more generally the society of classes. This distinction allows him to conceive of alienation as a historical or social fact, and not as having come about as a result of an original fall, or a metaphysical condemnation or a natural destiny. Thus, in Marx's view, redemption from alienation is possible. It should be remembered that since the 1930s

German existential philosophy has formulated a conception of alienation even more radical than that of Marx. Alienation is described as the condition of people, mortals thrown into a flimsy world which they do not, or cannot control and in which they are destined to live for the most part an inauthentic life. [U. M.]

Camporesi, C. (ed.) (1974) *Il concetto di alienazione da Rousseau a Sartre*, Sansoni, Firenze.
Marx, K. (1963) *Opere filosofiche giovanili* (1844), Editori Riuniti, Roma.
Marx, K. (1970) *Economic and Philosophic Manuscripts of 1844*, London, Lawrence & Wishart.
Melotti, U. (1974) *Marx*, Vallecchi, Firenze.

SOCIAL SCIENCE AND MIGRATION

Alienation, because of its wide range of application (separation or estrangement from the product of one's work, from oneself, from one's society, or from one's own culture) has become a concept which increasingly belongs to the discourse of the social sciences. In particular, in the field of migration studies, alienation has long been viewed as both the cause and result of migration.

As the cause of migration

Migration, as well as being approached as an economic, political or social phenomenon, has also been explored from a psychiatric perspective and from this perspective it has long been interpreted as the manifestation of a psychiatric pathology (Frigessi/Risso, 1982). Psychiatry uses the term 'alienation' for any type of mental disorder which renders the individual 'incapable of behaving normally in society' (Pieron and Poirier, 1978). Thus, the precondition

of alienation in one's native environment is perceived as a cause of migration. Consequently, the condition of being mentally alienated and that of being estranged from one's own native community tend to overlap, providing an interpretation of the migration process and related feelings of distress. The psychiatric conception of the migrant as alienated has contributed to host societies' transformation of the complex phenomenon of the presence of foreigner-migrants into a psychiatric problem. This latent concept of the migrant as mentally ill, or already alien from their own native society, has even entered our social unconscious (UNCONSCIOUS) and has contributed to intensifying discrimination and PREJUDICE against migrants.

As the result of migration

The psychiatric model described above – which treats alienation as a cause of migration – has gradually shifted emphasis, and the condition of alienation has more and more been perceived as the outcome of migration. The causes for the distress felt by migrants and foreigners have been increasingly sought for in the social, cultural and psychological rootlessness that came along with their condition. Handlin (1951) wrote that the history of immigration is the history of alienation. Solitude, isolation, estrangement, lack of available help, separation from the community, desperation as a result of the loss of meaning are the features of alienation which characterize the condition of immigrants. According to this viewpoint, immigrants live in a state of crisis because they have been uprooted. In this state of rootlessness, the old links have been lost while the new ones have yet to be established, and immigrants experience extreme distress. More recently, Cornell West has analysed the reasons for the detachment or alienation of African-Americans. This author suggests that the proper starting-point for the crucial debate about the prospects of black America is an examination of the nihilism that increasingly pervades black communities:

> Nihilism is to be understood here not as a philosophical doctrine that there are no rational grounds for legitimate standards of authority; it is, far more the lived experience of coping with a life of horrifying meaningless-ness, hopelessness and (most importantly) lovelessness. The terrifying result of all this is an unwitting detachment from others as well as a self-destructive attitude towards the world. A life without sense, without hope, without love generates a cold merciless vision of things, one which is destructive of the self and of others. In black America nihilism is nothing new. The first contact of Africans with the New World was marked by the Absurd. (West, 1994: p. 14)

From this perspective migrants can be seen as prisoners of two worlds and alien in each: they are estranged from their past and estranged from their present and future: they are lost in a hostile world, and may feel intense longing for the old and distant way of life, something which may become the object of agonizing idealization. Thus migrants are viewed as often afflicted with a particular kind of pathology: NOSTAL-GIA or homesickness (nineteenth-century psychiatry used the terms *lipemania* or *melancolia delirante*) which can be cured only when the migrants return to their place of origin.

Not all scholars agree or recognize that a major cause of alienation is the condition of being a foreigner *per se*: their position is that the prime cause of alienation is the extent of discrimination and marginalization present in the host society. Having studied the relationship between alienation as a result of work and other phenomena, Seeman (1959) found that ethnic hostility (ETHNICITY) contributed very little to the alienation of black Americans, which was more likely to be based on their lack of power. Seeman suggested that an analysis of alienation should be based on five factors. The first was lack of power, the impossibility of an individual to influence the outcome of events through their own behaviour; the second factor was lack of meaning, that is, difficulty in predicting the results of one's behaviour; the third was a lack of norms, or a situation in which norms and rules have been broken; the fourth was isolation, the attribution of low-level values to goals and beliefs cherished by society; and the fifth was self-estrangement, that is, becoming estranged from oneself. Indeed, it is not surprising that K. B. Clark and M. P. Clark (1947) in their celebrated and controversial 'doll study', found that African-American four- and five-year-olds were showing aversive reactions to the colour of their own skin (DIVERSITY–SIMILARITY).

The concept of estrangement or alienation as one of the consequences of the history of slavery is closely related to Franz Fanon's interpretation of the concept of alienation in *The Wretched of the Earth* (1963). He treats alienation as being the particular condition of those who have been colonized (COLONIAL-ISM). [M. B.]

Bastide, G. (1971) *Anthropologie appliquée*, Payot, Paris.

Clark, K. B., Clark, M. P. (1947) 'Racial identification and preference in Negro children', in Newcomb, T. M., Hartley, E. L. 1958, *Readings in Social Psychology*, Holt, New York.

Devereux, G. (1978) *Ethnopsychoanalysis: Psychoanalysis and Anthropology as Complementary Frames of Reference*, University of California Press, Berkeley.

Fanon, F. (1963) *The Wretched of the Earth*, Grove, New York.

Frigessi Castelnuovo, D., Risso, M. (1982) *A mezza parete*, Torino, Einaudi.

Handlin, O. (1951) *The Uprooted*, Little, Brown, Boston, MA.

Lichtheim, G. (1968) 'Alienations', in Sills, D. (ed.) *International Encyclopedia of the Social Sciences*, Macmillan and Free Press, New York, I.

Pieron, H., Poirier, J. (1978) 'Aliénation culturelle et hétéroculturelle', in Michaud G., (ed.) *Identités collectives et relations interculturelles*, Complexe, Paris.

Seeman, M. (1959) 'On the meaning of alienation', *American Sociological Review*, 24: 786.

West, C. (1994) *Race Matters*, Vintage Books, New York.

ALTRUISM

(It. *altruismo*; Fr. *altruisme*; Ger. *Altruismus*) The term derives from the French *altruisme* (from the spoken Latin *alter*, other), and was first coined by Auguste Comte, as a contrast to 'egoism'. He also put forward the maxim on which it was based: 'live for others', and used the term to describe an action which brings an advantage to a person other than the performer of the action, at some cost or risk to the latter.

With regard to the social and cultural heritage left by humanity throughout the course of evolution, much mention is made of AGGRESSION but little of altruism. As Hinde (1974) put forward, this is not related to the scarcity of altruistic behaviour in animals (altruism in this case having exactly the same connotations as when referring to humans), since altruistic behaviour is far more common than aggression among members of the same species. It is connected to the ideological position of the study as is often the case in the social sciences. In sociology, the same function had already been attributed to 'social constraints' (*contrainte sociale*), which Durkheim (1893) considered indispensable to the development of 'mechanical solidarity' and not – unlike 'organic solidarity' which was based on the division of labour – the result of egoistic considerations.

Altruistic behaviour is widespread both in humanity and in many species of animals. Among the 'social insects' (bees, ants and termites), it is a rule for sterile members of society. The phenomenon of altruism is so important that even Darwin (1871) had cause to think that his theory of evolution through natural selection (EVOLUTION) was fatally flawed. Evolutionary biologists seek to attribute aggression, male dominance, selfishness and other similar phenomena to genetic biological causes. Altruism is treated as an expression of latent self- or group interest. When evolutionary psychological explanations take an extreme reductionist form in which the gene is the prime actor and the organism is simply its carrier, altruism becomes incomprehensible. Social scientists recognize a complex relationship between human biology and CULTURE, rendering altruism understandable both in terms of human values and human need. Altruism is also a problem for rational choice theory action. Learning theories state that altruism is learned through reinforcement and imitation. According to cognitive development theories, however, it is the development of cognitive structures which leads to altruistic choices. With the discovery of the UNCONSCIOUS, psychoanalysis showed that all humans' actions, gestures, words and thoughts are supradetermined, i.e. the result of many stimulations, often contradictory with regard to one another and the chosen gesture of behaviour, thought or word. Moral and social values have not escaped this debunking analysis, and neither has altruism. Some writers have based their ideas on an individualistic concept of the human being; others on a relational concept. [U. M.]

Boorman, S. A., Levitt, P. R. (1972) *The Genetics of Altruism*, Academic Press, New York and London.
Darwin, C. (1871) *The Descent of Man*, John Murray, London.
Durkheim, E. (1960[1893]) *The Division of Labour in Society*, Glencoe, Free Press.
Hinde, R. (1974) *Biological Bases of Human Social Behavior*, McGraw-Hill, New York.
Melotti, U. (1985) 'Competition and cooperation in human evolution', *Mankind Quarterly*, Washington, 25(4).
Nagel, T. (1970) *The Possibility of Altruism*, Princeton University Press, Princeton.
Trivers, R. (1971) 'The evolution of reciprocal altruism', *Quarterly Review of Biology*, Baltimore, 46(4).

AMNESTY (It. *sanatoria*; Fr. *loi d'amnistie*; Ger. *Amnestie*) The

term 'amnesty' refers to the legalization of an illegal situation through renunciation by the authorities of prosecution of those responsible for breaking administrative and legislative provisions. In the case of MIGRATION, an amnesty allows foreigners who have entered or live in a country illegally (ILLEGAL ALIEN) to legalize their position. In recent years in Europe, the most important amnesties have been those of 1985–86 and 1991 in Spain; the 1981 amnesty and the amnesty of 1998 for *sans papiers* (undocumented migrants) in France; the amnesties of 1986 (Law n° 943), 1998 (Law n° 39, known as the Martelli Law), 1995 (Law Decree n° 489), 1998 (Law n° 40) and 1999 in Italy. Perhaps the most important amnesty in the history of modern migration was the 1996 amnesty which accompanied the passing of the Immigration Reform and Control Act in the USA by which more than 3.5 million undocumented migrants achieved the legal status of resident. [Gu. B.]

Colman, H. L., Harding, S. K. (1995) 'Citizenship, justice and political borders', in Schwartz, W. F., Schwartz, W. A. (eds), *Justice in Immigration*, Cambridge University Press, Cambridge.
Reyneri, E. (1996) *Sociologia del mondo del lavoro*, Il Mulino, Bologna.

ANTICIPATED SOCIALIZATION (It. *Socializzazione anticipatoria*;

Fr. *socialisation anticipatrice*; Ger. *antizipierte Sozialisation*) This term was first used by Merton (1951) to describe the acquisition of a behaviour pattern relevant to a specific context before the reasons for its adoption have been created. In studies of the migratory process, the term is used to describe how the values and behaviour of the destination country are acquired before the subject leaves his or her own country. It is used in this sense, for example, in Alberoni and Baglioni's studies (1965) of MIGRATION within Italy after the Second World War. However, these two authors maintained that anticipated socialization could only take place in the case of internal migration. Later studies, on the other hand, show that the process happens, to some extent, even in the case of today's international migrations (Melotti, 1985). [M. V.]

Alberoni, F., Baglioni, G. (1965) *L'integrazione dell'immigrato nella società industriale*, Il Mulino, Bologna.
Melotti, U. (1985) *La nuova immigrazione a Milano*, Mazzotta, Milano.
Merton, R. K. (1951) *Social Theory and Social Structure: Toward the Codification of Social Theory*, Free Press of Glencoe, Glencoe, CA.

ANTI-RACISM: see RACISM

ANTI-SEMITISM (It. *antisemitismo*; Fr. *antisémitisme*; Ger. *Antisemitismus*) Although other Semitic populations – as well as Jews – have experienced RACISM and victimization, the term 'anti-Semitism' is used to refer to PREJUDICE, hatred and attacks on Jews *qua* Jews. The term 'anti-Semitism', which did not come into use until the nineteenth century, is a curious word insofar as 'Semitism' – the glorification of Semitic as opposed to non-Semitic cultures – has never existed, although the word 'philo-Semitism' *is* used. This oddity notwithstanding, anti-Semitism has proved to be not merely a persistent phenomenon, but also a phenomenon with severe and genocidal consequences (GENOCIDE). Long-lasting historical phenomena such as anti-Semitism are difficult to understand precisely because of the seemingly different connotations and manifestations they assume over the centuries. Nevertheless, Jewish intellectual interpretation appears to treat the phenomenon as a single entity (Poliakov, 1966), although this runs the risk of creating abstract or mythical theories almost as illogical as anti-Semitism itself (such as 'eternal hatred' or 'chosen victims').

Anti-Semitism can be discerned in various eras, ranging from the moment of meeting of the Greek and Jewish civilizations (5–6 cent. BC), throughout Christianity and in many racist movements in the nineteenth and twentieth centuries. Though its most extreme manifestation was the Nazi Holocaust (SHOAH), anti-Semitism did not disappear with the defeat of Nazi Germany, but has been a significant force in Eastern Europe both under communist regimes and since their collapse.

Anti-Semitism is not a continuous phenomenon – it was almost imperceptible in the Late Middle Ages, in Europe and Byzantium before the Crusades (twelfth century) – and it comes in various intermittent, though often long-lasting forms. There is, however, no comparison between the scale and depth of anti-Semitism in Christian countries and the much weaker form found in Islamic countries prior to Western colonization (nineteenth and twentieth centuries) (COLONIALISM). Indeed, in Moorish Spain, especially under Ommaiadi dominion (and the independent Emirate of Cordoba, 755–1031), Islam and Judaism not only existed side by side, but actually became allied religions. However, anti-Semitism has existed in certain Arab countries, where it is nowadays fuelled by anti-Zionism (ZIONISM). For example, in a speech welcoming the Pope to his country, the President of Syria, though he did not specify Jews by name, spoke of Palestinians being murdered by 'those who killed the principle of equality when they claimed God created a people distinguished above all other peoples. . . . They try to kill all the principles of divine faiths with the same mentality of betraying Jesus Christ and torturing him, and in the same way that they tried to commit treachery against the Prophet Mohammed' (*Daily Telegraph*, 7 May 2001).

The first seeds of hostility against Jews in Eastern Mediterranean countries under Greek dominion were probably sown during the clash between East and West which began during the Persian wars and this was passed on through Greek culture to the Roman intellectual community. For example, Apion was an Egyptian of Greek culture whose libellous writings contested the scriptures of the Bible, in particular the Exodus (8 cent. BC). He claimed that Jews were a bunch of wretches with numerous illnesses, including leprosy, and his writings seem to have helped to persuade the Pharaoh to expel the Jews from Egypt. Similarly, the Roman historian Tacitus (AD 55–120) did not hesitate to show his dislike for the Jews.

Anti-Semitism has been linked to Christianity since the latter's very inception, as is evident in the writings of the Founders of the Church. This hostility probably began as a result of rivalry between the two semi-clandestine religions – very similar to one another and both ready to take advantage of the end of the classical world in order to gain supremacy. Christianity, the overwhelming winner of this battle, continued to despise the loser, although Christian hate of Judaism was fuelled by the equally strong – though contrary – feeling of filiation of Christianity to Judaism.

Sculptures showing the victorious Church and the defeated Synagogue – the latter blindfolded and damaged (as in two sculptures at one of the entrances to Strasbourg Cathedral) – are a concrete illustration of this phase of anti-Semitism. Nevertheless, there were opposing feelings in the Christian world that Jews were to be both protected and destroyed: Jews were regarded as both living witnesses to the historical truth of Christ's existence and as the population which had caused Christ's death, and as such they were seen as responsible for what was viewed by the Church as the worst crime in human history. In addition, there was the accusation that the Jews did not acknowledge Jesus Christ as the Son of God, notwithstanding biblical prophecies of the coming of the Messiah (Isaiah, 7 cent. BC). This conflict led to Jews being isolated and denied certain privileges (e.g. they were not allowed to own land or testify in legal proceedings). For example, in 1555 Pope Paul IV forbade Jews to practise medicine, to pursue 'high commerce' or to own real estate. Conversely, Jews were forced to carry out jobs that, though they were essential, were portrayed as somehow despicable (such as money-lending and trade), persecuted for performing the very tasks they were often forced to do and, finally, compelled to live in ghettos, such as that established by Paul IV in Rome in 1556, and to wear a badge (JEW, GHETTO).

According to popular belief, Jews were responsible for poisoning drinking water, spreading disease, killing individuals in their beds, using Christian blood in their religious rituals and planning the destruction of the entire Christian world. These superstitions and their use in repression of Judaism by the Church and the laity led to the trials, burning and slaughter of Jews in many parts of Europe, especially between the eleventh century and the end of the eighteenth century.

The French Revolution, which led quickly to full civic rights being extended to all French Jews (1791) and the French military victories under Napoleon, which resulted in the emancipation of the Jews in, for example, Prussia (1812), proved crucial turning points in Jewish history. Despite the temporary setback marked by Napoleon's defeat in 1815, gradually, and in many countries, Jewish liberty began to advance: for example, rabbis in France were put on the same footing as Christian clergymen in respect of salary (1831) and Jews, if elected, could take their seats in the British Parliament once the oath 'On the True Faith of a Christian' was no longer obligatory (1858).

One consequence of this new environment was that during the nineteenth century, Jews became leading players in liberal modernization and development movements, though in retaliation Christian churches launched furious campaigns against them through their most reactionary factions, widely supported by right-wing intellectual groups.

The Russian Revolution in 1917 led to new accusations of Jewish responsibility for and involvement in Bolshevism and further strengthened the already existing myth of a worldwide Jewish plot. Subsequently, Jews were, paradoxically, often depicted as the creators of both capitalism and communism. Adolf Hitler's rise to power in Germany laid the foundations for the Holocaust, which was the result of an amalgamation of all the superstitions, prejudices and crimes deriving from 2,000 years of history and led to the destruction of an entire Eastern European CIVILIZATION. [A. Z.] [P. B.]

Flavius, J. (1999) *The New Complete Works of Josephus Flavius*, trans. W. Winston, Kregel Publications, Grand Rapids, MI.
Poliakov, L. (1974) *The History of Anti-semitism*, Routledge, London.
Sartre, J-P. (1946) *Réflexions sur la question juive*, Paul Morihien, Paris.
Schwartz-Bart, A. (1959) *Le Dernier des justes*, Le Seuil, Paris.
Shirer, W. (1960) *The Rise and Fall of the Third Reich*, Simon & Schuster, New York.
Singer, I. B. (1950) *The Family Moskat*, Alfred Knopf, New York (English version; originally published in Yiddish).
Wistrich, R. (1989) *The Jews of Vienna in the Age of Franz Joseph*, Oxford University Press, Oxford.

APARTHEID: see RACIAL SEGREGATION

ART AND ETHNICITY (It. *arte ed etnia*; Fr. *art et ethnie*; Ger. *Kunst und Ethnizität*) There are three generally accepted meanings of the term 'art': (1) any human activity which depends on artistry or craftsmanship; (2) a use of skills and creative imagination in the production of 'aesthetic objects'; and (3) fine arts. We shall consider the second definition given above. The study of the feelings, concepts and judgements related to 'beauty' in the broadest sense is the field of the philosophical discipline of 'aesthetics' which, in the West, dates back to ancient Greece. Throughout most of European history the definition of art has been applied solely to the Western tradition, while excluding non-Western productions, discounted as 'PRIMITIVE' or 'exotic' (EXOTICISM).

The Romantics considered the art they produced to be the highest expression of Western culture, although somewhat contradicting this notion by exalting Greek classical art as an unattainable ideal at the same time. Art was seen as the expression of the Absolute: 'Art brings the *whole man* as he is to that point, namely to a knowledge of the highest, and this is what underlies the eternal difference and the marvel of art' (Schelling, 1978: 233). The romantic conception of art still quite aptly expresses the intangible and profound essence of artistic expression which applies to every era and every people. No historical period, no CULTURE and no CIVILIZATION can be properly understood without a comprehension of the art it produces. Although art has been, and continues to be, an object of commerce, as well as a means to express religious, philosophical, political and civil ideals, it is in itself none of these things.

In the West it has always been believed that art is governed by precise rules (e.g. Rameau's various treatises codifying the rules of harmony of eighteenth century music), while ascribing a freer, more 'spontaneous', creative expression to other cultures. In reality, however, even the most spontaneous, allegedly free and 'primitive' form of art is subject to more or less decipherable rules, and the sense of spontaneity perceived by Westerners in the artistic expressions of other cultures may be due to their difficulties in understanding these internal rules, particularly from the often markedly ethnocentric (ETHNOCENTRISM) standpoint of Western culture.

While improvisation and spontaneity are indeed elements in forms of artistic expression such as DANCE, MUSIC, etc., especially in traditional arts, improvisation techniques are governed by strict rules which performers and artists abide by. For example, improvisation plays an important role in jazz music, where it is nonetheless ruled by precise conventions.

At the end of the nineteenth century CULTURAL EVOLUTIONISM postulated the universality of artistic expression, recognizing as art non-Western creative expressions, although it continued to evaluate them according to Western standards. In opposition to cultural evolutionism, twentieth-century anthropology has considered art to be culturally determined. Marcel Mauss (1872–1950), one of the founders of modern ethnology, defined as art any phenomenon, activity, production or manifestation which is recognized as such by a given group, independently from any possible aesthetic judgement (CULTURAL RELATIVISM). Hence the study of the relations between art and society has developed into a sociology of art which studies the social and cultural roots of artistic expression, by analysing both the aesthetic values historically present in a given society – given that art, in all its forms, is a cultural fact, and it is impossible to fully understand a historical period without grasping the meaning of the art it produces – and that society's peculiar form of language and specific system of production and use of 'art objects'.

More recently scholars have begun to take an interest in art as a system through which every community celebrates its own ethnic identity. Art contributes in specific and crucial fashion to defining the identity of an ethnic group in the same way as do its language, its religion and its customs. In this sense, MULTIETHNIC societies, as well as being multilingual and multireligious, are also multi-artistic. Diversified artistic production in multiethnic societies serves the double function of providing each group with its own user niche while promoting reciprocal knowledge between different groups. However, the encounter of different artistic expressions is also at the origin of various cultural misunderstandings and, potentially, even of racist attitudes. Approaching the artistic languages of cultures different from one's own can be difficult in that failure to understand their internal rules can easily lead to misinterpretation and oversimplification. That said, it is possible to move beyond these barriers and approach art produced by different cultures from the standpoint of humanity's common psychic structure, both conscious and UNCONSCIOUS, regardless of differences in time and place, language and civilization. A musical or Noh theatre piece from ancient Japan, or a statuette from central Africa, can be understood by those who are willing to do so on this basis, although penetration of their deeper meanings requires a scientific application and determination which go far beyond a superficial appreciation of the exotic. While no 'universal' art can be said to exist – given that even music uses specific languages which are hard for non-specialists to understand – any work of art can be understood in its essential lines by those who approach it without prejudice. [S. G., R. R.].

Benjamin, W. (1999) *Selected Writings*, Harvard University Press, Cambridge, MA.
Croce, B. (1995) *Guide to Aesthetic*, Hackett, New York.
Kant, I. (1997) *Critique of Practical Reason*, Cambridge University Press, Cambridge.
Kierkegaard, S. (1980) *Writings*, Princeton University Press, Princeton, NJ.
Schelling, F. W. J. (1978) *System of Transcendental Idealism* (1800), transl. P. Heath, University Press of Virginia, Charlottesville.

ASSIMILATION

(It. *assimilazione*; Fr. *assimilation*; Ger. *Assimilation*) From the Latin *adsimilare*, to render similar, the term 'assimilation' was first applied by French and Portuguese colonial systems in Africa to the relationships between populations and cultures (CULTURE). The basic assumption was that colonized peoples could become citizens of the colonizing state – acquiring official citizenship – provided they had a certain income, a good level of education, a good knowledge of the language and that they kept a standard of behaviour adequate to the status of citizenship under consideration. In this case assimilation was partial. Total assimilation, which saw the inhabitants of the colonies treated in the same way – with the same rights and duties – as the colonizers, was rarely applied (COLONIALISM).

The term 'assimilation' has been also used to describe both the model and the process of absorption of people from different countries and different cultures, brought together as the consequence of the MIGRATION process. In this context, assimilation is often interpreted as a process of progressive ADAPTATION (leading towards inclusion in the host society) whose final outcome should be the disappearance of cultural differences. This unidirectional process is considered the 'natural' way for migrants to adjust gradually to their new environment by absorbing the values of the dominant culture. The model of assimilation is a precise political strategy which intends to keep the national COMMUNITY as homogeneous as possible by endeavouring to ensure that the same basic values are shared by the whole population (NATION, NATIONAL CHARACTER).

Implementation of a model of assimilation sees the host country set up specific policies to assimilate newcomers and thus encourage them to become citizens (ETHNIC POLITICS). In many cases, both the process and the model of assimilation have failed, partly because of the perceived 'unwillingness' of certain groups to relinquish their cultural specificity. In the past this led to such groups being defined as 'unassimilable' (e.g. the Poles in France, the Turks in Germany), although such a concept has now become obsolete as a result of the emphasis placed by scholars and politicians on reciprocal aspects of cultural differences (INTEGRATION, MULTICULTURALISM). Assimilation may also be uneven for several reasons: (a) because a national minority is not necessarily a local minority, so pressure locally to assimilate is less than normal or even absent; (b) because assimilation may be achieved in one sphere (e.g. language), but resisted in another (e.g. religion); and (c) because some groups are seen as much less 'amenable' and easy to assimilate than others which are more distant from the dominant culture and values.

Historically speaking, a detailed analysis of the process of assimilation can be found in the work of Park and Burgess (1921), according to whom assimilation is a process of interpenetration and fusion in which persons or groups substitute for their own cultural models those of their host society, taking on its attitudes, ways of thinking and memories and even coming to share its historical memory in such a way as to become part of a common cultural life. Assimilation is mentioned in Redfield, Linton and Herskovits' *Memorandum* (1936) on ACCULTURATION and it was also the subject of a seminar organized by the British Social Science Research Council in 1954. As used by sociologists in reference to immigrant groups, the term 'assimilation' refers to a unilateral process of absorption of the values of another culture and is distinguished from cultural processes which involve a bilateral and reciprocal influence between two cultures. Thus assimilation implies the passive attitude of one culture with respect to another, dominant culture. The concept of assimilation of immigrant groups was set forth by Gordon in 1964. Gordon suggested that the degree of assimilation of an immigrant group could be determined according to seven variables and argued that assimilation can only be said to have been accomplished when all seven conditions are satisfied: (1) substitution of the migrant group's cultural models with those of the host society; (2) a high rate of primary group participation in host society groups and associations; (3) a high rate of mixed marriages (MIXED MARRIAGE); (4) development of a feeling of belonging and citizenship of the host country exclusively; (5) absence of prejudices (PREJUDICE); (6) absence of discrimination (RACIAL DISCRIMINATION); (7) absence of value and power conflicts. In Gordon's model, complete assimilation presumes that no trace of separate social structures, based on ethnic rules or values different from those of the host society, remains between persons of different ethnic origins (ETHNICITY). This does not account for the influence of subdominant or minority cultures on the dominant culture during the process of assimilation. Some scholars consider that one social group cannot conform to the customs and values of another social group without some such change taking place. According to Bastide (1967), assimilation – understood as a spontaneous process of identification with an external culture and a renunciation of NATIVE culture – is a phenomenon of little importance within the context of anthropology unless the situation under examination involves cultural changes enforced upon ethnic and cultural communities. Furthermore, spontaneous assimilation is only expressed by individuals and family groups in a new host environment. While the assimilation process can used to describe the phenomena occurring when a dominant and a minority culture enter into contact, the generic term 'assimilation' can very often be substituted by terms such as 'Americanization' or 'Europeanization' which are considered more accurate in describing the two prevalent processes and models (EUROCENTRISM). According to this interpretation, assimilation is a process by which one or more groups of various ethnic, racial and cultural origins from outside Europe and North America abandon their native culture in order to assume the models of the Western civilizations with which they have come into contact (Bastenier and Dassetto, 1993). While assimilation in the Americas (Americanization) has mainly taken place in the United States and Brazil, assimilation in Europe has been strongly promoted in France. Since the beginning of the nineteenth century France has absorbed (and assimilated) immigrant minorities from several different areas, including Belgians, Poles and Italians. Assimilation was originally considered the only possible means of integration, with the only way for immigrants to live peacefully in the host country being to renounce their IDENTITY and become nationalized: an approach which, on the contrary, often exacerbated the tensions between minority groups and the host society. Indeed, a forced process of assimilation may provoke strong reactions from ethnic groups intent on saving their identities and values and may increase stereotypes, prejudice and rejection of the minority group by the host society. The repeated stereotyping of different groups is closely connected to the fact that countries of immigration tend to prefer certain groups of immigrants over others and helps to demonstrate the weakness of the assimilation model.

As a result of the economic crisis of the 1970s the French assimilation policy began to fail at the beginning of the 1980s and the improvement of social conditions for migrants became increasingly difficult, provoking MARGINAL-IZATION, refusal and profound changes in the structure of the immigrant population, a population which had become ever more diverse as a result of post-war migration from former French colonies and Algeria (Falga et al., 1994). As a result, more recently the predominant approach has been to encourage respect for diversity and voluntary integration and the establishment of a multicultural society in order to induce national loyalty and peaceful coexistence. From this perspective, imposing the host country values is not the only way of achieving the goal of political solidarity and loyalty (as originally conceived). The same objective can be achieved through the inclusion of other values in the host society in order to advance social integration by the creation of a multicultural society. A recent review of the French assimilation policy (Schnapper, 1991) showed that previously immigrants had needed to assume the values of Western culture in order to be assimilated, while the new integration policy leaves immigrants free to retain the values of their culture of origin. This recognizes and legally protects cultural differences in order to create a multicultural society similar to the Anglo-Saxon model. The United Kingdom too has seen a move from a policy of assimilation to an official government policy of cultural pluralism and equal opportunities for ethnic minorities in an attempt to create a pluralist society in which differences are recognized and protected by law. The Council of Europe has decided to abandon all assimilation policies and now merely expects immigrants to share the fundamental values of Western societies such as democracy and the distinction between civil law and religious law (this position is still considered by many to be highly Eurocentric). This new model of integration does not intend to provide a solution to all cultural conflicts, but attempts to suggest a means of mediation or reconciliation – based on reciprocal respect and conditions of substantial social EQUAL-ITY – aimed at providing safer ground for the creation of a peaceful, multicultural Europe. New countries of migration such as Italy, Spain, Greece and Portugal, seem to have favoured this policy for the integration of migrants over any idea of the implementation of assimilation policies. [L. Za.]

Bastenier, A., Dassetto, F. (1993) *Immigration et espace public: la controverse de l'intégration*, L'Harmattan, Paris.

Bastide, R. (1967) *Les Amériques noires*, Payot, Paris.

Falga, B., Wihtol De Wenden, C., Leggewie, C. (eds) (1994) *Au Miroir de l'autre. De l'immigration à l'intégration en France et en Allemagne*, Les Éditions du Cerf, Paris.

Gordon, M. M. (1964) *Assimilation in American Life: The Role of Race, Religion and National Origin*, Oxford University Press, Oxford.

Park, R. E., Burgess, E. W. (1921) *Introduction to the Science of Sociology*, University of Chicago Press, Chicago.

Redfield, R., Linton, R., Herskovits, M. J. (1936) 'Outline for the study of acculturation', *American Anthropologist*, n.s. 38.

Schnapper, D. (1991) 'La France de l'intégration – Sociologie de la nation en 1990', (ed.) Bibliothèque des Sciences Humaines, Gallimard.

ASYLUM SEEKER: see POLITICAL ASYLUM

AUSLÄNDER (It. *Ausländer*; Fr. *Ausländer*; Ger. *Ausländer*)

This term is mainly applied to differentiate between *Inländern* (citizens) and *Ausländern* (non-citizens). The former are citizens of the country in which they live; the latter are citizens of another country (CITIZENSHIP). There are various problems connected to the term 'Ausländer' in relation to the German question. The first problem concerns those persons who, according to the Constitutional Law of the Republic of Germany and the various legal regulations based on their 'ethnic affiliations', are potential *Inländer* (ETHNICITY, ETHNIC POLITICS). Section 116, subsection 1 of the Constitutional Law of the Federal Republic of Germany states: 'Subject to further legal regulations, a German is a person who has German citizenship or who has been admitted to Germany as a refugee or expellee of German ethnic affiliation or spouse of such person or descendant in the regions of the Deutsche Reich according to the situation on December 31, 1937.' Subsection 2 states: 'Former German citizens, whose citizenship was revoked for political, racial or religious reasons between January 30, 1933 and May 8, 1945, and their descendants may be granted citizenship once more (*wieder einzubürgern*) upon application. They are not deemed expatriates if they took up residency in Germany after May 8, 1945 and did not express a contradictory intention.'

According to these legal regulations there is a privilege for DIASPORA Germans with regard to their rights as citizens. This population does not need to be naturalized. A second question of problematic nature arises from the situation of the former GASTARBEITER population as well as various groups of refugees (REFUGEE) and other types of immigrants. In this case the result has certainly been a rather open policy of naturalization; however, it has been limited to two levels. Firstly, strict attention has been and is being focused on avoiding DUAL CITIZENSHIP although various federal institutions and authorities in the Federal Republic of Germany have secretly allowed dual citizenship. Secondly, this policy has limited naturalization in such a way that authorities have ensured that families do not get separated. This situation, which was strengthened especially because of the Turkish population which has very strong, national Diaspora ties to Turkey, also resulted in the growth of a third generation of Ausländer in some other European countries. A DENIZEN population developed that was largely excluded from parliamentary and political process and treated as second-class citizens. Based on the Ausländer situation, discussions arose about local voting rights, the foreigners' right to vote in Europe and especially about discrimination against residents by the promotion of foreigners in state programmes for economic advancement (FOREIGNER). The term 'Ausländer' developed into a collective term for all immigrants, so that the question of origin became a decisive element in discourses concerning discrimination. 'Hostility against Ausländer' became a typical subject in German politics. The political participation of Ausländer was nonetheless strengthened through various organizations: the setting up of foreigner advisory boards, committees and ombudsmen for foreigners – so-called 'representatives for foreigners' – was not only the beginning of an improvement in the social condition of many immigrants and their personal situation but also an attempt to achieve more comprehensive social participation and INTEGRATION. A new policy for naturalization has been developed since the Social Democrat–Green (*rot–grün*) coalition government took office in 1998. In particular, naturalization of second- and third-generation (SECOND GENERATION) families was made easier. But the double citizenship problem could not be solved. New obstacles were embodied in the procedure, such as the requirement of proficiency in the language of the country of immigration. [J. B.]

Hammar, T. (1990) *Democracy and the Nation State. Aliens, Denizens and Citizens in a World of International Migration*, Avebury, Aldershot.
Hammar, T. (1990) 'Denizens' political interest and participation: voting rights in the Nordic countries', in Barouh, S., Simon, I., Jean, P. (eds), *Les étrangers dans la ville. Le regard des sciences sociales (Communications présentées au colloque internationale de Rennes 14–15–16 décembre 1988)*, Paris, pp. 222–223.

BILINGUALISM

(It. *bilinguismo*; Fr. *bilinguisme*; Ger. *Zweisprachigkeit*) From the Latin *bi* (two) and *lingua* (tongue), in its common meaning the term indicates equal fluency in two languages on the part of an individual or group, or the use of two languages within a geographical or political area (region or state). When referred to the status of a region or state, the definition of bilingualism takes on historical and political connotations and does not merely define the presence of different linguistic groups in a given area. Rather it refers to a more specific condition whereby two languages enjoy official status in a country or region. For example, states such as Canada, or certain regions of Italy, such as Val d'Aosta or Trentino, are bilingual by virtue of the fact that they formally recognize two official languages (OFFICIAL LANGUAGE). Bilingualism is thus ensured through administrative and social measures, such as, for example, the adoption of double place names, the right to early bilingual education, and particular obligations or facilitations as regards fluency in both languages for access to state employment. Bilingualism differs in meaning from 'diglossia' (Fishman, 1967) – although literally the two terms both signify 'two tongues', the first being of Latin and the second of Greek derivation – in that the latter is used to refer to the use of two languages within the same COMMUNITY. This is the case of groups which use both a 'higher' and a 'lower' language, which are granted different levels of prestige and reserved for separate functions and

contexts, one being used more widely and enjoying a more official status, the other having a more restricted, local and informal usage. Some authors (Hamers and Blanc, 1984) propose to restrict the use of 'bilingualism' to the social context and to use 'bilinguality' to indicate the various individual conditions of knowledge of two languages.

Clearly the mere definition of individual linguistic competence in two languages can include so many variants as to make it impossible to consider this as a single phenomenon. For this reason it is more usual to define those people who are also able to communicate in one or more foreign languages – presuming that they have learned their mother tongue by exposure to it and other languages through formal learning, generally scholastic – as 'polyglots'. The adjective 'bilingual' is generally used for those who have grown up speaking two languages through contact with a double linguistic background. Strictly speaking, therefore, bilingualism applies either to a state which formally recognizes two languages, or, analogously, to individuals who recognize themselves as having two languages of origin and who have roots in both cultures. In this light the definition of 'bilingual' has long been applied to a restricted category of people – and to those states with two official languages, which currently comprise less than one fourth of the countries of the world.

The condition of bilingualism, whether applied to a political community or to individuals, was long considered somewhat unnatural, given the prevailing view that the normal status of a community is to have one language and the normal status for an individual is to have one mother tongue. Particularly on an individual level, bilingualism was considered to imply a certain level of psychological distress, inasmuch as it might prevent the complete acquisition of one language and increase the risk of feelings of disorientation. Nowadays this view has been dramatically altered, and the mastering of two languages is seen as a positive factor, not only in terms of linguistic competence, but also because such a condition is considered to imply a more flexible and open psychological attitude.

Issues concerning bilingualism and bilingual children are increasingly relevant in many Western European countries due to the large numbers of SECOND-GENERATION migrant children to be found there. Many of these children are bilingual, being exposed to their mother tongue within family circles and to the majority language at school and in early socialization. This has led to the highly debated question of whether the school system should provide specific bilingual education programmes to ensure the proper teaching of the mother tongues of such children. Some countries have preferred to run education programmes in the majority language only, in order to ensure proper education in this language, leaving the responsibility of teaching the mother tongue to the families. This policy has the goal of fostering rapid ASSIMILATION and a fast bridging of the linguistic gap these children might experience, in order to prevent them from encountering social and working problems. Conversely, other countries have started bilingual education programmes aimed at granting equal dignity to the cultures and languages of origin of second generation migrants, in order to reinforce their cultural identification with their families of origin and lessen generational conflicts

based on widening cultural gaps. The main criticisms addressed to such policies in international literature and declarations on the matter are that they might increase phenomena of social segregation and result in some children failing to master the majority language of the country they live in. It is considered that linguistic gaps could be created by bilingual education programmes, which could in turn result in social discrimination and disadvantage for these children. Finally, the costs of these programmes are a source of concern, particularly for countries where linguistic minority groups are extremely fragmented. [A. B., R. B.]

Amati Mehler, J., Argentieri, S., Canestri, J. (1990) *La babele dell'Inconscio. Lingua madre e lingue straniere nella dimensione psicoanalitica*, Cortina, Milano.
Crystal, D. (1997) *The Cambridge Encyclopaedia of Language*, Cambridge University Press, Cambridge.
Fishman, J. A. (1967) 'Bilingualism with and without diglossia: diglossia with and without bilingualism', *Journal of Social Issues*, 2: 29–38.
Hamers, J. F., Blanc, M. (1984) *Bilingualité et bilingualisme*, Mardaga, Bruxelles.
McArthur, T. (1992) *The Oxford Companion to the English Language*, Oxford University Press, Oxford and New York.
Skuttnabb-Kangas, T. (1984) *Bilingualism or Not: the Education of Minorities*, Multilingual Matters, Clevedon.
Titone, R. (ed.) (1996) *La personalità bilingue*, Bompiani, Milano.
Tosi, A. (1984) *Immigration and Bilingual Education*, Pergamon Press, Oxford.

BIOETHICS AND ETHNICITY (It. *bioetica e etnia*; Fr. *bioéthique et ethnie*; Ger. *Bioethik und Ethnizität*) The term 'bioethics' was coined in 1971 by the American oncologist V. R. Potter, who aimed to create a new, biologically based, ethics. However, this original

sense was soon to be replaced by the current meaning of the word, that is, 'the systematic study of human conduct in the area of life sciences and health care, in so far as this conduct is examined in the light of moral values and principles' (Reich, 1978). Current bioethics addresses issues such as clinical research, abortion, medically assisted reproduction, cloning, genetic research, euthanasia, palliative care, organ transplants, animal experimentation, and priority setting and allocation of resources in health care.

The development of bioethics has been profoundly influenced by debates on ethnicity. First of all, the rise of bioethics was marked by the protest against racism and the unjust treatment of ethnic minorities (ETHNIC MINORITY) in medical research. In 1974, as a reaction to the infamous Tuskegee Syphilis Study (a 40-year study sponsored by the US Public Health Service involving 399 black men whose syphilis was left untreated in order to investigate the 'natural course' of the disease), the US government created the National Commission for the Protection of Human Subjects of Biomedical and Behavioral Research, a milestone in the history of bioethics. One of the Commission's tasks was to identify some basic ethical principles that should govern biomedical and behavioural research involving human subjects. The Belmont Report, issued in 1978, attempted to summarize the basic ethical principles identified by the Commission in the course of its deliberations. Three basic principles were considered particularly relevant to bioethics: respect for the person (which includes the requirements to acknowledge autonomy and to protect those with diminished autonomy), beneficence (and non-maleficence) and justice. The application of these principles aims to create a common language between diverse cultures living side by side in the same society. This approach is now known as 'principlism' and is probably the main example of universalism in bioethics (other examples come mainly from Roman Catholic teachings). In this sense, ethnicity has deeply influenced the field of bioethics also in another respect. In contemporary multicultural societies (MULTICULTURALISM) the bioethical discourse is addressed to diverse communities (COMMUNITY), each one possessing its own cultural features and different, sometimes apparently irreconcilable, moral understandings. Therefore, bioethics has had to face the fundamental contradictions which exist between the rules and values of different cultures living together. The key issue is whether, in the field of biomedicine, it is possible to identify certain common moral values which exist across different cultures. Bioethics has been accused of being culture-bound and suspected of 'ethical imperialism' (CULTURAL IMPERIALISM). Critics argue that bioethics places too much emphasis on the individual at the expense of the community. They claim that ethicists have focused on Western biomedicine and have failed to provide sufficient discussion on the implications of cultural pluralism. Indeed the clash between CULTURAL RELATIVISM and universalism has conditioned the bioethical debate since its beginning, e.g. regarding the controversy on female circumcision (INFIBULATION). The debate on bioethics and multiculturalism also has practical implications. Ethnic minorities and local communities increasingly demand to participate in medical decisions that may affect their members. As a consequence ethics committees have been taking their views into account. It is now quite usual for group leaders or other prominent persons in a community to be actively involved in the design of medical research as well as in the ethical review of medical care and public health policies.

In the 1990s, the attention of international bodies turned to the global nature of many questions involving ethics. This resulted in international regulations (e.g. the European Convention on Biomedicine and Human Rights – enacted in 1998 – which was the first international bioethics document to be binding for the states signing it). One of the main causes of this new trend was a substantial change in US regulations, allowing researchers and sponsors to conduct medical research abroad in order to test and evaluate the safety and therapeutic efficacy of drugs, biologics, devices, and various other health-related interventions on human populations. As a consequence, in less than 10 years the clinical trials conducted in developing countries – but sponsored by Western countries – increased from just a few cases to thousands. A number of these trials have raised serious concerns because they were performed without respecting Western ethical standards (informed consent, positive benefit/risks ratio, etc.). It has been argued that medical research conducted in developing countries exploits nations that are poor and already burdened by diseases, and that such countries carry all the onus and risks of medical research without being able to take advantage of its results, as the new drugs are unaffordable for them, especially following the World Trade Organization's decision in 1994 to extend property rights on new drugs for a period of 20 years. As a result of this developing countries were no longer able to produce patented drugs unless they paid property rights, which in most cases is impossible for them. However, in 1997 the South African government enacted a ground-breaking law enabling the Health Minister to import generic versions of patented drugs or to license their domestic production without paying property rights to drug companies. Other DEVELOPING COUNTRIES, such as Brazil, soon began to follow South Africa's example. [Em. M.]

Brewster, A. (1993) 'Cross-cultural medicine', *New England Journal of Medicine*, 329: 26.

Dodson, M., Williamson, R. (1999) 'Indigenous peoples and the morality of the Human Genome Diversity Project', *Journal of Medical Ethics*, 25: 204–208.

Emanuel, E. J., Wendler, D., Grady, C. (2000) 'What makes clinical research ethical?', *Journal of the American Medical Association*, 283: 2701–2711.

Engelhardt, T. H. (1986) *The Foundation of Bioethics*, Oxford University Press, New York.

Lane, S., Rubinstein, R. A. (1996) 'Judging the Other: responding to Traditional Female Genital Surgeries', *Hasting Center Report*, 26(3): 25–30.

Macklin, R. (1998) 'Ethical relativism in a multicultural society', *Kennedy Institute of Ethics Journal*, 8: 1–22.

Macklin, R. (1999) 'International research: ethical imperialism or ethical pluralism?', *Accountability in Research*, 7: 59–83.

Mbidde, E. (1998) 'Bioethics and local circumstances', *Science*, 279: 155a.

Pellegrino, E., Mazzarella, P., Corsi, P. (1995) *Transcultural Dimensions in Medical Ethics*, University Publishing Group, Washington, DC.

Potter, V. R. Van (1971) *Bioethics: a Bridge to the Future*, Prentice Hall, Engelwood Cliffs, NJ.

Reich, W. T. (ed.) (1978) *Encyclopaedia of Bioethics*, Free Press, New York, Vols 1–3.

Turner, L. (1998) 'An anthropological exploration of contemporary bioethics: the varieties of common sense', *Journal of Medical Ethics*, 24: 127–133.

US Congress, Office of Technology Assessment (1993) *Biomedical Ethics in US Public Policy – Background Paper*, US Government Printing Office, Washington, DC.

Wikler, D. (1997) 'Presidential address: bioethics and social responsibility', *Bioethics*, 3–4: 185–192.

Continent: Themes and Outline, Weidenfeld & Nicolson, London.
Suret-Canale, J. (1959) *Afrique Noire*, Editions Sociales, Paris.

BLACK AFRICA (It. *Africa nera*; Fr. *Afrique noire*; Ger. *Schwarzafrika*) - Black Africa is a general term used to describe the African countries located south of the Sahara. Setting aside the historical, cultural and social differences of the populations in this area, the term is based on a distinction between inhabitants' skin colour (COLOURED, WHITENESS). Thus 'Black Africa' as opposed to 'Arab Africa' – a term used to describe the countries located north of the Sahara whose inhabitants have lighter-coloured skin and whose cultures present a strong Arab influence. A large number of French scholars began talking about Black Africa in the 1940s and 1950s; many of these scholars subsequently participated in the NEGRITUDE movement. However, this distinction was often criticized by those who supported the theory of a single Africa. According to other authors, European or African colonialists (COLONIALISM) – with a tendency towards RACISM – and the followers of the *divide et impera* motto mainly divide Africa into Arab and Black.

In America, emphasis was placed on Black Africa in the 1920s via Marcus Mosiah Garvey's highly contested 'Back to Africa' movement (BLACK MUSLIMS). Originally founded to encourage black pride, the movement urged black people in America to return to Africa and be proud of their RACE and origins. [M. V.]

Balandier, G. (1963) *Sociologie actuelle de l'Afrique Noire*, PUF, Paris.
Davidson, B. (1968) *Africa: History of a*

BLACK MARKET LABOUR: see SEASONAL MIGRANT WORKERS, ILLEGAL ALIEN

BLACK MUSLIMS (It. *Musulmani neri*; Fr. *Musulmans noirs*; Ger. *schwarze Muslime*) The term 'Black Muslims' refers to a predominantly black religious organization in the United States, that follows the teachings of Islam. Black Muslims follow Islamic religious rituals and pray five times a day as well as following strict codes of diet, dress, discipline and relationships. They are the largest and most significant sectarian movement in the USA and of increasing significance in Britain and other countries. Their importance, and the reason they continue to be supported by many black people lies in their contribution to black people's economic and social life; their effective resistance to RACISM; generosity to impoverished members and their contribution to the education of black young people and their ability to keep many away from drugs and violence. The organization's leaders advocate economic co-operation and self-sufficiency and enjoin a strict Islamic code. Black Muslims have established accredited schools in more than 45 US cities and own various farms from which they send produce throughout the United States using their own trucks and aeroplanes. Their weekly, *Muslim World News* (formerly *Muhammad Speaks*), is a widely circulated black newspaper. In addition, they rehabilitate convicts, drug addicts and alcoholics through their 'doing-for-self' philosophy and police some black neighbourhoods and housing projects in order to prevent drug-related violent crime. Although no membership records are kept, the movement is estimated to have at least 100,000 followers in the US alone. Their most well-known branch is the Nation of Islam.

The current activities of the movement arise from their origins in black self-improvement movements that began in Chicago and New York shortly before the First World War. One of these was the Universal Negro Improvement Association, founded in 1914 by Marcus Garvey (1887–1940), a Jamaican-born black nationalist leader who created the 'Back to Africa' movement. He started a weekly newspaper, the *Negro World* and urged American black people to be proud of their RACE and to aim to return to Africa, their ancestral homeland. He founded the Black Star Line in 1919 to provide steamship transport, and the Negro Factories Corporation to encourage black economic independence.

Another root of the Black Muslims was the Moorish Science Temple of America, founded in 1913 by Timothy Drew (1886–1929) who was later referred to as Prophet Drew Ali. This temple was based on Islamic principles and its members believed that their origins lay in the ancient Moors. They believed that black people had been the original Muslims, but that their religion had been stripped from them by white people who had robbed them of their land and exploited them. They saw black people not as a 'race', but as a NATION. As a result, Black Muslims are black nationalists (or African nationalists) (NATIONALISM). When Ali was murdered in 1929, leadership of the move-

ment passed to Wallace D. Fard (also known as Walli Farad, Master Farad Muhammad or the Great Mahdi to Black Muslims). In 1930 Fard, a silk salesman, established the Temple of Islam No. 1 (later known as a mosque) in Detroit. This was the beginning of the Nation of Islam. He taught his followers that their 'true religion' was not Christianity, but Islam, the 'religion of the black man' of Asia and Africa. Fard stressed 'knowledge of self' as a requirement for achieving black liberation.

The Chicago branch of the Nation of Islam was founded in 1933. In 1934, after the mysterious disappearance of Fard, the leader of the Chicago mosque became the Nation's leader. He was Elijah Muhammad (1897–1975), known as Holy Prophet and Messenger of Allah, who had been born in Georgia and was originally named Elijah Poole. Until his death in Chicago in 1975, Muhammad was the supreme leader of the Nation of Islam. In keeping with its black nationalist philosophy influenced by Marcus Garvey's ideas, Elijah Muhammad's programme for the Black Muslims included the creation of separate hospitals, schools, industries, farms and shops and he aimed to create a separate African-American state. He instituted self-help programmes designed to support Black Muslim independence from the industrial and financial corporations which effectively excluded black people and other minority ethnic groups from power.

Malcolm X (1925–65), the most famous member of the Nation of Islam, developed worldwide links and popularized the movement. He was born in Nebraska, as Malcolm Little. Malcolm's father, a Baptist minister, was an outspoken follower of Marcus Garvey who was murdered by the KU KLUX KLAN when Malcolm was six years old. Malcolm converted to Islam when he was introduced to the teachings of Elijah Muhammad while in prison for burglary in 1946. This provided the impetus for him to educate himself and, when released in 1952, he joined a Black Muslim temple in Detroit and took the name Malcolm X, symbolically replacing the name derived from the heritage of SLAVERY with an X to represent the unknown name of his African ancestors – a common practice for Black Muslims. By the early 1960s, the Nation of Islam had become well known and Malcolm was their most prominent spokesperson and head of the New York City mosque. In 1963, however, the Black Muslims ordered Malcolm to be silent for his remark that the assassination of United States President John F. Kennedy was like 'the chickens coming home to roost'. In the following year, Malcolm broke with the Nation of Islam and formed a secular black nationalist group, the Organization of Afro-American Unity (OAAU). In 1964 Malcolm made a *hajj* (pilgrimage) to the Islamic holy city of Mecca, Saudi Arabia. As a result of this trip, and others to Africa and Europe, he began advocating racial solidarity, and adopted the Arabic name El-Hajj Malik El-Shabazz. On 21 February 1965, while addressing an OAAU rally in New York, Malcolm was assassinated by men allegedly connected with the Nation of Islam.

Warith Deen (formally Wallace) Muhammad succeeded his father Elijah Muhammad as leader of the Nation of Islam in 1975. He played down black nationalism, admitted white people (who were no longer referred to as 'Devils') as members and enforced strict Sunni Islamic practices. In 1976 the movement's name changed from Nation of Islam to the World Community of Al-Islam in the West, then to American Muslim Mission. His followers are now known simply as Muslims. The movement has a decentralized structure of independent places of prayer called *masjids*.

In 1977, Louis Farrakhan led a group of discontented followers in resurrecting the Nation of Islam. The group has continued the black separatist and nationalist teachings of Elijah Muhammad. The term 'Black Muslim' is now most aptly applied to members of the Nation of Islam. Farrakhan has come to public notoriety for outspoken anti-Semitic pronouncements about Jews' economic control (ANTI-SEMITISM) – pronouncements which have fuelled existing tensions between Jewish people and black people in some New York neighbourhoods. Farrakhan has been debarred from entering Britain on the grounds that he is likely to incite racial hatred (RELIGION AND ETHNIC CONFLICTS). Nonetheless, the self-help programmes of the Nation of Islam, and perhaps the worldwide proliferation of Islam, ensures that they continue to recruit followers in Britain and are increasingly visible in British and other cities. In October 1995 Farrakhan organized the Million Man March in Washington, DC. At the march, hundreds of thousands of black men vowed to renew their commitment to family, community and personal responsibility. Although the march renewed criticism of Farrakhan's anti-Semitic statements and some black leaders refused to participate, it was widely regarded as a successful display of black solidarity. It helped Farrakhan move closer to the political mainstream, and some people also saw it as indicating the strength of Farrakhan's appeal to a significant segment of the black population. [A. P.]

Lincoln, E. C. (1993) *The Black Muslims in America*, Africa World Press, New Jersey.

Malcolm X, Haley, A. (1965) *The Autobiography of Malcom X*, Hutchinson and Collins, New York.

Marsh, C. E. (1996) *From Black Muslims to Muslims: The Resurrection, Transformation and Change of the Lost-found Nation of Islam in America, 1930–1995*, Scarecrow Press, Scarecrow, MD.

Smith, C. E. (1993) 'Black Muslims and the development of prisoners' rights', *Journal of Black Studies*, 24(2): 131–146.

BLACK POWER (It. *Black Power*; Fr. *Black Power*; Ger. *Black Power*) -

Although first used by American black activists in the 1950s (Wright, 1954), the term 'black power' is more generally attributed to Stokely Carmichael, leader of the Student Nonviolent Coordination Committee (SNCC), following its adoption as a slogan during the celebrated Mississippi civil rights march of June 1966. Subsequently, the term was used to help to define the coalition founded in Oakland in October 1966 between the SNCC, the Student Organization for Black Unity and the Black Panther Party.

The Black Power movement in the USA included some of the most important black American political activists of this period (Carmichael, James Foreman, Rap Brown, Willie Ricks, Angela Davis). Although the coalition broke up in 1968, until that date this movement represented the central point of reference for the whole – and not just the American – black revolutionary movement.

Black Power as a political and ideological movement was founded in the years in which reformist attempts to achieve civil rights – led by Dr Martin Luther King, Jr. and others (RACIAL SEGREGATION, JIM CROW) – were apparently making little progress. In the view of the proponents of revolutionary change, the time was therefore ripe for a new type of politics, based on opposition, if necessary violent opposition, to dominant White Power – opposition that aimed at achieving a radical transformation of the existing power structure. The fight was no longer a struggle for equal civil rights (EQUALITY), but a struggle for power: 'The concept of black power . . . is a call for black people in this country to unite, to recognize their heritage, to build a sense of community . . . to begin to define their own goals, to lead their own organizations and to support those organizations . . . to reject the racist institutions and values of the society' (Carmichael and Hamilton, 1967: 44).

This revolutionary connotation led the movement to oppose not only national RACISM but also, insofar as they saw white power as being hand in hand with neo-colonialism (COLONIALISM) and imperialism (CULTURAL IMPERIALISM), also to oppose racism internationally. Seen from this perspective, the concept of Black Power inevitably applied not just to the situation of black people in the USA, but equally to that of other non-white peoples and for this reason it could be seen as a freedom movement for oppressed people everywhere.

The idea of Black Power developed a significant following not just in the USA, but also in Britain, where its supporters argued that the people to whom Black Power referred included not just Africans and African-Caribbeans, but also 'Asians' – Indians, Pakistanis, Bangladeshis and Chinese – as well as Arabs and, indeed, all 'non-white peoples' living in the UK. Though this approach to 'blackness' had some influence for a time, the term 'black' has since tended to lose whatever inclusivity it temporarily commanded and has since gradually fragmented, allowing a recognition of more discrete 'minority' entities: thus it has become commonplace not simply to distinguish in some contexts between 'black' and 'Asian', but also between different elements within such broader entities.

According to Rudolph Vecoli (1978), as well as affecting black Americans, the Black Power movement in the USA also encouraged an increase in awareness of ETHNICITY among other minorities. Inspired by the example of Black Americans, certain white ethnic minorities started to commit themselves to a similar fight to free themselves from the brand and weight of ascribed inferiority, and thus Black Power succeeded in creating ideas of 'Irish Power', 'Polish Power', and so on. However, the overall white reaction to the Black Power movement was negative and, indeed, often intensely hostile and frequently violent as, perhaps for the first time, whites saw their presumed superiority questioned (WHITENESS). As this conflict intensified, the Black Power movement had to endure a series of attacks on its leaders and followers – including homicide, armed raids by the authorities and what amounted to 'show trials' – and these attacks eventually contributed to its demise as a significant political movement.

The relatively short life-span of Black Power as an active coalition of forces did not prevent the idea of Black Power having an influence long after its demise as a formal organization, and so the slogan 'Black Power' came to be adopted by many leading civil rights and protest movements in the USA, such as CORE, the Congress for Racial Equality. Nevertheless, the exact meaning of Black Power was uncertain and it came to be interpreted in different, and often contradictory, ways in following years. It was the basis for, *inter alia*, the development of a black IDENTITY – as expressed in new ways of dressing (*dishikis*), new hairstyles (*afros*) and new means of self-identity – ranging from the rejection of the term 'Negro', to the adoption of African names (Stokely Carmichael himself later taking the name Kwame Ture). It also came to be associated with, on the one hand, ideas of a separatist nationalism based on a form of black racism that opposed any suggestion of living together with whites, and, on the other hand, 'black capitalism' – a concept embraced by President Nixon in 1969, perhaps because, through encouraging the growth of a black bourgeoisie, it represented an attempt to contain part of the rebellion of Black Power within a capitalist logic.

Even though the term Black Power has lost much of whatever influence it once had – being replaced or overtaken by concepts such as AFROCENTRISM – it has nevertheless remained a significant concept within many black civil and equal rights movements. Moreover, when Carmichael and Hamilton's book *Black Power* was reissued in 1992, the authors declared that the gains made by blacks over the previous 25 years were mere window-dressing. In their eyes this not only confirmed the fundamental importance of the concept of Black Power, and the force of the arguments that lay behind it, but also emphasized the need for greater collaboration between black politics in the USA and the various revolutionary movements in Africa, as well as the need to focus on class rather than RACE. From their perspective, the Black Power movement continues to provide a positive point of reference for the development of black pride and the strengthening and expression of black identity [M. V.]

Biko, S. (1978) *Black Consciousness in South Africa*, Random House, New York.

Carmichael, S. and Hamilton, C. (1967) *Black Power*, Jonathan Cape, London; reprinted 1992.

Vecoli, R. (1978) 'The coming of age of the Italian-Americans: 1945–1974', *Ethnicity*, 5: 20.

Wright, R. (1954) *Black Power*, Harper & Brothers, New York.

BOAT PEOPLE

BOAT PEOPLE (It. *Boat people*; Fr. *Boat people*; Ger. *Boat people*) The term 'Boat people' is used to define migrants (MIGRANT) who leave their country of origin illegally by sea using makeshift vessels, often encountering great danger.

Historically speaking, the term became widely used on an international basis when the Saigon regime crumbled during the second half of the 1970s, resulting in a mass exodus by sea from Vietnam. In 1979, another wave of expatriation from Vietnam saw hundreds of thousands of boat people try to reach the coasts of Thailand, Malaysia, Singapore, Hong Kong and Indonesia. Many died as a result of adverse weather conditions, while others were the victims of pirates who murdered, mistreated, tortured, raped and robbed the migrants as they fled. Often, those migrants who managed to reach foreign shores were not allowed to disembark and were either towed back out to sea or attacked as soon as they set foot on land. The seriousness of the situation led to the first Conference of Indo-Chinese Refugees (in 1979) which established that migrants from Vietnam could benefit from REFUGEE status and be allowed to disembark in a country of first asylum (POLITICAL ASYLUM) in South-East Asia before settling in a third country (the first time in the history of modern political asylum that all expatriated boat people were granted the right to settle).

This agreement led to the settling of approximately 700,000 people in Western countries over subsequent years. Mass departures from Vietnam recommenced in the second half of the 1980s, although the exodus was no longer stimulated by political persecution. However, a second International Conference on Indo-Chinese Refugees – held in 1989 to discuss the large number of boat people in flight, the ever-decreasing willingness of Asiatic countries to accommodate them and the fact that Western countries were not keen to allow Indo-Chinese migrants to settle – outlined a Comprehensive Plan of Action (CPA) with the intention of counteracting the phenomenon at various levels. This not only made it more difficult for people to leave the country by increasing controls over the granting of refugee status, implementing campaigns to establish that individuals could not automatically transfer to another country and abolishing the general right to settle in third countries, but also encouraged repatriation by guaranteeing acquittal for repatriating refugees and support and economic compensation for voluntary repatriation as well as organizing legal departures from Vietnam.

The abolition of compensation for repatriation in 1991, the main – if not only – reason for expatriation, drastically reduced the number of boat people arriving from Vietnam and Laos. In June 1996 UNHCR abolished the Comprehensive Plan of Action, although at least 24,700 individuals were still living in refugee camps (RECEPTION CENTRE) in Hong Kong, Thailand, Indonesia and the Philippines. Over a period of 20 years, at least 850,000 individuals had left their country of origin, although the exact figure is impossible to estimate as many boat people were lost or killed at sea.

The term 'boat people' was also used in September 1991 when Haitians headed for the United States by sea following the military coup during which President Jean-Bertrand Aristide was removed from power. In the summer of 1994, around 36,000 Cuban 'boat people' (*balseros* – a Spanish word meaning 'raft people') left the island by sea on makeshift vessels heading for the coast of Florida. In 1996, the term was again used to describe the desperate attempt by illegal Somali immigrants (ILLEGAL ALIEN) to flee to the Yemen by sea regardless of pirate attacks, while in May of the same year, refugees escaping the civil war in Liberia by boat raised much consternation, as some individuals were not granted permission to land in Ghana for ten days and then only following international pressure. Another 900 refugees were accommodated in Sierra Leone. In 1991 the Italian mass media used the term 'boat people' to describe the continuous arrival of boats full of migrants (MIGRANT) from Albania (around 50,000 men, women and children came to Italy from Albania in less than six months), although different measures were adopted to deal with this influx of people. The high number of arrivals made it impossible to check each individual application for political asylum, so the Italian government adopted a generalized policy allowing all Albanians arriving on makeshift boats who agreed not to apply for political asylum to be regularized and thereby obtain a temporary permit of stay – also valid as a work or study permit – for humanitarian reasons. The policy changed on 31 July 1991 and large numbers of migrants arriving after that date were immediately repatriated (DEPORTATION). Logistically, legally and administratively unprepared for such a large number of migrants, the Italian government was forced to overcome the difficulties encountered in integrating Albanian migrants – and reducing the increasing tension between local inhabitants and refugees – by implementing several policy amendments. The flow of boat people to Italy – mostly from Albania and Tunisia – has fluctuated in numbers in recent years, although there has been an increase in the number of people arriving from Kurdistan, Pakistan and China. The desperate conditions in which these people arrive – often applying for entry as asylum seekers – seem to indicate that the finding of an alternative to the terrifying sea voyages arranged by criminal organizations is of fundamental importance. The question of how to implement humanitarian actions which both fight and counteract the criminal activity and respect the immigration laws is still very much open to debate. [M. V.]

Perlmutter, T. (1998) 'The politics of proximity: the Italian response to the Albanian crisis', *International Migration Review*, 32.

UNHCR, *The State of the World's Refugees*, 1992, 1993, 1994, 1995.

Zolberg, A., Suhrke, A., Aguayo, S. (1990) *Escape from Violence*, Oxford University Press, Oxford.

BORDER: See FRONTIER

C

CASTE (It. *casta*; Fr. *caste*; Ger. *Kaste*) The term 'caste' comes from Portuguese *casta*, 'breed, kind'. Despite the fact that caste systems occur in a number of African and Polynesian civilizations, the term is more specifically used to describe religious, political, military and economic organizations in India. In modern India, the more common word for caste is the indigenous term *jati*, which means RACE. The term was originally used to describe the colour of the Aryans (of Indo-European origin) who conquered India and enslaved the native ethnic groups (ETHNICITY). However, in time, it was transformed into a rigid classification system which distinguished conquered individuals from their conquerors and which prevented fraternization between these two groups. The influence of Hindu principles on the manner in which the world was viewed became decisive. The four initial castes were generated by different parts of Brahma's body: priests or *Brahmans* came from his mouth, warriors or *Kshatriyas* from his arms, farmers and breeders or *Vaishyas* from his thighs and *Shudras* (i.e. the untouchables), the natives with the most humble tasks and with whom fraternization was strictly forbidden for all Aryan descendants, from his feet. A number of sub-castes were added at a later date, bringing the total number of castes to over 100. Buddhism has fought against the caste system and modern independent Indian politics have tried to eliminate caste-based PREJUDICE. However, outbreaks of inter-caste violence in India have been a practical consequence of the system and many believe that it has greatly hindered India's ability to modernize by effectively suppressing any possibility of meritocracy-based progress. Nevertheless, despite the criticism advanced in recent times, whether by politicians anxious to modernize Indian society or from a religious perspective, the caste system has proved remarkably resistant to attack.

From a metaphorical point of view, the term 'caste' is also used in Western societies where there are no real caste systems to describe a closed system where social and cultural improvement is hindered by pre-set and unchangeable formulas. Here castes indicate closed professional associations aiming to defend their own privileges from outside change, thereby becoming expressions of cultural and social endogamies which run the risk of ending up in rigid bodies closed to new influences and therefore acting as harbingers of social conflict. [M. C.]

Pitt-Rivers, F. (1971) *On the Word 'Caste'*, Tavistock, London.
Sharma, U. (1999) *Caste (Concept in the Social Sciences)*, Open University Press, Milton Keynes.

CHAUVINISM (It. *sciovinismo*; Fr. *chauvinisme*; Ger. *Chauvinismus*) In relation to nations the term describes a fanatical form of extreme nationalism which denies the value of any other population or NATION. It is also used to indicate the exclusive and arrogant self-favouring fanaticism of any faction or group (NATIONALISM). It derives from the French *chauvinisme*, from N. Chauvin, a soldier who fought in the Napoleonic wars and whose allegiance to the Emperor never wavered. His allegiance is depicted in caricatures, songs and plays about fanatical patriots. The current meaning of the word was introduced to the humanities by W. G. Sumner in 1906 in order to describe how patriotism can degenerate to the point where it blemishes and perverts both thought and judgement. In his analysis of chauvinism, Sumner (1974) draws attention to the way in which a chauvinist ideology uses a few, simplified formulas to influence and even control the behaviour of people and thus overrides their ability to behave on a rational and logical basis. [G. H.]

Sumner, W. G. (1974) *Folkways and Mores* (1906), Ayer, New York.

CIRCUMCISION (It. *circoncisione*; Fr. *circoncision*; Ger. *Beschneidung*)

From the Late Latin *circumcisio*, from *circumcidere* (to cut around), as far as males are concerned, the term 'circumcision' indicates the total or partial removal of the foreskin by means of a circular incision. The practice is extremely ancient in origin, dating from Egyptian times. For Jews it was – and still is – a symbol of belonging to the people of Abraham and divine allegiance. In addition to its function of religious initiation for two great monotheist religions, Judaism and Islam, circumcision is sometimes also practised for reasons of hygiene. Female circumcision refers to the far more controversial practice of making a surgical incision into the skin covering the clitoris or the real and proper removal of the clitoris (INFIBULATION, MUTILATION). [S. G.]

Chebel, M. (1992) *Histoire de la circoncision des origines à nos jours*, Balland, Paris.

CITIZENSHIP (It. *cittadinanza*; Fr. *citoyenneté*; Ger. *Staatsbürgerschaft*)

From the Latin *civis*, citizen, via the ancient Italian form, *cittade*, the term 'citizenship' defines a legal status, i.e. the belonging of an individual to a political unit (usually a state) which awards him or her a particular status and a series of rights and duties.

The implications of citizenship (i.e. rights and duties) naturally change with time and differ according to the legal system concerned. The rights conferred by citizenship can usually be divided into three areas: civil, political and social. According to Theodor H. Marshall (1950), civil citizenship includes the rights required for individual freedom (personal freedom, freedom of speech, freedom of thought, property rights and the right to stipulate valid contracts, as well as the right to obtain justice); political citizenship includes the rights which permit citizens to participate in political power; and social citizenship includes the rights regarding safety and economic welfare (which may range from the guarantee of a minimum protection of one's possessions to all that is required for full PARTICIPATION in civil life as understood in the context of the state). Extension of this sequence of 'rights of citizenship' characterizes the development process of modern democracies. According to this theory, civil rights were gained in the eighteenth century, political rights in the nineteenth century and social rights in the twentieth century. It has recently been hypothesized that there is a need for a further stage in development, involving the passage from a 'state-centred' to a sociocentric conception of citizenship.

Citizenship can be acquired by birth or by adoption. Citizenship by birth may be acquired by descent (*jus sanguinis*), or by place of birth (*jus soli*), that is, by birth on the territory of a state. Citizenship can be acquired by adoption, either owing to changes in the boundaries of a state, or by legal benefit, marriage to a citizen or naturalization. The conditions required for the acquisition of citizenship (both by birth and by adoption) are established by law. The laws governing the acquisition of citizenship depend in large measure on the political culture of the country in question and, more particularly, on the distinction that is made in the country between citizenship and nationality, as well as the country's concept of NATION. Broadly speaking, the acquisition of citizenship by descent is the most widespread and most ancient. Dating from the feudal era, acquisition by place of birth later found important applications in countries with high immigration (MIGRANT), as it allows the children born of immigrant parents to become citizens of the state in which they were born (SECOND GENERATION). The extent and facility (or otherwise) with which citizenship is granted by adoption depends on the states concerned.

In France, where immigration has performed an important economic and demographic function, and where a policy of ASSIMILATION of immigrants has long been adopted, ample room is given to the acquisition of citizenship by *jus soli* and by naturalization.

In Germany, where the country's transformation into one with high immigration is still denied on an ideological level, *jus sanguinis* citizenship is most frequently applied; naturalization is difficult and even children born in Germany of immigrant parents have trouble obtaining German citizenship, despite relaxation in the law in 1993.

In the United Kingdom, citizenship has proved to be an extremely contentious issue as a result of alarm relating to the fact that under the 1948 Nationality Act, New Commonwealth immigrants possessed rights of entry as well as other rights as citizens. Beginning with the 1962 Commonwealth Immigrants Act, various Acts have addressed citizenship, not just restricting it, but also demarcating different degrees of citizenship and introducing concepts such as 'patrial' to identify those entitled to citizenship via their antecedents.

In Italy, the application of *jus sanguinis* citizenship is still prevalent, and has, in addition, ensured Italian citizenship for children who were born abroad of migrant parents.

On the theme of citizenship, the Treaty of Maastricht (1992) reinforces distinctions between citizens and non-citizens of the European Union. New and fundamental rights, restricted to European Union citizens, have emerged, as contained in the articles of the Treaty and the jurisprudence of the European Court of Justice. These regard the freedom of movement, the right to exercise dependent or autonomous work, and the right to settle in a state other than that of their nationality, and have access to its social services. [U. M.]

Gross, F. (1999) *Citizenship and Ethnicity: The Growth and Development of a Democratic Multiethnic Institution*, Greenwood Press, Westport, Connecticut.

Marshall, T. H. (1950) *Citizenship and Social Class*, Cambridge University Press, Cambridge.

Miller, D. (2000) *Citizenship and National Identity*, Polity Press, Cambridge.

Veca, S. (1990) *Cittadinanza. Riflessioni filosofiche sull'idea di emancipazione*, Feltrinelli, Milano.

Withol De Wenden, C. (ed.) (1988) *La Citoyenneté*, Edilig, Paris.

CIVILIZATION

(It. *civiltà*; Fr. *civilisation*; Ger. *Zivilisation*) A civilized society is a society characterized by the development of town and city life. Civilized societies are normally based upon trade, commerce or manufacture. The production of *surpluses* enables such societies to support elaborate political structures and elites dedicated to politics, religion, science, scholarship and the arts. The concept of civilization has therefore long been closely linked to ideas of progress and CULTURE. 'Civilization' has often been used as a synonym for societies at a more advanced stage of development than others. Civilization was contrasted with backwardness, barbarism and savagery (SAVAGE). In modern times terms such as 'civilization' and 'to civilize' have been used in a Eurocentric and racist manner; Westerners are the only people to be considered 'civilized' (EUROCENTRISM), to have attained the peak of human progress and to be the embodiment of progress itself. As from the sixteenth century, the West seized power and exercised colonial authority in terms of 'civilization' or a civilizing mission and used the idea of civilization as a justification for modifying cultures and dominating or enslaving peoples. COLONIALISM and imperialism (CULTURAL IMPERIALISM) destroyed or modified the cultural systems of subject countries as part of the processes of economic and political domination. The most effective form of the subordination of subjugated peoples requires that their value systems be replaced with Western value systems and that they carry in their heads beliefs in the backwardness of their own people and the cultural superiority of the dominant power (Fanon, 1970). Colonial officials, missionaries and schoolteachers were in the forefront of the civilizing mission.

The concept of civilization (i.e. to be civilized) as a *corpus* of good manners and good taste and of the progress of science and learning when formulated by Westerners was mainly attributed to their own culture. The notion of a civilizing process was developed within sociology by Norbert Elias (1982). His work describes the historical process in which people developed codes of interpersonal etiquette, emotional restraint and good manners; society becomes more peaceful and rule-governed. Even wars come to be conducted according to rules that respect non-combatants and prisoners and minimize the destruction of civilian populations. This view of human progress has been challenged by Bauman (1989), who argues that the Holocaust (SHOAH) was essentially the product of an advanced society. The bureaucratic division of labour and the detachment and depersonalization characteristic of modern industrial societies, as described by Max Weber, were prerequisites for the organization of systematic mass killings of people held ('scientifically') to be racially inferior. Thus the essentially progressive and optimistic view of Western civilization has been challenged and made part of a radical critique of Western society. This critique is taken up in other forms as part of the anti-colonial and anti-racist struggles, which require subordinated people to rediscover and celebrate their own civilization. [R. M.]

Bauman, Z. (1989) *Modernity and the Holocaust*, Polity Press, Cambridge.

Elias, N. (1978) *The History of Manners*, Blackwell, Oxford.

Elias, N. (1982) *The Civilising Process: State Formation and Civilisation*, Blackwell, Oxford.

Fanon, F. (1970) *Black Skin, White Masks*, Paladin, London.

Malik, K. (1996) *The Meaning of Race*, Macmillan, London.

COLONIALISM

(It. *colonialismo*; Fr. *colonialisme*; Ger. *Kolonialismus*) The term 'colonialism' (from the Latin *colonia*, and from *colonus*, colonist) was introduced at the end of the nineteenth century to define the position of the supporters of colonization, but is nowadays generally used to indicate, with an implicit negative connotation, the process whereby certain European societies extended their political, economic and cultural dominion to the rest of the world. Colonialism began with the great geographical 'discoveries' of the modern era and accelerated and became more entrenched with the changes brought about by the industrial revolution. It reached its apex between the end of the nineteenth century and the First World War and began to decline after the Second World War, with the rise of indigenous nationalist movements (NATIONALISM) and as independence was achieved in one colony after another. Colonialism, however, was often followed by neo-colonialism, in which unequal power relationships with these countries were still maintained, although in a situation of formal political independence. One of the main effects of colonialism was the creation of the great colonial empires of modern history: the Spanish empire in the Americas, with some colonies in Asia (Philippines) and Africa; that of Portugal in Brazil, Angola, Mozambique, Guinea-Bissau, Capo Verde, Macao and part of Timor; the British empire, which extended first to North America and to the Caribbean, then to India, Australia, New Zealand and to a large number of other Asian and African countries; that of France in North Africa, in West Africa, in Madagascar, in the Middle East, in Vietnam, in some islands of the Antilles (Haiti, Guadalupe and Martinique) and in the Pacific; that of Holland in Indonesia and in part of the Antilles and of Guyana; and that of Germany in Cameroon, Togo, south-west Africa and Tanganyika. Italy also had colonial dominions of a certain significance in Eritrea, Somalia, Libya, and, for a brief period, in Ethiopia.

Colonialism led to the 'colonial situation', which has been the subject of many sociological, anthropological and psychological studies. The impact of the West on colonized societies was analysed by Bronislaw Malinowski, Georges Balandier (1970) and Franz Fanon (1963), among others. These authors highlighted in particular the destruction of the colonized countries' traditional communities (COMMUNITY) by colonizers and the conditions of institutional inequality which existed in these countries. Inequality was in many cases exacerbated by RACISM, whether explicit or implied, and by the actual or latent violence which characterized colonial relationships and resulted in depersonalization and ALIENATION (RACE AND INEQUALITY). Other authors (Galli della Loggia, 1977) have analysed the cultural background of colonialism, which they identify with the inability of Europeans to establish non-destructive and non-subjugating relations with other civilizations (CIVILIZATION). According to these researchers, the historical significance and the essence of colonialism lie in the indiscriminate wish to extend European civilization to the world, by eliminating any different civilizations. Nevertheless, mention should be made of the objective conditions (economic, technological and military) which allowed Europe to develop and impose colonialism, with the result of creating – to quote Marx, who was one of its first critics – 'a revolutionary phenomenon despite itself' (Melotti, 1972). [U. M.]

Balandier, G. (1970) *The Sociology of Black Africa: Social Dynamics in Central Africa*, Deutsch, London.

Bertola, A. (1956) *Storia e politica coloniale e dei territori non autonomi*, Giappichelli, Torino.

Fanon, F. (1963) *The Wretched of the Earth*, Grove, New York.

Galli della Loggia, E. (1977) 'Colonialismo e colonizzazione', *Enciclopedia Europea*, Garzanti, Milano, Vol. III: 561–569.

Melotti, U. (1972) *Marx e il terzo mondo*, Il Saggiatore, Milano.

COLOUR BAR

COLOUR BAR (It. *Barriera di colore*; Fr. *barrière de couleur*; Ger. *Rassenschranke*) The term 'colour bar' indicates any kind of social and economic separation between different groups based on differences in skin colour, and constituting a barrier towards achieving real EQUALITY. This kind of separation can be actuated either through a clearly defined legal system – such as of Apartheid in South Africa – or through explicit or implicit social discrimination (RACISM). In many societies, phenomena of exclusion from social services, certain urban areas or employment opportunities, or from education and housing possibilities – either through explicit social refusal or owing to the fact that an unfair proportion of black people hold low-skilled jobs or reside in the poorest areas of cities – are evidence that black people encounter obstacles to integration associated with their skin colour. Even when such obstacles are not founded in a legal system or rigid caste-like society (CASTE), the final outcome is the creation of actual or virtual ghettos (GHETTO). In the United States, the awareness of the fact that the colour bar (color line) actually prevented black people from becoming fully integrated citizens has resulted in the implementation of AFFIRMATIVE ACTION policies in an attempt to counter the phenomenon.

The term 'colour bar' first began to be used in Great Britain after the Second World War, when a considerable number of COLOURED British citizens from various continents migrated to the United Kingdom following approval of the 1948 Nationality Act, pursuant to which all Commonwealth citizens were considered British subjects (MIGRANT, MIGRATION). Despite being British citizens, with the same rights as British residents, black British subjects were discriminated against in employment, education and housing – allegedly owing to the fact that their skin was darker than that of most autochthons – and even barred from entering clubs, shops, churches, pubs and dance halls (WHITENESS). In an attempt to counter the effects of this symbolic colour bar, the British government approved a number of Race Relations Acts (1968, 1976) (RACE RELATIONS), following the cue of the American affirmative action policies. The Acts expressly prohibited discrimination and facilitated the employment of black people in sectors such as banking and insurance, as well as improving their access to education and professional training. They also established that a body be set up to control and manage the problems linked to racial discrimination. While it is difficult to assess the success of these measures, it has become evident that measures which confine themselves to addressing legislative aspects tend to diminish in effectiveness over time.

Although an obvious source of racial tension between the white and black populations of Britain, the existence of the colour bar can be said to have indirectly contributed towards the strengthening of the 'racial' IDENTITY of many black British citizens, thus unwittingly helping to change the fundamental approach of government policies from the promotion of ASSIMILATION to the respect of racial minorities. [M. V.]

Rose, J. B. (1969) *Colour and Citizenship*, Oxford University Press, Oxford.
Solomos, J. (1989) *Race and Racism in Contemporary Britain*, Macmillan, London.

COLOUR-BLIND SOCIETY (It. *color-blind society*; Fr. *société ignorant la couleur*; Ger. *'farben-blinde' Gesellschaft*)

The term 'colour-blind society' is widely used in Anglo-Saxon countries to describe a non-racist society which pays little attention to skin colour (COLOURED, WHITENESS). The strongest supporters of this approach were black intellectuals and civil rights leaders (Walter White, Roy Wilkins and Bayard Rustin) at the beginning of the twentieth century, who maintained that racial categories would be socially irrelevant in the future, and thus countered white supporters of white supremacy and blacks who based their political struggles on the awareness of RACE and separatism. [M. V.]

Gennaro Larda, V. (1990) *From 'Melting Pot' to Multiculturalism. The Evolution of Ethnic Relations in the United States*, Bulzoni, Roma.

COLOURED (It. *coloured*; Fr. *gens de couleur*; Ger. *Farbiger*)

The term 'coloured has been primarily used in the UK and the USA to distinguish those with dark skin from those who are defined – or who define themselves – as 'white', as in the case of 'coloured immigrant'. The label 'coloured' is also often implied when reference is made to ethnic minorities (ETHNICITY), just as it is with now more discredited concepts such as half-caste or half-breed.

Already in use in the nineteenth century, the term replaced other terms whose use came to be considered derogatory such as 'Sambo', 'Blackamoor' and 'Black'. However, although the term 'coloured' appears to have been used originally to avoid negative labelling, it was often employed in a negative way. For example, according to Cesare Lombroso (1898), differences in skin colour are an evident and unequivocal sign of a human hierarchy, with whites at the apex and coloured people below. Thus coloured people were considered less genetically developed than non-coloured individuals, i.e. Whites (RACE).

However, the term is also used in a completely different, and to many extents contrary, manner. The political aim of the positive grouping of non-white populations led to the term being used throughout the twentieth century by various movements whose mission was to protect the rights of ethnic minority groups (ETHNIC MINORITY). These movements include the National

Association for the Advancement of Colored People, (NAACP), founded in 1909 following the riots in Springfield, Illinois. Open to a variety of minority ethnic groups, this is still one of the most important movements of its kind in the United States. Furthermore, the United Colored People's Association was established in the late 1960s to advance the BLACK POWER movement – a specifically *non-white people's* movement – by reuniting what it defined as all coloured populations in order to counter the white (or non-coloured) population.

During the 1970s use of the term 'coloured' was overtaken by use of the term 'black' which had once more become acceptable as a result of the success of the Black Power movement. More recently the term 'African-American' has come into use. Finally, 'coloured' has become popular in certain environments, e.g. among Pan-Africanism supporters, but has lost most of its political meaning. [M. V.]

Banton M. (1957) *White and Coloured: The Behaviour of British People towards coloured Immigrants*, Cage, London.
Bastide R. (ed.) (1977) *Schiava, la donna di colore in America Latina*, Mazzotta, Milano.
Fanon F. (1986) *Black Skin, White Masks* (1963), Pluto Press, London.
Lombroso C. (1898) *L'uomo bianco e l'uomo di colore*, Bocca, Torino.
Low, W. A., Cliff V. A (eds) (1980) *Encyclopedia of Black America*, A. Da Capo, New York.

COMMISSION FOR RACIAL EQUALITY (It. *Commission for Racial Equality*; Fr. *Commission for Racial Equality*; Ger. *Commission for Racial Equality*)

In a given society, legislation designed to eradicate or ameliorate racial inequality implicitly addresses three issues. First, what is the existing position of racial or ethnic minorities (ETHNIC MINORITY)? Secondly, what would the 'just' society look like? Thirdly, as far as these minorities are concerned, how do we progress from the existing position to a position of 'justice'? (McCrudden et al., 1991).

The 1976 Race Relations Act altered the way RACIAL DISCRIMINATION was conceived in the UK in two ways: it extended the concept of discrimination by including indirect or unintentional discrimination within the remit of the law; and it strengthened enforcement of the law. The 1976 Act also established the Commission for Racial Equality (CRE) and gave it a strategic role in enforcing the law (in England, Wales and Scotland; there is a separate organization for Northern Ireland) and equipped it with considerably more powers than those possessed by its two predecessors, the Race Relations Board and the Community Relations Commission.

The CRE was given several tasks. The first and more specific task was to combat racial discrimination. Here the CRE could assist individual complainants; it was empowered to mount formal investigations of the policies and practices of organizations and, if necessary, it could issue legally enforceable non-discrimination notices; it also has the sole power to act against discriminatory advertisements. More widely, the CRE was required to monitor the way the 1976 Race Relations Act was working and to recommend improvements to it. The second and more diffuse, though no less important, task was to encourage good relations between 'people of different racial and ethnic backgrounds' and to promote equal opportunity, for example through publicity and educational initiatives. Among many CRE publications are the following: a 10-point plan to help employers develop equal opportunity polices; a guide to achieving racial equality in the provision of services by local government; and an investigation of racial equality in education. The CRE has also published a number of Codes of Practice (covering areas such as employment, education, housing, maternity services and health care services) which, though neither legally authoritative, nor legally binding,' nevertheless offer useful guidance as to which actions or practices may contravene the law.

The weight of empirical evidence is that, despite successive Race Relations Acts in 1965, 1968 and 1976, and the widening definition in these Acts of what constitutes unlawful racial discrimination, such discrimination has continued at high levels in the UK. However, it does not follow from this that the CRE must have largely failed in its myriad tasks, even though it has been heavily criticized from a number of influential sources, including the House of Commons Sub-Committee on Race Relations and Immigration, which attacked what it perceived as the Commission's lack of cohesion and direction and its consequent ineffectiveness.

Certainly much attention has been directed to poor performance by the CRE. But there are other important factors that should be considered. For example, there may be limitations of legal enforcement in establishing standards of conduct, organizational procedures and general expectations about identifying and tackling racial discrimination. In addition, the CRE may have inadequate powers of intervention to combat discrimination and/or contradictions between anti-discrimination legislation and other legislation. For instance, in 1987 a mother demanded that her local education authority (LEA) should arrange a transfer for her young daughter out of a school which proclaimed its commitment to a multiracial and multi-faith education and where white children were in a minority, to a school where there was an overwhelming majority of white children. The LEA found itself confronted by two, apparently conflicting, pieces of legislation. On the one hand, according to Section 18 of the 1976 Race Relations Act it was unlawful for an LEA complying with its duties as provided for under various Education Acts to do anything that would constitute discrimination under the 1976 Race Relations Act. On the other hand, under the 1980 Education Act, LEAs were obliged to comply with parental preference as to choice of school (subject to certain exceptions which were irrelevant in this case), provided that vacancies existed. The Secretary of State for Education ruled that the provisions of the 1980 Education Act with regard to parental choice were inviolable and thus took precedence over the provisions of the 1976 Race Relations Act. The CRE contested this and sought a judicial review of the decision of the Secretary of State, partly on the grounds that to accede to the parent's request would be to accept what amounted to a condition of segregation between white and minority children. The judge ruled against the CRE, saying that while transferring from one school to the other moved the child apart from minority children, it did not amount to segregation; and that the obligations of the LEA to comply with parental choice did not depend on the nature of the choice or the reasons underlying it. In this case then, if there was a 'failure', it lay in the drafting of the 1976 Race Relations Act or in the way it was interpreted by the courts, rather than in any deficiency on the part of the CRE.

Lustgarten and Edwards (1992) have ascribed the ineffectiveness of the 1976 Race Relations Act to the following causes: incompetence on the part of the CRE and those who have represented those complaining of discrimination; lack of familiarity with the legislation (at least in its early years); hostility towards the Act (whether explicit or tacit) on the part of tribunals and judges; and the deficiencies in the legislation itself. Though they accepted that the effectiveness of the CRE could be increased if its powers were enhanced, they point to other complications that act to reduce the CRE's effectiveness. For example, the very fact that the CRE was given unusual, not to say unique, powers of enforcement in that it was accorded both the power to investigate and the ability to impose a sanction through the issue of a non-discrimination notice has given rise to some resistance on the part of judges, who have taken a restrictive view of CRE investigations.

The 2000 Race Relations (Amendment) Act extended anti-discrimination measures and imposed new obligations on over 300 UK public authorities to promote racial equality. The Act was seen by the CRE as playing an important role in creating what it described as 'the most positive and favourable climate for [its] work . . . ever seen in the UK' and the CRE claimed that the Act owed much to the recommendations that it had made in its periodic reviews of the 1976 Race Relations Act (CRE, 2000b). Though the CRE endorsed the general approach and the nature of the proposals contained in the consultation document that had preceded the Act, it took the view that in order to produce what it described as a 'joined-up' approach to racial equality, the obligations set out in the Act ought to be applied to *all* public authorities with functions relevant to racial equality.

The CRE's Annual Report for 2000 gives a good indication of the range of its anti-discrimination activities: it describes the initiation of formal investigations into the Ford Motor Company, the Crown Prosecution Service (Croydon) and the Prison Service. For example, the terms of the investigation into the Prison Service concerned, *inter alia*, the elimination of unlawful racial discrimination and the way in which complaints of such discrimination were investigated and acted upon by prison governors and others within the Prison Service (CRE, 2000b). The Report also reviewed progress made under a Partnership Agreement signed two years previously by the CRE and the Ministry of Defence. This dealt with a number of issues, such as the achievement of ethnic minority recruitment goals in the three armed services and the barriers to ethnic minority promotion within the armed forces (CRE, 2000b). The Report gave details of cases of alleged discrimination in which the CRE had offered legal advice and support to complainants. Thus in 2000 about 11,000 people had approached the CRE for advice, of whom just over 1,500 had applied for assistance to pursue their complaint. In addition to settling 83 cases at an early stage (for a total sum exceeding £400,000), the CRE secured more than £1.3 million in out-of-court settlements and of those cases heard at tribunals, 18 succeeded and 22 were dismissed (CRE, 2000b: 13–14).

Yet these activities received far less attention than did the CRE's attempt to keep 'race' out of the 2001 general election campaign. The CRE had arranged for the party leaders to sign an anti-racism pledge in a public ceremony at the House of Commons, but when individual candidates were invited to follow suit, three Conservative MPs refused to do so, whereupon the

CRE decided to publish their names on its website. In an editorial *The Times* accused the CRE of having provoked 'a destructive controversy' and of harming 'its own reputation by permitting an otherwise worthy, if vacuous, statement on race to become a vehicle for partisan sniping' (*The Times*, 23 April 2001). [P. B.]

Commission for Racial Equality (1981) *BL Cars Ltd: A Report of a Formal Investigation*, CRE, London.
Commission for Racial Equality (1988) *Learning in Terror*, CRE, London.
Commission for Racial Equality (1993) *Racism through the Nineties*, CRE, London.
Commission for Racial Equality (1998) *Racial Equality Means Quality: a Standard for Racial Equality for Local Government*, CRE, London.
Commission for Racial Equality (2000a) *Learning for All: Standards for Racial Equality in Schools* (for schools in England and Wales), CRE, London.
Commission for Racial Equality (2000b) *Annual Report*, CRE, London.
Lustgarten, L., Edwards, J. (1992) 'Racial inequality and the limits of the law', in Braham, P., Rattansi, A., Skellington, R. (eds), *Racism and AntiRacism: Inequalities, Opportunities and Policies*, Sage, London.
McCrudden, C., Smith, D., Brown, C. (1991) *Racial Justice at Work*, Policy Studies Institute, London.
Brown, C., Gay, P. (1986) *17 Years after the Act*, Policy Studies Institute, London.

COMMUNITY

(It. *comunità*; Fr. *communauté*; Ger. *Gemeinschaft*) From the Latin *communitas*, a unified body of individuals, the term 'community' is one of the most important words in the modern and contemporary political, philosophical and sociological lexicon. A community is any large or small group of people sharing a common history, language, set of values or goals (CULTURE). In its basic meaning, the term 'community' refers to our life together, and the bonds which sustain that life together. Indeed a 'community' can be a small group of people living in the same village or a group of citizens sharing a common goal. The term can also apply to very large groups, such as a NATION, whose members, despite their diversity, share common political institutions, symbols and memories. A community is 'constitutive' when its members' IDENTITY is chiefly constituted by their belonging to that community. Ethnic minorities (ETHNIC MINORITY) or other strongly culturally defined groups are undoubtedly constitutive communities; however, local communities, self-help groups, gay people, female workers, foreigners seeking political asylum, people suffering from the same chronic disease or the same disability – to cite a few – can also be seen to comprise, or may easily form, constitutive communities.

Throughout history, the term 'community' has been used in a wide variety of ways. During the Romantic period it was used by Schleiermacher to indicate a form of social life characterized by an organic, intrinsic and perfect bond between its members, while Tönnies contrasted the concept of community (*Gemeinschaft*) with that of society (*Gesellschaft*). Tönnies' definition of *Gemeinschaft* is particularly relevant to RACE and ETHNICITY as it represents a crucial development in the school of thought which, at the end of the nineteenth century, compared 'modern Western' society with 'other' societies. According to Tönnies, a *Gemeinschaft* is a social group in which the collective will prevails over the egoistic interests of its individual members, harmony prevails over competition, co-operation prevails over conflict and nature prevails over artifice. The model example of the *Gemeinschaft* is the rural village, which Tönnies contrasts with the industrial city. Nevertheless, even in large industrial metropolises the typical bonds of SOLIDARITY of the *Gemeinschaft* can be found in areas with a high concentration of individuals belonging to the same ethnic group or the same social class. Other sociologists (Simmel, Cooley, Weber, Durkheim) mitigated the positive prejudice in favour of the *Gemeinschaft*, until, by the middle of the twentieth century, the term 'community' came to be used mainly in reference to an area in which social relations of a localized type were prevalent, and in contrast to relations of a cosmopolitical type (COSMOPOLITISM). The Chicago School of Sociology proposed the term 'natural area ' to indicate areas in which subcultures – defined in terms of race and ethnicity (white, black, Hispanic, oriental, etc.) and social class (manual workers, sub-proletariat, etc.) – are concentrated as if a sort of village within the city. The importance of the values of land and blood ties to the concept of *Gemeinschaft* eventually led to its association with Nazi ideology and so to it becoming seriously compromised. During the second half of the twentieth century, empirical sociology (Merton, 1967) preferred to refer to the concept of 'group of reference' – a term with no spatial or localized relations – as opposed to *Gemeinschaft*. The term 'group of reference' refers to any group which makes a considerable contribution to determining the identity of its individuals and so ethnic groups are undoubtedly to be considered 'groups of reference'.

The term 'community' is now seeing a new wave of popularity thanks to the theory of communitarianism. Central to communitarianism is the concept of 'inclusive communities', based on 'the three communitarian principles of co-operative enquiry, mutual responsibility, and citizen participation' (Tam, 1998: vii). In this sense, inclusive communities are those which are open to newcomers, so long as they subscribe to their basic values. Even if the idea of inclusive communities is based on values very close to those which underlie the notion of *Gemeinschaft*, there is a basic difference between the two concepts: while the source of values in the *Gemeinschaft* is local tradition and culture, values in inclusive communities spring from informed community consent: questions about values are dealt with by the citizens themselves deliberating through public debate. Each individual may belong to several overlapping inclusive communities (a neighbourhood, a professional group, a co-operative enterprise, a region, a country), each one operating under the principle of 'subsidiarity', that is to say that any decision should be taken at the most decentralized level compatible with that decision. The concept of inclusive communities has been proposed as a viable alternative to both integrationist and segregationist approaches to multiethnic societies (MULTICULTURALISM). [Em. M.]

Etzioni, A. (1995) *The Spirit of Community*, Fontana, London.

Lawler, P. A., McConkey, D. (1998) *Community and Political Thought Today*, Praeger, New York.

Merton, R. K. (1967) *On Theoretical Sociology; Five Essays, Old and New*, Free Press, New York.

Tam, H. (1998) *Communitarianism. A New Agenda for Politics and Citizenship*, Macmillan, London.

Tönnies, F. (1988) *Community and Society/ Gemeinschaft und Gesellschaft*, Transaction Books, New Brunswick, NJ.

Walzer, M. (1999) *On Toleration*, Yale University Press, New Haven, CT.

COMPLEMENTARISM (It. *complementarismo;*
Fr. *complémentarisme;* Ger. *Komplementarismus*) The notion of complementarity – from the Latin *complementum,* deriving from *complere,* to fill – taken from Bohr's theory, was applied to ETHNOPSYCHIATRY by Georges Devereux (1972). As it is impossible to integrate knowledge acquired through ethnology and the methods of interpretation offered by psychoanalysis into a single theory, the complementarity method can be conceived as a possible scientific 'meeting point' for the two disciplines. For Devereux, the psychoanalytic experiment not only elicits the behaviour which it studies, but also creates it – as the opponents of psychoanalysis told the psychoanalyst all along (though he refused to listen). This is the reason why – according to Devereux – one can never be certain whether data provided by 'native healers' represent authentic scientific facts or whether they are mere fantasies derived from a model of cultural thinking. [Ar.C.]

Devereux, G. (1972) *Ethnopsychanalyse complémentariste,* Flammarion, Paris.

CONCENTRATION CAMP AND DEATH CAMP (It. *campo di concentramento e di sterminio;* Fr. *camp de concentration et d'extermination;* Ger. *Konzentrations und Vernichtungslager*) - Concentration camps and death camps are locations in which individuals considered dangerous enemies to national security for political, ethnic, racial, religious, etc. reasons are placed in forced racial segregation. Camp prisoners hardly ever receive fair trial.

According to their purpose, camps may be distinguished into concentration camps (where prisoners are simply segregated), labour camps (where prisoners are both segregated and forced to perform hard labour) and death camps (where the killing of the prisoners is the fundamental aim). The common objective of all camps is to neutralize their prisoners' personality through humiliation and terror. Prisoners may be stripped, shaved, forced to wear a uniform, identified by a number rather than a name, deprived of privacy, threatened with punishment and made to fight for survival.

The first concentration camps were built by the British in the late nineteenth century in order to contain prisoners and civilians at the time of the Boer War. The most notorious modern concentration camps were those organized by the Nazi regime (*Lager*). Over 2,000 camps, subcamps, external *Kommandos,* collection and transit centres were built in various parts of Germany and the occupied territories between 1939 and 1945. The main camps were Auschwitz (the largest death camp), Dachau (in 1933, the first camp to be opened), Buchenwald, Treblinka and Mauthausen. Millions of Jews (JEW) were imprisoned in these camps (ANTI-SEMITISM) although prisoners also included gypsies (ROMA), homosexuals, Jehovah's Witnesses, Allied prisoners of war and political activists of various nationalities – including Germans – who had opposed the Nazis: all of these prisoners were considered 'enemies of the Aryan RACE'.

A number of concentration camps and transit centres (Borgo San Dalmazzo, Bolzano, Fossoli di Carpi) were set up in Italy, mostly in the north, although there was also a death camp (Risiera di San Sabba) in Trieste. From these concentration camps prisoners were subsequently deported to camps under Nazi control.

Concentration and labour camps were also built under many communist regimes in a large number of colonies. They were often euphemistically referred to as 're-education' or 'correction' camps. The concentration camps built under Stalin in the former Soviet Union were known as *gulags* – a mnemonic of the title *Glavnoe Upravlenie ispravitel'no – trudovych Lagerei* (Corrective Labour Camps Headquarters), a term which became popular following publication of *The Gulag Archipelago* (1973) by the dissident A. I. Solzhenitsyn.

Concentration camps have once more become a topic for debate following the actions of various Asiatic, African and South American dictators and, more recently, during the war in ex-Yugoslavia. [M. V.]

Various authors (1995) *Voci dalla Shoah. Testimonianze per non dimenticare*, La Nuova Italia, Firenze.

Amery, A. (1987) *Intellettuale a Auschwitz*, Bollati Boringhieri, Torino.

Armaroli, A., Grattarola, A. (1988) *Razzismo di ieri, razzismo di oggi*, Thema, Bologna.

Bender, B. (1995) *L'ombra dell'Olocausto. Ricordi di due vite*, La Giuntina, Firenze.

Boursier, G., Converso, M., Iacomini, F. (1996) *Zigeuner. Lo sterminio dimenticato*, Sinnos, Roma.

Levi, P. (1947) *If This is a Man*, Penguin, London.

Mitscherlich, A., Mielke, F. (1960) *Unmenschliche Medizin*, Suhrkamp, Frankfurt am Main.

Picciotto Fargion, L. (1945) *Il libro della memoria. Gli ebrei deportati dall'Italia (1943–45)*, Mursia, Milano.

Poliakov, L. (1955) *Il nazismo e lo sterminio degli ebrei*, Einaudi, Torino.

Solzhenitsyn, A. (1973–1978) *The Gulag Archipelago*, trans. Whitney, T.P., Willets, H. (1999), Harvill Press, London.

CONFORMISM (It. *conformismo*; Fr. *conformisme*; Ger.

Konformismus) The term 'conformism' derives from the verb 'to conform' – from the Latin *cum* and *forma* – and describes a social process in which an individual complies with the behavioural, moral and legal standards of a group or society. Although conformism is often scorned in Western society as a type of behaviour which destroys an individual's creativity and reduces his or her freedom of choice, it is also acknowledged as a process fundamental to the existence of society. In order to create an organized society, its members must adapt to certain common rules, thereby ensuring that their behaviour is at least partly predictable and co-ordinated and that the division of society into groups – characterized by genre, generation, employment, etc. – is 'natural', accepted and admitted, even if such divisions seem unjust.

Experimental psychology and anthropological research establish that conformism is influenced by two elements: information and norms. Although both are superimposed in a wide range of situations and condition individual behaviour, they must be kept separate from a methodological point of view. The influence of information leads a group to define the perception and, therefore, social reality of the individual, i.e. the situation is defined by the way it is perceived by the majority of the group. Even if an individual has doubts as to the correctness of this definition, it is painful and/or difficult for the individual to disagree and oppose. This type of influence mostly concerns social representations, opinions and moral judgements.

The laws of the society in which he or she lives force an individual to adapt to the behavioural patterns and lifestyles of the majority of the group in order to receive economic and social reward and/or to avoid being condemned and excluded (ADAPTATION). Many research projects (Berkman and Syme, 1979; Russell, Cutrona, Rose and Jurko, 1984) have demonstrated the difficulties encountered by individuals when faced with the risk of social isolation. Eccentricity and personalized behavioural patterns are rarely admired and often condemned.

Although a number of well-known studies (Berry, 1967; Cooper, 1979; Turner, 1991) state that an individual's personality influences his or her tendency to conform, such conformity is certainly determined and/or heightened by cultural factors such as the attractive appeal of the bond of the group, the need to choose behavioural patterns, make judgements and affirm opinions before a large number of people. In such cases, the group may exercise its social control effectively and define the reality shared by its members. Conformism is induced by the unanimity and resoluteness of group expression, rather than sheer size.

Gender is another element which apparently influences this social process. Although little and rather vague research has been carried out on this aspect, women are claimed to be more conformist than men. This is probably due to the different status of women in comparison with men in most societies: women are generally expected to be diligent and obedient while men are encouraged to be independent and autonomous.

Total adaptation to the behavioural patterns, opinions and morals of the group tends to make an individual rather 'invisible', and if he or she wishes to gain prestige and social elevation, he/she must know how to balance his/her independence and autonomy very carefully.

In a complex industrialized society each social, generational or gender group includes various statuses which make conformism more dynamic and create a situation in which individuals of a higher social level become anti-conformist and are penalized less than other members of a lower social level. A series of research projects (Hollander, 1985; Moscovici and Paicheler, 1983) has demonstrated that as long as the privileged members abide by the more general rules of the group, anti-conformist behaviour actually increases their level of influence, i.e. their prestigious status among the majority means they are allowed to be innovative if they abide by the group's basic rules.

The capacity of mass media to spread almost without limits is an experience unique to our species, which has never been reached in such a general way and by such a large amount of messages with similar contents and, above all, communication structures. Its homologating force (HOMOLOGATION) and the differential action it probably exercises when it reaches the diverse cultures and societies of its users is still uncertain. However, it is an extremely powerful means of distributing the models to which mankind must adapt and conform. [M. C. G.]

Benedict, R. (1934) *Patterns of Cultures*, New American Library, New York.

Berkman, L. F., Syme, S. L. (1979) 'Social networks, host resistance, and mortality: a nine years follow-up study of Alameda County residence', *American Journal of Epidemiology*, 109: 186–204.

Berry, J. W. (1967) 'Independence and conformity in subsistence-level societies', *Journal of Personality and Social Psychology*, 7: 415–418.

Cooper, K. M. (1979) 'Statistically combining independent studies: a meta-analysis of sex differences in conformity research', *Journal of Personality and Social Psychology*, 37: 131–146.

Gellner, E. (1974) *The Legitimation of Belief*, Cambridge University Press, Cambridge.

Hollander, E. P. (1985) 'Leadership and power', in Lindzey, G., Aronson, E. (eds), *Handbook of Social Psychology*, vol. II, Special Fields and Applications, III ed., Random House, New York, pp. 485–538.

Moscovici, S., Paicheler, G. (1983) 'Minority or majority influences: social change, compliance, and conversion', in Blumberg, H. H., Hare, A. P., Kent, V., Davies, M. F. (eds), *Small Groups and Social Interactions*, Vol. 1, Wiley, New York, pp. 215–224.

Russell, D., Cutrona, C. E., Rose, J., Jurko, K. (1984) 'Social and emotional lonliness: an examination on Weiss's typology of lonliness', *Journal of Personality and Social Psychology*, 46: 1313–1321.

Turner, J. C. (1991) *Social Influence*, Brooks/Cole, Pacific Grove.

COSMOPOLITISM

(It. *cosmopolitismo*; Fr. *cosmopolitisme*; Ger. *Kosmopolitismus*) From the Greek *kosmos* (world) and *polis* (city), the term 'cosmopolitism' refers to a concept which considers all human beings to be the citizens of one nation, implying a spirit of universal fellowship which goes beyond differences in nationality (NATION) and RACE. Cosmopolitism was first theorized in the fourth century BC by the cynics, who rejected the institution of individual states which, in their opinion, prevented human beings from exercising their highest right – individual freedom.

The same attitude was a precept of the universalism which took hold during the Enlightenment in the eighteenth century, and which, inspired by the law of nature determined through human reason, contemplated universal brotherhood between free and equal persons (EQUALITY) as – Kant states – the destiny of human beings justified by a natural tendency in this direction.

Both the recognition of the universal human rights of man and the utopia originating from the misinterpretation of historical events are based on this concept. In any case, cosmopolitism remains a principle to be defended, as it is based on the respect of the dignity of all human beings without distinction and on the search for a better quality of life.

Cosmopolitism should be distinguished from the universalism of the Catholic Church and of many other religions, which is founded on metaphysical principles rather than reason. [S. G.]

Kant, I. (1974) *Anthropology from a Pragmatic Point of View* (1798), Martinus Nijhoff, The Hague.

Scarpetta, G. (1981) *Eloge du cosmopolitisme*. Grasset, Paris.

CREOLE

(It. *Lingua creola*; Fr. *langue créole*; Ger. *kreolisch*) Mixed linguistic systems, generally originating in ex-colonial areas as a result of contact between a European language and other native or imported languages, Creole languages have developed to such an extent as to become mother tongues.

Creole languages first developed as secondary languages – much reduced and simplified – known as PIDGIN languages, yet they differ from these latter in that (1) they have been passed on from generation to generation within the family (as a mother tongue); and (2) their vocabulary and internal structure have been enriched to such an extent that they have become a distinct variant of the European language in which they found their roots. Creole languages can be classified on the basis of their lexical derivation into Portuguese, Spanish,

English, French and Dutch. However, alongside the obvious colonial origins of the languages, they also show traces of many other influences – phonetic, lexical and structural – deriving from other autochthonic languages or languages imported during the complex ethnolinguistic changes caused by the slave trade (SLAVERY) and COLONIALISM.

Modern usage of the term 'Creole' (from the Portuguese *criuolo* meaning 'a servant born in the master's house') refers to the descendants of both European colonists and slaves born in the New World. Since the nineteenth century the meaning of term has also been broadened to encompass cultural expressions (e.g. Creole cuisine), languages and literature.

Paradigmatic examples of the development of Creole languages can be seen in the Creoles of the Antilles and the Caribbean, and especially the Creole of Haiti. Originally a French-based pidgin language spoken by the indigenous population and people of mainly African origins deported as slaves to the Caribbean plantations, Creole was the only language spoken by the majority of the population of Haiti until the proclamation of independence in 1807. Since 1987, Creole – alongside French – has been an OFFICIAL LANGUAGE of the state. According to the linguists Dillard (1971) and Labov (1971), an interesting evolution of the Creole and pidgin languages originally spoken by the African slaves is African-American Vernacular English (EBONICS).

The expression 'Creole language' can also be applied to mixed linguistic systems in areas not influenced by European languages (for example Swahili, which probably originated as the result of contact between Arabic and the Bantu language); however, such an interpretation would lead to almost all languages being considered mixed or

Creole languages – a phenomenon which can be compared with the biological interbreeding of human beings. [A. B., R. B.]

Crystal, D. (1997) *The Cambridge Encyclopedia of Language*, Cambridge University Press, Cambridge.
Dillard, J.L. (1971) 'The Creolist and the study of Negro non-standard dialects in the continental United States', in Dell Hymes (ed.), *Pidginization and Creolization of Languages*, Cambridge University Press, Cambridge, pp. 394–408.
Encyclopaedia Britannica (1997) www.eb.com.
Holm, J. (1988) *Pidgins and Creoles*, Cambridge University Press, Cambridge.
Journal of Pidgin and Creole Languages, www.siu.edu.
Labov, W. (1971) 'The notion of "system" in Creole studies', in Del Hymes (ed.), *Pidginization and Creolization of Languages*, Cambridge University Press, Cambridge, pp. 447–72.
McArthur, T. (ed.) (1992) *The Oxford Companion to the English Language*, Oxford University Press, Oxford.
Mounin, G. (1993) *Dictionnaire de la linguistique*, PUF, Paris.

CROSS-CULTURAL MEDIATION (It. *mediazione linguistico culturale*; Fr. *médiation linguistique interculturelle*; Ger. *interkulturelle Vermittlung*) Cross-cultural mediation describes a varied and wide-ranging set of participation strategies used to facilitate communication between individuals or communities (COMMUNITY) from different cultures. The aim of cross-cultural mediation is to reduce risks of intercultural conflict, and/or to avoid the phenomenon of MARGINALIZATION, which may result from lack of awareness of the linguistic or behavioural codes of the cultures involved.

The term is also used to describe the introduction of legislative or procedural changes aimed at producing a greater understanding of the cultural, linguistic and religious differences present in a multicultural society (MULTICULTUR-ALISM).

So cross-cultural mediation can refer to both specific integration strategies involving a third party (the mediator) – whose familiarity with the language and culture of both the MIGRANT and host communities allows her/him to act as an interface between the two parties – and a point of reference and political repre-sentation for ethnic and cultural mino-rities.

Cross-cultural mediation can be divided into three areas of activity. The most immediately obvious cross-cultural mediator is the interpreter, who is often not merely required to provide linguistic translation but also called upon to interpret cultural differences. Many groups in European countries provide professional interpreting services (on-line, live, in municipal offices, and during specific legal cases). These agen-cies are staffed either by members of the minority or immigrant community in question, or by people from the host community with a full knowledge of the particular immigrant or minority cul-ture, who are able to communicate in the native language of the group concerned or by means of a third, common language (VEHICULAR LANGUAGE). Many examples of this type of media-tion, both public and private, can be found in reception centres (RECEPTION CENTRE), national health services, schools, job centres, social security offices, post offices, voluntary associa-tions, law enforcement agencies, frontier police, courts and prisons. However, should the services offered by the interpreter merely concern linguistic problems and provide no intercultural

or interethnic contribution, the inter-preter can no longer be considered a cross-cultural mediator but is merely a party able to ensure the smooth running of services and the breaking down of barriers (creating so-called *user-friendly* services).

The ETHNICIZATION of services, although not strictly speaking a form of cross-cultural mediation, should also be mentioned. This involves the modifica-tion of existing services to reflect the growing ethnic diversity within a given society, and more specifically, the attempt to make these services more sensitive to the differing ethnic, cultural and religious needs of various commu-nities, especially ETHNIC MINORITY or immigrant groups. It should be empha-sized that prior to ethnicizing a service in this way, some form of cross-cultural mediation is required in order to recognize the legitimacy of the demands consequent upon the establishment of significant ethnic communities in a particular society (as in the case of CIRCUMCISION or the Muslim diet).

Political or legislative cross-cultural mediation is necessary when common ground must be found in order to reconcile conflicting cultural demands and values and thus permit the coex-istence of different ethnic communities. Obviously this kind of mediation goes far beyond direct participation in meet-ings either between individuals and the community or even between commu-nities of different cultural backgrounds; instead it becomes an exclusively poli-tical phenomenon.

Although there is no doubt about the value of the work of interpreters in improving communication between immigrants and the host community, the term 'mediation' suggests a concept which goes beyond mere establishment of linguistic understanding between two cultures. In fact, the attempt to solve conflict arising from cultural differences by means of mediation based on a linguistic interpretation alone could lead to absurd conclusions. According to this interpretation there ought to be no cultural conflict between the Mahgreb and the French, and, even if there were, nothing could be done as there are no real linguistic barriers. Obviously, experience has shown not only the presence of considerable cultural conflict but also a real and proper need to implement strategies of mediation. [A. B., R. B.]

Blanchard M. M. (1999) 'Médiation familiale et contexte interculturel: articulation du travail social et de la dynamique associative', *Vie Sociale*, 2.

Castiglioni M. (1997) *La mediazione linguistico culturale. Principi, strategie, esperienze*, Franco Angeli, Milano.

Cohen-Emerique, M. (1997) 'La négociation interculturelle, phase essentielle de l'intégration des migrants', *Hommes et Migrations*, 1208, July–August: 923.

Kaufert, J. M. (1990) 'Sociological and anthropological perspectives on the impact of interpreters on clinician/client communication', *Santé, Culture, Health*, 7(2–3): 209–235.

Klugman, J. (1992) 'Negotiating agreements and resolving disputes across cultures', *Mediation Quarterly*, special issue (Diversity. Some implications for mediation), 9(4) summer: 387–390.

Legault, G. (ed.) (2000) *L'intervention interculturelle*, Gaëtan Morin Éditeur, Montréal and Paris.

Smith, M. (1995) 'Mediation for children, youth and families: a service continuum', *Mediation Quarterly*, special issue (Victim and offender mediation: international perspectives on theory, research and practice), 12(3) spring: 277–283.

CROSS-CULTURAL MEDICINE (It. *Medicina transculturale*; Fr. *médecine interculturelle*; Ger. *transkulturelle Medizin*)

Advocates of 'cross-cultural medicine' wish to draw attention to the extent to which medical science combines knowledge and actions strongly related to the specific culture in which it is practised with the result that medical treatment differs according to culture. Indeed, they would argue that the close relationship between medicine and CULTURE and the specific symptoms of disease mean that certain pathological conditions cannot be adequately cured by a therapeutic approach which does not recognize cultural differences.

The most challenging aspect of cross-cultural medicine is the need to focus on understanding the concept of health and illness according to the patient's cultural background. In this sense cross-cultural medicine, which embraces contributions from various cultures and disciplines such as anthropology, sociology and psychology, stands in sharp contrast to the prevailing positivistic approach, with its mechanical view of the human body and its concept of medicine as a neutral scientific model able to interpret and treat any disease.

Cross-cultural medicine takes a very different theoretical and practical approach to medical treatment: its advocates wish first to recognize and draw benefit from other, often highly sophisticated, medical systems developed in other cultures, and then to apply this knowledge to the practical problems involved in understanding and treating people from different cultures. [A. B., R. B.]

Augé, M., Herzlich, C. (eds) (1983) *The Meaning of Illness: The Anthropology, History and Sociology of Illness* (Social Orders, Vol. V), Hanwood Academic Publishers, Australia.

Cassel, E. J. (1976) *The Healer Art: A New Approach to the Doctor–Patients Relationship*, Lippincott, New York.

Corin, E., Bibeau, G., Martin, J. C., Laplante, R. (1990) *Comprendre pour soigner autrement*, Les Presses de l'Université de Montréal, Montréal.

Del Vecchio Good, M., Brodwin, P. E., Good, B. J., Kleinman, A. (1992) *Pain as Human Experience: An Anthropological Perspective*, California University Press, Berkeley.

Kleinman, A. (1980) *Patients and Healer in the Context of Culture*, California University Press, Berkeley.

Voltaggio, F. (1992) *L'arte della guarigione nelle culture umane*, Bollati Boringhieri, Torino.

CULTURAL AREAS (It. *aree culturali*; Fr. *aires culturelles*; Ger. *Kulturgebiete, Kulturräume*)

The expression 'cultural areas' is used to indicate geographical regions within which shared cultural traits are found. These mainly concern common characteristics such as language, similar artistic traditions (ART AND ETHNICITY) and analogous social and cultural systems. Various schools of thought have used the concept of cultural area, although it was first formulated by Franz Boas (CULTURAL RELATIVISM) with regard to the Indian populations of America. [Al. C.]

Boas, F. (1962) *Anthropology and Modern Life* (1929), Norton, New York.

CULTURAL DETERMINISM (It. *determinismo culturale*; Fr. *déterminisme culturel*; Ger. *kultureller Determinismus*)

The philosophical doctrine of 'cultural determinism' assumes that every event, human action and choice is determined by the CULTURE within which preceding events and states of affairs have taken place, with the consequence that freedom from the influence of culture is illusory. The doctrine denies the element of chance or contingency and is opposed to indifference, or indeterminism, which maintains that preceding cultural circumstances do not definitely determine subsequent ones. As cultural determinism is generally assumed to be true of all events except volition, the doctrine is of greatest importance when applied to ethics. In modern anthropology, the theory was first affirmed by Franz Boas and his school (CULTURAL RELATIVISM). According to this school, cross-culturally valid terms and categories are not possible. Boas also maintained that cultures and their component traits and institutions cannot be subjected to comparative conclusions or generalizations and that each culture represents a particular configuration of elements and must be understood only in terms of its uniqueness. Boas' school is sometimes referred to as historical particularism, as it is critical of generalization.

Cultural determinism should not be confused with three other kinds of causal explanation of cultural patterns: material determinism, social determinism, and ideological determinism – which ultimately reflect different philosophies of which human needs are the most basic. Ideological, or more appropriately cognitive, determinists believe that the most basic human need is to establish some system of ordering an infinitely variable and chaotic natural, social and internal world. Accordingly, culture is mainly a system of ideas or cognitive (thought) categories and principles that helps to reduce confusion by neatly classifying and interrelating raw experience. Technology, subsistence, social organization, and other cultural systems are a further consequence of mental ordering. Social determinists maintain that population patterns, social groupings and especially the need to maintain a social order form the fundamental underpinnings of human existence. Ideology, technology and other cultural systems develop in relation to their importance in upholding social institutions. Material determinists or materialists hold that cultural institutions are most important because they meet basic needs for stable and efficient subsistence production. Accordingly, the development of technologies and the exploitation of the natural environment to provide food and other necessities constitute a central human concern and determine other aspects of culture, including social institutions and their beliefs and values. [S. G.]

Boas, F. (1911) *The Mind of Primitive Man*, Macmillan, New York.
Herskovits, M. (1972) *Cultural Relativism: Perspectives in Cultural Pluralism*, Random House, New York.
Shweder, R. A. (1991) *Thinking through Cultures*, Harvard University Press, Cambridge, MA.
Spiro, M. (1986) 'Cultural relativism and the future of anthropology', *Cultural Anthropology*, 1: 259–286.

CULTURAL EVOLUTIONISM (It. *evoluzionismo culturale*; Fr. *évolutionisme culturel*; Ger. *kultureller Evolutionismus*)

From the Latin *evolutionem*, from *evolvere*, formed of *ex-*, from, and *volgere*, to turn, to roll – the term 'evolutionism' was first used in a negative sense by the American culturalist school of Franz Boas (CULTURAL RELATIVISM) and the English school of functionalism to define the beliefs and methods of many anthropological schools of the second half of the nineteenth century. 'Evolutionist' theories can be said to be those which presume the existence of a single model of CIVILIZATION and a single and necessary evolutionary path for mankind comprising different stages, culminating in modern European society. In this context, the term is often used as a synonym of 'positivism', the theoretical foundations of which can be traced back to the evolutionist positivism of Herbert Spencer (1820–1903), and which privileges the idea of a constant progress involving the whole of humanity.

As from the 1950s, the evolutionist view found renewed vigour in the American current known as neo-evolutionism, multilinear evolutionism or cultural ecology. Claiming that this descended from nineteenth-century evolutionism, Leslie White founded a school of cultural evolution in the United States based on principles that rejected the racial determinism and rationalism of Victorian anthropologists, and in some ways advocated a Boasian view of culture. Leslie White's (1959) main thesis was that the driving force in culture and human affairs was technology and its ability to transform natural resources into energy available for human use. Cultures and societies assumed different forms and institutions to the extent that they were able to capture different amounts of energy from the natural environment. Each society could be assigned a figure for the energy that its particular tool kit could produce. This energy could be more broadly identified in terms of technological categories defined by one of a limited number of subsistence technologies. Cultural ecology was founded by another American, Julian Steward (1955), who adopted some of White's ideas but observed that a culture's subsistence base was as dependent upon its local environment as it was on its technology. Accordingly, he proposed a local ecology model which emphasized the influence of technology, natural resource availability and certain social variables, such as population and inter-group relationships. Steward actually referred to his theory as one of multilineal rather than unilineal evolution and reflected some of the historical particularist influences from his mentor Alfred Kroeber, one of Boas' main disciples. [Ar. C.]

Geertz, C. (2000) *The Interpretation of Cultures*, Basic Books, New York.
Laburthe-Tolra, P., Warnier J. P. (1993) *Ethnologie et anthropologie*, PUF, Paris.
Steward, J. H. (1955) *Theory of Culture Change. The Methodology of Multilinear Evolution*, University of Illinois Press.
White, L. (1959) *The Evolution of Culture*, McGraw-Hill, New York.

CULTURAL IMPERIALISM (It. *imperialismo culturale*; Fr. *impérialisme culturel*; Ger. *Kulturimperialismus*)

This idea gained currency in the decades between the mid-1960s and the mid-1980s, allied with the then popular theories of economic dependency and world systems. Dependency theory, and later, the concept of cultural imperialism, originated in the concerns of radical economists and sociologists in Latin America regarding US domination of their economies and societies. The central economic thesis of the *dependistas* is summed up in the argument that the development of the metropolitan powers continuously underdevelops the poorer countries. The process was said to be the result of the poorer countries' reliance on the export of primary commodities, a dependence produced by previous histories of COLONIALISM and imperialism, and their consequent need to import manufactured goods from the metropolitan powers. A transfer of economic surplus from the poorer to the richer countries was thereby ensured, and in addition the direction of development in the poorer countries was said to be too strongly influenced by multinational corporations which imposed a consumption pattern unsuitable for poor countries whose priority should have been the production of low cost basic necessities rather than the import of expensive consumer goods which were largely geared to the lifestyles of elites who were, in turn, linked by economic and cultural ties to the metropolitan countries (Frank, 1967; Schuurman, 1993). World-systems theory developed the main insights of the dependency view by positing a self-sustaining circle of global production and consumption in which the 'core' countries of the West dominated the economies of the 'peripheral', poorer countries which were forced to participate in an unequal system of world trade (Schuurman, 1993).

The cultural imperialism argument has never been as easy to set out as its economic counterpart, mainly because a number of different emphases were always part of the claims being advanced. The thesis, depending upon who was articulating it, varied from the view that the key issue was domination of an increasing part of the globe by an individualist and money-fixated 'American way of life' via cultural products connected to mass communications – films, television programmes, comics, news flows – stemming from the United States of America, to the argument that the real problem was the cultural swamping of all poorer regions by Western ideologies of capitalist consumerism (Tomlinson, 1991). The differences between the two claims are significant, for the former posited an affinity of interests between, say, Chile and France, while the latter resulted in a wide-scale opposition to all Western (capitalist) cultural products. Critics of cultural imperialism have also differed according to whether they focused more narrowly on the mass media or more broadly on all forms of Western technology and expertise which dominated the economies and institutions of poorer countries. Protests against 'Coca-Colonization' and 'McDonaldization' have managed to combine a variety of these concerns (Ritzer, 1996).

The cultural imperialism thesis is problematic in many respects, but it has been particularly weakened by the inability of researchers to demonstrate that cultural products such as television programmes and films are consumed and absorbed in an uncritical manner by audiences. Empirical studies, for example of the globally popular American TV series *Dallas*, have tended to suggest instead that viewers, while enjoying the narrative, were nevertheless less enthusiastic about the values and lifestyles portrayed in the programmes (Ang, 1985; Liebes and Katz, 1993). Similarly, with regard to the American comic *Donald Duck*, which was the centrepiece of a famous critique of cultural imperialism by Dorfman and Mattelart (1975), subsequent readings have revealed the variety of possible interpretations, some hostile to American capitalism, which are enabled by the narratives and characters in the texts (Barker, 1989).

Although Dorfman and Mattelart did point to derogatory racial stereotypes as a feature of *Donald Duck*, issues of racism and ethnicity have played little part in debates on cultural imperialism. Two major re-evaluations of the debates, Tomlinson's *Cultural Imperialism* (1991) and *Beyond Cultural Imperialism* (1997) edited by Golding and Harris, fail to provide any consideration of questions of 'RACE'. This is curious, given that a major feature of modern Western imperialism has of course been the elaboration and transmission of racial concepts and doctrines in which white, European peoples have been portrayed as superior to non-Western populations. Western cultural products, from advertisements to complex dramatic fiction, have been suffused with notions of white superiority (McKenzie, 1984; Shohat and Stam, 1994) (EUROCENTRISM), yet they have been largely ignored in the debates on cultural imperialism. This may perhaps be explained by the complex ethnic configurations of the Latin American countries – where the cultural imperialism thesis was initially formulated – and their relatively longer period of formal independence from COLONIALISM. The Marxist derivation of the theories of dependence also probably contributed to the overemphasis on class and capitalism and the neglect of factors to do with ethnicity and racism. It is noteworthy, too, that writers on cultural imperialism have neglected the massive cultural impact of colonialism which occurred in earlier periods via the imposition of Christianity and the setting up of Western systems of education in the colonies.

It is undeniable that portrayals of the attractiveness of Western cultures and their lifestyles in the cultural products of America and Western Europe have always contained subtexts and often overt messages regarding the superiority of white cultures, and that 'Western' cultural products have been suffused with derogatory racial stereotyping, including a denigration of European peoples not regarded as white enough, for example Italians, Spanish and the Irish (WHITENESS). Given the neglect of these issues in the discourse of cultural imperialism, and now that dependency theory has definitely had its day, it is not surprising that the concept of cultural imperialism has also largely lost currency in current debates.

The thrust of the cultural imperialist theses has also been blunted by the demonstration within the field of postcolonial studies that European cultures and the 'West' have in fact always been a syncretic mix of Western and non-Western elements (POSTCOLONIAL STUDIES), and by the acknowledgement that in a new phase of GLOBALIZATION, with major flows of migration from the former colonies into the metropolitan countries, Western societies in the late twentieth century and beyond have themselves been transformed into more complex multicultural and multiethnic entities such that the definitions 'Western' and, to some degree, 'American' are significantly different to what they were when the cultural imperialist theses were formulated.

Indeed, to the extent that the concept of cultural imperialism has been replaced by the notion of globalization, the previous debate has now taken a more sophisticated and productive turn, although one still marked by serious disagreement.

A major attraction of the concept of globalization, over cultural imperialism, is its acknowledgement that the relationship between the economic and cultural dimensions of global flows is too complicated to be captured by notions which assume that cultural domination is an almost automatic consequence of economic power in the international arena. Also, most conceptions of globalization display an awareness of the constant resistance to cultural homogenization that characterizes global processes (Scott, 1997), as well as the significance of migration and the development of diasporas in the transformation of national cultures in a new global age (Held et al., 1999). For example,

Tomlinson (1999), in shifting his attention from cultural imperialism to globalization, regards 'complex connectivity' as intrinsic to globalization. Waters (1995) argues that the definition of globalization should be restricted to the idea of social processes being less constrained by geography, together with an awareness by people that such constraints are receding. Moreover, he stresses that the three global arenas of the economy, polity and culture are related but 'structurally independent'. Held, McGrew, Goldblatt and Perraton (1999) argue that globalization should refer to a stretching of social, political and economic relations across frontiers, an intensification of interconnectedness, a speeding up of global interactions and a magnification of the impact of distant events, and suggest that the process is historically contingent and contradictory. Appadurai in an influential contribution (1990) argues that globally there exist 'fundamental disjunctures between economy, culture and politics' and conceptualizes globalization as consisting of a number of disjunctive flows: ethnoscapes, mediascapes, technoscapes, finanscapes, and ideoscapes (1990: 296).

Questions of racism and ethnicity continue to be a peripheral concern for most major writers on contemporary patterns of globalization. Appadurai (1990) is an exception, pointing to the manner in which deterritorialization, for example of Sikhs from India, has led to the formation of diasporic communities (DIASPORA) which in turn have played important roles in the emergence of ethnic conflicts in the countries of origin.

However, it also appears that specialist researchers on race, ethnicity and culture treat globalization as a taken for granted backdrop to their main interests, which seem to focus on particular nation states or to regions such as the Northern

Western. Castles (2000) has made one of the few contributions to a more systematic engagement with issues of globalization in relation to racism in an analysis which shows interesting links with the debates on cultural imperialism. Castles' theorization is less multidimensional than that of the other writers cited above, for he views the present process primarily as an extension and continuation of the Western capitalist expansionism that began in the fifteenth century (Castles, 2000: 164). Thus globalization for him is essentially a diffusion of Western modernity and values, including the racism which has been intrinsic to this modernity. As far as the present period is concerned Castles' primary emphasis is on the way in which globalization is restructuring various sectors of the industrial economies of the West and also undermining previous forms of national IDENTITY. In an analysis that draws upon the work of the French sociologist Michel Wieviorka (1995), Castles argues that globalization leads to economic and social crises of de-industrialization, perceived threats to the NATION and the significant weakening of labour movements, all of which allow racist ideologies and movements to re-emerge in place of earlier Left politics. In other parts of the globe, the newer nation states, formed out of previous colonial administrations, often find themselves engulfed by violent ethnic conflicts as they struggle with severe economic difficulties (exacerbated by global patterns of neo-colonial trade relations), weak political structures and the legacy of colonial state boundaries which took scant account of ethnic loyalties (Castles, 2000: 176).

Castles' view of globalization is akin to that of Sklair (1995), for whom the spread of an ideology of capitalist consumerism is the key feature of present global flows. This conception was pre-figured in the cultural imperialist theses of writers such as Schiller (1985) who combined critiques of Americanization with a concern over the global hegemony of the capitalist system.

A systematic multidimensional analysis of the relation between contemporary globalization, the spread of Western culture and patterns of racism and ethnic conflict is yet to be written. [A. R.]

Ang, I. (1985) *Watching Dallas*, Routledge, London.

Appadurai, A. (1990) 'Disjuncture and difference in the global cultural economy', in Featherstone, M. (ed.), *Global Culture: Nationalism, Globalization and Modernity*, Sage, London.

Barker, M. (1989) *Comics: Ideology, Power and the Critics*, Manchester University Press, Manchester.

Castles, S. (2000) *Ethnicity and Globalization*, Sage, London.

Dorfman, A., Mattelart, A. (1975) *How to Read 'Donald Duck': Imperialist Ideology in the Disney Comic*, International General Editions, New York.

Frank, A. G. (1967) *Capitalism and Underdevelopment in Latin America*, Monthly Review Press, London.

Golding, P., Harris, P. (eds) (1997) *Beyond Cultural Imperialism*, Sage, London.

Held, D., McGrew, A., Goldblatt, D., Perraton, J. (1999) *Global Transformations*, Polity Press, Cambridge.

Liebes, T., Katz, E. (1993) *The Export of Meaning: Cross-Cultural Readings of 'Dallas'*, Polity Press, Cambridge.

McKenzie, J. M. (1984) *Propaganda and Empire*, Manchester University Press, Manchester.

Ritzer, G. (1996) *The McDonaldization of Society*, revised edn, Pine Forge Press, London.

Schiller, H. (1985) 'Electronic information flows: new basis for global domination?', in Drummond. P., Paterson, R. (eds), *Television in Transition*, BFI Publications, London.

Schuurman, F. J. (1993) 'Development theory in the 1990s', in Schuurman, F. J. (ed.), *Beyond the Impasse: New Directions in Development Theory*, Zed Press, London.

Scott, A. (ed.) (1997) *The Limits of Globalization*, Routledge, London.

Shohat, E., Stam, R. (1994) *Unthinking Eurocentrism: Multiculturalism and the Media*, Routledge, London and New York.

Sklair, L. (1995) *The Sociology of the Global System*, 2nd edn, Prentice-Hall/Harvester Wheatsheaf, Hemel Hempstead.

Tomlinson, J. (1991) *Cultural Imperialism*, Pinter, London.

Tomlinson, J. (1999) *Globalisation and Culture*, Polity Press, Cambridge.

Waters, M. (1995) *Globalisation*, Routledge, London.

Wieviorka, M. (1995) *The Arena of Racism*, Sage, London.

CULTURAL RELATIVISM

CULTURAL RELATIVISM (It. *relativismo culturale*; Fr. *relativisme culturel*; Ger. *Kulturrelativismus*) Cultural relativistic theories date back to Herodotus and the sophistry of Ancient Greece, but the expression 'cultural relativism' should be reserved to a social-anthropological theory first implemented by Franz Boas (1858–1942) and his disciples. Born in Germany, Boas studied geography at Kiel before embarking on expeditions to the Arctic and British Columbia, which shifted his interest to the study of the indigenous tribes and motivated his emigration to the USA in 1886. In 1899 he was appointed Professor at Columbia and became a dominant figure in establishing modern anthropology in the USA. He and his school established new and complex concepts of culture and race, as outlined in his writings. The theory of cultural relativism is also known as CULTURAL DETERMINISM and sets forth the view that all morals, rules and needs must be judged in the context of the society and culture which produce them and observed from that society and culture's point of view. Judgement from the point of view of the observer may lead to ETHNOCENTRISM.

Debates among anthropologists about cultural relativism have had two periods of vogue. The earlier relativist position, as formulated by Boas and his school, was a response to Social Darwinism and was largely a plea for tolerance. Cultural relativism emerged in reaction to CULTURAL EVOLUTIONISM, a theory which affirmed that human societies progressed in stages from 'primitive' to 'modern', assuming that European society was the furthest advanced (EUROCENTRISM). The current debate on cultural relativism is largely influenced by postmodern philosophy. In its most extreme version, it embodies a form of cognitive relativism assuming that it is impossible for anyone outside a CULTURE to understand any internal element within that culture. A less extreme version states that outsiders may come to understand other cultures, but that any attempt to judge diverse cultures is arbitrary. Some anthropologists have criticized relativistic theories, affirming that it is possible to identify a number of different universals. Melford Spiro (1986), for instance, claims that it is reasonable to assume the existence of a set of universal psychobiological traits in the human species, such as pain avoidance, object constancy, attachment behaviours, and others. Universals rooted in human neurobiology include the 'formal' deep structure of language put forth by Noam Chomsky, and the processes involved in human bonding described by R.F. Fox (1988). Cultural relativism can be criticized also from an ethical point of view: although cultural relativism states that all cultures are equal and none is inferior or superior to the others – seemingly giving an impression of openness and TOLERANCE – the concept often hides: (a) the risk that observers and judges become mentally lazy and therefore merely compile personal types of catalogues; (b) any hypothesis of interaction through a refusal to compare different cultures; (c) sophistic cowardice and weakness in observers who avoid judging and are therefore unable to interact; (d) implicit RACISM deriving from the indifference of anthropological theories. According to Reginald Bibby (1990), pluralism may lead to cultural relativism with the result that there are no real shared values, no inviolable standards and little on which to construct a distinct nationality (MULTICULTURALISM). Such hypotheses are also pursued in the work of Richard Gwynn (1990), who cites crime and the range of legal defences based on cultural differences as examples of the threat to society posed by cultural pluralism. However, cultural relativism can be seen as a positive phenomenon, when individuals are willing to look at things from the point of view of the other. [S. G.]

Bibby, R. (1990) *Mosaic Madness*, Stoddart, Toronto.
Boas, F. (1911) *The Mind of Primitive Man*, Macmillan, New York.
Fox, R.F. (1988) *Energy and the Evolution of Life*, W.H. Freeman, New York, p. 43.
Gwynn, R. (1990) *Nationalism without Walls: The Incredible Lightness of Being Canadian*, Stoddart, Toronto.
Shweder, R.A. (1991) *Thinking through Cultures*, Harvard University Press, Cambridge, MA.
Spiro, M. (1986) 'Cultural relativism and the future of anthropology', *Cultural Anthropology*, 1: 259–286.

CULTURE (It. *cultura*; Fr. *culture*; Ger. *Kultur*) 1 From the Latin verb *colere*, to cultivate and the noun *cultura*, the term 'culture' is used today mainly with two meanings; the first and most ancient of these, taken up at the beginning of the seventeenth century by Francis Bacon, refers to the body of knowledge and manners acquired by an individual, while the second describes the shared customs, values and beliefs which characterize a given social group, and which are passed down from generation to generation.

Many scholars in the socio-anthropological and psychological fields have striven to explain the concept of culture, the classical anthropological definition of which was provided in 1871 by Tylor (1994), who describes it as 'that complex whole which includes knowledge, belief, art, morals, law, custom, and any other capabilities and habits acquired by man as a member of society'.

According to a more recent definition by Kroeber and Kluckhohn (1944), culture is 'an abstraction from concrete behaviour but is not in itself behaviour'.

Lévi-Strauss (1977) opposes the particularity of culture to the universality of nature, believing that 'everything universal in man derives from the order of nature and is characterized by spontaneity', . . . while 'everything which is subject to a norm belongs to culture and presents the attributes of the relative and the particular'.

Others, such as Geertz (1973) and Weber, have preferred to focus on the problematic aspect of culture rather than on its definition, and regard the human condition with reference to culture as that of 'an animal suspended in webs of significance he himself has spun'. Therefore, they consider the analysis of culture to be 'not an experimental science in search of law but an interpretative one in search of meaning'.

Further elements towards the understanding of culture have been provided by psychoanalysis, including the influence of the UNCONSCIOUS life on creativity (Freud, 1964), the connection between social organization and the control of sexual drives (Freud, 1930), studies on the universality of myths and symbols (Jung, 1936) and the deep interconnection between language and the unconscious (Lacan, 2001). Unconscious cultural patterns may manifest both at an individual and at a social level, for example in the style with which one expresses oneself and in social habits and customs. The unconscious element of culture tends to be most evident in those deep-rooted needs, thoughts and values of a society which elude rational explanation. Thus it may be said that although culture comprises evident and comparable products and contents, its structure is not obvious, as it originates in the social unconscious. In order to truly understand a culture, therefore, it is necessary to trace the origins of the deep-seated needs and feelings expressed in its customs and values, as well as its history and the environmental factors which have contributed towards shaping it.

All definitions of culture imply an opposition to the idea of nature, inasmuch as culture is considered to be a body of acquired elements that can be learned and taught – and which are therefore seen to be somewhat artificial – while nature is seen as a manifestation of a set of elements caught in a dialectic tension – elements which are not man-made, and that human beings can only attempt to understand. However, as even nature can be manipulated to a certain extent, any strict distinction between culture and nature could be seen to be ambiguous and ill-founded. To envision natural elements in their purest form is merely speculation; even so-called natural instincts are the result of a 'cultural' modification superimposed on 'natural' elements – if these indeed can be said ever to have existed in the first place – the origins of which have been lost in time.

2 The oldest definition of the term 'culture' refers to the cultivation of soil or the raising of plants or animals. However, two different meanings of the term are most in use today. The first of these, 'the training, development and refinement of mind, tastes and manners' (*Oxford English Dictionary*) had already begun to take precedence over the old Latin meaning by the 1950s. The second, which has grown in common usage since the nineteenth century, chiefly owes its increase in popularity to the sciences of sociology and anthropology and is best explained by Edward Tylor's famous definition, quoted earlier.

In the first instance, culture is seen to be a universal value, generally ascribed to the realms of cultural production such as MUSIC or art or to the scientific field, and frequently defined in opposition to the lack thereof. In 1873 Matthew Arnold wrote that to have culture is to 'be acquainted with the best that has been known and said in the world'. Today, this concept is more often termed 'high culture' to indicate the artistic and cultural expressions valued by a given society's elite, and as such frequently opposed to popular culture.

Tylor's definition, on the other hand, while it still describes culture as a singularity, by focusing on the distinguishing characteristics of each social group already carries within it the implication of relativity. Nevertheless, it was Franz Boas who first provided a pluralistic definition of culture as something that always characterizes a specific group and like a group, exists only in plurality. Thus he laid the foundations for CULTURAL RELATIVISM, which rejected the developmental stages of evolutionism (CULTURAL EVOLU-TIONISM) in favour of a view of cultures as each having their own standards, and as not subject to being judged by the point of view of another culture.

After the Second World War, the concept of culture superceded the concept of 'RACE' as the main term of comparison in anthropological discourse:

> 'Culture' instead of 'race' as fundamental difference between humans was meant to be a different kind of difference: difference was no longer a question of descent, of heritage, of differential positioning on the steps of evolution, of unalterable, virtually natural-biological endowment with differential abilities. Cultural differences are acquired differences, acquired by socialization in specific cultural contexts.

However,

> Especially in two aspects, the concept of culture assumes the problematical heritage of racism and the concept of race. The first aspect is a tendency of determinism. Just as belonging to a race determined in certain ways the individual, culture now was understood as something (however defined) that shaped the thoughts and behaviour of individual human beings. (Sökefeld, 1998)

The second way in which the concept of culture inherited the legacy of 'race', is in the danger of hierarchization it implies. A pluralistic view of culture necessarily carries with it the concept of 'cultural difference', which in turn implies the drawing of comparisons. However, if one culture is viewed in opposition to another, it is also viewed through the distorting lens of the culture which is analysing it.

On the other hand, culture as a relative concept – i.e. intended as the body of learned beliefs and behaviour of a given group or society – in losing its universal quality also by necessity loses its absolute positive value, and therefore it must be considered that each individual culture will comprise trivial and negative aspects alongside its more positive products. In the light of this awareness, the culture which analyses another culture must also come under scrutiny, in the knowledge that some of its constructs may not be positive or indeed even logical.

This self-critical attitude is evident today in the Western world in the growing mistrust of culture – in particular scientific and technological culture – seen as something which alienates man from nature. The culture versus nature duality is a constant of Western thought, with culture often being thought of as the dimension which elevates human beings above the animals.

> . . . the opposition between culture and nature . . . is congenital to philosophy. It is even older than Plato. It is at least as old as the Sophists. Since the statement of the opposition – *physis/nomos, physis/technè* [nature/culture, nature/art of making] – it has been passed on to us by a whole historical chain which opposes 'nature' to the law, to education, to art, to technics – and also to liberty, to the arbitrary, to history, to society, to the mind, and so on. (Derrida, 1972)

However, this view necessarily implied a unified conception of culture as a straightforward evolutionary progress common to the whole of humanity, of which European culture was seen to be the highest point (CULTURAL IMPERIALISM). With cultural relativism, Western culture began to question itself, and certain cultures previously considered to be 'primitive' from a Eurocentric (EUROCENTRISM) standpoint, are now sometimes seen to be more harmonious in that they are closer to nature.

Nevertheless, the question remains as to whether it is possible to judge another culture at all and according to which parameters. For example, can what to one culture appears to be an obvious violation of basic human rights be dismissed as the mere product of a cultural difference? If our own culture has a bias in its understanding of other cultures, it should be asked whether it is possible to speak of a universal cultural, intellectual and moral standard, or of a universal capacity to communicate in this respect. This bears a significance both with respect to cohabitation in multicultural societies (MULTICUL-TURALISM) and to wider issues relative to human rights.

3 The debate surrounding culture is obviously one of great relevance to the social and political discourse of multi-cultural societies. Nowadays most Western societies recognize the need to promote multiculturalism through the implementation of programmes and policies aimed at fostering, protecting or even promoting cultural diversity. However, the current debate on multi-culturalism has not shed light on the definition of 'culture'. While it has been claimed that every homogeneous group has a culture of its own and that culture should be ranked alongside terms such as 'race' and 'ethnicity' in identifying the various groups making up homogeneous communities (COMMUNITY), the same difficulties encountered with the definition and use of the concepts of 'race' and ethnicity are also found when establishing the boundaries of individual cultures and of the various sub-groups making up each culture.

Cultural boundaries are more often defined along the lines of racial, geographical, national or linguistic divisions. Indeed, in everyday language, and even in academic circles, it is not unusual for references to be made to national cultures, such as the Italian culture or the French culture, yet far from being homogeneous phenomena, national cultures are composed of a number of minority cultures. Even the apparent linguistic unity of many nations is a by-product of national unity, as linguistic homogeneity was sought as a means to strengthen the formation of nation states.

Multicultural education programmes often focus on language as a defining cultural factor. But although the implementation of bilingual schemes is relatively unproblematic from a theoretical point of view, in practice in many societies it is hard to cater for all linguistic minorities and to establish which are those cultural elements which should be protected and fostered. When multicultural programmes extend beyond the basic promotion of linguistic diversity they often run the risk of attempting to represent all possible cultures in clearly defined units, thereby inadvertently stressing the opposition between cultures and cultural differences. In order to combat such rigid definitions, which could perpetuate the idea of the irreconcilability of different cultures, multicultural education should also focus on promoting understanding between cultural, racial or religious groups, with the aim of fostering tolerance, inclusion and positive diversity (INTERCULTURALISM). [S. G.]

Arnold, M. (1925) *Culture and Anarchy* (1869), Macmillan, New York.

Derrida, J. (1972) 'Structure, sign and play in the discourse of the human sciences', in Macksey, R., Donato, E. (eds), *The Structuralist Controversy: The Language of Criticism & the Sciences of Man*, Johns Hopkins University Press, Baltimore and London.

Freud, S. (1910) *Leonardo da Vinci and a Memory of his Childhood*, edited by J. Strachey, trans. Alan Tyson, Norton, New York (1990).

Freud, S. (1930) *Civilisation and its Discontents*, trans. J. Strachey, W.W. Norton (1961).

Freud, S. (1964) *Leonardo da Vinci and a*

Memory of his Childhood, trans. Alan Tyson, Norton, New York.

Geertz C. (1973) *Interpretation of Cultures*, Basic Books, New York.

Jung, C. G. (1936) *The Archetypes and the Collective Unconscious: The Collected Works of C.J. Jung*, Vol. 9, Part 1, Princeton University Press.

Kroeber A. L. and Kluckholm, C. (1944) *Configuration of Culture Growth*, University of California Press, Berkeley.

Lacan, J. (2001) *Ecrits* (1966), Routledge, London.

Lévi-Strauss, C. (1977) *The Elementary Structures of Kinship* (1949), Beacon Press, Boston, MA.

Sökefeld, M. (1998) 'The concept of culture between politics and social anthropology: from difference to continuity', *Ethnologie Heute*, 3, available online: http://www. uni-muenster.de/EthnologieHeute/eh3/culture.htm

Tylor, P. B. (1994) *Collected Works*, Routledge, London.

CYBERNAZIS (It. *Cybernazisti*; Fr. *Cybernazis*; Ger. *Cybernazis*) The term 'cybernazis' is relatively new and has been used by the press to indicate individuals and organizations who use the Internet to openly promulgate neo-Nazi messages, proclamations and cartoons. Cybernetic neo-Nazis (also referred to as 'Net Nazis') first appeared in North America and Europe, particularly in Germany, at the beginning of the 1990s. By 1996 the phenomenon had become so widespread that the Simon Wiesenthal Center in Los Angeles – an international human rights association – claimed it had found more than 600 sites on the Internet that it considered to be racist, compared with just over 300 detected only a year earlier. A formal request for stricter controls on Internet access led to widespread debate and many opposed the Center's contentions, stating that maximum freedom of expression in 'cyberspace' must be guaranteed and that the only way to counter such messages is public criticism. Although the Internet offers individuals and groups new and perhaps more effective ways of interacting with other groups and individuals, it is also more difficult for authorities to keep under surveillance than 'traditional' means. Indeed, as the Internet and similar networks expand, it is quite possible that more new means of racist (RACISM) propaganda will appear and that racist movements may use the Internet to recruit young people, so that appropriate legislation will most certainly become necessary.

In November 1997, a global conference dealing with racism on the Internet was held in Geneva. Conference participants said global restrictions were unlikely to be implemented in the near future, because technology is changing faster than efforts to police it. Furthermore, legal differences between countries make it very difficult to require service providers to take responsibility for preventing offensive material from being published on the Internet. This idea has received more support in Europe than elsewhere; while some European countries such as Sweden and Germany have implemented controls to make service providers responsible for content, such limitations are unlikely to be adopted in the United States, where in accordance with the First Amendment few, if any, limitations can be applied to what can be published on the Web. In Germany, France and other European countries it is illegal to incite to or to promote racial hatred, and to defend 'negationist' or 'revisionist' theories that deny the Holocaust ever happened. Consequently, many neo-Nazi websites – approximately 100 according to estimates published by some online magazines in August 2000 – have started to transfer their web pages to the USA, a fact which could lead to America becoming a sort of free port for perpetuators of racial hatred (RACE AND THE MEDIA). Many articles on ANTI-SEMITISM and white racial supremacy are published on the American network – e.g. the website of World Wide White Pride – as well as mailing lists, chat rooms and links, ranging from those of the KU KLUX KLAN to those of skinhead movements.

The problem of controlling the cyber-nazi phenomenon came to the attention of the general public following the so-called *affaire Yahoo*. While, in May 2000, the G8 conference in Paris discussed Internet crime, the French judge Jean-Jacques Gomez approved a petition filed by various anti-racist associations in which the Internet provider Yahoo was requested to take suitable technical action to prevent French Internet users from accessing neo-Nazi websites selling collectors' items considered offensive to the national memory. The websites in question were removed from the French portal, but Yahoo appealed to the freedom of speech sanctioned by the US Constitution and claimed that it was technically impossible to prevent access to the site. In recognition of the technical complexity of the problem, Judge Gomez requested that a commission of experts be set up to identify a possible solution.

The experts found that it was possible to prevent access to the site on the basis of the geographic origin of the request for access, although with just 80 per cent effectiveness. On the basis of this Judge Gomez ordered Yahoo to block access to the Neo-nazi online sales websites by users in French territories, and France thus became the first Western country ever to censor the Internet. In view of the need to discourage the promotion of racial hatred and racist ideologies, this prohibition was considered a reasonable and necessary limitation of the right to freedom of speech and expression. In the USA, certain organizations – such as the Anti-Defamation League – are currently attempting to counteract cybernazism by registering as many potential hatred-inspired Internet domain names as possible, so as to prevent their being adopted by hate groups and racist individuals. [M. V.]

Chroniques de cybérie (2000) Montréal.
EC, *Council Directive 2000/43/EC of 29 June 2000 implementing the principle of equal treatment between persons irrespective of racial or ethnic origin.*
EUMC (European Monitoring Centre on Racism and Xenophobia) (1999) *Diversity and Equality for Europe, Annual Report.*
Quotidiano.net, 21 agosto 2000.

D

DANCE (It. *danza*; Fr. *danse*; Ger. *Tanz*) The Mexican Zuni say they dance both for their own pleasure and for the good of the city (Sachs, 1933). Dancing is found in all cultures, and it is impossible to say exactly when human beings began to dance; like music, dance has probably always been a part of human behaviour. Images of dancers are found in prehistoric rock paintings. Animals also dance, at important times in their biological and social lives, from courtship to death.

Indeed, just as it would be naive of musicologists to maintain that music emerged as an imitation of birdsong, it would be crude and simplistic to assume that dancing – both individual and in groups – was caused by some external factor. Dance, like music, is connected to the rhythm of the human heartbeat; it is an experience of coenesthesis – the body's gaining awareness of itself as a living and moving entity. The unborn foetus is swathed in the sensations, rhythms and sounds of its mother's womb, to which it responds with movement. Our first dance then is our first attempt to adjust to our surroundings in the womb, while at the same time attempting to communicate with the outside world.

In the beginning dance was a means to narrate events, a RITE, an exorcism and an allurement. Other dances were more symbolic, expressing possession over someone or something. In any case, whether it was symbolic or narrative, dance has always been an expression of sexuality, autoerotic or seductive. A good example of this is belly-dancing, which can be found in all Muslim countries, as well as in other countries, and which is probably all that remains of ancient fertility dances in honour of the Mother goddesses. In belly-dancing female dancers perform a series of repetitive, undulating movements, displaying their rounded bellies as a symbol of fertility and eroticism. However, erotic dancing is not just the prerogative of women. In some North African countries male dancers also perform sexually suggestive hip movements.

In Western societies dance developed into ballroom dancing and ballet. Until the beginning of the twentieth century, ballroom dancing was divided into popular and aristocratic-bourgeois forms, performed by amateurs for pure pleasure. Dancing today – individually, in pairs, or in groups – is mainly perceived as a form of entertainment and release, although its still maintains sexual connotations and undertones of courtship. In the West popular dancing is nowadays mainly confined to night clubs, while most traditional folk dances survive only as tourist attractions. [R. R., S. G.]

Highwater, J. (1996) *Dance: Rituals of Experience*, Oxford University Press, Oxford.
Lievre, V. (1987) *Danses du Maghreb*, Karthala, Paris.
Sachs, C. (1937) *World History of the Dance*, Bonanza Books, New York.

DENIZEN (It. *denizen*; Fr. *denizen*; Ger. *Denizen*) An antiquated English word once used to indicate a resident as opposed to a full citizen.

The word was reintroduced at the end of the 1980s by Thomas Hammar to indicate a group of permanent immigrants residing in certain European countries. According to Hammar (1990), denizens are not citizens of the country in which they live, but are foreign citizens with the legal status of permanent residence, who enjoy full social and economic rights, are often well integrated into the host country and may enjoy some political rights (CITIZENSHIP). However, because they are not citizens they are not normally represented politically.

In Europe, the modern figure of the denizen is the result of a process of MIGRATION which began at the end of the Second World War, when many Central and Northern European countries imported migrant workers to fuel industrial development. On the basis of their continued economic and demographic utility, and as a result of various struggles since the 1980s, immigrants have changed their status from worker (GASTARBEITER) to resident – denizen – and thus are able to enjoy numerous rights as well as higher earnings, a fact which may indicate the end of their generally precarious and insecure situation. Although the prevailing law varies throughout Europe, the status of permanent resident is awarded if certain specific conditions are satisfied. Thus once an individual can prove that they have legally lived and worked in a country for a certain amount of time (usually over five years), verify that they have sufficient and stable financial resources, and demonstrate their INTEGRATION into the host society (in terms of, for example, knowledge of the local language and possessing suitable accommodation), they may be awarded denizen status. In order to maintain such status, they must avoid leaving the country for long periods of time, abstain from burdening the welfare state and, above all, commit no serious crimes. The essential difference between a denizen and a naturalized citizen is that the latter is obliged to give up all their rights in their country of origin. DUAL CITIZENSHIP has become more common in recent years.

Denizens have an ambiguous relationship with both their country of settlement and their country of origin. They may claim and receive certain important rights in the host country, but they can also refuse to become fully assimilated (ASSIMILATION) and maintain not only their original citizenship, but also certain behavioural patterns with regard to religious, ideological and traditional beliefs which differ from those of the host country (DOUBLE CONSCIOUSNESS). In many respects, denizen status is the highest legal recognition a FOREIGNER can expect to receive in a country, other than full citizenship. However, as the migration scenario has completely changed over the last two decades and integration models in the more important European countries of immigration have reached a crucial turning point (in France, Germany and the UK), denizens appear to be torn between the obligation to change citizenship and the risk of MARGINALIZATION, a phenomenon which continues to reduce the few certainties a denizen can count upon. The experience of denizens illuminates some of the problems faced by multicultural societies (MULTICULTURALISM). For example, even in those countries in which citizenship is awarded on the basis of the expectation of assimilation, some immigrants will continue to refuse to change, preferring to demonstrate their differences. [M. V.]

Hammar, T. (1990) *Democracy and the Nation State: Aliens, Denizens and*

Citizens in a World of International Migration, Avebury, Aldershot.

DEPORTATION (It. *Espulsione dello straniero*; Fr. *expulsion*; Ger. *Abschiebung, Ausweisung*)

Enforced removal of an alien from a country in which he/she is resident to the country of his/her origin. Formal expulsion, by persuasion or by an executive agency, is usually imposed on aliens whose presence in a country is deemed unlawful (ILLEGAL ALIEN) or detrimental (for instance aliens who become public charges, commit crimes of moral turpitude, or engage in subversive activities). Deported aliens are barred from re-entering the deporting country without specific authorization. Deportation differs from exclusion in that the latter involves the refusal on the part of a governing authority to admit an alien (see below).

Historically speaking, the term 'deportation' has been used with a broad range of meanings not exclusively related to the removal of aliens, including the banishment of citizens (EXILE), the transportation of criminals to penal settlements and the displacement of enslaved populations (SLAVERY). Until the modern era, deportation proceedings were more often used as a formal means of expelling aliens who were considered undesirable for political reasons. In modern European countries the concept of deportation has played an important role in protecting totalitarian governments and, in this context, can be easily related to policies of GENOCIDE (CONCENTRATION CAMP AND DEATH CAMP) and ETHNIC CLEANSING. Deportation has also become an instrument of national policy with regard to MIGRATION, closely associated with immigration policies and varying according to political events and economic developments.

Technically speaking, modern expulsion measures are classified either as 'security measures', adopted by authorities following the conviction of a foreigner for serious crime, or as 'police measures' autonomously implemented by police authorities. Police measures are those more frequently adopted in order to counter illegal immigration. Such measures may be adopted at ports of entry, or at borders and in their vicinity, for aliens arriving in, attempting to enter, or who have entered a country at unauthorized points; or they may be applied though controls carried out in the country, and might lead to the deportation of those aliens living there without a residence permit. The legal systems of some countries consider illegal immigration a crime to be dealt with according to the procedures of the criminal code, while some view it as a situation which may be resolved by the implementation of simple administrative measures leading to the exclusion or repatriation of illegal aliens. These administrative measures vary: some countries impose a time limit within which such cases must be processed, while others extend such procedures until the moment of deportation. The time factor is one of the most difficult problems to be addressed as far as strategies aimed at countering illegal immigration are concerned, as it is difficult for authorities to verify the IDENTITY and country of origin of suspected illegal aliens within the allowed time limits, yet such a time period cannot be extended *ad infinitum* without infringing the suspects' fundamental human rights. While the right of a state to deport an alien remains unchallenged, removal proceedings should be carried out while respecting human rights, that is, deportation should take place within modalities which are non-injurious and aliens must be granted a reasonable amount of time to wind up their affairs and leave the deporting country. In addition, the right to deport aliens cannot be separated from the duty to ensure that those deported are admitted to another state, generally that of origin (CITIZENSHIP, STATELESS).

The free circulation pacts for EU citizens in member states have led to an increase in controls for foreign citizens (FOREIGNER, FREE MOVEMENT) at European borders. According to certain authors, exclusion measures are considered more effective and less problematic than deportation (Holliefield, 1992). In addition, strategies of collaboration with the police forces of the countries of origin and transit of illegal immigration flows have been adopted. These include intergovernmental bilateral agreements aimed at limiting the numbers leaving their countries of origin and controlling borders and repatriation treaties to facilitate the repatriation of expelled aliens.

In Anglo-American law, enforced removal proceedings may similarly be based on grounds of inadmissibility or deportability. Inadmissibility applies when an alien seeking admission at a port of entry does not meet the required criteria. This may result in either an expedited removal (see below) or in removal proceedings taking place before an immigration judge. Under certain circumstances, an inadmissible alien may be allowed to withdraw his/her application for admission. Voluntary retraction of the application means that no hearing before an immigration judge is necessary and no expedited removal enforced, and such cases are not filed among non-immigrant admission data.

Deportability applies to any alien illegally present in the country, regardless of whether they entered by fraud or misrepresentation, or entered legally but subsequently violated the terms of their non-immigrant classification or status. Deportation is ordered by an immigration judge, and does not entail any punishment. For instance, in the United States, expedited removal proceedings cover both aliens who are inadmissible because they have no entry documents or because they have used counterfeit, altered, or otherwise fraudulent or improper documents, and aliens who arrive in, attempt to enter, or have entered the country without having been admitted by an immigration officer at a port of entry. The Immigration and Naturalization Service (INS) has the authority to order the removal, and the alien is not referred to an immigration judge except after he/she makes a claim to legal status in the United States or demonstrates a credible danger of persecution if he/she returned to his/her home country. Both in the United States and in European countries, restrictions are established with regard to the exclusion and expulsion of foreigners to whom REFUGEE status has been awarded pursuant to Section 1 of the Geneva Convention (POLITICAL ASYLUM). In this case removal proceedings may only be ordered for reasons of public order and national security and, in any case, the expelled refugee must be guaranteed a reasonable period of time to find another state in which to live. [A. B., R. B.]

Bonetti, P. (1993) *La condizione giuridica del cittadino extracomunitario*, Maggioli, Rimini.
Brochmann, G., Hammar, T. (eds) (1999) *Mechanisms of Immigration Control*, Berg, Oxford.
Britannica on line (2000) Deportation, http://britannica.com.

D'Orazio, G. (1993) 'Straniero (condizione giuridica dello) (diritto costituzionale)', in *Enciclopedia Giuridica Treccani*.

Holliefield, J.F. (1992) *Immigrants, Markets and States: The Political Economy of Postwar Europe*, Harvard University Press, Cambridge, MA.

Microsoft Encarta Online Encyclopedia (2000) Deportation, http://encarta.msn.com.

Nascimbene, B. (1984) *Il trattamento dello straniero nel diritto internazionale ed europeo*, Giuffré, Milano.

Sassen, S. (1996) *Guests and Aliens*, New Press, New York.

US Immigration and Naturalization Service (2000) Glossary & Acronyms, http://www.insusdoj.gov/graphics/glossary.htm

DEVELOPING COUNTRIES (It. *Paesi in via di sviluppo*; Fr. *Pays en voie de développement*; Ger. *Entwicklungsländer*)

The term 'developing countries' was first used during the first United Nations Conference on Trade and Development (UNCTAD), which was called in the early 1960s in order to discuss the problems relating to international commodity markets and to trade as a primary instrument for economic development. In the field of immigration (MIGRATION), developing countries are considered to be, for example, non-European countries which present strong push factors (PUSH FACTORS – PULL FACTORS) for emigration to Western Europe (EXTRACOMUNITARIO, FLOWS). Developing countries display little homogeneity (being located in Latin America, Africa and Asia, and their populations differing by race, religion and culture) but they are lumped together because of their similarly precarious economic situations.

From the economic point of view, for example in the analysis of the World Bank, the main criterion for classifying economies is the gross national product (GNP) per capita, as a constant relationship is found to exist between a summary assessment of well-being and economic variables. Economies are classified either as low income, middle income, or high income. Low-income and middle-income economies are sometimes referred to as 'developing economies'. The term is used for convenience purposes; it is not intended to imply that all economies in the group are experiencing similar development or that other economies have reached a preferable or final stage of development. Classification by income does not necessarily reflect development status. Income and other economical variables are certainly the easiest to assess, but development is a very complex phenomenon which also has sociological and anthropological aspects. In the perspective of the UN's *Human Development Report*, human development is nowadays conceived as the process of attaining a wider range of choices for people. Income is certainly one of the main means of increasing choices and well-being, but the choices available should also be increased by developing human capabilities and functioning (for example, by helping people live longer lives, keeping them healthy and well nourished and promoting proper integration with others in the community).

At all levels of development the three factors essential for human development are: the possibility of leading long and healthy lives; the opportunity to acquire knowledge; and access to the resources needed for a decent standard of living. According to this perspective, the Human Development Index (HDI) measures the overall achievements of countries in these three basic dimensions. If these capabilities are not achieved, many choices are simply not available and many opportunities remain inaccessible. However the realm of human development stretches further, ranging from the political, economic and social opportunities available, to issues concerning self-respect, empowerment and a sense of belonging to a COMMUNITY.

While the HDI measures the overall progress of countries in terms of human development, the Human Poverty Index (HPI) measures the backlog of deprivation that still exists. The HPI measures poverty in developing countries in the same dimensions of basic human development (percentage of people expected to die before age 40; percentage of adults who are illiterate; percentage of people without access to health services and safe water; and percentage of underweight children under five). From this point of view, development is conceived as closely linked to the realization of human rights. Taking an integrated view of all human rights – beyond a narrow and exclusive civil and political focus – it provides a framework in which advancing human development is commensurate with the realization of human rights.

At present the main goals of UNCTAD are to help developing countries, particularly the least developed, to achieve a sustainable development, and to help them face challenges arising from GLOBALIZATION so that they can integrate into the world economy on an equitable basis. Forty-eight countries (totalling about 614 million inhabitants between them) are currently designated by the United Nations as 'Least Developed Countries' (LDCs) on the basis of the following criteria: a low income; weak human resources (life expectancy at birth, per capita calorie intake, school enrolment and adult literacy); and a low level of economic diversification. The list is reviewed every three years and criteria are also subject to continuous review. The Committee for Development Policy has recently recommended that the Economic Diversification Index be replaced by an Economic Vulnerability Index reflecting the main external shocks to which many low-income countries are subject. In the early 1990s there was a widespread expectation that the globalization of production systems and finance, and the liberalization of economic activity, would promote diminishing income disparities between countries within the global economy. The 1990s saw an accelerating process of economic liberalization in many LDCs. However, overall progress in human and social development has been disappointingly slow, except for a few cases. The number of people living in poverty is increasing in various regions of the world, and the poorest countries are failing to catch up with developed and other developing countries, and some are getting stuck in vicious circles of economic stagnation and regress. At present the development prospects of most LDCs still critically depend on aid relationships and associated external debts dynamics. LDCs represent the hard core of the problem of MARGINALIZATION in the world economy, as they run the risk of becoming persistent pockets of poverty in the global economy. As stated in the UNCTAD *Least Developed Countries 2000 Report*: 'with continued international commitment to a two speed liberal economy order, in which policies to facilitate the free movement of goods and capital are vigorously pursued whilst equivalent measures to facilitate the free movement of labour are discouraged, the citizens of LDCs will increasingly face an unenviable choice between either poverty at home, or social exclusion abroad, as illegal workers or second class citizens in other countries'. [A. B., R. B.]

United Nations Conference on Trade And Development (UNCTAD) (2000) *The Least Developed Countries 2000 Report*, New York and Geneva.

United Nations Development Program (UNDP) (2000) *Human Development Report*, New York and Geneva.

DIASPORA

(It. *diaspora*; Fr. *diaspora*; Ger. *Diaspora*) Though the image of a journey is central to the idea of diaspora, not every journey can be conceived as constituting a diaspora. The concept of diaspora, which means dispersion, from the Greek verb *dia-speirein* to scatter, from *dia-* and *speirein* to sow, suggests a particular type of journey, one usually involving some degree of compulsion. To illuminate the concept further, we first need to specify not just who is travelling, but when, how and under what circumstances travel is undertaken. Secondly, we need to differentiate one diasporic formation from another. Diasporas might be created as a result of, *inter alia*, conquest, colonization, SLAVERY, systems of indentured labour, expulsion, persecution, political conflict or war, as well as by economic migration flows (Brah, 1996: 182).

The crucial aspect is, however, not simply a function of a community being relocated, dispersed or separated from an original centre to other locations by means such as these; this community must have a sense at the end of their journey of not being truly settled or completely accepted in what can be described as the 'host society'.

At one time the term 'diaspora' referred almost exclusively to the exile and dispersion of the Jewish people and also to their continued scattering throughout the world outside Palestine and, later, Israel, a condition which has continued into the modern era. The Hebrew word for diaspora, *Galut*, means exile (ANTI-SEMITISM), and, indeed, the Jewish diaspora began with the EXILE from Babylon in 586 BC and continued after the destruction of the Second Temple in AD 70; it is estimated that by the first century AD at least 5 million Jews lived in various provinces of the Roman empire outside Palestine. In the context arising from the special relationship between the Jewish people and the biblical Land of Israel, the term 'diaspora' carries philosophical, political, religious and eschatological connotations.

We can discern two contrasting characteristics of the Jewish diaspora. On the one hand, Jews continued to think of themselves as a single people and so we can speak of a core of Jewish culture and values that has held Jews together over many centuries despite their dispersal (JEW). On the other hand, through ASSIMILATION, Jews developed substantial ties with the individual countries of the diaspora in which they lived (for instance, Persia, Spain, Portugal, Italy, France, Germany, Poland, Russia, the UK and the USA). Nevertheless, such assimilation did not prevent Jews from being regarded as 'strangers' – in Simmel's terminology, the 'archetypal stranger' (Simmel, 1908) – that is, as people who, even if they had the right to stay in a given country and even if they had lived there for centuries, continued to be regarded as 'outsiders' and who thus remained somehow 'peripheral' (FOREIGNER). These contrasting elements of a diasporic condition – of being 'outsiders', of having a shared history, of being displaced from an original location – come together in the following way:

> The diasporic community experiences a real or believed feeling of not being accepted in the host community. It

cherishes a MYTH of the original homeland which is seen as a place of return and is committed to the restoration of this homeland. This commitment and continuing relationship with the homeland is essential to group solidarity and identity within the diasporic community. (Westin, 1998)

Given the circumstances of their removal and the conditions that Jews were subsequently to endure in the countries in which they had settled, the concept of diaspora inevitably became associated with notions of loss, victimization, persecution and discrimination (GHETTO). In keeping with this, an important dimension of diaspora is encapsulated in the contrast between the conditions that had apparently prevailed in the original location and those suffered in the present location: this contrast is symbolized insofar as diasporic communities do not control territory and certain diasporas, notably Jewish communities, have not been allowed to own land in various countries in which they have settled.

There is another vital component of diasporas: 'In a mythic sense their identities are tied to events outside the temporality of the nation state [in which they live]. Past events of great significance explain their present situation and their difference' (Westin, 1998: 22). In certain instances – the most notable being the Jewish prayer of 'Next Year in Jerusalem' – these past events give rise to the idea of 'return' to the place of origin.

Cohen suggests that the concept of diaspora encompasses a wide range of exiled communities and that the following features usually apply to a diaspora:

(i) Dispersal from an original homeland (sometimes traumatically); or

(ii) The migration from a homeland for reasons of work, trade, or colonization;

(iii) The collective memory of a homeland;

(iv) The idealization of the ancestral homeland;

(v) The development of a return movement;

(vi) A strong ethnic consciousness and a sense of distinctiveness;

(vii) A troubled relationship with host societies;

(viii) A sense of solidarity with co-ethnics in other countries;

(ix) The possibility of a distinctive, creative life in pluralistic host societies. (Cohen, 1997, quoted in Westin, 1998)

To this list we might add the concept of what are termed 'first nation' diasporas – diasporas created by the colonization and acquisition of land by dominant settler communities that may result in a processes of dispersal of First Nation peoples and their confinement to specified locations or reserves and, more generally, their relegation to the lowest echelons of the newly formed society. Obvious examples of this are the Australian Aborigines and the Native Americans in North America. Indeed, if we conclude that First Nation peoples come to form what amounts to an internal diaspora, this might cause us to re-evaluate classic diasporas (whether resulting from exile or forced migration) as constituting what amounts to 'First Nation people in exile'. In addition, where return from the diasporic condition to the homeland occurs, this may precipitate serious and seemingly intractable conflict if two peoples dispute the same land (INTIFADA).

Several modern ethno-national migrations – such as those of the Moroccans in France, Spain and Germany; the South Koreans in the USA and Canada; and the Russians in former Soviet republics – look as if they will become permanent, well-organized diasporas. Despite the fact that these modern diasporas are more the result of voluntary than forced migration, these communities share several characteristics of the original Jewish diaspora in terms of the conscious maintenance of their original ethno-national identities, their organization into transnational, horizontal networks and the maintenance of strong ties with their homelands.

The concept of diaspora encourages us to reconsider certain key aspects of ETHNICITY, as it throws doubt on the common assumption that territoriality is the essential and determining condition for ethnicity: thus it is widely held that common traits, CULTURE, language, religious belief and so on are derived from a common origin, and this, in turn, is connected to a given territory. Yet, because as Rex (1994) points out, 'ethnic communities are often concerned precisely with their *detachment* from a territory', the notion of diaspora allows us to explore the way in which displacement (and perhaps also, return) is maintained in the 'collective memory' of an ethnic community and helps to define certain ethnic groups.

Notions of diaspora are changing as GLOBALIZATION acts to 'deterritorialize' social identities (IDENTITY) and thus may be seen as modifying some of the conventional wisdom about ethnicity. One consequence of this change is that minority ethnic communities (ETHNIC MINORITY) in countries of immigration are no longer as dependent as they once were on conditions in the country in which they have settled. Not only is it now much easier for diasporic communities to constitute transnational communities with common identities, cultural characteristics and lifestyles but they can much more easily form transnational *economic* networks thanks to developments in communications, such as cheap air fares, satellite TV, the Internet, electronic data interchange, fax and email.

One contribution of diasporic studies is to draw attention to the importance of transnational 'imagined communities' and to help students of migration to move away from the view that international migration consists of a unidirectional flow of people from one location to another which, moreover, inevitably involves migrants abandoning their culture of origin and accepting – through assimilation – the culture of the country in which they settle. The 'corrective' which the concept of diaspora brings to migration studies should not, however, be exaggerated: migration studies have had no difficulty in encompassing, for example, exploration of remittances sent by migrants to family members who have not migrated or exploration of the eventual wish on the part of many migrants to return to the country of origin when sufficient savings have been accumulated.

In some circles – especially nationalist and right-wing circles – the existence of a diasporic community gives rise to deep concern and suspicion about the community's double and divided loyalties (DOUBLE CONSCIOUSNESS) towards the homeland and the host country (Sheffer, 1995). It is precisely this sense of shared origins and ties with a 'homeland' which, though it may constitute a strong cementing element for diasporic communities, is capable of arousing ambivalent or hostile feelings in the wider, host society. Jews have been particularly susceptible to such suspicions, often being regarded as disloyal to their host country and not infrequently being accused of espionage and conspiracy against it. [P. B., A. Z.]

Angelo, M. (1977) *The Sikh Diaspora: Tradition and Change in an Immigrant Community*, Garland Publishing, New York.

Brah, A. (1996) *Cartographies of Diaspora: Contesting Identities*, Routledge, London.

Cohen, R. (1997) *Global Diasporas: an Introduction*, UCL Press, London.

Rawidowicz, S., Ravid, B. J., Meyer, M. A. (1997) *State of Israel, Diaspora, and Jewish Continuity. Essays on the 'Ever-Dying People'*, published by the University Press of New England, Hanover, NH, USA.

Rex, J. (1994) 'The nature of ethnicity in the project of migration', *Innovation. The European Journal of Social Science*, 7(3): 207–217.

Segal, R. (1996) *The Black Diaspora*, Noonday Press, New York.

Sheffer, G. (1995) 'The emergence of new ethno-national diasporas', *Migration 28/95*, special issue, ed. Sheffer, G.: *Nationalism and Diaspora*.

Simmel, G. (1908) *Soziologie. Untersuchungen über die Formen der Vergesellschaftung*, Dunker & Humblot, Leipzig.

Vertovec, S. (2000) *The Hindu Diaspora: Comparative Patterns (Global Diaspora)*, Routledge, London.

Westin, C. (1998) 'Temporal and spatial aspects of multiculturality: reflections on the meaning of time and space in relation to the blurred boundaries of multicultural societies', in Bauböck, R., Rundell, J. (eds), *Blurred Boundaries: Migration, Ethnicity, Citizenship*, Aldershot, Ashgate.

DIFFERENTIALISM

(It. *differenzialismo*; Fr. *différentialisme*; Ger. *Differentialismus*) The term 'differentialism' refers to the view that it is important to protect differences (DIVERSITY–SIMILARITY), especially those of an ethnic or cultural nature against the processes of homogenization.

This view was expressed with clarity and force in a document written for UNESCO by Claude Lévi-Strauss in 1952. According to Lévi-Strauss, world civilization cannot be other than a worldwide coalition of cultures – each of which maintains its own originality. He warned against the dangers of cultural homogenization, and asserted that CIVILIZATION implied the coexistence of cultures (CULTURE) of the maximum diversity and, indeed, that civilization even *depends* on such a coexistence (Lévi-Strauss, 1952).

In keeping with its long-standing resistance to the homogenization that results from GLOBALIZATION, the French Left has traditionally taken a differentialist line. Henri Lefebvre, a noted French Marxist scholar, published a 'differentialist manifesto' which advocated resistance to the great homogeneous powers operating in the modern world, first among which were capitalist production methods (Lefebvre, 1970). However, the Left seemed to reverse its position in respect of the French state's approach to immigration. It saw in French immigration policy an attempt to promote ASSIMILATION (or *Gallicization*) rather than accept cultural diversity – with the aim of including immigrants within a single notion of 'Frenchness' – in accordance with the prevailing model of French Republicanism. The Left unwittingly helped to create a new form of RACISM, which rested on the assumption that races and cultures are unequal and uncompromisingly different. These accusations, which were more ideological than scientific, had the paradoxical effect of suggesting that Lévi-Strauss was an advocate of the differentialist approach, even though Lévi-Strauss had always been a sworn enemy of any form of racism and a supporter of the importance of dialogue between cultures, as well as of the need to protect cultural differences.

By contrast, the New Right in France criticized French immigration policy, not merely because, in their view, certain kinds of immigrants threatened

'Frenchness', but also because, through assimilation of such immigrants, official policy sought to deny what the New Right saw as the fundamental and fixed differences between what it regarded as discrete cultures.

Similarly, some left-wing scholars have interpreted the politics of movements such as the Northern League in Italy as differentialist or new racist insofar as they attempt to preserve their cultural IDENTITY from 'improper' contamination by immigrants and foreigners. [U. M.]

Balbo, L., Manconi, L. (1990) *I razzismi possibili*, Feltrinelli, Milano.
De Benoist, A., Béjin A., Taguieff, P. A. (1986) *Racisme et antiracisme*, Méridians Klincksieck, Paris.
Lefebvre H. (1970) *Le Manifeste différentialiste*, Gallimard, Paris.
Lévi-Strauss, C. (1952) *Race et histoire*, UNESCO, Paris.

DISCRIMINATION: see RACIAL DISCRIMINATION

DIVERSITY - SIMILARITY (It. *Diversità–somiglianza*; Fr. *Diversité–similitude*; Ger. *Verschiedenheit–Gleichartigkeit*) Diversity and similarity are the opposite extremes of a relationship which is often used to explain phenomena connected with ETHNICITY and RACISM. The term 'diversity' derives from the Latin *diversum*, meaning 'facing the opposite direction', and is used to describe the quality or condition of someone or something which is different. The term 'similarity' derives from the Latin *similis*, meaning similar, and is used to describe someone or something bearing a 'likeness' to another. Psychological analysis of racism has often made use of the diversity–similarity pairing. Indeed, this pairing plays a positive role in encouraging child development and stimulating individuation processes, i.e. those processes during which a human being becomes an individual who is aware of his or her individuality. Margaret Mahler's description of the symbiotic stage and her concept of separation-individuation makes wide use of the diversity–similarity pairing. However, intensification of these processes can lead to real and proper psychopathologies of the sensation of diversity–similarity.

Discovering the diversity and similarity between one individual and another can be both gratifying and disturbing. While similarity may reassure an individual and guarantee his or her belonging to a group, this sense of inclusion may also be rejected for both conscious and UNCONSCIOUS reasons. Should this occur a conflict is created within the self and with others which may lead to racist behaviour. On the other hand, diversity often helps build and consolidate the IDENTITY of both individuals and groups. When individuals are able to recognize the diversity of other individuals, they are also able to clearly outline the limits of their psychic and existential space. However, should an individual perceive his or her diversity in a moment of particular psychological weakness, he or she may try to react to this perception by paranoid exaltation of diversity. The individual then disparages the others and, failing to recognize them as diverse, sees them as inferior. Thus the perception of diversity may lead to racist behaviour.

Social psychology has shown that analogous mechanisms can also be used to explain group behaviour and attitudes, including XENOPHOBIA and racism. The identity of any group is the result of several processes of recognition of interior similarity and exterior diversity. An understanding of the meaning of diversity may help a group unite and build its essential structures, regardless of whether the individual chooses this group consciously or voluntarily, or whether he or she automatically becomes part of an established set. When a group discovers it is different to others, it tends to recognize how members of the community conform to the principles held by the group, while the individual recognizes the common characteristics of the group as his or her own (CONFORMISM). However, a group may suffer from pathological identity crises leading to its destruction, or crisis in individual members leading to the group's disintegration or inclusion within another group, or even individual identity crises (ADAPTATION, ALIENATION). The more a group is able to distinguish itself from others, the more united it will be. Groups may even close in on themselves in order to ensure protection from the negative aspects of diversity that might engulf their members in totalitarian HOMOLOGATION. In this case anything outside the group is demonized or denied. The positive aspects of diversity form one of the fundamental principles on which group identity is based. Such aspects come to the fore in dialogue with others; however they may become negative when used as a pretext for groups to close in on themselves in order to disparage others, consequently producing racism and xenophobia.

The diversity–similarity pairing is also considered relevant to the debate on ethnicity from a biological point of view. Modern biology recognizes the substantial similarity (based on the universality of the genetic code) of all beings living on the planet Earth. It emphasizes that diversity does not contradict this similarity but enriches it. The term 'biodiversity' has been used to describe the huge variety of life forms existing at all biological levels. Various estimates set the number of living species at between 10 and 100 million, of which no more than 1.5 million have been identified and classified by biological science. Both the genetic variety of the various species and the genetic variety within each species are the result of an ongoing process of ADAPTATION involving the individual and the environment and make the development of future adaptation mechanisms possible. Biologists see biodiversity as a crucial resource for all the organisms living on our planet. The protection of biodiversity from the threats resulting from the increase in the human population – such as pollution, intensive farming and, more recently, the introduction to the environment of genetically modified organisms – has been one of the most important features of ecological struggles over the last few years. In 1992 the United Nations adopted an international convention on biological diversity. This affirms that the conservation of biological diversity is a responsibility of humankind and its sustainable use is crucial to meeting the food, health and other needs of a growing world population.

The concept of biological diversity also refers to genetic variation within the human species (GENOTYPE). In this case, the opposing elements of the diversity–similarity pairing are inverted. Biologists have highlighted that the most important feature of the human species is the uniformity of its genetic heritage. After years of debate about the monogenetic (the human species derives from a single group of ancestors) and plurigenetic (the human species has its origins in various groups which then converge to form the different ethnic and racial stocks) theories, the results of the Human Genome Diversity Project seem to confirm the monogenetic hypothesis (MONOGENISM), refusing to admit that any theory which sees the division of the human species into races can have genetic foundations. Genetic diversity between the various human 'races' seems to be largely a myth (RACE). [S. G.]

Cavalli-Sforza. L., Cavalli-Sforza, F. (1996) *The Great Human Diasporas: The History of Diversity and Evolution*, Perseus Publishing, Cambridge, MA.

Ehrenfeld, D. (ed.) (1995) *To Preserve Biodiversity: An Overview*, Blackwell, Oxford.

Mahler, M. S. (1968) *On Human Symbiosis and the Vicissitudes of Individuation*, International University Press, New York.

Rex, J. (1973) *Race, Colonialism and the City*, Routledge, London.

Wieviorka, M. (1991) *L'Espace du racisme*, Seuil, Paris.

Wilson, E. O., Peter, F. M. (eds) (1988) *Biodiversity*, National Academic Press, Washington, DC.

DOUBLE CONSCIOUSNESS (It. *doppia co-scienza*; Fr. *double conscience*; Ger. *doppeltes Bewußtsein*)

The concept of 'double consciousness' with regard to RACE RELATIONS was developed by the intellectual black activist William E.B. Du Bois (1868–1963). Referring to the situation in the United States, he maintained that in order to create a non-racist society, black Americans should simultaneously maintain their American and their African identities. Du Bois often stated that no people represented the spirit of the Declaration of Independence more faithfully than black Americans, that there was no truly American music except that deriving from the black slaves (SLAVERY) and that the legends of American folklore originated in the more ancient Indian and African cultures. Furthermore, black Americans had fought in America's battles and played an active role in her social and political experiments, mixed their blood with that of other Americans – from generation to generation – and urged a stubborn and uncaring people not to despise justice, compassion and truth.

Du Bois' statements show that the problem of double consciousness is strongly connected to the condition of MARGINALIZATION and inferiorization experienced by African-American people, yet the condition of double belonging is also a common feature among many other members of American society, as clearly expressed by the need for such terms such as 'hyphenated citizen' and 'hyphenated identity'. The pervasiveness of this special condition of doubleness throughout American mythology results from the fact that the United States has always been described as a country open to all human beings, regardless of their cultural diversity (DIVERSITY–SIMILARITY). To be American requires nothing more than to share the same universal principles and, as a consequence, it is possible for migrants to become American without losing any elements of their culture of belonging, unless such elements constitute a threat to the safety of the nation. However, although the condition of double consciousness is relatively unproblematic in a political sense, from a psychological point of view the feeling of disorientation experienced by migrants can be extremely disturbing (ALIENATION). Indian political leader Jawaharlal Nehru, whose studies in the West had turned him into a 'strange mixture of East and West, out of place everywhere and never at ease' (Nehru, 1941: 65), describes how he had adopted the thoughts and outlook on life of the Western model but was unable to detach himself from racial memory of generations of Brahmans that was ingrained in his UNCONSCIOUS and thus felt a foreigner and a stranger in the West yet an exile in his country of origin. [M. V.]

Du Bois, W. E. B. (1968) *Dusk of Dawn: An Essay toward an Autobiography of a Race Concept*, Schocken Books, New York.

Nehru, J. (1941) *Toward Freedom. Autobiography of Jawaharlal Nehru*, John Day, New York.

Park, R. (1928) 'Human migration and the marginal man', *American Journal of Sociology*, 33: 881–893.

Stonequist, E. V. (1937) *The Marginal Man: A Study in Personality and Culture Conflict*, Scribner's Sons, New York.

Turner, V. (1987) 'Betwixt and between. The liminal period in rites of passage, in Mahdi, L., Foster, S., Little, M. (eds), *Betwixt and Between: Patterns of Masculine and Feminine Initiation*, Open Court, Lasalle, IL.

DUAL CITIZENSHIP (It. *doppia cittadinanza;* Fr. *double nationalité;* Ger. *doppelte Staatsbürgerschaft*) The term 'dual citizenship' refers to the status of a person who is simultaneously the citizen of two countries. Dual citizenship can be obtained by birth or acquisition of new CITIZENSHIP which allows maintenance of the citizenship of origin. Regulations governing dual citizenship are based on a Convention signed in Strasbourg on 6 May 1963, concerning the reduction of cases of multiple citizenship. Generally speaking, it is still possible to obtain dual citizenship within all European and non-European countries. [Gu. B.]

Colabianchi, A. (ed.) (1997) 'Cittadinanza dell'Unione Europea, il diritto di voto e di elegibilità alle elezioni comunali', *I quaderni dell'Anide*, Roma.

Lippolis, V. (1994) *La cittadinanza europea*, Il Mulino, Bologna.

EBONICS

(It. *Ebonics*; Fr. *Ebonics*; Ger. *Ebonics*) Coined in 1975 by the American linguist Robert L. Williams, the term 'Ebonics' derives from the words 'ebony' (referring to blackness) and 'phonics' (the sound quality and musicality of the phonation of a language) which identifies the originality and autonomy of the language spoken by African-Americans as opposed to Standard English. As well as providing a verbal communication system (also known as *Pan-African Communication Behaviours* or *African Language Systems*), Ebonics has long since been used in African-American literature as an expression of ethnic pride (ETHNIC). According to black linguists, Ebonics is based on an African perspective which differs radically from Euro-Western views of nature and reality, and, although controversial, ideas about the significance of Ebonics (which also lie at the heart of an unresolved controversy over Afrocentric education) should not be glossed over lightly.

> There is a continuing need to disseminate the facts about the relationship between Standard English and Non Standard Varieties such as Black Vernacular English, as the principle of mutual recognition and respect is constantly being challenged. . . . These days there is an increasing understanding of the educational issues: but an enlightened approach to the problem is by no means universal. (Crystal, 1997: 35)

The linguistic form which has spread through black urban working-class communities is generally known as Afro-American Vernacular English (AAVE) or Black English Vernacular (BEV). It is widely accepted (Dillard, 1972; Labov, 1982) that this language largely derives from the PIDGIN and Creole languages originally spoken by African slaves in the plantations of the Southern United States (Plantation Creole). Following the abolition of SLAVERY, this language continued to be used in the urban ghettos (GHETTO) in which African-American people migrating towards the Northern States chose to settle. Thus, as a result of its Creole origins (CREOLE LANGUAGE), the African-American language still preserves traces of the original merging of West African (Igbo, Yoruba, Ewe) and Caribbean languages, despite the influence of the English spoken by white people which has progressively obscured its roots (decreolization).

The term 'Ebonics' takes on special relevance for ethnic or racial groups in the promotion of their CULTURE and activities designed to overcome discrimination and inferiorization. An intense debate has developed in the United States regarding the right to cultural and linguistic independence of African-American communities, of which Ebonics is an important expression. Insistence upon the use of Ebonics reflects the view that language patterns are the lens through which a cultural group looks at the world. Thus, the debate on Ebonics has become part of the process of promotion and confirmation of black culture – a current also known as 'Black Renaissance' or AFROCENTRISM.

There is a careful balance to be achieved between recognizing the links between West African languages and Ebonics and attending to the major goal of black students of becoming fluent in

Standard English. Nevertheless, teachers and administrators would do well to understand that Black English Vernacular – in both its verbal and its non-verbal aspects (body language) – is not some form of whimsical, transient or popular slang. Instead it is an evolving system of communication that, at least in the past, proved adaptive in enabling black people to function in a marginalized African-American world (MARGINA-LIZATION). That this is a controversial view is shown by the fact that a resolution passed in December 1996 by the School Board of Oakland, California made headlines across the USA. This was directed at developing improved methods for teaching Standard English to students of African-American descent and spoke in terms of recognizing the worth of Ebonics as a 'language' rather than a 'dialect'. This is not to diminish the need for black people to become proficient in the language of the dominant culture if they are to become integrated into mainstream society. Rather it is to underline the importance of accurately disentangling the complex web of social and cultural phenomena – the putative causal factors – associated with academic underachievement.

Saving Ebonics is not a matter of cultural pride, but a means of preventing total ASSIMILATION. The same word differs in meaning in Standard English and in Black English Vernacular, evoking different images and bringing a whole range of inherent cultural factors into play. Thus, cultural behaviour is related not only to cultural background but also to the language spoken. The possibility of introducing Ebonics into the school system should be considered not naïve homage but an attempt to give academic dignity to a linguistic system in such a way as to improve that system's chance of survival, free from discrimination and devaluation.

According to Alondra Oubré (1997), the modern challenge is to convince the youth who speak Ebonics that their identity within the wider COMMUNITY will not be compromised or ridiculed if they take the steps to learn and adopt Standard English as their primary tongue. As a corollary, educators and policy-makers ought to realize that all of these students are quite conscious of the fact that taking these steps will, to some degree, alter the very way in which they perceive the world around them. [A. B., R. B.]

Crystal, D. (1997) *The Cambridge Encyclopedia of Language*, Cambridge University Press, Cambridge.

Dillard, J. L. (1972) *Black English: its History and Usage in the United States*, Random House, New York.

Labov, W. (1982) 'Objectivity and commitment in linguistic science: the case of the black English trial in Ann Arbor', *Language in Society*, 11(2): 165–201.

La Page, R. B., Tabouret-Keller, A. (1985) *Acts of Identity: Creole-based Approaches to Language and Ethnicity*, Cambridge University Press, Cambridge.

Oubré, A. (1997) *Black English Vernacular (Ebonics and Educability): A Cross-cultural Perspective on Language, Cognition and Schooling*, online http://www.phaelos.com/oubre.html.

ECO-RACISM (It. *eco-razzismo*; Fr. *écoracisme*; Ger. *Ökorassismus*)

The term has come into use in Germany in relatively recent times to describe specific types of hostile views about migrants (MIGRANT). Although rooted in classic racist thinking, its special property is that this form of RACISM is presented in ecological terms, thus giving the impression of neutrality and distancing it from more conventional expressions of xenophobic ideology (XENOPHOBIA). The origins of eco-racism can be traced back to two factors: (a) the development of a 'new interpretation' of ecological problems, which appeared in the late 1950s and was characterized by an extremely reactionary view of the relationship between people and their environment; and (b) the growing hostility towards foreigners (FOREIGNER) in what was then the Federal Republic of Germany, especially in the wake of the changed economic conditions which followed the oil crisis of 1973. (Hostility took on much more violent aspects in the early 1990s following German reunification and the arrival of growing numbers of asylum seekers.)

From the eco-racist point of view, irrespective of any economic benefits it may bring, immigration is unwelcome simply because it is seen as having dire environmental consequences for the country of immigration. From such a perspective, a large concentration of immigrants increases the population density of a city (INVASION), produces refuse which must be disposed of and causes depletion of available land. In some cases, the eco-racist argument is even more specific (or convoluted), claiming that as immigrants generally come from countries with a warmer climate, once they have settled in Germany or other Northern European countries they supposedly make greater use of central heating systems, consume more oil and thus increase atmospheric pollution.

The language of eco-racism is evident in mass media coverage of race and immigration (RACE AND THE MEDIA). In Italy, for example, a study of the language of the daily newspapers (Ter Wal, 1996) demonstrated that immigration is often described in terms of ecological disasters: immigrants are compared to 'a human avalanche' or 'the foam of the five seas'; migratory movements are 'floods', 'tides', 'waves', 'deluges' and 'avalanches'.

Though eco-racism may appear distinct in its reliance on the modern preoccupation with the environment as a pretext for hostility towards immigrants, closer inspection reveals that it merely repeats traditional anti-immigrant expressions of feelings which so often blamed immigrants for housing shortages or the deterioration in the quality of life in a given locale and which also depicted the arrival of immigrants in terms of 'tides' and 'floods'. Two examples illustrate this point, both from the UK – one from the 1960s, the other from 1906. Foot quotes the secretary of an anti-immigrant organization in Birmingham as saying: 'Edgbaston Road used to be a *lovely* road . . . it was a pleasure to walk in that area. Now *they've* [black immigrants have] taken over, and the place is like a slum. These people are ruining our town. . . . The houses are falling apart, and they have a pretty high rate of TB. Their habits are pretty terrible. They use their front gardens as a rubbish dump and heavens knows what they do in the toilets' (1965: 36). Similarly, the arrival of Jewish immigrants in certain parts of the East End of London at the end of the nineteenth century and the beginning of the twentieth century was depicted in the election address of one parliamentary candidate as follows: 'Whitechapel, standing as it does, at the very gates of the City of London, the centre of the Empire, was never destined to become a foreign pauper settlement. It is intolerable that we should have unblushingly dumped down among us the very scum of the unhealthiest of continental nations . . . an outrage to the district' (*East London Observer*, 6 January 1906, quoted in Garrard, 1971: 60). Thus if eco-racism is a recent development, it nevertheless draws on a long tradition. [P. B., M. V.]

Ehrich, P., Ehrich, A. (1972) *Population, Resources, Environment*, Freeman, San Francisco.

Foot, P. (1965) *Immigration and Race in British Politics*, Harmondsworth, Penguin.

Garrard, J. (1971) *The English and Immigration, 1880–1910*, Oxford University Press for the Institute of Race Relations, London.

Hardin, G. (1969) *Population Evolution and Birth Control. A Control of Controversial Ideas*, Freeman, San Francisco.

Ter Wal, J. (1996) 'The social representation of immigrants: the Pantanella issue in the pages of *La Repubblica*', *New Community*, 22: 39–66.

EMANCIPATION
(It. *emancipazione*; Fr. *émancipation*; Ger. *Emanzipation*) From the Latin *emancipare* (to set free), the term describes the process by which an individual or an entire population previously subjected to restrictive constraints – social, economic, cultural, etc. – gains recognition of certain important rights. This empowerment (EMPOWERMENT–DISEMPOWERMENT) is usually the result of legislative measures, often arising from assertive initiatives on the part of ethnic, religious or cultural minorities (ETHNIC MINORITY). Emancipation goes hand in hand with the abolition of segregationist (RACIAL SEGREGATION) and discriminatory laws (RACIAL DISCRIMINATION) and marks a movement towards a more democratic form of coexistence. More recently, the emancipation process has come to mean desegregation. The concept of emancipation could be applied to all struggles for liberation by social groups suffering oppression or discrimination (slaves, colonized populations, women and, more recently, homosexuals). Notable among the historical events concerning migratory and racist phenomena is the emancipation of the Jews in Europe between the end of the eighteenth and the nineteenth centuries (JEW). This resulted in the abolition of ghettos (GHETTO) and the ending of forbidden professions and bans on the ownership of property, and permitted Jews to take up public office and to travel freely. The emancipation of black people in the United States began in the latter half of the nineteenth century, concentrating first on the abolition of SLAVERY, then on the recognition of EQUALITY in civil rights. Another important emancipatory process can be seen in the activities of the many liberation movements fighting against COLONIALISM. In South Africa, the most significant landmark in emancipation for black people was the abolition of apartheid.

Emancipation may be a long-drawn-out process, and it must be realized that in many cases – through the impositions of the dominant group or the wishes of the minority – it leads to shifts in cultural practices, greater or lesser ASSIMILATION of the values of the dominant group and, sometimes, perpetuation of racial PREJUDICE. For example, a study of the rising black middle class in the United States (Frazier, 1957) shows that the emancipation process coincides with the acceptance of a cultural model which not only holds fairness of skin in high esteem, but has led to racist attitudes towards those black people who have not managed to gain a certain economic status. [M. V.]

Bonazzi, T., Dunne, M., (eds) (1994) *Cittadinanza e diritti nelle società multiculturali*, Il Mulino, Bologna.

Cooper, F., Holt, T. C., Scott, R. J. (2000) *Beyond Slavery: Explorations of Race, Labour, and Citizenship in Postemancipa-*

tion Societies, University of North Carolina Press, Chapel Hill.

Frazier, F. (1957) *Black Bourgeoisie*, The Free Press, New York.

Klein, M. (1993) *Breaking the Chains: Slavery, Bondage, and Emancipation in Modern Africa and Asia*, University of Wisconsin Press, Madison.

EMIGRATION: see MIGRANT, MIGRATION

EMPOWERMENT - DISEMPOWERMENT

(It. *Empowerment–disempowerment*; Fr. *Empowerment–disempowerment*; Ger. *Empowerment–disempowerment*) The concept of empowerment refers to a process whereby people who are oppressed are enabled to gain some power and control over their lives (Bystydzienski, 1992). It is, therefore, the opposite of disempowerment – a process by which people are socially excluded because they are denied access to such power and control. Empowerment and disempowerment can be said to occur at three interconnected levels: personal, COMMUNITY and political. At a personal level, empowerment refers to the process whereby people are enabled to gain the resources that enable them to live in optimal conditions, in ways that they would choose. While these resources are partly psychological, they are also educational, economic and political. People can have self-confidence, self-esteem and the knowledge necessary to influence their environments but be disempowered by the community or political system in which they live. However, as Sudbury points out, 'the concept of individual empowerment is an important one within social movements which aim to counter the internali-

zation of the dominant mode of social interaction' (1998: 61).

RACISM, ETHNICIZATION, religious, gendered and social class discrimination are all sources of community and political disempowerment in that they reduce people's life chances and the economic and social possibilities open to them (Small, 1994). With increasing recognition of, and opposition to, oppressive practices and COLONIALISM throughout the world, empowerment has been on the political agenda since the 1960s (Yuval-Davis, 1994). Notable examples of attempts to empower communities include: the pioneering work of Paolo Freire (1972) who used community-based pedagogic techniques in order to enable people living in poverty in Brazil to become literate; the liberation theology of some Roman Catholic priests in South America who aimed to assist poor people in resisting the socio-economic circumstances and oppressive regimes under which they lived; credit unions which lend money to their members (who are usually in the same organization) at lower rates of interest than would otherwise be possible; and the work of various charities and of many self-help groups which aim to help make communities self-sufficient. The BLACK MUSLIMS can be seen as a controversial community-level organization which has empowered many of its members by its emphasis on black people's self-sufficiency and mutual support.

At a political level, anti-discriminatory legislation and economic strategies designed to promote EQUALITY (including policies of AFFIRMATIVE ACTION) can be seen as strategies for empowerment. Yet the concept of empowerment is not as straightforward as it appears to be at first sight. The very idea is in itself problematic since the notion of empowering other people is only possible if those doing the empowering are more powerful than those to be empowered. The question then arises as to who should decide which groups should be empowered and in which ways. Many would argue that this can only be decided by groups and communities themselves. This is because the imposition of strategies for empowerment is itself disempowering in treating people in relatively powerless positions as if they have no agency or competence. In effect, it denies them participation in the process that is supposed to empower them and, instead, offers them inclusion only on the terms of the socially included. In discussing THIRD WORLD development (DEVELOPING COUNTRIES), Singh and Titi point out that 'the powerful may appear to be conceding power, but they do so in order to manage the *powerless*. Empowerment, therefore, is a contradiction in terms; there can only be *self empowerment*' (1995: 34). This is particularly the case since strategies for empowerment may require economic resources which governments may be reluctant to give (Craig and Mayo, 1995).

The underlying assumption behind strategies for empowerment is often that those identified as socially excluded wish to be socially included and so want the strategies for empowerment being offered to them. Yet there is evidence that many of those who are less powerful in society 'if given a chance to reflect and act collectively, would want to change that system and "to make it their own" by addressing structural issues of their choice' (Shanahan and Ward, 1995: 72). This has been an issue in some strategies designed to address issues raised by MIGRATION. Policies of ASSIMILATION, INTEGRATION and MULTICULTURALISM, in the USA and Britain, have all been criticized on the grounds that they have been imposed on minority ethnic groups (ETHNIC MINORITY) in the interests only of the white ethnic majority and, as such, have reinforced unequal power relations (Rattansi, 1992). As Yuval-Davis points out, an even greater difficulty with the concept of empowerment is 'the ideology of the community' which underpins it (1994: 180), because the perception of 'the community' as a natural social unit – 'a given collectivity with given boundaries' (p. 181) – ignores the fact that the boundaries of, for example, ethnic groups are constructed and permeable, changing over time and according to circumstance. Perhaps even more importantly, it ignores the power imbalances and ETHNIC POLITICS inside racialized and ethnicized groups or that people can be members of more than one community. When outsiders seek to empower particular ethnic groups, they often consult with those whom they consider the 'most authentic' members of that ethnic group and these are often fundamentalists. As a result, by ignoring gender (RACE AND GENDER), as well as social class and other internal differences, strategies for empowerment can serve further to disempower the least powerful even as they allow power to some within ethnic collectivities. Although, for example, some young black children find black teachers empowering (Callender, 1997) and some black teachers put a great deal of effort into attempting to empower their black students (Casey, 1993) care should be taken in generalizing from specific examples. Despite these difficulties, the notion of empowerment continues to be popular. There has, for example, been a European working group on 'Empowering the Excluded' (1995–2000) which aimed to reduce social exclusion and to promote active social inclusion by allowing members of excluded groups to lead the strategies.

However, the very fact that this focused on labour-market strategies indicates that there is, necessarily, an outsider-imposed agenda. In considerations of empowerment–disempowerment, political agendas on 'race', ethnicity, gender etc. must not be: 'taken forward successfully by simplistic notions of empowerment of · the oppressed' (Yuval-Davis, 1994: 182). [A. P.]

Bystydzienski, J. (ed.) (1992) *Women Transforming Politics: Worldwide Strategies for Empowerment*, Indiana University Press, Bloomington.
Callender, C. (1997) *Education for Empowerment*, Trentham Books, Stoke-on-Trent.
Casey, K. (1993) *I Answer with My Life: Life Histories of Women Teachers Working for Social Change*, Routledge, New York.
Craig, G., Mayo, M. (eds) (1995) *Community Empowerment: A Reader in Participation and Development*, Zed Books, London.
Freire, P. (1972) *Pedagogy of the Oppressed*, Penguin, London.
Rattansi, A. (1992) 'Changing the subject? Racism, culture and education', in Donald, J., Rattansi, A. (eds), *'Race', Culture and Difference*, Sage, London.
Shanahan, P., Ward., J. (1995) 'The university and empowerment: the European Union, university adult education and community economic development with "excluded groups"', in Craig, G., Mayo, M. (eds).
Singh, N., Titi, V. (eds) (1995) *Empowerment for Sustainable Development: Toward Operational Strategies*, Zed Books, London.
Small, S. (1994) *Racialized Barriers: The Black Experience in the United States and England in the 1980s*, Routledge, London.
Sudbury, J. (1998) *'Other Kinds of Dreams': Black Women's Organizations and the Politics of Transformation*, Routledge, London.
Yuval-Davis, N. (1994) 'Women, ethnicity and empowerment', in Bhavnani, K. K., Phoenix, A. (eds), *Shifting Identities: Shifting Racisms*, Sage, London.

ENCULTURATION (It. *inculturazione*; Fr. *enculturation*; Ger. *Inkulturation*)

The term 'enculturation' derives from the word 'culture' and indicates the ASSIMILATION of the contents, practices and values of the cultural traditions of a group by the individuals belonging to the group. The term was introduced into social sciences by M. J. Herskovits (1948), in order to indicate the complex interaction between an individual and the particular CULTURE of which this person is both creation and creator. It is clear that when cultural models are passed on from one generation to another they are never exactly the same, as they are continuously subject to additions and innovations. Margaret Mead defined this phenomenon, which is emphasized in the industrial society, as the 'generation gap' (1970). According to Herskovits, the process of enculturation lasts a lifetime, changing with each different stage in an individual's life, making it necessary to distinguish between the infancy stage (where enculturation is imposed and arbitrary), the adolescent stage (in which it is orientated towards social integration, beginning with socialization in informal groups with the adolescent's peers), and the adult stage (when it is an aware and critical form of acceptance or refusal of the values and choices of the person's group).

Other approaches focus on the complementarity of socialization and enculturation, with enculturation being considered a process which comprises conscious and UNCONSCIOUS moments experienced by an individual throughout his or her life with different levels of intensity (Callari Galli, 1993). Following a careful study of the process of individual cultural acquisition, anthropologists have defined an 'antiracist' theory according to which, when every other element of a group apart from RACE is the same, similar enculturational teachings automatically lead to a similar social and cultural repertoire. According to Marvin Harris (1968), even if it is not possible to prove that all major groups of *Homo sapiens* have the same ability to learn all types of responses, there is no doubt that most of the repertoire of responses of any human population can be learned by any other population. [G. H.]

Callari Galli, M. (1993) *Antropologia culturale e processi educativi*, La Nuova Italia, Firenze.

Harris, M. (1968) *The Rise of Anthropological Theory. A History of Theories of Culture*, Crowell, New York.

Herskovits, M. J. (1948) *Man and His Works*, Knopf, New York.

Kluckhohn, C. (1949) *Personality in Nature, Society and Culture*, Knopf, New York.

Linton, R. (1945) *The Cultural Background of Personality*, Appleton-Century-Crofts, New York.

Mead, M. (1970) *Culture and Commitment: A Study of the Generation Gap*, Natural History Press, Garden City, NY.

EQUALITY

(It. *uguaglianza*; Fr. *égalité*; Ger. *Gleichheit*) In the field of ethics, the principle of equality is generally ascribed to the Ancient Greek Stoic school of philosophy, as far as the rationality and morality of human beings is concerned, and to Jewish-Christian thinking with regard to the idea of equality between citizens as an essential principle of any democratic regime based on majority rule. The ethical value of equality – which generates the legal principle of equality – implies a need to consider the interests and desires of all human beings on an equal basis as all such interests and desires have an equal dignity. Thus,

morally and legally, any difference in treatment must be justified. On the other hand, the legal principle of equality is, by its very nature, relative, as the fundamental purpose of any regulation is to introduce distinction and thus inevitably propose inequality.

The principle of equality of the citizens of a state was first set forth in the *Unanimous Declaration of the Thirteen United States of America* (1776), better known as the Declaration of Independence: 'We hold these truths to be self-evident, that all men are created equal, that they are endowed by their Creator with certain unalienable Rights, that among these are Life, Liberty and the Pursuit of Happiness'. This document greatly influenced the French *Declaration of the Rights of Man and of the Citizen* adopted in Paris in 1789, the first article of which reads: 'Men are born and remain free and equal in rights. Social distinctions may be founded only upon the general good.' Legal confirmation of the principle of equality between citizens was an expression of the rule of law which was gradually taking hold and was manifest in the texts of the liberal constitutions introduced in various European settings during the revolutionary and Napoleonic period and throughout the nineteenth century. These late eighteenth-century ideas of equality attacked a more traditional idea of privilege based on rank, wealth, religion or social class. They are normally taken to imply equality of treatment and opportunity, but not for example, except in certain socialist recastings, equality of wealth. They applied, however, primarily to white men. The history of women's movements over the past two centuries has largely been one of the attempt to achieve equal treatment for women (legally, politically, economically and so on). Similarly, various racial and ethnic groups have, in both Western and postcolonial contexts (POSTCOLO-NIAL STUDIES), engaged in struggles to achieve similar sorts of equality.

The concept of equality, while it has come to be generally accepted, has not been without its challengers. The French text cited above contains the very ingredients for its undermining. That text allows for social distinctions insofar as they contribute to the general good; no society, for example, advocates that murderers be treated the same as other citizens. But it is in the definition of the general good that one can find the justification for denying equality. The maintenance of a traditional political, economic and social order can for example justify systems as profoundly unequal as the JIM CROW laws once in force in the American South or South African apartheid (RACIAL SEGREGA-TION). And if a specific (possibly ethnic) group is identified as a threat to the common good (for example Jews in Nazi Germany) then the common good can be invoked to justify so-called crimes against humanity (ANTI-SEMITISM).

Enlightenment ideas on equality were reiterated in the United Nations' 1948 *Universal Declaration of Human Rights*: 'Article 1. All human beings are born free and equal in dignity and rights.' That document, however, goes a step further than those cited above in specify-ing the grounds upon which equality should *not* be denied: 'Article 2. Every-one is entitled to all the rights and freedoms set forth in this Declaration, without distinction of any kind, such as race, colour, sex, language, religion, political or other opinion, national or social origin, property, birth or other status.' In keeping with this expanded conception, the late twentieth century saw the proliferation of movements for equality in the interests of groups traditionally discriminated against in various ways: racial or ETHNIC groups, homosexuals, persons with phy-sical or mental handicaps, non-citizens (EXTRACOMUNITARIO, DENIZEN) and so on. In that period the issue of equality also became inextricably bound up with a global discourse on human rights. In reaction to historic situations which subsequently came to be recog-nized as unequal and unjust, for exam-ple the inferior status of African-Americans, various attempts have been made to 'level the playing field' and speed up the process of establishing equality (for example of educational and economic opportunity). The most nota-ble and debated of these attempts has been AFFIRMATIVE ACTION, a form of reverse discrimination which seeks to accelerate the upward socio-economic mobility of the targeted group. Not surprisingly, affirmative action has been attacked as violating the principle of equality and, most notably by its opponents among the targeted groups, for creating a syndrome of dependence. The UN document cited above also signalled a new attitude with regard to immigrants (MIGRANT) and non-citi-zens. Liberal national constitutions have traditionally guaranteed the equality of *citizens* before the law, while non-citizens (until they are naturalized) have been subject to different and discriminatory regimes (with regard to rights of residency and employment, criminal prosecution, access to services, voting rights and so on). Recent decades have witnessed a reaction against such regimes and the progressive expansion of the rights of equal treatment regarded as the patrimony of all individuals who find themselves (legally) in the national territory. [S. P.]

Cerri, A. (1994) 'Eguaglianza (principio costituzionale di)', in *Enciclopedia giur-idica*, Treccani, Roma.
Cruse, H. (1987) *Plural but Equal: Blacks*

and Minorities and America's Plural Society, Morrow, New York.

Fisk, M. (1980) *Ethics and Society*, New York University Press, New York.

Kristol, I. (1968) 'Equality as an ideal', in *International Encyclopaedia of the Social Sciences*, Macmillan, New York.

Paladin, L. (1992) 'Eguaglianza', in *Enciclopedia del diritto*, Giuffré, Milano.

Touraine, A. (1997) *Pourrons-nous vivre ensemble?*, Fayard, Paris.

ETHNIC

(It. *etnico*; Fr. *ethnique*; Ger. *ethnisch*) The adjective 'ethnic' qualifies the features which are characteristic of, relate to, or are peculiar to a given people. An ancient Judaeo-Christian meaning referred the term to non-monotheistic populations. However, more generally, both the adjective and the corresponding noun ETHNICITY, although useful descriptive tools, remain scientifically ambiguous and vague. [S. G.]

ETHNIC CLEANSING

(It. *pulizia etnica*; Fr. *nettoyage ethnique*; Ger. *ethnische Säuberung*) 'Ethnic cleansing' is a literal translation of the Serbo-Croat *etnicko ciscenje*. The origins of the expression are difficult to trace; however, it is used to describe warlike conduct against civilians who are targeted solely because of their nationality, RACE or religion (RELIGION AND ETHNIC CONFLICTS), and made the objects of persecution and terrorization, mass murder, rape, torture, plunder or even castration. The actual expression 'ethnic cleansing' was first used in 1981 to describe the decision to render a number of areas in Kosovo 'ethnically pure zones', but the policy itself has

been applied outside the former Yugoslavia, often with terrible consequences in all areas inhabited by populations of different ethnic origin, especially where the problem of redefining borders is involved (FRONTIER). In these cases AGGRESSION is directed towards sections of the civilian population who are seen to be the enemy, rather than unleashed between opposing armies. There are many examples of ethnic cleansing all over the world, such as the extreme cases of conflict between the Hutus and Tutsis in Rwanda and Burundi. [S. G.]

Niemegeers, M. (1997) *Qui veut la mort du Burundi?*, Harmattan, Paris.

Gashi, A. (ed.) (1992) *The Denial of Human and National Rights of Albanians in Kosovo*, Illyria Publishing, New York.

Grmek, M., Gjidara, M., Simac, N. (1993) *Le Nettoyage ethnique. Documents historiques sur une idéologie serbe*, Fayard, Paris.

Levy Vroelant, C., Joseph, C. (1997) *La Guerre aux civils*, Harmattan, Paris.

ETHNIC ENTERPRISE

(It. *imprenditoria etnica*; Fr. *entreprise ethnique*; Ger. *ethnisches Unternehmen*) The term 'ethnic enterprise' is a polyvalent expression used to describe a wide array of socio-economic phenomena. Its coinage responds to the obvious economic impact that accompanies social diversification (DIVERSITY–SIMILARITY). Such diversification created new specific needs deriving from ETHNIC and national origins and made available specific skills connected to national origins. Ethnic enterprise may, and indeed does, vary from one group to another according to differences in social capital or family organization. The starting point for the study of ethnic enterprise is that migrants (MIGRANT) often have a higher entrepreneurial rate than the indigenous population. This can be interpreted as the product of two convergent forces. First, migrants tend to be members of a select group of people with a high entrepreneurial aptitude (one of the factors which leads them to migrate). This can be considered the positive force. By contrast, migrants often experience difficulties in entering the job market of the host country – especially in the state sector, which may exclude non-citizens (CITIZENSHIP). Few jobs are therefore available to migrants, and this constitutes a push factor inducing migrant workers to set up their own businesses. The term refers to many categories and populations, including foreigners (FOREIGNER), migrants and ethnic groups (ETHNIC MINORITY). Although it is extremely difficult to offer a single definition of an ethnic enterprise, attempts have been made to provide a classification of ethnic enterprise. Zucchetti (1995) lists five kinds of independent business run by foreigners, migrants or members of ethnic minorities: (1) typically ethnic enterprises which supply products and services specifically to satisfy the special needs of an immigrant community and which are not available in the host country; (2) intermediary enterprises offering products and services which are not typically ethnic but which require mediation in order to be exploited by the immigrant population; (3) exotic enterprises offering specific products from the country of origin to consumers of migrant origin and indigenous origin alike (EXOTICISM); (4) open enterprises less closely connected to the ethnic roots of the entrepreneur operating on the competitive market; (5) refugee enterprises whose products and market are difficult to identify as a result of their marginal position (REFUGEE).

In various countries, such as France, Germany, Holland and the UK, enterprises set up by immigrants or ethnic minorities often occupy positions of considerable social and economic significance. In France, only 4 per cent of the widely varied immigrant population is involved in ethnic enterprise, the majority of these migrants being North Africans operating in the retail food industry (bars or restaurants) in Paris. Chinese immigrants involved in ethnic enterprise are concentrated in the Parisian Chinatown. Indeed, 40 per cent of the shops in the 13th *arrondissement* are Chinese-owned and there is a thriving textile industry. The residential factor thus plays a fundamental role. One group of migrants involved in ethnic enterprises outside Paris are the Senegalese, who generally make their living as independent street pedlars.

In Germany, a large number of ethnic enterprises were set up by Italian, Greek and Yugoslav migrants in the food industry during the 1960s. Greek minority enterprises have also flourished in the fur and clothing sectors and more recently in sea transportation activities. These business mainly served the autochthon community. By contrast, enterprises set up by Turkish immigrants mainly aimed to serve the local migrant community and the growth of these businesses went hand in hand with the increase in residential numbers, eventually leading to the creation of an ethnic enclave. More recently, some Turkish-run enterprises have begun to operate on the open market in the food, construction and transport sectors.

In Holland, only Turkish, Surinamese and Greek immigrants seem to be involved in ethnic enterprise, with Turks favouring activity in the textile industry and the Surinamese focusing their efforts in the food sector.

In the UK the setting up of ethnic enterprises by migrants from New Commonwealth countries was helped by marked residential segregation and the development of ethnic markets. Small, medium and large Asian enterprises now operate in many wholesale and retail sectors, especially clothing. In contrast, African-Caribbean enterprises have been slower to emerge. [R. B.]

Light, I. (1972) *Ethnic Enterprise in America*, University of California Press, Los Angeles.
Light, I., Bonacich, R. (1988) *Immigrant Entrepreneurs: Koreans in Los Angeles*, University of California Press, Los Angeles.
Waldinger, R., Aldrich, H., Ward, R. (1990) *Ethnic Entrepreneurs. Immigrant Business in Industrial Society*, Sage, London.
Wilson, P. (1987) *Growth Strategies in Minority Enterprise: Case Studies in Corporate Growth of Asian and Afro-Caribbean Business in Britain*, SBRT, London.
Zucchetti, E. (1995) 'L'imprenditoria etnica', in ISMU, *Primo rapporto sulle migrazioni*, Franco Angeli Editore, Milano.

ETHNIC MINORITY (It. *Minoranza etnica*; Fr. *minorité ethnique*; Ger. *ethnische Minderheit*)

The concept of 'minority' is obviously closely connected with that of 'majority'. With regard to RACE, ETHNICITY and CULTURE, the term 'minority' often refers to representation and power rather than numbers and proportions. The definition of 'ethnic minority' can apply to various kinds of groups, which may be self-defined, separatist, regionalist or autonomist movements, or foreign ethnic groups residing in countries of immigration (FOREIGNER, MIGRATION). The concept of minority is linked to that of IDENTITY, as perceived by the self or as imposed from an external source. Minority groups may have a strong perception of their identity which does not correspond to that ascribed to them by the surrounding majority. Furthermore, the concept of ethnicity – in the same way as that of PEOPLE, race or NATION – is extremely ambiguous. Many issues affect minorities which are part of complex, stratified societies, particularly ethnic minorities. Such issues range from the institutional mechanisms which control – or attempt to control – relations between governments and minorities to the definition of the ethnic 'philosophy' underlying such mechanisms (ETHNIC POLITICS).

Currently we are facing a new phenomenon, namely the rediscovery – sometimes even the actual creation – of ethnic identities within the framework of a vast cultural process. This cultural process is one which entails a cultural identity crisis where what Barth defined as 'ethnic borders' are continuously shifting and changing between old and new closures, and stretched to include previously unthinkable new identities. The concepts of minority and majority are also changing, as ethnic minority groups may at the same time come to belong to a vaster whole.

Issues surrounding ethnic minorities have today become crucial, not only because of the interests and aspirations underlying them, but also owing to the conflicts involved in the current process of redefinition of the categories of DIVERSITY–SIMILARITY, singularity/universality and globality/locality (GLOBALIZATION), all of which must find new meaning and a new cultural balance. [M. V.]

Barth, F. (ed.) (1969) *Ethnic Groups and Boundaries: The Social Organisation of*

Culture Difference, George Allen & Unwin, London.

Smith, A. D. (1995) *Nations and Nationalism in a Global Era*, Polity Press, Cambridge.

Tentori, T. (1987) *Il rischio della certezza*, Studium, Roma.

ETHNIC POLITICS (It. *Politica etnica*; Fr. *Politique ethnique*; Ger. *ethnische Politik*)

The meaning of 'ethnic politics' must always depend upon the context in which the expression is used. The term may refer to politics that promote or defend the central values of an ethnic group; the Salman Rushdie affair in 1989 in the UK is a conspicuous example of Muslim minorities mobilizing – with transnational support – in response to what they believed to be a blasphemous attack upon their religion. In the 1960s and early 1970s Sikhs campaigned in Britain for the wearing of turbans in occupations where employers either sought to ban them or required a standard form of headwear. Debate about the wearing of scarves in French schools entails 'ethnic politics' on the part of both Muslims and the French authorities.

Ethnic politics can, secondly, embody the promotion of the material interests of an ethnic group without necessarily bringing it into direct conflict with others (ETHNICITY). For example mobilization by minority groups around the demand to be counted separately in the US and UK censuses is intended to ensure that these groups are visible when discrimination is monitored or when government resources are allocated. Material interests may, however, have to be pursued on an ethnic basis at the expense of others. Moore described examples of UK trade unions failing to support immigrant workers in the 1960s and 1970s, even when the disputes were plainly trade union issues. But when unions went further and sought to *exclude* immigrant workers from promotion in their occupations the immigrants were forced to organize as an Asian workforce, relying on the resources of the Asian community rather than their unions (Moore, 1975: 73–94). Material interests had to be defended through ethnic mobilization and therefore ethnic politics.

A more limited usage of the term 'ethnic politics' describes situations where migrants mobilize and compete with one another over 'home' issues; Kurds and Turks in Germany, Greek and Turkish Cypriots in the UK, etc. The political issues may be relatively obscure to the local population and the debates encapsulated within the minority population seldom (if ever) impinge upon the majority population.

Ethnic associations will seldom engage in ethnic politics alone. Rex's summary description of the politics of the Indian Workers' Association shows that an organization needs to strike a balance, and perhaps a series of compromises, between the types of ethnic politics described above, whilst simultaneously mobilizing a wider constituency on the basis of shared *material* interests (1991: 94–97).

Finally, ethnic politics may be the *politics of ethnicity*, a transformation of 'race' politics into ethnic politics. In this case the assumptions underlying debates about migrants 'fitting in' or assimilating (ASSIMILATION) shift from crude scientific racism to assertions about irreconcilable incompatibilities between cultures. This has been the major shift in the politics of 'race' and immigration in post-war Europe; scientific racism was discredited and mainly associated with the Nazi regime. The terms of racist debates have shifted towards a more respectable-seeming discourse on culture. Thus 'race' politics come to be conducted in 'ethnic' terms.

In its weakest form the politics of ethnicity seeks to celebrate diversity rather than confront inequality. [R. M.]

Banton, M. (1983) *Racial and Ethnic Competition*, Cambridge University Press, Cambridge.

Glazer, N., Moynihan, D. (eds) (1975) *Ethnicity*, Harvard University Press, Cambridge, MA.

Institute of Race Relations (1987) *Policing against Black People*, IRR, London.

Modood, T., Werbner, P. (eds) (1997) *The Politics of Multiculturalism in the New Europe: Racism, Identity, and Community*, St Martin's Press, London.

Moore, R. (1975) *Racism and Black Resistance in Britain*, Pluto Press, London.

Rex, J. (1991) 'Ethnic identity and ethnic mobilisation in Britain', *Ethnic Relations*, Monographs in Ethnic Relations No. 5, Centre for Research in Ethnic Relations, University of Warwick, Coventry,pp. 1–129.

Smith, A. D. (1981) *The Ethnic Revival*, Cambridge University Press, Cambridge.

ETHNICITY (It. *etnia*; Fr. *ethnie*; Ger. *Ethnizität*)

1. The term 'ethnicity' derives from the Greek *ethnos*, meaning people, but also stock, multitude, crowd or nation. Many claim that the Greek word in turn derives from the Sanskrit *sabbah*, community. Until the late nineteenth century and beginning of the twentieth century, the concept of ethnicity was often linked to those of RACE, PEOPLE and NATION, and traces of this ambiguity still remain today. The term was first used by G. Vacher de la Pouge in 1896 to describe the cultural (CULTURE), psychological and social characteristics – which he defined as 'natural and counterfeit' – of a population, and in order to distinguish the latter from the concept of race, which he identified as referring to a series of physical characteristics. According to de la Pouge, a single ethnicity could include individuals of different races brought together by historical factors, but was not to be confused with the concept of nation, which required a deeper brand of solidarity. Max Weber later distinguished clearly between the concepts of race, ethnicity and nation, and saw the first as being founded on the COMMUNITY of origin, the second on a subjective belief in shared origins and the third as characterized by a more intense political 'passion'. In Weber's view (1922), ethnic groups are groups of humans who have a subjective belief in shared origins, a belief which is founded on a similarity of habits, customs or both, or on collective memories of migrations or colonization. Such a belief is important for the creation of a community spirit, irrespective of whether blood ties exist. The concept of ethnicity implies three factors: (1) membership of a group, either from personal choice or as an external imposition, but which nonetheless implies the existence of an 'us' and a 'them', and therefore the concept of 'other'; (2) the search for a common IDENTITY on the part of the group members; and (3) the perception on the part of other groups of more or less coherent stereotypes ascribed to the ethnic group in question.

The term 'ethnicity' came into frequent use in the field of social sciences in America during the 1970s (partly due to the publication of the magazine *Ethnicity*) owing to the explosion at the time of conflicts and movements among ethnic minorities (ETHNIC MINORITY), both in MULTIETHNIC and supposedly monoethnic industrial societies, and in THIRD WORLD countries. According to Cohen (1978) the problem of 'belonging' is a constant in the modern world, where belonging to an ethnic group is no longer defined in religious and cultural terms, but is structured around political and economic factors. Accordingly, belonging to ethnic groups appeared to replace class distinctions. Brass (1991) asserted that ethnic communities are an alternative form of social class organization and that ethnicity as a form of identification is an alternative to class consciousness. In the 1970s, studies also began on the linguistic structures of so-called ethnic groups. Today the issue of ethnicity is universal and addressed in all fields. It is an issue related to modernity, as ethnic groups have recently begun to rediscover their cultural roots, as opposed to previous trends towards cultural hegemony.

Since the 1980s a new trend has emerged whereby ethnicity is viewed not so much as an isolated entity but as the result of the constant encounters between different peoples. This view, however, risks restricting the application of the concept of ethnicity to less industrially advanced peoples, to distinguish them from the more industrially developed populations. On the other hand, there is a tendency to abandon concepts such as 'tribe' or 'tribalism', as they are considered to be derogatory. Ideally, it is preferable not to refer the concept of ethnicity to stable groups, but to groups which share certain economic, social, cultural and religious characteristics at a given moment in time. Thus, ethnicity can apply universally and without bias to all models of society, past and present, advanced and 'primitive' (Hannertz, 1974; Wolf, 1982).

According to a current of contemporary anthropological thought, societies and nations are expressions of the industrialized world, while tribes and ethnicities concern PRIMITIVE groups. From this point of view ethnicity is a construction of Western colonial culture (COLONIALISM) according to which elements of presumed homogeneity or difference are ascribed from above.

Various theories on ethnicity have been developed since the beginning of the twentieth century. According to the *primordialist* theory, certain archetypal primordial features exist which define the essential characteristics of each human group. All later criticism has been aimed at refuting primordialist theories. The *modern* debate focuses on the relational and dialogic aspects of ethnicity which lead to ethnic characteristics, that is, each 'us' is created in relation to a 'them'. Membership of a group implies the designation of 'others' who are excluded from that group. Ethnicity asserts a collective ego to the exclusion of others (Comaroff, 1987). Each ethnic group perceives the greatest differences in its nearest neighbours (Alber, 1992) according to *mobilizationists*; separation and interaction are the building blocks of ethnicity, and competition and conflict between ethnic groups are of particular importance. Thus ethnicity is not a situation of isolation, but one of dynamic exchange and conflict with others; culture is the communication or opposition between different semantic structures, which sets social relationships in motion.

These three basic theories have created two opposing camps; for some, ethnicity is a tool for the fulfilment of needs and the struggle for power (EMPOWERMENT–DISEMPOWERMENT), while others claim it is manifest in the continuous rebuilding – often symbolically – of social relationships. Barth does not see ethnic groups as developers of cultural structures, but as coolly calculating operators intent on promoting their own material interests. Common values are important not because they contribute to an ethnic identity, but because they necessitate the formation of roles and interactions.

Barth (1969) highlights the concept of continuously changing 'borders' – a principle which is at the same time real and abstract – within which the principles that structure a group operate. Ethnology, anthropology and sociology are not clear on the concept of ethnicity. The same can also be said regarding the concept of RACE, although confusion in this field is more damaging, owing to the presumed and false objectivity which the sustainers of the concept attribute to genetic and evolutionist theories (EVOLUTION), with serious political and social repercussions. At least the concept of ethnicity, in its ambiguity, may be used without assigning value scales to the definition of different groups on the basis of social and cultural characteristics. Ethnicities are universal, are created across boundaries (FRONTIER), are changeable and moving, and are dynamic and not necessarily stereotypical. The cultural debate under way today has not yet managed to prevent ethnicity from being associated with foreign (FOREIGNER) and somewhat marginal situations in the social UNCONSCIOUS of the more or less educated West. In Europe the terms 'ethnicity' and ETHNIC are often used with reference to non-European social and cultural groups. Ethnic MUSIC, ethnic art (ART AND ETHNICITY) and ethnic cooking (FOLKLORE) are all definitions used when speaking of exotic (EXOTICISM), foreign cultures. A deeper understanding of the meaning of the concepts of 'folkloristic' and 'ethnic' is desirable, extending them to all those cultural-artistic forms which can be identified as belonging specifically to a particular group in a particular context, and with the understanding that folklore refers to those expressions which are more closely linked to a popular tradition and are

less acculturated. These definitions, however, should still be used with the awareness that they are abstract concepts ascribed for purposes of convenience. [S. G.]

Alber, J. L. (1992) *Métissages*, Université de la Réunion, L'Harmattan, Paris.
Barth, F. (ed.) (1969) *Ethnic Groups and Boundaries: The Social Organisation of Culture Difference*, George Allen & Unwin, London.
Brass, P. (1991) *Ethnicity and Nationalism. Theory and Comparison*, Sage, London.
Comaroff, J. L. (1987) 'Of totemism and ethnicity: conciousness, practice and the signs of inequality'. *Ethnos*, 52(1/2): 303–323.
Cohen, A. (ed.) (1974) *Urban Ethnicity*, Tavistock, London.
Cohen, R. (1978) 'Ethnicity, problem and focus in anthropology', *Annual Review of Anthropology*, 7: 379–403.
Copans, J. (1996) *Introduction à l'ethnologie et à l'anthropologie*, Natan, Paris.
Epstein, A. L. (1978) *Ethnos and Identity, Three Studies in Ethnicity*, Tavistock, London.
Hannertz, U. (1974) 'Ethnicity and opportunity in urban America', in Cohen A. (ed.).
Poutignat, P., Streiff-Fenart, J. (1995) *Théories de l'ethnicité*, PUF, Paris.
Vacher de la Pouge, G. (1896) *Les Sélections sociales*, Thorin, Paris.
Weber, M. (1922) *Wirtschaft und Gesellschaft*, Mohr, Tübingen.
Wolf, E. R. (1982) *Europe and the People without History*, University of California Press, Berkeley.

2. The term 'ethnicity' suffers from having both common and technical usages. In popular discussion ethnicity may be used as a euphemism for 'race'. Thus the press and politicians may speak of ethnic groups in order either to avoid discredited ideas of race or to distance themselves from crude racism when making points hostile to minorities. Similarly the idea of ethnicity may be used by commentators who wish to celebrate diversity without confronting the social reality of race and RACISM: this is sometimes referred to as MULTI-CULTURALISM. Thus multiethnic may be used as a substitute for multiracial to describe the diversity (DIVERSITY–SIMILARITY) of a population. Popular usages should be avoided, not least because they deflect attention from underlying complexities and ambiguities in the concept of ethnicity. In sociology and anthropology ethnicity refers to particular forms of group membership. Banton has suggested that ethnicity may better be understood by starting with how a group sees itself, rather than how others see it (1988). This alerts us to the possibility that people may be assigned to ethnic groups by more powerful others, and that ethnicity may be imposed rather than self-defined.

Authors have tended to stress either the inherited or the contingent nature of ethnicity. Geertz treated ethnicity as one of the givens of social existence deriving from birth into a particular community of language, belief and social practices:

> These congruities of blood, speech, custom and so on, are seen to have an ineffable, and at times overpowering, coerciveness in and of themselves. One is bound to one's kinsman, one's neighbor, one's fellow believer *ipso facto*, as the result not merely of personal attraction, tactical necessity, common interest or incurred moral obligation, but at least in great part by virtue of some unaccountable absolute import attributed to the very tie itself. (Geertz, 1962: 109)

This formulation echoes the view of the French sociologist Emile Durkheim (1963) who suggested that the subject matter of sociology is *social facts*. These social facts are tangible and should be treated as things, they are external to and constraining upon the individual. Ethnicity is a social fact; we are born into an ethnic community in which relationships with proximate others are experienced as real and tangible: they become *ties* to others. This usage of 'ethnicity', commonly found in traditional anthropology-based analyses, sharply contrasts ethnicity with relationships based upon common interests, as in class relations, or the claims to and recognition of honour found in status relations. It is because ethnic ties cannot be reduced to any others that Geertz calls them 'primordial'. Individuals may 'stubbornly continue to unite' (Rex, 1991) with those with whom they have ethnic ties even where there may be rationally calculable incentives to unite with others on the basis of shared interests.

Social actors do not consciously live their lives as members of ethnic groups. Their ethnicity is latent, a resource capable of mobilization or exploitation in specific contingencies. Thus, according to Barth (1969) ethnicity is related to interests and provides one basis for mobilizing in pursuit or defence of interests (ETHNIC POLITICS). Writing about Birmingham in the later 1960s, Rex and Moore (1967) described how immigrants to the Sparkbrook district of the city were able to mobilize the resources provided by the presence of kin, co-villagers and co-religionists in dealing with a hostile social and political environment. In pursuit of interests ethnicity may be deployed to meet others' expectation rather than being a 'truthful' expression of cultural identity. This may be seen in the contrast between the creation of an ethnic ambiance in Chinese and Indian restaurants and the utilitarian style in which the same entrepreneurs construct take-away food shops. Ethnicity becomes a resource that can be manipulated and exploited for economic purposes (ETHNIC ENTERPRISE).

For the consumer, ethnic signifies the exotic, foreign or (paradoxically) authentic. Ethnicity may also be exploited in the labour market by individuals seeking advancement in agencies that are publicly committed to the development of equality of opportunity. Aspirant members of the middle class may, for example, stress their membership of a minority ethnic group by seeking professional and white-collar employment in government agencies or NGOs. The malleability of ethnicity or ethnic identities may be seen in the proliferation of hyphenated identities in the USA (Italian-American, African-American, etc.) or the use of new UK census categories (Asian British, Black British) and in debates about new ethnicities. New ethnicities and ethnic syncretism have become part of the subject matter in the analysis of GLOBALIZATION, global culture and diasporas (DIASPORA) (Hall, 1996). Young members of minorities create new identities through, for example, musical syncretisms and, in contrast, through mobilization in response to political issues surrounding police violence. Ethnicities are thus to be found in the process of formulation and negotiation, dissolution and renewal. It is futile to argue whether ethnicity is basically a politically determined or a cultural phenomenon. The cultural 'givens' are one resource for confronting political problems and new cultural resources can be formed in the confrontation. The complexity and contingent nature of debates about ethnicity and identity can be epitomized by attempts to create or define black group identity. Whilst many Asians in Europe resent being identified with African and African-Caribbean people the term 'black' has nevertheless been extended to include Asians, and especially Asian youths, in the process of mobilizing around issues of racial violence and political exclusion. But the term 'black' is by no means accepted or uncontested as an 'ethnic' identity. 'We'

may be black in one context, Asian in another and Punjabi in a third, whilst ill at ease with the application of any category singly when applied in, for example, censuses and surveys.

In the contemporary European context the idea of ethnicity has taken on new levels of meaning in the resurgence of ETHNO-NATIONALISM and the emergence of the idea of ETHNIC CLEANSING.

Historical conflicts that were to some extent held in check (or regulated) by the Soviet bloc states have resurfaced in the modern era. Appeals to the antiquity of the injustices for which redress or revenge are claimed gives ethnicity a 'primordial' aspect, as when conflicts between Christians and Muslims in the Middle Ages are cited (RELIGION AND ETHNIC CONFLICTS). We cannot readily resolve the problem of whether it is material interests and political contingencies that make it possible for these appeals to ethnicity to be effective, or whether primordial appeals to past wrongs and the thirst for revenge combined with a strong sense of ethnic group identity are sufficient. The 'stubbornness' of the ethnic loyalties that can lead to people killing their former friends, schoolmates and neighbours is a particular challenge to sociology and social sciences wedded to an essentially progressive view of human history (CIVILIZATION). [R. M.]

Banton, M. (1988) *Racial Consciousness*, Longman, London.

Barth, F. (ed.) (1969) *Ethnic Groups and Boundaries*, George Allen & Unwin, London.

Cohen, P. (ed.) (1999) *New Ethnicities, Old Racisms*, Zed Books, London.

Connor, W. (1994) *Ethnonationalism: The Quest for Understanding*, Princeton University Press, Princeton, NJ.

Delanty, G. (1995) *Inventing Europe: Idea, Identity, Reality*, Macmillan, Basingstoke.

Durkheim, E. (1963) *Les Règles de la méthode sociologique* (1895), Alcan, Paris.

Geertz, C. (1962) *Old Societies and New States. The Quest for Modernity in Asia and Africa*, Free Press, New York.

Hall, S. (1996) 'New ethnicities', in Morley, D., Hsing Chen, K. (eds), *Stuart Hall. Critical Dialogues in Cultural Studies*, Routledge, London.

Rex, J. (1991) 'Ethnic identity and ethnic mobilisation in Britain', *Ethnic Relations*, 5: 1–129, Centre for Research in Ethnic Relations, University of Warwick.

Rex, J., Moore, R. (1967) *Race, Community and Conflict: A Study of Sparkbrook*, Oxford University Press, Oxford.

third approach argues that race and ethnicity are distinct, but not mutually exclusive concepts. Because members of racial and ethnic groups make similar kinds of claims about the distinctive aspects of group membership, this new ethnicity approach contends that conceptual overlap is theoretically necessary. The new ethnicity perspective agrees that different historical processes create different race and ethnic categories, and that societies assign individuals to groups according to different rules. Hence, concepts of race and ethnicity must be distinct. Nevertheless, racial and ethnic groups assert their respective identities by making identical claims about who they are.

ETHNICITY AND RACE (It. *etnia e razza*; Fr. *ethnie et race*; Ger. *Ethnizität und Rasse*)

The central problem animating theoretical debates among American sociologists who study race identities and inequalities is profound disagreement over the concept of RACE. American scholars differ little on the concrete definition of race; all include phenotypical differences among racial groups as a key component of the definition. The debate turns on the conceptual distinction between 'race' and ETHNICITY. Three different approaches can be distinguished. The traditional approach conflates the concepts of race and ethnicity, treating them as if there were no substantively important conceptual difference between them. This approach is now in decline although it was common before 1965. A popular and relatively new approach views race and ethnicity as conceptually distinct. This racial formation approach (Omi and Winant, 1994) claims that race and ethnic IDENTITY formation displayed different historical patterns in the United States that require different theoretical explanations. The

THE TRADITIONAL APPROACH

Scholars at the University of Chicago initiated modern race theory in the United States in the 1920s in an attempt to understand the social adjustment process of European immigrants to the United States. Robert Park and other members of the Chicago School maintained that race and ethnicity were mutable social categories. The decline in the salience of the ethnic identities of European immigrants (MIGRANT, MIGRATION) and their descendants appeared to validate that view. Immigrants from different parts of Europe formed distinct ethnic enclaves where they maintained their NATIVE culture, but ethnic differences declined over time and over generations through the process of assimilation. By the late twentieth century, ethnic identity among the descendants of European ethnics was an option rather than an imperative (Waters, 1990; Alba, 1990). According to Park (1950: 138–152), assimilation proceeded in stages. During the contact stage, immigrants settled in cities and neighbourhoods where previously arrived immigrants were located. Along with tensions that developed because of the clash between immigrant and American cultures, competition for jobs, housing and education also developed. Despite these tensions, Park found that each succeeding ethnic group found its niche and adjusted to the mores and values of the dominant American society, a process he called accommodation (ADAPTATION). In the last stage, immigrant groups incorporated the norms, values and beliefs of the dominant group, thus becoming fully assimilated (ASSIMILATION). Park argued that these stages more accurately described the process that European immigrants went through than did the earlier Social Darwinist theories which suggested that there were genetic differences between racial and ethnic groups that predicted their failure or success.

Gordon (1964, 1978) rejected Park's idea that assimilation followed stages, but agreed that the social processes shaping the boundaries of racial and ethnic groups were identical. He conceived of assimilation as a multidimensional process, which left open the possibility that different dimensions of assimilation develop with different speeds for different groups. Black Americans might assimilate structurally and culturally, for example, but encounter obstacles to marital assimilation with whites. Other scholars who adopted the ethnicity approach to race grappled with the same problem (e.g. Banton, 1983; Horowitz, 1985; Schemerhorn, 1978). If there are no meaningful theoretical differences in the processes that create racial and ethnic groups, how can one explain the apparent failure of American racial groups to assimilate at the same rates enjoyed by European immigrant groups? Does the immigrant analogy apply to American racial groups, or not?

THE RACIAL FORMATION APPROACH

An influential new approach rejects the core assumption that race and ethnicity are equivalent conceptually and denies the assumption that the immigrant analogy can be applied to racial groups. Based upon their analysis of the historical forces that shaped race and ethnic inequalities in the USA, Omi and Winant (1994) conclude that race inequalities cannot be explained by theories designed to explain the transformation of ethnic boundaries. Race is not just another variety of ethnicity. Instead, race is 'an autonomous field of social conflict, political organization, and cultural/ideological meaning' (Omi and Winant, 1994: 48). The historical forces that shaped race inequalities in the USA differ qualitatively from those that shape ethnic inequalities. Europeans voluntarily immigrated to North America. Despite the grim circumstances that motivated European emigration, the choice to migrate expressed agency, a self-defining action denied to racial groups. Many European immigrants faced high levels of discrimination in the USA, but most assimilated successfully. They and their descendants (SECOND GENERATION) became white Americans (WHITENESS). The experiences of racial groups were dramatically different. Africans were brought to America involuntarily, Asians faced various forms of exclusionary laws, and American Indians were colonialized or exterminated in genocidal wars with white Americans (COLONIALISM, GENOCIDE). Immigrants to North America from the British Isles created a *racialized social structure*, where the phenotypical and cultural attributes of groups were used as racial markers that determined their life chances.

Winant (2000) argues that the sociopolitical context constructed racial categories for blacks, Asians and American Indians (ETHNICIZATION, RACIALIZATION). The racial, rather than ethnic, constructions of these groups distinguished them from white ethnics. Racial formation, 'the socio-historical process by which racial categories are created, inhabited, transformed, and destroyed', provides a better explanation than ethnicity for the persistence of racial inequalities in America (Omi and Winant, 1994: 55). A major contribution of racial formation theory is the importance attributed to social movements in transforming racial identities. Social movements produce new cultural representations or 'racial projects' (Omi and Winant, 1994: 56) that redefine race identities of group members. Hence, race identities and inequalities are not completely determined by social, economic and political contexts as the traditional ethnicity perspective presumes. Race is a social construct that changes constantly depending upon circumstances and the self-defining agency of group members.

THE NEW ETHNICITY APPROACH

Most studies of race inequalities agree that American social and political institutions are racialized (RACIALIZATION), as Omi and Winant argue. European immigrants and their descendants were transformed into white Americans as the boundaries between white ethnics diminished in importance over time. By contrast, boundaries between racial groups were tenaciously maintained by social institutions, sanctioned by state policies, and legitimized by race ideologies. The historical social forces assigning individuals to race categories in the United States were consistently more powerful than those assigning individuals to ethnic groups.

Despite differences in the historical processes of social assignment to race and ethnic groups, such groups express identities in similar ways. Ethnic groups are self-consciously ethnic (DOUBLE CONSCIOUSNESS). Members express their common ethnicity through claims of shared kinship, belief in a shared history, and shared symbolic representations of their peoplehood (Cornell and Hartmann, 1998). Racial groups make claims about race identities that are identical in form to those made by ethnic groups. For example, Black Americans claim descent from African ancestors, are familiar with the history of SLAVERY and race discrimination that limited the life chances of blacks, and recognize skin colour as the ultimate symbol that defines racial group membership (COLOUR BAR, COLOURED).

The new ethnicity approach incorporates the strengths of the traditional view and the racial formation perspective. The distinctiveness of race and ethnicity is preserved by allowing for differences in the process of social assignment. Arguing that racial groups are self-consciously ethnic once ethnic language is adopted to describe the experience of racial group membership incorporates the similarities of race and ethnicity. The malleability of race and ethnic identities is emphasized by positing a dynamic relationship between the social assignment of race categories and the assertion of identities by racial and ethnic groups. Race identities emerge as social movements and other racial projects resist or accommodate to the social forces assigning individuals to racial groups.

Most American sociologists have abandoned the assimilationist model suggested by traditional ethnicity theory, but are still divided on the relative merits of the racial formation and new ethnicity approaches to the conceptualization of race. The traditional ethnicity approach, including its Marxist variants (e.g. Bonacich, 1976; Miles, 1993), appears to exaggerate the importance of the assignment process and undervalue or ignore the ability of groups to shape their own identities. Similarly, now-abandoned primordialist (e.g. Shils, 1957; Isaacs, 1975) and nationalist theories (e.g. Cruse, 1967) exaggerate the capacity of groups to maintain their identities in spite of changing circumstances. Because of its exclusive focus on the history of race inequalities in America, the racial formation approach ignores the similar forms that race and ethnic identity construction processes display in a cross-national, comparative context (e.g. Marx, 1998). The new ethnicity perspective offers a more balanced approach than the traditional approach. Indeed the focus on dynamic links between social assignment and the ability of groups to assert their identity represents a new theoretical framework which can also incorporate other approaches as special cases. The new ethnicity perspective offers a more balanced approach than traditional ethnicity theory and incorporates the sensitivity of the racial formation approach to the abilities of racial groups for self-definition in opposition to powerful social assignment processes. [M. O.], [D. R. J.]

Alba, R. D. (1990) *Ethnic Identity*, Yale University Press, New Haven.

Banton, M. (1983) *Racial and Ethnic Competition*, Cambridge University Press, Cambridge.

Bonacich, E. (1976) 'A theory of ethnic antagonism: the split labor market', *American Sociological Review*, 38: 583–594.

Cornell, S., Hartmann, D. (1998) *Ethnicity and Race: Making Identities in a Changing World*, Pine Forge Press, Thousand Oaks, CA.

Cruse, H. (1967) *The Crisis of the Negro Intellectual*, Morrow, New York.

Gordon, M. M. (1964) *Assimilation in American Life: The Role of Race, Religion, and National Origins*, Oxford University Press, New York.

Gordon, M. M. (1978) *Human Nature, Class, and Ethnicity*, Oxford University Press, New York.

Horowitz, D. L. (1985) *Ethnic Groups in Conflict*, University of California Press, Berkeley.

Isaacs, H. R. (1975) *Idols of the Tribe*, Harvard University Press, Cambridge MA.

Marx, A. W. (1998) *Making Race and Nation: A Comparison of South Africa, the United States and Brazil*, Cambridge University Press, New York.

Miles, R. (1993) *Racism after 'Race' Relations*, Routledge, London.

Omi, W., Winant, H. (1994) *Racial Formation in the United States: From the 1960s to the 1990s*, Routledge, New York.

Park, R. (1950) *Race and Culture* (1926), The Free Press, Glencoe, IL.

Schemerhorn, R. A. (1978) *Comparative Ethnic Relations*, University of Chicago Press.

Shils, E. (1957) 'Primordial, personal, sacred and civil ties', *British Journal of Sociology*, 8: 130–145.

Waters, M. (1990) *Ethnic Options: Choosing Identities in America*, University of California Press, Berkeley.

Winant, H. (2000) 'Race and racial theory', *Annual Review of Sociology*, 26: 169–185.

ETHNICIZATION

(It. *etnicizzazione*; Fr. *ethnicisation*; Ger. *Ethnitisierung*) This term indicates the tendency to provide explanations or interpretations based on ETHNICITY for tensions and conflicts caused by other factors, particularly by social problems. Its use is widespread in Anglo-Saxon literature, where the problems linked to immigration (MIGRATION) are often discussed from an ethnic or 'racial' point of view. [U. M.]

Fourier, M., Vermès, G. (1994) *Ethnicisation des rapports sociaux*, L'Harmattan, Paris.

ETHNOCENTRISM

(It. *etnocentrismo*; Fr. *ethnocentrisme*; Ger. *Ethnozentrismus*) This term indicates the tendency of members of an ethnic group to privilege their group above all others and to judge outsiders according to the group's own values and ideas. This term was introduced, duly illustrated by examples, by William G. Sumner (1906), who quoted several examples of its use. Sumner pointed out the fact (often repeated in literature on the subject) that many ethnic groups tend to define themselves using terms meaning 'good', 'beautiful', 'brave', 'excellent', 'rich' and even, *tout court*, 'men', while often the members of other groups are defined in derogatory terms (such as 'ugly', 'cowards', 'lice'). Similar trends also exist in complex societies. The Jews consider themselves to be the 'chosen people' (JEW). The Greeks defined all foreigners (FOREIGNER) as 'barbarians' (literally: babbling). This word was passed down to present generations with all its well-known negative implications as the result of the strong ethnocentric approach on the part of the Greeks, who used it to define all those who spoke a language different from their own. The Chinese, who considered their country to be the centre of the world, despised foreigners. As is witnessed by the reports of the first European diplomatic missions to that country, ambassadors were regarded as delegations sent by the barbarian sovereigns of the West to submit to the Son of Heaven and implore him to allow them to be part of the superior CIVILIZATION of the 'Empire of the Centre'. When referring to complex societies, the object of assessment is not so much their population (PEOPLE) as their CULTURE. In this case it would be more appropriate to speak, not of ethnocentrism, but of cultural centrism. [U. M.]

Melotti, U. (1968) 'Razzismo ed etnocentrismo nella cultura italiana di oggi', *Terzo Mondo*, 2: 29–68.
Sumner, W. G. (1906) *Folkways*, Ginn, Boston.
Tentori, T. (1987) *Il rischio della certezza. Pregiudizio, potere, cultura*, Studium, Roma.

ETHNOCIDE

(It. *etnocidio*; Fr. *ethnocide*; Ger. *Genozid*) This recently coined term, associated with a re-evaluation of the concept of ETHNICITY, refers to the total destruction of an ethnic group or its civilization. In a wider sense, the concept also applies to conflicts currently taking place on several continents (a few examples being former Yugoslavia, Burundi and Rwanda), where the ultimate objective is not the complete elimination of ethnic groups, but the creation of MONOETHNIC STATES, involving the expulsion of minority ethnic groups from a particular territory. [M. V.]

Cerulli, E. (1977) *Tradizione e etnocidio*, Utet, Torino.

ETHNO-NATIONALISM

(It. *etnonazionalismo*; Fr. *ethnonationalisme*; Ger. *Ethnonationalismus*) This term refers to a particular type of NATIONALISM and concerns populations which are already part of a constituted NATION, yet who claim autonomy and/or independence in the name of their real or presumed ethnic and cultural IDENTITY (ETHNICITY, CULTURE). This ideology may be motivated or strengthened by economic or social factors.

There has been a significant increase in ethno-national movements in Europe since the Second World War. At first such movements occurred mainly in Western Europe (for example in Catalonia and the Basque provinces in Spain, Corsica and Brittany in France and the northern regions of Italy in which the Northern League [*Lega Nord*] has strongly supported the founding of the state of Padania), while more recently the situation has exploded – with occasionally tragic consequences – in the countries of Eastern Europe following the collapse of the collective bureaucratic system (especially in the ex-Soviet Union and ex-Yugoslavia). Ethnonationalist movements can also be found in many non-European countries, for example the ethno-nationalism of Kurds scattered over an area divided into five different nations. [U. M.]

Besikçi, I. (1990) *Kurdistan, An Interstate Colony*, Alan Press, Isp, Frankfurt am Main.

Connor, W. (1994) *Ethnonationalism: The Quest for Understanding*, Princeton University Press, Princeton, NJ.

Melotti, U. (ed.) (2000) *Etnicità, nazionalità e cittadinanza*, Seam, Roma.

ETHNOPSYCHIATRY (It. *etnopsichiatria*; Fr. *ethnopsychiatrie*; Ger. *Ethnopsychiatrie*)

Broadly speaking – therefore including related terms such as transcultural or cross-cultural psychiatry, ethnopsychology, ethnopsychoanalysis, psychoanalytical anthropology – this term refers to the study of the intersections between anthropology and the psychological sciences. In a strict, and possibly overly limiting, sense, its field of inquiry has been defined as the study of mental illness from an intercultural perspective.

Despite the fact that ethnopsychiatry as a field of interest is but a century old, its historical context deserves description. The major clinical and research perspectives of the term will be discussed subsequently. Ethnopsychiatry has changed over the last hundred years. At the start of the twentieth century, ethnopsychiatry focused on the description of remote and exotic cultures (EXOTICISM). The comparative studies of that time were performed from a Western point of reference, and were Western-centred in nature (ETHNOCENTRISM). A major change was introduced by Freud in his monumental *Totem and Taboo* (1913). In this theoretical study, Freud systematically outlined the application of his theories to the field of anthropology. By working not in the field, but on literary material (mainly provided by the works of J. G. Frazer [1890]), he searched for 'correspondences' and 'correlations' between the manifestations of various cultures. In this sense he linked elements observed during his clinical practice (such as desires, impulses, defence mechanisms, symptoms and thought organization) with tribal organizations, beliefs, magic rites and taboos of the culture of so-called 'savages' or 'primitives' (SAVAGE, PRIMITIVE). C. G. Jung, through his definitions of the 'collective unconscious' and of 'archetypes', introduced the concepts of comparison and contamination between the various cultures, a substantial addition to the ethnopsychiatry of that time (Jung, 1936) (UNCONSCIOUS).

In the mid-twentieth century, the major effort in the field of ethnopsychiatry was explanatory. More specifically, researchers attempted to integrate psychoanalytic concepts into anthropological works. M. Mead and B. Malinowski were the two main figures in this effort. Both approached ethnopsychiatry with their anthropological expertise and examined the psychoanalytic concept that adult personality is largely determined in childhood. Malinowski, based on his studies of sexuality in Trobriand Islanders, opposed the notion that existed in his time that the Oedipus complex is universal (1927). Mead argued against the necessity of adolescent turmoil that was widely accepted at her time (1928). She observed that this seemingly universal phase does not exist in the Samoan culture, and related this to the non-possessive sexual relationships among adolescents there. Her original (and strongly criticized) study advocated cultural determinism, and was innovative. Although nowadays her approach is unacceptable to most behavioural researchers, it balanced the biological determinism (CULTURAL DETERMINISM) commonly accepted at that time and thus stands as a cornerstone of contemporary ethnopsychiatry. G. Devereux (1973), a Hungarian psychoanalyst, ethnologist and Hellenist, defended the thesis of the psychic unity of humanity, claiming, against Malinowski and 'culturalism', that the Oedipus complex is, despite its varied manifestations, universal. A scholar of epistemology, he noted that it is impossible to integrate the reciprocal contributions of psychoanalysis and ethnology and that the specificity of the two studies requires a 'double discourse method'. Using a complementary approach combining the psychological and ethnological methodologies, ethnopsychiatry was a double science (i.e. a science which makes usage of terminological and methodological systems taken from more than one science) in order to provide a method which better explores boundaries and limits. This was actualized in the studies of T. Nathan, a student of Devereux. Nathan's work (1993) is based on his clinical activity in the now multiethnic city of Paris, a context in which it is quite normal for a Western therapist to treat non-Western patients. This kind of therapeutic relationship challenges psychoanalytic theory as the psychotherapist has to be continuously ready to overcome the limitations of his own theory – which is inevitably an expression of western culture – and to rely on intellectual flexibility in order to reshape the relationship between the therapist and the patient on an ongoing basis and thus understand the functioning of the human mind and its pathologies.

In the last four decades, efforts in ethnopsychiatry have been aimed at several issues. The transition from universalistic (Western-centred), non-introspective perspective to culturally specific perspective is, perhaps, one of the most important movements in the field. Additional issues are related to methodology (e.g. developing valid cross-cultural instruments for epidemiological research). Another front, which is of current interest, is the practical importance of ETHNICITY (in its broader sense) in the therapist–patient relation. This include aspects such as assessment, language, mental status examination and therapies (psychological-oriented, pharmacological and culturally specific therapies). Yet another theoretical transition in contemporary ethnopsychiatry is related to the conception of CULTURE. Traditionally, culture was perceived as a top-down covering that fits over the real. Present theoreticians (such as A. Kleinman, 1980) view culture as a bottom-up process that both makes up the local world and is made up by it at the same time.

The perception of ethnopsychiatry fundamentally affects classification methods in modern psychiatry. Western scientific thought proclaimed itself as a body founded on indisputable axioms. This assumption, by definition, rendered non-Western views of mental health as mere 'beliefs' or as cultural variations of the 'norm', rather than critically challenging the very assumption behind Western psychiatry. The American Psychiatric Association's *DSM*, in its avid attempt to be highly specific, neglects to consider those clinical manifestations of psychiatric disorders that are culturally specific and consequently is of limited sensitivity (e.g. depression is characterized by emptiness, irritability, 'loss of soul' as opposed to sadness and worthlessness). This bias also allows for the classification of illness in a particular cultural setting according to the diagnostic categories provided by another, without determining the cross-cultural validity – the so-called category fallacy. According to the existing *DSM-IV* definitions and categorization, culture-bound syndromes (CBS) are defined as 'recurrent, locality-specific patterns of aberrant behavior and troubling experience . . . indigenously considered to be "illnesses" or at least afflictions . . . generally limited to specific society or culture areas and are localized, folk diagnostic categories that frame coherent meanings for certain repetitive, patterned and troubling sets of experience and observations'. The current representation of CBS in *DSM-IV* is composed of a heterogeneous group of exotic CBS (such as *Koro*, *Amok*, *Pibloktoq* etc.), thus encouraging the misconception that the CBS are rare psychological curiosities.

The last decade of the twentieth century witnessed several attempts to apply ethnopsychiatry in the everyday clinic (CROSS-CULTURAL MEDICINE). It thus recommends that the psychiatrist (a) pay special attention, not only to the cross-cultural variation in phenomenology, but also to the importance of the cultural context in prevalence, risk factors, attributed aetiology, help in seeking choices, course and treatment response; (b) appraise the patient in his/her cultural context and the impact it exerts on the clinical encounter. For instance, how appearance, dress style, speech modalities and thought patterns may reflect cultural differences should be considered. The above were not incorporated into the final version of *DSM-IV*, but the adjusted version of the originally proposed 'Glossary of Culture Bound Syndromes and Idioms of Distress' was accepted. The term 'idiom of distress' was stricken and the three Western culture-bound syndromes (anorexia nervosa, chronic fatigue syndrome and dissociative identity disorder) were excluded from it. A proposal urging the inclusion of dissociative trance disorder in this section was dismissed; however, it was listed in the appendix of 'Criteria Sets and Axes Provided for Further Study'.

The recent research development in ethnopsychiatry is typified by the mixing of previously disparate methodologies (Lewis-Fernandez and Kleinman, 1995). Methods adapted from psychiatry, psychology, epidemiology and anthropology blend in a combined effort to simultaneously achieve cultural validity and research reliability. Bridging the gaps between adjacent disciplines is of obvious theoretical importance, but also has significant practical implications. Recent studies thus focus on the diagnostic, therapeutic and mental health care cost derivatives of ethnicity and cultural identity. Special attention is paid to the relevance of these issues for immigrants and minorities. [A.C., S.M.]

American Psychiatric Association (1994) *DSM-IV Diagnostic and Statistical Manual of Mental Disorders*, Washington, DC.

Devereux, G. (1973) *Éssais d'ethnopsychiatrie générale*, Gallimard, Paris.

Frazer, J. G. (1890) *The Golden Bough*, Macmillan, London.

Freud, S. (1913) *Totem and Taboo*, in Strachey, J. (ed.), *The Comple Psychological Works of Sigmund Freud*, Hogarth Press and the Institute of Psychoanalysis, London, 1953, XIII, pp. 1–161.

Jung, C. G. (1936) *The Archetypes and the Collective Unconscious: The Collected Works of C.J. Jung*, Vol. 9, Part 1, Princeton University Press.

Kleinman, A. (1980) *Patients and Healer in the Context of Culture*, University of California Press, Berkeley.

Lewis-Fernandez, R., Kleinman, A. (1995) 'Cultural psychiatry: Theoretical, clinical and research issues', in *The Psychiatric Clinics of North America*, Saunders, Philadelphia.

Malinowski, B. (1927) *The Father in Primitive Psychology*, Norton, New York.

Mead, M. (1928) *Coming of Age in Samoa*, William Morrow, New York.

Nathan, T. (1993) *Fier de n'avoir ni pays ni amis, quelle sottise c'était . . . Principes d'ethnopsychanalyse*, Editions La Pensée Sauvage, Grenoble.

EUROCENTRISM (It. *eurocentrismo*; Fr. *eurocentrisme*; Ger. *Eurozentrismus*)

The term is based on ETHNOCENTRISM – the tendency to assess 'other' ethnic groups in comparison with the ethnic group of the judge – and indicates the conviction that Europe is an inevitable and necessary global reference point as it is the cultural, political and economic centre of the world. According to Ella Shobat and Robert Stam, 'Eurocentrism . . . envisions the world from a single privileged point. It maps the world in a cartography that centralizes and augments Europe . . . and bifurcates the world into the "West and the Rest"' (1994: 2). Along with the meaning of ethnocentrism usually attributed by anthropologists, Eurocentrism must also be considered both a form of 'European egocentrism' and the result of modernity and the universal development of the European logic of egalitarianism and HOMOLOGATION.

The definition of a coherent and homogeneous CULTURAL AREA is a very difficult and ambiguous task, so any attempt to define a presumed homogeneous European culture is a highly complex process which often results in a highly contradictory outcome. Ever since the time of the Roman empire the culture of the geographical area of what is currently known as Western Europe – all of which finds its origins in Ancient Greece – has been unified by same underlying cultural roots and values. Other cultures in different geographical locations have been strongly influenced by Western European culture. The influence of other cultures has often been weighted in very different ways, with Western eyes at times undervaluing or neglecting the importance of the culture of origin or even failing to consider the existence of an autonomous culture in other geographical areas (ACCULTURATION).

Europeans first discovered the differences (DIVERSITY-SIMILARITY) of other human beings during expansion which began in the fifteenth and sixteenth centuries following numerous explorations and the discovery of the New World – events which came well after 'Arab and Asian understanding of previous centuries' (Maget 1968: 1257). It should not be forgotten that so-called Eastern cultures had a strong influence on other cultures, e.g. the influence of Indian culture on Greek philosophy; of Eastern culture on the Roman Empire; of Judaism on Christian values and of China on European culture at the beginning of the twentieth century. Although the culture modernly conceived as European has always been open to absorbing and including influences from other cultures, it has nevertheless had a strong tendency to impose its own values on other cultures (especially since the Age of Enlightenment). Numerous and varying European social and cultural problems began to take on a planetary dimension as European domination progressively extended through the process of colonialism to include all the peoples and countries throughout the world and the assumption has always been that this would lead to the gradual extension of European values to the entire human race through the spreading of technology and the development of a new type of Man who has been emancipated from barbarism to reach equality and freedom. In this perspective, Europe may be considered as having 'played the role of city, market and factory' (Sauvy, 1977: 71). The controversial and often dramatic historical development of Western countries striving for democracy has, of course, had a strong influence on the attitude of Western culture towards other cultures. For instance the utopian dream of the Age of Enlightenment which achieved equal dignity for all people and full respect for freedom (EQUALITY), may have been useful to those seeking justification for the destruction of other cultures and political systems or those wishing to justify the implementation of a new kind of colonization which was more acceptable to the democratic awareness of the time. However, the spreading of Western culture should not merely be interpreted in exclusively

negative terms, highlighting such effects as the exploitation of resources or colonization (COLONIALISM). On the contrary, many positive aspects – such as democratic values, freedom and technological advancement – also contributed to its successful global extension. Interpreting the worldwide distribution of some of the best Western values merely as a means of imposing force, disregarding or failing to recognize the fashioning power of the Western model could belie a rather simplistic approach towards the phenomenon. Modern-day concern regarding the spreading of Americanization – implemented through the forces of the global market (GLOBALIZATION) – is increasing on a daily basis as this new kind of colonization leads to the denial of other cultures not as a result of a lack of cultural values but as the result of such cultures' inability to compete in economic terms. Americanization can be seen as congruent with, stemming from, or even the same as, Eurocentrism.

Even though anthropological studies have familiarized the idea that a kind of ethnocentrism is present in all cultures, and traces of ethnocentrism can be found in all human societies (Leach, 1978), it is striking to note that Eurocentrism is endemic in present-day thought and education and has become a commonly shared concept. Europeans passively accept that history means history as seen from the European point of view (European referring not only to Europeans of Europe *per se*, but also to neo-Europeans of the Americas, Australia and elsewhere) while philosophy and literature are assumed to be European philosophy and literature. The pervasive influence of Western culture and its negative effects raise considerable concern. As a result of the elusive nature of Eurocentrism and the difficulty in counteracting the phenomenon, some scholars such as Samir Amin (1989) consider that rather than being a social theory integrating various elements into a global and coherent vision of society and history, Eurocentrism is a PREJU-DICE that distorts social theories, drawing from a storehouse of components according to the ideological needs of the moment. Eurocentrism can thus be considered much more than the pure and naive attitude of a culture which considers itself the epitome of mankind and regarded as a far more elusive and aggressive project of global power and domination. [G. H.]

Amin, S. (1989) Eurocentrism, Zed Press, London.
Callari Galli, M. (1974) Gli altri noi, Ghisoni, Milano.
Herskovits, M. J. (1948) Man and His Works, Knopf, New York.
Kroeber, A. L. (1948) Anthropology, Harcourt Brace & World, New York.
Leach, E. (1978) 'Etnocentrismi', in Enciclopedia Einaudi, Vol. V, Torino.
Levine, R. A., Campbell, D. T. (1972) Ethnocentrism. Theories of Conflict, Ethnic Attitudes and Group Behavior, John Wiley & Sons, New York.
Maget, M. (1968) 'Problèmes d'ethnographie européenne', in Poirier, J. (ed.), Ethnologie générale, Gallimard, Paris.
Sauvy, A. (1977) L'Opinion publique, PUF, Paris.
Shobat, E., Stam, R. (1994) Unthinking Eurocentrism: Multiculturalism and the Media, Routledge, London.
Tentori, T. (1987) Il rischio della certezza, Studium, Roma.
Van der Berghe, P. L. (1967) 'Pluralisme social et pluralisme culturel', Cahiers Internationaux de Sociologie, 43: 67–69.

EVOLUTION (THEORY OF) (It. *teoria dell'evoluzione*; Fr. *théorie de l'évolution*; Ger. *Entwicklungslehre*)

From the Latin *evolvere*, formed of *ex-*, from, and *volgere*, to turn, to roll. Until the middle of the nineteenth century, the study of living forms was dominated by theories fundamentally based on Plato's conception, according to which variations within species were imperfect manifestations of ideal Forms (*eidos*, or Ideas), or 'accidents', and the Platonic/Aristotelian view of the world which saw different species as fixed and unchangeable. It was not until Charles Darwin (1809–82) that this fundamentally static interpretation of the natural world was seriously challenged, and variation came to be seen as the result of an evolutionary process rather than accidental, and not necessarily as involving divine intervention. Darwin set out his fundamental ideas in *The Origin of Species*, published in 1859, which outlined for the first time a theory which could explain the mechanism of evolution, i.e. that evolution is a gradual process, that all species descend from a common ancestor and species continue to exist or disappear as a consequence of environmental selection. While some of these theories had been advanced by thinkers before him, Darwin's originality lay in his intuiting the selective function of the environment. The same conclusions were drawn by A. R. Wallace (1823–1913), completely independently from Darwin. Both were influenced by the economist T. R. Malthus (1766–1834), and his theory that poverty was the result of the increase in population rate exceeding the availability of food and other resources. Darwin and Wallace extended Malthus' theory to all living organisms, most of which generate more offspring than can survive, thereby leading to competition for the available resources.

The concept of 'natural selection' – the survival of those individuals and species most suited to a particular environment – however, could not alone sustain a theory which did not require the idea of transcendent intervention. If we compare the process of natural selection to the work of a breeder or of a farmer, who select the most suitable animals and plants for their specific needs through cross-breeding, then evolution could still be understood to be the work of a supreme Being above nature. Hence Darwin introduced the idea of a 'struggle for survival', according to which it is competition between the members of the same species, between species and with the environment that is the driving force of evolution processes. He borrowed this concept from H. Spencer's (1820–1903) principle of the 'survival of the fittest', which is so obvious as to be tautological, unless we assume the fittest to be identifiable *a posteriori*; in fact, the fittest is the one who survives and the one who survives is the fittest.

Thus variation was no longer considered to be accidental, as in Plato's and Aristotle's conceptions, but came to be seen as an essential characteristic of living beings and of evolution, which cannot occur without variation as this would make differential environmental selection impossible. However, evolution does not just operate through variation, it also produces it – especially with regard to the more important changes that occur over a long period of time – as it is responsible for diversification of the species and therefore for increases in variation. Evolution is thus both the cause and effect of variation.

When the theory of evolution through natural selection was first developed, there was no understanding of the mechanisms governing hereditary variations. Although formulated by G. J. Mendel (1822–84) in 1865, the laws of heredity were not particularly influential until 1900 when they were independently rediscovered by C. Correns, E. von Tschermark and H. de Vries.

Further developments in evolutionary theories occurred at the beginning of the twentieth century when statistical and mathematical analysis were applied to the study of genetics. This field of study considers genes to be not just the hereditary factors which give origin to each individual, but also as the elements common to a given group of individuals – i.e. a population – among whom they are distributed and recombined. The first theoretical developments of this approach were made by R. A. Fisher, J. B. S. Haldane, S. Wright and S. Chetverikov. Other scientists such as T. Dobzhansky, E. Mayr, G. G. Simpson and G. L. Stebbins subsequently provided experimental evidence for the proposed mathematical models. These new studies led to interpretation of the theory of organic evolution, a neo-Darwinian theory which, in 1942, the English biologist Julian Huxley called 'modern synthesis' or 'the synthetic theory'. This new theory described evolution as a process consisting of two distinct phases, the production and redistribution of variation – whose mechanisms were explained by genetics (PHENOTYPE, GENOTYPE) – and the action of natural selection on variation, as expounded by Darwin. According to Darwin, the evolution process comprises the appearance of new forms of life from pre-existing life forms (macro-evolution), over a long period of time. This view describes the result of the evolutionary process, which is obtained only by the cumulation of the many minor changes which occur in every generation. It follows that, in order to fully understand evolution, we must study the small events that occur over a short period of time (micro-evolution). Having carried out his work before the discovery of genetics, Darwin was not able to fully comprehend the mechanisms of evolutionary change. Modern science can detect the changes occurring in all living beings from one generation to the next, and thus can formulate hypotheses on how the evolution process takes place.

From a genetic point of view, evolution can be defined as 'a change in the gene frequencies from one generation to another'. The role assigned to a population and its structure in the development of new species is fundamental to this conception of the world. The variation recorded among the individuals comprising a population is the condition required to ensure the existence of individuals pre-adapted to the changes that occur in an environment over time. These individuals are those who will be more likely to survive such environmental changes and/or leave behind more offspring, so that from generation to generation, the number of individuals who are more similar to them will increase. Therefore, a population adapts to changes in the environment, while the individual is adapted to the environment.

The synthetic theory met with two challenges during the 1960s and 1970s. The first was a consequence of the development of studies on molecules carried out by Japanese scientist M. Kimura, who, in 1968, developed a 'neutral theory of molecular evolution'. Later on, following the debate between pan-neutralists and pan-selectionists, Kimura reformulated a theory of 'mutation-genetic drift', which suggested that most mutations are sufficiently neutral from a selective point of view and that whether they are perpetuated in a population depends on random processes, in other words, on genetic drift. The second challenge came from the new studies on fossils, which led to the theory that evolution was not a continuous process, as supported by 'phyletic gradualism', but rather occurred irregularly, in leaps. This theory, formulated by N. Eldredge and S. J. Gould in 1972, is known as 'evolution by punctuated equilibrium', based on an idea expressed in the 1950s by G. G. Simpson, according to whom the main evolutionary changes occur through *evolution quantums*. These theories, unlike criticisms voiced by Creationists, do not attempt to deny that evolutionary mutations occur or that current species descend from a common ancestor, or that Darwin's natural selection plays a role in the evolutionary process. The dispute involves the evolutionary school of thought and a revision of the traditional concepts and contrasting theories and allows ideas of neutrality and punctuated evolution to be included in a global vision of the synthetic theory.

Starting from the 1970s, developments in evolutionary theory have supported the findings of other sciences which prove the falseness of conceptions based on presumed differences in biological races in man. Subsequent molecular studies have provided valuable evidence that our species (*Homo sapiens*) originated as one, in Africa, in relatively recent times (about 100,000 years ago). [G. B., O. R.]

Dawkins, R. (1976) *The Selfish Gene*, Oxford University Press, Oxford.

Eldredge, N. (1995) *Reinventing Darwin*, John Wiley & Sons, New York.

Eldredge, N., Gould, S. J. (1972) 'Punctuated equilibria: an alternative to phyletic gradualism', in Schopf, T. J. M. (ed.), *Models in Palaeobiology*, Freeman, Cooper, San Francisco.

Greene, J. C. (1959) *The Death of Adam*, Iowa State University Press, Ames.

Huxley, J. (1963) *Evolution: The Modern Synthesis*, George Allen and Unwin, London.

Kimura, M. (1983) *The Neutral Theory of Molecular Evolution*, Cambridge University Press, Cambridge.

Mayr, E. (1963) *Animal Species and Evolution*, The Belknap Press of Harvard University Press, Cambridge, MA.

Simpson, G. G. (1960) *This View of Life*, Harcourt, Brace & World, New York.

EXCLUSION: see DEPORTATION

Marzano, F. (1989) 'Esilio (diritto costituzionale)', in *Enciclopedia giuridica Treccani*, Vol. XIII, Roma.

EXILE (It. *esule*; Fr. *exilé*; Ger. *Exil*)

From the Latin *exul-ulis*, referring to soil, and *solum*, referring to individuals who have been permanently or temporarily banned from their state of belonging, owing to crimes committed or following sentence by the authorities who consider their presence within national territory to be a destabilizing factor for established order.

The main characteristics of exile are the fact that it is designated by public law (i.e. a condition of exile is decided by state representatives) and its prevalently political character (it is a condition inflicted in order to defend and preserve the political regime by which it is applied). The figure of the exile differs from that of the deportee (DEPORTATION) or of a person in forced residence in that in the latter cases the person concerned must be banished from the territory. Owing to its individual character, exile should be distinguished from collective and general exodus, which consists in the forced MIGRATION of ethnic or social groups (DIASPORA), a phenomenon which has, moreover, often been accompanied by the physical elimination of people. Exile was adopted in order to remove the enemies of the French Revolution and from that moment onwards similar measures against political adversaries have often been adopted during revolutions and coups during the nineteenth and twentieth centuries. [S. P.]

Bon Valvassina, M. (1966) 'Esilio', in *Enciclopedia del diritto*, Vol. XV, Giuffrè, Milano.

EXOTICISM (It. *esotismo*; Fr. *exotisme*; Ger. *Exotismus*)

The term derives from the Greek *exo* – meaning outside, from distant lands, foreign – and the French *exotisme*, *exotique* (Montaigne, 1992). It was initially used in connection with cultural research (CULTURE) regarding distant civilizations (CIVILIZATION) and countries, with aesthetic tendencies. Following elaboration of the concept of FOLKLORE, it has now acquired a more sociological meaning.

The term 'exoticism' can be used to describe the way in which Western culture understands occasional waves of fascination experienced by artists and scholars regarding distant cultures. The term finds early use in such ancient works as *The Odyssey* and reiteration in Marco Polo's *The Million*. During the sixteenth and seventeenth centuries, Turkish and oriental exoticism became extremely popular and in the eighteenth century the phenomenon was also mentioned in Montesquieu's *Persian Letters* (ORIENTALISM). Furthermore, exoticism became one of the important aesthetic categories of the Romantic period, conquering authors such as Byron and Flaubert and the painter Delacroix. Although exoticism recognizes the force of attraction of distant cultures it nevertheless looks at them as transient phenomena often impregnated by a form of naiveness (ART AND ETHNICITY). While the discovery of the New World, which was mainly of economic interest, did not create any particular forms of exoticism, still, in the nineteenth and twentieth centuries, exoticism developed with regard to the subject of the 'Indios' and tropical paradises, as can be seen in such successful works as Offenbach's *La Périchole* and Gauguin's paintings. At the beginning of the twentieth century, exoticism began to take the form of a taste for Chinese and Japanese products, with the MUSIC of Puccini being particularly successful in Italy.

As with any cultural phenomenon, exoticism has also been recognized as an evolutionary movement: as a shift in the interest of Western culture towards different, far-off countries and their cultures. During the 1960s, movements opposing the conformist consumerism of the Western world were intrigued by India and her neighbouring countries finding an alternative to the affirmative religions of the West, which had been compromised by power, in the metaphysical philosophies of this cultural area. The pronounced esotericism of a large number of yoga-based rituals and the spiritualism of many forms of associationism, together with a fascination with artistic expressions uncommon in Western culture, led many to make pilgrimages to the East. There was also an attempt to export these religious, health-oriented, meditative and spiritual forms to the West, above all by those involved in the world of entertainment. The relationship between the mentor and his disciple greatly preoccupied the Western world and the guru became a popular means of spreading ideologies, while prophets and holy men led their followers to spiritual and religious regeneration. Nevertheless, it could be argued that the acritical and rather superficial approach to these cultures shown by Western culture was merely an expression of a hidden form of RACISM based on the presumption that Western culture is in some way more artificial and therefore less natural. [S. G.]

Montaigne, M. (1992) *Les Essais* (1571), PUF, Paris.
Montesquieu, de C. L. (1973) *Persian Letters* (1721), Penguin Books, London.
Villari, R. (1971) *Storia dell'Europa contemporanea*, Laterza, Bari.

EXTRACOMUNITARIO (It. *extracomunitario*; Fr. *extracomunitario*; Ger. *Extracomunitario*)

This word has its origins in bureaucratic terminology employed within the European Community where it was used to refer to non-European Community individuals resident and/or employed within the community. Such individuals had previously been referred to as 'Third Country Nationals'. In its bureaucratic usage the term encompassed all those within the Community (and later the Union) who were not citizens of one of the member countries. For example, it applied equally to Turkish, Swiss and American citizens who worked in one of the member states. Because it incorporates the word 'community', the term 'extracomunitario' became technically inaccurate the moment that the European Community was renamed the European Union. Nowadays all official documents use the term 'non-EU citizens', though in some documents certain non-EU states may be distinguished as countries of 'high migratory pressure' from other countries that are designated as 'advanced' or 'developed'. Subsequently, this term enjoyed a wider circulation, being used in the media – especially in Italy – as a synonym for MIGRANT. In this capacity it often carried negative connotations. This was because the media used the term only in respect of migrants from poorer countries, such as Albania, who were more readily associated with problems of one kind or another. [R. B.]

FAMILY (It. *famiglia*; Fr. *famille*; Ger. *Familie*) A family is a social nucleus formed of two or more people, linked to each other by matrimony, blood ties, affinities and/or other ties (legal, economic, religious, etc.). Its main functions are biological reproduction and socialization, that is, the INTEGRATION of individuals within a given social context.

The concept of 'family' varies greatly from culture to culture and even from era to era within the same CULTURE. Furthermore, roles and relationships within the family change according to both time and social situation. The values underpinning the idea of family are often a reason for the contrast between MIGRANT groups and the host society and between ethnic minorities and majority groups (ETHNIC MINORITY). Modern cultural anthropology has largely abandoned the concept of the unilinear development of the family (from the primitive horde to the modern monogamous family), which was widely accepted in the nineteenth century, and instead has adopted the position that there is a series of socially and geographically defined family models independent from each other (Linton, 1936). In other words, the current view is that there is no such thing as a natural and universal family model; instead, various forms of families are seen as closely related to, and indeed dependent on, the social and political organization, industrial production system and property laws of a given society.

A distinction can be drawn between *extended* and *nuclear* families, the former being typical of the pre-industrial societies of the past, based on a prevalently agricultural economy, and the latter belonging mostly to modern urban-industrial societies. Extended families are characterized by a large number of family members – including several generations – living in the same home. In the past, this family model played an important economic and productive role; all those who worked within it were part of the family irrespective of blood ties, and various kinds of relationships existed within it (affection, solidarity, work, etc.). Nuclear families consist of few members (usually two parents and a limited number of children) and fulfil a smaller number of functions, as such functions are increasingly absorbed by the external society. In industrial societies families retain, above all, reproductive and emotional support roles, while functions related to economic, educational and social relations are diminished.

Even though the contemporary family model cannot, strictly speaking, be considered a productive unit, it nevertheless continues to make a significant contribution to the economy, producing and transforming goods and services for the satisfaction of its members. Unpaid domestic work allows the family to use resources provided by society which would otherwise be unusable. Therefore, the family not only provides material support and affection but also represents the private space in which individuals can live and reproduce. At the same time, the family carries out the function of ideological reproduction – transmitting the values of the society of belonging. The family can be considered a private sphere which plays a public role, as it takes on social requirements (e.g. of the reproduction of consensus). Althusser (1986) defines the family as 'a state ideological tool', as a result of its role in educating in individualism, select intimacy, negation of the collective dimension and the reproduction of consensus and social stratification.

Although the nuclear family model is the most widespread in all Western countries, other family models exist in cities of THIRD WORLD countries with which the Western world has come into contact through foreign MIGRATION. The countries of origin of many immigrants provide examples of extended families although there are significant differences from one country to another. In Central and, to a lesser extent, South America, it is not uncommon to find a family model centred around a female figure who is far more important than the (often absent) male figure in terms of the economic and educational responsibilities undertaken towards the offspring. In the agricultural world and among the working classes of the city, extended families and common-law families, with no legal or religious ties, are quite widespread. In Arab countries there are many differences between the rural and urban situations. In rural areas extended families are widespread, with several family units living under the same roof. In contrast, nuclear families are prevalent in cities, although relatives often look for homes near each other (e.g. in the same building). In both contexts extended families have important support functions and provide a social network for women. In most cases, women who marry live with their husband's parents. Female and male roles are different and distinct, the women being expected to care for the family and family relations while the men take on public roles. Family groups

prevail over individuals and the greater part of marriages are arranged or at least approved by the families.

The Chinese family model usually consists of an extended family based on the father's authority. Families also include ancestors, to whom an area of worship is dedicated in every home. Families have a clearly defined hierarchy (such a system may seem incredibly complex to Western observers) in which every person, including the ancestors, has a precise role. The role of each family member is based on his or her seniority, gender and productive role. Families are considered to be, and often are, economic units, in which relationships are not based solely on affection and are usually more formal than those of Western families. In China too, marriages are arranged by the family group, and women, by marriage, become part of their husband's family and owe obedience to their in-laws. Muslim families are also based on a rather rigid hierarchy and on male authority; parental authority belongs, by law, to the father only – as is also the case in China and Japan – and, in his absence, to the eldest male child or to other male relatives. Family relationships are regulated, in most Arab countries, by the Personal Statute Codes, which refer to the laws and doctrine of the Koran. The code which departs furthest from Islamic law is the Tunisian code. Islamic family law requires women to hold a subordinate position with respect to men. Muslim women often manage only the private area inside the home, with the result that youths only slightly older than schoolchildren come to discuss their brothers and sisters' progress with teachers. The Chinese tend to recreate extended families in immigration situations, although they do not necessarily share the same roof, and Chinese women, in most cases, work in the family or quasi-family business. This is much less common among Muslim families and is a further element of distress for many women who do not work and who were used, back home, to collectively managing the home, the children and the relations within the family group. To these women, emigration means, above all, social isolation.

These traditional family models, which mostly apply to the less wealthy classes and to the more traditional middle classes, are often reproduced by foreigners in an immigration context. Obviously, some immigrants move away from these family models and sometimes the models linked to the country of origin meet with a crisis when confronted with Western family models, or in the SECOND GENERATION of immigrants, who are more likely to identify with the host society.

Immigration often increases the importance of the role of the extended family as a support to its members (economic support, help in finding work, etc.) and also as a vehicle to pass down the culture of origin. Information on this is provided by many surveys carried out in Europe and in the USA, which reveal a systematic and daily relationship with relatives in the organization of life in the country of emigration, whether members live together or not. This could be interpreted both as a re-creation of the typical family models of the country of origin and as an answer to the needs which arise in an immigration context, and which require increased solidarity between relatives or compatriots. Families, when they emigrate, also play a very important role in the maintenance of their culture of origin, in particular that of sexual and generational roles, through the socialization process. It is particularly with regard to the transmission of the values of the society of

provenance that conflicts arise between parents and children, as the latter are more in contact with the values of the host society.

Emigration can also have the effect of calling traditional family roles in question and of changing them in consequence. This happens for three principal reasons: (1) the absence of a father figure; in this situation women take on the role of head of the family and their first-born takes on the maternal role; (2) contact with different behavioural and family models, which may facilitate the abandoning of part of one's traditions and the taking on of other cultural traits (for example, a certain number of female immigrants shift their behaviour towards that of native women); and (3) the difficulty for mothers to fulfil their role as expected in Western societies, because they do not speak the language of the host country and/or because they prefer not to be involved in public matters. In this event, as is often the case with Arab women immigrants, their elder children come to fill the role of maternal substitutes and interpreter-translator, even in situations when they would normally be thought to be too young (for example, they may substitute for their parents in dealings with schools and they may accompany them and act as interpreters in their dealings with social and health care institutions, such as family planning clinics). [Le. Z.]

Althusser, L. (1986) *Essay on Ideology*, Columbia University Press, New York.
Burguière, A., Klapisch-Zubar, C., Segalen, M., Zonabend, F. (1986) *Histoire de la famille*, Armand Collin, Paris.
Linton, R. (1936) *The Study of Man*, Appleton, New York.
Melotti, U. (1981) 'Toward a new theory of the origin of the family', *Current Anthropology*, 22(6): 625–638.

FAMILY REUNIFICATION (It. *ricongiungimento familiare*; Fr. *réunification familiale*; Ger. *Familienzusammenführung*)

Family reunification refers to the bringing together of FAMILY members who have been separated for one reason or another. The term is frequently used by sociologists and social workers in reference to families that are divided because of divorce, abandonment, abuse, or the arrest of a family member. In the context of MIGRATION, family reunification concerns involuntary or undesired separation across political frontiers (FRONTIER), a problem which can be alleviated or hindered by the states involved. Although family reunification may be as old as the family itself and can be encountered throughout the globe, it became an important political issue in the United States following the immigration restrictions of the 1920s and in Western Europe following the Second World War and this continues to be so because those two regions are the major international poles of attraction for immigration.

The United States introduced immigration restrictions with the quota Acts of 1921 and 1924. Subsequently aliens wishing to join family members in the USA had to be admitted as part of a national quota (QUOTA SYSTEM) (though for many Asian nations immigration was simply barred). From its inception, the US national origins system did incorporate special preferences for wives, parents, brothers, sisters, children under 18 years of age, and fiancées of US citizens and aliens who had applied for CITIZENSHIP or served in the US armed forces. By 1924 alien wives and dependent children of citizens were included in the non-quota category (i.e. those who might be admitted regardless of whether quotas had been filled). Clearly the conception of family reunification was that of a male head of household being joined by his various dependants. Following the Second World War, the so-called War Brides Act facilitated the immigration of a large group of European wives and children of US servicemen. The 1952 Immigration and Naturalization Act further expanded the non-quota class to include relatives of permanent-resident aliens and so allowed for thousands more spouses from Europe and Asia to reunify in the USA (alien husbands joining US-resident wives were also explicitly recognized). The US national origins system was eventually replaced, in 1965, by both a universal quota and a uniform per-country ceiling. Within the new system, two categories of immigrants were specifically recognized as welcome: those with special occupational skills, and family members of US citizens and permanent residents. Since that time, family reunification has represented as much as 80 per cent of legal migration to the USA. It has not, however, been a system without problems, and waiting times for family reunification applications have reportedly stretched out as long as a decade.

Family reunification became an important issue in Europe following the Second World War, the aftermath of which saw millions of refugees traversing the continent (REFUGEE). It was in this context that the Geneva (1949) and the United Nations (1951 and subsequent) Conventions made specific references to the reunification of refugee families. Aside from refugees, who might be involuntarily separated from their families, reunification was not a major issue in the years of economic growth and relatively free immigration characterized the 1950s and 1960s. Those decades saw the beginning of migration to Europe from, especially, South Asia, the Caribbean, North Africa, sub-Saharan Africa, and Turkey (much, but not all, of this immigration came from former colonies of the European powers). Then, beginning with the UK in the 1960s and in the other immigration-receiving countries in the 1970s, restrictive and zero-immigration policies were introduced. At that point family reunification became an issue for labour immigrants as well as for refugees (just as it had been in the USA since the 1920s). Each European state pursued its own policy, though reunification was generally permitted under certain circumstances.

Family reunification normally finds its justification in the so-called family principle, which has been expressed as follows: 'The family is the natural and fundamental group unit of society and is entitled to protection by society and the state' (1966 International Covenant on Civil and Political Rights). The family principle has found its way into a number of widely subscribed international instruments as well as various national legislations and constitutions. In the case of refugees (itself a contested category), the family principle has generally translated into unrestricted encouragement and facilitation of reunification. For non-refugee (including labour) migration, the same cannot be said. For while the International Labour Organization (from 1949) and the UN (from at least 1977) have encouraged migrant-receiving countries to facilitate family reunification for migrant workers – as early as 1961, the European Social Charter referred to the need to 'facilitate *as far as possible*' (emphasis added) reunification of legal migrant worker families, a position reiterated subsequently by the OECD, the Council of Europe and the EU's 1993 Resolution on the Harmonization of National Policies on Family Reunification – individual countries (and the EU) have been more reluctant.

The European proposal to harmonize family reunification policy raises several problems. The first of these is how to define the family. In addition to spouses and biological children, various national legislations recognize reunification for parents, grandparents, adopted children, siblings, aunts, uncles, nephews and nieces. The second problem is how far the notion of the family needs modification given that unmarried partners, both same and opposite sex, have also been admitted under the family reunification rubric.

The question of allowing reunification for labour immigrant families 'as far as possible' is also a vexed one. Insofar as most immigrant-receiving countries are seeking to severely limit immigration, there is a strong temptation to limit family reunification, a temptation based on political considerations rather than humanitarian ones or the family principle. This is not to say that humanitarian reasons cannot be found for limiting family reunification. It can be argued, for example, that it is contrary to the best interests of the joining family members, especially if they are children, to be introduced into a situation of sub-standard housing, transient lodging, or extreme poverty. To this end a number of requirements are generally made relative to the already legally resident migrant family member. These might include minimum income, quality of housing, and length of stay and of VISA. With regard to the joining family members it is frequently stipulated that they must not present a security or health risk to the host country.

There is considerable concern in immigration countries regarding the possible abuse of family reunification provisions, in particular fraudulent marriages contracted solely for the purpose of immigration. Some immigration legislations stipulate periods following reunification (from one to several years) during which, should a married couple *not* cohabit, the 'reunified' spouse will be deported. The United States is particularly attentive in this regard, but its example is beginning to be followed in Europe. However it should be noted that such policies can create captive situations and foster spousal abuse.

In any context of immigration restriction, family reunification becomes a sensitive political issue. On the one hand, there may be a strong humanitarian argument in favour of family reunification, while, on the other, political and public opinion may call for greater restriction of immigration. The criteria determining regulation may indeed have little if anything to do with the family principle, the rights of married couples, or the best interests of children; and that disjuncture can constitute a glaring inconsistency in family reunification policies. [C. I.]

Bernard, W. S. (1980) 'Immigration: history of US policy', in Thernstrom, S. (ed.), *Harvard Encyclopedia of American Ethnic Groups*, Harvard University Press, Cambridge, MA.

De Sipio, L., De la Garza, R. O. (1998) *Making Americans, Remaking America: Immigration and Immigrant Policy*, Westview Press, Boulder, CO.

Intergovernmental Consultations on Asylum, Refugee and Migration Policies in Europe, North America and Australia (1997) *Report on Family Reunification*.

FLOWS (It. *flussi*; Fr. *flux*; Ger. *Strö-me*) From the Latin *fluxus*, from *fluere*, to flow. The term 'flows' is used with reference to MIGRATION in its universal application – i.e. independently from individual national situations – to indicate mass migrations of people from poorer areas of the world more strongly affected by economic or political problems, towards so-called industrialized countries, in search of better living conditions, work opportunities, or protection from war or persecution. The causes of this phenomenon mainly lie in the gap which exists between the economies of DEVELOPING COUNTRIES and those of more developed countries, as well as in the growth in population in THIRD WORLD countries. Recent studies in North America have shown that migrants create a demand for further migration and an opportunity structure for later migrants (MIGRATION CHAIN).

Other examples of 'flows' can be found in the daily or weekly commuting across BORDERS (and even across whole continents or oceans) for employment reasons. [S. P.]

Cohen, R., Deng, F. M. (1998) *Masses in Flight: The Global Crisis of Internal Displacement*, Brookings Institution, Washington, DC.

EEC (1993) *Abhandlungen zu Fluchtingsfragen Band – Vol. XXII*, Association for the Study of the World Refugee Problem, Roma.

FOLKLORE (It. *folclore*; Fr. *folklore*; Ger. *Folklore*) The term 'folklore', coined in 1846 by the English archaeologist W. J. Thoms, combines the words *folk* (people) and *lore* (tradition) to indicate popular traditions and their study.

To begin with, the study of folklore was limited to the songs and stories of oral traditions. However, it soon began to include all popular customs, arts and traditions. Such a comprehensive study presents two problems. The first problem lies in finding a criterion to define the object of study, i.e. to distinguish which aspects are legitimate, anonymous, popular expressions and which are the product of academic CULTURE, as established authors often take inspiration from the former. Another problem concerns the vastness of this potential field of study. Popular expressions include DANCE, figurative arts (ART AND ETHNICITY), MUSIC and literature which are part of complex religious and social rituals (RITE), and which, together with clothing and cookery, comprise the primary cultural and social background of a population. To what extent, therefore, should the study of folklore – intended as the study of the traditions and communication abilities of a PEOPLE – be concerned with these expressions? It is interesting to note that, oddly enough, the culture currently known as *pop* (from popular), is in actual fact completely alien to popular culture. Some crafts have been replaced by the moulding of plastic materials, and other practices, such as the cooking of traditional meals, have become rare. The real and popular cookery of today is fast food, while traditional dishes are served alongside exotic foods (EXOTICISM) under the comprehensive label of 'ethnic cuisine' (ETHNICITY), which is increasingly less related to anything 'popular'. Another example of this trend is the clothing industry, where it is worth noting the 'social' evolution of *denim*, which to begin with marked the wearer as belonging to the lower classes and later took on a 'universalistic' character which goes beyond social distinction. Today folklore is, possibly implicitly, almost entirely managed by the media. It has lost its 'popular' character and has become a mass production. One example of surviving modern folklore can be found in the musical field, in the output of singer-songwriters, while the rest of popular music has become crystallized into a series of exhibits to be displayed at tourist and religious events, most of which maintain only the trappings of ancient forms. [S. G.]

Hazlitt, W. C. (1995) *Faiths & Folklore*, Bracken Books, London.

Hoggart, R. (1992) *Oxford Encyclopaedia of Peoples and Cultures*, Oxford University Press, Oxford.

Niles, J. D. (1999) *Homo Narrans: The Poetics and Anthropology of Oral Literature*, University of Pennsylvania Press, Philadelphia.

FOREIGNER (It. *straniero*; Fr. *étranger*; Ger. *Ausländer*)

This term is used to denote a person travelling through or staying in a country other than his/her country of CITIZENSHIP (the term 'citizenship' being interpreted in the modern sense to mean a legal condition stemming from an individual's belonging to a particular nation state). Legally speaking, 'foreigner' (or alien) denotes a person who resides in one country while being the citizen of another. According to the modern nation-based world political system, to be 'foreign' means not to be a citizen of one's country of residence, usually implying that one is granted somewhat limited general and political rights. However, often foreigners who are citizens of countries having reciprocal agreements with their host countries enjoy the same civil rights as citizens. Over the last 30–40 years, the increased recognition of human rights in many Western democracies has resulted in fewer differences in legal status between foreigners and citizens. Most countries distinguish between temporary aliens and those who wish to reside in the country permanently. Entry requirements are generally stricter for foreign migrants (MIGRANT) looking for work than they are for foreigners wishing to enter a country on a temporary basis as tourists or students. In any case, any foreigner wishing to enter a country for any purpose must hold a valid passport and, where required, a VISA.

The legal definition of the term 'foreigner' (or alien) is intrinsically connected with the concept of CITIZEN-SHIP, and is relatively recent, its development being contemporaneous and correlated to that of the national state (NATION). On a more general level, the experience of being foreign extends beyond mere legal status and is independent from a person's citizenship or passport or, even, nationality. In this sense the wide range of meanings inherent in the experience of being a 'foreigner' is perhaps best deduced from an etymological analysis of its synonym 'stranger', which stems from the same Latin root *extraneus* as 'strange' and 'extraordinary' – a peculiarity common to many European languages – showing that historically foreignness has been associated with 'strangeness' to a certain extent. To be foreign, or a stranger, is to be in some way extraneous to, or outside, a given political or cultural COMMU-NITY. Failure to be part of, or exclusion from, a community may depend on a variety of factors, including differences in language, traditions or habits, or even simply of values.

Georg Simmel (1908) provides one of the most striking definitions of strangeness, with reference to those arriving in a foreign country to stay. He highlights the paradox inherent in the experience of being a stranger, which implies nearness and remoteness at the same time, as in order to be defined as a stranger one must come from elsewhere and yet find oneself close to or immersed in the culture defining one as such. In this sense migrants become in a way permanent strangers; once the umbilical cord with the homeland has been severed, complete reconnection is no longer possible. They are uprooted, their sense of stability permanently undermined. In addition, their 'leaving' the mother country may be viewed with suspicion both at home and abroad. So migrants set out on a never-ending journey, and are 'condemned' to being viewed as strangers for the rest of their lives. A poignant example of this permanent state of foreignness could be that of the Jewish people. From the archetypal point of view, we are reminded of the figure of the wanderer, and the mythological journey of the Greek hero Odysseus.

The experience of being foreign – whether for a day or for life – is always psychologically distressing. Obviously the distress experienced by persons who have been forced to migrate in conditions of extreme poverty, or as a result of war, famine or disaster, such as labour migrants or refugees, can in no way be compared to the experience of a modern-day tourist. Many scholars have spoken of 'transcultural shock' with reference to immigrants' experience of being strangers in their host countries. Psychopathological studies have long tried to describe the psychological distress related to the feeling of being a stranger, with particular attention to specific syndromes affecting those staying in a foreign country for extended periods. The disorientation caused by the encounter with a new language, new customs and a new moral code can at times have serious consequences. This emotional and intellectual state affecting those persons who are faced daily with the encounter with foreignness is described as one of disorientation, frustration, rejection, rebellion and anxiety (Camilleri and Cohen-Emerique, 1989). Such problems may be accentuated by the host society's erroneous interpretation of foreigners' behaviour, owing to basic differences in expression. Behaviour considered normal in one culture may even be viewed as pathological in another. Without attempting to justify such misinterpretations by resorting to the CULTURAL RELATIVISM explanation, any individual who is adjusted to his/her native society will inevitably face an identity crisis when his/her behaviour is received differently by a new host society. Such individuals face the double task of acquiring the respect of their host society – with regard to both their origin and their status within the new country – and reconciling the mores of their native country with those of the host country. On the part of the host society, it is important that TOLERANCE (INTOLERANCE) does not turn into indifference, and that foreigners are made to feel part of a society which accepts their wish to establish good relations with its native inhabitants, and their willingness to reconsider their original values (DIVERSITY-SIMILARITY). [S. G.]

Camilleri, C., Cohen-Emerique, M. (eds) (1989) *Chocs de cultures: Concepts et enjeux pratiques de l'interculturel*, Harmattan, Paris

Harman, L. D. (1988) *The Modern Stranger: On Language and Membership*, Mouton De Gruyter, Berlin.

Kristeva, J. (1994) *Strangers to Ourselves* (1988), Columbia University Press, New York.

Simmel, G. (1908) *Soziologie Unterzuchungen über die Formen der Vergesellschaftung*, Dunker & Humblot, Leipzig.

FORTRESS EUROPE (It. *Fortezza Europa*; Fr. *forteresse Europe*; Ger.

Festung Europa) A term used to designate: (a) a sense of being under siege which the citizens of Europe feel with regard to the phenomenon of immigration (MIGRATION) and, generally speaking, with regard to poorer countries (DEVELOPING COUNTRIES; THIRD WORLD); (b) the resurgence of a EUROCENTRIC conception of the world, according to which Europe is viewed by the FOREIGN citizen as a longed-for destination, a fortress to be stormed, and not, as is more likely, a place in which to find work; (c) policies restricting migrant FLOWS which were adopted by the European Union.

The term implies an UNCONSCIOUS attitude: the fear Europeans feel of losing a 'treasure' accumulated after decades of development and abundance. [Gu. B.]

Council of Europe (1991) *Community and Ethnic Relations in Europe*, Final Report, Council of Europe, Brussels.

Schnapper, D. (1992) *L'Europe des immigrés*, F. Bourin, Paris.

FREE MOVEMENT (It. *libera circolazione*; Fr. *libre circulation*; Ger. *Freizügigkeit*) The expression 'free movement' defines one of the basic objectives of the European Union which, in the first deed following its inception, signed in 1957, placed as its main aim the free movement not only of goods, services and capital, but also of people. The main aspect of 'free movement' sees workers from member countries as having the freedom to settle in any Community country. However, for many immigrants (MIGRANTS) – even if they have been legally settled in a country of the European Union for many years – the only form of free movement allowed is movement for tourism purposes which cannot exceed

a duration of three months. A high incidence of cases of violation of the right to free movement is reported in many countries as the right to move and settle freely – established by the law – is often neglected *de facto* as a result of the arbitrary and abusive practices of many national administrations.

The concept of free movement also declares illegal any form of discrimination between indigenous workers and those from other community countries. The subject of freedom of movement was taken up again in 1986 in the Single European Act, Section 8a, which envisaged the implementation, by 1 January 1995, of an area with no internal frontiers for goods, services or people. In 1992, the Maastricht Treaty returned to the subject, only changing the numbering, so that in the new text the Section is now 7a. It must be emphasized that although the items were dealt with at some speed, the principle of free movement has not fully come into force, since some countries (the United Kingdom, Ireland and Denmark) continute to apply a restrictive interpretation, limiting the principle to the abolition of internal border controls (FRONTIER) only to Community citizens, and not to those of third countries. A few years before, in 1985, five states with common borders (France, Germany, Belgium, Holland and Luxembourg) signed an agreement at Schengen to abolish controls at common internal frontiers, and started negotiations for the drafting of a Convention, signed in 1990, which contained the measures necessary to put it into action. In November of that year, Italy formally joined the Schengen agreement, followed by Spain and Portugal in 1991 and Greece in 1992. [Gu. B]

Nascimbene, B. (1995) *Da Schengen a Maastricht*, Giuffrè, Milano.

FRONTIER (It. *frontiera*; Fr. *frontière*; Ger. *Grenze*) Deriving from the Latin *frons* (front), through the ancient French *frontiere*, the term 'frontier' has two main meanings: the first referring to the boundary line which defines the territory of a state, i.e. which surrounds that portion of the earth, including the waters – lakes, rivers – over which a state has territorial sovereignty; and the second denoting an area of transition, passage or communication between two states. Of course, any border is always an arbitrary line, whether such boundary refers to legal, cultural or geographic matters.

Frontiers – or national boundary lines – define each state's independence from another. However, no precise boundaries are required in order for a state to be considered a subject of international law. The temporary nature of certain frontiers, where their determination is conditioned by future agreements, does not exclude the existence of a state's territory, even if sovereignty over certain areas is uncertain. Boundaries can be established by states either through conventions, or, in exceptional cases, unconventionally, on the basis of actual territorial configurations and other spatial criteria regulations. In the majority of cases, sea, air and land frontiers are established through agreements between the interested parties, so that their determination does not remain subject to the changing wishes of the states involved. Conventional regulations governing the matter are contained in the territorial cession treaties, as well as in the specific treaties for the resolution of peaceful controversies arising on such matters. Newly formed states maintain the frontiers of the states which preceded them, unless otherwise stipulated with the interested neighbouring nations. Boundaries can be natural, where they correspond to physical characteristics, or artificial, their identification depending on delimitations generated by humankind. With regard to the criteria used to identify natural frontiers – as it is impossible to speak of any pre-set criteria for the definition of artificial boundary lines, as none exist – and where the issue is not mentioned in the conventions in question, some authors claim the existence of international customs (e.g. in the case of a frontier consisting of a navigable river, the *Thalweg* criterion, referring to the deepest point, would apply).

Frontiers are not just a dividing line between neighbouring states and a means to identify the territory of individual nations, but are also a place of transition and a point of contact. The presence of boundaries creates the so-called frontier zones, or international frontiers. As the vicinity of states to each other is often a source of conflict, it is usual for the nations involved to attempt to reconcile their opposite and mutual interests by collaborating and co-operating. Thus a series of rights and duties – 'good neighbours' principles – have emerged and apply to matters of international law. These regulate the various legal situations which arise in the areas of contact between two or more territories. In order to achieve better co-operation in frontier activities, neighbouring states generally stipulate agreements covering several areas, including frontier traffic – which includes the traffic of people – customs operations, combined national checks, co-operation across the border, etc. European Union member states are now looking to achieve even greater collaboration through the creation of a true 'common area without frontiers', within which the FREE MOVEMENT of goods, people, services and capital is ensured (Section 7a, Maastricht Treaty). [S. P.]

Spatafora, E. (1989) 'Frontiera (zona di)', in *Enciclopedia giuridica*, Treccani, Roma.

FUNDAMENTALISM (It. *fondamentalismo*, *integralismo*; Fr. *fondamentalisme*, *intégralisme*; Ger. *Fundamentalismus*) From the Latin *fundamentum*, foundation, the term 'fundamentalism' refers to an attitude which emerged at the beginning of the 1900s among Protestant circles, particularly in North America. It was first applied to a theological current which opposed any liberal interpretation of Christianity and established certain fundamental, and, therefore, 'non-negotiable' points, whereby an individual could define him/herself as a Christian. Animated by a strong conservative spirit, fundamentalists opposed – both in national Protestant churches and in their missions abroad – the liberal brand of Christianity which attempted to reconcile traditional doctrines with the new theories elaborated by natural scientists. In particular, fundamentalists believed that the Darwinian philosophy, based on 'survival of the fittest', would destroy the Christian foundations of American civilization.

Today fundamentalism is more generally understood to refer to extreme conservatism as applied to any faith which founds and justifies a fanatical attachment to a specific and totalizing vision of the world (RELIGION AND ETHNIC CONFLICT). For example, Islamic fundamentalists accuse modernist thinkers of being purveyors of Western morality and believe that the emancipation of women as conceived by the West is responsible for the disintegration of the family and for permissive sexual morality. Furthermore, the bitter resentment Muslims feel towards Western COLONIALISM has made many of them regard everything Western as evil, and this, in turn, has contributed to the growth of Islamophobia (XENOPHOBIA) in many non-Muslim states, a development that has caused serious difficulties for Muslim communities in these countries. In assuming an attitude of inflexible superiority, and in making religion the only reference point in human life, fundamentalists oppose pluralism (MULTICULTURALISM) and totally reject anyone and anything outside their *Weltanschauung*, or world vision. They reject those who are 'different' (DIVERSITY–SIMILARITY), by eliminating and sometimes even physically destroying them, on the basis of a split conception of the world into good and evil, legitimate and illegitimate and believers and infidels. To a certain extent, it can be said that fundamentalism places itself outside or above history or any comparison or criticism, and that its followers fight for the restoration of their religion, which they consider should also be imposed, at any price, as a political power. Fundamentalists belonging to any religion refuse dialogue as a principle and use religion as a tool of power. They consider that their church, sect or movement should prevail at all costs. [A. D. S.]

Amin, S. (1989) *Eurocentrism*, Monthly Review Press, New York (originally published as *L'Eurocentrisme: Critique d'une idéologie*, Anthropos, Paris).

Burgat, F., Dowell, W. (1992) *The Islamic Movement in North Africa*, University of Texas, Center for Middle Eastern Studies, Austin.

Eisenstadt, S. N. (1994) *Fondamentalismo e modernità*, Laterza, Roma-Bari.

Ferjani, M. C. (1991) *Islamisme, laïcité et droits de l'homme*, L'Harmattan, Paris.

Friedman, M., Sivan, E. (1990) *Religious Radicalism and Politics in the Middle East*, State University of New York Press, Albany.

Gellner, G. (1992) *Postmodernism, Reason and Religion*, Routledge, London.

Laroui, A. (1987) *Islam et modernité*, La Découverte, Paris.

Marty, M. E., Appleby R. S. (eds) (1991) *Fundamentalism Observed: A Study Conducted by the American Academy of Art, Part of the Fundamentalism Project*, University of Chicago Press, Chicago.

Watt, W. M. (1989) *Islamic Fundamentalism and Modernity*, Routledge, London and New York.

G

GASTARBEITER (It. *lavoratore ospite straniero [temporaneamente presente]*; Fr. *Gastarbeiter*; Ger: *Gastarbeiter*) In Germany the word 'Gastarbeiter' is a colloquial euphemism that has replaced the former term 'AUSLÄNDER' since the 1950s. Nevertheless 'Gastarbeiter' implies that the immigrant worker is understood as being a 'guest': namely a person for whom the country of immigration fulfils a duty and who, after a certain amount of time, leaves the country again (MIGRANT, MIGRATION). This system of temporary admission has a long tradition in Germany (Dohse, 1985) and was introduced again in the mid-1950s in a 'rotation policy'. The Gastarbeiter system was copied in various Western European countries. In the Republic of Germany, from 1955 until 1973, a complex system of recruitment of Gastarbeiter developed that was organized on the basis of bilateral contracts between the various countries of immigration and emigration. The specific organization was different in each country of immigration, although, as a rule, it dealt with recruiting single persons, who were tested and checked with regard to their skills and health. Arrangements were then made to send them to particular companies.

Gastarbeiter immigration classically deals with the recruiting of rural workers for employment in the construction, coal, iron and steel industries and assembly plants. These were usually known as the three D jobs – dark, dirty and dangerous. Moreover, Gastarbeiter were enlisted for traditional service jobs. The post-industrial revolution and general crisis led to the number of working Gastarbeiter sinking dramatically and being limited more or less to the construction and service industries. At first, Gastarbeiter in the Federal Republic of Germany came from the south-western periphery of Europe (Italy, Spain and Portugal); later also from Greece and then Turkey, Morocco and other semi-peripheral countries. In the 1960s the working-class population in Germany was no longer able to supply employees for large scale enterprise. Due to this, international migration was intensified and Gastarbeiter immigration was concentrated on the working classes from the THIRD WORLD. Since the 1970s, this situation has fundamentally changed. New kinds of people have immigrated. This can be traced to restrictive migration policies and is also due to worldwide economic and political changes. Gastarbeiter have established families and settled in the country of immigration (SECOND GENERATION), but most of them remain foreigners (FOREIGNER). [J. B.]

Althammer, W. (1975) 'Das Gastarbeiterproblem. Rotation? Integration? Arbeitsplatzverlagerung? Jugoslawien, Griechenland, Türkei. Ergebnisse einer Fachtagung', in Althammer, W. (ed.), *Südosteuropa-Studien*, 23, München.

Castles, S., Booth, H. and Wallace, T. (1984) *Here for Good – Western Europe's New Minorities*, London, Pluto Press.

Dohse, K. (1985) *Ausländische Arbeiter und bürgerlicher Staat. Genese und Funktion von staatlicher Ausländerpolitik und Ausländerrecht. Vom Kaiserreich bis zur Bundesrepublik Deutschland*, Königstein/Ts.

Kammerer, P. (1991) 'Some problems of Italian immigrant organizations in the

Federal Republic of Germany', in Ostow, R., Fijalkowski, J. et al. (eds), *Ethnicity, Structured Inequality, and the State in Canada and the Federal Republic of Germany*, Lang, Frankfurt am Main, New York.

Reimann, H. and Reimann, H. (eds) (1987) 'Gastarbeiter. Analyse und Perspektiven eines sozialen Problems' (2., völlig neu bearb. Aufl.), *WV-Studium*, 132, Opladen, 2 Aufl. 1987.

GENOCIDE (It. *genocidio*; Fr. *génocide*; Ger. *Genozid*) The systematic destruction of a human group by the extermination of all members of the group and destruction of their cultural heritage. Coined by Raphaël Lemkin in 1946, the term is a combination of the Greek *ghenos* (race) and the Latin *cidium* (from *caedere*, meaning to cut, in the sense of to kill). Although this crime against humanity and contravention of human rights has been repeated several times throughout human history, only in 1948 was the term defined and brought into use in international law through the Universal Declaration of Human Rights, approved by the General Assembly of the UN (Lemkin, 1946). [A. B., R. B.]

Lemkin, R. (1946) 'Genocide: a new international crime, punishment and prevention', *Revue Internationale de Droit Pénal*, 17: 371–386.

GENOME see GENOTYPE

GENOTYPE (It. *genotipo*; Fr. *génotype*; Ger. *Genotypus*) A composite term, deriving from the Greek *ghenos*, race, generation, and *typos*, character, indicating all the genes which constitute the heredity of an individual, and which may be passed down to descendants, 'genotype' may be used either as a synonym of *genome* or to define a single *locus* of a specific chromosome. Conceptually related to PHENOTYPE – its physical equivalent and indicator of the external physical characteristics which are the direct manifestation of the information contained in the genotype – the genotype can be considered to be the individual's 'plan', while the phenotype represents the externally identifiable type, the result of the interaction between the genotype and the environment. An individual's genotype remains unchanged for the duration of his or her life, with certain exceptions. With regard to the intersections between the concepts of genotype, RACE and RACISM, it may be said that the study of genotypes, first at protein level (undertaken since the 1950s–1960s), then directly on *DNA* (undertaken since the 1980s), has further undermined the concept of race, which has always been based on phenotypic – and rudimentary – parameters, such as skin colour, body structure, skull shape, etc.

In 1989, the Human Genome Organization (HUGO) – an international organization of scientists – was established in order to perform a complex coordinating role within the Human Genome Project (HGP), a global initiative to map and sequence the human genome. The activities of the HUGO range from supporting data collation for the construction of genetic and physical maps of the human genome to the organization of workshops to promote the consideration of a wide range of ethical, legal, social and intellectual property issues. By the end of the year 2000, more than 5.8 million cDNA sequences, representing over 90 per cent of the human genome, were identified. In 1991, another project – the *Human Genome Diversity Project* (HGDP) – was set up. The HGDP is an international scientific endeavour which complements the HGP by examining the genomic variation of the human species, through analysis of DNA from populations, families and individuals worldwide. The mission of the HGDP is to analyse and raise awareness of the fundamental unity of humankind, human biological history, population movements, and susceptibility or resistance to various human diseases.

The HGP, the HGDP, and other genetic research initiatives have given rise to a number of concerns, especially the fear that genome research could lead to discrimination against and stigmatization (STIGMA) of individuals and populations and be misused to promote racism. In order to address these concerns, the General Conference of UNESCO of 1997 adopted a proposal of the International Bioethics Committee (BIOETHICS AND ETHNICITY), thus approving the *Universal Declaration on the Human Genome and Human Rights* and affirming that: 'The human genome underlies the fundamental unity of all members of the human family, as well as the recognition of their inherent dignity and diversity. In a symbolic sense, it is the heritage of humanity' (article 1). [Ar. C.]

Dobzhansky, T. (1973) *Genetic Diversity and Human Equality*, Basic Books, New York.

Human Genome Organization (2000) *Statement on Benefit-Sharing*, Vancouver, BC.

McKusick, V. A. (1989) 'The Human Genome Organization: history, purposes, and membership', *Genomics*, 5: 385–387.

UNESCO (1997) *Universal Declaration on the Human Genome and Human Rights*, Paris.

GHETTO

(It. *ghetto*; Fr. *ghetto*; Ger. *Ghetto*) The term 'ghetto', from the Venetian dialect *ghetto*, originally and principally refers to a street, an area or even a complete city, used as an enforced permanent residence for JEWS. Today, the term is applied – especially in the USA and not least in American popular culture – to run-down, though no longer walled-in, areas where ETHNIC MINORITIES, or other disadvantaged members of society, languish in comparative misery.

The segregation (RACIAL SEGREGATION) of Jews into ghettos was a physical expression of a long history of religious hatred and persecution. It arose from the fear of the Jews' influence on the Christian faithful and was also a way of satisfying the demand by influential Christian businessmen and corporations that economic sanctions should be imposed on their Jewish competitors (ANTI-SEMITISM). The ghetto was, however, also portrayed by municipal authorities as a way to protect Jews from attacks by non-Jews.

The name 'ghetto' probably derives from a foundry on one of the islands which was used to segregate the Jews in Venice in 1516, though the Venetian Ghetto was not the first to be created. Ghettos were established in the following cities: Breslau (1266); Palermo (1312); Barcelona (1350); Valencia (1390); Turin (1400); Frankfurt (1460); Prague (1473); Kasimierz (1494); Rome (1556); Vienna (1570); Florence (1571); Verona (1605); Mantua (1612); Ferrara (1624) (Gilbert, 1992: 44). Ghettos were not confined to Christian countries: a ghetto was established in Fez (1450) and one of the most ancient examples of segregation of the Jews was in Morocco, where in 1280 the Jews were moved into areas called *mellahs*. However, Jews were not subjected there to the same degree of indignity or restriction as they were in Christian Europe (ibid.). The structure of the Venetian ghetto, with its walls, gates and Christian guards, became the model for other Italian ghettos. Inside the ghettos, the Jews enjoyed a degree of autonomy, with their own religious, judicial, charitable and recreational institutions. Since it was impossible to increase the area of the ghetto, more accommodation could only be created by building upwards, which resulted in inevitable congestion, heightened the risk of fire and encouraged the deterioration of sanitary conditions.

Ghettos were abolished in Western Europe during the nineteenth century, the last to be abolished being the Roman Ghetto – on 20 September 1870 – on the occasion of the unification of Italy and the ending of Papal temporal power. Ghettos were recreated by the Nazis during the Second World War as holding areas prior to the extermination of the Holocaust (SHOAH). Most of these ghettos were in Eastern Europe, but on 16 October 1943, in the Roman Ghetto (the name which is still applied today to the area in Rome where once Jews were forced to live) the Nazis rounded up 1,200 Jewish Roman citizens, who were then deported to Auschwitz. [A. Z., P. B.]

Gilbert, M. (1992) *Jewish History Atlas*, 4th edn, Weidenfeld & Nicolson, London.
Poliakov L. (1966) *The History of Anti-Semitism*, Elek Books, London.
Various authors (1995) *Atlante storico del popolo ebraico*, Zanichelli, Bologna.

GLOBALIZATION (It. *globalizzazione*; Fr. *mondialisation*; Ger. *Globalisierung*) The term 'globalization' was used for the first time in

1968 by Marshall McLuhan in his famous *War and Peace in the Global Village*. Analysing the role of television in the unfolding of the events linked to the war in Vietnam, McLuhan showed how the media in the 1960s had begun to play an important part in current affairs by shaping public opinion, and more generally predicted the decisive role which modern communication technologies were to play in the world in the acceleration of progress.

The word was taken up again by Theodore Levitt in 1983, in his article, 'The globalization of markets', to describe the vast changes which had taken place over the past two decades in the international economy with the convergence of world markets. In Latin countries the term 'mondialisation' is also often used in lieu of globalization (Nadoulek) and although some authors – particularly in the Francophone world – distinguish between the two, attributing a more critical meaning to the first, etymologically speaking they are synonymous, and there does not appear to be enough evidence that clear distinction between them can be made.

According to Chakravarthi Raghavan (1995), the term globalization 'is also being used synonymously for "liberalization" and "greater openness"; of economies – implying both liberalization of the domestic economy and external liberalization'. Increasing economic integration and interdependence means that NATION states no longer play a major role in world economy in the face of the growing power of multinational and transnational corporations operating as horizontal, decentralized networks.

Given this scenario it is obvious that advances in transport, communications and information technology are a determining factor in the globalization process. While the liberalization of capital and trade flows is creating a global economy, the liberalization of telecommunications – which can bring high-quality medical, education and business services to every village in the world – stands to globalize human society itself.

The pre-eminent role of information in the globalization process has also contributed to the concept's gradual extension from the economic sphere to several political, sociological and cultural phenomena (CULTURE), affecting several areas, including human rights, CITIZENSHIP, democracy, local and global identities, MULTICULTURALISM and the 'clash of cultures'. It follows that globalization implies a world system in which different cultures are interconnected on several levels. In this sense Held (1991) described globalization as 'the intensification of worldwide social relations which link distant localities in such a way that local happenings are shaped by events occurring many miles away and vice versa'.

Of course the process of globalization does imply the profound restructuring of economic and labour markets and consequently of political systems.

There is much evidence of significant social and economic phenomena occurring as a result of this. Although the positive aspects of globalization can hardly be denied, some of the changes can be traumatic. If this is true for 'developed' countries, which have to face radical restructuring of their labour and welfare systems, it is even more so for DEVELOPING COUNTRIES. Consider the effect that the liberalization of the economy is having in the countries of the Eastern bloc and China. The fall of the Berlin Wall triggered a complete reorganization of the social and political equilibrium, the far-reaching consequences of which are still unforeseeable. The collapse of the previous system has left a situation of political instability in

the Balkans and the former Soviet Union, with the result that dramatic conflicts have flared up, although the feared mass invasion of Europe by millions of migrants from the East has not happened.

Along with these dramatic political changes the sometimes perverse impact of globalization on local economies should also be mentioned. This includes exploitation of human resources, pollution, exploitation of natural resources and the sale of unsafe products, and other aspects that have sometimes been called 'the dark side of globalization'. It is hardly surprising that there are many critics of globalization and its role in the present crisis. But globalization is not a policy to be judged right or wrong. It is a process, driven by the realities of economic and technological change. Two hundred years ago, steam power launched the first industrial revolution. A hundred years later, mass production and mass transport launched a second industrial revolution. Each led to a fundamental change in the organization of production and in the role of governance. Now a revolution in communications and informatics – the digital revolution – is reshaping the global economic landscape in equally powerful ways.

The advent of a borderless economy has enormous potential to generate growth, to spread the benefits of modernization, and to build a more stable and secure planet. But it also challenges the status quo. It demands that we adapt. The real issue before us is not the debate about globalization but to see how technological progress can be better channelled to promote more growth, more trade and greater modernization – and so help the world economy to emerge from its present difficulties. This is a complex challenge – a challenge that will require vision and patience, and the awareness that e-commerce could be a very powerful tool.

The reality of globalization is the reality of interdependence, an interdependence that extends far beyond trade or strictly economic criteria. But trade remains a key element in sustaining and spreading the benefits of interdependence. Over the past 50 years, trade has been a powerful engine for growth. In 1950 its ratio to global GDP was 7 per cent. Now it represents 23 per cent, and a third of the 25 largest trading countries are now developing countries. Between 1948 and 1997, merchandise trade increased 14 times, while world production increased 5.5 times. In the same period world GDP increased by 1.9 per cent per year at constant prices and taking account of overall population growth. Seen in a historical context, this figure is extremely high.

Of course the benefits of development are not evenly shared, and MARGIN-ALIZATION remains a real threat for too many. The least-developed countries have 10 per cent of the world's population but undertake less than half of 1 per cent of world trade. This marginalization is dangerous and it risks worsening if these countries are left behind by the next wave of globalization.

Another challenge is posed by the need to widen the knowledge base of people, especially in the developing world, so that everyone has the potential to be part of the information economy.

Another criticism concerns the danger of cultural homogenization and the destruction of local and national identities (IDENTITY) implied in the globalization process, which is seen as a new form of CULTURAL IMPERIALISM imposed by the West through economic domination. However, many scholars are convinced that the globalization process already contains within it the seeds to counteract this kind of action, in that a dialectic tension exists between the global and the local, and the process in itself tends in any case to reproduce diversity. In addition, the globalization process would allow the emergence of local identities, previously suppressed in the name of national homogeneity:

> Globalization has also its ambiguities. . . . Does it imply cultural homogenization, cultural synchronization or cultural proliferation? What does it say about the direction of cultural flows? Is it the interaction of the local and the global, with the emphasis on the former, or vice versa? (King, 1998)

The extremely significant role played by the media in this new context cannot be overlooked, along with the risk of the possible manipulation of information on the part of powerful multinational companies owned by individuals who are not controlled politically. On the other hand, the increasing availability of information concerning the world situation, with its areas of injustice and violation of human rights, can stimulate greater awareness and responsibility on the part of the world community. The opportunities offered by globalization should not be underestimated, in that it entails an even more active social and political participation in which the responsibility of every citizen stretches well beyond the boundaries of their local community or country, and extends to the entire planet.

Finally the role of migration flows (FLOWS) should also be mentioned, as they play a part in increasing the interaction of peoples from different countries – forcing the redefinition of the idea of citizenship itself – and in producing new and emerging phenomena such as the new ethno-national diasporas (DIASPORA). Globalization, therefore, also brings with it the need to deeply rethink many of our traditional categories, such as those of *ethnie* and state:

> For quite some time the nation state has been regarded as a norm of state formation, that is to say, as the final stage of an *ethnie*'s political autonomy and achievement. Currently, however, in the age of globalization and transnational connections, the nation state ideal may be regarded as a special case of the relationship *ethnie*-state. (Westin, 1998)

It should also be stressed that awareness of the problems posed by globalization should not prompt us to attempt to arrest what is an inevitable process as well as an inestimable potential source of richness for world economy. Instead we should accelerate the process with the creation of effective representative bodies to ensure a better response to these problems on a global scale.

This is even more crucial after the terrorist attacks on New York and Washington of 11 September 2001 and the creation of a broad worldwide coalition against international terrorism. Today there is a growing awareness and willingness to accept the need for stronger governance to tackle the problems deriving from globalization. Increasing and more effective international governance today appears the only sensible solution and goal. Yet, if enhanced international co-operation is the method, the community of nations is still seeking to establish the nature of the unavoidable global response. New strategies are emerging, based on what can be better explained by the reflections of the Indian economist and Nobel Prize winner Amartya Sen; that is, that individuals and their fundamental rights are more and more becoming the starting point of any sensible initiative to turn a worldwide free market into a machine that produces justice instead of blind opulence. [R. Ru.]

Held, D. (ed.) (1991) *Political Theory Today*, Stanford University Press, Stanford, CA.

King, A. D. (1998) 'Introduction: spaces of culture, spaces of knowledge', in King, A. D. (ed.), *Culture*, Aldershot, Ashgate.

Levitt, T. (1983) 'The globalization of markets', *Harvard Business Review*, 1 May 1983: 92–102.

McLuhan, M., Fiore, Q. (1968) *War and Peace in the Global Village*, Hardwired, San Francisco.

Nadoulek, B. (2001) 'Les enjeux de la mondialisation', in *Vox Latina*, online at www.voxlatina.com.

Raghavan, C. (1995) 'What is globalisation' (extract from a lecture delivered at the University of Lausanne), online at www.twnside.org.sg/title/what-cn.htm.

Sen, A. (1999) *Development as Freedom*, Anchor Books, New York.

Westin, C. (1998) 'Temporal and spatial aspects of multiculturality: reflections on the meaning of time and space in relation to the blurred boundaries of multicultural societies', in Baubóck, R. and Rundell, J. (eds), *Blurred Boundaries: Migration, Ethnicity, Citizenship*, Aldershot, Ashgate. pp. 53–84.

GYPSY: see ROMA, SINTI

H

HEALTH AND IMMIGRATION (*It. salute e immigrazione; Fr. santé et immigration; Germ. Gesund und Immigration*) It is difficult to establish any precise relationship between health and immigration as: a) people involved in the migratory process are not part of a homogeneous group according to health, sociological or anthropological classifications; b) although it is possible to identify health conditions that are characteristic of different ethnic groups (such as a genetic predisposition to certain illnesses or health risk factors connected to hygienic or eating habits), there is no evidence of a specific health condition that is associated with the immigrant population and distinguishes it from the non-immigrant population; c) there are common, non-specific health risks induced by travelling, environmental change and living conditions in the host country, but it is very difficult to truly understand the effect of migration on a migrant's general health condition (the psychological and physical hardships that migration causes in each migrant) because migration itself, along with the very status of being a migrant, is a fleeting phenomenon that is ill-defined and far from clear. The identification of a suitable reference theoretical model used in approaching the relationship between health and migration is made even more difficult because a narrow-minded traditional view has prevailed in the recent past.

Historically, the approach to the health of people involved in migration has developed along two traditional lines, which in many ways, must be treated with speculation. The first is the 'medical' (or rather, medicalizing) approach, which focuses on the social control of migrants and aims to check the possible negative psychological and physical effects that they may have on the health of the autochthonous population. The second approach, which is based on a culture of solidarity, aims to provide assistance to people involved in moving and resettlement. The first approach has often been characterised by stigmatisation (STIGMA) and the segregation of migrants through the quarantine system and the enforcement of health controls (HEALTH CHECKS AT FRONTIERS). There is testimony from the Ellis Island Museum that exemplifies this aspect of immigration: From the end of the nineteenth century to the middle of the twentieth century, immigrants passed through the 'immigrant stations' there in order to be checked before being allowed into the US. Another example of the 'medicalizing' approach – from a psychological and psychiatric point of view – can be found in the psychiatric theory, which has linked the desire to emigrate with a psychopathic personality (Frigessi Castelnuovo and Risso, 1982). This theory developed in the second half of the nineteenth century with the identification of the *'aliénés voyageurs ou migrateurs'* proposed by the neurologist A. Foville, and was widely endorsed between the 1930s and the 1960s. The best description of it is seen in the famous monography *Emigration and insanity. A study of mental disease among the Norwegian-born population of Minnesota*, published in 1932 by the Norwegian psychiatrist O. Ødegaard.

The origins of the second approach – humanitarian assistance – date back to the Middle Ages, and persist in the Renaissance and Baroque periods. For example, Italy played host to many migratory phenomena, and its hospital institutes were founded with the purpose of providing hospitality and assistance for travellers and pilgrims. The institutes were thus situated along main roads and in the most popular destinations, and there are still traces of these institutes, despite having been greatly altered over the years to meet changing needs.

At present, the best way to approach the relationship between immigration and health seems to be through a clear understanding of the migration process. In taking as a starting point both the reasons for migration as well as the motivations behind migration projects, it is important to try to understand: a) the complex circumstances involved in migratory processes; b) the equally complex consequences resulting from immigrants' initial impact on the social order of the host countries, as well as the effects of their long-term presence in the context of changes that are occurring in the host societies. In going beyond merely providing simplistic and stereotypical explanations, the 'medicine of migration' focuses on identifying the effects that migratory processes may have on the health and social status of immigrants, who are perceived as people who may share very similar experiences, but do not form a single community according to social, anthropological or health classifications. (Beneduce, et al., 1994).

Typical descriptions of immigrants' health profiles are based on non-specific criteria, which nevertheless identify problems of importation, adaptation and acquisition (Favaro, Tognetti Bordogna, 1988). 'Importation' refers to aspects of migrants' health stemming from the health situation in the country or geographical area from which they come, and includes factors such as hereditary traits in the country of origin (i.e. sickle-cell anaemia, thalassemia, rickets), injuries caused by the cultural practices in the countries of origin (for example genital MUTILATION or poisoning from the use of certain cosmetics) and diseases endemic in the countries of origin (malaria, tuberculosis, intestinal parasites, sexually-transmitted diseases). It is important to realise that, especially with regard to infectious diseases, these maladies are not confined to immigrants, since immigration and human mobility are not one and the same thing. The speed of modern air travel means that vacationers and business travellers also pose a major threat for transmitting disease. The problems of 'adaptation' take many forms that derive from the various hardships connected with ALIENATION, which are brought on by the process of migration and immigrants' status. Such hardships cover a whole range of mental illnesses, from mild symptoms to psychosomatic problems, drug addiction and complete mental breakdown. Although many psycho-pathological or alienating factors are inherent to immigrants' status, it is impossible to establish a definitive relationship between immigration and the problems caused by ADAPTATION. The problems of 'acquisition' – which are not always distinguishable from those of adaptation – are manifested in changes in the health condition of immigrants, which are normally caused by exposure to the risks posed by unhealthy living conditions, a lack of safety in the workplace, and difficulty in accessing public health services. These environmental factors are not specific to immigrants and may be found at any disadvantaged level of society where the autochthonous population shares conditions of poverty or MAR-GINALIZATION. Nevertheless, stereotyping immigrants as the carriers of disease is part of RACIST and anti-immigrant rhetoric that creates an image of immigrants as disease carriers. (parasites) threatening the host society (PREJUDICE).

These observations strongly suggest that understanding the relationship between immigration and health is found in the problem of inequality. In this way, the health care of immigrants is a question of EQUALITY rather than the identification of specific diseases. [A. B., R. B.]

Beneduce, R., Costa, G., Favretto, A. R., Frigessi, D., Gogliani, F., Lemma, P., Pastore, M., Rossignoli, F. (1994) *La salute straniera, epidemiologia culture diritti*, ESI, Roma.

Bollini, P., Siem, H. (1995) 'No real progress toward equity: health of migrants and ethnic minorities on the eve of the year 2000', *Social Science and Medicine*, jg 41, nr 5:819–823.

Favaro, G., Tognetti Bordogna, M. (eds.) (1988) *La salute degli immigrati*, Unicopli, Milano.

Frigessi Castelnuovo, D., Risso, M. (1982) *A mezza parete. Emigrazione, nostalgia, malattia mentale*, Einaudi, Torino.

Garret, C.R., Treichel, C.J., Ohmans, P. (1998) 'Barriers to health care for immigrants and nonimmigrants: a comparative study', *Minnesota Medicine*, 81(4): 52–5.

Hopkins, A., Bahl, V. (eds.) (1993) *Access to Health Care for People from Black and Ethnic Minorities*, Royal College of Physicians of London.

Mares, P., Henley, A., Baxter, C. (1985) *Health care in multiracial Britain*, Health Education Council, London.

Meledandri, G. (2001) 'Modelli di approccio epidemiologico', in Bianchini, C., Marangi, M., Meledandri, G., Morrone, A. (eds.) *Medicina internazionale*, SEU, Roma.

Navarro, V. (1990) 'Race or class versus race and class: mortality differences in the United States', *Lancet*, 336: 1238–1240.

Thomas, S.B. (1990) 'Community health advocacy for racial and ethnic minorities in the United States: issue and challenges for health education', *Health Education*, 17: 13–19.

HEALTH CHECKS AT FRONTIERS (It. *controlli sanitari alla frontiera*; Fr. *contrôles médicaux à la frontière*; Ger. *ärztliche Kontrollen an der Grenze*) Health checks at frontiers are the compulsory medical checks or documents certifying the absence of illness requested by certain countries before a VISA is granted. They are not usually necessary for tourist visas or short stays. Although there is no standard strategy or simple reason for the implementation of such procedures, in the majority of cases the aim is to identify the presence of any disease which might result in the carrier being refused admission to the country. In other cases such checks are intended to help set up programmes for the prevention and cure of communicable diseases.

Australia, Canada, New Zealand and the United States have clear legislative provisions which establish that obligatory health checks must be carried out – at the relevant embassy – before visa applicants leave their country of origin, or any other country. Such certification is issued only after a full medical examination, laboratory analyses of samples and other tests carried out according to precise and well-defined procedures set forth in forms devised for the compilation of medical reports by qualified medical teams. American legislation (Code of Federal Regulation, Title 8, Aliens and Nationality) sets forth the following reasons for ineligibility for entry to the country on health grounds:

(a) evidence of a communicable disease considered dangerous to public health (tuberculosis and some sexually transmitted diseases are typical examples, although the list of diseases included in this category changes continuously); (b) evidence of mental disorders, conditions associated with drug addiction and socially dangerous behaviour. Should the only obstacle to entry be a medical certificate stating the applicant's inability to work, an entry visa to the United States may be granted provided that a personal fund is set up to cover any future public health service expenses. Australia is more explicit, refusing to grant entry visas to applicants whose health problems could burden public health services as well as posing a threat to public health (King, 1992). Such restrictive legislation is justified in two main ways: (a) protection of public health; (b) avoidance of burdening the public health service with the treatment of people who have not contributed in economic terms to public health service funds (appealing to the principle of retributive justice based on the fact that no individual should take from the COMMUNITY more than he or she has contributed).

One argument against the implementation of obligatory health checks is that it can be seen as a form of immigrant control that is harassing or even degrading to would-be immigrants. Indeed, from this perspective, health checks – not always a valid means of protecting public health (McCance, 1992) – could be used to justify discrimination and limit the granting of entry visas in favour of individuals who are able to work and unlikely to burden the welfare system of the host country. From this point of view, health controls – which may be seen as a real and proper human resources selection mechanism – could be used to enrich the host country to the detriment of the immigrants' countries of origin.

Right up until the 1950s, American health legislation established that immigrants had to be detained in the Ellis Island reception centre, Manhattan Bay, before being allowed to enter United States territory. In Europe, regulations vary from country to country and are nowhere nearly as clearly defined as in 'countries of immigration' such as the USA, Australia, Canada and New Zealand. For example, French legislation provides that the granting of a visa for work purposes depends on the outcome of a medical examination carried out in the country of origin by the health department of the Organization for International Migration or by doctors approved by the French Consulate (in the case of countries where the OIM is not represented). These examinations consist of a general clinical examination and a chest X-ray, unless the doctor responsible advises otherwise (*Code du travail*, article L341–2–9, R341–3; Decree of Ministry of Social Affairs 30 June 1986 and 7 November 1994). In 1995, Italian legislation established that non-EU citizens (EXTRACOMUNITARIO) wishing to enter Italy were required to exhibit to border guards approved documentation proving the absence of diseases dangerous to public health (contagious or infectious diseases) – a provision which has not been renewed in more recently approved law decrees. At present, Italian law on immigration requires no obligatory health checks – apart from those set forth in the provisions of international law – which could jeopardize the granting of permission to enter the territory.

There is much debate about the morality of health checks at frontiers. Although mandatory, many examinations are not always completely safe for the individual involved nor even particularly precise in their results. For example, state laws generally prevent the expulsion of immigrant minors, yet proof that an individual is under the age of 18 years is extremely difficult to obtain. In case of doubt, an individual may be subject to X-ray analysis – involving exposure to radiation – although the results of such testing are not very reliable and the determination of the individual's age – and consequent right to stay in a country – remains open to debate. Furthermore, in cases of FAMILY REUNIFICATION, in order to avoid fraudulent entry of individuals into a country, virginity tests may be required to prove that a marriage has been consummated. Again, the methodology used and the reliability of the results are very much open to ethical debate regarding the breach of privacy related to the test and its controversial results: interpretation of the results depends on a culturally bound concept of marriage (FAMILY). The inclusion of a negative HIV test result among the conditions of entry to some countries (e.g. Australia and the United States) at the end of the 1980s gave rise to many arguments in medical, ethical and political circles – arguments which have led to wider discussion of the discriminatory implications and scientific value of compulsory health checks (Gellert, 1993). On many occasions, the World Health Organization has explicitly condemned this measure with the accusation that such requirements totally obstruct the global strategy of the fight against AIDS (WHO Resolution 41.24, 13 May 1988: *Avoidance of discrimination in relation to HIV – infected people and people with AIDS*). [A. B., R. B.]

King, K. (1992) 'Medical screening of migrants in Australia', *International Migration*, 30: 233–237.
McCance, C. (1992) 'Medical screening of migrants: current national requirements in the United States', *International Migration*, 30: 215–221.
Gellert, G. A. (1993) 'International migration and control of communicable diseases', *Social Science and Medicine*, 37(12): 1489–1499.

HEALTHY MIGRANT EFFECT (It. *effetto migrante sano*; Fr. *effet migrant sain*; Ger. *Positiver Migranten Beitrag*)

Frequently used in epidemiology and sociology, this expression highlights the fact that, on reaching a decision to migrate (MIGRATION), individuals are subject to selection procedures which also consider health factors. Even if the decision to emigrate is often a group or family initiative, individual consideration of the physical and psychological obstacles to be overcome plays an extremely important role for anyone facing this high risk activity – migrants must consider their current state of health adequate to stand up to the risks and stress of emigration. Thus the epidemiological profile of emigrants – compared with the health of those who stay in their country of origin – is characterized by a healthy migrant effect (Beneduce et al., 1994: p. 20).

The healthy migrant effect can be compared with two specific aspects of the migratory process: (a) emigration is a dramatic and highly risky undertaking mainly involving individuals capable of facing great psychological and material difficulties; (b) good health and, therefore, the ability to work are the main assets a migrant is able to bring to the host country. With regard to this latter aspect, the healthy migrant effect can be seen as a 'health drain', similar to the so-called 'brain drain', in which the best available resources are removed from the emigrant's country of origin. Emigrants are generally healthy individuals – those in poor health decide not to face the difficulties of migration – and are generally young people who can withstand poor living conditions and stress. From another point of view, the healthy migrant effect can be considered a result of specific selection policies imposed by the countries traditionally known as 'countries of immigration', where the granting of a VISA depends on the outcome of a detailed medical examination – a means of reassuring public opinion in the host country that xenophobic fears (XENOPHOBIA) of immigrants and disease are groundless (PREJUDICE). Thus the natural selection process is reinforced by HEALTH CHECKS AT FRONTIERS. [A. B., R. B.]

Beneduce, G., Costa, G., Favretto, A. R., Frigessi, D., Gogliani, F., Lemma, P., Pastore, M., Rossignoli, F. (1994) *La salute straniera, epidemiologia culture diritti*, ESI, Roma.

HETEROPHOBIA (It. *eterofobia*; Fr. *hétérophobie*; Ger. *Heterophobie*) The term was introduced by A. Memmi (1982) to define attitudes of rejection which are not dictated by biological differences. It can be used to define all fears caused in reaction to the 'other', i.e., to that which is different (DIVERSITY–SIMILARITY), and, more particularly, XENOPHOBIA and MIXO-PHOBIA. [U. M.]

Melotti, U. (1993) 'Xenofobia e razzismo. Concetti, dati, analisi', in Gindro, S. (ed.), *La xenofobia*, Guida, Napoli.
Memmi, A. (1982) *Le Racisme, description, définition, traitement*, Gallimard, Paris.

HOLOCAUST: see SHOAH

HOMOLOGATION (It. *omologazione*; Fr. *homologation*; Ger. *Homologisierung*) The term 'homologation', from the Greek *homologos* (composed of *homos*, equal, similar, and *logos*, discourse) can have various meanings. It is most commonly used to refer to the official validation of acts or facts subject to a norm or determined discipline and may be used in legal circles and fields of sport (e.g. homologation of a record). Other meanings of the word and its derivatives are found in geometry, where polygons having the same angles but different surfaces are defined as 'homologous'; biology, to define anatomical structures (and, in ethology, behaviour) having the same phylogenetic origin but different functions; archaeology; and anthropology, to define those stages of development which always occur in the same relative order, even if in very different times (this use of the term was introduced by Gordon Childe, 1951). The term also defines several mathematical and chemical concepts.

'To homologate' also means 'to make similar to a model'. This meaning applies mainly in social sciences, particularly when it is referred to values or behaviour. In this meaning, the term is more commonly heard in modern Italian (*omologazione*) than in other European languages. This is probably due to the fact that the Italian Pier Paolo Pasolini (1975) used it extensively in daily newspapers, although in vague and evocative terms and with no precise definition, albeit with clear negative implications. In social science, the term mainly indicates a negative judgement, although the founders of the discipline warned against the danger of confusing judgements of reality with judgements of value (Émile Durkheim) and theorized the importance of a type of analysis which was at least potentially free from the latter (Max Weber). Many authors consider the safeguarding of differences (biological and, above all, cultural differences) as an important factor in its own right and as a condition for the further development of CIVILIZATION (DIF-FERENTIALISM). Among these authors, particular mention should be made of Claude Lévi-Strauss (1952).

The strong denunciations of homologation on the part of certain GLOBA-LIZATION theorists (for example, Anthony Giddens, 1990) and critics of the so-called 'Westernization of the world' (for example, Serge Latouche, 1996) can be seen to stem from such anthropological positions. In many cases these positions are equivocal and abstract. In reality it is difficult to judge negatively the fact that, for example, in a development process certain structures are homologated to certain standards, even if this involves a certain international homogeneity. Even the strongest critics of homologation, for example, when travelling to a THIRD WORLD country (possibly to study the process in

a critical light), would certainly prefer to land at an airport which fulfils certain international safety *standards*, rather than at one built exclusively according to the standards of the local CULTURE. This example might appear too easy, as it refers to technical matters relative to important questions of safety. However, one could quote many other situations (from telecommunications to computers) where homologation has important functions. For the most part, in a great number of cases, technical, social and cultural aspects are inextricably connected. [U. M.]

Childe, G. V. (1951) *Social Evolution*, Watt, London.

Giddens, A. (1990) *The Consequences of Modernity*, Stanford University Press, Stanford, CA.

LaTouche, S. (1996) *The Westernization of the World: The Significance, Scope, and Limits of the Drive towards Global Uniformity*, Polity Press, Cambridge.

Lévi-Strauss, C. (1952) *Race et histoire*. UNESCO, Paris.

Pasolini, P. P. (1975) *Scritti corsari*, Garzanti, Milano.

IDENTIFICATION WITH THE AGGRESSOR

(It. *identificazione con l'aggressore*; Fr. *identification à l'agresseur*; Ger. *Identifizierung mit dem Aggressor*) Identified and applied to the field of psychoanalysis by Anna Freud in 1936 (Laplanche and Pontalis, 1967), the psychological process of identification with the aggressor occurs when individuals find themselves in a subordinate or uneasy position as the result of severe criticism or admonition by an authoritarian figure and thus defend themselves – either consciously or unconsciously (UNCONSCIOUS) – by adopting the attitudes, values and symbols of power of the authoritarian figure as well as the same aggressive function: for example, children who assume the most feared psychological and behavioural traits of their parents and use them as their own. Similar to other incorporative processes, identification with the aggressor, together with other individual and collective psychological processes (SELF-FULFILLING PROPHECY), is often used in the interpretation of social behaviour to explain causes of racial PREJUDICE, or other negative attitudes towards ethnic minorities (ETHNIC MINORITY). The psychosociological attitude to this subject is more or less directly influenced by concepts derived from psychoanalysis and stresses that racial prejudice and hostility towards minorities, usually by weaker people, are a means by which individuals – either consciously or unconsciously – defend themselves against their own inner conflicts. Two widely recognized theories regarding the phenomenon are the theory of frustration-aggression (AGGRESSION), developed in the 1930s by a group of psychologists at Yale University, led by John Dollard (1938) and the theory of the authoritarian personality put forward by Theodor W. Adorno and his team (1950).

MIGRATION, discrimination and the need for ADAPTATION by immigrant populations to the implicit or explicit difficulties and attacks encountered in many areas of the host society (ALIENATION) create ideal environments for the implementation of the process of identification with the aggressor (Frigessi Castelnuovo and Risso, 1982: 69). Insofar as immigration and integration policies are strongly oriented towards ASSIMILATION of minorities, immigrants – as well as any other individuals who are disadvantaged, discriminated against or made to feel inferior – not only acquire an undervalued opinion of themselves, but might even be persuaded to adopt the racial stereotypes and negative prejudices connected with immigration. The result is that often, and in many ways paradoxically, a special emphasis on the stigmatization (STIGMA) caused by their difference is found even among the immigrant population. In this regard, Sandro Gindro (1985) suggests use of the term 'parody' to describe the psychological identification processes – implemented by fear – which cause people to, pathologically, adopt the violent behaviour of others in the hope of exorcizing it. Thus, the weak or marginalized (MARGINALIZATION), those who fear the strong, adopt brutal behaviour towards those whom they perceive as weaker than themselves, even treating them with a ruthlessness far more cruel than that of those who instil fear in them – a phenomenon which simply contributes to the greater spread of hatred and violence. [A. B., R. B.]

Adorno, T. W., Frenkel-Brunswik, E., Levinson, D. J., Sanford, R. N. (1950) *The Authoritarian Personality*, Harper, New York.

Dillard, J. (1938) 'Hostility and fear in social life', *Social Forces*, 17.

Frigessi Castelnuovo, D., Risso, M. (1982) *A mezza parete. Emigrazione, nostalgia, malattia mentale*, Einaudi, Torino.

Gindro, S. (1985) 'La via del riconoscimento', *Psicoanalisi Contro*, 18: 1–13.

Laplanche, J., Pontalis, J. B. (1967) *Vocabulaire de la psychanalyse*, PUF, Paris.

IDENTITY

IDENTITY (It. *identità*; Fr. *identité*; Ger. *Identität*) Contemporary politics and the social sciences appear to be preoccupied with questions of identity. There are good reasons why this is the case. Issues of identity come to the fore when there is a crisis of identities, and there did indeed seem to be such a crisis in the last part of the twentieth century, and will be for the foreseeable future into the new millennium. The crisis is a product of a number of changes that have engulfed the planet, especially the richer countries of the North, which have led to the disembedding of hitherto relatively settled identities at both a personal and social level. These transformations are variously referred to as leading to a new period of 'late modernity' (Giddens, 1990, 1991) or 'postmodernity' (Lyotard, 1986; Bauman, 1987, 1991) or a new Global Age (Albrow, 1997). Rapid social change is said to be a key feature of this new era, affecting not only the highly industrialized countries but also poorer regions, all of them caught up in a set of forces drawing all parts of the globe into closer ties of interdependence and continuous social transformation on a scale never experienced before. National identities, in many cases newly formed after struggles against colonial rule (POSTCOLONIAL STUDIES), have become vulnerable to erosion by transnational forces such as multinational corporations and international communities such as the European Union. The de-industrialization of the richer regions has led to a shrinking manufacturing working class and thus to a weakening of labour movements and working-class solidarities. At the same time, gender identities have undergone a transformation, partly as a consequence of greater participation by women in the workforce, but also spurred on by the emergence of a 'second wave' of feminism. Other new social movements, such as the Greens and gay liberation, have combined with the increasing significance of consumption in fashioning individual identities to lead to a further loosening of earlier forms of identification, especially those based around social class.

New forms of articulation between the global and the local have led to what have come to be called 'hybrid' or syncretic identities (SYNCRETISM), especially among young people (Rattansi and Phoenix, 1997), a process aided by the formation of diasporic communities in the metropolitan countries (see DIASPORA). These new identities combine elements from a variety of cultural sources, and are particularly evident in a complex mixing of musical styles (MUSIC), literary genres and cinematic expressions (Hall, 1992a). The exact nature and significance of this 'hybridity' are a matter of some debate (Young, 1995; Brah and Coombes, 2000), but there is little doubt that ever more complex new formations of identity are going to be a more or less permanent global phenomenon.

These transformations have inevitably impacted on the forms which ethnicities and racisms are now taking in various parts of the globe (CULTURAL IMPERIALISM). An acute understanding of this emerges from the development of newer theorizations of identity (see Hall, 1992b; Rattansi, 1994; Hall and du Gay, 1996; Rattansi and Phoenix, 1997). Partly under the intellectual influence of poststructuralism and postmodernism, identities are increasingly being conceptualized as more decentred, ambivalent, contradictory, provisional, contextual and de-essentialized than before. Each of these elements can be seen to have a bearing on rethinking racialized (RACIALIZATION) and ethnic identities (Rattansi, 1994).

Decentring involves a move away from the notion of social actors as fully rational and self-aware to a view of actors as subject to the play of emotions and unconscious motivations as well as defined by relational elements. Thus identifications with and against ethnic and racialized groups are likely to be affected by UNCONSCIOUS projections on to these groups, for example of sexual anxieties, as well as by the inability of individual identities to be defined except in relation to others – white identities, for instance, cannot occupy 'the centre' but can only be defined in relation to non-white, 'Western' in relation to 'non-Western'. 'Self' is always haunted by an 'Other'. Identities are thus conceptualized as not self-contained. In turn, this has led to a view of white, Western racial identities as historically formed by a superimposition of such divisions as Christian/pagan, civilized/SAVAGE, male/female, adult/infant, rational/ irrational on to a perceived white/black dichotomy. Such forms of identification are seen as always the product of power relations, and moreover relations in which the second term in the relation, for example irrational or black, is made to occupy an inferior and more marginal location.

The decentring is also understood as manifesting itself in contradictions and ambivalences. Complex friendship patterns with otherwise despised ethnic groups as well as envy of and desire for the attributes of the Others that occupy the margins are some of the consequences. Good examples here are the friendships among young people of different ethnicities, the ways in which black bodies function in Western cultures and the attractions of the 'Orient', especially its women (see ORIENTALISM), whether at home or abroad (Rattansi, 1994: 43–46, 68).

The significance of context as well as provisionality are evident in the shifting nature of ethnic alliances, as documented in research on schools and other urban locales (Rattansi, 1992; Back, 1996), and the instability of racialized political identifications, as is evident, for instance, in the turnover of membership of extreme right-wing racist movements.

De-essentialization leads to a conceptualization of racism and ethnicity as forms of identification which take plural forms. Neither race nor ethnicity is viewed as having a fixed meaning irrespective of context or historical location; both are seen as drawing on a variety of features of individual and group attributes – skin colour, religion, regions of geographical origin, nationality, cuisine, language – thus giving rise to complex racisms (RACISM) and ethnicities (ETHNICITY).

The closure of identities, such as ethnic or racial identities, by processes of strict boundary formation, is now being seen not as a 'natural' or 'primordial' fact, but as one which also depends crucially on strategies of mobilization.

Relative degrees of closure are seen as, broadly, political achievements, secured by strategies such as the 'invention of tradition' the rewriting of group narratives via 'myths' of origin and other symbolic events, and the construction of imaginary unities through media of representation such as photographs, film, music and novels (Ranger and Hobsbawm, 1983).

'Social constructionist' and 'mobilizationist' accounts of identity formation have elements in common with this framework, and have had a particularly strong influence on analyses of ethnicity, which they see as the product of active strategies of boundary closure (Jenkins, 1997). Some important caveats need to be entered here. It is easy to exaggerate the extent to which identities are malleable; stability as well as flux obviously characterize individual and group identities. Moreover, it is a common mistake to underestimate the degree to which identities in the period before 'late modernity' were unsettled and subject to change (Calhoun, 1994: 4). Also, anti-essentialist positions appear to rely on a number of essentialisms in order to make their arguments (Fuss, 1989).

Nevertheless, and despite the misgivings that have also been expressed regarding the rise of so-called 'identity politics', 'identity' is now such a significant issue that it cannot but occupy an important place in analyses of race, ethnicity and culture. [A. R.]

Albrow, M. (1997) *The Global Age*, Polity Press, Cambridge.
Back, L. (1996) *New Ethnicities and Urban Culture*, UCL Press, London.
Bauman, Z. (1987) *Legislators and Interpreters: On Modernity, Postmodernity and Intellectuals*, Polity Press, Cambridge.
Bauman, Z. (1991) *Modernity and Ambivalence*, Polity Press, Cambridge.
Brah, A., Coombes, A. (eds) (2000) *Hybridity and Its Discontents*, Routledge, London.

Calhoun, C. (1994) 'Preface', in Calhoun, C. (ed.), *Social Theory and the Politics of Identity*, Blackwell, Oxford.
Fuss, D. (1989) *Essentially Speaking: Feminism, Nature and Difference*, Routledge, New York.
Giddens, A. (1990) *The Consequences of Modernity*, Polity Press, Cambridge.
Giddens, A. (1991) *Modernity and Self-Identity*, Polity Press, Cambridge.
Hall, S. (1992a) 'The new ethnicities', in Donald, J., Rattansi, A. (eds), *'Race', Culture and Difference*, Sage, London.
Hall, S. (1992b) 'The question of cultural identity', in Hall, S., Held, D., McGrew, J. (eds), *Modernity and Its Futures*, Polity Press, Cambridge.
Hall, S., du Gay, P. (eds) (1996) *Questions of Cultural Identity*, Sage, London.
Jenkins, R. (1997) *Rethinking Ethnicity*, Sage, London.
Lyotard, J-F. (1986) *The Postmodern Condition*, Manchester University Press, Manchester.
Ranger, T., Hobsbawm, E. (1983) *The Invention of Tradition*, Cambridge University Press, Cambridge.
Rattansi, A. (1992) 'Changing the subject? Racism, culture and education', in Donald, J., Rattansi, A. (eds), *'Race', Culture and Difference*, Sage, London.
Rattansi, A. (1994) '"Western" racisms, ethnicities and identities in a "postmodern" framework', in Rattansi, A., Westwood, S. (eds), *Racism, Modernity and Identity*, Polity Press, Cambridge.
Rattansi, A., Phoenix, A. (1997) 'Rethinking youth identities: modernist and postmodernist frameworks', in Bynner, J., Chisolm, L., Furlong, A. (eds), *Youth, Citizenship and Social Change in a European Context*, Ashgate, Aldershot.
Young, R. (1995) *Colonial Desire: Hybridity in Theory, Culture and Race*, Routledge, London.

ILLEGAL ALIEN (It. *clandestino*; Fr. *clandestin*; Ger. *illegaler Einwanderer*) In the field of MIGRATION the term 'illegal alien' refers to foreigners (FOREIGNER) who have illegally entered a country, or who have entered a country legally but do not hold a valid residence permit. A distinction should therefore be made between: (a) illegal aliens, who are migrants who infringe controls when leaving their country of emigration and/or when entering a country of immigration, e.g. by crossing a border (FRONTIER) in a fraudulent fashion or at an unauthorized point; and (b) irregular immigrants, who have not crossed the border of an immigration country illegally, but are resident in such country under false pretences, for example a foreigner who enters a country as a tourist but then remains in that country for longer than the allowed period and works there illegally; or a foreigner whose residence permit has expired and no request for renewal or conversion is presented, or where it has been cancelled or revoked by police authorities. In the latter case, the residence permit declares the individual to be involved in an activity which does not correspond to the truth.

The phenomenon of illegal immigration has existed throughout the history of migrations, the illegal status is usually the consequence of the limits imposed on foreigners in the country of destination, as in many cases, even if such persons have the right to immigrate, they are often forced to fulfil certain requirements or possess specific documents (such as a VISA, a specific occupational profile, proof of psychological and physical fitness, certification of knowledge of the language, etc.) which may be difficult to comply with. Therefore, illegal immigration often appears to be the result of discrepancies between controls in the country of destination and the needs of the migrant. The International Organization for Migration (IOM) estimates that about 30 million people who are actively involved in the economies of countries other than those of their origin have irregular status, as they immigrated illegally or because they work illegally in countries of immigration (Castles and Miller, 1998).

One of the most significant hypotheses is that illegal immigration is quite normal in many Western countries. According to Jaques (1989), the inequalities between rich and poor nations lead to an increase in migratory flows from the THIRD WORLD which are mainly illegal (PUSH FACTORS – PULL FACTORS). This is also the consequence of the behaviour of those countries in which illegality is tolerated: trade unions and associations founded specifically to safeguard foreign migrants have often complained of the tendency to turn a blind eye to illegal immigration with a view to its exploitation. This is because illegal immigrants – who cannot claim rights, for obvious reasons – easily fall victim to exploitation and often end up competing not so much with local manpower, but with legal immigrants. As early as the 1970s, many authors defined the phenomenon of illegal immigration as the twentieth-century slave trade (SLAVERY). This phenomenon often involves entire families, with the obvious negative repercussions affecting their more vulnerable members. However, it appears that illegal immigration is not tolerated purely for economic reasons. According to David North (1991), democratic countries cannot effectively control international migration FLOWS as they are not willing to invest the necessary financial, diplomatic, intellectual and, above all, emotional resources. In other words, many democracies are not prepared to invest the funds required to manage international migration, and to submit the needed numbers of diplomatic requests for repatriation, which often involve countries with which they are generally on friendly terms. At the same time many states are reluctant to inflict further suffering on otherwise law-abiding disadvantaged persons. Nevertheless, in recent years many states have been adopting strict regulations aimed both at stopping illegal immigrants from entering a country (exclusion) and at facilitating the DEPORTATION of immigrants who are illegally present on their territories. This has resulted partly from the growing demands made by various sections of the receiving societies and the belief that illegal immigration has several negative consequences. However, expulsion is no real answer to illegal immigration – especially where it is performed solely to demonstrate that the country in question deals with illegal immigration with firmness – unless it is backed by other legislative reforms. Since enforced removal proceedings are often unpopular and unsuccessful in preventing illegal immigration, receiving countries generally prefer to have recourse to amnesties (AMNESTY), which are the only way illegal aliens can rectify their illegal status and remain in their chosen country of destination. But amnesties often mean that illegal aliens have to face the difficult choice of accepting the chance to change their illegal status – which would allow them to obtain a regular residence permit but often result in loss of employment – or remaining in a situation in which they are exploited, but are nevertheless employed. It is clear that unitary measures at an international, or at least at a European, level must be adopted, also in order to avoid the application of unethical measures on the part of individual countries.

From the legislative point of view, Convention 143 of the International Labour Organization (ILO, 1975a) is the first attempt on the part of the international community to deal with the problem of irregular migration and labour, which had become acute at the beginning of the 1970s. The Convention contains a series of provisions aimed at ensuring a basic level of protection for migrant workers who have an irregular status with regard to immigration regulations, or those who have been employed irregularly and whose situation cannot be regularized. The Convention does not limit the sovereign powers of each state to allow or refuse entry to a foreign citizen – nor to regulate migration flows – but aims to affirm the right to protection of migrant workers, whatever their status, regardless of whether they entered the country legally or illegally.

As regards EU countries, measures to combat illegal immigration, and its often tragic results, are defined among the union's main objectives as part of its effort to establish an area of freedom, security and justice for its members. The Schengen agreement permitted the standardization of detection systems and the creation of databanks. The responsibilities of passenger carriers have been increased, with fines set not only for airlines and shipping companies but also for road transport companies who facilitate illegal immigration. These actions are part of a general strengthening of restrictive and repressive measures, which has led to a debate on the risks involved in criminalizing immigration from non-EU countries (FORTRESS EUROPE). Increasingly, it is argued that one of the prerequisites for the control of the phenomenon is a global immigration policy established through partnerships with the countries of origin of immigrants, the fair treatment of citizens of third countries and the careful management of migration flows, in order to make more legal immigration channels available for migrant workers. As highlighted in the Communication of 2 November 2000 of the Council of the European Parliament:

There is a growing recognition that, in this new economic and demographic context, the existing 'zero' immigration policies which have dominated thinking over the past 30 years are no longer appropriate. Programmes to regularize the position of illegal migrants, which often give rise to difficult internal political debate, are developing in a number of Member States. Tragic incidents, such as the one in Dover in July 2000 in which 58 Chinese nationals trying to enter illegally into the United Kingdom lost their lives, which are taking place in almost all Member States, point not only to the importance of the fight against the trafficking of human beings, but also to the existence of a demand for clandestine manpower and the exploitation of such undocumented migrants. (Commission, 2000: 6)

Thus, in order to control illegal immigration, it is necessary to ensure international police co-operation between member states and third countries and stricter border controls (visa controls) as well as to complete determined actions to counter the exploitation of illegal immigrants. However, these actions must also offer assistance to the victims of such exploitation, the protection of fundamental human rights and repatriation on a humanitarian basis. In such a framework a fundamental role can be played by information campaigns aimed at raising awareness among potential immigrants regarding the actual possibilities of legal immigration, what they can expect in the countries of arrival and the dangers involved in illegal immigration and human trafficking.

When confronted with the growing complexity of the mechanism of illegal immigration, the worrying forms of systematic exploitation become a central issue, as they are an infringement of the most basic human rights, and their victims often end up being involved in those same illegal activities. Particularly serious phenomena are those of the smuggling of migrants, which involves facilitating their illegal entry, stay and employment in a country in exchange for payment, and of the trafficking in human beings, where vulnerable individuals are implicated in illegal immigration and faced with threats and violence as in the sadly exemplary cases of the exploitation of prostitution and actual trafficking of minors. [A. B., R. B.]

Castles, S., Miller, M. J. (1998) *The Age of Migration. International Population Movements in the Modern World*, Macmillan, London.
Collinson, S. (1993) *Europe and International Migration*, Pinter, London.
Commission of the European Communities (2000) *Communication from the Commission to the Council and the European Parliament on a Community Immigration Policy. COM (2000) 757 final*, Brussels, 22.11.2000, http://digilander.iol.it/euroinfo/index.htm.
ILO (International Labour Organization) (1975a) *Convention C143: Migrant Workers*, http://ilolex.ilo.
ILO (International Labour Organization) (1975b) *R151: Migrant Workers Recommendation*, http://ilolex.ilo.
Jaques, A. (1989) 'Alle radici delle grandi migrazioni', in *Rapporto sul Terzo Mondo*, Edizioni Associate, Roma.
North, D.S. (1991) 'Perché i governi democratici non riescono a eliminare l'immigrazione illegale?', in Presidenza del Consiglio dei Ministri, *Atti della Conferenza Internazionale sulle migrazioni*, Roma, 13–16 marzo, Editalia, Roma.
Sassen, S. (1996) *Guests and Aliens*, New Press, New York.

IMMIGRATION: see MIGRANT, MIGRATION

INDIGENOUS: see NATIVE

INFIBULATION (It. *infibulazione*; Fr. *infibulation*; Ger. *Weibliche Beschneidung*)

From the Latin *fibula* (buckle), the term 'infibulation' refers to the MUTILATION of the female genital apparatus by the reduction of the lower orifice of the vagina, usually with the added practice of the extirpation of the clitoris, the small labia and most of the large labia. The two sides of the vulva are sewn together, leaving only an orifice in the lower part to allow the flow of urine and of menstrual blood. The permanent damage and suffering provoked by this kind of mutilation and the cultural significance of ritual oppression (RITE) inferred from this have led feminist and other activists to campaign for the banning of mutilation practices throughout Western countries and even in countries in which they are more widespread. Furthermore, traditional methods of infibulation often imply a medical risk of infection resulting from the poor and often unsafe conditions in which the operations are performed. Condemnation of such methods – in order to avoid exposing young women to risk – has resulted in heated debate where certain ethnic minorities (ETHNIC MINORITY) may request infibulation as medical treatment. The ethical problem lies in the fact that other types of ritual mutilation such as CIRCUMCISION are allowed and therefore denying infibulation could be seen as an expression of cultural centrism or discrimination.

Infibulation is practised above all in East Africa, where it is considered to be a form of prevention of sexual promiscuity. [S. G.]

Kopelman, L. M. (1994) 'Female circumcision/genital mutilation and ethical relativism', *Second Opinion*, 20(2): 55–71.

Toubia, N. (1994) 'Female circumcision as a public health issue', *New England Journal of Medicine*, 331(11): 712–716.
World Health Organization (1997) *Female Genital Mutilation: A Joint WHO/UNICEF/UNFPA Statement*, Geneva.

INSTITUTIONAL RACISM (It. *razzismo istituzionale*; Fr. *racisme institutionel*; Ger. *institutioneller Rassismus*)

The expression was first defined by Stokely Carmichael (later to be known as Kwame Ture) and Charles Hamilton in their 1967 book *Black Power* (BLACK POWER). In using this term they sought to draw attention to pervasive and systemic racism in the USA which, they argued, influenced and affected all aspects of society. Institutional racism is a conception of RACISM as a stable and long-standing structural feature of society, rather than a psychological or cultural trait of individuals and groups. The constituent elements of institutional racism can include assumptions, customs and informal culture, routine practices, as well as procedures, rules and regulations.

Carmichael and Hamilton treated the distinction between individual and institutional racism as akin to the distinction between overt and covert racism. While individual racism can be seen and heard, institutional racism is 'less overt, far more subtle, less identifiable in terms of specific individuals committing the acts . . . [it] originates in the operation of established and respected forces in the society' (Ture and Hamilton, 1992: 4). This latter aspect is important because it draws attention to racism emanating from powerful groups, and to racism operating through bureaucratic procedures. To differentiate between the individual/overt and the institutional/ covert forms they provide this illustration. Individual and overt racism can be seen where a black family is racially attacked for moving into a white neighbourhood. However, it is institutional racism that keeps black people locked into slum housing, through exploitation and discrimination by landlords and estate agents. This situation is either ignored by society or thought to be unchangeable. This example indicates a number of ways in which institutional racism operates. First, dominant groups may simply be indifferent to patterns of inequality in society, such as slums. Secondly, there may be a feeling that it is simply too difficult to change the social conditions that give rise to slums and so no meaningful response is ever contemplated. In both these instances there is little active discrimination, but the effects or consequences can be seen as the product or outcome of institutional racism. A third way in which institutional racism can operate is by rejecting the view that racism is structural and by reverting to cultural explanations instead. Some dominant social and political discourses may suggest that slum housing is largely the fault of the poor themselves.

Carmichael and Hamilton also saw institutional racism as based upon 'active and pervasive' (Ture and Hamilton, 1992: 5) anti-black attitudes and practices. They maintained that whites believed themselves to be superior as a group to blacks and that this racist attitude operated on both individual and institutional levels, and overtly and covertly (WHITENESS). They considered institutional racism a form of INTERNAL COLONIALISM in the USA, in that although blacks had the same CITIZENSHIP status as whites, they stood as colonial subjects in relation to white society.

The distinction between individual/ overt and institutional/covert forms of racism can be mapped on to the division between direct and indirect racism made in the 1976 Race Relations Act (RACE RELATIONS) in the UK. The 1976 Act aimed to make unlawful conditions that disproportionately affect particular racial minorities, for example height requirements in employment that cannot be justified by the nature of the job. Another example of indirect racism was evident in patterns of allocation to public housing in the UK in the 1960s and 1970s. While the housing rules did not bar black and Asian people, they did specify that applications for public housing could not be considered from those who had recently arrived in a local authority area (Rex, 1987). In the private sector, the restriction on loans and mortgages for the purchase of homes in areas with significant ETHNIC MINORITY populations was also found to be a form of indirect discrimination. In the field of education cultural bias has been shown to be operating in supposedly objective proficiency or academic tests. In all these cases, there is no explicit policy or statement of discrimination against ethnic and racial minorities, but they clearly produce disadvantageous outcomes for some of these minorities. Institutional racism is usually treated as something hidden or concealed. Its underlying causes may be difficult to detect; it may not even be based on overt prejudicial attitudes (PREJUDICE), or on any intention to discriminate.

The distinction between intentional and unintentional forms of racism is evident in two differing definitions of institutional racism in the UK. Both definitions are from official inquiries which were concerned with issues of race (specifically with young blacks of

African-Caribbean origin) and policing in the inner city. One – the Scarman Report – was an inquiry into the public disorders or riots in Brixton, south London in 1981. The other, chaired by Sir William Macpherson, was concerned with police failure to solve the racist murder of the black teenager Stephen Lawrence in a different part of south London in 1993. Lord Scarman rejected the charge that the police were institutionally racist, because he found no evidence that there was any policy or intention to discriminate, or that their actions were knowingly and as a matter of course discriminatory. In contrast, Macpherson specifically ruled that the police's failures were due to institutional racism and came up with this new definition of it as 'the collective failure of an organization to provide an appropriate and professional service to people because of their colour, culture or ethnic origin. It can be seen or detected in processes, attitudes and behaviour which amount to discrimination through unwitting prejudice, ignorance, thoughtlessness, and racist stereotyping which disadvantage minority ethnic people' (1999, § 6.34).

The concept of unwitting racism is significant. It means that institutional racism arises unintentionally and thoughtlessly, though its effects or manifestations are considered to be visible in the treatment of particular groups, and in the social and economic patterns of contemporary societies. The Macpherson Inquiry's view remains contested and highly controversial. The conclusion of the inquiry and its definition of institutional racism is rejected by some right-wing newspapers and many police officers. Most of that opposition rests on two interlinked pillars. For some in the police, the finding is seen as a blanket accusation that all police officers are racist. Similarly, for sections of the media the rejection is based on the view that Macpherson's definition brands the whole of British society as racist. The first of these erroneously elides individual and structural (or institutional) forms of racism. The second however touches on an important issue about the 'catch-all' nature of the term 'institutional racism', which lacks precision in determining the extent of racism in the UK, and in differentiating between stronger and weaker forms of racism.

Following Macpherson the existence of institutional racism has been acknowledged in a number of governmental and other organizations. Measures to address it include recruitment and training programmes and reviews of organizational polices and practices for forms of indirect racism. However, some critics maintain that these actions are superficial and do not address deep-seated power imbalances within organizations. There are a number of problems with the ways in which the term institutional racism has been defined and used. First, the view that it refers to covert forms of racism is questionable. Institutionalized racism can be both overt and covert. For example, apartheid and other systems of RACIAL SEGREGATION have been an open part of official ruling ideology and governmental programmes. Another example is immigration legislation in the UK, which has not explicitly articulated an aim to discriminate though this has certainly been its effect and intent. Both of these can be regarded as examples of institutional racism, though it is arguable that the latter could better be described as 'institutionalized discrimination', particularly where class and gender divisions intersect with racial and ethnic ones.

There is also a good deal of confusion about how to account for unintended institutionalized racism. While it is possible that institutional practice may embody assumptions and values that are not explicitly discriminatory, in some cases an institution's own acknowledgement of racism seems to be a device to obviate individual responsibility. Alternatively, individual racist behaviour is sometimes taken as a sign of institutional responsibility. While the term was intended to shift attention away from individual and subjective forms of racism as prejudicial attitudes, and while it seeks to account for the persistence of racial inequalities (COMMISSION FOR RACIAL EQUALITY, RACE AND INEQUALITY) even in societies with formal and active commitments to EQUALITY, in practice it has been used to describe both, even though distinct policies and interventions may be required according to whether racism is judged to be intentional or unintentional.

The distinction between individual and institutional forms is dubious since it places individuals outside institutions, 'thereby severing rules, regulations and procedures from the people who make and enact them, as if it concerned qualitatively different racism rather than different positions and relations through which racism operates' (Essed, 1991: 36).

In addition there is a problem of asserting that it is racism or institutional racism that accounts for all racially biased outcomes or effects. The use of 'institutional racism' in this way overlooks other possible causes, such as social class and gender inequalities. It also risks treating institutions as homogeneously racist. An alternative view would stress the different ways that racism works and examine its articulation with other forms of subordination and inequality. There may be multiple racisms in organizations, their operation dependent on context. A blanket description of an organization as institutionally racist is not sensitive to this.

The relationship between the idea and effects may not be straightforward. Ideologies and practices may not match up, either positively or negatively. Institutional racism is largely treated as a case of white (institutional) power over blacks. This is not sensitive to variations in power within and between whites and blacks, and it concentrates on inter-racial differences rather than intra-racial and ethnic differences.

The stretching of the meaning of institutional racism is an instance of what Miles (1989) more broadly regards as the 'conceptual inflation' of the term 'racism' to encompass both ideas and actions. Linking it to consequences or outcomes makes it impossible to isolate the specificity of racism from class and gender relations. For example, recruitment policies that rely on informal hiring practices may also be designed to exclude women and so could not be treated as instances of institutional racism. Miles argues that 'institutional racism' should be restricted to those instances where a racialized (RACIALIZATION) discourse or a racist ideology is invoked or implied. In spite of these difficulties the term can be useful in highlighting the institutional production of outcomes or patterns that are racially discriminatory, and in accounting for indirect and implicit forms of racism that produce persistent forms of discrimination. It suggests the need for greater self-examination of institutional practices. Examples of issues that are at the forefront of debates about the nature of institutional racism in the UK include the differences in the treatment of racial and ethnic minorities in the following areas: employment and promotion patterns; school exclusions; stop and search operations by the police; the treatment of prisoners; differential sentencing of ethnic groups by the courts; and differences in diagnosis of schizophrenia and other mental illnesses (RACISM AND MEDICINE). In these and other cases, the term 'institutional racism' ought to act as a prompt to examine the ways in which organizational policy and practice help to produce distinctive racial and ethnic patterns. Instances where such outcomes are not acted upon or addressed by relevant authorities are likely to confirm the suggestion of institutional racism. As Goldberg says, 'where there is a recognizable, institutionally governed pattern of racially predicated discrimination or exclusion, ongoing because unrectified, the presumption must be that continuing exclusions are considered permissible by those institutionally able to do something about them' (1993: 99). Institutional racism should be applied to the interactions between subjective and institutional processes, and to outcomes not reducible to individual racism. This needs to be complemented with an awareness of the process of institutionalization, as a way in which social activities become routine, persistent and stable features of social structures. [K. M.]

Essed, P. (1991) *Understanding Everyday Racism*, Sage, London.
Goldberg, D. (1993) *Racist Culture*, Blackwell, Oxford.
Macpherson, W. (1999) *The Stephen Lawrence Inquiry*, The Stationery Office, London.
Miles, R. (1989) *Racism*, Routledge, London.
Rex, J. (1987) *Race and Ethnicity*, Open University Press, Milton Keynes.
Scarman, L. (1981) *The Brixton Disorders*, HMSO, London.
Ture, K. (originally Carmichael, S.), Hamilton, C. (1992) *Black Power* (1967), Vintage Books, New York.

INTEGRATION (It. *integrazione*; Fr. *intégration*; Ger. *Integration*) The concept of integration, from the Latin *integratio* (from *integratus*, integrated), indicates the sociological process by which divisions and heterogeneous factors within a society are overcome in order to create a new, balanced whole. Integration, therefore, is an essential dynamic factor in the creation of a society based on co-operation between individuals and groups.

Sociological studies of the concept of integration by Comte, Pareto, Durkheim and Parsons assign various meanings and emphases to the phenomenon. Parsons' contribution is especially significant, underlining the role of regulations in the fostering of social cohesion and highlighting the importance of the interiorization of cultural and value models – and regulations – by the members of a group. This type of integration process has permitted the formation of national states (NATION), creating a common model with which all the heterogeneous groups forming national societies can identify. Over the last 50 years, the term 'integration' has been particularly used with reference to migration FLOWS and the subsequent integration of both individual immigrants into a social structure and various ETHNIC groups into a national structure. In the sociology of immigration (MIGRATION), integration refers to the gradual process which leads foreign and autochthon groups to live together, characterized by mutual processes of ADAPTATION and acceptance and dependent on the capacity of two groups to compare and exchange values and behavioural models. The term is normally used in contradistinction to ASSIMILATION – which implies a situation in which a minority group or groups are forced to abandon their behaviour in order to adopt that of the majority – and in association with the concept of cultural pluralism, which implies acceptance of the existence of different cultures within the same society (MULTICULTURALISM).

The integration process is characterized by a mutual exchange between the MIGRANT and the host society, and generally involves various stages (e.g. accommodation, adaptation and even conflict), without, however, following an established order. Significant differences come to light on a case by case basis.

The integration process normally results in a renewed equilibrium of the social system – the integration of immigrants leading to the acceptance of some of the values of the host society and confirmation of the culture or cultures of origin. Integration can be divided into various kinds: economic, political, cultural and associative. In some cases integration involves all the aforementioned areas and allows new citizens (CITIZENSHIP) to participate actively in all aspects of the life of the host society, while in other cases it only contains certain aspects. Relationships between immigrants and host societies vary in relation to individual immigration plans. Temporary immigration, for example, might impel foreign workers to choose a greater involvement in the economic field and a lesser integration from the linguistic and cultural point of view. The immigrant's willingness to adapt to the rules of the host society may be restricted to the strictly necessary (e.g. respect of laws) or the immigrant may aim for a greater involvement in social life, and consequently the acquisition of less conflictual behaviour. Generally speaking, political integration – the active and passive right to vote and the possibility of exercising political power – is the most difficult to achieve. In many European countries, laws regarding

political rights are restrictive and limit the participation of foreigners (FOREIGNER) in political activities, thus emphasizing the role of governments in the integration process.

In the majority of cases integration is not spontaneous, unless considerable economic resources are available or a country is sparsely populated, e.g. the migration flows which populated the United States and Australia.

At present political and economic powers lead the integration process by planning the distribution of resources, establishing laws, social rules and adequate education policies (ETHNIC POLITICS, INTERCULTURALISM), as well as using any other tools necessary to guide the process.

The degree of integration achieved partly depends on immigrants and their choices – the duration of their stay abroad, their acceptance of the values of Western societies and the relationships established with institutions operating in these countries – as well as other factors, such as the level of cohesion of a given ethnic group. However, more often than not, the dominating factor is social and economic mobility. The impossibility of improving social and economic standing and the social MARGINALIZATION experienced by many immigrants are often responsible for failure to integrate, closure towards the host society, reliance on the ethnic group and even deviant behaviour. The expectation of social advancement is one of the main reasons for emigration, so the integration of immigrants in Western society requires careful planning of flows and appropriate accommodation policies.

Another important aspect of integration is the definition of rules with regard to compatibility and social harmony, in order to prevent friction and conflict between foreigners and marginal autochthon groups, as well as the education of both majorities and minorities – i.e. whole indigenous and immigrant groups – in such a way that they can communicate and live with one another in peace. New generations (SECOND GENERATION) have to be taught to live in a multifaceted social and cultural fabric, while adults must be encouraged to overcome limitations imposed by their ethnocentric education (ETHNO-CENTRISM). Majority and minority groups must therefore be educated in communication and interaction with those who are different (DIVERSITY–SIMILARITY) and in mutual respect. A state integration policy implemented in Great Britain in the 1960s attempted to eliminate certain forms of social and racial discrimination by declaring them unlawful. It aimed to promote equal opportunities both from the legal point of view and through the creation of special institutions, such as the COM-MISSION FOR RACIAL EQUALITY, and also attempted to educate the autochthon population with regard to the problems and interests of the immigrant communities. [Le. Z.]

Banton, M. (1985) *Promoting Racial Harmony*, Cambridge University Press, Cambridge.
Landecker, W. S. (1961) 'Types of integration and their measurement', *American Journal of Sociology*, 56: 4.
Parsons, T. (1964) *The Social System*, Free Press, New York.

INTERCULTURALISM (It. *intercultu-ralismo*; Fr. *interculturalisme*; Ger. *Interkulturalismus*)

A composite word deriving from the Latin *inter* (between) and *cultura* (CULTURE), the term 'interculturalism' is often used as a synonym of – or confused with – such terms as MULTI-CULTURALISM and pluriculturalism which have specific meanings depending on the cultural areas in which they are used. In America the term follows the usage made in intercultural anthropology and linguistics and interethnic communications, while the French use the word to indicate the confluence of multidisciplinary approaches.

In the field of intercultural educational science in particular, teaching inevitably has a formative value as regards a young person's IDENTITY, and this formative process should be based on the communication of an appropriate attitude towards other peoples (PEOPLE), towards those who are different (DIVER-SITY– SIMILARITY). This is especially obvious when individuals of different ethnicities (ETHNICITY) meet, or clash, within a group or class. In such a context it is useful to approach the problem first of all by trying to understand ethnicities which are different from one's own from the cultural point of view, and then to always bear in mind that 'different' does not mean 'inferior', and that all human beings share certain UNCONSCIOUS elements. A teacher's approach to this type of problem could be either to minimize or to accentuate the difference so as to facilitate understanding. The difficulties of the practical management of an intercultural context lead back to the problems which lie at the heart of the theoretical debate on the subject, such as the contradictions and limitations posed by the principles of CULTURAL RELA-TIVISM and universalism (COSMO-POLITISM). According to the former, all phenomena and individuals should only be judged within the context of their culture of belonging: no external judge-ment is possible. A possible contra-diction inherent in this principle – which shows the maximum respect for diversity – is the recognition of the impossibility of communication between different cultures and the consequent negation of any possible comparison. On the other hand, according to universalistic principles, certain non-variable data can be identified – whether mental structures, thought patterns or 'values' – which are present in all cultures, and which permit the comparison and understanding of diversity. However, this attitude risks transformation into a kind of 'covert' cultural imperialism, on the basis of which exportation of the Western model continues.

Only TOLERANCE of diversity and interaction with other cultures can result in interculturalism. The concept of diversity is rooted in the fact that all individuals in some way experience the feeling of being FOREIGN or not fully known to themselves. The strong feeling of instability that results can be seen as the basis of a pathological reaction of refusal and AGGRESSION towards the 'other' or foreigner. [Ar. C., S. G.]

Abou, S. (1981) *L'Identité culturelle*, Anthropos, Paris.

Lewis, R. D. (2000) *When Cultures Collide*, Nicholas Brealey Publishing, London.

Paige, M. R. (1993) *Education for the Intercultural Experience*, Intercultural Press, Yarmouth, Maine.

INTERCULTURAL PEDAGOGY: see INTERCULTUR-
ALISM

INTERNAL COLONIALISM (It. *colonialismo interno*; Fr. *colonialisme interne*; Ger. *interner Kolonialismus*) This expression has been used in reference to many different situations,

to describe the relationship between various groups in a country whose subjugated status is similar to that of the colonized in the colonial system model (COLONIALISM). Referring to the situation in the United States, Robert Blauner (1972) describes how some groups, such as blacks and Native Americans, find their freedom limited or are forced into a condition in which their culture is depreciated or undervalued and, thus, experience a profound feeling of lack of INTEGRATION into society. The result is that these groups assume a position inferior to that of the majority, similar to the relationship between a colonized population and the colonizers (INSTITUTIONAL RACISM).

The same is not true for voluntary migrants (MIGRANT) to the United States, who, able to integrate into the American creed, are capable of getting out of the GHETTO – the urban expression of the internal colony – where only second-class citizens live. The Blauner analogy seems to offer a powerful interpretation of

the contemporary Northern ghetto [in the USA] which, like European colonies, existed as a world apart, administered by politicians, police, social workers, educators, and others whose primary relationship to the community was one of social control. . . . If ghettos constituted a kind of colony, then it followed that the so-called riots were actually a form of 'revolt', analogous to uprisings in the third world. (Steinberg, 1995: 88)

Blauner's analysis refers to the explosive situation of the 1960s and, indeed, the analogy with the revolt in the colonies provides the violence experienced in the ghettos with a new and completely different meaning. Such violence is not merely urban violence but a dramatic battle for freedom and dignity.

The peculiar nature of the history of the Native American, black and Hispanic populations in the United States – a history riddled with violence, MARGIN-ALIZATION and powerful exploitation – differs profoundly from the experience of European migrants. Yet in these very peculiarities lies the reason why the experience of the Northern ghetto populations should be considered a new version of colonialism and imperialism – complete with a similar burden of violence and exploitation – which no longer involves subjugation in the colonies, but rather directly in the country of destination. From a certain point of view, all migration FLOWS (both domestic and international) can be interpreted (as they are by many Marxist economists) as a new form of imperialism and colonialism and thus as a consequence of economic GLOBALIZATION and the crisis in traditional COLONIALISM. The migrant is considered a neo-colonized individual who, contrary to a traditionally colonized individual, emigrated to another country. This interpretation – clearly supported by the heavy migration flows from former colonies to the mother lands (Great Britain and France) – has also been applied to countries that did not have a colonial history in order to highlight the fact that the expression derived from the new method of organization of multinational labour. According to Delia Castelnuovo Frigessi (1974), in the 1970s the status of SEASONAL MIGRANT WORKERS in Switzerland was the most resounding example of domestic colonialism which forced foreign working classes to accept political inexistence, economic discrimination and social segregation while exploiting them by assigning them a precise role (the heaviest, most humiliating and most poorly paid work) in the production cycle in exchange for a job which could be lost at any moment.

The term 'internal colonialism' has also been used to describe regional imbalance within a single country. For example, the imbalance between northern and southern Italy has frequently been analysed in terms of such colonialism.

By contrast, 'internal colonization' instead has been used, primarily in historical contexts, to describe the efforts of states to populate low-density (and often reclaimed) regions within the national frontiers (FRONTIER). [M. V.]

Blauner, R. (1972) *Racial Oppression in America*, Harper & Row, New York.
Castelnuovo Frigessi, D. (1974) 'Colonialismo a domicilio: i lavoratori stranieri in Svizzera', *Il Ponte*, November–December. pp. 1447–1478
Rex, J. (1977) *Race, Colonialism and the City*, Routledge, London.
Steinberg, S. (1995) *Turning Back*, Beacon Press, Boston.

INTERNATIONAL LANGUAGE

(It. *lingua internazionale*; Fr. *langue internationale*; Ger. *internationale Sprache*) The term 'international language' refers to any languages tacitly or deliberately adopted as a means of communication between people of different nationalities or mother tongues. Both existing languages spoken by a certain linguistic community (English, Russian, Arabic, Chinese, etc.) and artificial languages specially created for use in international communications in diplomatic or scientific circles (Esperanto, uninflected Latin or Interlingua) can be used as international languages, although use of the former is far more frequent. Guidelines regarding the choice of the OFFICIAL LANGUAGES used to ratify the decisions of international assemblies are provided by international law and by specific treaties, conventions and protocols. [A. B., R. B.]

> *Britannica on line*, http://www.eb.com.
> *Dizionario enciclopedico italiano*, Treccani, Roma.

INTIFADA

(It. *Intifada*; Fr. *Intifada*; Ger. *Intifada*) From the Arab verb *nafâda* (present tense, *yantafidou*) the word 'Intifada' literally means to revolt, struggle, square one's shoulders against too heavy a burden, or to stand or rise up against an intolerable situation. By extension, it has also come to mean an explosion of rage, the breaking of limits, disorder, spontaneous demonstration, uprising and unplanned agitation.

But the action of the Intifada has become a political metaphor for a specific problem, occurring in a well-defined area, Palestine, and more specifically in the Occupied Territories and certain areas officially under the control of Palestinian authorities.

One peculiar characteristic of the Intifada is the great number of youths taking part in it. No adults, no guns – at least to begin with – just stones and catapults. Most of these youths are from REFUGEE camps. They are not *petit bourgeois*, most of them have little hope for the future and, often, no job. They express their fury and frustration by hurling stones at the Israeli soldiers and police. The stones are thrown to provoke and hurt; the aim is to force the occupiers to retreat from Palestinian territories.

The word 'Intifada' first appeared in the Western press in the autumn of 1987. The historical causes of the movement date from the months following the Arab defeat of June 1967, when Israel occupied the territories, and, in particular from the battle of Karamé, on 21 March 1968, in the course of which the main Palestinian organization, the Fatah lost many of its number. The burial of those referred to as the Karamé martyrs carried out by a dense crowd of angry mourners, was a ritual that came to be repeated often. Such demonstrations catalysed the Palestinians' will to resist. For Israel, they were a destabilizing force and a form of resistance which was hard to prevent.

At the time there was as yet no mention of the Intifada. Palestinians were still seeking means to express their rejection of the occupation, and the funerals offered a chance to vent their profound suffering and frustration.

Palestinian leaders, while continuing armed combat on the field, explored possible new avenues of resistance. Beginning with Amman in November 1984, the Palestinian leader Abou Jihad reorganized the internal networks that would later give birth to the Intifada.

Before adopting the term Intifada to describe what was happening on the field, the media had used words such as 'clashes', 'confrontations', 'encounters' 'troubles', 'incidents', 'disorders' and 'agitations', later to be replaced by terms like 'crisis', 'insurrection', 'civil war' and 'revolt'. On 22 December 198 the French daily, *Libération* spoke of 'Stone-throwers' revolution'. The word Intifada appeared a few weeks later.

The trigger for the Intifada can be dated from the dispatch of 10 December 1987 which read: 'A Palestinian youth was killed and several others wounded yesterday near the Jabaliya refugee camp, in the Gaza Strip, following violent clashes between Israeli soldiers and Palestinian demonstrators.' The young rebels – backed and at times accompanied by women – had known nothing but the refugee camps and the occupation. Using rudimentary tools such as stones – they opposed an army equipped with sophisticated precision weapons. Here lay the originality of this movement. The Israeli army was caught unprepared and did not know how to react.

On 18 December 1987 *Libération* correspondent Shalom Cohen wrote:

What strikes one most when walking the streets of Gaza is the absence of fear. There is much hatred, bitterness and excitement in the eyes of the youngsters mounting guard at the barricades, but no detectable trace of fear. They have taken their destiny into their own hands and are no longer afraid of the consequences.

The Palestinian historian Elias Sanbar lists five lessons to be learned from the Intifada:

1. The occupation has lasted too long; the population has moved to a deeper level of resistance.
2. Innovation in the art of war: the use of apparently laughable weapons, of using stones, has deprived the adversary of the possibility of using its military capacities.
3. The traditional self-defence of Arab societies is in the hands of its youth.
4. The movement has managed to unite and awaken the various dispersed groups of the Palestinian people.
5. The fifth lesson touches on diplomacy: the Intifada has not only forced Israel to negotiate with the Palestinians, but has made such negotiations possible.

From these confrontations was born the mystique of the resistance of the poor. This mystique is possibly what has developed into the tragic and serious phenomenon, that of ultimate sacrifice commonly known as kamikaze or suicide bombing.

Another peculiarity of the Intifada is that it has seemed to follow no designated chief. For a long time the media asked who was behind the riots.

This first Intifada ended immediately following the Madrid meeting of October 1991, a prelude to the Oslo agreement. About 1,000 young Palestinians had died during the uprising. There followed a four-year interlude during which there was a widespread belief that peace, or at least the peace process, would continue. This interlude lasted until the assassination of Yitzhak Rabin in November 1995, after which hopes were dashed once again and resistance resumed.

The second Intifada – more violent than the first as this time the youths were armed with guns, rockets, mortars and grenades, as well as stones – began in September 2000. It is an uprising of all strata of Palestinian society, including the Islamists, whether or not affiliated to the Hamas. The first year there were 815 dead, mostly Palestinians. In response to the second Intifada the Israeli government and military launched a full-scale military offensive in 2002 under Prime Minister Ariel Sharon.

In the climate that has followed the Twin Towers attack of September 11, 2001, the Israelis justify their actions as a response to carefully orchestrated Palestinian terrorism. Those actions have inspired still greater Palestinian resistance including a spate of Kamikaze or suicide bombings in Israel carried out by young Palestinian men and women. At the time of this writing the violence continues to spiral out of control.

The term Intifada has now been used beyond the borders of Palestine/Israel.

In April 2001, Kabylie (Algeria) was shaken by several demonstrations, which were violently suppressed by the police. The Algerian and French press labelled the demonstrations of the

Kabylie youths the Algerian Intifada, an Intifada against the *hogra*, that is the contempt shown towards these youths by those in power. Today, whenever a popular uprising erupts in an Arab country, the image of the Intifada is conjured up. However, the term remains linked to the history of the Palestinian revolution. [T. B. J.]

Revue d'études palestiniennes, Winter 1989 issue, Editions de Minuit, Paris.
Sanbar, E. (1994) *Les Palestiniens dans le siècle*, Découvertes Gallimard, Paris.

INTOLERANCE (It. *intolleranza*; Fr. *intolérance*; Ger. *Intolleranz*)

The term 'intolerance' derives from the Latin *intolerantia*, composed of the negative *in* and *tolerantia*, from *tolerare*, meaning to bear, to endure. Any institutions, ways of thinking, behaviour, individual or collective attitudes, or character and personality traits which involve PREJUDICE against, repression or elimination of those people who are considered not to fit the accepted norm can be qualified as intolerant. Intolerance may be expressed due to differences in religion, 'RACE', gender etc., or towards behaviour, values, ideas or desires which are considered to be false or wrong, again because they do not conform (CONFORMISM).

In a general discussion on intolerance, one should also consider its 'microphysics', the seemingly insignificant but widespread forms of intolerance which occur in families, schools, offices, football grounds, discotheques, on the road and in newspapers, and which cause as much suffering as intolerance in the name of official ideology and political authority. Seemingly innocent acts, like everyday RACISM, demonstrate and spread intolerance, serving both to establish a fixed habit and to allow such intolerance to take root in the social UNCONSCIOUS. The psychological roots of intolerance are just as important as its economic, social, political and ideological background. Psychoanalysts maintain that the roots of intolerance are to be found in: (1) overly frustrating early relationships; (2) the creation of an internal emptiness, which can only be endured by a retreat into NARCISSISM or sadomasochistic (SADOMASOCHISM) attacks; (3) the projection of irresistible desires on to another, who thus becomes the incarnation of the enemy; and (4) the creation of a fictitious IDENTITY which denies the 'plurality' of the persona.

While there are many studies on the social history of racial, moral and political intolerance (e.g. Cohen, 1999), few attempts have been made to conceptualize the theoretical issues underlying the history of intolerance in the West. Indeed, although intolerance has hardly ever been claimed to be a value *per se*, TOLERANCE has its limits and so certain events are, by definition, 'intolerable'. John Stuart Mill first dealt with this issue in 1869 by affirming the so-called 'harm principle', according to which no event which causes another harm should be tolerated. However, the notion of harm is quite a vague one, and does not permit a boundary between the tolerable and the intolerable to be clearly established.

The principle of tolerance has become a cornerstone of liberal thought since the seventeenth century through the work of thinkers such as Spinoza, Locke, Voltaire and John Stuart Mill. The nineteenth century saw the peak of the belief that tolerance (at least religious and political tolerance) was destined to grow and to spread. At the beginning of the century the German philosopher Hegel claimed the ultimate goal of history was the freedom of man. From the idea of negative freedom – in the words of Isaiah Berlin – which focused on external constrictions, Hegel developed the idea of freedom as self-realization, the full accomplishment of human potentiality ('positive freedom', according to Berlin). A nation state, Hegel predicted, would be essential to secure this development given that freedom is the condition of living self-consciously in a fully rational community. Ironically, Hegel's system was the model adopted by all social, philosophical and political movements in the 1900s that denied freedom and the primacy of the principle of tolerance. Popper, one of the most influential liberal philosophers of our age, even accused Hegel of being – along with Plato and Marx – one of the theorists of the totalitarian state.

The most radical attack on the principle of toleration did in fact come from a philosopher educated in the Hegelian circle, the founder of communism, Karl Marx. Marx argued that liberal thought was an ideological justification for the rise of capitalism, and its defence of tolerance and individual liberty was nothing but the exaltation of the market.

Marxism is the most comprehensive modern political philosophy which opposes individuals' freedom and tolerance. Its political success resulted in Marx's original ideas being interpreted at their most extreme, and in its Leninist and Stalinist forms, communism became primarily involved in the total seizure of political power, leaving no room for personal liberty. The Marxist criticism of the concept of tolerance has even been echoed in the contemporary debate on academic free speech and the so-called 'hate speeches' (racist, sexist and other discriminatory speeches) in the USA. Since the late 1970s, a movement aiming to introduce speech codes has developed in American academia. This movement has its roots in the work of the Marxist philosopher H. Marcuse who, in an essay of 1965 entitled *Repressive Tolerance*, argued that true tolerance is always partisan, because it is intolerant of those who support the repressive status quo. Marcuse suggested that a new 'liberating tolerance' would include 'the withdrawal of toleration of speech and assembly from groups and movements which promote aggressive policies, armament, chauvinism, discrimination on the grounds of race and religion, or which oppose the extension of public services, social security, medical care, etc.' (Marcuse, 1965: 85).

In the 1900s another important current besides Marxism opposed tolerance: NATIONALISM, according to which one's own nation was not only important, but invested with unique qualities which made it superior to others. Nationalism can be thought of as the major source of intolerance, XENOPHOBIA, RACISM and ANTI-SEMITISM in continental Europe. So while in the first part of the nineteenth century it was the Hegelian philosophers who were the major critics of the principle of tolerance, at the end of the century, nationalist, anti-liberal, anti-individualistic, and authoritarian movements took the floor.

At the beginning of the twentieth century the influence of Nietzsche's seminal critiques of Western morality was also felt. Nietzsche has been accused of being a precursor of Nazism, but he actually despised German nationalism, anti-Semitism and the authority of the state. However, he also despised the mass, and believed that democratic liberalism could only create cynicism and nihilism. According to Nietzsche, liberal doctrines, including the respect for tolerance, not only caused people to stop believing in religious and moral truths, but also caused them to stop wanting to believe in a general sense. He called this state of affairs 'passive' nihilism, and he saw it as a sign of weakness; he considered that some superior individuals might adopt an 'active' nihilism that is the expression of the 'will of power', in response to this.

Nietzsche's deconstruction of Western ideals was followed by that expounded by another German philosopher, Spengler, in his influential book *Decline of the West*, published just after the First World War, in 1918. According to Spengler, all history is a struggle among nations, and each nation's future will be decided by its power relationships with other peoples. In his view, a healthy CIVILIZATION should be organic, cohesive and intolerant of any foreign element.

This appeal to local traditions remains important even in contemporary Europe. The terrible bloodbath of the First World War closed the first period of European nationalism. The second period was marked by the birth of Fascism, an extreme nationalist movement created by the Italian politician Benito Mussolini, which became widespread throughout Europe between the two world wars. Fascism rejected the heritage of the Enlightenment with its emphasis on liberty and on the equality of human beings and exalted the supreme sovereignty of the nation as an absolute principle.

In Germany, the Fascist movement was embodied by National Socialism and the Nazi Party founded by Adolf Hitler. Together with communism, Nazism was probably the modern political movement most imbued with the ideal of intolerance. Hitler expounded the main ideas of his movement in *Mein Kampf*, which he wrote between 1924 and 1926. These included the total rejection of all miscegenation and the necessity of conquering a vast land base in Eastern Europe for German settlement. Intolerance of Jews was the cornerstone of

Hitler's theory. Nazism rejected all liberal theories and promoted the most aggressive, anti-Semitic and intolerant policy ever seen in Europe. The Nazi search for a Western identity unsullied by the Enlightenment and liberalism was shared by certain European influential thinkers, such as the German legal philosopher C. Schmitt. He is known above all for his theory of conflict, believing that European identity should be sought for in the Middle Ages. In Schmitt's view, any government should be able to guarantee its nation's survival by identifying its enemies – in particular internal enemies – and then restraining them. Liberalism, by undermining this basic function of the government in the name of discussion, pluralism and democratic rights, would have the effect of making conflicts worse and less manageable. However, the end of Nazi and Fascist regimes did not bring about an end in the history of intolerance in the West. This was not only because the Soviet system survived for over 40 years following the Second World War before finally collapsing in 1989, but, paradoxically, because intolerance is a concept which is inherent in that of toleration.

In post-war Europe, nationalism and nationalist parties have found new expression, and as the traditional nation state is gradually eclipsed by supranational organizations it has found a complement in regionalism and regional parties – the Front National in France, Northern League in Italy and Freedom Party in Austria – organizations that claim to uphold the integrity and value of tradition. These movements see society as an integrated body held together by shared conceptions of the common good and a common ETHNICITY. In this light, all those elements that differ from local, regional values, and that may erode the common regional heritage, are considered to fall outside the boundaries of what is tolerable. These movements represent, among other things, a reaction to what has been perceived as excessive European tolerance of non-European immigration.

The issue of what is 'intolerable' is also crucial in the current debate on 'zero tolerance'. This concept is based on a theory advanced in the 1980s by two criminologists, J. Q. Wilson and R. J. Herrenstein, who claimed that authorities could create a climate in which serious crime would find it impossible to flourish if they refused to tolerate minor infractions of the law, such as the painting of graffiti on walls or dropping of litter on the sidewalk. They called this the 'broken window' phenomenon; if one window in a building is broken, all the others will soon suffer a similar fate. If, however, one fixed the broken window rapidly, the situation will not deteriorate. This policy was first adopted in New York City by Mayor Rudolph Giuliani. [Em. M., M. B.]

Altemeyer, B. (1996) *The Authoritarian Specter*, Harvard University Press, Cambridge, MA.
Berlin, I. (1990) *Four essays on Liberty*, Oxford University Press, Oxford.
Brown, D. (2001) *Contemporary Nationalism: Civic, Ethnocultural and Citizenship*, Oxford University Press, Oxford.
Cohen, M. N. (1999) *Culture of Intolerance: Chauvinism, Class, and Racism in the United States*, Yale University Press, New Haven and London.
Farganis, S. (1977) 'Liberty: two perspectives on the women's movement', *Ethics*, 88: 62–73.
Fukuyama, F. (1992) *The End of History and the Last Man*, Free Press, New York.
Gellner, E. (1994) *Conditions of Liberty*, Allen Lane, New York.
Gress, D. (1998) *From Plato to Nato*, Free Press, New York.
Hagendoorn, A., Csepeli, G., Dekker, H. (eds) (2000) *European Nations and Nationalism: Theoretical and Historical Perspectives*, Ashgate, Aldershot.
Hitler, A. (2000) *Mein Kampf*, CPA Books.
Hobsbawm, E. J. (1992) *Nations and Nationalism since 1780*, 2nd edn., Cambridge University Press, Cambridge.
Marcuse, H. (1965) *Repressive Tolerance*, Beacon Press, Boston, MA.
Marx, K. (1998) *The German Ideology*, Prometheus Books, New York.
Mussolini, B. (1932) *What is Fascism?*, http://www.fordham.edu/halsall/mod/modsbook.html (15 February 2001).
Nietzsche, F. (1989) *Beyond Good and Evil*, Prometheus Books, New York.
Noel, L. (1994) *Intolerance: The Parameters of Oppression*, McGill Queens University Press, Montreal.
Pareto, V. (1991) *The Rise and Fall of the Elites: An Application of Theoretical Sociology*, Transaction Books, New Brunswick, NJ.
Popper, K. (1945) *The Open Society and Its Enemies*, Routledge, London.
Wilson, J. Q., Herrnstein, R. J. (1985) *Crime and Human Nature*, Simon & Schuster, New York.

INVASION
(It. *invasione*; Fr. *invasion*; Ger. *Invasion*) The term 'invasion', from the verb *invadere*, dates back to the 'dark ages' (Barbarian invasions) and is used to describe the occupation of a new country – often with the use of military force – on the part of a large mass of people. Thus, from many points of view, invasions can be considered to be a form of MIGRATION and have been an important and recurrent form of population flow (FLOWS). Inherent in the term is the idea of violence, and its use in the migration debate expresses the widely held perception that migrations which are no longer influenced by a demand for employment in the country of destination, but by demographic, economic and political situations in the countries of origin, risk becoming unsustainable for the host country (PUSH FACTORS – PULL FACTORS).

The term 'invasion' has often been used in the media to infer an irrational and fearful reaction to the arrival of migrants which bears no relation to the number of migrants arriving nor to the material risks ensuing for the host society (RACE AND THE MEDIA). Such a reaction is frequently based on the conviction that the arrival of new-comers places an unbearable economic burden on the host society or that the habits and behaviour of the migrants could contaminate the cultural PURITY of the hosts, thus leading the host society to poverty, destruction or a complete loss of cultural IDENTITY (DIVERSITY–SIMILARITY).

This negative and ominous stance has characterized much of the European debate on migration since the 1960s, and forms a central component of many right-wing positions, from that of Enoch Powell in the UK to that of Le Pen in France or, more recently, of Haider in Austria. Even the concept FORTRESS EUROPE, referring to the zero-migration policies implemented in Europe since the mid-1970s, has been mirrored in the media image of migrants as possible 'invaders'. [E. R.]

Bohning, W. R. (1984) *Studies in International Labour Migration*, Macmillan, London.

Livi Bacci, M., Martuzzi Veronesi, B. (1990) *Le risorse umane nel Mediterraneo*, Il Mulino, Bologna.

Palidda, S. (1992) 'Pour une approche des réalités effectives des migrations', *Migrations et société*, 24: 7–24.

Reyneri, E. (1979) *La catena migratoria*, Il Mulino, Bologna.

Sayad, A. (1991) *L'Immigration ou les paradoxes de l'altérité*, De Boeck-Wesmael, Bruxelles.

Schnapper, D. (1992) *L'Europe des immigrés*, Éditions François Bourin, Paris.

JEW (It. *Ebreo*; Fr. *Juif*; Ger. *Jude*) The word 'Jew' refers to members of the Semitic people who are notionally descended from the ancient Israelites and who, although they are spread throughout the world, have remained linked by cultural and/or religious ties. As Jewish descent is from the maternal line, a Jew is a person born to a Jewish mother. But in a wider sense, a Jew is anyone who, through descent or conversion, belongs to a worldwide group that constitutes a continuation of the Hebrews of the Old Testament. The term 'Hebrew' derives from the Latin *hebraeus* and the Greek *hebraios*, which in turn are derived from the Hebrew *ivrì*. The original meaning of the Hebrew word *ivrì* was FOREIGNER or outsider – not unlike the word *falasha* in the Ethiopian language. Indeed, in ancient times, people referred to Jews as 'those who come from elsewhere'.

The Jews as a people originated from the group of 12 tribes who settled in the land of Canaan in the thirteenth century BC and were eventually united in a single kingdom under Saul in about 1000 BC. After the reign of Solomon this kingdom was split into two parts, Israel and Judah (or Juda). Judah was subsequently conquered by the Babylonians who carried many of the Jews into exile in 586 BC, though they were able to return after a lengthy captivity in 539 BC thanks to the permission given by Cyrus for the exiled Jews to return to Judah, where they settled chiefly in the neighbourhood of Jerusalem. However, after the conquest of Jerusalem by the Emperor Titus Vespasian Augustus in AD 70 many Jews were massacred and hundreds of thousands were banished. A Roman garrison subsequently occupied the ruins of Jerusalem specifically to prevent its reconstruction by religious Jews. Later, under the sovereignty of the Emperor Hadrian, a new city, Ælia Capolitana was founded on the site of Jerusalem and no Jew was allowed either to reside there or to approach its environs.

Following their banishment from Jerusalem in AD 70, the history of the Jews both under Roman rule and after the fall of the Roman empire more often was one of persecution and inequality than favourable treatment. Above everything, however, their experience was to be one of dispersal and forced movement. For example, in 1492 Jews were expelled from Spain, despite having lived there successfully and in relative peace for several centuries, and they were obliged to seek refuge in North Africa, Turkey – where they were hospitably received – Holland and France. Such expulsion and 're-expulsion' helped to create the myth of the Wandering Jew.

Englander therefore describes the 'Jewish enigma' as confronting the question of how and why:

> Stateless for more than two millennia, scattered across the four corners of the earth, living under different regimes, diverse in status, occupation, education and culture, varying in the degree of acculturation and assimilation, the Jewish people have nevertheless contrived to retain a distinct identity. (Englander, 1992: ix)

The idea that for Jews a life outside what was defined as the historical birthplace of the Jewish people was 'a life of exile' formed a central component of Zionist thinking (ZIONISM). Yet even after the establishment of the State of Israel in 1948, which marked the end of an EXILE that had lasted 2,000 years, only a minority of Jews chose to live there. The total number of Jews in the world today is estimated to be about 14 million – of whom close to 6 million live in the USA, 4.5 million in Israel, 1.5 million in the former USSR, approximately 600,000 in France, 360,000 in Canada, 250,000 in Argentina and less than 300,000 in the UK. This suggests that for many Jews what was important was the knowledge that a Jewish state in Israel existed, and thus any prior sense of rootlessness that they may have felt was not primarily a matter of physical relocation or even of the social or political circumstances in which they lived (DIASPORA).

Like Christianity and Islam, Judaism is a monotheistic faith, i.e. a religion which believes in only one God. The Torah (law), the Nevi'im (prophets), the Ketuvim (writings), the Talmud (interpretation) and oral traditions constitute all that remains of the enormous body of ancient Jewish writings – works which document the complex universal and humanitarian development of Jewish culture and religion. Jewish religious practice reflects the different histories consequent upon the expulsions that Jews had endured – the most notable difference being between Ashkenazi Jews (from Eastern Europe) and Sephardic Jews (from Iberia and North Africa) – and takes many forms: orthodox, conservative and reform.

Since the days of the Roman empire, the relationship between Christianity and Judaism (RELIGION AND ETHNIC CONFLICT) has been a principal source of anti-Jewish persecution and of deep-rooted prejudice towards Jews (ANTI-SEMITISM), at least until very recent times. The roots of the anti-Semitism of the Christian Church were several-fold: a belief that the Jews were eternally cursed by their refusal to accept Jesus Christ as the Messiah and by their alleged part in Christ's death; and the Church's view of itself as the 'new Israel'. Moreover, the fact that by the fourth century AD Christianity had become the official religion of the Roman empire encouraged it to see Judaism as an anachronism and this led to the demand that Jews be isolated socially, that the practice of Judaism be circumscribed and that Jewish communities be kept in a position of subservience (Alexander, 1992: 172, 175).

One notable consequence of Christian anti-Jewish prejudice is that in all European languages the word 'Jew' came to be identified with strongly negative characteristics, notably cheating and avarice, and many dictionaries still include various pejorative meanings of the term 'Jew' such as a miser, a person who drives a hard bargain, or a money-lender. These negative connotations stem from medieval times when, because of restrictions imposed on them as religious outsiders which denied them access to many occupations and professions, Jews were often obliged to act as money-lenders and, moreover, were often encouraged or compelled to do so by the authorities. More generally, not only has Jewish 'vice' been routinely contrasted with Christian 'virtue', but the word 'Jew' also came to be associated with notions of treachery insofar as the name 'Judas' – the disciple who betrayed Jesus Christ and whose name stems from the territory of 'Judaea' – is still used as the classic epithet to describe a traitor. It is noteworthy that the phrase 'treacherous Jews' was used in Catholic Easter prayers as recently as 1960, when this wording was finally abolished by the Second Vatican Council (1962–1965).

However, despite the strength and depth of anti-Jewish stereotyping, it is simplistic to say that Jews have been depicted only in negative terms in all Western societies. In fact, the picture is much more complex. For example, in his analysis of 'the Jew' in English literature and society, Cheyette discerns

a Semitic discourse which constructed 'the Jew' as both within *and* without; a stranger *and* familiar; an object of esteem *and* odium; a progressive universalist *and* a racial particularist. . . . Jews could be represented as: 'Eastern', 'Oriental', 'European', 'Asian', 'modern', 'medieval', 'pagan', 'prophetic', 'degenerate', 'regenerate', 'proletarian', 'bourgeois', 'aristocratic', 'tribal', 'assimilated', 'orthodox', 'heretical', 'rational', 'deranged', 'vengeful', 'orderly'. (Cheyette, 1993: 268, original emphasis)

Although anti-Semitism has represented a serious threat to Jews in that it has led to persecution, segregation (GHETTO), restriction, expulsion, and GENOCIDE (SHOAH), Jewish existence is also threatened by the diminution of anti-Semitism characteristic of post-Enlightenment and post-Emancipation periods – for example, through intermarriage or loss of Jewish identity in societies that are increasingly secular. Diminution of Jewish numbers in the post-enlightenment Diaspora – via both conversion and intermarriage – has long been discernible in Jewish communities. In the USA only one out of 23 original Jewish families of 1654 still had Jewish members 100 years later. Yet the problem was masked in that diminution through ACCULTURATION and conversion was more than matched by immigration from elsewhere. For example, between 1881 and 1914 120,000 Eastern European Jews settled in the UK and millions settled in the USA and in each case the size of the Jewish community multiplied.

Jews who left the community in, say, nineteenth-century Russia did so under often considerable pressure: when a prominent nineteenth-century Russian archaeologist was asked whether his decision to convert to Christianity was a matter of pragmatism or conviction, he replied that he had been baptized entirely as a matter of conviction, namely the conviction that it was preferable to be a professor in the Academy in St Petersburg, rather than a teacher in the local Jewish school or *heder* (Sacks, 1996: xx).

In contemporary Western societies, by contrast, leaving the Jewish community is, pre-eminently, a choice which reflects a decline in religious belief, a diminishing sense of ETHNICITY, or both – not a matter of coercion. The change relates to the diminishing pressure to conform (Sacks, 1996: xxi). The very removal of once impervious residential, occupational and social barriers permits a degree of ASSIMILATION, via intermarriage and other mechanisms, that is seen to threaten the existence and viability of Jewish communities (Nettler, 1992: xiii). In recent years there has therefore been growing debate within Jewish communities about how to maintain Jewish distinctiveness in conditions of freedom, choice and increasing secularization. [P. B.] [A. Z.]

Alexander, P. (1992) 'The origins of religious and racial anti-Semitism and the Jewish response', in Englander, D. (ed.), *The Jewish Enigma*, The Open University in association with Peter Halban and the Spiro Institute, Milton Keynes.

Cheyette, B. (1993) *Constructions of the 'Jew' in English Literature and Society*, Cambridge University Press, Cambridge.

Englander, D. (ed.) (1992) Preface to *The Jewish Enigma*, The Open University in association with Peter Halban and the Spiro Institute, Milton Keynes.

Gilbert, M. (1992) *Jewish Historical Atlas*, 4th edn., London, Weidenfeld & Nicolson.

Glick, L. (1999) *Abraham's Heirs: Jews and Christians in Medieval Europe*, Syracuse University Press, Syracuse, NY.

Kaplan, J. (ed.) (1984) *International Bibliography of Jewish History and Thought*, K. G. Saur, Jerusalem.

Nettler, R. (1992) Introduction to Englander, D. (ed.), *The Jewish Enigma*, The Open University in association with Peter Halban and the Spiro Institute, Milton Keynes.

Poliakov, L. (1971) *Harvest of Hate*, Greenwood Press, London.

Sacks, J. (1996) 'Jewish discontinuity' (one of several 'Centenary Essays') in Massil, S. (ed.), *The Jewish Year Book*, Centenary 1996 edition, Valentine Mitchell, London.

Seltzer, R. (2001) *Jewish People, Jewish Thought*, Prentice-Hall, New Jersey.

JIM CROW (It. *Jim Crow*; Fr. *Jim Crow*; Ger. *Jim Crow*) Originating with a character in a popular minstrel show of the 1830s, 'Jim Crow' as a term grew to encompass a wide variety of laws and customs mandating RACIAL SEGREGATION between African-Americans and whites. Laws enforcing racial segregation and black oppression can be traced to the early nineteenth century when the problem of free blacks began to bedevil communities in all regions of the country. In the South, their status was hardly discernible from that of slaves (SLAVERY). For example, Virginia, Georgia, Tennessee and Mississippi required free African-Americans to register with local authorities. In all Southern states, ex-slaves faced restrictions on voting, freedom of movement, owning property, and finding employment.

In the North, many if not most of the same restrictions prevailed. In New York and Pennsylvania, voting was limited to ex-slaves who owned more than $250 worth of property, while white males faced no such test. In Boston, the school authorities established a separate school for African-Americans in 1820. Other towns and cities across the North followed suit. By the 1850s, some communities in Ohio and Illinois reacted to free blacks in hostile and violent ways. Regardless of the setting, laws were enacted to control the free African-American population, to keep them from mixing with whites, and to deny them political and economic agency in their own lives.

Following the Civil War, Southerners redesigned laws governing the behaviour of slaves and followed the example of Northern jurisdictions. Instituted in 1866, the Black Codes called for strict racial separation and denial of opportunities for African-Americans. These codes were eventually challenged by an alarmed Republican Party majority in the US Congress, which saw them as an attempt by an unrepentant South to reimpose the old order. The Civil Rights Acts of 1866, 1867 and 1875 and the fourteenth and fifteenth Amendments to the US Constitution banned the codes and were intended to rid the South of the residual effects of slavery. By the late 1870s, however, the nation had grown tired of the South's racial problems, and the courts had begun to rule against federal efforts to ban discrimination (RACIAL DISCRIMINATION). As a result, by the 1890s, numerous states in the South had passed laws which were essentially updated versions of the Black Codes, and their endeavours were legitimized in 1896 by the US Supreme Court's *Plessy* v. *Ferguson* decision that endorsed the principle of separate but equal facilities for blacks and whites.

While ostensibly following the law, in actuality the Southern states maintained two separate and unequal systems in education, public recreation, transportation and employment. The terms 'Jim

Crow' and segregation increasingly found their way into the nation's vocabulary by the early twentieth century and both came to mean racial oppression for African-Americans. In both the public and private spheres, African-Americans were denied the same or similar opportunities offered to white Americans. For example, for every two dollars Southern schools spent on black children in 1930, on average seven dollars were spent on each white child. Not content with segregation in most areas of American life, several communities such as Louisville, Kentucky and Baltimore, Maryland attempted to pass laws forcing blacks to live in certain areas of their cities. In the North, although few segregation laws were in place, racial separation existed by custom and private arrangement and was enforced legally. By the middle of the twentieth century, Northern cities such as Chicago, St Louis, New York City and Philadelphia contained highly segregated and densely populated black neighbourhoods that rivalled the South. The existence of racial segregation began to break down as African-Americans moved from the rural South into urban areas to take advantage of job opportunities created by industrialization and the Second World War. Although civil rights groups such as the NAACP had attacked Jim Crow for years, sustained efforts at the grassroots level could not begin until blacks had developed churches, COMMUNITY organizations, schools and businesses that helped provide the necessary leadership and funds for an overall assault on segregation. With the US Supreme Court's *Brown* v. *Board of Education* ruling in 1954 overturning the *Plessy* decision, community-centred struggles immediately increased. In cities and small towns such as Birmingham, Alabama, Little Rock, Arkansas, and Farmville, Virginia,

black organizations mounted protests against what historians called the 'peculiar institution'. Their endeavours led to the first congressional acts since the Civil War to overturn segregation, such as the 1957 and 1964 Civil Rights Acts, the 1965 Voting Rights Act, and the 1968 Fair Housing Act.

While the nation could claim to have abolished Southern-style segregation by the 1970s, it found *de facto* segregation in the North to be a more intractable problem. Statistics from the US Census Bureau show that racial segregation actually increased in Northern cities between 1950 and 2000. Many social scientists argue that racial segregation remains the most important and vexing problem for Americans. Unfortunately, few resources at the federal level have been devoted to dismantling the vestiges of Jim Crow, and the courts have similarly adopted a *laissez-faire* attitude. Until RACE becomes as significant an issue as the environment, economic growth or military spending, racial segregation is likely to continue to exist for many years to come. [D. W. F.]

McMillen, N. R. (1989) *Dark Journey, Black Mississippians in the Age of Jim Crow*, Urbana, University of Illinois Press.

Vann Woodward, C. (1955) *The Strange Career of Jim Crow*, Oxford University Press, New York.

Williamson, J. (ed.) (1968) *The Origins of Segregation*, D.C. Heath, Boston, MA.

JUS SANGUINIS: see CITIZENSHIP

JUS SOLI: see CITIZENSHIP

K

KU KLUX KLAN (It. *Ku Klux Klan*; Fr. *Ku Klux Klan*; Ger. *Ku Klux Klan*) The end of the American Civil War and the establishment of Radical Reconstruction resulted in the elimination of many Southern white men from public life. Determined to guide their own destiny and control the newly freed slaves (SLAVERY), many whites resolved to carry on a kind of guerrilla warfare against both African-Americans and whites who represented the federal government in the South. As a result, scores of coercive, violent organizations, such as the Regulatros, the Jayhawkers and the White Brotherhood, were formed between 1866 and 1876 to 'keep the Negro in his place'. The most infamous and longest-lasting organization created was the Knights of the Ku Klux Klan.

In some ways, the Klan may be the world's oldest and most persistent terrorist organization, although the intensity of its activity has ebbed and flowed for nearly a century and a half. Begun by a group of six former Confederate soldiers in a lodge near Pulaski, Tennessee in 1866 (the exact date is uncertain), the club's title came from the Greek word *kuklos*, meaning 'circle'. In 1867, the group quickly spread, engaging in scare tactics: members would dress in white sheets with hoods designed to scare superstitious African-Americans. Originally conceived of as a fun but harmless diversion, participants quickly realized the Klan's potential to reimpose white supremacy across the defeated South.

White Southerners already had a long history of using violence in the exercise of political, social and economic power. Beginning in the 1600s, the white South passed laws and implemented slave patrols designed to keep African-Americans in an enslaved status. Free blacks as well were circumscribed in their actions by the sanction of law and custom. With the end of slavery, white Southerners successfully reinstated the plantation regime through a bewildering set of laws known as the Black Codes, backed by the threat and use of violence.

In April 1867, the Klan convened in Nashville, Tennessee to draft a new constitution and elect a new leader, former Confederate general and slave trader Nathan Bedford Forrest. Led by a group of former plantation owners, Confederate officers, attorneys and politicians, the Klan established itself in 12 states and gained half a million members over the next two years. Their targets were those in the South who represented the federal government, the Union Army, Northern industrial interests and active members of the Republican Party. Their most venomous attacks, however, were directed at African-Americans who attempted to learn to read, establish a school or business, buy land and, worst of all, vote or run for political office. Using guns, swords, arson and knives, Klan members intimidated, bribed and drove Republicans from power across the former Confederate states plus Kentucky. The Southern Democratic Party, eager to regain control, sheltered and encouraged Klansmen to carry out through violence what they could not achieve peacefully. Nonetheless, by January 1869, news of Klan exploits in gang rapes and out of control burning and looting sullied the organization's reputation, and Forrest called for an end to all Klan activity.

The announcement seemed to strengthen the more violent elements of the Klan, as the organization quickly split into factions based in the various states. In Georgia, Alabama, Mississippi, Florida, South Carolina and Louisiana (all states still under military occupation in 1870), decentralized Klansmen launched a new wave of terror intending to permanently remove all vestiges of federal government control from the South. Although the US Congress held hearings into Klan terrorism and eventually passed laws in 1870 and 1871 to outlaw Klan activity, whites in the North grew tired of the South's political crisis and desired a more peaceful region where industrial interests could grow and prosper. At the same time, many Northern whites shared the beliefs of white Southerners that blacks were unfit for politics and should be racially segregated (RACIAL SEGREGATION). Finally, the Democrats regained control of the US House of Representatives in 1874; by 1876, one-party rule had been effectively restored in the South. The first phase of the Klan had done its job and, as a result, faded into Southern memory as a glorious movement.

From the 1880s to 1910, white vigilantes and politicians continued to impose law and order in the South through disfranchisement, racial segregation and lynching. Simultaneously, the national culture had begun to change as the result of growing numbers of immigrants (MIGRATION) from Southern and Eastern Europe. The onset of the First World War led to both an increase in black migration to Northern and Western states and a new intolerance of ethnic Americans (partly due to American propaganda against Germany) who clung to their native languages. Finally, the growing rebellion by some citizens against Victorian-era values worried many Americans. Into this fertile territory stepped a revitalized version of the Klan. In 1915, film director D. W. Griffith adapted novelist Thomas Dixon's *The Clansman* into America's first epic motion picture, *Birth of a Nation*. The film romanticized the Klan as a protector of Southern white virtue, and with endorsements from President Woodrow Wilson and the Chief Justice of the US Supreme Court, *Birth of a Nation* quickly became the accepted view of the Reconstruction period. Discussions were held nationwide about the prospects for a Klan revival, and on Thanksgiving night in 1915, several hundred whites gathered at Stone Mountain, Georgia, where the new Knights of the Ku Klux Klan pledged themselves to defend Christianity, the country and white womanhood.

Electing William Simmons, a former minister from Atlanta as their first leader, the Klan added immigrants, Catholics, Jews and radical labour unions to their enemies list. In the West, Southwest, and Plains states, Asians, Mexicans and American Indians were subject to their wrath. In addition, the Klan impressed many Christians with its advocacy of the prohibition of alcohol and encouragement of marriage. The group also led many Americans to believe that it was a bulwark against the spread of communism. As a result, the Klan could boast 4 million members by 1924; larger chapters in Ohio, Indiana, Illinois and California than in any other states; governorships in Alabama, Georgia, Colorado and Indiana; and allies in Congress, state legislatures, city and county councils and judgeships. The group was especially adept at infiltrating sheriffs' offices and police departments from Norfolk, Virginia to Los Angeles, California. Indeed, the Klan was arguably America's third political party during the early 1920s.

As rapidly as the Klan gained power and influence over American politics, it also quickly lost power due to concern about its advocacy of violence, its record of criminal activity and its embezzlement of members' dues. By 1929 membership had sunk to 100,000, and many Americans had turned their attention to economic concerns with the onset of the Great Depression. Simmons had resigned many years earlier, but the Klan's new leader, Hiram Evans, proved ineffective in gaining new members and resigned in 1939. In 1944, the Klan officially disbanded when the Internal Revenue Service alleged that the group owed $685,000 in back taxes.

Although the third major phase of the Klan did not really begin until the mid-1950s, there were various attempts to resurrect it during the late 1940s and early 1950s. The 1954 *Brown* v. *Board of Education* decision ordering an end to racially segregated schools, however, prompted the Klan's resurgence. In all probability, *Brown* was simply the spark that lit a smouldering fire. African-Americans had made many advances since 1941, beginning with the establishment of the federal Fair Employment Practices Commission. By 1948, President Harry Truman had ordered the desegregation of the armed forces, a federal judge had ruled that whites-only primary elections were unconstitutional, and restrictive covenants in private housing were also deemed illegal. At the same time, African-American political and economic power had steadily increased until substantial numbers of black churches, businesses, schools and other institutions could provide the leadership and money to sustain an all-out assault on white supremacy. The Klan's revival in the 1950s merely reflected what whites saw and feared happening around them.

Other anti-black but ostensibly more moderate organizations were also created in the wake of *Brown*. The National Association for the Advancement of White People and the White Citizens' Councils, sometimes known as the 'uptown Klan', were established across the South and used the threat of economic reprisal against African-Americans who supported civil rights activism. The movement received a true shot in the arm when more than ninety members of Congress from the South signed the 'Southern Manifesto', a document that declared their opposition to school desegregation and in all likelihood encouraged some whites to take matters into their own hands. Further stoking the fire was the movement by white officials in several Southern states to label the NAACP and other civil rights organizations as 'subversive'.

Although energized, Klansmen found themselves in a decentralized organization during the 1950s with no fewer than 15 rival groups. Nevertheless, this fact perhaps made them even more dangerous, for no one leader could order a halt to Klan violence. Between 1952 and 1968, Klansmen were implicated in hundreds of bombings, arson attacks, beatings and assassinations, such as the 1963 murder of Mississippi NAACP president Medgar Evers. In fact, Birmingham, Alabama became so well known and feared for its bombings and Klan violence that it was renamed 'Bombingham' by the press. Synagogues also received attention because of the widespread belief that Jews and communists were behind the NAACP.

The existing rivalries created confusion and dissension among many whites, until 1961, when the United Klans of America was formed to unify various groups. Based in Tuscaloosa, Alabama, the United Klans failed to become an umbrella organization, although it succeeded in gaining 30,000 members and had chapters in 18 states. However, the violence of the 1960s finally led the US Justice Department to crack down on Klan activities, as they realized that all-white local juries in the South would not convict a white man for beating or killing an African-American. With the threat of increased federal involvement during the late 1960s, and newly enfranchised black voters who would throw out of office those authorities who did nothing about the Klan, many white office-holders began to look unfavourably on the organization. Since the early 1970s, Klan membership has roughly varied between 1,500 and 12,000, although those figures are deceiving. Many whites who abhor interracial contact have joined or organized other white supremacist groups, such as the American Nazi Party, the Aryan Nations and the Christian Identity Movement. Many have also formed militia or survivalist groups as innocuous-sounding rifle and hunting clubs. As the Southern Poverty Law Center, a Klan-watch group, has argued, violent white supremacy may be even more dangerous because it has been pushed underground. Despite the low numbers, the ideas represented by the Klan remain its most enduring and ominous contribution to the future of American society. [D. W. F.]

MacLean, N. (1994) *Behind the Mask of Chivalry. The Making of the Second Ku Klux Klan*, Oxford University Press, New York.

Trelease, A. W. (1971) *White Terror. The Ku Klux Klan Conspiracy and Southern Reconstruction*, Harper & Row, New York.

Wade, W. C. (1987) *The Fiery Cross, The Ku Klux Klan in America*, Simon & Schuster, New York.

LANGUAGE SHIFT (It. *sostituzione linguistica*; Fr. *remplacement linguistique*; Ger. *Sprachsubstitution*)

The expression describes a situation in which the spread of a language causes the weakening or disappearance of another language. In the 1960s, the American linguist J. A. Fishman (1989) proposed a dual theory of linguistic conservation and linguistic substitution. His purpose was to show how, within the same country, or where there is contact between populations, a language which plays a minor role (from an economic, political or cultural point of view) is subjected to pressure from what might be thought of as a majority language. The first may survive despite the influence of the second, or it may yield and become progressively weaker until extinction. [A. B., R. B.]

Crystal, D. (1997) *The Cambridge Encyclopaedia of Language*, Cambridge University Press, Cambridge.

Fishman, J. A. (1989) *Language and Ethnicity in Minority Sociolinguistic Perspective*, Multilingual Matters, Philadelphia.

Summer Institute of Linguists, www.sil.org.

LINGUA FRANCA (It. *lingua franca*; Fr. *lingua franca*; Ger. *Lingua Franca*)

While the actual Lingua Franca was a language that developed in the eastern Mediterranean basin – probably around the time of the first Crusades (1095) – following early commercial and military relations between Europeans and Arabs, the general term 'lingua franca' refers to any language used for communication among people of different mother tongues.

The specific Lingua Franca can trace its etymology back to the Arabic expression *lisan al-ifrang* (the language of Europeans), in which the term *ifrang* – literally, *frankish*, or French – was used by the Arab world to include all the peoples of Christian Europe. The Lingua Franca was characterized by: (a) an extremely simple grammatical structure; (b) a lexis mainly deriving from the vocabulary of southern Romance languages and a few Arab words. Lingua Franca is the oldest known example of a PIDGIN or Creole language (CREOLE languages) deriving from European languages, but texts in Lingua Franca are rare. The earliest known text was written on the island of Djerba, in 1353 (Holm, 1988).

More generally, whenever any language takes on a vehicular function (VEHICULAR LANGUAGE) – regardless of the context – it can be considered a lingua franca. The role of linguae francae is especially important in geographic areas of great linguistic diversity. [A. B., R. B.]

Crystal, D. (1997) *The Cambridge Encyclopaedia of Language*, Cambridge University Press, Cambridge.

Holm, J. (1988) *Pidgins and Creoles*, Cambridge University Press, Cambridge.

McArthur, T. (ed.) (1992) *The Oxford Companion to the English Language*, Oxford University Press, Oxford.

M

MARGINAL MAN (It. *uomo marginale;* Fr. *homme marginal;* Ger. *Aussenseiter*) The term 'marginal man' is used in connection with the study of MIGRATION, and was coined by the American sociologist Robert Ezra Park (1928) – a major figure of the so-called Chicago School in the 1930s – to identify a person who is neither a newly arrived immigrant (MIGRANT) or FOREIGNER nor a person completely assimilated (ASSIMILATION) into the new society. A 'marginal man' is a person somewhere between the two conditions. Faced with a new social reality, in which strongly held beliefs are challenged or derided, a marginal man is a product of change and is forced to live in two different cultural groups, as a result of which his personality becomes unstable and assumes particular behavioural patterns. According to Park, he cannot be other than a 'split personality', since he is torn between the security of his own traditions and the attraction of the MELTING POT. A marginal man is a cultural hybrid, the type of person who lives according to, and participates in, the CULTURE and traditions of two different peoples, living on the border. This type of person lives on the border of two cultures and two societies which have never completely merged. Living in two worlds, but as a stranger to both, the positive side of marginality involves being a cosmopolitan citizen of the world (Park, 1928).

For Park, marginality (MARGINALIZATION) becomes an illness when the marginal man is unable to take part in the 'fusion' of cultures and cannot assimilate. In this sense, the concept of marginal man has rather negative connotations, as such a person remains excluded in their new environment, while also being excluded from their original COMMUNITY because they now adopt behaviour which has no meaning in their original society.

Park's analysis was continued by his student Everett Stonequist (1937), who postulated that this person – who could easily become the victim of a profound identity crisis (DOUBLE CONSCIOUSNESS) as a result of this life being suspended between two worlds – is strongly drawn to reflection and critical analysis. According to Stonequist, migration not only leads to a change of old customs and habits, when someone is faced with a new and different economic and geographical situation, but gives rise to accelerated thought processes, the awakening of more advanced mental functions. Persons suspended between two groups need mental agility: they have no time to rest or vegetate. In this regard at least, Stonequist's analysis offers a less negative view than does that of Park.

More recent analyses have identified and emphasized the positive aspects of the dual personality involved in marginality: for example, the work developed by Turner (1987) on 'liminal' man, and Leed's work on the traveller. However, dual personality in immigrants must be understood as both the decision of the migrant to keep a certain distance from the two worlds of belonging and also the result of attitudes adopted in the former and the new society. In addition, the possibility of being able to conceive a person as having a well-constructed identity is nowadays frequently challenged. According to Stuart Hall,

> the logic of identity is, for good or ill, finished. It's an end for a whole range of reasons. It is an end in the first instance because of some of the great de-centrings of modern thought. . . . We have the notion of identity as contradictory, as composed of more than one discourse, as composed always across the silence of the other, as written in and through ambivalence and desire. (1997: 43–49).

[M. V.]

Hall, S. (1997) 'Old and new identities, old and new ethnicity', in King, A. (ed.), *Culture, Globalization and the World-System. Contemporary Conditions for the Representation of Identity*, University of Minnesota Press, Minneapolis.

Leed, E. J. (1991) *The Mind of the Traveller. From Gilgamesh to Global Tourism*, Basic Books, New York.

Park, R. E. (1928) 'Human migration and the marginal man', *American Journal of Sociology*, 33: 881–893.

Stonequist, E. V. (1937) *The Marginal Man: A Study in Personality and Culture Conflict*, Scribner, New York.

Turner, V. (1987) 'Betwixt and between. The liminal period in rites of passage', in Mahdi, L., Foster, S., Little, M. (eds), *Betwixt and Between*, Open Court, Lasalle, IL.

MARGINALIZATION

(It. *emarginazione*; Fr. *marginalisation*; Ger. *Ausgrenzung*) The term 'marginalization' refers to two main issues. The first issue is the significant reduction in involvement in society and the considerable loss of opportunities experienced by certain groups or individuals within a specific society, with a consequent breakdown of ties either in terms of social control or in terms of reciprocal SOLIDARITY. Such reduction leads to a progressive decline in social PARTICIPATION, an increase in the level of poverty and ongoing exclusion from social agencies such as schools, the job market, political communities and so on. When taken to the extreme, this process results in people becoming dropouts or *clochards* and completely refusing the social values and ties of the society. The other issue – which although connected to the former does not completely overlap with it – is that even in such *seemingly* fluid structures as democratic societies, in which all players have equal opportunities to move within the social context, and especially to move up and down the social ladder, there are relatively rigid or semi-rigid elements which considerably reduce the social mobility of the members of some groups, condemning them to a future of marginalization. In other words, such group members do not share the same opportunities to improve their condition in society as others due to being denied access to positions of power, prestige and wealth.

The marginalization of ETHNIC and racial groups (RACE) is often seen as being a special case of marginalization which results from the way the wider society treats those identifiable by their ethnic origin or skin colour (COLOURED). Marginalization of these groups is usually characterized by social segregation, such as their concentration in the poorer areas of cities, and social indicators associated with poverty and underperformance in society – such as low school attainment, higher proportions of employment in low-skilled jobs and in 'secondary' rather than 'primary' employment, as well as by their underrepresentation in professions such as journalism, law, accountancy and medicine. In the case of MIGRATION, there is strong evidence to suggest that marginalization may be passed on to subsequent generations (SECOND GEN-ERATION). To the extent that this holds, it conflicts with the expectation that the second or third generation of migrants will be better placed than the first generation.

According to George Borjas' review (1999) of the social performance of ethnic national groups of migrants to the United States during the twentieth century, 'the historical record shows that the skill differentials across ethnic groups . . . did not disappear within one generation. It is also remarkable that the intergenerational correlation between the average skills of immigrants and their children was roughly constant through the entire twentieth century' (Borjas, 1999: 139). Ethnicity matters and it matters for a very long time. Indeed, it matters because it reduces social mobility and therefore can be considered another possible reason for marginalization. [R. B., P. B.]

Borjas, G. J. (1999) *Heaven's Door: Immigration Policy and the American Economy*, Princeton University Press, Princeton, NJ.
Demarchi, F., Ellena, A., Cattarinussi, B. (eds) (1987) *Nuovo dizionario di sociologia*, San Paolo, Milano.

MELTING POT (It. *melting pot*; Fr. *creuset*, *melting pot*; Ger. *melting pot*)

This expression refers to the idea, long cultivated in the United States, that FLOWS of people from different origins arriving in America merge in this 'country of immigrants' to give life to a *quid novi et pluris*: the good American. The term was first used in a comedy at the beginning of the twentieth century (*The Melting Pot*, by Israel Zangwill in 1909). The idea also inspired the motto *E pluribus unum*

(from many, one) which is still inscribed on American coins today. It should be said that the melting pot, as depicted by Zangwill, i.e. a process of reciprocal ADAPTATION on a more or less equal basis, never actually came about, owing to the dominance of the *WASP* (White, Anglo-Saxon Protestant) component of the country, which determined and encouraged Anglo-conformity (CONFORMISM) from its beginnings. Following the Second World War, faith in the integrating capacity of the American society was drastically reduced, and the situation which effectively existed in the country began to be illustrated by another image, that of the *salad bowl*, in which the various ingredients maintain their specific characteristics. The growing numbers of 'Hyphenated Americans' (those who continue to define themselves as Italian-Americans, Hispanic-Americans, Russian-Americans, etc.) (DOUBLE CONSCIOUSNESS), the recent ethnic revival – which has re-proposed and revalued original identities – and, above all, the arrival of new immigrants (MIGRANT) who are more obviously resistant to the expected melting pot effect (the so-called *unmeltable ethnics*) are expressions of this phenomenon.

Although the existence of an American model which recognises the influence of different populations on the dominant Anglo-Saxon structure cannot be denied, the melting pot may be nothing more than a MYTH. Instead of the happy and unproblematic mixing of peoples implied by the term imagined in St John de Crèvecœur's *Letters from an American Farmer*, published in London in 1782 – a work fundamental to understanding the first American approach to the migratory phenomenon, according to Albert Bastenier and Felice Dassetto (1995: 19–36). The process of merging and ASSIMILATION has often been violent and extremely problematic, and has frequently resulted in MARGIN-ALIZATION. Not only has this process never been fully accomplished, but the continuous reappearance of new ETHNIC diversities (DIVERSITY–SIMI-LARITY) and the efforts made by distinct ethnic groups to preserve their cultural specificity could be seen as proving the complete failure of the melting pot model in America.

That the persistence of different groups, such as Italians, Puerto Ricans, Mexicans, Cubans, Russians, Poles, Chinese, Koreans and Vietnamese, can easily be used to demonstrate the inconsistency of the American model and therefore the failure of the melting pot may, of course, be simply a problem of perspective. The fact that the modern approach focuses on either uniformity or diversity within the same cultural context may simply mean that the melting pot is not currently fashionable either as a social paradigm by which to interpret the American experience or as a political and cultural programme based on the overcoming of diversities in the production of one single model. [U. M.]

Bastenier, A., Dassetto, F. (1995) *Immigration et espace public. La controverse de l'intégration*, CIEMI L'Harmattan, Paris.
Crèvecœur, J. H. St John de (1782) *Letters from an American Farmer*, Fox, Duffield 1904, New York.
Glazer, N., Moynihan, D. P. (1963) *Beyond the Melting Pot*, Harvard University Press, Cambridge, MA.
Hirschman, C. (1983) 'America's melting pot reconsidered', *Annual Review of Sociology*, 9: 397–423.
Noblet, P. (1992) *L'Amérique des minorités*, L'Harmattan, Paris.
Noiriel, G. (1998) *Le Creuset français*, Seuil, Paris.
Novak, M. (1972) *The Rise of Unmeltable Ethnics*, Free Press, New York.
Schlesinger, A. Jr. (1991) *The Discounting of America: Reflections on Multicultural Society*, Norton, New York.
Zangwill, I. (1925) *The Melting Pot* (1990), Macmillan, New York.

MIGRANT (It. *migrante*; Fr. *migrant*; Ger. *Migrant*) Reduced to its essentials migration simply denotes a permanent change of residence. This suggests that a move to a new house within a town or city could be described as migration, but more usually migration is defined as a permanent or semi-permanent move from one part of a country to another or from one country to another. Thus a journey to work is not classed as migration, whereas the seasonal movement of, say, Irish labourers to harvest crops in Britain would be classed as migration. Migration within the nation state is referred to as "in-migration" or "out-migration", whereas movement of people to take up permanent residence in another state is described as "emigration" or "immigration". It is migration across a national boundary by individuals, families or groups that concerns us here (Pryce and Drake, 1994: 5).

While immigration denotes the movement towards a receiving country, society or state, emigration denotes the movement away from a sending country, society or state; the emigrant is the person moving away from his previous place of residence. The receiving country sees the influx of persons of foreign origin in terms of immigration. The sending country sees the loss of persons regarded as regular members of its population in terms of emigration. Migrants may see themselves both as emigrants and immigrants, or place emphasis on one of these two categories depending on the motives and factors that triggered the move (PUSH FACTORS – PULL FACTORS), the process of incorporation or ACCULTURATION, reactions migrants encounter and their sense of loyalty to one or the other society. An international migrant is a person who moves from one country to another in order to settle there, if not permanently, at least for a prolonged period of time. Various words in everyday use indicate that a person is not born in the country of residence or is not a citizen of that state. 'Immigrant' and 'FOREIGNER' are two examples. These words have different connotations, denotations and applications. The word 'foreigner' applies to someone who is present in a country other than his/her country of CITIZENSHIP. A foreigner is thus a person who is not a citizen of the country. The word foreigner conveys nothing about a person's length of stay in the country or about intentions to stay. Neither does the word foreigner say anything about a change of place of residence. A foreigner is (usually) required to leave the country within a certain limited period of time. There is no verb corresponding to the noun foreigner.

The receiving country does not regard return migrants belonging to the country's own population (through birth in the country or citizenship) as immigrants. Nor does the sending country regard persons of foreign origin who leave the country as emigrants.

Migrants may also be classified according to the grounds upon which residence permits are issued. Only those with legal residence status are counted. Those who are not registered as residents of the country are foreigners on temporary visits for leisure, business, studies or diplomatic service. This latter category also includes asylum seekers whose applications are being processed

(POLITICAL ASYLUM), seasonal workers and artistes on tour.

Illegal or undocumented migrants whose status in the country is not officially accepted represent a third category (ILLEGAL ALIEN).

Migrants face a process of reorientation and readjustment during the resettlement phase (ADAPTATION). This may involve learning a new language, accepting or understanding basic value orientations in the society of resettlement, building up social networks and organizations and acquiring skills of importance to function in the economy and labour market. There are no reliable statistics on the number of international migrants. Castles and Miller (1998) cite an estimate from the International Organization for Migration of 120 million in 1994. This represents less than 2 per cent of the world population. While OECD countries monitor migration FLOWS and keep track of individual migrants, border controls in developing countries are less well equipped to monitor and record migratory flows. International MIGRATION between countries in the developing world is estimated to be of a much larger magnitude than migration to and between OECD countries. [C. W.]

Castles, S., Miller, M. J. (1998) *The Age of Migration. International Population Movements in the Modern World*, 2nd edn, Macmillan, London.
Pryce, W. T. R., Drake, M. (1994) 'Studying migration', in Pryce, W T. R. (ed.), *From Family History to Community History*, Cambridge University Press, Cambridge.

MIGRATION (It. *migrazione*; Fr. *migration*; Ger. *Migration*) The word 'migration' is derived

from the Latin word *migratio*, which means to move, to wander. It pertains to individual mobility. Migration is purposive and instrumental. Migration may take place within the boundaries of a state (internal migration) or across state boundaries (external or international migration) (FRONTIER). Practically all over the world today there is a large shift of population from rural regions to cities and urban areas where there are more job opportunities. In many places people flee from ecological disasters and political oppression. Migratory FLOWS (internal as well as international) are part of the GLOBALIZATION processes and these are linked to flows of capital and goods, ideas and images, information and remittances. Migration has become a central issue in international relations. It is a major factor of economic and political change. It is one of the most important questions of domestic politics in both sending and receiving countries.

All forms of migration have effects on individuals and societies. Sending regions tend to become economically impoverished, while receiving regions will experience the establishment of 'new' ethnic minorities (ETHNIC MINORITY), social tensions and problems of social cohesion. On the individual level, moving from one's home town or village means being cut off from social networks, associations and a social structure that one was part of (ALIENATION). It usually takes some time before migrants become established in the receiving region's networks, markets and associations (ADAPTATION). Changes of this kind occasioned by migration will inevitably affect migrant identities (IDENTITY). International migration involves all this but also questions pertaining to rights of residence, rights of access to welfare systems and jobs, CITIZENSHIP, often language and communication problems, and in many cases social exclusion and discrimination (MARGINALIZATION).

The concepts of immigration and emigration apply to international migration, not to internal migration. Immigration denotes the move *to* and settlement in a particular country. Emigration stresses the move *from* a country of previous settlement. Voluntary migration means moving from one's original place of residence for reasons of work, family reunification, etc. Forced migration represents situations of flight in which the individual has little or no choice but to flee in order to avoid persecution, imprisonment or maltreatment. Another classification focuses on time planning, whether the migrant intends to settle permanently in the receiving country or only on a temporary basis with the aim to return to his/her country of origin. In cases of forced migration, the receiving country may decide to grant permanent or temporary residence permits. A third classification of migration pertains to alleged reasons for migrating (economic, political, environmental, family, etc.).

While most states do not prevent citizens from leaving the country they strictly control and monitor the entry of non-citizens. This gives rise to the distinction between legal and illegal migration. Illegal migration is about entering and residing in a country without official permission of the receiving country's immigration authorities (ILLEGAL ALIEN).

Migration theory focuses on factors in sending countries that trigger migratory flows (push-factors/political and economic), factors in receiving countries (pull factors/political and economic), and the transnational field that develops between sending and receiving countries (PUSH FACTORS – PULL FACTORS). Migration theory may also focus on the macro situation of economy, politics, communities and information flows as well as on the micro situation of individual decision-making and motivation. [C. W.]

Castles, S., Miller, M. J. (1998) *The Age of Migration. International Population Movements in the Modern World*, 2nd edn, Macmillan, London.
Cohen, R. (ed.) (1995) *The Cambridge Survey of World Migration*, Cambridge University Press, Cambridge.
Hammar, T., Brochmann, G., Tamas, K., Faist, T. (eds) (1997) *International Migration, Immobility and Development. Multidisciplinary Perspectives*, Berg, Oxford.
King, R. (ed.) (1993) *Mass Migration in Europe. The Legacy and the Future*, Belhaven Press, London.
Straubhaar, T. (1988) *On the Economics of International Labour Migration*, Verlag Paul Haupt, Bern.
Zolberg, A., Suhrke, A., Aguayo, S. (1989) *Escape from Violence. Conflict and the Refugee Crisis in the Developing World*, Oxford University Press, Oxford.

MIGRATION CHAIN (It. *catena migratoria*; Fr. *chaîne migratoire*; Ger. *Migrationsverbund*) This expression indicates both the relationship between migrants (MIGRANT) and their families and friends back home, and an evolving pattern that characterizes the phenomenon of MIGRATION. Both aspects reveal how migratory movements have their own dynamics, which, to some extent, are unrelated to the demographic or economic situation in the country of origin or the destination country. That these movements are brought about by a 'vacuum' on one end, and an 'overflow' on the other, is a model based on a mistakenly mechanical vision of the phenomenon. Given the fact that such population growth is not a natural phenomenon, as might be supposed from the use of a term like 'population bomb', the most enlightened demographers have concluded that the best way to understand migratory pressure from the THIRD WORLD is to move away from demographic variations to factors related to living standard and economic development; however, the conclusions reached should be seen as tentative rather than unequivocal.

What migratory movements do show us is that there are complex mechanisms at work; among these the so-called push and pull factors (PUSH FACTORS – PULL FACTORS) play a significant part. The presence of push factors is considered to be a necessary condition, though in and of itself not enough to set off a migratory flow (FLOWS). The decision to emigrate is a choice made by an individual or a family and concerns only those who are prepared to bear the monetary or emotional costs of leaving, and who possess the financial and cultural resources needed to face hardship: migration is always a selective process. It is no coincidence that processes of economic development enlarge the pool of potential emigrants even when their per capita income rises. One need only think of the poverty in overcrowded cities in all the countries of the Third World today. To be able to emigrate a 'migratory knowledge' is required, that is to say, access to a network of relationships in the destination country. Emigration reaches large proportions only if a 'migration chain' develops between a local COMMUNITY or a family network in the country of origin, and a family network or community in the country of arrival. The size of the pool of potential emigrants is also associated with the image that the developed society projects through channels of personal relations (for example letter writing or telephone) and the mass media. An ever-present pull factor is the MYTH of an affluent, open and free society which offers possibilities for EMANCIPATION and consumption to everybody.

Once a migration chain has formed it can prolong the movement of individuals even after the mechanisms which originally generated it are no longer operative. In addition, a migration chain is an essential condition for irregular entry because it makes it easier for controls and restrictions to be avoided (ILLEGAL ALIEN). This chain is also the reason behind the transformation of temporary immigration into permanent immigration, something which characterized Northern and Central Europe during the 1970s and 1980s. When in 1974 measures were taken to discourage or restrict the entry of immigrant workers in a number of European countries, the reduction in immigrant populations was less than had been predicted because many immigrants, when faced with the prospect of not being able to regain entry to France and Germany, decided to settle there and bring their families to join them. Previous to this, the numbers of those who had settled permanently was already on the rise, but this new development accelerated the 'maturation of the migratory process', which Bohning (1984) divided into four stages. In the first stage immigrants are almost entirely composed of workers who plan to go home after a few years. Most of them are single men, because single men are the most enterprising and the freest to leave, and they come from the least backward areas of the country where there is a better knowledge of employment opportunities abroad. The second stage is one of transition: in this the average age of the immigrants rises as well as the number of married men,

even if they are unaccompanied by their spouses. The length of stay grows longer and the turnover is slower. The effect of 'imitation' in the country of origin means that culturally deprived people with fewer skills and qualifications also emigrate. In the third stage the changes are more evident: the immigrants' average age rises even further, as well as the number of women in the population, whether wives who join their husbands bringing their children with them, or couples who decide to leave together. Activity rates slow down while a significant demand appears for services and social infrastructure. Return rates diminish while the length of stays and the probability of permanently settling increases. The fourth stage is the mature phase of the migratory flow. Immigrants continue to stay longer and FAMILY REUNIFICATION increases, but the population of foreign residents reaches noticeable proportions, generating both a high demand for recognition of their cultural IDENTITY and for social services. Problems related to immigration become problems related to ethnic minorities (ETHNIC MINORITY).

According to some experts, this sequence does not apply to the migrant flows which occurred during the 1990s in those countries of Europe where immigration is a recent phenomenon; this is because the various stages seem to overlap and follow each other in much more rapid succession. In Italy high activity rates and the low level of family reunification would tend to weaken this hypothesis. Rather than being the original aim of new emigrants, the increased tendency to settle down permanently may have directly resulted from the closed border policies that the countries of Southern Europe adopted in the wake of an initial period of *de facto* free entry because they had not been prepared for the phenomenon. [E. R.]

Bohning, W. R. (1984) *Studies in International Labor Migration*, St. Martin's Press, New York.

Reyneri, E. (1979) *La catena migratoria*, Il Mulino, Bologna.

Sayad, A. (1991) *L'Immigration ou les paradoxes de l'altérité*, De Boeck-Wesmael, Bruxelles.

MIXED MARRIAGE (It. *matrimonio misto*; Fr. *mariage mixte*; Ger. *Mische-he*)

This expression describes a marriage where the partners belong to two different national, ethnic, racial or religious groups (ETHNICITY, RACE). It is one of the most important indicators of the degree of INTEGRATION of immigrant communities into the host society, and consequently an interesting area for research in the study of interethnic and intercultural relations. At the same time, this type of marriage acts as a sort of 'laboratory' for research into the dynamics which characterize marriage itself. Historically speaking, racially mixed marriages have often been explicitly forbidden, as in the case of mixed-race marriage in South Africa or in Nazi Germany. However, even in less extreme circumstances, society may place various obstacles in the path of inter-religious marriages.

From a sociological point of view, it is important to consider the 'distances' between the marriage partners' countries of origin. These distances are cultural (this can be located only approximately along the continuum between the poles of 'tradition' and 'modernity'); economic (which can be evaluated through their position in the hierarchy of the current international division of labour); political (totalitarianism versus democracy, although the heritage from possible past colonial relations (POSTCOLONIAL STUDIES) between the two countries is also relevant); demographic (that is, demographic growth differences between the North and South of the world, inaptly cited as one of the main reasons for migratory movements); religious; and based on skin colour. Within the FAMILY unit, these distances can translate into a union between individuals who may have been socialized into different ideas of the roles of the sexes, the education of children, and relationships with the extended families.

It could be said that whereas marriage normally involves partners of similar age, financial standing and social status, union between an indigenous partner (a citizen) and a FOREIGNER may be significantly different. For example, such unions may involve the choosing of a partner who is different in some key respect such as being younger or better off, but in many cases are distinguished by being primarily a means of providing entry to a country (FAMILY REUNIFICATION) or regularizing an individual's legal status in the country of immigration. Thus, for quite different reasons each partner can be thought to have made some sort of social conquest by marrying, even if unknowingly. Such marriages can be seen as a kind of 'reciprocal compensatory exchange'.

From a legal point of view, mixed marriages present the problem of international personal rights. The seriousness of this becomes especially clear in the event of separation, where decisions must be made over custody of young children. All these matters have obvious correlations with inter-religious marriages, especially with regard to the marriages between Catholics and Muslims, two religious traditions with marriage rights deriving from very different anthropological conceptions. The difficulties caused by interethnic marriages, together with the negative reactions the couples often experience from their families and communities, make such marriages relatively rare events, even among to immigrants from second, and later, generations.

Nevertheless, the cohabitation of citizens of different nationalities, whether institutionalized or otherwise, is a growing phenomenon which bears witness to a move away from mainly economic migration, with the temporary and functional aim of working to earn money, towards an immigration (MIGRATION) aimed at settling in the country of arrival. This 'populating' immigration thus leads to the formation of family units. [L. Z.]

Barbara, A. (1990) 'Les Mariages mixtes (fait migratoire et familial)', *Colloque International 'Métissages'*, Saint Denis de la Réunion.
Cahill, D. (1990) *Intermarriages in International Contexts*, Scalabrini Migration Center, New York.
De Paolis, V. (1992) *Il matrimonio misto*, ISTRA/CADR, Milano.
Delcroix, C., Guyaux, A. (1992) *Double mixte. La rencontre de deux cultures dans le mariage*, L'Harmattan, Paris.
Streiff-Fenart, J. (1989) *Les Couples franco-maghrebins en France*, L'Harmattan, Paris.

MIXED RACE (It. *razza mista*; Fr. *race mixte*; Ger. *gemischte Rasse*) Used to define a person whose parents belong to different races, this has come to replace older derogatory and racist (RACISM) terms such as half-caste, half-breed, mulatto, octoroon, etc. However, such a definition remains contentious and bound by limited and untenable concepts in that it implies that a pure 'RACE' exists.

Nevertheless, as societies become more diverse, it has become increasingly important to positively recognize the identities of those who define themselves as 'mixed race', 'métis/se', of 'mixed parentage' and of 'dual heritage', as a source of richness, and to map emerging identities (IDENTITY).

In view of this, for want of a better definition the term 'mixed race' is recognised and included in the Censuses of the United States and now (since 2001) the UK, to indicate those persons who fall under two or more of the different classifications listed, and who previously had had no other alternative than to tick the box labelled 'other'. [F. P.]

MIXOPHOBIA (It. *mixofobia*; Fr. *mixophobie*; Ger. *Mixophobie*) The term derives from the Greek *mìxis* (mixture, blend) and *phobos* (fear). First coined by Pierre-André Taguieff (1987), the term 'mixophobia' refers to an unconditional fear of mixture and describes the dominant form of RACISM associated with NATIONALISM. Mixophobia can be divided into three types: intra-national (regionalism, autonomism and independentism), national (nationalism in the strict sense of the word) and supra-national (Europeanism).

The concept of mixophobia includes the tendency to demonize others and treat them as deviants from the norm, repulsion at any contact or mixing with anyone considered different (DIVERSITY–SIMILARITY), obsessive defence of PURITY, the resultant fear of cultural or biological hybridization and the uncompromising defence of a pure racial lineage and thus a primordial identity which is assumed to have lasted from time immemorial. [M. B.]

Taguieff, P. A. (1987) *La Force du préjugé*, La Découverte, Paris.

MONOETHNIC STATE (It. *stato monoetnico*; Fr. *état monoethnique*; Ger. *monoethnischer Staat*)

The concept of 'monoethnic state' envisages a NATION inhabited by a single ethnic group (ETHNICITY), and which consequently is monocultural, monoreligious, etc. A similar concept, which can be found in the aspirations of totalitarian systems such as Nazism, was applied to the situation in former Yugoslavia in the 1990s, where, through the practice of ETHNIC CLEANSING, attempts were made to create nations which were ethnically pure (PURITY).

Attempts at the creation of monoethnic states are inevitably accompanied by violence and tragedy, since existing nations are made up of many ethnic groups, of which one or more are generally in a dominant position, while others form subordinate minorities (ETHNIC MINORITY). In other words, even if it is difficult to imagine that MULTIETHNIC nations may become reality, it is even more difficult to conceive of a monoethnic, monocultural society. [M. V.]

Vešović, M. (1994) *Smrt je majstor iz Srbije*, Bosanska Knjiga, Sarajevo (Italian trans.: *Chiedo scusa se vi parlo di Sarajevo*, Sperling & Kupfer, Milano, 1996).

MONOGENISM (It. *monogenismo*; Fr. *monogénisme*; Ger. *Monogenismus*)

The term 'monogenism' derives from the Greek *mónos* meaning one, alone, single, and *génesis* meaning birth. The theory of monogenism – according to which all human beings descend from Adam and Eve – derives from the emphasis placed by Western culture on the Bible in attempting to explain the origins of mankind. Starting in the sixteenth century, a heated debate developed between the advocates of monogenism and those who professed opinions to the contrary (POLYGENISM). Among the many books written during this time on the accepted origins of humankind are *The Primitive Origination of Mankind Considered and Examined According to the Light of Nature*, by the English scholar Matthew Hale and published in 1677, and the *Dissertatio critica de hominibus orbis nostri incolis, specie et ortu avito, inter se non differentibus quam in auditorio gymnasii*, published by the German philosopher Vincent Rumpf in 1721.

Modern science supports the theory that humanity shares a common evolution, and that we do not descend from a same pair of progenitors – as held by Creationists – but from a population of a different species which underwent very rapid evolutionary changes (EVOLUTION) resulting in the development of humanity as we know it today. [G. B., O. R.]

Greene, J. C. (1959) *The Death of Adam*, Iowa State University Press, Ames.

MULTICULTURALISM (It. *multiculturalismo*; Fr. *multiculturalisme*; Ger. *Multikulturalismus*)

1 The term 'multiculturalism' refers to the coexistence of a range of different cultural experiences within a group or society. It is often used as being synonymous with 'PLURICULTURALISM', or 'cultural pluralism',

resulting in a certain amount of theoretical and conceptual confusion. More recently, the trend in literature has been to use similar terms, such as INTERCULTURALISM and 'transculturalism', with far more precise meanings.

All human societies throughout history can to a certain extent be said to be multicultural, as differences in gender, generation, type of occupation or ethnic group of belonging – no matter how slight or simple – have always been expressed through a wide range of cultural codes deriving from different experiences.

Currently terms such as multiculturalism are generally used with reference to those societies, or segments of society, in which – for political, economic or social reasons – groups of different cultures (CULTURE), originally formed independently of each other owing to historical or geographical factors, have come to cohabit. As such, multiculturalism may be the sociocultural manifestation of multiethnicity (MULTIETHNIC). While in and of itself multiculturalism is value-free, when it is extended beyond the conceptual sphere to the application of policies aimed at preserving and promoting cultural diversity in the politically and socially charged context of ethnically evolving societies, there is a danger that such policies could in fact prove an obstacle to true multiculturalism (and INTEGRATION), as the cultural fabric may become woven in such a way that different groups and cultures do not truly interact with each other, possibly depriving some groups of social mobility. During the 1970s, faced with substantial immigration FLOWS, many Western countries such as the Netherlands, Sweden and Great Britain were keen to apply multicultural policies aimed at helping specific groups to maintain their language and culture of origin and strengthen their cultural identity, thus also hoping to improve RACE RELATIONS. However, the results of many such policies have proved to be anything but uncontroversial, as emerges for example from a review of the Swedish case:

> Some analysts are highly critical of the way in which multicultural programmes are implemented. For example, Sweden adopted an immigration policy in the 1970s that was to reinforce the position of immigrant minorities with regard to social, economic and political rights without forcing them to assimilate (Hammar, 1985). This policy was intended to bring out a society in which cultural diversity is seen as a strength. This, however, is not the way things have turned out. Instead there has been a marked increase in racist actions, discrimination, segregation and unemployment. The foreign born population has been especially hard hit. (Westin, 1998: 59)

Nowadays it is recognized that some multicultural policies could unwittingly encourage cultural conflict and exacerbate the phenomena of segregation (RACIAL SEGREGATION), and the idea that race relations can be improved through their application is less universally accepted, not least because of the difficulties involved in taking into account all the complexities and dynamics of cultural exchanges.

Another area of concern in this respect is the process of GLOBALIZATION of culture, which on the one hand ensures that each country of the world is able to communicate with other countries, while creating a culture of inequality on the other. Worldwide communication is mostly in the hands of the media, while the economic gap between rich and poor countries, as well as between the richer and the poorer classes within individual states, is becoming more marked. In addition, it is worth considering that the kind of cultural

.egregation which could be produced by multicultural policies could be exploited by allowing certain elites to monopolize the most productive forms of culture and knowledge (CULTURAL IMPERI-ALISM). This means multicultural policies and the related cultural models and education programmes could conceivably limit the application of standard education systems, thus depriving large groups of people of the opportunity to compete. In such a situation cultural exchanges often stop at the more 'volatile' and transient expressions which, as they do not operate at the structural level of the education system, are not able to influence cultural models and education programmes. Consequently, the same marginality which increasingly large social groups already experience at an economic level is reflected in cultural production (MARGINALIZATION).

The risks presented by the application of rigid multicultural policies might be counteracted by adopting a pluralistic approach to cultural diversity (DIVERSITY–SIMILARITY), geared towards cultural exchange rather than compartmentalization. An international colloquium convened by UNESCO in Paris in 1999, entitled 'Towards a Constructive Pluralism', with the participation of scholars and experts in various aspects of cultural pluralism, made the following recommendations: (a) religious, ethnic, linguistic and other groups should be encouraged to emphasize those aspects of their traditions that foster mutual respect and understanding; (b) where appropriate and requested, assistance should be given to individuals and communities (COMMUNITY) in reconstructing their identities where these have been disrupted by MIGRATION and urbanization; (c) a range of educational processes should be developed to support interaction and

encourage respect between communities; (d) academics, policy-makers and practitioners should be encouraged to engage in dialogue with each other to inform the debate on pluralism. [M. C. G.]

Forbes, J. D. (1977) *Racism, Scholarship, and Cultural Pluralism in Higher Education*, University of California Press, Davis.
Hammar, T. (1985) *European Immigration Policy*, Comparative Ethnic and Race Relations Series, Cambridge, Cambridge University Press.
UNESCO (1999) *Towards a Constructive Pluralism*, UNESCO, Paris.
UNESCO (2000) *World Culture Report 2000. Cultural Diversity Conflict and Pluralism*, UNESCO, Paris.
Westin, C. (1998) 'Temporal and spatial aspects of multiculturality: reflections on the meaning of time and space in relation to the blurred boundaries of multicultural societies', in Bauböck, R. and Rundell, J. (eds), *Blurred Boundaries: Migration, Ethnicity, Citizenship*, Ashgate, Aldershot.

2   In sociological and political debate, multiculturalism refers to a particular political system or specific policies aimed at granting and ensuring equal dignity (EQUALITY) to different cultures and at fighting discrimination against those belonging to specific ethnic/cultural minorities.

From this perspective the principles associated with multiculturalism – namely protection of the right of all persons to see their values and culture respected – fall within the scope of the universal principles which form the core values of Western democracies, as set out as early as in the French Revolution charter and the American Declaration of Independence.

Nevertheless, from another perspective multiculturalism can appear to be at odds with some of democracy's basic values, which tend to consider institutions as value-free and neutral, and blind to cultural diversity:

> our lack of identification with institutions that serve public purposes, the impersonality of public institutions, is the price that citizens should be willing to pay for living in a society that treats us all as equals, regardless of our particular ethnic, religious, racial, or sexual identities. . . . On this view, our freedom and equality as citizens refer only to our common characteristics – our universal needs, regardless of our particular cultural identities. (Gutmann, 1994: 4)

In reality, given that cultural diversity does not exist in a vacuum, minority values have less chance of survival, because of the sometimes implicitly imposed ASSIMILATION of persons belonging to ethnic minorities and of migrants. In this sense the adjustment process tends to produce cultural and linguistic homogeneity, which can be experienced by members of minority groups as a devaluation of their culture and thus of their IDENTITY by the majority culture:

> I experienced first-hand the influence exerted by poverty, discrimination, and the perception of one's culture and language as inferior. Speaking only Spanish when I entered first grade, I was immediately confronted with the arduous task of learning a second language while my already quite developed native language was all but ignored. Over 40 years later, I still recall the frustration of groping for words I did not know to express thoughts I could say very capably in Spanish. Equally vivid are memories of some teachers' expectations that, because of our language and cultural differences, my classmates and I would not do well in school. (Nieto, 1996: 2)

Sociological and psychological literature contains many such experiences. The growing awareness of harassment – as exercised by the majority towards ethnic, sexual or handicapped minority groups – triggered civil rights movements in the 1960s and 1970s, which started the process of political recognition of the need for the empowerment of minorities (EMPOWERMENT–DISEMPOWERMENT), of which multiculturalism is such a fundamental aspect.

Studies in this area have shown that rapid assimilation of members of cultural minorities – with the associated devaluation of their culture of origin and pressure to take on new values – can be experienced as traumatic and have disruptive effects in sociological and psychological terms for both the individuals and groups involved (SOCIAL DISORGANIZATION).

> A new land requires a new life, new ways of life. But in learning the new ways, the immigrant is slow, awkward, a greenhorn, quickly outpaced by his own children. He is likely to feel inferior, and his children are likely to confirm the feeling. But this sense of inferiority, so painful to him, is also a disaster for them. It cuts them adrift in a world where they are never likely to feel entirely at home. (Walzer, 1982: 15)

Such devaluation or even strong rejection of minority cultures can obviously be considered to be at the root of many phenomena of marginalization and social deviance. Studies similar to the above have also been carried out in France on second generation migrants from North Africa; these show comparable dramatic effects on family and social disorganization, with a consequent growth in juvenile delinquency and marginalization.

The natural conclusion to be drawn from this is that promoting the value of the cultural and social organization of young people's original homeland could have a positive social impact and counteract the effects connected to exposure to discrimination, the under-rating of their cultural values experienced by newcomers, the fragmentation of their social and family structures, and the undermining of their self and group identity.

It is obvious that the goals of multicultural policies and education programmes are to counteract precisely such effects. However, while the aim to create an environment in which all cultures are treated with equal respect – provided they do not expound any values which could be threatening to the freedom and safety of others – may seem relatively straightforward, their implementation seems to pose more problems than it solves:

Apart from ceding each of us the same rights as all other citizens, what does respecting people as equals entail? In what sense should our identities as men and women, African-Americans, Asian-Americans, or Native-Americans, Christians, Jews, or Muslims, English or French Canadians *publicly* matter? (Gutmann, 1994: 4)

The application of multicultural schemes is particularly controversial in the area of education, where students belonging to ethnic minorities may be discriminated against on the grounds of lack of proficiency in the language and culture of the majority (BILINGUAL-ISM). This not only limits the chances of minorities of climbing the social ladder and escaping conditions of inferiorization, but also tends to reinforce the hierarchy of values which grants lesser relevance to minority cultures. From this perspective, changes in curricula need to be implemented as a strategy to recognize the proper academic value of the cultures and expressions of minority groups, which may not be the same as those of the hegemonic groups. However, objections are often raised to

changes in core courses on the grounds that these could lower education standards by subjecting curricula to the 'standardlessness of relativism, the tyranny of the social sciences, light-weight trendiness, and a host of related intellectual and political evils' (Gutmann, 1994: 13). [R. B.]

Gutmann, A. (ed.) (1994) *Multiculturalism*, Princeton University Press, Princeton, NJ.
Nieto, S. (1996) *Affirming Diversity*, 2nd edn, Longman, New York.
Thomas, W. I., Znaniecki, F. (1918–20) *The Polish Peasant in Europe and America*, University of Chicago Press, Chicago and Boston.
Walzer, M. (1982) 'Pluralism in political perspective', in Walzer, M., Kantowicz, E. T., Higham, J., Harrington, M. (eds) (1982), *The Politics of Ethnicity*, The Belknap Press of Harvard University Press, Cambridge, MA and London, UK.

MULTIETHNIC (It. *multietnico*; Fr. *multiethnique*; Ger. *multiethnisch*)

The term 'multiethnic' from the Latin *multus*, (much, many) and the Greek *ethnikós* (from *éthnos*, people), describes a social whole made up of ETHNIC components that interact with each other and organize their behaviour on the basis of a perceived ethno-cultural diversity (DIVERSITY–SIMILARITY), claimed from within the group or imposed from outside. Closed groups such as families (FAMILY), school classes, trade unions, associations or similar, can be defined as multiethnic when they contain individuals who attach some importance to ethnic factors in their social interactions.

According to some writers, ETHNICITY is primordial (Geertz, 1973), i.e. made up of inherited elements which in turn form the nucleus of social identity. Other writers maintain that, on the contrary, ethnicity is situational, i.e. that individual or collective behaviour is organized on an ethnic basis in only some contexts, and this factor coexists with other elements (Mitchell, 1956; Barth, 1969; Wallman, 1980). With this interpretation, 'multiethnic' can be applied to many cases of identity which arise from those ACCULTURATION processes where members of different cultures meet. These shades of meaning make the concept problematical as by its very nature it is continually being redefined to fit new social structures (Banks, 1996).

As far as Western Europe is concerned, the adjective 'multiethnic' is commonly understood to describe a new phenomenon, that of the coexistence of different ethnic groups as a result of the immigration (MIGRATION) processes which affected various countries during the 1960s. As the history of Europe shows, this continent has long since been characterized by migratory movements which have created an extraordinary mix of PEOPLE and cultures, obstructed more by the political restraints of NATION states than by any natural barriers (Foucher, 1993). Basques, Catalans, Friesians, Bretons, Saami, Romani (ROMA), Corsicans and Sardinians are just some of the ethnolinguistic minorities (ETHNIC MINORITY) whose aspirations, together with those of their immigrants and their descendants, create the need to confront the questions posed by multicultural societies (MULTICULTURALISM) (Rex, 1996). [P. S.]

Banks, M. (1996) *Ethnicity: Anthropological Constructions*, Routledge, London.
Barth, F. (ed.) (1969) *Ethnic Groups and Boundaries: The Social Organisation of Culture Difference*, George Allen & Unwin, London.
Foucher, M. (1993) *Fragments d'Europe*, Fayard, Paris.
Geertz, C. (1973) *The Interpretation of Cultures*, Basic Books, New York.
Mitchell, C. (1956) *The Kalela Dance: Aspects of Social Relationships among Urban Africans in Northern Rhodesia*, Manchester University Press, Manchester.
Rex, J. (1996) *Ethnic Minorities in the Modern Nation State*, New York St Martin's Press/Basingstoke, Macmillan in association with Centre for Research in Ethnic Relations, University of Warwick.
Wallman, S. (1980) 'The boundaries of "race": processes of ethnicity in England', *Man*, 13: 200–217.

MUTILATION (It. *mutilazioni*; Fr. *mutilation*; Ger. *Verstümmelung*)

The term derives from the Latin adjective of unknown origin *mutilum* (cut, truncated) and indicates the 'crude and disfiguring removal' of a part of the body, and the permanent, invalidating or painful alteration of certain organs. The most widespread mutilation, practised for cultural or religious reasons, is connected with initiation rites (RITE), which are therefore acceptable to and desired by those who receive them and their social group, although such acceptance may be due to the inability to resist or to revoke consent owing to the youth of the subjects involved. In addition to CIRCUMCISION, another kind of initiation to puberty involves the sub-incision or longitudinal incision of the penis from the urinary meatus to the scrotum, up to the urethra. This initiation is practised by Australian Aborigines. Another form of initiation mutilation of the male genital apparatus is the extirpation of a testicle, which creates an artificial monorchidism, a practice which was widely in use, for example, among the *ianejro* people of western Ethiopia.

Mutilation is also carried out on the female body, the most widespread type being clitoridectomy and INFIBULATION. As well as in some African countries, these mutilations are practised in Malaysia, Indonesia, the Philippines, Pakistan and among the Indian populations of Venezuela and Peru.

Mutilation with different significances, which does not involve the sexual organs, is also practised among other peoples. Some indigenous Australian populations ritually extract the incisor teeth of adolescent males. Some criminal associations, such as the Japanese *yakuza*, amputate the phalanx of a finger from the hands of their affiliates. Practices by which the heads of newborn babies are artificially deformed by means of special apparels and bonds, such as those in use in Melanesia and Central Africa, can also be classed as mutilation. For reasons of aesthetics and of social prestige, the feet of upper-class Chinese girls used to be bandaged to impede their growth. Practices such as tooth filing and the piercing of the nasal septum, the nostrils, the earlobes and pinna and the lips – sometimes coupled with the introduction of sticks or disks, such as in the case of the 'labret women' of the basin of Chari, in Chad – are carried out for the same reasons. Tattoos, which – for aesthetic and cultural reasons – are becoming widespread in Western society, are a derivation of a similar practice which has long been in use among Eskimos and American Indians, and may also be considered a kind of mutilation as they involve the irreversible colouring and/or stripping of the skin.

All mutilations imply multiple determination, involving religious symbolism, sexual symbolism and the enhancement of certain physical characteristics for exhibitionism or exaltation of power. Other reasons behind mutilations can be seen in adults' hostile drives towards children; furthermore the fear that their minors might escape impels adults to mark them irreversibly with symbols of belonging. Western CULTURE has generally chosen not to mark the human body, attempting instead to perfect it through gymnastics and aesthetic treatment. Many ritual and symbolic functions in the West have instead been fulfilled by clothing, from the priest's habit through the uniforms of soldiers to the universal or particular impositions of fashion. Although it can be said that Western culture has abandoned early practices requiring the mutilation or permanent marking of the body, some practices, such as ear-piercing, have continued in the name of fashion rather than for any religious belief. Modern Western societies are currently witnessing a new and increasing tendency to mark or in some way mutilate the body as a sign of cultural diversity (DIVERSITY–SIMILARITY). Extreme kinds of piercing mixed with tattoos and other forms of body mutilation are now commonly used among young people as a symbol of their radical opposition to society or as a way of showing their support of a form of fashion strongly influenced by African black culture and Rastafari. Western culture considers some of these practices to be purely exotic (EXOTICISM), while others give rise to problems regarding their acceptance or refusal on cultural, moral or even sanitary bases. Mutilation practices which may be considered unacceptable when employed by an ethnic group (ETHNIC MINORITY) living in a society which regards such mutilation as bizarre, undesirable or barbaric, may have quite a different significance when seen as the dominant practice of a country or region. Thus, mutilation may be an important factor in the way immigration is perceived and in ethnic or RACE RELATIONS. In this sense, the way mutilation is viewed might be compared with the way in which certain minority religious rituals, such as the slaughtering of animals for food or religious purposes, are perceived by the majority. The problem which emerges lies in the contrast between the dangers of ETHNOCENTRISM and those of a noncommittal CULTURAL RELATIVISM. [S. G.]

Macklin, R. (1999) *Against Relativism*, Oxford University Press, Oxford.
Van Gennep, A. (1961) *The Rites of Passages* (1911), University of Chicago Press, Chicago.

MYTH (It. *mito*; Fr. *mythe*; Ger. *Mythus*) From the Greek *mythos* (narration, story-telling). Although the term has several meanings, that which is most relevant to the socio-psychological field refers to those tales which narrate human and supernatural events, and which, although they may sometimes overlap with fairy tales or legends, are ostensibly explanatory or historical in nature, generally with reference to events in the distant past of which all trace has disappeared.

All cultures possess a more or less organic mythological tradition, which often serves as an inestimable source of artistic inspiration for the production of works of great value, as exemplified by the heritage of Greek mythology. In the same way all religions, including the positive religions (those religions – Christianity, Islam and Judaism – which trace their origins to the teachings of great religious innovators who spoke as the organs of a divine revelation), originate in mythology, and only later develop into organized theological thought and dogma.

According to Müller, myths could be explained as a by-product of the development of language, and mythmaking is a 'disease of language' arising at the early stages of linguistic evolution, where words that illustrated particularly important concepts were elevated to mythological proportions (e.g. sky = Father Sky [Zeus]). Other scholars, such as Cassirer, sought to explain myths as the product of a kind of pre-logical, anti-empirical thinking, distinct from scientific thought. More recently, the relationship between myth and RITE has become the object of scientific debate in an attempt – which has proved to be fruitless – to determine which originated from the other.

Psychoanalysis – as is evident from the work of its founding fathers – has granted much attention to myths, seeing them as the conscious manifestation of fantasies and desires locked in the UNCONSCIOUS. According to Freud,

> Like Oedipus, we live in ignorance of these wishes, repugnant to morality, which have been forced upon us by Nature, and after their revelation we may all of us well seek to close our eyes to the scene of our childhood. . . . To-day, just as then, many men dream of having sexual relations with their mothers, and speak of the fact with indignation and astonishment. It is clearly the key to the tragedy and the complement to the dream of the dreamer's father being dead. The story of Oedipus is the reaction of the imagination to these two typical dreams. (1900: 263–264)

Jung believes that myths express archetypal figures: 'the libido that will not flow into life at the right time regresses to the mythical world of the archetypes, where it activates images which, since the remotest times, have expressed the non-human life of the gods, whether of the upper world or of the lower. . . . Herein lay the vital importance of myths: they explained to the bewildered human being what was going on in his unconscious and why he was held fast' (1952: 308).

Thus myths do not just play an important role in the early or 'PRIMITIVE' stages of a society, but retain a permanent and active presence in contemporary societies. Here they are expressed through rituals which, although they may no longer hold any conscious significance for individuals, are able to evoke the unconscious mythological memories of a society. This has led many scholars to consider the ways in which myths and representations continue to shape social phenomena in contemporary societies. The semiologist Roland Barthes views myth as a metalanguage which gives contingency the appearance of eternity and historical intention natural justification. In this sense, according to Barthes, myth is depoliticized speech, which serves to purify and render innocent that which it speaks of by providing a 'natural' image of historical reality.

Myths are a powerful element of group cohesion, providing a strong feeling of belonging. The power attributed to myths goes well beyond the fact that they are a shared cultural element; their strength lies in the capacity to fascinate and to access the deeper unconscious of individuals. In particular, myths obviously play a vital role in shaping national, group and ethnic identities (IDENTITY) and in ethnic and RACE RELATIONS; although not all myths can be said to be xenophobic (XENOPHOBIA), often one of the strengthening factors for group cohesion is an element of opposition to other groups – which may be based on a myth of origins that presumes the superiority of the group in question over other peoples, with obvious racist implications.

A prime example of this is the Aryan myth on the origin of the NATION, which contributed to the rise of ANTI-SEMITISM (Poliakov, 1971). Similar myths continue to appear or to be revived creating different, inevitably sectarian, forms of RACISM. According to Poliakov, there is no national representation which is not a symbolic bringer of conflict.

Many authors have pointed out the fact that all nations seem to create their own myth of origins in an attempt to provide a sense of common identity and cultural uniformity and continuity. According to Homi K. Bhabha (1997), the boundaries of nations are defined by myth and as such are only constructions of the mind.

On the other hand, some comparativist scholars have found in myth yet another indication of the essential oneness of humanity. Malinowski sees myths as having the function of justifying the structures of social relationships, rooting them in a mythical and sacred past. These socio-anthropological theories were also taken up by Lévi-Strauss (1955, 2000), whose structural analyses of myth in relation to social organization led him to conclude that the mythologies of different geographical areas all shared common structures or forms. This he considered an indication of the essential similarity of all human beings and therefore a refutation of racist ideologies based on differences between human races. [S. G.]

Barthes, R. (1993) *Mythologies*, Vintage Books, London.
Bhabha, H. K. (ed.) (1997) *Nation and Narration*, Routledge, London.
Cassirer, E. (1955) *Philosophy of Symbolic Forms: Mythical Thought*, Yale University Press, New Haven.

Freud, S. (1900) *The Interpretation of Dreams*, SE, 4–5. (See reference on p. 332)

Jung, C. G. (1952) *Symbols of Transformations*, Routledge & Kegan Paul, London.

Jung, C. G., Kerenyi, C. (1969) *Essays on a Science of Mythology*, Princeton University Press, Princeton, NJ.

Lévi-Strauss, C. (1955) *Myth and Meaning*, Schocken Books, New York.

Lévi-Strauss, C. (2000) *The Structural Anthropology*, Basic Books, New York.

Malinowski, B. (1992) *Magic, Science and Religion*, Souvenir Press, London.

Müller, F. M. (1861) *Lectures on Science of Language*, Longman, London.

Poliakov, L. (1971) *The Aryan Myth: A History of Racist and Nationalist Ideas in Europe*, Greenwood Press, London.

NARCISSISM

NARCISSISM (It. *narcisismo*; Fr. *narcissisme*; Ger. *Narzissmus*) The love of an individual for him or herself or his or her own image, with reference to the myth of Narcissus (see below). The psychoanalytic usage of the term, now in widespread use, refers to a pathological way of relating which can be seen to be at the root of UNCONSCIOUS refusal and inferiorization mechanisms and of certain manifestations of INTOLERANCE.

The term 'narcissism' was introduced in psychiatry at the end of the nineteenth century – later to be adopted in the field of psychoanalysis – by Havelock Ellis (1898), to describe a form of sexuality based on the individual's own body, with reference to the Greek myth of Narcissus, a handsome shepherd who fell in love with his own image reflected in a pool and subsequently drowned trying to kiss it. Freud (1914) spoke of a primary narcissism of children, beginning at birth when their *libido* is concentrated on themselves before being directed outwards. Although at first Freud distinguished the libido from *self-eroticism*, where sexuality is directed towards a particular part of the body, he later (1922) eliminated this distinction, stating that an individual's narcissism actually began in the uterus when the foetus has no sense stimuli and is thus incapable of object relationships. Freud then postulated that a secondary narcissism, when the individual turns his/her libido towards him/herself rather than outwards, follows the initial primary form. Melanie Klein (1950) opposed the idea of newborn children being incapable of object relationships, affirming that they immediately distinguish between *good* and *bad objects*. According to Lacan (1949), narcissism occurs during the *mirror stage*, when the child's *Self* sees its own image as that of another and structures his/her understanding of his/her body through this perception. Kohut (1971) speaks of a narcissistic phenomenon called the *Great Self*, which he sees as an indication of fragility of the ego resulting from a lack of harmonization between the Self and the social group. However, Kohut does not deny that narcissism also has a positive function as a source of creativity. Other authors describe narcissism as a defence mechanism common to all human beings (Gindro, 1993), which operates to shield the person from the frustrations of the world by negating the latter and shifting the focus on to the self. If exaggerated to a pathological degree, this mechanism can result in a perverted relationship to the world.

The earlier use of the term 'narcissism' in psychoanalysis – as strictly connected with the psychosexual development of the individual – was later extended, even by Freud himself, to include certain processes which have been identified as bearing a relevance to social phenomena:

> all the relations which have hitherto been the chief subject of psycho-analytic research may claim to be considered as social phenomena; and in this respect they may be contrasted with certain other processes, described by us as *narcissistic*, in which the satisfaction of the instincts is partially or totally withdrawn from the influence of other people. (1921: 69)

Despite being an intrinsic element of relationship dynamics, narcissistic processes are one of the factors of disintegration which hinder positive interaction between human beings and as such must be considered if an understanding is to be reached of the unconscious dynamics underlying perverse and inauthentic means of relating to others, of which intolerance is a prime example:

> In the undisguised antipathies and aversion which people feel towards strangers with whom they have to do, we may recognize the expression of self love – of narcissism. This self love works for the self assertion of the individual, and behaves as though the occurrence of any divergence from his own particular lines of development involved a criticism of them and a demand for their alteration. . . . But the whole of this intolerance vanishes . . . as the result of the formation of a group, and in a group. . . . Such a limitation of narcissism can . . . only be produced by one factor, a libidinal tie with other people. Love for oneself knows only one barrier – love for others, love for objects. (Freud, 1921: 102)

From a psychoanalytical point of view, intolerance is an expression of the inability of an individual to cope and interact positively with the differences made manifest by another person (DIVERSITY–SIMILARITY). Contact with differences is perceived as an invasion of the narcissistic sphere, and the individual who feels thus threatened reacts by establishing distance from those who display such differences, in the first place by depicting them as strangers (FOREIGNER), and often exalting him/herself by belittling the other.

The narcissistic sphere which the individual is thus moved to protect is all the more vulnerable when his/her subjectivity is precarious. In this sense Daniel Sibony (1997) describes racial intolerance ('l'horreur de voir le même devenir différent') as IDENTITY hatred deriving from a narcissistic impasse,

symptomatic of the racist individual's (or racist group's) inability to find a better solution to the feeling of profound precariousness of his or her origins and the painful instability of his or her sense of belonging – the original 'wannabe', or lack of being. Being confronted with another who comes from a different country, belongs to a different sex, displays a different sexual preference, or belongs to a different ethnic or religious group, are all situations which can trigger unconscious denial mechanisms, of which intolerance is the most obvious expression. However, in contradiction to what might be assumed, psychoanalytic research has shown that the greatest threat to the narcissistic sphere in which the individual recognizes him/herself – and which is strengthened in the group – seems to be posed by minor differences in a context of general resemblance. The fact that indefinable differences lead to intolerance and violent PREJUDICE was repeatedly stated by Freud in his references to 'narcissism of minor difference'. He says that 'It would be tempting to pursue this idea and to derive from this "narcissism of minor difference" the hostility which in every human relation we see fighting successfully against feelings of fellowship and overpowering the commandment that all men should love one another' (1918: 199).

Sociological research has also highlighted the disproportionately high number of clashes which arise from relationships of proximity (a model is provided in the chapter dedicated to contrasts in Simmel, 1908) and has shown how differences are the object of fascination when they lie within the realm of distant EXOTICISM, but give rise to violent forms of conflict when incarnate in individuals or groups with whom a relationship of proximity is to be established. Thus, as such intolerance does not stem from absolute difference but rather from affinity, it is manifest in those situations where it is more difficult for individuals or groups to distinguish themselves from other individuals or groups who have become less strange, which is when the narcissistic sphere feels most threatened. In such cases, acceptance of the other, i.e. TOLER-ANCE, would be tantamount to the individual accepting facets of him or herself which he or she does not accept: the disturbing image of our 'double' mentioned by Jean Bertrand Pontalis (Jaquard and Pontalis 1984–85), or the unconscious *per se* mentioned by Julia Kristeva (1988). According to this premise, the reaction of hostility and refusal of the other, as occurs with RACISM, is manifest when there is a substantial similarity with the other: a perception which produces a sort of narcissistic checkmate (Gindro, 1991). [S. G.]

Freud, S. (1914 *On Narcissism*, SE, XIV, pp. 69–102.
Freud, S. (1918) *The Taboo of Virginity (Contributions to the Psychology of Love III)*, in Strachey, J. (ed.), *The Standard Edition of the Complete Psychological Works of Sigmund Freud [SE]*, Vol. XI, pp. 191–208, The Hogarth Press, London.
Freud, S. (1921) *Group Psychology and the Analysis of the Ego*, SE, XVIII, pp. 67–143.
Freud, S. (1922) 'Two encyclopedia articles', *SE*, XVIII, pp. 235–262.
Freud, S. (1934–38) *Moses and Monotheism*, SE, XXIII, pp. 3–137.
Gindro, S. (1991) 'Inconscio sociale e diversità', in Gindro, S., Melotti, U. *Il mondo delle diversità*, Edizioni Psicoanalisi Contro, Roma.
Gindro, S. (1993) *L'oro della psicoanalisi*, Alfredo Guida Editore, Napoli.
Havelock Ellis, H. (1898) *Autoerotism, a Psychological Study*.
Jaquard, A., Pontalis, J. B. (1984–85) 'Entretien: une tête qui ne convient pas', *Le Genre Humain*, 11: *La societé face aux racisme*, S.15–28, Paris.
Klein, M. (1950) *Narrative of a Child Analysis*, Basic Books, New York.
Kohut, H. (1971) *The Analysis of the Self*, Int. Univ. Press, New York.
Kristeva, J. (1988) *Étrangers à nous-mêmes*, Fayard, Paris.
Lacan, J. (1949) 'Le stade du miroir comme formateur de la fonction du Je, telle qu'elle nous est révélée dans l'expérience psychanalytique', *Revue Française de Psychanalyse*, 13(4): 449–455.
Sibony, D. (1997) *Le 'Racisme' ou la haine identitaire*, Christian Bourgois Éditeur, Paris.
Simmel, G. (1908) *Soziologie. Untersuchungen über die Formen der Vergesellschaftung*, Dunker & Humblot, Leipzig.

NATION

(It. *nazione*; Fr. *nation*; Ger. *Nation*) From the Latin *natio* (tribe, race), the term 'nation' is usually taken to mean a group of people united by culture, language, traditions and common interest. Such a definition can only be tentative, though, as it merely explains how the term is used in everyday language, and suggests some of the echoes it has in the social UNCONSCIOUS. The many different uses of the word, and the political, social and psychological importance it has taken on, combine to make the concept of 'nation' one of the most problematic in political science.

In the Middle Ages, the term referred to a range of groups: university students coming from the same area; the delegates from various European territorial areas attending the Council of Constance in 1414; an administrative area; a city; and finally the members of a guild. According to historian Federico Chabod, it was in the eighteenth century that the concept of 'nation', in its modern sense, came of age (through the defence of liberty and other Helvetic traditions put forward by Swiss historians such as von

Muralt and Bodmer). In the latter half of the eighteenth century, the German philosopher Herder proposed a definition of 'nation' as a distinct entity having certain characteristics, of which the most important were blood, territory and language. French Enlightenment thinkers like Rousseau used the concept to contest authority, and subsequently the French Revolution caused legitimate sovereignty to pass from the monarchy to the nation (as embodied in the National Assembly). The revolutionary period also saw an active programme to create a sense of national COMMUNITY, for example by means of language, schooling and national ceremonies, which met with considerable success. As the defence of the Revolution, the Napoleonic victories and the reactive nationalism that emerged in Britain and elsewhere revealed, the French, by appealing to the 'nation', had tapped into a potent force for political mobilization. Indeed the issue of nation has been at the centre of political conflicts and developments ever since (though there are some signs that we may, in the twenty-first century, be moving into a post-national age).

In the Romantic period, the idea of 'nation' firmly took root and became a watchword of organizations and political movements. According to Chabod, 'nation' came to be understood in two possible ways, naturalistic and voluntary (1967: 31). In its naturalistic form, it easily came to be identified with RACE and an integral form of NATIONALISM that saw nations as biological communities struggling against one another for survival. The Nazi vision was, of course, an extreme example of this view. In its voluntary form, the nation was recognized as a group sharing traditions and language, but also legitimate political aspirations to self-rule. In 1861 the Italian nationalist Giuseppe Mazzini wrote that a nation is a set of principles, beliefs and aspirations towards a common end, accepted as a basis of brotherhood by the great majority of citizens (1972: 946–947). A similar idea of nation inspired Woodrow Wilson's 14 points of January 1918: in the aftermath of the First World War, Wilson called for self-determination of nationalities and a redrawing of European boundaries along national lines. As subsequent history in Europe and elsewhere has shown, this noble principle is vexed by the very problem of determining what a nation is (and the fact that nations, however defined, often overlap geographically).

There have been countless attempts to define 'nation' over the past two centuries. To take one example, Ernest Gellner proposes two conditions for identifying a nation: (a) two people are of the same nation if and only if they share the same CULTURE, where culture in turn means a system of ideas and signs and associations and ways of behaving and communicating; (b) two people are of the same nation if and only if they recognize each other as belonging to the same nation (1983). Gellner's definition attempts to get at that general perception of nation implied in the opening of this entry without reference to territory, history, race or other elements often considered essential to a nation (BORDER, ETHNICITY). In the recent debate over nation Gellner falls in the modernist camp of those who see nations as inventions or constructs, entities based on perception rather than blood or history. According to the modernists, people come to believe they are part of a nation in response to schooling, propaganda, television, political leaders and so on. Benedict Anderson's *Imagined Communities* is perhaps the most important modernist statement in this regard. Its title well sums up the modernist characterization of nation. The alternative or primordialist view, more typical of late nineteenth- and early twentieth-century thinkers, sees nations as real things, based in common traditions, common language and a shared homeland, as well as possibly having common genetic and racial characteristics. A compromise position is that of the 'ethnic continuationists' who agree with the modernists that nations really only came into existence in the past couple of centuries, but also recognize deeper historical roots. A. D. Smith, for example, identifies six components: (a) a collective name; (b) a common myth of descent; (c) a shared history; (d) a distinctive shared culture; (e) an association with a specific territory; (f) a sense of solidarity, which form the basis of an *ethnie*, and it is out of the *ethnie* that a nation is formed (1986) (MYTH). [M. B., C. I.]

Anderson, B. (1991) *Imagined Communities: Reflections on the Origin and Spread of Nationalism*, Verso, London and New York.
Chabod, F. (1967) *L'idea di nazione*, Laterza, Roma and Bari.
Cohen, W. (1996) 'Nationalism in Europe', in Bodnar, J. (ed.), *Bonds of Affection: Americans Define their Patriotism*, Princeton University Press, Princeton, NJ, pp. 323–339.
Gellner, E. (1983) *Nations and Nationalism*, Cornell University Press, Ithaca, NY.
Mazzini, G. (1972) 'Dell'unità italiana' (1861), in *Scritti politici*, UTET, Torino.
Smith, A. D. (1986) *The Ethnic Origins of Nations*, Blackwell, Oxford and New York.

NATIONAL CHARACTER (It. *carattere nazionale*; Fr. *caractère national*; Ger. *Nationalcharakter*) 'National character' refers to all those traits, behaviour, attitudes and ways of thinking which are common to most of the adults comprising a given nation's population, as distinguished from those of the populations of other nations.

The belief that every population has its own character is an ancient one, and was certainly already common among the ancient Greeks and Romans; Herodotus and Thucydides thought that every *ethnos* (people) (ETHNICITY) had its own *ethos* (character), and the same belief is expounded in Caesar's *Commentaries* and in Tacitus' *Germania*. However, although these works do describe the characteristics of various peoples, they do not describe 'national' characteristics, being prior to the concept of NATION itself.

The idea of national character as we intend it today only began to take shape in the eighteenth century, when the modern idea of nation was defined and later as anthropology began to structure itself as a science. National character was the object of Montesquieu's ethnopsychological studies, while Hume devoted an essay to the subject and Kant addressed the issue in his *Anthropology from a Pragmatic Point of View*. This line of study continued up to Herbert Spencer's *Descriptive Sociology* (1873–81) and Wilhelm Wundt's *Volkerpsychologie* (1900–20).

During the Second World War, the study of both friends and foes became intensified and the analysis of national characters developed into a field of study in its own right. The anthropologist Margaret Mead recalls that a great number of anthropologists working for the US government in 1943 concerned themselves with the study of national character. The contributions of anthropology to the study of the relationship between CULTURE and character and on national characteristics, although debated and criticized, nevertheless remain a point of reference in the field. Concepts such as those of the basic personality structure and the modal personality still bear great relevance to the study of national character in anthropology and social psychology.

According to Linton (1945), the basic personality structure is the common denominator of the characters of the people sharing a culture, while the modal personality, as described by Du Bois (1944), is the type of character most frequently found in a given group. In 1949, Gorer and Rickman, taking as a starting point the theories of Freudian psychoanalysis, postulated a correlation between educational systems and adult personality. In addition, several studies were carried out on the character of individual nations, for example of the Japanese (Benedict, 1946), the French (Métraux and Mead, 1954), the Americans and the English (Gorer, 1948, 1955), and the Russians (Gorer and Rickman, 1949).

Various definitions of the characters of different peoples can be often heard in everyday conversation, e.g. the English are reserved, the Spanish high-spirited, the Germans disciplined. At Princeton, when asked to describe Italians, students answered without much hesitation: 'artistic, impulsive, passionate' (Bollati, 1979: 950).

These kinds of judgements go to form 'national stereotypes', often perpetuated through sayings or proverbs, and they 'are born of particular circumstances, of specific political situations, or of widespread perceptions in a given context. Once formed, these judgements are those which tend to be adopted by conformist public opinion' (Tentori, 1987: 131).

The distinction between 'national stereotype' and 'national character' is rather blurred and hard to define.

Tentori, for example, quoting the differences in national characters defined by Kant in his *Anthropology from a Pragmatic Point of View*, maintains that it is

> difficult to speak of one's own people and of other peoples without falling into stereotyping and being swayed by likes and dislikes, as in this we are influenced not only by our own ethnicity, but also by our own social position and particular cultural formation. This means that it is impossible to give an unprejudiced description of the overall characteristics of any people, as all nations are multiform and comprise different social and cultural parts, and are the result of complex actions and reactions to historical events. (Tentori, 1987: 139)

Several objections have been raised to the concept of national character, starting with the impossibility of generalizing and the need to take into account variations within national groups, as well as changes in national characteristics occurring over time. Such categorizations are regarded as encouraging ethnocentric attitudes (ETHNOCENTRISM), by perpetuating inflexible and undiscriminating definitions of national character and inherently racist conceptions of national psychological characteristics. In this light national character is considered to be nothing more than a stereotype adopted in order to stigmatize, discriminate or exploit, and to ignite and justify hostility (Harris, 1968; Tentori, 1987). [M. B.]

Benedict, R. (1946) *The Chrysanthemum and the Sword*, Houghton Mifflin, Boston.

Bollati, G. (1979) 'L'italiano', in *Storia d'Italia*, Vol. I, *I caratteri originali*, Einaudi, Torino.

Du Bois, C. (1944) *The People of Alor: A Social-Psychological Study of an East Indian Island*, University of Minnesota Press, Minneapolis.

Gorer, G. (1948) *The American People, A Study in National Character*, Norton, New York.

Gorer G. (1955) *Exploring English Character*, Criterion Books, New York.

Gorer G., Rickman, J. (1949) *The People of Great Russia: A Psychological Study*, Cresset Press, London.

Harris, M. (1968) *The Rise of Anthropological Theory*, Crowell, New York.

Inkelees, A., Levinson, D. J. (1969) 'National character: the study of modal personality and sociocultural systems', in Linzey, G., Aronson, E. (eds), *The Handbook of Social Psychology*, Vol. IV, Addison-Wesley, Cambridge, MA.

Linton, R. (1945) *The Cultural Background of Personality*, Appleton-Century-Crofts, New York.

Metraux, E., Mead, M. (1954) *Themes in French Culture*, Stanford University Press, Stanford, CA.

Tentori, T. (1987) *Il rischio della certezza. Pregiudizio, potere, cultura*, Studium, Roma.

NATIONAL PREFERENCE (It. *preferenza nazionale*; Fr. *préférence nationale*; Ger. *nationale Bevorzugung*)

The expression 'national preference' is a French coinage and describes an attitude or policy which favours autochthons at the expense of immigrants (MIGRANT) or foreigners (FOREIGNER). It was introduced into contemporary political language by the Nouvelle Droite's Club de l'Horloge in the 1980s and gained general notoriety when picked up by Jean-Marie Le Pen and his right-wing party, the Front National (FN); it was included in that party's 1991 '50 measures against immigration'. Le Pen and his followers argue that French policy should reflect 'national preference' in areas like housing, unemployment and the awarding of social benefits (for example child subsidies). The 'French' should be hired before the non-French, receive preferential treatment from municipal administrations, and so on.

National preference raises a series of problems. The first is that it requires a definition of who is French, as Le Pen's ideas clearly extend beyond simple questions of CITIZENSHIP to a national or racial conception. The second problem is that the introduction of such a policy would violate both international agreements to which France is a signatory and French laws (a problem FN administrators recognize). Thirdly, national preference is fundamentally at odds with French egalitarian and republican traditions (and also with the often discredited French model of immigrant ASSIMILATION), though FN politicians contest this point. In some sense the concept received official sanction in 1998 when former Gaullist Prime Minister Edouard Balladur called for a special commission to consider the FN's proposed policy of national preference.

National preference is uniquely French of course only in name. It might well describe other examples of XENOPHOBIA or discrimination (RACIAL DISCRIMINATION) present in the politics and policies of Europe and elsewhere. The distinction between indigenous citizen and foreigner is already enshrined in legislation that ensures a sort of national preference in a number of areas; for example, citizenship is required for many posts in the public sector and almost always in order to enjoy voting rights. A degree of discrimination between nationals and foreigners then already exists, though it is the position of those favouring national preference that introduction of discrimination to much broader areas is a solution to the problems besetting the nation, such as unemployment and housing shortages.

If it is accepted that certain equal rights exist for all people (EQUALITY), irrespective of citizenship (as laid down in the various European constitutions – including the French – and international instruments), then national preference easily verges on discrimination based on ETHNICITY, nationality (NATION), RACE or religion. [C. I.]

Ben Jelloun, T. (1984) *Hospitalité française*, Le Seuil, Paris.

Camus, Y., Monzat, R. (1992) *Les Droites nationales et radicales en France*, Presses Universitaries de Lyon, Lyon.

Club de l'Horloge (1985) *La Préférence nationale. Réponse à l'immigration*, Albin Michel, Paris.

Griffin, R. (2000) 'Plus ça change! The Fascist legacy in the metapolitics of the Nouvelle Droite', in Arnold, E. (ed.), *The Development of the Radical Right in France 1890–1995*, Routledge, London.

Revelli, M. (1996) *La Destra Nazionalista*, Il Saggiatore – Flammarion, Milano.

Taguieff, P. A. (1987) *La Force du préjugé*, La Découverte, Paris.

NATIONALISM

(It. *nazionalismo*; Fr. *nationalisme*; Ger. *Nationalismus*) The term refers to an ideology which emphasizes the formation and assertion of a NATION by making it the main objective of political action. Furthermore, just as there are many different kinds of nation – modern, pre-modern and postmodern, rationalistic, romantic and positivist (Melotti, 2000) – there are also many different forms of nationalism.

It can be said that nationalism entered the European political scene with the French Revolution in 1789. During this period, the MYTH of the *Grande Nation* fuelled the many – first defensive and then offensive – warlike initiatives of the 'armed population'. This myth soon extended like a great revolutionary force to other countries of the European continent ranging from Spain to the nations of Central Eastern Europe, where the great multinational empires (Habsburg, Russian and Ottoman) existed, and passed through Italy and Germany which were still divided into a large number of small pre-modern states. At first (1789–1871), the prevailing objective was the construction of national states (independent from foreign domination with all units being politically united and conceived as belonging to one nation often romantically understood as having the same cultural background), such as Greece, Italy, Germany and Poland. Later (1871–1945), the main objective became the extension of the power of national states – be they of ancient or recent constitution – through colonial conquest (France, Great Britain and Italy) and imperialist domination (United States of America, Germany, Japan) (COLONIALISM). As a result of this connection, the term 'nationalism' acquired new and negative connotations and became increasingly differentiated from the term 'patriotism', which, for many, still embodied positive values. Even recently, the 'Republican' version of patriotism, re-proposed in Italy, has a positive connotation, and is clearly differentiated from nationalism, which has a negative meaning that is very close to CHAUVENISM. During the first period of history mentioned above, nationalism was often associated with liberalism and the first democratic processes, while during the second period it fuelled irrationalist and warlike movements of reactionary orientation and even entered into an ill-fated synergy with the racist ideologies of authoritarian regimes between the two wars (Italy, Germany, Japan).

According to Giuseppe Mazzini, the great apostle of the 'principle of nationality', the nation should never become the ultimate purpose of political action, but rather should be an instrument – and one of extra-ordinary importance – of such action which serves as an intermediary between individuals and humanity. This principle became the guiding purpose of the *Giovine Italia* Society. Later, however, the nation became for many the ultimate value to which all political and ethical actions were subordinate (according to the principle of 'Right or wrong, this is my country' or the still more sinister German formula 'Deutschland über alles', now rejected even in Germany).

Very distinct from the type of nationalism described above is ETHNO-NATIONALISM, the ideology behind locally based movements inspired by a real or presumed ETHNICITY and which claims, in various forms (autonomy, separation, secession), the recovery or achievement of the independence of certain territorial units with real or presumed ethno-cultural characteristics from the national state. This phenomenon saw a revival following the Second World War. In Western Europe, cases of ethno-nationalist activity include the movements in Catalonia and the Basque provinces in Spain, Corsica and Brittany in France and the movement politically expressed by the supporters of the Northern League (*Lega Nord*) in Italy, which, for a few years in the 1990s, boasted of its intent to gain the independence of the northern regions and bring them together in the new national state of Padania. In Eastern Europe, ethno-nationalism exploded – with occasionally tragic consequences – after the collapse of the system of collective bureaucracy (in particular in the areas of the ex-Soviet Union and ex-Yugoslavia).

The situation of many non-European countries subjected to colonial domination stands in marked contrast to the European experience. In such countries nationalism inspired clearly progressive and even revolutionary independence movements (India, Algeria, Cuba, Angola, Mozambique, Guinea-Bissau, Eritrea). However, in some cases, these movements eventually degenerated and led to the strengthening of authoritarian and illiberal regimes, often inclined towards internal repression, military activities and long-lasting and devastating wars.

Another form of nationalism which has also seen two distinct stages – although such stages significantly lag behind the aforementioned European experiences – is ZIONISM, the ideology which has shaped the construction of Israel as a Jewish state.

Due to the complexity of the issue, it is not really possible to summarize all the issues connected to the idea of nation conceived as a natural entity or entity entitled to protect human beings. Nevertheless, mention should be made of the right of every individual or group of individuals to their own place in the world as a result of birth or shared values as well as the faculty of individuals or groups to impede the settling of others on the same piece of land. Interpreted in this way, nationalism may easily lead to a narrow-minded practice which sees countries close their doors to all foreigners or migrants (FOREIGNER, MIGRANT) yet this ideology obviously enters into conflict with universalistic ideas. Often the effort to find the right balance between the need to protect national IDENTITY and national community and the need to recognize such universal rights as freedom of movement and the human right to a safe place and reasonable living conditions is extremely difficult.

An attempt to strike a reasonable balance can be seen in most European democracies which, despite tough legislation on MIGRATION in some cases, are committed to recognizing the right of asylum (POLITICAL ASYLUM) of all persons whose lives are endangered by persecution. [U. M.]

Chabot, J. L. (1995) *Il nazionalismo* (1986), Mondadori, Milano.

Connor, W. (1994) *Ethnonationalism: The Quest for Understanding*, Princeton University Press, Princeton, NJ.

Gellner, E. (1983) *Nations and Nationalism*, Blackwell, Oxford.

Kohn, H. (1967) *The Idea of Nationalism: A Study in its Origins and Background*, Collier Books, New York.

Melotti, U. (1965) *Premesse del sionismo nella storia delle dottrine politiche*, Centro Studi Terzo Mondo, Milano.

Melotti, U. (ed.) (2000) *Etnicità, nazionalità e cittadinanza*, Seam, Roma.

Rusconi, G. E. (1997) *Patria e nazione*, Il Mulino, Bologna.

Smith, A. D. (1995) *Nations and Nationalism in a Global Era*, Polity Press, Cambridge.

Viroli, M. (1995) *For Love of Country: An Essay on Patriotism and Nationalism*, Clarendon Press, Oxford.

NATIVE

NATIVE (It. *nativo*; Fr. *natif*; Ger. *Eingeborener*) Describing the specific link between an individual or group of individuals and their country or land, the term 'native' – commonly used as a substitute for the less frequently found nouns 'autochthon' and 'aborigine', and the adjective 'indigenous' – refers to people born in a specific country. There are subtle differences in meaning between the four terms: the term 'native' stems from the Latin *nativus* (innate, natural) and is used to indicate a person born in a specified place or area; 'autochthon' derives from the Greek *autòs* (self) and *chthon* (earth) and refers to the earliest known inhabitants of a country; 'aborigine', from the Latin *aborigines*, plural, from *ab origine*, meaning 'from the beginning', refers to an original inhabitant of an area, especially as opposed to an invading or colonizing people (when capitalized it refers to a member of the indigenous people of Australia); and 'indigenous' derives from the Latin *indo* (in) and *gena* (generate) and describes a person originating in a country or region. The term 'native' is commonly used in a neutral manner to refer to both people born or originating in a specific land and those populations who lived in a country prior to invasion by Europeans.

Acceptable current usage of the term 'native' requires clarification of the ethnic group name to which the person described belongs (e.g. *bororo, kayapò, lakota, maya*). In addition, the term 'native' should be used to identify the specific CULTURE or ethnic background of the person described, rather than adopted in a rather vague and imprecise manner implying reference to PRIMITIVE or SAVAGE. Furthermore, its use with no further specification can often be understood as implying an opposition between 'civilized' and 'native' (and a negative reference to nativism); a highly specific use of the term allows precise identification of the culture of belonging.

As well as removing linguistic offence to the dignity of populations and cultures conveyed by historically mistaken and often racially discriminatory terms like Indian, Indios, primitive, savage and redskin, the term 'native' also raises an important ethical and political problem, namely the recognition of the special bond that any person has with his or her homeland. This relationship implies that in one way or another the dominant culture must recognize the rights of the native people to – and in – their own country. On the basis of this right – despite its outright violation in the past, manifest in such events as the hunting and poisoning of natives pursued as sport by Europeans in Australia and the action against Native Americans in the United States – all democracies have set up policies aimed at awarding special rights to native populations, for example the Sami in Sweden, the Maori in New Zealand and Native Americans in the United States. Generally speaking, the aim of these policies is to protect the language, values and traditions of the native population (the Self Determination Act passed in 1975 in the United States not only ensures the education, social welfare and civil rights of Native Americans, but also reinforces their legal status as a distinct ethnic group (ETHNIC MINORITY)). However, the political use of such policies has often failed to limit discriminatory outcomes against ethnic minorities, and has, on occasion, even provided a way of perpetuating the inequality between native and invading groups. [M. C.]

Hymes D. (ed.) (1999) *Reinventing Anthropology*, University of Michigan Press, Ann Arbor.
Lévi-Strauss, C. (1969) *The Raw and the Cooked*, Basic Books, New York.
Tentori, T. (1968) *Civiltà indigene d'America*, Edition Ricerche, Roma.

NATIVE AMERICAN: see NATIVE

NATURALIZATION: see CITIZENSHIP

NEGRITUDE (It. *negritudine*; Fr. *négritude*; Ger. *Negertum*) The term 'negritude' was coined to emphasize the view that, apart from skin colour and other 'Negroid' physical features, there are other values and characteristics which typify individuals, or peoples, with black skin. Colour is only the façade of a difference which makes the black COMMUNITY significantly distinct from other communities, and especially white communities. Black uniqueness is extolled by one of the foremost black intellectuals of the last century, Edward Wilmot Blyden. Blyden maintained that every RACE has its own characteristics which must be protected from the danger of corruption, a viewpoint he shared with De Gobineau (1816–82), who is considered one of the forerunners of classic modern RACISM. However, unlike De Gobineau, Blyden challenged the concept of a hierarchical valuation of different races, refuting the supposed inferiority of the black race. Many movements, albeit with different motivations and objectives, were established on these assumptions in the early decades of the twentieth century: not just in the United States (Negro Renaissance, for example, founded by Du Bois, and the Back to Africa movement led by Marcus Garvey), but also in Haiti (Indigenism) and in Cuba (Cubanism).

The rediscovery of black CULTURE and psyche was also championed by many European, and especially French, artists and intellectuals (including the Surrealist André Breton). However, the cultural movement known as Negritude only really took off in the 1930s, with the publication of works by black writers such as the Martinican Aimé Césaire and the Senegalese poet Léopold Sédar Senghor. By the end of the 1940s, the

Negritude movement had attracted a steady stream of black writers, working in different continents, who documented the uniqueness of black people, often expounding anti-colonialist ideas. The conviction that the tragedy of the Second World War was a product of white CIVILIZATION, the aspirations which accompanied decolonization (COLONIALISM) and the election of Senghor as head of state of Senegal (1960) added a political dimension to the term. Indeed, Negritude offered an alternative to the social, economic and cultural values of both the East and the West (communism and capitalism). The Organization of African Unity (OAU) – founded in 1963 by 33 African states (in 1999 the number had risen to 53) – originally focused on decolonization but now deals with many of the problems which create instability in the continent.

The main point of reference became the black African tradition, or at least traditions rooted in Africa (BLACK AFRICA). Rediscovery of the past formed a basis for constructing the future. Among the most significant consequences of this approach was the establishment of the first important study of the history of Africa (Diop, 1955; Ki Zerbo, 1954, 1972) in modern times from which supporters of Negritude extrapolated and evaluated two particular elements: the existence of the historic and cultural past of the black peoples of Africa, as illustrated by the ancient histories of Egypt and Ethiopia, and confirmation of the existence of a pre-colonial society based on a system of COMMUNITY and collectivism. This, it was argued, distinguished Africa from the political, economic and cultural reality of other continents, and this necessitated a (re)evaluation to avoid *'the bogus progress of capitalism'* or *'the bogus freedom of socialist regimes'*. This second observation attracted much criticism, notably from African scholars of

Marxist extraction: for example Majhemout Diop's studies of pre-colonial African societies in Mali, Senegal and other countries demonstrated that SLAVERY was common at the time, so such societies could hardly be considered 'communitarian'.

In answer to these and other criticisms, the Negritude movement changed direction in favour of a celebration of black uniqueness. In a famous but also much-criticized work, Léopold Senghor stated that 'emotion is black, in the same way that reason is Greek', to some extent attempting to extol and delineate the black community. Furthermore, Senghor tried to link Negritude to specific, almost biophysical, features such as the different attitude of blacks with regard to the universe, based on naturalness, honour, sensuality, tactility, emotion, generosity and religious feeling, but also on rhythm and image – all qualities, Senghor argued, that were 'naturally' far more highly developed in blacks than whites. The difficulty in justifying these notions – which were strongly criticized by notable African intellectuals such as Fanon, Nkrumah and Sekou Touré – led the concept of Negritude to lose much of its original meaning in the 1960s, until it finally became the justification for purely nominalist movements (such as 'Melanism' or 'Negrism'). Even worse, it offered a theoretic basis for utterly totalitarian systems which justified their lack of democracy as a sort of return to ancient traditions (e.g., the *authenticité* movement in Zaire which coincided with 'Mobutuism', or the references to Negritude provided by dictators such as Amin and Bokassa).

The strand of Negritude closest to the spirit of the original movement – which is now fairly widespread – focuses on 'African Personality' and is based on an initial hypothesis by Blyden (who coined the term at the end of the nineteenth entury) of the existence and uniqueness of a personality common to all blacks. In its most modern form, proposed by Kwame Nkrumah in Ghana, African personality applies only to blacks living on the continent of Africa. Thus the issue is more a case of 'Africanism' (AFRO-CENTRISM) than Negritude.

The debate over Negritude has raised many questions, some of which are still important today, even after several decades. Notable among these, because of its implications, is Jean-Paul Sartre's observation in *Orphée noir*, the preface to Senghor's *Anthologie de la nouvelle poésie nègre et malgache* (1948), which contains the works of writers who were among the first supporters of the Negritude movement and which became its manifesto. In *Orphée noir* (Black Orpheus), the French philosopher defined Negritude as a kind of anti-racism (RACISM) in that it was an attempt to change a previously held stance based on the acceptance and justification of the attributes of a race (the black race) considered radically different from other races. This theme has been taken up again in modern times in so-called differentialist anti-racism. For Sartre, the only real justification for anti-racist racism was related to the ultimate goal the Negritude movement could reach – the conquest of the notion of race, which would inevitably result in the extinction of the movement. [M. V.]

Adotevi, S. (1972) *Négritude et Nérologues*, Union Générale d'Éditions, Paris.
Balandier, G. (1963) *Sociologie actuelle de l'Afrique Noire*, PUF, Paris.
Carrilho, M. (1974) *Sociologia della negritudine*, Liguori Editore, Napoli.
Césaire, A. (1956) *Cahier d'un retour au pays natal* (1939), Présence Africaine, Paris.
Diop, C.A. (1955) 'Nations nègres et culture', in *Présence Africaine*, Paris.
Diop, M. (1971–72) *Histoire des classes sociales dans l'Afrique de l'Ouest*, François Maspero, Paris.

Fanon, F. (1952) *Black Skins, White Masks*, Paladin, London.
Ki Zerbo, J. (1954) 'Histoire et conscience nègre', in *Présence Africaine*, Paris.
Ki Zerbo, J. (1972) *Histoire de l'Afrique Noire*, Hatier, Paris.
Kesteloot, L. (1970) *Négritude et situation coloniale*, Editions Clé, Yaoundé.
Senghor, L. (1948) *Anthologie de la nouvelle poésie nègre et malgache*, PUF, Paris.
Senghor, L. (1961) *Négritude et humanisme*, Éditions du Seuil, Paris.
Towa, M. (1971) *Léopold Senghor: Négritude ou servitude?*, Editions Clé, Yaoundé.
Wauthier, C. (1973) *L'Afrique des Africains. Inventaire de la négritude*, Éditions du Seuil, Paris.

NEGRO

NEGRO (It. *negro*; Fr. *nègre*, *noir*; Ger. *Schwarzer*, *Neger*) Deriving from the Latin adjective *niger* (the colour 'black'), the term refers to a person with black skin, of Negroid origin. Nowadays other terms (such as 'black') are preferred. This can be explained by the negative and sometimes offensive connotations of the word 'Negro' which date from the time of SLAVERY and exploitation, where the term was a synonym of 'slave'. Indeed, nowadays the word is, on occasion, applied to individuals who display negative qualities, failings or weaknesses associated with this era of prescribed racial inferiority (RACISM). Supposedly scientific discoveries, for example, that links between man and the apes had been found in the Hottentots or that the blood of Negroes was different from that of Whites, became stereotypical views in European literature in the seventeenth century. So-called discoveries of this kind led many writers, especially in France, to argue that Africans were a separate species (Davis, 1966: 454)

In the nineteenth century, scholars classified humanity racially on the basis of skin colour – De Gobineau (1816–82) in his *Essai sur l'inégalité des races humaines* (1853–55), maintained that there were innate differences, both moral and physical, between members of the three basic racial groups: white, yellow and black. Each race, immediately identifiable by skin colour, had certain characteristics, so hierarchical classification was also possible – the 'white race' was placed at the top of the hierarchy while the black race was considered to form a 'missing link' between humans and animals (Lombroso, 1871). Nevertheless, the expression 'Negro race' was widely used by certain black writers who, in an attempt to refute the supposed racial inferiority attributed to them, asserted a Negro uniqueness. This process, set in motion by Edward Wilmot Blyden, was taken up again by important movements such as the United Negro Improvement Association, founded in the United States in the 1920s and followed in later years by the cultural movement known as the Harlem Renaissance (AFRO-CENTRISM). The term was used again in the 1930s, with no pejorative connotations, in various sociological studies (Johnson, 1930; Frazier, 1939). It was only with the increasingly radical political developments in the 1960s in black communities in various parts of the USA that the term 'Negro' came to be replaced by 'black' (as in BLACK POWER, Black Panthers, BLACK MUSLIMS) and later by terms like Afro-American, African-American and African. It is worth noting, however, that the term 'nigger' (a more derogatory variant of the word 'negro') has come to be used in an ironic fashion by some black people, e.g. rappers. In France, a slightly different process is taking place: the term *nègre* has been freed, at least in part, from the disparaging connotations which separated it from the more neutral *noir*.

This happened mainly in the 1940s, following its acceptance by the NEGRITUDE movement.

With regard to new countries of immigration (MIGRATION), up until the last few decades at least, there has been no real difference in the use of the terms *nero* and *negro*, probably because of the absence of any significant black population and the different level of involvement with colonization (COLONIALISM). This is clear from the undiscriminating use of both terms even during the period of black struggle. With the arrival of immigrants from African countries, greater attention is being paid to the meaning of the two terms, and *negro* is now considered politically incorrect. [M. V.]

Davis, D. B. (1966) *The Problem of Slavery in Western Culture*, Ithaca, New York.

Lombroso, C. (1871) *L'uomo bianco e l'uomo di colore*, Tipografia F. Sacchetto, Padova.

Low, W. A., Clift, V. A. (eds) (1981) *Encyclopaedia of Black America*, Da Capo, New York.

Moore, R. B. (1992) *The Name 'Negro'. Its Origin and Evil Use* (1960), Black Classic Press, Baltimore.

NEO-COLONIALISM: see COLONIALISM

NEO-FEUDAL ADAPTATION (It. *adattamento neofeudale*; Fr. *adaptation neoféodale*; Ger. *neufedal Anpassung*) This expression was used by Hoffmann-Nowotny (1973) to describe a popular way of inserting immigrants (MIGRANT) into foreign countries. Following a study of the social and psychological condition of immigrants in Switzerland at the beginning of the

1970s, Hoffmann-Nowotny highlighted a mechanism that causes immigrants to feel inferior in many European countries. In neo-feudal adaptation, the immigrant accepts a status inferior to that of the autochthons, and thus renounces his or her initial expectations and is satisfied by less gratifying objectives. According to Hoffmann-Nowotny, such resignation is merely a reflex reaction to the impositions of the host society which proves to be closed or 'neo-feudal' and only accepts new arrivals who prove their willingness to accept and interiorize discrimination and even to live in an 'ethnic shell'. In some ways, the acceptance of subjection is the cost an immigrant has to pay in order to be accepted by the closed social system. This phenomenon can also be found in all situations where there is a strong system of segregation (RACIAL SEGREGATION).

Neo-feudal adaptation often characterizes first generation settlers, while it is generally bitterly criticized by the SECOND GENERATION whose members tend to adopt different forms of insertion. [M. V.]

Frigessi Castelnuovo, D., Risso, M. (1982) *A mezza parete*, Einaudi, Torino.
Hoffmann-Nowotny, H. J. (1973) *Soziologie des Fremdarbeitsproblems*, F. Enke Verlag, Stuttgart.

NOMAD (It. *nomade*; Fr. *nomade*; Ger. *Nomade*) From the Greek *nemo* (pasture) this term defines pastoral people as well as those populations which have no permanent abode or settlement. Nomadic groups are characterized by absolute or irregular mobility (not based on constant rhythms or itineraries). There are three main kinds of nomadism: hunter-gatherer nomadism, pastoral nomadism, and modern nomadism.

The hunter-gatherer type of nomadism, which follows the movements of wild fauna and the discontinuous distribution of the vegetation gathered, can be periodical and linked to seasonal cycles. Populations of hunters and gatherers can still be found in many parts of the world, although confined to marginal regions. Absolute mobility is also practised among *pastoral populations*, for example among the people of Mongolia. This type of nomadism tends to take the shape of regular migrations between mountains and plains according to the variations in climate and in the seasons such as in transhumance (movements of cattle according to the location of pastures), and these migrations have played a significant role, particularly in Europe. The main areas of nomadic livestock breeding are the tundra, the forest steppes, the savannahs, the desert steppes, the deserts of northern Asia, northern Africa, the Sahel and eastern and southern Africa, the desert areas of the Near and Middle East, and the regions from the Black Sea to Manchuria. Often these forms of nomadism are accompanied by agricultural practices (as in the case of the Bedouins of Arabia and of the Sahara). Thus various forms of *semi-nomadism* are created, in which the cultivation of products and movement for the pasture of cattle are equally important. In these cases movement is restricted to limited areas; in some populations only part of the COMMUNITY moves with the cattle while the rest of the group stays near water and the crops.

Clans are at the basis of the political organization of nomadic societies. Clans generally consist of groups of nuclear families (FAMILY), which are more or less linked by blood ties. They are not very large and normally consist of about 30 people. Clans are formed for the mutual convenience of their members. Internal harmony and a fertile territory are the bases on which a clan is founded. If either of these elements is lacking any one of the members may decide to abandon the clan, join another clan, or form a new clan together with their own family. Each clan member has decision-making powers. However, authority is conferred on a chief, who is chosen for the efficiency of his actions. Final decisions are left to the chief, but pre-eminence can easily pass to another should he be considered more effective. EQUALITY among members and in the distribution of the subsistence income is fundamental to the life of the clan. A distinct case and a modern form of nomadism is that of the Romani (ROMA) in Asia, Europe, North Africa and the Americas, whose nomadic culture is historically relatively recent (about eleventh century).

In general we cannot speak of an evolutionary development from nomadic forms of social life to settled civilized societies (CIVILIZATION). Nomadic societies have existed at all times and are not remnants of an earlier way of life but a highly flexible adaptation to specific geographical and social conditions. Many nomadic groups constantly shift back and forth between settlement and wandering, adapting to the current requirements of the group. This holds true for hunter-gatherer societies as well as for modern forms of nomadism as practised by the Romani people of Europe. [J. E., T. M.]

De Martino, E. (1972) *Magic*, T. Stacey.
Dyson-Hudson N. and Irons, W., (eds) (1996) *Perspectives on Nomadism*, Leidon, Brill.
Fabietti, V. and Salzman, P.C., (eds) (1996) *The Anthropology of Tribal and Peasant Pastoral Societies/Antropologia delle società tribali pastoriali e contadine*, Pavia, Ibis.
Fings, K., Heuss, H., Sparing, F. (1997) *From 'Race Science' to the Camps. The Gypsies during the Second World War*, Interface Collection 12, Hatfield.
Fromm, E. (1977) *Anatomy of Human Destructiveness*, Penguin.
Hund, W. D. (ed.) (1996) *Zigeuner. Geschichte und Struktur einer rassistischen Konstruktion*, DISS, Duisburg.
Laughlin, J. M. (1999) 'European gypsies and the historical geography of loathing', *Review*, Ferdinand Braudel Center, 22(1): 31–81.
Ratzel, F. (1896) *The History of Mankind*, New York, Macmillan.
Voltaggio, F. (1992) *L'arte della guarigione nelle culture umane*, Bollati Boringhieri, Torino.

NOMADIC CAMP (It. *campo nomadi*; Fr. *camp de nomades*; Ger. *Nomadencamp*)

An area allocated by a local administration as a semi-stable settlement for Romani (ROMA) groups, generally found at the margins of cities. In addition to the provision of essential services (water, electricity, etc.), in some cases education programmes for minors are implemented, on site or elsewhere. Dwellings consist of caravans, tents or other precarious constructions. The dwellings are generally situated around the camps according to blood or friendship ties, so that those nearest to each other are also those with whom relations are more friendly. Permanent inhabitants of the areas next to nomad camps almost always have hostile relations with the inhabitants of the latter. [J. E., T. M.]

'Casalino 700 addio, al suo posto un parco Smantellato il campo nomadi più grande d'Europa,' in *Corriere della Sera*, 17 October, 2000.

Chwgule, Ashok, (1999) 'A Gypsy Awakening', in *The Economist*, 11 September.

Gronfors, Martii (ed.) and Chris Powell and Marta Miklusakova (2001) *The Marginalisation and Criminalisation of the Roma (Gypsies) in Britain, the Czech Republic and Finland*, University of Hertfordshire Press.

Hund, W. D. (ed.) (1996) *Zigeuner. Geschichte und Struktur einer rassistischen Konstruktion*, DISS, Duisburg.

Laughlin, J. M. (1999) 'European gypsies and the historical geography of loathing', *Review*, Ferdinand Braudel Center, 22(1): 31–81.

'Nomadi, torna l'emergenza: "Smembrare i campi rom"' in *Il Messaggero*, 3 February, 2002.

Rossi, M. (1999) 'Gipsy women between modernity and tradition: Strategy of integration, dynamics and social change', *EUROFOR Conference 27*.

UNESCO (1984) *A Brief History of the Roma*, www.geocities.com.

'Un piano contro l'emergenza nomadi Saranno chiusi i campi pericolosi come quelli di Tor di Quinto e Vicolo Savini,' in *Il Messaggero*, 6 April, 2002.

Van de Port, M. (1999) *Gipsies, Wars and Other Instances of the Wild. Civilization and its Discontents in a Serbian Town*, Global Books, Amsterdam.

NOSTALGIA (HOMESICKNESS) (It. *nostalgia*; Fr. *nostalgie*; Ger. *Heimweh*) From the Greek *nostos* (voyage, return and, more particularly, return to one's country) and *algos* (pain, suffering, affliction), this term refers to a feeling of homesickness or longing for people, things or situations which are far away in space (for example one's family, home or country) or even in time (a lost love, youth or, generally, the past). Although this feeling is well documented in important literary works of the past (including Homer, Ovid and Dante Alighieri), the term is actually of quite recent invention. It was apparently introduced by a doctor from Basle, Johannes Hofer, author of a study (*Dissertatio curiosa-medica De Nostalgia, vulgo Heimweh oder Heimwehsucht*, 1678) on the strange sickness which affected many young people from Switzerland serving as mercenaries in foreign armies, or who left their homes and families to study or work abroad. According to Hofer, these young people suffered so much when they were unable to return home that they died in a foreign land, overcome by fever and consumption (Frigessi Castelnuovo and Risso, 1982). Hofer, who considered this condition to be a real disease (characterized by precise symptoms: loss of appetite, irritability, anguish, fever and progressive physical decline), and lacking a term to define it, invented the fortunate neologism, which was soon being used outside the medical world to indicate the sadness caused by leaving one's country and the desire to return to it.

The first studies of nostalgia tended to attribute the disease to physical causes (in the case of the aforementioned Swiss youths, the effects of the passage from a salubrious Alpine environment to the unhealthy plains and cities was highlighted). Later, increasing importance was given to 'moral' causes, or better, psychological, social and cultural causes, among them the breaking of ties with loved ones, uprooting, loneliness and the difficulties encountered in a foreign, sometimes hostile, environment. The forced exile of many patriots during the Romantic era, and the great transatlantic emigrations which took place from the second half of the nineteenth century until the First World War, provided ample material for the study of nostalgia (by then documented not only in important literary and musical works, but also in letters, songs and popular sayings).

The phenomenon attracted renewed attention because of the internal and international emigration which took place after the Second World War, especially in Italy, which, at the time, had the highest emigration rate (MIGRA-TION) in Europe (Frigessi Castelnuovo and Risso, 1982). Students of the nostalgia of immigrants (MIGRANT) point out that such a state cannot be ascribed to a pre-existing condition of depression, but that the depression which often accompanies immigration is caused by the distance from home and FAMILY, the difficulties encountered in adapting (ADAPTATION) to a new environment, partly owing to the lack of the necessary cultural skills, and by scarce social relationships, isolation, MAR-GINALIZATION or self-marginalization (Mellina, 1987). Empirical research has highlighted the ease with which these conditions can develop into real psycho-pathologies (Favaro and Tognetti Bordogna, 1998). [U. M.]

Ben Jelloun, T. (1977) *La Plus haute des solitudes*, Du Seuil, Paris.

Favaro, G., Tognetti Bordogna, M. (1998) *La salute degli immigrati*, Unicopli, Milano.

Frigessi Castelnuovo, D., Risso, M. (1982) *A mezza parete*, Einaudi, Torino.

Mellina, S. (1987) *La nostalgia nella valigia*, Marsilio, Venezia.

Pickering, J., Kehde, S. (eds) (1997) *Narratives of Nostalgia, Gender, and Nationalism*, New York University Press, New York.

OFFICIAL LANGUAGE (It. *lingua ufficiale;* Fr. *langue officielle;* Ger. *offizielle Amtssprache*)

An 'official' language is a language adopted by all the territories of a state pursuant to precise legal provisions. These provisions: (a) ratify the written and spoken use of the language in all areas of public life (education, administration and jurisprudence, legislation, place names, etc.) and (b) regulate the use of the language in relation to the use of foreign languages and other local languages (the dialects or languages of minority communities).

In many cases, the choice of the official language of a country emerges naturally from the history of the state and is based on the national language (NATION). In other cases the choice leads to much controversy, especially in multilingual states. The importance of the issue varies from one country to another, e.g. in Belgium choice of language affects the whole of national politics, while in the UK it mainly concerns Wales. Several European countries, such as the UK, Norway and Belgium, also have more than one official language. Many ex-colonial countries have preferred not to abandon the use of a European language, as this would result in a reduction of the country's linguistic competence, but instead revive the use of the NATIVE language as a means of expression of ethnic and cultural IDENTITY. Obviously, legislative control over the use of a language within a country gives rise to many problems, especially the need to protect the rights of minority language groups as well as cases in which linguistic conflicts within a country are related to a need to preserve cultural identity (ETHNIC MINORITY). Although – at least in principle – modern-day orientation tends towards unanimous acceptance of multilingualism, a mere glance at past history shows deep-rooted opposition to the concept: the imposition of the English language on the Indians of North America or the Aboriginal populations of Australia, restrictions governing public use of the Basque language (Euskera) in Spain, the linguistic battles between Anglophone and Francophone communities in Canada and the problem of linguistic policies in ex-Yugoslavia. More recently, legislative problems have arisen – for example in schools – regarding the use of Black English Vernacular (EBONICS) by young people in the United States, and Spanish in California; this has emphasized the fact that the preservation of ethnocultural identity is not always the result of the coexistence of different languages (e.g. the use of Albanian in some mountain communities in Italy or Tigrinya in Ethiopia, where the official language is Amharic), but may also depend on the presence within one country of variations of the same language developed internally according to social status and level of education (La Page and Tabouret-Keller, 1985).

As far as international relations are concerned, an 'official language' is a means of communication chosen, on a case by case basis, according to specific agreements between states (INTERNATIONAL LANGUAGE). The same is also true with regard to international organizations. For example, the Statute of the Food and Agriculture Organization of the United Nations (FAO) establishes

Arabic, Chinese, French, English and Spanish as the organization's official languages. The European Union has 12 official languages. [A. B., R. B.]

La Page, R., Tabouret-Keller, A. (1985) *Acts of Identity*, Cambridge University Press, Cambridge.
Tollefson, J. W. (1991) *Planning Language, Planning Inequality*, Longman, London.

ORIENTALISM

(It. *Orientalismo*; Fr. *Orientalisme*; Ger. *Orientalistik*) The term was originally used to describe two main historical movements. First, the scholarship and administrative practices of members of the Asiatic Society of Bengal in the latter part of the eighteenth century, especially Sir William Jones, who believed that the British East India Company should govern India in accordance with perceived Indian traditions. Jones and his associates attempted to make an intensive study of the languages and cultures of the populations that came within the Company's Indian territories. Jones is particularly well known for his research into India's classical past and for postulating links between the ancient Indian language, Sanskrit and the family of European languages, 'thus re-animating a resplendent past by identifying it as the source of Western civilization' (Singh, 1996: 66). There was open acknowledgement by these Orientalists, though, that this was not disinterested scholarship but part of a strategy of government (MacKenzie, 1995: 3).

The second group to be labelled Orientalists were the nineteenth-century French artists who painted scenes, real and imagined, of North Africa and the Middle East. Artists from many other European countries also made representations of these regions, and India, with the 'Oriental' woman becoming an alluring source of fascination for those who depicted these diverse cultures in art (Thornton, 1994). The period of decolonization in the second half of the twentieth century saw a major re-evaluation of Orientalist practices. An earlier relatively neutral usage gave way to a concept of Orientalism that stresses its tenuous connection with the realities of the cultures of South Asia, North Africa and the Middle East as represented in art, literature and historical studies and emphasizes the central role it played in assisting the European colonial domination (COLONIALISM) and exploitation of these regions.

Early critiques of Orientalism came from specialist scholars such as the historian A. L. Tibawi (1964) and Anouar Abdel-Malek (1963). Both identified crucial flaws in the way in which the Islamic world had been presented variously, and with weak evidence, as changeless, in decline, as dependent upon biblical and Jewish texts for its religious tenets, and as a minor contributor to science and philosophy (Sardar, 1999: 56–61; Said, 1985: 17). However, it was the publication of Edward Said's *Orientalism* (1978) which ignited a large-scale controversy, drawing in a wide range of disciplines and areas of research. According to Said, Orientalism is constituted by several elements: the academic study of the Orient as defined by specialist scholars of history, languages, art and so forth; a 'style of thought' which consistently differentiates the East from the West, regarding the former as inherently inferior to the latter; and as a 'corporate institution' for authorizing views of the Orient which enable power to be exercised over the range of territories and cultures encapsulated by the term. Furthermore, Said maintains that there is a systematic imbrication between Orientalism as a set of discourses and Orientalism as a form of institutional power and domination over those so designated. From an Orientalist point of view, the West not only produced what it regarded as knowledge of the Orient, but also produced the Orient itself in the image of this knowledge because the Orient was governed in conformity with the West's representations. The tragic irony was that the image of the Orient with which the West operated had little purchase on the realities of these cultures and territories. Western knowledge was as much the product of fantasy, wishful thinking, convenient projection and brutal legitimation of imperial power as any serious insight into 'Oriental' cultures. Furthermore, the Orientalist debate also includes the discourse that allowed European culture to manage and produce the Orient politically, sociologically, militarily, ideologically, scientifically, and imaginatively during the Enlightenment period'. According to Said, 'European culture gained in strength and IDENTITY by setting itself off against the Orient as a sort of surrogate and even underground self' (1978: 3). The French writer Flaubert's account of his encounter with an Egyptian courtesan is highly representative of the genre. Not only is the Oriental considered a sexually available and exciting female, but she is never allowed to speak for herself. Flaubert, being a 'foreign, comparatively wealthy, male', was in a position which allowed him to possess her physically and tell his readers in what way she was 'typically Oriental' (Said, 1978: 6).

Problems with the study of Orientalism arise from the fact that little of the corpus of research on the subject provides any real knowledge of the Orient and that substantial elements of the Orient were re-made by imperial powers in *their* image of the Orient. Orientalist scholars tend to polarize Orient and Occident in a manner which prevents an appreciation of the fact that there was also admiration for and imitation of the Orient in Western arts and humanities (Mackenzie, 1995). Finally, it has been argued that the East/West binary opposition is unable to recognize the ways in which the identities of both were formed by the imperial and colonial encounters.

The continuing relevance of the concept of Orientalism has recently been demonstrated in the notion of 'Techno-Orientalism'. This refers to the manner in which Japanese advances in technology and representations of their supposedly innate 'Otherness' (DIVERSITY–SIMILARITY) combine with products like Japanese computer games, involving animations, to produce Western images of Japan as 'cold, impersonal and machine-like, an authoritarian culture lacking emotional connection to the rest of the world' (Morley and Robbins, 1995: 169) (NATIONAL CHARACTER). Here again, a binary divide is being posited between a 'civilized', humane West and an Orient that is its opposite.

Despite its many problems, it is likely that the concept of Orientalism will continue to furnish a useful if somewhat blunt analytical tool for understanding the forms in which Western culture sustains its unitary identity as the most 'progressive' force on the globe (Sardar, 1999: 77–118). [A. R.]

Abdel-Malek, A. (1963) 'Orientalism in crisis', *Diogenes*, 44 (Winter): 107–8.
Ahmad, A. (1992) *In Theory: Classes, Nations, Literatures*, Verso, London and New York.
Bernstein, M., Studlar, G. (eds) (1997) *Visions of the East: Orientalism in Film*, I. B. Tauris, London.
Clifford, J. (1988) 'On orientalism', in Clifford, J. (ed.), *The Predicament of*

Culture: Twentieth Century Ethnography, Literature and Art, Harvard University Press, Cambridge, MA.

MacKenzie, J. M. (1995) Orientalism: History, Theory and the Arts, Manchester University Press, Manchester.

Mani, L., Frankenberg, R. (1985) 'The challenge of orientalism', Economy and Society, 14(2): 174–192.

Morley, D., Robbins, K. (1995) Spaces of Identity: Global Media, Electronic Landscapes and Cultural Boundaries, Routledge, London.

Said, E. (1978) Orientalism, Routledge, London.

Said, E. (1985) 'Orientalism reconsidered', in Barker F., Hulme P., Iversen M. (eds), Europe and Its Others, Vol. 1, University of Essex Press, Colchester.

Said, E. (1993) Culture and Imperialism, Chatto & Windus, London.

Sardar, Z. (1999) Orientalism, Open University Press, Milton Keynes.

Singh, J. G. (1996) Colonial Narratives/ Cultural Dialogues: 'Discoveries' of India in the Language of Colonialism, Routledge, London and New York.

Tibawi, A. L. (1964) English-Speaking Orientalists: A Critique of their approach to Islam and Arab Nationalism, Islamic Cultural Centre, London.

Thornton, L. (1994) Women as Portrayed in Orientalist Painting, ACR Edition, Paris.

P

PARTICIPATION (It. *partecipazione*; Fr. *participation*; Ger. *Teilnahme*)

The term 'participation' derives from the Latin *pars*, meaning part, and *capere*, meaning take, and is used to describe the way in which the various members of a company act with regard to the management of the enterprise. From this point of view, participation by the different social, sexual, generation and ETHNIC sections of a society in running common amenities becomes decisive in countering any possible forms of MARGINALIZATION. However, participation often means including marginal groups or individuals in order to ensure that a certain control is maintained. Participation also means sharing part of a company's profits. Although trade union leaders participate in management meetings, the real decision-making power remains firmly in the hands of the owners.

Participation in the generation of a given CULTURE, the production and diffusion of new morals and the creation of lifestyles is important. However, according to a number of observers, the problem that is yet to be resolved stems from the fact that participation has never meant decision-making, but merely making an appearance. [M. C.]

Featherstone, M. (1966) *Undoing Culture: Globalization, Postmodernism and Identity (Theory, Culture and Society)*, Sage, London.
Ferrarotti, F. (1961) *La sociologia come partecipazione*, Taylor, Torino.

PEOPLE (It. *popolo*; Fr. *peuple*; Ger. *Volk*)

The term derives from the Latin *populus*; it has a number of meanings and connotations which change from language to language. In English it refers first of all simply to the human race. It has also often been used to refer to the common people, the masses, or the proletariat, usually 'the people'. A clear and explicit sociopolitical definition of people is found in the banner of ancient Rome: SPQR (*senatus populusque romanus* – the senate and the Roman people) in which the State was defined as the assembly of nobility and people, to whom the tribunes guaranteed full rights. In municipalities of the Middle Ages, the *populus* became a political party, with its own leader. Later, the term was used to identify citizens of an inferior rank. Enlightenment thinkers – partially reacting to the idea of inherent differences between classes – embraced a more universalist idea of people that found expression in various American political documents. For example, the Declaration of Independence (1776) begins 'When in the Course of human events, it becomes necessary for one people to dissolve the political bands which have connected them with another . . .' while the US Constitution (1787) begins 'We, the people of the United States . . .'. It is however interesting to note that French and American statesmen referred to the rights of *man* and the equality of *men* rather than of people. 'People' is used in these documents to refer to a COMMUNITY of humans who share traditional roots, habits, customs, values, language and sometimes, but not always, religion; a population that shares certain common traits among themselves. In this sense, the concept of 'people' resembles that of a NATION. During the nineteenth century, the Romantic movement defined the 'people' as an entity embracing the spirit of the nation and the world. Geographical location alone, however, is not sufficient to define inhabitants within the same borders (FRONTIER) as a people. There are many geographical national areas, and even more political areas, inhabited by different peoples. The concept of a people as a nation free from outside domination was one of the main reasons for Romantic and revivalist ideology all over Europe (dating from about the time of the French Revolution). Many scholars believe that the concept of people also implies a wish to join together and a uniformity of interests. The impossibility of geographical definition of a people has constituted an inherent and at times tragic contradiction in the construction of modern states (in particular nation states). Sometimes physical traits are included among the common characteristics which serve to construct individuals as members of the same people or, in this case, ETHNICITY or RACE. The relationship, however, between the concepts of ethnicity or race and people is fluid, since according to the point of view, one category may be greater or more extensive than the other.

With the development of industrial societies, the term 'people' was endowed with another meaning, becoming identified with the oppressed classes (the proletariat). The population of each country was divided into the oppressor and the oppressed: the latter being the people. From this point of view, the term 'people' no longer coincided with the idea of nation, but as a result of the concept of universal brotherhood, came to be used to describe all oppressed peoples throughout the world. [S. G.]

Bobbio, N. (1983) 'Popolo', in *Dizionario di politica*, UTET, Torino.

PERMIT OF STAY: see ILLEGAL ALIEN, RECEPTION CENTRE

PHENOTYPE (It. *fenotipo*; Fr. *phéno-type*; Ger. *Phänoty-pus*) The term 'phenotype' derives from the Greek words *phainein*, meaning appear, and *typos*, model, and is used to describe the assessable characteristics of an individual. A number of these, such as proteins, can be discovered only through laboratory analyses and are simply the direct realization of the segment of self-sufficient information contained in the GENOTYPE – a project which becomes identifiable reality without mediation. On the other hand, complex characteristics such as height, weight, skin colour and intelligence are conditioned by external factors inter-connecting with genetic information in order to define their physical expression. In this case, it is said that the phenotype is the result of interaction of the genotype with the surrounding environment, for example diet influences weight and height and exposure to the sun influences skin pigmentation. Thus, similarities in physical characteristics between individuals and populations derive not only from people's genetic likeness to their ancestors, but also from the similar environmental conditions in which they live. Unlike the genotype, the complex phenotype of individuals changes in accordance with their stage of development. All human beings are the result of the interaction of genetic inheritance and environment. It is the interaction of nature and nurture which makes us what we are from a physical, behavioural and psychic point of view. [G. B., O. R.]

Cavalli-Sforza L. L., Bodmer W. F. (1971) *Genetics of Human Populations*, W. H. Freeman, San Francisco.
Vogel, F., Motulsky, A. G. (1982) *Human Genetics*, Springer-Verlag, Berlin and Heidelberg.

PIDGIN (It. *pidgin*; Fr. *pidgin*; Ger. *Pidgin*)

The term 'pidgin' describes a simplified language that results from extended contact between groups of people with no language in common. According to John Holm, pidgin evolves when there is a 'need for some means of verbal communication, perhaps for trade, but no group learns the native language of any other group' (1988: 5). Using a simple vocabulary and basic grammar, these mixed language systems see so-called substrata speakers (those holding less power) using words from the language of the superstratum (those holding more power), although often with subtle differences in meaning, while the superstratum speakers adopt these changes in meaning and simplify the language by dropping inflections and reducing the number of different words used. Pidgins are rarely a mother tongue, but are learned wherever and whenever their use becomes necessary.

Although spoken by millions of people, pidgin languages were long thought of as a corruption or aberrant form of the language from which they developed. Only in the second half of the twentieth century was their fundamental importance recognized. Following intense study of the formation, interaction and modification of pidgin and Creole languages (CREOLE language), the term 'pidgin' (which first appeared in literature around 1850) lost its original generic and disparaging meaning of 'bastard language' (interpreted as the linguistic expression of uncivilized people) and is now a technical term, used especially in the fields of history and sociolinguistics.

The origin of the word is uncertain. Some connect the term with the American Indian Pidians – the first NATIVE people encountered by English explorers around the estuary of the Orinoco River in the seventeenth century – while others attribute it to the pronunciation of the English word 'beach' by the peoples of the South Pacific; alluding to the place where this mixed language was spoken (Mühlhauser, 1986: 1). Others still suggest that the origin is Lusitanian, emphasizing the fundamental role played by the Portuguese in starting the spread of European languages during their commercial explorations (Holm, 1988: 9). A more widely held theory is that 'pidgin' is a phonetic rendering of the English word 'business' as pronounced in Chinese and that this Chinese Pidgin English term was consequently extended to include all the other mixed and simplified trading languages (*Oxford English Dictionary*).

Pidgin linguistic forms have developed in all ages and all continents ever since the identification of the concept of language. The first known pidgin languages were the ancient linguae francae of Mediterranean ports and the languages which sprang up in various regions of Africa as a result of the contact between Arabs and the indigenous populations in the eleventh century, as noted in 1068 by the geographer Abu

'Ubayd al-Bakri (Holm, 1988). However, the best-known forms of pidgin developed as a result of continuous and stable contact between people with different languages and cultures with the expansion outside Europe of Western European PEOPLE, CULTURE and language. Chinese Pidgin English serves as an illustration of all pidgins. Originating in Canton after the establishment of the first English trading base in 1664, Chinese Pidgin English was a mixed language formed from modified English lexis built on a Chinese grammatical base. It was soon established as the LINGUA FRANCA for trade between Europeans (mainly English) and Chinese, although it later developed into a less specific means of communication and was widely used by Chinese communities in the United States, especially in California. It became extinct as a result of the fact that the Chinese considered the use of such a language humiliating and demeaning – over the years the sound of the language had become comical to the ears of the Anglophone community – but it survived in Hong Kong until the end of the Second World War. A startlingly cutting reference to the use of Chinese Pidgin English can be found in the story of Lee, one of the characters in John Steinbeck's *East of Eden* (1952). A large number of pidgins, with lexical components derived from Portuguese, Spanish, English, French and Dutch, appeared in Africa, the Caribbean and the Americas (Atlantic Pidgins). These pidgins are directly connected with the history of trade, exploration, SLAVERY, religious missionary work and COLONIALISM. Many of them later developed into CREOLE languages (creolization). Other pidgins formed from English and Malay (Melanesian Pidgin, Beach-la-Mar, Tok Pisin) developed in the South Pacific, where they are still widely used today.

Because of their original specific use in the fields of trade and administration, most pidgins remain exclusively oral languages, which quickly die out when they are no longer needed as a means of communication, i.e. when contact between different linguistic groups ceases, when one group learns the language of the other, or where both groups begin to use a third common language with greater communicative value (VEHICULAR LANGUAGE). Lingua franca and Chinese Pidgin English remained in use for centuries, while the Franco-Annamese Pidgin (Tây bôy), which spread through Vietnam from 1860, paralleling the French colonial era (1887–1956) was used for about 100 years and then rapidly died out as a direct result of the withdrawal of the occupying forces and a large part of the Francophone community in 1956. Tây bôy survived until the end of the 1960s, when it was replaced by a new pidgin based on American-English lexical components, following American military intervention. This also died a rapid death with the end of the Vietnam War. In other areas, such as the Caribbean, the Americas and West Africa, many pidgins were adopted as mother tongues by entire communities and were thus transformed into CREOLE languages. These have constantly evolved and developed, remaining in use as both the spoken and written languages of several populations. Finally, in geographical areas characterized by wide linguistic diversity, some Pidgins have asserted themselves to a large extent as means of communication, attaining a high degree of stability and official acceptance (OFFICIAL LANGUAGE). Two examples are English Nigerian Pidgin in Nigeria and Melanesian Pidgin in Papua New Guinea. These languages allow communication between many linguistic groups, who otherwise would not be able to understand each other. Such languages are known as 'expanded Pidgins' as they are still largely used as auxiliary languages, rather than mother tongues (i.e. they are not learned or used to communicate within the family environment); however, their structures have been enriched and they are used in many fields – such as radio and the press – and some have even given rise to independent literary forms.

As well as providing models which are useful to the linguist as an explanatory tool, the linguistic processes involved in the development of pidgins (reduction, re-expansion, Creolization and de-creolization) also provide a continuum open to a great number of influences. For example, they can be used when there is a need to affirm ethnic and cultural IDENTITY, or to resist the various pressures imposed by other languages. However, there is not one comprehensive definition of the origin and evolution of the pidgin languages. [A. B., R. B.]

Crystal, D. (1997) *The Cambridge Encyclopedia of Language*, Cambridge University Press, Cambridge.
Encyclopaedia Britannica, www.eb.com.
Holm, J. (1988) *Pidgins and Creoles*, Cambridge University Press, Cambridge.
Journal of Pidgin and Creole Languages, www.siu.edu.
McArthur, T. (ed.) (1992) *The Oxford Companion to the English Language*, Oxford University Press, Oxford.
Mühlhauser, P. (1986) *Pidgin and Creole Linguistics*, Blackwell, Oxford.

PLURICULTURALISM (It. *pluriculturalismo*; Fr. *pluriculturalisme*; Ger. *Plurikulturalismus*)

From the Latin *plures*, several, and *cultura*, culture, the term 'pluriculturalism' is often used as synonymous with MULTICULTURALISM, to refer to a tolerant (TOLERANCE) and positive political and conceptual approach to the coexistence of different ethnic groups in the same society. In the Anglo-Saxon world the latter term is more generally used. However, a certain distinction between the two can be made. Some European scholars (Perotti, 1997) distinguish between 'pluriculturalism' – seen as a model of society where different cultural groups interact with each other and therefore create multiple cultural and religious points of reference – and 'multiculturalism', which they view as a more compartmentalized model where there is little exchange between the different groups. In France 'pluricultural' is often used with particular reference to the education system, to define the process whereby the various languages and cultures (CULTURE) of the ethnic groups which came to settle in the country were gradually introduced in the school curricula. [S. G.]

Perotti, A. (1997) 'Le pluriculturel n'a pas été inventé de nos jours', interview in *Ensemble*, 36/97.

POGROM (It. *pogrom*; Fr. *pogrom*; Ger. *Pogrom*)

Originally used to describe violent and often murderous anti-Jewish persecutions (the most important of which took place in Kishinev) in Russia following the assassination of Tsar Alexander II in 1881, more recently the term 'pogrom', from the Russian *pogrom* (total destruction, devastation) has also been used to refer to attacks on other groups.

The persecution of Jews in Russia continued until 1917 on the crest of a wave of ANTI-SEMITISM, causing the flight, especially to the United States, of more than 1.5 million Russian Jews (JEW). During the civil war which followed the Bolshevik Revolution, the anti-Communist White Army carried out many pogroms: it is believed that 100,000 people were killed in Ukraine alone. The Russian pogroms were carried out by non-official soldiers, such as the Cossacks, and the local populations with the tacit approval of government.

Kristallnacht (literally 'Night of Crystal') which occurred on the night of 9–10 November 1938 and in which Nazi-inspired attacks on Jewish premises caused widespread damage and injury, can be considered to mark the beginning of the Holocaust (SHOAH). Although many Jews had returned to Poland after the Second World War, thousands more fled after a series of pogroms, such as that in Kielce in July 1946. Many of these pogroms were carried out by a reactionary group, the National Armed Forces (*Narodowe Siły Zbrojne*).

In the face of pogroms and state repression, the Jewish population of Poland fell from 200,000 in the immediate post-war years to 50,000 by 1950. By the early 1980s it was a mere 6000. [A. Z.]

Kochan, L. (1992) 'East European Jewry since 1770' in Englander, D. (ed.) *The Jewish Enigma*, The Open University in association with Peter Halban and the Spiro Institute, Milton Keynes.
Poliakov, L. (1966) *The History of Anti-Semitism*, Elek Books, London.

POLITICAL ASYLUM (It. *asilo politico*; Fr. *asile politique*; Ger. *politisches Asyl*) The term derives from the Greek *ásylon*, inviolable; composed of *a* and *sýlon*, violence, theft. For the purposes of international law it is used mainly to indicate the refuge (REFUGEE) and protection granted by a state within its territorial boundaries – or equivalent areas (FRONTIER) – to individuals who have entered such areas in order to escape from religious, political, ethnic and other forms of persecution in their country of origin (territorial asylum). States can take on the protection of such individuals by refusing to comply with any requests for delivery or DEPORTATION made by the authorities of the states of which the individuals are citizens (CITIZENSHIP), or from whose jurisdiction they have escaped.

According to international law, the granting of political asylum is an expression of the freedom which rightfully belongs to all members of the international community within their own territory with respect to all those individuals who reside in or request admission there. In this respect, international law lacks regulations which limit freedom by imposing delivery of individuals who have sought refuge in a state to the government requesting their consignment (obligation of extradition) or, conversely, by obliging states not to render, or in any case, not to expel an individual, and thus to grant asylum. Therefore, all states are absolutely free to grant or deny asylum in their territory to individuals who have entered the state in search of refuge. In no case does the granting of asylum constitute an infringement of the legal obligations of a state towards other states, even when the individuals to whom asylum is granted are political adversaries of the state from which they have escaped. In such cases, asylum will be considered illegal only where the state of refuge does not adopt the necessary measures to ensure that such individuals do not use their territory as a base for offensive action against the government from which they have escaped. [S. P.]

Barontini, G. (1992) 'Sulla competenza per l'esame delle domande di asilo secondo le Convenzioni di Schengen e Dublino', Rivista di Diritto Internazionale, Giuffré, Milano.

Beghè Loreti, A. (1990) *Rifugiati e richiedenti asilo nell'area della Comunità europea*, CEDAM, Padova.

Esposito, C. (1958) 'Asilo (diritto di)', in *Enciclopedia del diritto*, Vol. III, Giuffré, Milano.

Martin, D. A. (1988) *The New Asylum Seekers in the 1980s, The 9th Sokol Colloquium*, Martinus Nijhoff, Dordrecht and Boston.

POLYGENISM (It. *poligenismo*; Fr. *polygénisme*; Ger. *Poligenismus*)

The term 'polygenism' derives from the Greek words *polýs*, meaning many or much, and *génesis*, birth. The principle of a single origin of humankind (MONOGENISM) was not challenged until the discovery of the American continent in 1492, when the Old World first encountered previously unheard-of new populations. This led to the idea that 'Red Indians', who were completely segregated from the rest of humanity, could not possibly have the same origins as Europeans, i.e. it was not possible for Adam and Eve to be their forefathers. This theory was extended to all other existing populations and became known as polygenism.

Theophrast Bombast von Hohenheim (Paracelsus), a German doctor and alchemist, was the first to contest the principle of a single origin of humanity, in 1520. Subsequently, in 1616, the Italian scholar Giulio Cesare Vanini stated in his *De admirandis naturae reginae deaeque mortalium arcanis* that primeval humans were not upright and that humankind was divided into lower and higher levels. This was regarded as so provocative that the author was judged to be a heretic and condemned to the stake (EVOLUTION). About 40 years later, in the *Prae-Adamitae* (1655), the Frenchman Isaac de La Peyrère argued that Genesis only referred to the world known by the Jews. In this case, luckily, the 'liberal thinking' of the Parliament in Paris only condemned the book to the stake, while its author was arrested. In 1695, a book by an anonymous author entitled *Two Essays sent in a Letter from Oxford to a Noble Man in London*, was published in London. The book stated that neither the American Indians nor the Africans from the regions south of the Sahara – whom the author called Negroes – descended from Adam and Eve.

The debate was naturally linked to the *vexata quaestio* of human 'races' – the existence of which was considered a postulate and not something to be proved – which persisted throughout the Age of Enlightenment. The hypothesis of distinct origins for mankind became less credible in the twentieth century, although it has never disappeared completely. Indeed, although anthropologists became increasingly interested in trying to 'scientifically' classify mankind into 'races', between the end of the 1960s and the beginning of the 1970s, it was demonstrated beyond doubt that classification of RACE does not apply to the human species, and in the 1980s the discussion over the origins of *Homo sapiens* took a different direction; palaeoanthropology and molecular anthropology have today contributed to shifting the debate to the origins of modern man. [G. B., O. R.]

Greene, J. C. (1959) *The Death of Adam*, Iowa State University Press, Ames.

POSITIVE ACTION: see AFFIRMATIVE ACTION

POSTCOLONIAL STUDIES (It. *studi postcoloniali*; Fr. *études postcoloniales*; Ger. *Postkoloniale Studien*) Also referred to as 'postcolonialism', the term identifies an area of research concerned with the colonial encounter and its aftermath. Its main interest is in the European imperial and colonial project symbolically inaugurated by Columbus' famous 'discovery' of the so-called New World at the end of the fifteenth century. In a sense 'colonial studies' would thus be a more accurate description. Although the 'post' is slightly misleading, as it appears to suggest that this field of research is primarily focused on the situation of nation states (NATION) and the world order after the end of formal colonialism in the second half of the twentieth century, it does have significance because the characteristics of this field are thoroughly marked by a variety of features that have emerged primarily during the period of decolonization beginning with the 1950s. This is particularly true of the intellectual resources that are drawn upon within this cross-disciplinary enterprise: French poststructuralism, especially the work of Michel Foucault and Jacques Derrida, itself partly a product of the traumatic effects of the Algerian anti-colonial struggle against the French, but also the structuralist-influenced psychoanalytic approach deriving from Jacques Lacan (Young, 1990); the culturalist Marxism of the Italian Antonio Gramsci (1891–1937) the significance of whose work has only been felt internationally from the 1960s onwards; second wave feminism, again a post-1960s development; and

the reappropriation of anti-colonial writers, especially the psychiatrist Franz Fanon (1925–61), who was born in Martinique but worked in what was then French Algeria and wrote brilliantly about the psychic economy of colonialism and the dehumanization of the colonized.

The field also deserves the appellation 'postcolonial' because central to its development have been the efforts of writers and researchers who have been crucially marked by the experience both of colonialism and the period after its formal demise and who, intellectually and politically, may be said to inhabit a 'hybrid' cross-cultural positionality. They are often from the former European – especially British – colonies, but deploy Western intellectual resources in an effort to provide novel understandings of the impact of the imperial and colonial eras on both the colonized and the colonizers. They are interested, too, in attempting to provide a distinctive 'postcolonial' politics, especially in the field of CULTURE and IDENTITY, appropriate to a new 'post-national' period in which the emergence of formerly colonized populations has spawned global diasporas (DIASPORA), especially in the former colonial countries, and in a context where the forces of GLOBALIZATION are generally eroding national identities and leading to the emergence of complex, 'hybrid', deterritorialized cultures (Gandhi, 1998: 122–140).

Edward Said, Homi Bhabha and Gayatri Spivak are often referred to as the 'holy trinity' of postcolonial studies and their personal biographies and intellectual approaches epitomize some of the key features of the subject. It is primarily through their work that the nature of postcolonial studies will be illuminated here.

Edward Said, displaced from Palestine and now an academic in the USA, is best known for his *Orientalism* (1978) (ORIENTALISM) which drew upon both Foucault and Gramsci to explore how the colonizers' conceptions of the colonized structured the institutions of rule by which subject populations were governed. In emphasizing this form of imbrication between power, hegemony and knowledge, Said's analysis posed a challenge to conventional Marxism and other forms of investigation which had seen the development of colonial knowledges, contained in anthropology, history, language studies, fiction and travel literature, as mere *post facto* legitimizations of colonial plunder and exploitation.

Postcolonialism has also developed from Said the insight that it was not merely the identity of the colonized, but also that of the colonizer that was formed by the colonial encounter. The European colonizers' conception of themselves as white, Christian, 'civilized', masculine, rational, adult and so forth, developed in tandem with a conception of Orientals and Africans as binary opposites of these qualities: as black or 'COLOURED', pagan, barbaric, feminine and over-emotional, irrational, and childlike: in short, as inferior in every way and requiring rational, Christian government and CIVILIZATION (Rattansi, 1997: 481–482).

This kind of understanding of the mutual imbrication of identity, which does not ignore the enormous asymmetry of power between the two, has been extended in a whole range of researches by scholars working within a postcolonialist framework. Viswanathan (1989), to take just one example, has demonstrated how the development of English literary studies in Britain was decisively influenced by their success in India where they were put in place to produce Anglicized Indians who could serve as intermediary civil servants in the British government of India (for other examples of typical postcolonialist research see Rattansi, 1997). English literature has itself become the site of a specific project for the understanding and creation of English national identity, thus connecting the colonizer and colonized in a mutual identificatory process which has subsequently seen the emergence of English as one of the most popular subjects for university study in India. Moreover, Indian writers of fiction, such as Salman Rushdie, Vikram Seth and Arundhati Roy, amongst others, are regarded as some of the most important in the English-speaking world.

Bhabha's writings have provided another of the most original insights of postcolonial studies: that the domination of the colonizer over the colonized suffered from chronic instability, deriving from the deep ambivalence that marked the psyche of the colonizer in their relation to the colonized. Bhabha's writing is notoriously opaque and what follows should be regarded as a particular reading of his work (see his collected essays, 1994). Basing his primary work on episodes in the history of British India, Bhabha documents the threat posed to the colonizer's superiority by the forced and voluntary internalizations of the colonizer's culture by the colonized, thus undermining the idea of the forever 'uncivilized native', while at the same time holding up to the colonizer a caricatured version of the colonizer which implicitly mocks colonial culture. The colonizer remains trapped in a conundrum deriving from the desire to turn some of the natives (NATIVE) into 'brown Englishmen', partly to provide a cadre of civil servants, but this is a process continually disrupted by the obdurate survival of elements of 'native' culture; however, for the colonizer to succeed completely in transforming the native would force the colonizer to drop the pose of superiority. The 'mimicry' of the native only produces a 'hybrid' culture that consistently slips away from the colonizer's desire for complete mastery and domination, a desire that can be fulfilled only by undermining the cultural basis of the colonizer's claim to rule in the name of 'civilization'.

Another element implicit in Bhabha, but developed by other commentators, concerns the destabilization of the colonizer/colonized relation by the ambivalence of desire in all its complexity. The disgust of the colonizer at the habits, especially the supposed sexual immorality, of the native is disrupted by the fascination and attractions of native sexuality for the colonizer, played out in sexual fantasies as well as actual sexual liaisons which unravel the strict binary dichotomy between colonizer and 'native' (see, for example, Hall, 1992: 302–303; Rattansi, 1994: 43–46; Hyam, 1990).

The coupling of anxiety and desire of the colonizer abroad mirrored, to some extent, the ambivalence of the dominant classes at home when confronted by internal Others, especially women and the growing urban working classes (Viswanathan, 1989; Rattansi, 1997: 485–488) but also, in Britain, immigrants (MIGRANT) such as the Irish, whose 'WHITENESS' was continually doubted (Dyer, 1997).

An interesting related theme is the fascination of postcolonialist researchers with the distinctive role of the many white women who flouted the restrictions of Victorian conventions and travelled in various parts of the colonies, writing travelogues which were informed by great empathy for the cultures and the plight of the colonized, again fracturing the simple, strict opposition between the colonizer and 'native'

inscribed at the heart of the colonial project (Pratt, 1992; Mills, 1991).

In all these researches postcolonial studies inevitably make assumptions about the ability of present-day researchers to capture the reality of the colonial encounter and, very importantly, the consciousness both of the colonizer and the colonized. Spivak, another Indian educated in India and the West, has been instrumental in interrogating such possibilities in a more problematizing mode, through an eclectic mix of feminism, Derridean poststructuralism and deconstruction, Marxism and psychoanalysis. She has questioned the degree to which the voice of the colonial subaltern, especially that of the female, can ever be rearticulated by postcolonial researchers, given the construction of the history of the colonies by the imperial powers, the continuing domination of the Western academy in such researches and the general global hegemony of the West in a regime of neocolonialism (Spivak, 1987, 1993, 1999). Much of her writing works through the epistemological and political dilemmas that continually face postcolonial research, while at the same time she engages in such research herself. A focus on literary texts is a hallmark of her work. One of her most influential analyses has been the demonstration of how, in canonical works of English literature, such as the nineteenth-century *Jane Eyre*, the construction and resolution of the narrative rely on the existence of marginal colonial figures and background colonial events which are taken for granted: in this novel a crucial but marginalized figure is the Creole wife of the central character Rochester, whom Jane Eyre eventually marries, and a rather important but underplayed event is Jane Eyre's inheritance of a fortune from the West Indies, thus making her financial freedom complicit with the slavery of people of African descent (Spivak, 1985). What Spivak's reading of the novel excavates is precisely the mutual imbrication of the identities and fortunes of the colonizers and the colonized which is such a key feature of postcolonial studies.

Through her interventions in the 'Subaltern Studies' project in India Spivak has highlighted the significance of both gender and poststructuralism to postcolonial studies (Spivak, 1988). This project is the work of groups of historians and other researchers committed to studying the role of subaltern, that is, non-elite, groups in Indian anti-colonial struggles (see Guha, 1997 for a useful selection of studies from the work of the group). The term 'subaltern' is adapted from the work of the Italian Marxist, Antonio Gramsci). Spivak's critique of the group's project (Spivak, 1988) has questioned the tendency of the researchers to attribute a unified consciousness to subaltern groups as well as their more naive assumption that the truth of this collective consciousness can be captured by projects of historical recovery. Using poststructuralist insights Spivak has insisted on the need to decentre the subaltern subject, thus undermining notions of subaltern group unity, and has pointed to the inevitability of the selectivity of readings of subaltern histories by the members of the project. This selectivity is particularly apparent in the group's MARGINALIZATION of women's role in subaltern struggles as well as the limiting of subaltern insurgency to a narrative of nationalist struggle.

This last point connects with another concern of postcolonial studies. Said, Bhabha and Spivak, together with other postcolonialist researchers, have attempted to provide resources for a present-day post-nationalist politics, thus drawing out the significance of the postcolonialist project for contemporary concerns. Contemporary global inequalities between North and South and the role of American economic and cultural hegemony (CULTURAL IMPERIALISM) play key roles in contextualizing the need for distinctive postcolonialist perspectives (Said, 1993: 341–367; Spivak, 1999: 357–394). The incorporation of national elites in the South into global capitalism and the collapse of state apparatuses in the new nation states formed out of nationalist (NATIONAL-ISM) anti-colonial struggles leads to pessimistic readings by the likes of Said and Spivak of the current prospects for radical economic, political and cultural change in these former colonies. Said's involvement in the struggle for a Palestinian state and Spivak's interventions in feminist struggles in Bangladesh, India and elsewhere have led both to a form of resistance thoroughly permeated by disillusionment. Said pins his hopes on the emergence of post-nationalist politics and anti-systemic movements out of the mass migrations (MIGRATION) and displacements that have accompanied a global hybridization started by the processes of colonization and kept alive by the very forces of unequal globalization that have also led to de-radicalization (Said, 1993: 402–408). This is paralleled by Bhabha's alignment with what he calls the politics of a 'Third Space' of hybridity which emerges with the collision of cultures in the colonial and postcolonial world (Bhabha, 1990: 211). This may be thought to point to a form of MULTICULTURALISM as the preferred mode of postcolonialist politics, but in fact existing forms of multiculturalism are severely criticized either for what is seen as an assimilationist agenda that underlies them (Bhabha, 1990: 207–209, 219) or for co-optation by the demands of multinational capitalism (Spivak, 1999: 396–402).

A consistent charge against postcolonial studies has been its neglect of political economy in the analysis of colonialism and its aftermath (see Parry, 1987, among many others). There is undoubtedly a great deal of truth in this criticism. Nevertheless, three points are relevant in mitigation. First, the aim of postcolonial studies has been to rectify the neglect or simplification of the identity-constituting effects of the colonial encounter by approaches that have privileged the brutal economic exploitation that has been the more obvious driving force in the colonial enterprise. Secondly, postcolonial studies is seriously concerned by the current global economic inequalities that have resulted from the period of direct colonization. Finally, many postcolonial researchers have been keenly interested in exploring the dimensions of class and gender inequalities and identities that were forged in the colonial process (Rattansi, 1997: 485–486). Overemphasis on the analysis of literary and other textual products of writers and scholars from the colonial powers in the constitution of the colonial project has been another persistent criticism. That this complaint is justified is undeniable. Said, Bhabha and Spivak all have their primary training and expertise in literary studies, which form the central core of their research agendas. Not surprisingly, their influence has been significant in giving postcolonial studies a distinctive literary bias. However, historians, sociologists and anthropologists have also made significant contributions to the field, often inspired by the seminal work of Said in particular (e.g. Chatterjee, 1986; Mitchell, 1988; Hall, 1996; Mudimbe, 1988, 1994).

Some critics have pointed to the paradox and perhaps impossibility of unmasking the colonial enterprise using the tools of Western theory such as poststructuralism, psychoanalysis and so forth (Loomba, 1991). But the extraordinary insights yielded by using these tools undermine the force of this reservation. Also, the work of Stoller (1995) has shown how the postcolonial studies gaze can be returned to interrogate the effects of Eurocentrism on key intellectual resources of postcolonial studies, for example the work of the French social historian and philosopher, Michel Foucault.

Another reservation, expressed particularly by Marxist critics, concerns the overwhelming metropolitan location of the researchers and their co-optation by lucrative academic posts, especially in the USA (Ahmed, 1992). This is certainly an ever present danger, and one that Spivak, for example, has attempted to face up to, especially in *A Critique of Postcolonial Reason* (1999). On the other hand, given the global collapse of socialism as a serious alternative to capitalism and the real loss of radicalism in the South it is not clear what alternatives are offered by Marxism which has now completely lost ground as a radical intellectual and political alternative (see Kaviraj's 1993 response to Ahmed). [A. R.]

Ahmed, I. (1992) *In Theory: Classes, Nations, Literatures*, Verso, London.
Bhabha, H. (1990) '"The third space": interview with Homi Bhabha', in Rutherford, J. (ed.), *Identity: Community, Culture, Difference*, Lawrence & Wishart, London.
Bhabha, H. (1994) *The Location of Culture*, Routledge, London.
Chatterjee, P. (1986) *Nationalist Thought and the Colonial World*, Zed Press, London.
Dyer, R. (1997) *White*, Routledge, London.
Ghandi, L. (1998) *Postcolonial Theory*, Columbia University Press, New York.
Guha, R. (ed.) (1997) *A Subaltern Studies Reader 1986–1995*, Minnesota University Press, Minneapolis.
Hall, S. (1992) 'The West and the rest', in

Gieban, B., Hall, S. (eds), *Formations of Modernity*, Polity Press, Cambridge.

Hall, C. (1996) 'Histories, empires and the post-colonial moment', in Chambers, I., Curti, L. (eds), *The Post-Colonial Question*, Routledge, London.

Hyam, R. (1990) *Empire and Sexuality*, Manchester University Press, Manchester.

Kaviraj, S. (1993) 'The politics of nostalgia', *Economy and Society*, 22(4): 525–543.

Loomba, A. (1991) 'Overworlding the "Third World"', *Oxford Literary Review*, 13(1–2): 164–191.

Mills, S. (1991) *Discourses of Difference: An Analysis of Women's Travel Writing and Colonialism*, Routledge, London.

Mitchell, T. (1988) *Colonising Egypt*, University of California Press, Berkeley and Cambridge University Press, Cambridge.

Mudimbe, V. (1988) *The Invention of Africa*, Indiana University Press, Bloomington.

Mudimbe, V. (1994) *The Idea of Africa*, Indiana University Press, Bloomington.

Parry, B. (1987) 'Problems in current theories of colonial discourse', *Oxford Literary Review*, 9(1–2): 27–58.

Pratt, M. (1992) *Imperial Eyes: Travel Writing and Transculturation*, Routledge, London.

Rattansi, A. (1994) '"Western" racisms, ethnicities and identities in a "postmodern" frame', in Rattansi, A., Westwood, S. (eds), *Racism, Modernity and Identity: On the Western Front*, Polity Press, Cambridge, pp. 15–86.

Rattansi, A. (1997) 'Postcolonialism and its discontents', *Economy and Society*, 26(4): 480–500.

Said, E. (1978) *Orientalism*, Routledge, London.

Said, E. (1993) *Culture and Imperialism*, Chatto & Windus, London.

Spivak, G. (1983) *Outside in the Teaching Machine*, Routledge, London.

Spivak, G. (1985) 'Three women's texts and a critique of imperialism', *Critical Inquiry*, 12(1): 243–261.

Spivak, G. (1987) *In Other Worlds*, Methuen, London

Spivak, G. (1988) 'Subaltern studies: deconstructing historiography', in Guha, R., Spivak, G. (eds), *Selected Subaltern Studies*, Oxford University Press, New York.

Spivak, G. (1999) *A Critique of Postcolonial Reason*, Harvard University Press, Cambridge, MA.

Stoller, A. (1995) *Race and the Education of Desire: Foucault's History of Sexuality and the Colonial Order of Things*, Duke University Press, London and Durham, NC.

Viswanathan, G. (1989) *Masks of Conquest*, Faber & Faber, London.

Young, R. (1990) *White Mythologies: Writing History and the West*, Routledge, London.

PREJUDICE (It. *pregiudizio*, Fr. *préjudice*; Ger. *Vorurteil*) Middle English term from Old French, from Latin *praejudicium*, from *prae*, in advance, and *judicium*, judgement. Prejudice refers to beliefs, opinions and attitudes that are characterized by inflexibility, dogmatism and narrowmindedness. These may be learned, copied or acquired beliefs about another group or other groups (or individuals seen as belonging to that group). Such prejudices are usually though not always: (a) acquired before meeting that group/those individuals; (b) negative opinions and judgements; and (c) distorted, misinformed and inaccurate beliefs. Because of this, prejudiced individuals can also be described as intolerant (INTOLERANCE), bigoted and doctrinaire. It is an outlook that is unjustified by facts and unlikely to be changed, even in the face of evidence to the contrary. Allport (1954) regarded it as an antipathy based on faulty and inflexible generalizations. The core elements of prejudice are well summed up by Goldberg (1993: 104) who states that a prejudice is an antipathic, hostile attitude, felt or expressed towards a person considered strictly as a member of a group. An individual object of the prejudice is presumed to bear those (usually reprehensible) characteristics supposed to define the group. The prejudicial judgement may be made in inexcusable ignorance of all the available facts, or it may involve the logical error of overgeneralization: persons expressing prejudices may either improperly judge the object of their prejudice a member of the group in question, or they may wrongly infer that an individual is characterized by the designated properties because he/she is a member of the group. Prejudice necessarily involves stereotyping.

Prejudice has both cognitive and affective dimensions, the former including beliefs and stereotypes, the latter active dislike and aversion. Prejudice is an attitude that may or may not map on to its behavioural equivalent: discrimination. For example, where aversion leads to avoidance and bias, the line between attitude and behaviour is crossed and discrimination occurs. But, where dislike remains an attitude or outlook, it remains at the level of prejudice. Allport (1954) identified five levels within an isosceles triangle to depict the ascending scale of prejudice. It begins at the base with anti-locution (verbal abuse and insults), rising to avoidance (actively ignoring specific individuals and groups), discrimination (exclusion and stigmatization (STIGMA)), physical attack (persecution) and ultimately to GENO-CIDE (extermination). While Allport's scale seeks to link prejudiced attitudes to discriminatory behaviour, Van der Berghe (1967) attempts to separate these and to indicate that there is no automatic link. In the 'prejudiced non-discriminator' the existence of prejudice may lead to no outcome, because the individual is either unable or unwilling to act on her/his prejudices. This is contrasted with the 'non-prejudiced discriminator' to indicate that absence of prejudice does not mean absence of discrimination. A non-prejudiced individual may simply conform to prejudicial group or societal norms and this would produce patterns of discrimination. This model is still used in some organizations, though the question of how prejudices may or may not be operationalized needs to be understood in specific contexts. An element of that is the issue of power and there has been a proposition that RACISM can be understood as prejudice plus power. This view maintains that prejudice is widespread and commonplace, but only some have the capacity or power to act upon their prejudices to produce discriminatory outcomes. Although this was influential for a time in the UK, it relies on a simplistic conception of power as a zero sum game. It does not account for unevenness in prejudicial attitudes, or the relationship between beliefs and actions. Nor does it define the basis of power. It is also weak in accounting for ways and times when the objects of prejudice challenge images and representations of themselves.

A number of explanations for prejudicial attitudes have been advanced, including that they are based on: (a) frustration, AGGRESSION, or that they are a means of displacing certain feelings (the frustration-aggression hypothesis); (b) projection and psychic discomfort (a reaction to, or denial of, tension); (c) a general hostility to others and to strangers (FOREIGNER). Some of these traits have been associated with the idea of the authoritarian personality. Adorno et al. (1950) sought to identify the core elements of the personality type they saw as typical of the most uncritical supporters of the Nazis in Germany in the 1930s and 1940s. Among the traits they identified were stereotyped thinking, submissiveness to authority, hostility to those regarded as different (DIVERSITY-

SIMILARITY), and an emphasis on traditional values, correct behaviour and conformist attitudes (CONFORMISM). Adorno et al. held that such views originated in specific types of families and child-rearing practices, particularly families (FAMILY) with a strict father, emotional rigidity and a general lack of love. Using Freudian psychodynamic theory, they argued that the child is forced to develop repression as a defence mechanism against the parenting style that denies the child self-expression. The authoritarian parenting style creates aggression, frustration and hatred, which is then directed at convenient scapegoats. Inability to deal with ambiguity or cognitive dissonance may lead to the creation of prejudice and stereotypes, especially of ethnic and racial minorities (ETHNIC MINORITY). Conformity and submissiveness make the authoritarian personality susceptible to racist or Fascist ideologies, particularly ANTI-SEMITISM for the period considered by Adorno et al. Their thesis has been extensively criticized, for instance for overstating the influence of parenting and family dynamics. Although devised as a means of explaining racial prejudice, the authoritarian personality theory is now rarely used in research studies.

Allport (1954) also identified faulty childhood training, and fear and frustration as causes of prejudice. But these were only some causes of prejudice. The list of factors includes sexual conflicts, the importance of group membership for individuals, and social structures and cultural patterns. This indicates that prejudices have a broader social context than just the family and childhood experiences. Nonetheless, a criticism of Allport's and other psychological accounts of prejudice would be that they tend to assume that prejudice is an abnormality and that it is confined to relatively small numbers of the population. Because of the notion of prejudgement, they also assume that prejudice is essentially irrational. The existence of prejudice is also often regarded as pathological and as an uncharacteristic aberration of liberal societies. However, studies of racist individuals and groups suggest that abnormality and irrationality are not necessarily useful ways of understanding their motivations and beliefs.

If prejudice is merely irrational this suggests that teaching and inculcation of 'the facts' could eliminate it, and this approach has been adopted in educational and training programmes. But such models do not address the uneven, ambivalent and sometimes contradictory character of prejudices. There are at least three aspects to this. First, prejudices may be maintained even though an individual knows and acknowledges them to be irrational. Secondly, they may be maintained against other groups and cultures even while there is some admiration of the other culture. For example, Jewish people (JEW) may be disliked for seeking to keep apart from the rest of society and admired for their sense of group IDENTITY. Thirdly, prejudiced individuals may dislike some members of a particular group but not others. For these reasons prejudices are not simply antipathy to all 'others', but can have complex and variable meaning and forms.

Prejudices could be seen as having a functional component in serving the needs of individuals, groups and societies by attaching blame or responsibility for social problems to 'out-groups', often racially defined. In this sense, prejudice could be connected to scapegoating, where both are seen as the product of a universal societal requirement for some 'other' to serve the needs of fostering and maintaining integration. There is, however, little evidence to support the idea that prejudice against out-groups is higher among individuals who are highly bonded into their own groups. The scapegoating or blaming of others for social and personal ills could also be seen as a defensive reaction by particular groups seeking to maintain boundaries at times of rapid social change in which the denunciation and demonization of others fosters a dichotomization of 'us' and 'them'. Some other explanations for prejudice include group position theory, which asserts that prejudice stems from racial ALIENATION, particularly a feeling that one's own group is being treated unfairly. Another view is that hostility increases the more that other groups are seen as competitive threats. This discussion suggests that there is a distinction between a general ETHNOCENTRISM (of 'us' versus 'them') based on prejudices against other societies and cultures, as well as a more specific prejudice against particular groups. These two elements may well overlap in practice but they may also diverge at times.

Prejudice in its racial or ethnic forms suggests that the objects of prejudice are chosen because they are identifiably 'different', for example because of the existence of external markers such as skin colour or some other bodily sign. This does not account for prejudice against those of similar appearance – for example in the case of Catholics and Protestants in Northern Ireland. Nor does it explain why some somatic features such as skin colour sometimes acts as markers, while others do not. Both assumed biological and cultural differences may be invoked in prejudices. Prejudicial attitudes and stereotypes may mean that biology and culture are called up in contradictory ways: for example black people may be seen as naturally lazy and, at the same time, as inclined to athleticism. In terms of intergroup relations there may be horizontal

hostility and prejudice between similar minority groups (e.g. Orthodox and liberal Jews). In other cases prejudice may be sustained by a negative interdependence where each group perceives the other as a threat to its own identity and existence, as in the Israel/Palestine conflict.

The impact of prejudice is difficult to determine, except in specific instances. It has been suggested that the targets of prejudice may be liable to internalize negative views and this may affect their performance. For example, the low expectations by teachers is held as a common explanation for the poorer educational performance of some black children in schools. A more general version is that the lower socio-economic position of racial minorities is due to the prejudices they encounter in the labour market and other areas of social life. [K. M.]

Adorno, T. et al. (1950) *The Authoritarian Personality*, Harper & Row, New York.
Allport, G. (1954) *The Nature of Prejudice*, Beacon Press, Boston, MA.
Goldberg, D. (1993) *Racist Culture*, Blackwell, Oxford.
Van der Berghe, P. (1967) *Race and Racism: Comparative Perspectives*, Wiley, New York.

PRIMITIVE (It. *primitivo*; Fr. *primitif*; Ger. *Primitiver*) Generated by evolutionist theories, the term 'primitive', from the Latin *primitivus* (from the beginning), has come to replace the inappropriate and blatantly discriminatory SAVAGE, in defining those people 'discovered' by the West who live outside technological and industrial CIVILIZATION. Nevertheless, even the term 'primitive' has strong derogatory connotations and is therefore not commonly used nowadays. As the conception of history as an obligatory set of progressive and identical stages is no longer accepted, the use of expressions such as 'primitive PEOPLE' and 'primitive society' is destined to give way to ostensibly more neutral and plausible definitions describing people and societies as nature-based', 'archaic', 'non-writing', pre-industrial', 'indigenous' or 'small-scale'.

The description of peoples or societies as 'primitive' implies a negative or reductive comparison with Western societies (EUROCENTRISM) and may be considered misleading insofar as it suggests the existence of some absolute primitive' people – independent of specific historical and cultural circumstances – who have, in reality, never existed. According to Cantoni, primitive people no longer live in any part of the world and the reconstruction of the primitive personality on the basis of the rather meagre and incomplete data available is either impossible or reduced to a level of simple generalization and imagination (1941: 3-4). The likeness DIVERSITY–SIMILARITY) of non-European or THIRD WORLD peoples to the first inhabitants of the earth assumed by early anthropologists stemmed from a desire to reconstruct – through a study of what they presumed to be their original, simple and elementary nature – the ways of life and the social structures of past or extinct civilizations. This approach was based on a false view of primitive peoples as 'survivors' of less evolved' populations, and thus destined to disappear with the progress of civilization.

In current usage the term 'primitive' is employed only in a *de facto* descriptive sense, and interpretative use of the term is condemned. Increasingly, refusal to recognize the historical dignity of 'primitive' peoples is coming to be seen as the result of a reductive approach to history by the ethnocentric West (ETHNOCENTRISM). Even the assumed simplicity of the vision of the so-called primitive world or the perceived crudity of 'primitive cultures' (CULTURE) – in contrast to the complexity which characterizes civilization and the concept of EVOLUTION – may be considered in a different light following examination of the many cases expounded in ethnologic writings. The culture of the Dogons of Mali, who, according to some BLACK MUSLIMS, are one of the most beautiful examples of savage primitiveness, and who were studied for a long time by Marcel Griaule in the 1930s and 1940s, was organized in an extremely complex mythical–religious (MYTH) structure and their world vision was the African equivalent of the great classical cosmogonies. According to Griaule in *Dieu d'eau* (1966) these people lived according to a cosmogony, a metaphysical concept and a religion which places them on the same level as ancient populations.

In an attempt to interpret the 'primitive world', Lucien Lévy-Bruhl (1966) formulated the notion of a 'prelogical mentality', a thought process which did not use the principles of causality and contradiction, as is the case with civilized humans, but prefers 'mystical participation'. Franz Boas' studies, on the contrary, led to the conclusion that there is no fundamental difference between the way in which primitive and civilized people think, nor has there ever been any confirmation of a close relationship between 'RACE' and personality (Boas, 1938). Many events have led to replacement of the original meaning of the term – which was deeply embedded in a specific value category – with a descriptive use. In accounting for the growing recognition that once-prevailing western attitudes were ethno-centric, mention should be made of the effect of studies and research in chan-ging the way in which the social structure and culture of these groups is assessed, i.e. the inaccuracy of evolu-tionist assumptions – criticized by the biological and social sciences – and the profound effect of decolonization. Indeed, the political controversies which followed the decolonization pro-cess were proof of the ethnocentric attitude inherent in Western civilizing campaigns and Western occupation of the Third World, during which descrip-tion of these people as inferior served as a basis for the tremendous exploitation implemented under the banner of civilization (COLONIALISM, POST-COLONIAL STUDIES). [A. D. S.]

Boas, F. (1938) *The Mind of the Primitive Man*, Macmillan, New York.
Cantoni, R. (1941) *Il pensiero dei primitivi*, Garzanti, Milano.
Lévy-Bruhl, L. (1966) *Primitive Mentality*, Beacon Press, Boston, MA.
Griaule, M. (1966) *Dieu d'eau* (1948), Librairie Arthème Fayard, Paris.

PURITY

PURITY (It. *purezza*; Fr. *pureté*; Ger. *Reinheit*) 'Purity' is freedom from added elements or contaminants, the absence or degree of absence of any-thing harmful, inferior, unwanted or of a different kind. Purity is in principle a religious concept and is the state of being ritually acceptable: before enter-ing into a relationship with the divinity one must free oneself from any element of contamination (RITE). Obviously each religion differs in what it considers to be causes of impurity and has differ-ent purification rites. For example, in Christianity 'purity' often refers to the abstinence from sexual contact.

Contemporary history is rife with examples of ideological movements which have borrowed the concept of purity and applied it to the preservation of a PEOPLE or of a COMMUNITY of peoples from contamination by other human groups (DIVERSITY–SIMILAR-ITY, MIXOPHOBIA). At the basis of these ideologies is the assumption that a given people are 'pure', in view of the fact that the individuals making it up share certain physical characteristics which designate a RACE that cannot be confused with other races, coupled with the surmise that this particular race is the bearer of abilities and values which grant it supremacy above all others. Thus a taxonomic principle of physical anthropology – which in the nineteenth century aimed to provide a precise classification of all the races and sub-races composing the human species – became a political tool. The Nazi ideology is possibly the most extreme case of this.

The ideological foundation of Nazism can be found in Adolf Hitler's *Mein Kampf* (1923). By defining the 'white race' as the superior phyletic (racial) group, and assuming the highest expression of this race to be found – at its most uncontaminated – in the German people, Hitler set out a political plan which would allegedly lead Germany to achieve the dominion of the European continent and thus fulfil its grandiose destiny. This was to be achieved through the infeudation of the Eastern European Slavs and the expulsion and later elimination of the Jewish people (JEW). Hitler's political activities from 1923 to 1933, and during his chancellery from 1933 to 1945, were an attempt to actuate the programme expounded in *Mein Kampf*. Anti-Semitism, in particular, was exalted to the point of a kind of mass religion, and resulted in the extermina-tion of about 6 million Jews (SHOAH). In many ways, ANTI-SEMITISM was the ideological glue which bound the various strands of the Nazi utopia together. Ideologies of racial purity, with adjustments for local situations, did not disappear with the defeat of Nazi Germany, but survived throughout the second half of the twentieth century, though undergoing a peculiar shift; in Eastern Europe purity is ascribed now to one, now to another of the populations making up the Slav community, providing a political justification for ETHNIC CLEANSING. Nazism, Nazi-Fascism or Fascist-like ideologies still have a following in many countries of Western Europe, and take on various guises, such as anti-Semitism, XENOPHOBIA and tendencies towards regional separatism, often with particularly violent manifestations.

A closer analysis of the vast phenomenon, which includes the many political programmes inspired by the ideal of 'purity' appears to reveal, in diverse and complex situations, a common trait: the exploitation of the ideal of 'purity' as an expedient in order to solve the problems posed by political or social anomalies. It can be argued that the roots of German anti-Semitism can be found in Germany's historical delay in forming a national state (NATION). This delay was explained in some quarters as being caused by contamination by the Jews, as well as by local particularism and by other countries, France in particular. The Jewish people were seen not only as the bearers of various elements of impurity, but also, in view of their historical condition which saw them in turn as guests of one or another country, as potential allies of all of Germany's traditional foes. Hence Hitler's project, sufficiently simplified to be assimilated by the masses: to expel and/or eliminate the Jews, thus strengthening the German people so as to allow them to constitute, within and without its traditional boundaries, a new, powerful national state – the 'millenary Reich' – which would be large enough to allow the 'great' destiny of the Germanic people to unfold. This explains why to political observers German reunification – which followed the dissolution of the USSR (1989–91) – appears to be an authentic paradox. The new German national state, the German Federal Republic, raises the possibility of a re-emerging anti-Semitic trend, accompanied by strong xenophobic tendencies. The political solution of 1989–91 should have prevented such a phenomenon precisely in so far as Germany is now reunified and also has the makings of a great Western democracy. This would indicate that what was once a political anomaly has now become a social anomaly. The *Osten*, that is the citizens of the *Länder* of *Ost-Deutschland* (what used to be East Germany), are in a distinctly weaker economic position than the citizens of the western provinces of the country, which means that they may be induced, through an obvious psychological mechanism, to identify in the 'other' (the GASTARBEITER or foreign worker [FOREIGNER]) the cause of their situation, as well as ascribing to the Jewish people the character of agents of a 'fierce' global capitalism. [F. V.]

Bartov, O. (2000) *Mirror of Destruction: War, Genocide and Modern Identity*, Oxford University Press, Oxford.
Douglas, M. (1993) *Purity and Danger*, Routledge, London.
Moore, B. (2000) *Moral Purity and Persecution in History*, Princeton University Press, Princeton, NJ.

PUSH FACTORS - PULL FACTORS (It. *fattori di espulsione/fattori di attrazione;*

Fr. *facteurs d'expulsion/facteurs d'attraction*; Ger. *Ausreisegründe/Einreisegründe*) The study of the causes of migration traditionally considers push factors to be those elements in the place of exodus which determine the choice to leave. Pull factors are those elements in the area of arrival which also influence the decision to emigrate, as well as the duration and character of the emigration process. In the case of current international migrations both push and pull factors are important, though it should be strongly emphasized that the causes of emigration are many and mainly involve large-scale social and economic phenomena.

Push factors are determined by the overall demographic, economic, social, political and cultural situation of a country. From a demographic point of view (which determines, at least in the first place, the migration potential of a country) the first matter to be examined is a concern with increases in population in the majority of poorer countries. The world's population more than doubled between 1950 and 1995, increasing from 2.5 billion to 5.7 billion people. In developed countries, the growth has been 400 million people (from 0.8 to 1.2 billion inhabitants), whereas the population of poorer countries has grown by about 2.8 billion people.

The population growth rate of poorer countries is partly due to a rapid fall in the mortality rate, even though it remains much higher than that of developed countries. This fall has been produced by access to clean water, better prevention of infectious diseases and by the introduction of highly efficient, although simple and economical, medical treatments. Furthermore, while the average age of the world population is falling (half of the world's population is under 25), in richer countries it is increasing as a result of low birth rates

and the lengthening of the average lifespan. This also involves a consistent relative reduction in the population of employable age in richer countries, while in poorer countries the 'reserve army' of actual or potential unemployed is growing. On the basis of these demographic trends alone, an increase in the migration pressure from the South to the North of the world is to be expected, in particular towards Western European countries, the United States, Australia, Canada and Japan.

The demographic growth of poorer countries would constitute a less powerful push factor without the accompanying deterioration in the standard of living of the majority of their populations. Rich or 'developed' countries today own almost 80 per cent of the world's assets while accounting for only 20 per cent of its population. This gap is widening and because of the internal disproportion determined by so-called 'development' processes, the number of people who live in absolute poverty has grown in poorer countries, as well as in many of those of medium affluence. According to United Nations statistics, almost 1 billion people in the world today suffer from famine, and at least 50 million people, of whom 13 million are children, die of starvation every year.

Rapid urbanization has led to the urban population of poorer countries increasing by over 1 billion people, equal to the total world population of the middle of the last century. In 1950 only two cities, New York and London, had more than 10 million inhabitants. By 1975 there were already seven cities with such numbers. New York was followed by Tokyo-Yokohama, capital of the third emerging world power, followed in decreasing order by Mexico City, Shanghai and São Paulo, with London following. This scenario has now changed and by the early years of the twenty-first century the most populated cities in the world will include, in addition to those already mentioned, Bombay, New Delhi, Cairo, Jakarta and Manila. It is estimated that 75 per cent of the Latin American population, 42 per cent of Africans and 37 per cent of Asians now live in cities. This has already resulted in further environmental problems and a crisis in transport, communications and other services such as health care and education. In turn, this has caused a serious deterioration in already precarious living conditions and therefore acts as a spur to migration.

Economic and social factors are accompanied by more specifically cultural elements (CULTURE). The widespread influence of Western cultural models (which came about first through colonial contact and the presence of Christian missions in these countries, then through the growing commercial and tourist relations and the pervasive messages of the media) is causing growing pressures towards consumerism which may be said to combine push and pull factors encouraging migration. On the political plane, it is clear that in many countries the response to dramatic economic-social problems and to demands for reform has been repression. In many poorer countries governments appear to be controlled by old oligarchies or new bureaucracies, which are above all interested in maintaining their privileges and positions of power, sometimes with the support of countries from the North of the world.

Military coups, as in Chile in 1973 and elsewhere in Latin America, as well as repressive regimes in the Philippines, Indonesia, Turkey, Iraq and many other countries have created millions of exiles around the world (EXILE). This situation has been severely exacerbated by international conflicts such as in the Middle East and by civil wars, often involving violent ethnic conflicts, in parts of Africa, in Sri Lanka, Afghanistan, Iran, South East Asia and in the former Yugoslavia. Refugees have therefore become a very significant element in recent migration movements (REFUGEE), and a considerable source of debate and policy-making in the EU under the general issue of 'asylum seekers'.

Pull factors are no less complex. An important pull factor is undoubtedly the brutal economic fact of the wide difference in wealth between 'developed' and 'developing' countries. This is one reason why even the relatively well educated may seek menial jobs in the richer countries, as for example the many Philippine and Latin American women who become domestic workers in Western Europe and the USA respectively.

Shortages of unskilled labour in Western Europe and the USA were crucial pull factors in the period after the Second World War. The second half of the twentieth century saw economic migrations from the Caribbean, South Asia, Africa, China, Turkey and many other countries to Western Europe and the USA which have transformed these into more complex multiethnic societies (MULTICULTURALISM). More recently, in the 1990s, shortages of skilled and professional workers in new economic sectors such as information technology gave rise to a new form of migration as the richer countries, such as the USA and Germany, encouraged migration and began to drain the pool of highly educated workers from the poorer countries of the world such as India.

In their economic effects these recent migrations are similar to earlier phases, where poorer countries were further impoverished and the richer countries gained workers whose initial costs of education, health care and general upbringing had been borne by the poorer countries, although it is also arguable that the absence of suitable employment opportunities in poorer countries as well as remittances sent to them by migrant workers have made emigration of some economic benefit to the labour-exporting countries. [U. M., A. R.]

Castles, S., Miller, M. J. (1998) *The Age of Migration. International Population Movements in the Modern World*, Macmillan, London.

Collinson, S. (1993) *Europe and International Migration*, Pinter, London.
Melotti U. (1992) *L'immigrazione, una sfida per l'Europa*, Edizioni Associate, Roma.
Organization for Economic Cooperation and Development (2000) *Trends in International Migration 2000 edition*, Paris.
Sassen, S. (2000) *Guests and Aliens*, New Press, New York.
United Nations Development Program (UNDP) (2000) *Human Development Report*, New York and Geneva.
United Nations Population Fund (UNPFA) (2000) *The State of World Population*, Paris.

Q

QUOTA SYSTEM (It. *quote*; Fr. *système de quota*; Ger. *Quote*) The term 'quota system' (from the Latin *quota*, quota, part) generally describes the adoption of contingencies and policies limiting the number of foreigners (FOREIGNER) who may enter a country, above all for the purpose of work, in countries which receive 'mass migration FLOWS'. This type of system is usually based on immigration policies adopted in the USA, Australia and Canada (MIGRATION). During the 1970s, 'quota programmes' were used in Western Europe to accept and offer protection to refugees (REFUGEE) from South-East Asia, Vietnam in particular, and Latin America. The increasing number of refugees from these areas required different solutions to those adopted by neighbouring or primary countries of EXILE. Europe made its own contribution by also adopting quota programmes' whereby European countries undertook to assist a previously established number of refugees, especially with regard to their journey, and subsequently accept them. Refugees were automatically offered protection under these circumstances, without having to prove that they were afraid of persecution pursuant to Section 1 of the Geneva Convention (POLITICAL ASYLUM).

In 1998, Italy adopted a quota programme for immigrants in search of regular work which meant that the number of immigrants (MIGRANT) allowed to enter the country for work purposes was set each year by decree of the Prime Minister. The number of immigrants entering Italy for family reunification with parents and sons is not included in the quota. According to the Italian Constitution, the right to FAMILY REUNIFICATION is a human right, not restricted by administrative decisions.

All European Union member states are required to fulfil international obligations according to national economic needs, the availability of funds and administrative structures designed to ensure appropriate acceptance of immigrants, requests for work permits from immigrants already in the host country for other purposes (tourism, study, etc.) and the number of immigrants already holding work permits who are registered with the unemployment office as they are currently unemployed. Furthermore, a programme has been outlined for social and economic support aimed at encouraging social and cultural INTEGRATION of foreigners, maintaining their cultural IDENTITY and their right to education and a home.

In Germany, following events in former communist East European countries which led to large numbers of immigrants moving to the West and the reunification of the country after the 'Berlin Wall' was destroyed, immigration policies became rather strict. No non-European citizens were allowed to enter the country for the purposes of work, unless a decree from the Ministry of Internal Affairs stated otherwise. This decree can only overturn the general ban on immigrants for the purposes of subordinate employment in certain sectors and for a specific period of time.

The term 'quota system' is also used for systems of AFFIRMATIVE ACTION and positive discrimination which allow ethnic minorities (ETHNIC MINORITY) to access jobs and other resources such as seats in legislative assemblies, and compensate for previous generations of exclusion. [S. P.]

Borjas, G. J. (1999) *Heaven's Door: Immigration Policy and the American Economy*, Princeton University Press, Princeton, NJ.

Martin, D. A. (1980) 'The new asylum seekers', in *The New Asylum Seekers: Refugees and Law in the 1980s*, Dordrecht, The Netherlands.

Reimers, D. M. (1992) *Still the Golden Door*, Columbia University Press, New York.

R

RACE (It. *razza*; Fr. *race*; Ger. *Rasse*) **1** In order to fully comprehend the development of the concept of race, the psychological mechanisms underlying the process of identification of racial differences should first of all be analysed. It is important that such mechanisms are properly understood as many race-related controversial and difficult issues are partly based on the fact that the perception of racial differences triggers certain deep-seated psychological reactions related to the wider context of the perception of diversity (DIVERSITY–SIMILARITY). Such reactions are particularly dangerous and difficult to address because they stem from emotion rather than from the logical mind.

The need to categorize events, objects and other humans, in order to identify and control them, is part of the psychological makeup of all human beings and plays a fundamental role in the definition of diversity and, by definition, also of racial diversity. The idea of race predates the actual origins of the term, which are rather obscure. Long before this word became part of our language, human beings had attempted to understand why various populations (PEOPLE) presented different somatic, psychic and cultural characteristics. However, had all the inhabitants of the earth been physically similar, spoken the same language, followed the same religion, moral standards and behavioural patterns, abstract, if not objective, theories – based on another form of distribution of diversity – would very likely still have been formulated in order to establish the differences between one individual and another. Human beings share a deep-seated psychological urge to identify diversity and similarity as terms of comparison in an effort to establish their essential IDENTITY. This urge implies a fundamental conflict, in that we require diversity in order to distinguish ourselves from others and therefore to individuate, while at the same time we find reassurance and comfort in the experience of similarity and belonging to the human race. It follows· that both experiences, of difference and of sameness, are desired and feared in equal measure, as sameness implies the risk of loss of individual identity while diversity is perceived as a threat to unity. Kierkegaard (1946) probably best expressed this ambivalence when he spoke of the irrational 'dread' which assails people when confronted with the feeling of precariousness engendered by the infinite possibilities presented by diversity, which on the other hand also enables them to envision a range of choices otherwise absent. These ambivalent feelings also come into play with the perception of racial diversity.

The need to establish terms of comparison means that human beings automatically tend to assign hierarchical and value scales to the categories which they define, with the obvious dangers implied when such a mechanism is applied to the categorization of different races. One possible way of establishing categories for human differences is through scientific method. However, the danger remains that the argument could be used to rationalize many other subconscious drives which are in actual fact aimed at the exploitation and domination of others. Still, at the beginning of the twentieth century, some scientists attempted to condemn a number of groups to a subordinate role in society and raise others to a dominating position by defining categories of alleged racial inferiority/superiority. In order to repel such ideologically based discrimination, other scientists attempted to question the concept of race itself.

Although modern sciences now agree that the diversities recognized in human beings are not founded on a biological definition of race, none of the findings of these sciences – genetic or otherwise – are such that they imply that it will not be possible for new, more controversial discoveries to be made in future, and new ways of categorizing race to be established. The tools are already available to provide evidence of the fundamental identity of human beings or the substantial uselessness of the concept of race, but there is no way of knowing how future developments may change our perception of it. Whatever such developments may be, the implicit danger is that any 'neutral' categories of race established by science may be exploited by the more subconscious urges in the human psyche, against which understanding remains the best defence. [S. G.]

Gindro, S., Melotti, U. (1991) *Il mondo delle diversità*, Psicoanalisi Contro, Roma.
Kierkegaard, S. (1946) *The Concept of Dread* (1844), Oxford University Press, London.

2 The concept of race, while it should not be treated as a creed, should not be treated as a taboo either. Although it is true that many reactionary ideologies exploit the concept of race to justify social and cultural inequality, many progressive ideologies aimed at combating RACISM, especially in some European countries, are affected by ideological distortions or are simply unaware of even the most elementary notions of biology, and actually strenuously deny that different human races exist. Arguably the best way to combat RACIAL DISCRIMINATION is not by denying the existence of different races, but by understanding the true nature of such differences, so as to bring clarity to an issue which is otherwise allowed to dwell in the darker sphere of irrational feelings, where it can be exploited as a powerful tool for social discrimination and political propaganda. However, even if it is inexact, as well as counterproductive, to affirm that 'there is no such thing as race', the modern concept of race is far removed from the typological concept adopted by nineteenth-century biologists, which classified the human species as consisting of four main races identifiable by certain physical features – in particular skin colour, defined as 'white', 'black', 'yellow' or 'red' – races which were considered to have originated in different continents. Modern genetics recognizes the existence of an infinite number of sub-populations within the human species which may be classed as 'races', and which are characterized by various different genetic elements. Theoretically any number of races may be classified, depending on the criteria adopted in their definition. The geneticist Theodosius Dobzhansky (1962), having stated beforehand that 'differences in race can be ascertained objectively, however the number of races an individual chooses to acknowledge is merely a question of convenience', defined a classification of races which is extremely indicative of the approach of modern genetics, and which defines 34 races in all, some of which (for example, neo-Hawaiians, Ladinos and coloured North Americans) may seem quite disconcerting to the ayman. Dobzhansky's classification implies acknowledgement of the fact that races, far from being strictly defined types', are in reality Mendelian populations which change through time, and which the scientist must approach as such, independently of their hybrid origin and more or less recent formation. As Dobzhansky himself stressed, 'race' is a process rather than a fact. [U. M.]

Dobzhansky, T. (1962) *Mankind Evolving*, Yale University Press, New Haven.

Dobzhansky, T. (1973) *Genetic Diversity and Human Equality. Facts and Fallacies in the Explosive Genetics and Education Controversies*, The John Dewey Society Lecture, Basic Books, New York.

Melotti, U. (1979) *L'uomo tra natura e storia: la dialettica delle origini*, Centro Studi Terzo Mondo, Milano.

Montagu, M. F. A. (1952) *Man's Most Dangerous Myth. The Fallacy of Race*, Harper & Brothers, New York.

3 At first sight, it may seem that the use of the term 'race' to denote the differences between groups of people is neutral, natural and scientific. Indeed, it is widely assumed, even today, that 'race' has a clear, unambiguous, single meaning. On the contrary, the term is now regarded by many social and natural scientists as highly problematic and contentious, and in consequence they elect to qualify its appearance with quotation marks to indicate this. To understand how the concept achieved its scientific status, however spurious this status turned out to be, it is necessary to examine the early contacts between European and non-European groups of people – chiefly Africans and Orientals – with whom they came into contact from the sixteenth century onwards, although precursors of fully fledged racial theories had also emerged independently in China and Japan (Dikotter, 1997) although probably not on the Indian subcontinent (Robb, 1997).

At this juncture in European history, the use of the word had no particular scientific status; race was employed to denote a class of persons *or* things. Admittedly, contact between Europeans and non-Europeans could draw on a deeply embedded form of colour symbolism, a symbolism that is evident at least as early as medieval times although the evidence is more equivocal for the Graeco-Roman world (Hannaford, 1996: 17–86). In this tradition, the colour *black* is associated with undesirable or fearful characteristics like dirt, ugliness, death, sin and the devil, whereas the colour *white* (WHITENESS) is associated with godliness, purity and beauty (Banton and Harwood, 1975: 14–15). In addition, there existed conceptions of (non-European) 'monstrous races', characterized in particular by rampant sexuality (Friedman, 1981), and conceptions of peoples distinguished chiefly by the quality of 'Otherness', where this property is an inversion of all that was held to be European, Christian and civilized. As Jordan remarked, 'for Englishmen the most arresting characteristic of the newly discovered African was his colour. Travellers rarely failed to comment upon it; indeed when describing Africans they frequently began with complexion and then moved on to dress (or, as they saw it, lack of it) and manners' (1982: 43).

There was, Jordan explains, much speculation about the origins of the blackness of Africans. This speculation centred on one of two probabilities: either it was the result of the climate, and in particular, the consequence of the sun blackening the skin; or it was to be explained in theological terms, as the sign of God's curse on Ham and his descendants. The biblical portrayal of physical and cultural differences between apparently distinct groups of people was extremely influential. This intermingled God's purpose in creating different peoples, descent from different ancestors and the effect of living in different parts of the world. At the same time there emerged the view that the contrast between black and white – and between Europeans and non-Europeans more generally – was not simply a matter of difference, but also a matter of hierarchy. This view is well represented by the eighteenth-century philosopher David Hume, who characterized the difference between black and white as follows:

> I am apt to suspect that negroes, and all other species of men (for there are four or five different kinds) to be naturally inferior to the whites. There was never a civilized nation of any other complexion than white, nor even any individual eminent either in action or in speculation. No ingenious manufacturer amongst them, no arts, no sciences. . . . Such a uniform and constant difference could not happen, in so many countries and ages, if nature had not made an original distinction betwixt these breeds of men. (cited in Fryer, 1984: 152)

Hume eschewed even a cursory anthropological account of non-European cultures, and explained and justified his ethnocentric evaluation (ETHNO-CENTRISM) by positing a hierarchy of natural differences, where what he described as the most barbarous of 'the white' still possessed a certain eminence and thus were superior to all black peoples. Hume's views serve to highlight the common belief in the eighteenth and nineteenth centuries that white groups were also biologically differentiated, with Saxons and Teutonic 'races' being considered as superior to Slavs, for example.

What is often regarded as the first scientific treatise on 'race' was published by the slave-owner Edward Long in 1774. In his widely quoted three-volume *History of Jamaica*, Long drew upon contemporary scientific sources to propose the theory that whites and blacks were different species. This theory was based on a combination of physical and cultural characteristics – as discerned by Long – that were supposedly present in blacks. These included having 'bestial fleece' (as distinct from hair) and an inferior intelligence to apes, and displaying excessive sexuality and cruelty to children (Banton and Harwood, 1975: 18–19). Views like those of Long did not go unchallenged. Indeed, three contrasting discourses may be cited. One was the idea of the Noble Savage (SAVAGE). A second was the suggestion that the physical and cultural characteristics (CULTURE) of Africans were the product of their environment: thus if they were transported to the different climate and habitat of the Americas, these characteristics could be transformed. A third was a version of Christianity that stressed a common humanity and the possibility of African (heathen) conversion to its doctrines.

These countervailing discourses, though they undoubtedly contributed to the anti-slavery movement (SLAVERY), were not sufficiently influential to displace the prevailing view of African and Oriental inferiority – a view accepted even by many abolitionists. Some Christian abolitionists perceived the African as, simultaneously, degenerate savage and potential convert. The belief that the grouping of human beings into several 'races' might be established as objective, scientific truth first emerged at the very end of the eighteenth century. But it was not until the nineteenth century that this opinion won wide acceptance. This development coincided with the application of scientific procedures to various fields of inquiry – notably in physiology and medicine (RACISM AND MEDICINE) – and the application of scientific methods to a wide range of industrial processes. The advance of scientific racism occurred in an era when science assumed growing legitimacy and when it promised to provide fundamental truths about nature and about society.

As far as scientific racism was concerned, the vital element was the growing belief in biological determinism, which represented perceived differences between groups of human beings as not merely innate, but also unchangeable. This was a fundamental departure from previous environmental theories, which treated presumed racial differences as the consequence of differences in climate and habitat. Key texts in the development of scientific racism were written by Robert Knox, whose *Races of Man* was published in 1850 and Joseph de Gobineau, whose four-volume work *Essai sur l'inégalité des races* (Essay on the Inequality of Human Races) appeared shortly thereafter, in the years 1853–55. Both works depicted racial typologies based on several types of physical marker, such as skin colour, type of hair, and, notably, size and shape of skull. According to Banton and Harwood, these and other racial doctrines had two main consequences on prevailing thought. The first was that the scientific world of the time accepted 'that in comparative morphology [the study of shapes and structures of the human body] it was a valid procedure to distinguish a variety of anatomical types and to call them races'. The second was that, henceforth, 'the initiative lay with arguments advancing physical causes as the explanation of all human differences. *Homo Sapiens* was presented as a species divided into a number of races of different capacity and temperament. Human affairs could be understood only if individuals were seen as representatives of races for it was there that the driving forces of history resided' (1975: 30). The title of de

Gobineau's text underlines a key aspect of these racial doctrines: that the races that these doctrines claimed to be able to delineate – and each contributor had a different classification which yielded a different number of races – were situated on a hierarchical scale on which black races were at the bottom and white races were at the top. In other words, scientific racism was ultimately a cloak for views of white superiority. This said, scientific racism was not stationary. For example, it became increasingly *medicalized* by being articulated with discourses concerning various kinds of natural and social pathology. In this process much attention was devoted to the supposed bestial and unrestrained nature of black sexuality. In addition, it should be realized that the questions addressed by scientific racism and the hypotheses that it formulated were part of an *ideological* process. That is to say, the production of this meaning and knowledge were part – and an important part – of the exercise of power. In particular, the interconnected ideas that it was possible to differentiate between 'races' that were fixed biological entities, that these races stood in relation to one another as superior and inferior, and that they constituted a prime explanation for human behaviour and human history – perhaps *the* prime explanation – provided a convincing justification for colonial exploitation as a civilizing mission (CIVILIZATION, COLONIAL-ISM). Scientific racism played a central role in the ANTI-SEMITISM and other racist practices of Nazi Germany.

The racial classifications that held sway in the nineteenth century and in the early part of the twentieth century were based primarily on what are referred to as *phenotypical* features, such as skin colour, physiognomy and type of hair. Even so, it proved difficult to produce a classification of mutually exclusive groups, to say nothing of a list of groups that met with any degree of consensus from others in the field. Thus lists and types grew exponentially. Moreover, it proved notoriously difficult to demonstrate any systematic connection between PHENOTYPE and social practices or individual behaviour. Yet what really undermined the belief that human beings could be divided into discrete racial groups, which was the fundamental belief of scientific racism, was the development of the science of genetics. The key finding of modern genetics as far as the concept of race is concerned is summed up by Lewontin as follows:

> Of all human genetic variation known for enzymes and proteins . . . 85 per cent turn out to be between individuals within the same local population, tribe or nation. A further 8 per cent is between tribes or nations within a major 'race', and the remaining 7 per cent is between major 'races'. That means that the genetic variation between one Spaniard and another, or between one Masai and another, is 85% of all human genetic variations, while only 15 per cent is accounted for by breaking people up into groups. . . . The result of the study of genetic variations is in sharp contrast with the everyday impression that major 'races' are well differentiated. Clearly, those superficial differences in hair form, skin colour, and facial features that are used to distinguish 'races' from each other are not typical of human genes in general. Any use of racial categories must take its justification from some other source than biology. The remarkable feature of human EVOLUTION and history has been the very small degree of divergence between geographical populations, as compared with the genetic variations among individuals. (1987: 206–207)

The science of genetics may be complex, but its lesson for the study of 'race' until recently has been straightforward. This lesson has been that while physical differences between groups certainly exist, these differences are comparatively trivial in genetic terms. The vital point is that there is much greater variation between individuals within any designated 'racial group' than there is between such designated racial groups. However, developments in genetics may not continue to offer the same foundation for 'scientific anti-racism' in the twenty-first century (Kohn, 1995). Data from the Human Genome Project (GENOTYPE) and other research emanating from the new genetics may be used to construct a new kind of racial science in which older concepts of 'race' are replaced by forms of population genetics which will be pressed into the service of novel kinds of scientific racisms, aided by arguments from evolutionary psychology (Rose and Rose, 2000).

There are other reasons why the concept of 'race' is unlikely to be of merely historical interest. In large measure, this is because 'race' is a *social construct* and, as social scientists recognize, it is a social construct that is capable of exercising great force. In this sense 'race', although appearing under the guise, for instance, of cultural difference, is often taken to refer to the same or similar criteria that once formed the basis of now-discredited racial typologies – notably skin colour and physiognomy. This incarnation of race follows from the frequency with which such characteristics are used by individuals and groups to identify themselves as belonging to a given 'race' and, more especially, by the propensity of gate-keepers to use such characteristics as a means of discriminating against such individuals and groups. In circumstances like these, where 'race' is the pretext for discrimination, the law may be invoked to combat it, as in Britain's RACE RELATIONS legislation, but in so doing it is obliged to give recognition to a concept that has no remaining scientific basis. [A. R.]

Banton, M., Harwood, J. (1975) *The Race Concept*, David & Charles, Newton Abbot.

Dikotter, F. (ed.) (1997) *The Construction of Racial Identities in China and Japan*, Hurst, London.

Friedman, J. (1981) *The Monstrous Races in Medieval Thought and Art*, Harvard University Press, Cambridge, MA.

Fryer, P. (1984) *Staying Power: The History of Black People in Britain*, Pluto Press, London.

Hannaford, I. (1996) *Race: The History of an Idea in the West*, Johns Hopkins University Press, Baltimore.

Jordan, W. D. (1982) 'First impressions: initial English confrontations with Africans', in Husband, C. (ed.), *'Race' in Britain*, Hutchinson, London.

Kohn, M. (1995) *The Race Gallery: The Return of Racial Science*, Jonathan Cape, London.

Lewontin, R. (1987) 'Are the races different?', in Gill, D., Levidos, L. (eds), *Anti-Racist Science Teaching*, Free Association Books, London.

Robb, P. (ed.) (1997) *The Concept of Race in South Asia*, Oxford University Press, New Delhi.

Rose H., Rose S. (2000) *Alas, Poor Darwin*, Jonathan Cape, London.

'RACE' AND GENDER (It. *razza e genere;* Fr. *Race et genre;* Ger. *Rasse und Geschlecht*) It is now common for those interested in the study of society to recognize that both RACE and gender are important features of most societies which differentiate people's experiences and life chances. A major impetus for the linkage of 'race' and gender was the dissatisfaction expressed by black feminists, primarily in the USA and the UK, with the constructions of 'women' made by white feminists and of 'black people' made by black men. These often took white women's experience as paradigmatic of gender and black men's experience as paradigmatic of 'race' so that black women's experiences were, for example, invisible while white men were taken for granted as the norm (Alcoff, 1998). For example, the US Combahee River Collective statement (1977) put racialized (RACIALIZATION) and gendered difference and the politics of alliance on feminist and black political agendas when they argued for recognition of differences (DIVERSITY–SIMILARITY), as well as of commonalities between black women and black men and black women and white women.

This simultaneous focus on 'race' and gender is far from new. In 1851 a black female ex-slave gave a speech at the Women's Rights Convention in Akron, Ohio (USA) which has become famous for her argument that, while she had worked hard and not been protected all her life (in contrast to how white womanhood was defined), she was nevertheless a woman. She thus made a powerful challenge to essentialist thinking that women are necessarily weaker than men and that black women slaves were not 'real' women. In addition, it raised the simultaneity of racialized and gendered power relations – an issue that black feminists were also to put on the feminist agenda 130 years later. See, for example, bell hook's (1981) book of the same title as Sojourner Truth's speech, *Ain't I a Woman?* and Hull, Scott and Smith's aptly titled edited collection, *All the Women are White, All the Blacks are Men, But Some of Us are Brave*, which argued that: 'We believe that sexual politics under patriarchy is as pervasive in Black women's lives as are the politics of class and race. We also often find it difficult to separate race from class from sex oppression because in our lives they are most often experienced simultaneously' (1982: 16). While black women played an important part in making the intersections of 'race' and gender visible, the processes of 'race' and gender had operated for centuries so that white, middle-class men, for example, had, for centuries, benefited from their power over women and black people (Elam, 1994; Hall, 1992; Ware, 1992). In challenging simple oppositions between 'black' and 'white'; 'man' and 'woman', black feminist writers also challenged bipolar constructions and insisted that it was illegitimate to deploy general constructs such as 'women' or 'black people' in ways which excluded black women.

In Britain (although not in the USA) 'black women' came to include women from the Indian subcontinent – those styled 'women of colour' (COLOURED) in the USA. In the 1970s and 1980s, a focus on the specificity of black women's, white women's, black men's and white men's experiences led some people to engage in IDENTITY politics where political action was based on the supposed unity of race/gender groups. This ensured that both 'race' and gender were kept on the social agenda and mentioned in research (Sudbury, 1998). However, it has been much criticized for treating groups such as 'black women' and white 'women' as if they constitute unitary, 'essentially fixed, oppositional categories' instead of 'historically contingent fields of contestation within discursive and material practices' (Brah, 1996: 95). More recent theorizing has attempted to treat both 'race' and gender as relational – recognizing that, for example, what it is to be a woman can only be understood in relation to what it means to be a man – and as a dynamic, changing process (Nicholson, 1998; Rattansi, 1994). ETHNICITY has also been recognized as a central feature of differentiation (Anthias and Yuval-Davis, 1992). A focus on the complexities of difference has allowed better analy-

tical understanding than was enabled by a dualist focus on difference as bipolar black/white or men/women.

An understanding of 'race' and gender was given added impetus in the 1990s by concerns in many countries around the world with boys' poor educational attainment in comparison with that of girls (Arnot et al., 1999). With increasing research attention devoted to masculinities, it has become clearer that masculinities are racialized in such a way that, in Britain and the USA, black men and boys are contradictorily positioned as hyper-masculine (and envied and desired for their style and assumed toughness) and as too tough and dangerous (Majors and Billson, 1992; Sewell, 1997). It will, therefore, only be possible to address what some have called 'a crisis of masculinity' if the intersections of 'race' and gender are addressed. Yet recognizing their simultaneity is the beginning rather than the end of a process, since 'there is still a paucity of material concentration on the interrelationship between "race" and gender' (Afshar and Maynard, 1994: 1) and, indeed, difference has sometimes been treated in tokenistic or marginalizing ways:

A nod in the direction of the panoply of gender, ethnicity and 'race' has now become the sine qua non of being a good sociologist. . . . The concern that all sociologists should always make at least a passing reference to 'women and ethnic minorities' [ETHNIC MINORITY] has become a form of 'political correctness'. . . . If such a concern has now become a received wisdom in the sociological fraternity (for this is still largely what it is . . .) what happens to a serious consideration of social divisions? What is so important about gender, ethnicity, 'race' (and class) that means we should not allow their analysis to be reduced to 'women and ethnic minorities', to that easy, homogenizing, guilt-allaying cliché of the modern sociology textbook or to a form of what some may see as an empty 'political correctness'? (Anthias, 1996: 1)

There have been some political advances as a result of recognizing that 'race' and gender are interlinked. For example, the post-apartheid South African Constitution has simultaneously to legislate for both 'race' and gender equality. It remains to be seen whether this will be achieved in practice. [A. P.]

Afshar, H., Maynard, M. (1994) *The Dynamics of 'Race' and Gender*, Falmer, London.

Alcoff, L. M. (1998) 'Racism', in Jaggar A., Young I. (eds), *A Companion to Feminist Philosophy*, Blackwell, Oxford.

Anthias, F. (1996) 'Rethinking social divisions: or what's so important about gender, ethnicity, "race" and social class?', *Inaugural Lecture*, University of Greenwich, Greenwich.

Anthias, F., Yuval-Davis, N. (1992) *Racialized Boundaries: Race, Nation, Gender, Colour and Class and the Anti-racist Struggle*, Routledge, London.

Arnot, M., David, M., Weiner, G. (1999) *Closing the Gender Gap*, Polity Press, Cambridge.

Brah, A. (1996) *Cartographies of Diaspora: Contesting Identities*, Routledge, London.

Combahee River Collective (1977/1997) 'A black feminist statement', in Hull et al. (eds) (1982).

Elam, D. (1994) *Feminism and Deconstruction: Ms en Abyme*, Routledge, London.

Hooks, B. (1981) *Ain't I a Woman? Black Women and Feminism*, South End Press, Boston, Mass.

Hall, C. (1992) *White, Male and Middle Class: Explorations in Feminism and History*, Polity Press, Cambridge.

Hull, G., Scott, P.P., Smith, B. (eds) (1982) *All the Women are White, All the Blacks are Men, But Some of Us are Brave*, The Feminist Press, New York.

Majors, R., Billson, J. (1992) *Cool Pose: The Dilemmas of Black Manhood in America*, Lexington, New York.

Nicholson, L. (1998) 'Gender', in Jaggar, A., Young, I. (eds), *A Companion to Feminist Philosophy*, Blackwell, Oxford.

Rattansi, A. (1994) '"Western" racisms, ethnicities and identities in a "post-modern" frame', in Rattansi, A., Westwood, S. (eds), *Racism, Modernity & Identity: On the Western Front*, Polity Press, Cambridge.

Sewell, T. (1997) *Black Masculinities and Schooling: How Black Boys Survive Modern Schooling*, Trentham Books, Stoke on Trent.

Sudbury, J. (1998) *Other Kinds of Dreams: Black Women's Organisations and the Politics of Transformation*, Routledge, London.

Ware, V. (1992) *Beyond the Pale: White Women, Racism and History*, Verso, London.

RACE AND INEQUALITY (It. *Razza e inugualianza*; Fr. *Race et inégalité*; Ger. *Rasse und Ungleichheit*) Malik (1996) in examining Enlightenment conceptions of RACE suggested that the idea became a basis for inequality late in European history, contrary to the claims of more radical commentators. The idea of race was needed (in part) to enable people with universalistic beliefs to account for persistent inequalities within and between populations. Malik also suggests that beneficiaries of the Enlightenment found that the ideas of EQUALITY that had underpinned their critique of the old regime were less helpful in maintaining their position in the new order. The idea of natural racial inequalities also formed part of the Romantic reaction to the Enlightenment. It is important, however, to note that the late eighteenth and the nineteenth centuries were a period in which 'race' applied to the 'white' population. The notion of degenerate strains within a population was one origin of eugenic policies in Europe and North America and, later, euthanasia in Nazi Germany, a scheme by which contaminants (PURITY) could be removed from society (Kevles, 1986; Kohn, 1996; Müller-Hill, 1988).

In the United States, although the majority of poor people are white, inequality became highly racialized (RACIALIZATION). Racial inequality (in effect, white dominance) was supported by the notion that inherent racial inferiority could not be overcome (in spite of evidence to the contrary). Banton suggested that the argument that race only became salient in opposing anti-slave trade campaigns 'is far from satisfactory'. In South Africa race became the basis for the deliberate construction of a highly unequal system of economic, social, legal and political relations (RACIAL SEGREGATION). Modern versions of inherent racial inequality are found in the work of psychologists (notably Jensen, 1969, who can be taken to symbolize the wider RACE AND IQ debate, and Gould, 1984) and were revived by Herrnstein and Murray in *The Bell Curve* (1994). Murray in his earlier work cited youth unemployment, decline in marriage and crime as symptoms of an 'UNDERCLASS'. William Julius Wilson replied to the Murray analysis by showing that the changing economic structure of the USA had marginalized (MARGINALIZATION) large sections of the urban black population. Also, paradoxically, equal rights legislation has removed role models from the former ghettos (GHETTO) and deprived them of effective leadership (Wilson, 1987). Fischer et al. replied in detail to *The Bell Curve* in their *Inequality by Design* (1996), demonstrating both the fragile (or spurious) scientific foundations of this best-selling volume and its ideological functions in promoting beliefs about race and racial inequality.

The political economy of racialized inequality has been studied by a number of authors who take the view that inequality is structured and not to be explained by the characteristics of the dominated groups. From this perspective, because certain (racially defined) groups can be discriminated against, they can be used to perform crucial functions in either providing low-cost labour or can be employed outside the transitional patterns of native workers, thus enabling employers to effect a smoother transition to new technologies (Castles and Kosack, 1973; Duffield, 1985; Fevre, 1984). The lack of CITIZENSHIP may make migrants (MIGRANT) (and their descendants) (SECOND GENERATION) especially vulnerable to this form of inequality (Moore, 1977, 1989).

There is also a more empirical and pragmatic approach to observed social, political and economic inequalities between migrants and native populations of Europe and North America. For example, there was a COLOUR BAR running through the American stratification system, with blacks over-represented in the bottom strata and under-represented in the upper strata. The policy problem is to tip the line until it is upright and minorities (or blacks) are equally represented at all levels of society. This is plainly a less radical approach than that rooted in political economy and does not treat the overall structure of society as problematic. Furthermore, discrimination is taken as a problem to be solved rather than as an intrinsic feature of society. Research in this approach entails measuring and documenting the extent to which racial or ethnic minorities (ETHNIC MINORITY) fall behind the NATIVE population in education performance and in the acquisition of higher-status jobs, income and property. Explanations are commonly framed in terms of the social and cultural capital that migrants bring to their host countries or acquire there and the extent to which they assimilate to the CULTURE, overcome cultural barriers to success and acquire the motives and ambitions of the native population. The differences remaining when all these factors have been taken into account can be attributed to discrimination and the facts thus established may become the basis for equal opportunities policies. In the course of this research differences may emerge both between minority groups and genders (RACE AND GENDER). For example, in the United Kingdom Chinese and Asian school-children are beginning to out-perform native English children. The performance of children of Afro-Caribbean origin is nearer 'white' children's, but with Afro-Caribbean boys falling behind (Modood and Berthoud, 1997). Such research may illuminate and explain the social mobility of particular groups but is inadequate in explaining, for example, why black Americans have remained concentrated in the lowest strata while successive waves of migrants have been economically successful. [R. M.]

Banton, M. (1977) *The Idea of Race*, Tavistock, London.

Banton, M. (1988) *Racial Consciousness*, Longman, London.

Castles, S., Kosack, G. (1973) *Immigrant Workers and Class Structure in Western Europe*, Oxford University Press, Oxford.

Duffield, M. (1985) *Race and Labour in Twentieth Century Britain*, Frank Cass, London.

Fevre, R. (1984) *Cheap Labour and Racial Discrimination*, Gower, London.

Fischer, C. S., Swidler, A., Lucas, S. R. (1996) *Inequality by Design*, Princeton University Press, Princeton, NJ.

Gould, S. J. (1984) *The Mismeasure of Man*, Pelican, London.

Herrnstein, R. J., Murray, C. (1994) *The Bell Curve: Intelligence and Class Structure in American Life*, The Free Press, New York.

Jensen, A. R. (1969) 'How much can we boost IQ and scholastic achievement?', *Harvard Educational Review*, 39: 1–123.

Kevles, D. J. (1986) *In the Name of Eugenics*, Pelican, London.

Kohn, M. (1996) *The Race Gallery: The Return of Racial Science*, Jonathan Cape, London.

Malik, K. (1996) *The Meaning of Race*, Macmillan, London.

Modood, T., Berthoud, R. (1997) *Ethnic Minorities in Britain*, Policy Studies Institute, London.

Moore, R. (1977) 'Migrants and the class structure of Western Europe', in Scase, R. (ed.), *Industrial Society: Class Cleavage and Control*, George Allen & Unwin, London.

Moore, R. (1989) 'Ethnic divisions and class in Western Europe', in Scase, R. (ed.), *Industrial Societies: Crisis and Division in Western Capitalism and State Socialism*, Unwin Hyman, London.

Müller-Hill, B. (1988) *Murderous Science*, Oxford University Press, Oxford.

Murray, C. (1984) *Losing Ground: American Social Policy, 1950–1980*, Basic Books, New York.

Wilson, W. J. (1987) *The Truly Disadvantaged: The Inner City, the Underclass and Public Policy*, University of Chicago Press, Chicago.

RACE **AND IQ** (It. *razza e QI*; Fr. *Race et QI*; Ger. *Rasse und IQ*) RACE and IQ (where IQ refers to 'Intelligence Quotient') is a shorthand term for a long-running debate which centres on the issue of whether black people are genetically predisposed to be less intelligent than white people. The first systematic intelligence test was devised by the French psychologists Alfred Binet and Theophile Simon in 1905. This was designed to assess, in order to help, children who were lagging behind their peers. The IQ score is obtained by comparing the score gained by an individual on a test with the range of scores obtained by a group of people of a similar age on whom the test has been standardized. The average score obtained by most people is standardized as the norm and assigned a score of 100. Someone who scores 145 or more would be considered to be particularly gifted, while those who score 75 or less would be considered to have special educational needs.

A formal link between race and intelligence was made during the First World War, when mass intelligence testing was carried out for the first time on the US army. This provided data showing that black recruits scored less on IQ tests than their white counterparts. The area of race and IQ was underpinned by essentialist arguments about black people's genetic intellectual inferiority to white people because, in a historical context where some academics were also enthusiastic eugenicists, genetic explanations of this kind were widely accepted and, indeed, taken for granted (Lewontin et al., 1984; Evans and Waites, 1981). This form of essentialism predated the development of IQ tests since it had, for centuries, been accepted as fact that white 'races' were naturally superior to black 'races' (Miles 1989). Such long-standing beliefs helped to provide the conditions within which black people's inferior performance on IQ tests was accepted as natural (Gould, 1981).

Although PREJUDICE and stereotyping concerning the superiority of one race over another exist in many countries, the academic debate on the connection between intelligence and race, especially as measured through IQ, has been most vigorous in the USA and the UK. One of the reasons for this may be that when the discussion on race and IQ commenced – at the time of the Second World War – many European countries were experiencing directly the effects of extreme racist theories (RACISM). In the aftermath of the war in many countries the use of the term 'race' was banned from any academic context. Racist theory seemed to be completely discredited.

Recent controversy over 'race' and IQ began with a lengthy paper written by Jensen in 1969, which basically suggested that it was a waste of time and money to try to increase black children's IQ scores since, genetically, they were intellectually inferior. Jensen's explicit aim was to get the funding for the USA Head Start preschool intervention programme halted (and, indeed, President Nixon did stop it). Within British and US academia, a lot of time and energy was spent, by white academics and black academics alike, on careful refutations of Jensen's arguments and detailed examinations of the shortcomings of the 'evidence' on which the hereditarian case was built (Rose and Rose, 1978; Guthrie, 1976). While not denying that human characteristics are inherited, such refutations contest the notion of inheritance of intelligence by race and demonstrate the contribution of environmental factors to test scores (Lewontin et al., 1984). However, there was also some support for Jensen's position from psychologists such as Richard Lynn and Hans Eysenck and the physicist William Shockley. Eysenck (1971) also argued that there should be political consequences of black–white differences in IQ in relation to what he termed 'sensible' policies on immigration (MIGRATION). For those who support hereditarian notions of 'race' and IQ, skin colour is constructed as a major signifier of genes for high or low intelligence. Shockley argued that 'Nature has colour-coded groups of individuals so that statistically reliable predictions of their adaptability to intellectually rewarding and effective lives can easily be made and profitably be used by the pragmatic man in the street' (Shockley, 1972: 307).

Outside the academy, much political activity was undertaken in opposition to the implications of hereditarian arguments. There were successful attempts by groups of black parents in the USA (supported by some black psychologists) to have standardized IQ tests for educational diagnosis of ETHNIC MINORITY children legally banned on the grounds that they were racially and culturally biased (CULTURE) (McLoughlin and Koh, 1982; Hilliard, 1992). With concerted opposition to the hereditarian position espoused by Jensen and the loss of credibility following Kamin's (1974) demonstration that the British psychologist Cyril Burt had manufactured the separated twin study data on which the hereditarian position was founded, the hereditarian argument seemed to be in decline. However, hereditarians continued in productive work, some of which was aimed at clearing Burt's name, and the British Psychological Society did eventually reinstate Burt. The race and heredity debate resurfaced in Britain with the official publication in the bulletin of the British Psychological Society of a paper by Rushton which argued that black people and white people had different reproductive strategies associated with different IQs, genitalia and family forms (Rushton, 1990). Though many psychologists protested strongly against its publication, Rushton's article showed how social concerns about the demise of the 'traditional FAMILY', then current in British society, could be incorporated into old hereditarian arguments and influenced by sociobiological ideas.

Hereditarian claims also raised fresh controversies a few years later when the US scholars Richard Herrnstein and Charles Murray (1994) published *The Bell Curve*, which argued that intelligence was declining in the USA. This work not only reiterated Jensen-type arguments about black people being less intelligent than white people, but also resurrected ideas that social class differences result from differences in intelli-

gence. As with the original Jensen paper, this book received some support, but was also the subject of hundreds of careful refutations (Currie and Thomas, 1999; Levine and Painter, 1999; Reser, 1998; Simon, 1997; Stankov, 1998). The fact that such arguments have continued to resurface since the 1930s necessarily raises the issue of why this is so. Academics come to differing conclusions about this question. For example, Odling-Smee remarked:

> how little seems to have changed, and how little advance has been made since the days of Galton and Binet, in spite of a century of accumulating biological knowledge, the advent of quantitative genetics, and the potency of modern molecular biology. Why is this? Why can't we do better? Leaving aside the wilfull [sic] and pernicious misinterpretations of data, there appear to be two principal sources of confusion. The first is a widespread failure to understand what biology cannot yet tell us. The second is an equally widespread failure to understand what it can. (Odling-Smee, 1990: 653–654).

Richards argued that

> under normal circumstances (whatever they are!), the controversy would have reached closure by about 1980 on the strength of the 'internalist' anti-differences case. . . . Adopting a cinematic metaphor . . . what we really need now is not so much an explanation of population differences in mean intelligence, but of America's cultural addiction to this series and the 'studios' which fund it. (1997: 265–285)

It seems clear that debates on 'race' and IQ are informed not only by psychology, but by irreconcilable political and ideological commitments – although these are consistently denied by hereditarians (Wachtel, 1999). Questions of whether or not IQ differences are transmitted through 'race' are, arguably, so familiar that the debate is akin to flogging a dead horse (Brush, 1990). They will, no doubt, continue to surface as knowledge of human genes becomes more sophisticated and failure to counter hereditarian arguments in race and IQ – however specious they are – would be seen by many to confirm their truth. [A. P.]

Brush, F. R. (1990) 'Why does an already dead horse need to be flogged again?: commentary on "Are Intelligence Differences hereditarily transmitted?"', *European Bulletin of Cognitive Psychology*, 10(6): 595–598.

Currie, J., Thomas, D. (1999) 'The intergenerational transmission of "intelligence": down the slippery slopes of *The Bell Curve*', *Industrial Relations*, 38(3): 297–330.

Evans, B., Waites, B. (1981) *IQ and Mental Science: An Unnatural Science and its Social History*, Macmillan, London.

Eysenck, H. (1971) *Race, Intelligence and Education*, Temple Smith, London.

Flynn, J. R. (1990) 'Explanation, evaluation and a rejoinder to Rushton', *Psychologist*, 3(5): 199–200.

Glymour, C. (1998) 'What went wrong? Reflections on science by observation and *The Bell Curve*', *Philosophy of Science*, 65(1): 1–32.

Gould, S. J. (1981) *The Mismeasure of Man*, Norton, New York.

Guthrie, R. (1976) *Even the Rat was White: A Historical View of Psychology*, Harper & Row, New York.

Herrnstein, R., Murray, C. (1994) *The Bell Curve: Intelligence and Class Structure in American Life*, Free Press, New York.

Hilliard, A. (1992) 'IQ and the courts', in Hurlew, A. K. H., Banks, W. C., McAdoo, H. P., Azibo, D. A. (eds), *African American Psychology: Theory, Research and Practice*, Sage, Thousand Oaks, CA.

Hirsch, J. (1997) 'Some history of heredity-vs-environment, genetic inferiority at Harvard(?), and the (incredible) *Bell Curve*', *Genetica*, 99(2–3): 207–224.

Jensen, A. (1969) 'How much can we boost IQ and scholastic achievement?', *Harvard Educational Review*, 19: 1–123.

Kamin, L. (1974) *The Science and Politics of IQ*, Wiley, New York.

Levine, D. I., Painter, G. (1999) 'The NELS Curve: replicating *The Bell Curve* analyses with the National Education Longitudinal Study', *Industrial Relations*, 38(3): 364–406.

Lewontin, R. C., Rose, S., Kamin, L. (1984) *Not in Our Genes*, Pantheon Books, New York.

McLoughlin, C., Koh, T. H. (1982) 'Testing intelligence: a decision suitable for the psychologist', *Bulletin of the British Psychological Society*, 35: 308–311.

Miles, R. (1989) *Racism*, Routledge, London.

Odling-Smee, F. J. (1990) 'The mistreatment of diversity. Commentary on "Are Intelligence Differences Hereditarily Transmitted?"', in Roubertoux, P., Capron, C., *European Bulletin of Cognitive Psychology*, 10(6): 653–658.

Reser, J. P. (1998) 'Contested representations of psychology and science: the use and abuse of psychological arguments and evidence in the race debate', *Australian Psychologist*, 33(1): 50–52.

Richards, G. (1997) '*Race*', *Racism and Psychology: Towards a Reflexive History*, Routledge, London.

Rose, H., Rose, S. (1978) 'The IQ myth', *Race and Class*, 20(1): 63–74.

Rushton, P. J. (1990) 'Race differences, r/k theory, and a reply to J. R. Flynn, *The Psychologist*, 3(5): 195–198.

Shockley, W. (1972) 'Dysgenics, geneticity, raceology: a challenge to the intellectual responsibility of educators', *Phi Delta Kappa*, pp. 297–307.

Simon, J. L. (1997) 'Four comments on *The Bell Curve*', *Genetica*, 99(2–3): 199–205.

Stankov, L. (1998) 'Intelligence arguments and Australian psychology', *Australian Psychologist*, 33(1): 53–57.

Stepan, N. L., Gilman, S. L. (1993) 'Appropriating the idioms of science: the rejection of scientific racism', in Harding, S. (ed), *The 'Racial' Economy of Science: Toward a Democratic Future*, Indiana University Press, Bloomington.

Wachtel, P. (1999) *Racism in the Mind of America: Breaking the Vicious Circle between Blacks and Whites*, Routledge, New York.

RACE AND THE MEDIA (It. *razza e mass media*; Fr. *Race et mass media*; Ger. *Rasse und Media*) In *An American*

Dilemma, first published in 1944, Gunnar Myrdal described press coverage of race in the USA in this way:

> The press, with remarkable exceptions, ignores the Negroes, except for their crimes. There was an earlier unwritten rule that a picture of a Negro should never appear in print, and even now it is remarkably rare. The public affairs of community and state are ordinarily discussed as if Negroes were not part of the population. (Myrdal, 1964: 37)

This observation is not simply an interesting historical curiosity. For example, 'black crime' still attracts special attention. According to a study of coverage in several English newspapers carried out in the mid-1990s, ETHNICITY was one of the factors that made a search for a rapist newsworthy. This study found that the London *Evening Standard* was three times more likely to refer explicitly to the ethnicity of rapists being sought by the police if the suspect came from an ethnic minority background rather than being white (Grover and Soothill, 1996: 572–573).

There have been significant changes in recent years, however. For example, newspaper editors in the UK have drawn up codes which specify under what circumstances the racial origin or ethnicity (ETHNICITY AND RACE) of an individual may be mentioned and, more importantly, where it would be judged to be irrelevant. Moreover, ethnic minorities appear on television in the UK and the USA in a variety of roles – as news presenters and news correspondents, in advertisements, in comedy and drama – which were once reserved more or less exclusively for whites.

Nevertheless, ethnic and racial minorities remain under-represented in the media and they are also *misrepresented* by being depicted stereotypically and negatively. Two kinds of research have been employed to demonstrate this – content

analysis and discourse analysis. Content analysis is useful because it establishes the frequency with which certain topics appear (for example illegal immigration (ILLEGAL ALIEN)) and the words or terms that are typically used in connection with various topics (for example, 'Race Clash', 'Race Row', 'Race Riot'). However, content analysis by itself would miss some of the more subtle aspects of the way the media portrays ethnic groups that discourse analysis may illuminate.

Coverage of ethnic or racial issues can best be understood in terms of three interconnected elements: historical associations that have shaped perceptions of race and ethnicity; prevailing perceptions of contemporary 'RACE RELATIONS' or 'ethnic relations'; and the operation of normal 'news values', which explains, at least in part, why race-related and ethnic-related stories are often portrayed in a context of conflict, tension, violence and crime. It is the interaction of these three elements that will largely determine whether a given race-relations story is published, and if it is published how it is portrayed and what prominence it receives.

At one time, most attention was given to the role of the media in creating or reinforcing PREJUDICE and in influencing behaviour directly, not excluding their part in provoking civil disorder involving minority groups. Nowadays, more attention is devoted to the media's role in setting the agenda as to what the major issues are in the area of immigration (MIGRATION), race and ethnicity – and to the overall way the media represents these issues. In the UK a great deal of media coverage was once devoted to the scale of black immigration and, subsequently, much attention has been given to the social problems allegedly posed by the black presence, especially problems involving the

SECOND GENERATION, who have been born or brought up in Britain.

More recently, particular attention has been paid to the role of the media in giving credence to the belief that a substantial minority ethnic or racial presence poses a significant threat to national IDENTITY. This is especially well illustrated by coverage of the so-called Rushdie Affair in 1989, which followed publication of *The Satanic Verses*. Over a protracted period the British press published hundreds of articles about different aspects of the affair, especially: the *fatwah* issued against Rushdie by the Iranian religious authorities, the protests about the book in the UK and in many other countries, and, above all, the conduct of British Muslims and the implications that their conduct had for the tradition of free speech in Britain. In this coverage British Muslims appeared not merely as fundamentalists (FUNDAMENTALISM), intolerant (INTOLERANCE) of the views and rights of others, but as an undifferentiated mass of *outsiders* – that is, as alien to the British way of life, though whether this was inevitably so because they could not become acculturated (ACCULTURATION), or a deliberate choice on their part was unclear (Cottle, 1993; Henry, 1992: 172; Van Dijk, 1995: 98; Braham, 1999: 144–145).

In addition to all this, the media have the ability to provide constructions of issues and events about which most of their (white, indigenous) consumers may have little direct knowledge. Van Dijk has suggested that even the material that forms the basis of white resentment in 'everyday talk is largely borrowed from media reporting of ethnic affairs' (Van Dijk, 1995: 88). So if prevailing views held by the majority population about black people are negative, there may be some degree of 'selective perception' at work and the proposition is that selective perception serves to exaggerate unfavourable media coverage about them. The corollary is that any *favourable* coverage of ethnic minorities may be seen as evidence that the media are biased, or simply discounted in the belief that the media are suppressing 'the truth', for example about the actual size of the black population or black involvement in violent crime.

Though most analysis of race and the media has focused on either the press or broadcasting, the exponential growth of the Internet has introduced a new element, especially in the context of race hatred. The first extremist hate site was *Stormfront* (1995) and the number of such sites has grown dramatically: the European Union's Racism Monitoring Unit estimates that by the year 2000 there were more than 2,100 Internet sites promoting racism and anti-Semitism (CYBERNAZIS) (*Guardian*, 24 November 2000). Moreover, even if this estimate was accurate at the time it was made, the figure will have grown since then and will continue to do so. On its own *anti-racist* website, the Anti-Defamation League (2001) concluded its review of websites that 'promoted bigotry, extremism and violence' by saying

combating online extremism presents enormous technological and legal difficulties. Even if it were electronically feasible to keep sites off the Internet, the international nature of this medium makes legal regulation virtually impossible. Furthermore, in the United States, the First Amendment [of the Constitution] guarantees the right of freedom of speech to all Americans, even those whose opinions are reprehensible.

According to the European Union's Racism Monitoring Unit most race hatred sites were based in the USA, but in Germany alone the internal security service recorded 300 registered hate sites in 2000, an increase of 100 on the figure for 1998. A listing produced by the Anti-Defamation League gives some indication of the wide variety of these sites. They include many devoted to Holocaust Denial (SHOAH), sites produced by the KU KLUX KLAN, as well as sites catering for 'Aryan Women', which the ADL describes as appropriating feminism in order to spread intolerance online (Anti-Defamation League, 2001). In its Annual Report for 2000, the European Union's Racism Monitoring Unit remarked of these sites that

what was undercover, shameful and liable to prosecution in the past is today readily available and viewable on the net . . . movements which were in decline in both Europe and the US have received a new lease of life thanks to the sites they have created. (quoted in *Guardian*, 24 November 2000)

[P. B.]

Anti-Defamation League (2001) *Poisoning the Web: Hatred Online: Internet Bigotry, Extremism and Violence*, http://www.a-dl.org/poisoning_web/poisoning_toc.html.
Braham, P. (1998) 'I cambiamenti avvenuti nell'immagine delle minoranze etniche nei media inglesi: l'uso dei termini "razza" e "immigrazione"', in Bracalenti, R., Rossi, C. (eds), *Immigrazione: L'accoglienza delle Culture*, EDUP, Roma.
Cottle, S. (1993) 'Reporting the Rushdie Affair: a case study in the orchestration of public opinion', *Race and Class*, 32(4): 45–64.
Dines, M., Humez, J. (1995) *Gender, Race and Class in Media*, Sage, London.
Grover, C., Soothill, K. (1996) 'Ethnicity: the search for rapists and the press', *Ethnic and Racial Studies*, 19(4): 567–584.
Hall, S., Critcher, C., Jefferson, T., Clarke, J., Roberts, B. (1998) *Policing the Crisis: Mugging, the State, Law and Order*, Methuen, London.
Hartmann, P., Husband, C. (1974) *Racism and the Mass Media*, Davis-Poynter, London.
Layton-Henry, Z. (1992) *The Politics of Immigration*, Blackwell, Oxford.
Myrdal, G. (1964) *An American Dilemma, Two Volumes (The Complete Twentieth Anniversary Edition)*, McGraw-Hill, New York.
Van Dijk, T. (1991) *Racism and the Press*, Routledge, London.
Van Dijk, T. (1995) 'Elites, racism and the press', *Zeitschrift für Literaturwissenschaft und Linguistic*, 97: 86–115.

RACE RELATIONS (It. *relazioni interrazziali*; Fr. *relations raciales*; Ger. *Rassenbeziehungen*)

It can be argued that the ultimate justification for the emergence of 'race relations' as a specialized field of study within social sciences generally and sociology in particular lies – as in the formulation adopted by Rose in *Colour and Citizenship* – in the widespread uncertainties about the significance of race and the tenacious myths (MYTH) about racial differences. In other words, the study of race relations, dealing with, *inter alia*, RACIAL DISCRIMINATION, racial PREJUDICE and the occupational and educational profiles of different ethnic groups, is founded not on the acceptance by academics that there are objective racial differences, but on their observation of the popular belief that such differences are deep and even uncrossable (Rose, 1969: 34).

According to Miles, the argument in favour of 'race relations' is essentially twofold. First, there is the idea of 'race relations' as a notion that is applied by people in their everyday life. Typically, an incident reported in the media may be described as leading to a deterioration or improvement in 'race relations'. The logic of such a description is that the incident involves interaction between two or more groups who can be

255

considered 'races', or who define themselves as such. Secondly, 'race relations' is a employed by social scientists to refer to such widespread perceptions and to certain social processes that might engender a specific structure of social relations. From this perspective it does not matter in the least that the concept of discrete 'races' (RACE) has been discredited scientifically. What counts is that this discrediting has had little impact on popular consciousness. It is this consciousness that continues to impute great significance to phenotypal differences (PHENOTYPE) and the relations constructed on this basis (Miles, 1982: 280).

Social scientists can therefore reject 'race' as a scientifically valid concept, but maintain the study of 'race relations' as the study of interaction, conflict, allocation of resources and stratification, and so on, in which a belief in racial differences or a belief that the meaning of 'race' is clear and unambiguous plays an important role. Here race relations encompass the study of racism (RACISM) and the belief that inequalities between different ethnic groups can be accounted for by genetically based differences (GENOTYPE); the role played by racial ideologies in maintaining various social structures, including those associated with COLONIALISM and segregation (RACIAL SEGREGATION); the extent of racial disadvantage, racism and discrimination in the labour market; and the racialization of immigration policies in specific countries.

The idea of 'race relations' as the systematic study of relations between groups utilizing the *idea* of 'race' in their interactions with other groups originated in the output of a number of eminent social theorists working in the United States from the 1920s to the 1950s. These theorists – of whom Robert Park, Lewis Worth, Charles Johnson, E. Frank-

lin Frazier, Oliver Cromwell Cox and Gunnar Myrdal are among the most notable – not only increased the salience of race in the analysis of US society, but directed specific attention to segregation, immigration (MIGRATION) and race consciousness, as well as developing concepts that were eventually to constitute the sociology of race relations (Solomos, 1989: 5). The studies of Park and others focused especially on the inequalities experienced by black people in the USA, and by extension on the cultural and psychological characteristics of black Americans and on their family relations.

The underlying assumption of much of this work was that at the heart of 'race relations' was the consciousness of racial differences. As Park put it:

Race relations . . . are the relations existing between peoples distinguished by marks of racial descent, particularly when these racial differences enter into the consciousness of the individuals and groups so distinguished, and by so doing determine in each case the individual's conception of himself as well as his status in the community. (Park, 1950: 81, quoted in Solomos, 1989: 6)

In Park's work the focus is less on the conditions that precipitated racial consciousness and more on the nature of the relationships between groups that racial consciousness is depicted as producing, as well as on the conflicts that ensue. Park visualized a cycle of race relations consisting of four successive stages: contact, conflict, accommodation and ASSIMILATION (Park, 1950: 82–84). The view that race relations involved a sequence of stages was bolstered by the impact of Myrdal's magnum opus, *An American Dilemma*, published in 1944. Myrdal's belief that racial integration and assimilation would come to replace the racial segregation and racial conflict that he observed and recorded rested on he eventual upholding of what Myrdal visualized as an 'American Creed' of social justice (Solomos, 1989: 6).

An early attempt to construct a theoretical framework of race relations was contained in Michael Banton's *Race Relations* (1967). As Solomos explains, this concentrated on situations of cultural contact, beliefs about 'race', and on the relations erected on the basis of racial categorization. In the light of his global and historical analysis, Banton discerned six orders of race relations: institutionalized contact, ACCULTURATION, domination, paternalism, INTEGRATION and PLURALISM (Banton, 1967: 68–76). Using this framework, Banton examined post-war immigration to Britain and British race relations as they developed in the 1950s and 1960s.

Yet the very concept of race relations as being concerned with the outcome of racial interaction and conflict has been a matter of some dispute. The dispute centres not so much on how far racial differences – notably phenotypal differences – define what are termed race relations, but on the degree to which this distinguishes such relations from other kinds of social relations. The idea that race relations are, indeed, a distinct form of social relations is expressed particularly well in the work of John Rex, who was quite aware that the interconnections of social class and race raised the question of how far racial inequalities could be subsumed by more general inequalities. His response was that race relations denoted a particular kind of inter-group conflict wherein groups categorized racially come to be located in a distinctive way in an overall system of stratification. In Rex's analysis of race relations in the UK, he found that differences in 'life chances' between black and white groupings, which themselves reflected the extent and persistence of racism and racial dis-

crimination, caused blacks to be located not just at the bottom, but outside the (white) class structure, resulting in the creation of a black underclass. This, together with the distinctive forms of racial consciousness that emerged in consequence lent support, Rex argued, to the perception that race relations were, indeed, distinct forms of social relations. As he put it:

> Race relations situations . . . refer to situations in which there is a high degree of conflict between . . . (two or more) groups . . . true race relations may be said to exist when the practices of ascriptive allocation of roles and rights. . .are justified in terms of some kind of deterministic theory, whether this theory be of a scientific, religious, cultural, historical, ideological or sociological kind. (Rex, 1983: 159–160)

According to Rex, social relations are more likely to be definable as race relations in a number of specific circumstances: for example, where there is unfree, indentured or slave labour (SLAVERY); where there is cultural diversity (DIVERSITY–SIMILARITY) but restricted interaction between different cultural groups; and where migrant labour is concentrated in less desirable and socially stigmatized (STIGMA) types of employment. In Rex's view, we may speak of race relations where there is what he calls a 'racially structured social reality' – a reality that consists of both structural conditions (such as those just mentioned) and the definitions of those involved in these relations (Rex, 1983: 74). As Parekh remarks, as a general principle, '(w)hen outsiders come to a country, they can be conceptualized in several different ways. They can be described as foreigners, as immigrants, by their national or ethnic origins, by their religion, and so on' (2001: 3). However, what distinguished the British response to post-war immigration from that in, say, (West) Germany was that in the UK the idea of race gained immediate currency and was at the centre of political discourse. As Parekh argues, 'the British approach to Commonwealth immigrants has from its very beginning been articulated in racial terms' (Parekh, 2001: 21).

In post-war Britain the conceptualization of immigration in terms of race relations reflected two mutually reinforcing chief influences. One influence was the conceptualization of race relations extant in the American literature, which portrayed them as a distinct type of social relations. The other influence was the reaction to post-war immigration (MIGRATION) into the UK which was seen by the indigenous population, politicians and the media, as well as by many academics, primarily in terms of 'race' and 'colour', a perception that was itself conditioned by British colonial history (COLONIALISM). The debate in the UK about this immigration and its aftermath reveals a general framework within which immigration was automatically coupled with race and colour. This helps to explain why in the immediate post-war period immigration to the UK from Eastern Europe attracted relatively little controversy. The nature of 'race relations' in this era is conveyed by what is cited in the index to *Racial Disadvantage in Britain*, which set out to describe the situation of racial minorities in Britain in the mid-1970s (Smith, 1977): under 'Race Relations', as well as specific mention of the 'Climate of (race relations)', the reader is invited to see under 'Conflict'; 'Disadvantages, racial'; 'Discrimination'; 'Incitement'; 'Polarization'; and 'Prejudice'. Of course, the specific subject matter listed under the heading 'Race Relations' might vary from one book to another, according to the author's approach. For example, at the

moment of the passing of the second and third (UK) Race Relations Acts, Rex advocated a study of the relative life chances of members of 'different races or ethnic groups' because such a study was in keeping with what was recognizably a main task of sociology (Rex, 1979: 297). It is worth adding that whereas the index of many books on 'race' and immigration published in the UK once included entries under 'race relations', nowadays there is often no such entry and entries for 'racism', 'racialization' and 'racial violence' seem to be preferred.

It might seem that there are only two views that can be adopted in response to the argument that treats race relations as real on the basis that 'race' is widely seen to explain and determine the capabilities of members of different groups. One view is that although people may often act in line with the way in which they define their social world – perhaps by treating immigration and relations between certain groups in racial terms – it does not follow that independent scientific analysis must accept this definition as valid. Indeed, Miles suggests that sociology tends *not* to accept everyday definitions of social phenomena in its analytical reasoning. Social scientists try to establish and measure analytical categories independently of popular beliefs. It is precisely Miles' contention that 'race relations' represents an instance where sociologists in contradistinction to normal practice 'actively construct a discrete field of enquiry primarily on the basis of . . . everyday notions' (Miles, 1982: 281).

On the other hand, it can be argued that to treat race relations as 'real' because people erroneously give credence to the significance of 'race' does not exclude the study of subject matter which is outside everyday notions about race. Thus race relations can encompass objective measures of the extent of discrimination or the scale of immigration, as well as the reasons why such objective information might be overlooked or disbelieved. In particular, the study of race relations can focus on the willingness of gatekeepers to employ notions of 'race' to discriminate against members of certain groups perceived as racially distinct.

To treat race relations as a distinct sub-category of inter-group relations has a number of potential consequences, not all of them desirable. For example, the very process of constructing a sociology of 'race relations' that proceeds from the categorizations which impute significance to phenotypal differences such as skin colour inevitably emphasizes the way in which such relations are assumed to differ from other social relations. Ethnic minorities often tend to be studied as if they exist in social structures separate from the wider society and 'race' is often accorded an explanatory power. The ramifications of such an approach can be discerned in the way that explorations of racial discrimination in employment often proceed as if selection and promotion are invariably based on meritocratic principles *except* where racial minority workers are concerned. In this way racial discrimination is treated as exceptional or even unique, whilst other types of discrimination are ignored.

There are further objections to a separate study of race relations where this is grounded in the belief that such relations are qualitatively different from other kinds of group relations. One objection is that racial ascription of capabilities and characteristics is merely an ideological process and to take such ascription as the basis of a study of race relations is to reify an ideological construct. Another objection is that not only does the idea of 'race

relations' help to maintain the erroneous perception that humanity consists of separate races, it also causes religious and cultural underpinnings of racism to be neglected (Parekh, 2000: xxiv). [P. B.]

Banton, M. (1967) *Race Relations*, Tavistock, London.

Miles, R. (1982) 'Racialism and nationalism in Britain', in Husband, C. (ed.), *'Race' in Britain: Continuity and Change*, Hutchinson, London.

Myrdal, G. (1944) *An American Dilemma*, McGraw-Hill, New York.

Parekh, B. (2000) *The Future of Multi-Ethnic Britain* (The Parekh Report), Profile Books, London.

Parekh, B. (2001) *Integrating Minorities* (The ICA Diversity Lecture, 2000), London, Institute of Contemporary Arts.

Park, R. (1950) *Race and Culture*, Free Press, New York.

Rex, J. (1979) 'Sociology, theory, typologies, value standpoints and research', Appendix 1 in Rex, J., Tomlinson, S. *Colonial Immigrants in a British City: A Class Analysis*, Routledge & Kegan Paul, London.

Rex, J. (1983) *Race Relations in Sociological Theory*, 2nd edn, Routledge & Kegan Paul, London.

Rose, E. (1969) *Colour and Citizenship*, Oxford University Press, London.

Smith, D. (1977) *Racial Disadvantage in Britain: The PEP Report*, Penguin, Harmondsworth.

Solomos, J. (1989) *Race and Racism in Contemporary Britain*, Macmillan, London.

RACIAL DISCRIMINATION (It. *discriminazione razziale*; Fr. *discrimination raciale*; Ger. *rassistische Diskriminierung*)

To comprehend racial discrimination adequately it is important to be clear about the distinction between PREJUDICE, RACISM and discrimination. In the context of 'race' and ethnicity, prejudice – literally, 'prejudging' –

involves having or expressing adverse beliefs about individuals based on their membership of a specific ethnic or 'racial' group. Racism goes further by ascribing superiority or inferiority to groups – and thus to individuals on the basis of group membership – by asserting a connection between physical characteristics or ETHNICITY and shared capabilities or characteristics.

By contrast, racial discrimination occurs where someone is *treated* less favourably on grounds of group membership signified by skin colour, 'race', national or ethnic origin and so they find their access to scarce resources or opportunities restricted or denied. In early social scientific accounts racial discrimination is depicted as a deliberate, practical expression of ETHNOCENTRISM: a dislike of people who are 'different' (DIVERSITY–SIMILARITY). Later accounts make a distinction between discrimination which is intentional – being based on prejudice or racism – and that which is unintentional. This 'evolution' of the concept of discrimination is reflected in the difference between the first UK Race Relations Acts (1965 and 1968), which treated discrimination as something entirely deliberate; and the 1976 Race Relations Act, where the definition of racial discrimination was extended to encompass unintentional discrimination (referred to in the Act as indirect discrimination).

Direct discrimination occurs when on racial grounds a person is treated less favourably than someone else in similar circumstances. Indirect discrimination, by contrast, occurs when a person is either unable to comply with a requirement that cannot be justified on other than racial grounds, or is less likely to be able to do so than those from other 'racial groups' – or, though the requirement can be justified on non-racial grounds, these grounds are irrelevant to the task

or matter in question. Recognition of this distinction helps to explain why in practice someone who is prejudiced or a racist may be a *non-discriminator* and why – simply by following established rules and procedures – someone who is neither prejudiced nor racist may be a *discriminator*. In recent years attention has focused more and more on unintended and indirect discrimination and so analysis of racial discrimination has increasingly overlapped with discussion of INSTITUTIONAL RACISM – as in the way large-scale enterprises discriminate by adhering unthinkingly to existing unspoken assumptions, norms, rules and procedures, or in the way that standardized academic and vocational tests may be attuned to the majority and so discriminate against specific minorities (as well as being poor indicators of relevant skills and subsequent performance).

A well-established way to assess the extent of racial discrimination in employment has been to use controlled experiments. One frequently used in the UK involves 'testers' – identifiable as belonging to different 'racial' or ethnic groups – applying for a range of jobs in writing, by telephone and in person, but doing so in such a way that the success rates of each group can be compared. This type of experiment was first used in Britain in 1966 and, with minor variations, has been utilized in the following decades. For instance, testing carried out by Political and Economic Planning (PEP) in the early 1970s covered recruitment of different racial groups for unskilled, semi-skilled and skilled manual jobs and several types of white-collar employment (Smith, 1977: 105).

The 1966 tests clearly indicated that racial discrimination in employment was widespread and this finding was one factor which gave impetus to the second UK Race Relations Act. Despite the fact that this Act outlawed racial discrimination in employment and housing, subsequent tests have shown that racial discrimination in employment remained substantial. Replication in 1984 and 1985 by the Policy Studies Institute of tests carried out in the 1970s demonstrated that at least one third of private employers in the UK discriminated against either African-Caribbean or Asian applicants or against both (Brown, 1992).

The contrasting experiences of black applicants and Greek immigrant 'testers' included in one of these tests suggested that much of the discrimination encountered by 'non-white' applicants (WHITENESS) amounted to a crude response to skin colour, rather than to 'foreignness' *per se*. In the UK, unfavourable attitudes to black applicants had become entrenched partly because until 1968 racial discrimination in employment was lawful. Before this date explicitly discriminatory advertisements appeared frequently, and it was common for employers to specify a refusal to employ black or Asian workers (Brown, 1992: 47). According to the 1966 PEP Report, employers would hire black workers only where it was impossible to recruit and retain white workers at an economic rate, so they were overwhelmingly employed in jobs where work was dirty, pay was poor and hours were unsocial (Daniel, 1968: 94, 120). In addition, their prospects for promotion were severely limited because it was invariably taken for granted that a black worker could not be placed in authority over a white worker (Wright, 1968: 108). This might explain why in the 1960s the degree of racial discrimination in employment experienced by black applicants of recent immigrant origin was greatest for those who possessed *British* qualifications (Daniel, 1968: 69).

Racial inequalities in the employment market were, of course, not simply the product of immediate and direct discrimination, they were also the outcome of structural factors. Ethnic minorities (ETHNIC MINORITY) had entered the British labour market from the late 1940s onwards as a 'replacement', to fill vacancies where indigenous labour was insufficient. Endemic labour shortages that had arisen in Britain in the years after the Second World War also occurred in other Western European countries, such as France, Germany and Switzerland. Immigrant labour therefore played an important part in perpetuating and deepening a 'dual labour market'. Immigrants occupied 'secondary jobs' – where wages were lower, where there was little security of employment, training was minimal and prospects for promotion were poor, rather than 'primary jobs' – where pay, conditions and job security were reasonably good.

The 1966 PEP Report also recorded widespread and persistent racial discrimination in the UK housing market, and it was common to see notices about available accommodation specifying 'no coloureds' (Daniel, 1968). Similar discrimination was equally evident in the experiences of foreign workers in obtaining housing in, for example, Germany, Switzerland and France. Advertisements in German local newspapers routinely stipulated *Gastarbeiter unerwünscht* (foreign workers not desired) and *nur für Deutsche* (Germans only) and in Switzerland advertisements often specified *kein Italiener* (literally meaning no Italians, but implying no foreigners) or *für ruhige Schweizer Bürger* (for quiet Swiss citizens). In certain cases discrimination was official policy. One local French council released funding to a housing society only with the proviso that no Algerians were to be housed on a new estate (Castles and Kosack, 1973: 268, 310). There is also evidence of *indirect* discrimination in housing. For example, in the UK it was once argued that immigrants, even though they were citizens, had a lesser entitlement to council (i.e. public) housing because they were newly arrived in Britain and had not paid taxes for as long as the indigenous population. This view was institutionalized by applying residence qualifications that the local indigenous population could meet, but which few immigrants could satisfy. Similarly, there has been considerable controversy over the practice known in the UK and the USA as 'red-lining', where banks and building societies refrained from financing the purchase of houses in inner-city areas where the minority ethnic groups were heavily concentrated.

Between the mid-1960s and 1976 three Race Relations Acts were passed in Britain. The 1965 Act prohibited direct racial discrimination in public places such as public houses and restaurants, but it did not cover discrimination in either employment or housing. This was remedied by the 1968 Act; and the 1976 Act included indirect discrimination. In addition, the 1976 Race Relations Act established the COMMISSION FOR RACIAL EQUALITY, giving it power not only to mount formal investigations of organizations suspected of racial discrimination, but also to issue non-discrimination notices where the law had been breached (Brown, 1992: 55). These different interventions were important because they set a standard by which public and private behaviour could be measured and judged; they constituted an unequivocal declaration of public policy; and they assured majority and minority groups that important issues of concern were now being addressed (McCrudden et al., 1998: 4). Where possible, the CRE's preferred policy has been to try to resolve complaints of institutional discrimination by working

with potential respondents, rather than by taking legal action. Nonetheless, in some cases the CRE has felt obliged to use its powers of formal investigation to eliminate discrimination and to promote equal opportunity. For example, in 2000 the CRE embarked on three new formal investigations – into the Ford Motor Company, the Crown Prosecution Service (CPS) Croydon and Her Majesty's (HM) Prison Service. In the case of HM Prison Service, the terms of the formal investigation included the elimination of unlawful racial discrimination, with specific reference being made to complaints by staff and prisoners, to any barriers that prevented such complaints being made and recorded and to the way that such complaints were treated by those in authority (CRE, 2001: 17–18).

There are several reasons why assessing the extent of racial discrimination may be complicated. First, past discrimination often affects present-day life chances. For example, previous restrictions on the employment of black workers may mean that they are more vulnerable to being laid off than their fellow-workers simply through the operation of normal rules of seniority. Secondly, although it is now commonplace for organizations to have an Equal Opportunity policy in place, support at senior levels for this policy is often undermined by discriminatory practice and attitudes at local and junior levels. Such disparities between policy and practice have been noted not just in the case of employers or within the trade unions, but also and especially in relations between the police and minority ethnic communities (COMMUNITY) (Smith and Gray, 1985). Much of the argument about police–minority relations concerns alleged 'over-policing' – saturation policing of areas in which minority ethnic groups are concentrated, as well as excessive, aggressive and disproportionate use of police powers of arrest, 'stop and frisk' (or 'stop and search' as it is referred to in the UK) and the use of deadly force. Perhaps the clearest contemporary example of. alleged racial discrimination by the police has occurred in the USA and concerns what is termed 'racial profiling', specifically what has become known as 'Driving While Black' (often shortened to DWB). Racial profiling which encompasses 'stop and frisk') is a matter of fierce argument between the police, who contend that they are merely responding to 'crime patterns', and their critics, who contend that blacks and Hispanics are unfairly targeted by the police. In the USA the issue of racial profiling has been the subject of growing media interest (RACE AND THE MEDIA), several statistical reports, lawsuits and legislation. Harris argues that racial profiling

is based on the premise that most drug offences are committed by minorities. The premise is factually untrue, but it has nonetheless become a SELF-FULFILLING PROPHECY. Because police look for drugs primarily among African Americans and Latinos, they find a disproportionate number of them with contraband. Therefore more minorities are arrested, prosecuted, convicted and jailed, thus reinforcing the perception that drug trafficking is primarily a minority activity. This perception creates the profile that results in more stops for minority drivers. At the same time, white drivers receive far less police attention, many of the drug dealers and possessors (of drugs) among them go unapprehended, and the perception that whites commit fewer drug offences than minorities is perpetuated. (Harris, 1999)

One of the most precise and authoritative statistical analyses of racial profiling was designed by John Lamberth to test whether the Maryland State Police patrolling Interstate I-95 searched significantly higher numbers of black motorists than would be anticipated on the basis of the racial make-up of motorists and the racial make-up of traffic violators travelling on this Interstate. The conclusion of this research was unequivocal: it found that there was 'without question a racially discriminatory impact on blacks and other minority motorists' (Lamberth, quoted in Harris, 1999).

A similar attention to detail can be found in Hood's analysis of whether 'race' – and thus racial discrimination – has been a factor in the sentences imposed in the Crown Courts of England (Hood, 1992). The two main explanations that might account for the over-representation of African-Caribbeans in English prisons mirror those applied to racial profiling: that this group is more likely to be guilty of criminal behaviour; or that they suffer discrimination at successive stages of the criminal justice process, from disproportionate attention by the police to heavier sentences by judges. Though Hood certainly found disturbing differences in several respects, for instance in the resort to custodial sentences, in the length of sentences and in the resort to non-custodial sentences, he took care not to overstate the position. His findings included the following: there were significant race differences in the distribution of sentences in terms of both imprisonment and alternatives to imprisonment; probation officers recommended probation orders less frequently for blacks (and Asians) than for whites; and though African-Caribbeans formed less than 4 per cent of the local male population aged 16 to 64, in 1989 they accounted for between 15 and 21 per cent of those found guilty in West Midlands Crown Courts. But as Hood's analysis indicates, we should hesitate before accepting such findings at face value and he therefore posed a crucial question: to what extent did observed race differences in the proportion of blacks, whites and Asians *disappear* when a combination of factors summarizing the *probability of custody* (a score summarizing the probability of an offender with a given combination of attributes receiving a custodial sentence) was taken into account? Hood calculated that if race had had no effect at all in the cases surveyed then 479 instead of 503 blacks would have received a custodial sentence – which, although a significant disparity, he describes as being 'not as large a "residual race difference" as many commentators have suggested' (Hood, 1992: 194–204).

Apart from these complexities, whether racial discrimination has occurred is not always clear-cut and may therefore be much more a matter of interpretation than measurement. For example, in 1989 a major controversy arose in France over the right of Muslim schoolgirls to wear the *hijab* (headscarf) at school. The French Education Minister eventually ruled that the *hijab* was unacceptable not because – as many French people probably believed – it contravened the secular ethos of French state education, but on the grounds that, unlike the cross worn by Christian pupils, it could not be classed as a *discreet* religious symbol.

Although the principle of equal treatment for all may seem identical to the idea of an absence of discrimination, in certain cases EQUALITY may actually result in discrimination against specific minority groups. When in 1972, to comply with road safety requirements, motorcyclists in the UK were for the first time compelled to wear crash helmets, Sikhs objected that this was discriminatory because it would prevent them fulfilling their religious obligation to wear a turban. Following a legal judgment that turbans did, in fact, meet the necessary safety standards, UK law was amended to exempt turban-wearing Sikhs from wearing crash helmets even though this requirement continued to apply to all other motorcyclists (Parekh, 2000).

Without underestimating the significance of discrimination we need to balance racial discrimination, exclusion and inequality with the skills, qualifications, orientations and preferences of different minority groups. We would be well advised to keep in mind Miles' warning:

> The obsession of 'race relations' research with the extent and impact of racial discrimination to the exclusion of most other factors encourages a perspective in which . . . (minority ethnic groups) come to be viewed unidimensionally as the objects of other people's beliefs and behaviour. (Miles, 1982: 65)

[P. B.]

Brown, C. (1992) 'Same difference: the persistence of racial disadvantage in the British labour market', in Braham, P., Rattansi, A., Skellington, R. (eds), *Racism and Antiracism: Inequalities, Opportunities and Policies*, Sage, London.

Castles, S., Kosack, G. (1973) *Immigrant Workers and the Class Structure in Western Europe*, Oxford University Press, London.

Commission for Racial Equality (2001) *Annual Report, 1 January 2000 to 31 December 2000*, CRE, London.

Daniel, W. (1968) *Racial Discrimination in England* (based on the PEP Report), Penguin, Harmondsworth.

Harris, D. (1999) *Driving While Black: Racial Profiling on Our Nation's Highways*, an American Civil Liberties Union Special report, ACLU, June, USA.

Hood, R. (1992) *Race and Sentencing: A Study in the Crown Court, a Report of the Commission for Racial Equality*, Clarendon Press, Oxford.

McCrudden, C., Smith, D., Brown, C. (1998) *Racial Justice at Work: Enforcement of the 1976 Race Relations Act*, Policy Studies Institute, London.

Miles, R. (1982) *Racism and Migrant Labour*, Routledge & Kegan Paul, London.

Parekh, B. (2000) *Rethinking Multicultural-ism, Cultural Diversity and Political Theory*, Macmillan, Basingstoke.

Smith, D. (1977) *Racial Disadvantage in Britain* (The PEP Report), Penguin, Harmondsworth.

Smith, D., Gray, J. (1985) *Police and People in London*, Policy Studies Institute, London.

Wright, P. (1968) *The Coloured Worker in British Industry*, Oxford University Press, London.

RACIAL HARASSMENT (It. *molestie razziali*; Fr. *harcèlement racial*; Ger. *rasistische Gewalttätigkeiten*) The term 'racial harassment' is employed to denote offensive, derogatory, violent or otherwise unacceptable behaviour that is judged to be racially motivated. It can be applied to the behaviour of individuals or groups of one ethnic group against an individual or individuals of another ethnic group and may refer to a single event or to a sequence of events. In practice, even if such harassment is not in itself violent, it may make the victim or victims conclude that they may be the target or potential target of violent, racially motivated attack.

Racial harassment was described in a 1989 report of the Home Affairs Committee of the House of Commons as 'one of the frightening realities' of life for black people and their children living in the UK. Such harassment may affect minority ethnic communities (ETHNIC MINORITY) as a whole, not just specific individuals belonging to these communities. It is therefore more than an impediment to the creation of an inclusive multiracial or MULTIETHNIC society; it has the capacity to engender deep and genuine fear in minority communities. The Home Affairs Committee Report lends support to the view that in the UK racial harassment is experienced much more often by black people than it is by white people. For this reason alone it might be better to describe the racial harassment suffered by black people on the streets, in their neighbourhoods and at school as 'racist harassment'.

Perpetrators of racial harassment and violence were found by a Home Office report to be of all ages and they included not just youths and adults, but also very young people and even pensioners. They were both male and female and often acted together as a group of friends or as families (Sibbitt, 1997: vii). The Home Office report's most significant conclusion was that

> The views held by all kinds of perpetrators towards ethnic minorities are shared by the wider communities to which they belong. Perpetrators see this as legitimizing their actions. In turn, the wider community not only spawns such perpetrators, but fails to condemn them and actively reinforces their behaviour. The reciprocal relationship between the two suggests that the views of the 'perpetrator community' also need to be addressed in efforts to reduce racial harassment. (Sibbitt, 1997: viii)

Even the perpetrators of violent racial assaults do not act in a 'social vacuum', but operate in areas

> in which all age groups across the local community share common attitudes to ethnic minorities, where people regularly express these views to each other and where people of all ages, including the very young and older adults, regularly engage in the verbal abuse and intimidation of ethnic minorities. Indeed, such communities, with their own entrenched problems of socio-economic deprivation and crime, appear to 'spawn' violent perpetrators. (Sibbitt, 1997: 101)

The contention here is that there is a mutual relationship between the individual perpetrator and the wider community in which the community helps to shape and reinforce the views of individual perpetrators. This relationship manifests itself in various ways, notably in a refusal to co-operate with the authorities in identifying those who have carried out serious racial attacks, including murder. In such communities individual acts of racial harassment and violence and levels of RACISM combine with a pre-existing aversion to co-operation with the police so that responsibility for racial harassment extends to the wider community and it is possible to refer to a 'perpetrator community'. In addition, there are strong grounds to suggest that ethnic minorities serve a particular *function* for some individuals within this community, providing a focus for the discontent, injustice and grievance that they feel about other aspects of their lives (Sibbitt, 1997: 101–102). In other words, though the origins of the hostility they attract may be varied, foreigners and ethnic minorities serve as *scapegoats* (PREJUDICE).

Particular attention should be given to the role of the police. The police themselves are frequently accused of racial harassment (for example, where black individuals are disproportionately subject to 'stop and search' or where black motorists are stopped disproportionately for questioning (RACIAL DIS-CRIMINATION). There is also concern that black and Asian police officers are often victims of racial harassment by white police officers (where the 'canteen culture' in the police force encourages racism). On the other hand, the police have a critical role in combating racial harassment (Smith and Gray, 1985).

In the UK the term 'racial harassment' is used to describe 'minor' racially motivated incidents, even though such incidents often involve violence. The police define a 'racial incident' as one where the victim, the attending police officer or a witness attests to its racial nature. Using this measure, the annual number of reported racial incidents – ranging from assault to arson – which result in physical injury in the UK has been put as high as 14,000. However, given that the British Crime Survey suggests that reported incidents account for only 10 per cent of the true level of crime, the actual number of such incidents is likely to be considerably greater than official figures suggest (Home Office, 1994; Ruddock, 1994).

Defining a racial incident only as a physical attack on an ethnic minority group, on an individual belonging to an ethnic minority group, or on their property, is a narrow view. A broader view would encompass a wide range of actions that, though non-violent, may be variously demeaning, offensive, intimidatory or threatening. Such actions may include derogatory name-calling, insulting remarks and teasing, racist jokes, ridicule, racist graffiti, victimization and bullying, and verbal abuse and threats. Viewed from this wider perspective racial harassment can occur at work as well as on the street or in the neighbourhood and can be perpetrated in a variety of ways by seemingly 'normal' people. This should be enough to remind us that though in many cases racial harassment is deliberate and direct, in other cases it is more subtle and indirect and arises because social signals are complex and differences in attitude and outlook are easily misunderstood. In the workplace racial harassment is being increasingly recognized as behaviour by a co-worker or manager that is racially offensive and/or intimidating, and which would be recognized as such by any reasonable person. As is evident from the following list, definitions of racial harassment at work often overlap with definitions of racial discrimination. Such harassment includes: exclusion from normal workplace conversation or social events;

lifferential treatment in career progres-
;ion; unfair allocation of work duties;
)ersistent and unfounded criticism of
vork performance; and intimidation that
mpacts on work performance or induces
ear, anxiety, stress or sickness; and
acist jokes and remarks (CRE, 1995: 8).

The COMMISSION FOR RACIAL
:QUALITY has noted with concern the
;rowing number of cases of racial
1arassment at work that reach industrial
ribunals. Such complaints may be made
igainst the employer as well as the
)erpetrator, not simply because under
he 1976 Race Relations Act employers
ire liable for discriminatory actions by
heir employees, but because it is no
lefence for the employer to say they
vere unaware of such actions. As the
:RE points out, because most people
vho experience racial harassment at
vork simply put up with it, such
omplaints represent just the 'tip of the
ceberg' (CRE, 1995: 5). According to a
ormal investigation of the largest com-
)anies in the UK conducted by the CRE,
l6 per cent had formal procedures to
leal with racial harassment at work.
)ther CRE investigations also indicate
hat the great majority of employers
vere unaware of the statutory *Race
Relations Code of Practice in Employment*,
)ublished by the CRE to help enforce the
l976 Race Relations Act (CRE, 1984).
This observation is important because,
hough the 1976 Race Relations Act did
1ot include the term 'racial harassment',
ndustrial tribunals are increasingly
ikely to conclude that racial harassment
it work is 'less favourable treatment on
·acial grounds' – which constitutes
unlawful racial discrimination (CRE,
l995: 14).

For a number of reasons, assessing the
level of racial harassment is not easy.
First, there is disagreement and confusion over what constitutes racial harassment. As a consequence, attempts to

document, and measure the extent of
racial harassment are inconsistent, not
least because it is unclear where the
boundaries lie between racial incidents,
racial crimes, racial attacks, racial bullying, racial conflict and racial discrimination in general. There is then a tendency
either to define racial harassment too
narrowly, so excluding many forms of
harassment, or too broadly, so rendering
the term virtually meaningless. Even if,
for example, we take only what are
defined as individual 'racial incidents',
not all such incidents are reported and
the threat to a group – as opposed to
individuals within a group – is overlooked. This reservation notwithstanding, data from the 1990s show an
unmistakable upward trend right
across Europe in acts of violence against
members of various ethnic and racial
minorities, much of which has been
linked to activities of the Far Right. For
example, it was reported by the Campaign Against Racism and Fascism that
there had been 52 'racist killings' in
Germany in 1993 and, according to the
German government, in 1994 the
number of anti-Semitic attacks recorded
in Germany exceeded the level in the
period 1926–31, when the Weimar
Republic was collapsing and the Nazi
push for power was intensifying. There
are similar developments in other European countries. In the Netherlands
recorded incidents of racial violence
rose from a mere four in 1988 to 279 in
1993, in which year there were also 123
attacks on asylum centres. In France,
according to official figures contained in
the fifth annual report of the Consultative Commission for Human Rights, 25
people were killed in racially motivated
episodes between 1980 and 1993. In Italy
in the period 1993–95, the National
Observatory on Xenophobia recorded
approximately 300 violent acts committed each year by Italians against

foreigners. A valuable and up-to-date assessment of the level of racist incidents across Europe (including the UK) appears in the *Race Relations Bulletin* published quarterly by the Institute of Race Relations (see, for example, IRR, 2000: 'The dispersal of xenophobia').

Racial harassment should be seen not just in terms of individual acts, but also in terms of the wider elements that may encourage such acts. Particularly significant in this context are three interconnected factors. One is the role of the media (RACE AND THE MEDIA) in reporting RACE RELATIONS and reinforcing notions of difference (DIVERSITY–SIMILARITY), exclusion and 'otherness'. Equally significant is the role of politicians in defining immigration (MIGRATION) and asylum (POLITICAL ASYLUM) issues in a negative fashion and in raising racial tensions. The third element in producing a climate in which racial harassment may thrive is public opinion in general. In the UK a British Attitudes Survey conducted by MORI revealed increasing resentment of black and Asian people and a heightened intolerance of refugees (REFUGEE) and immigrants (National Centre for Social Research, 2000). One third of respondents freely admitted to being racially prejudiced and nearly half believed that attempts to provide equal opportunities for blacks and Asians had 'gone too far'. The Parekh Report, *The Future of Multi-Ethnic Britain*, also noted a rising trend of racial intolerance.

The final element is the reaction of various authorities to defining and dealing with racial harassment. This reaction may fluctuate over time and from country to country: there may be a refusal to acknowledge racial harassment or to take it seriously; it may be defined too narrowly; and it may be defined too widely. [P. B.] [M. V.] [R. S.]

Commission for Racial Equality (1984) *Race Relations Code of Practice: for the Elimination of Racial Discrimination and the Promotion of Equal Opportunities in Employment*, CRE, London.

Commission for Racial Equality (1995) *Racial Harassment at Work: What Employers Can Do About It*, CRE, London.

Home Office (1994) *British Crime Survey: Research and Planning Unit, Paper 82*, HMSO, London.

Institute of Race Relations (2000) 'The dispersal of xenophobia', *European Race Bulletin*, Special Report, Bulletin Nos 33/34 August, pp. 1–59.

National Centre for Social Research (2000) *17th British Attitudes Survey*, London.

Parekh Report (2000) *The Future of Multi-Ethnic Britain*, Profile Books, London.

Ruddock, J. (1994) *Racial Attacks: The Rising Tide*, The Labour Party, London.

Sibbitt, R. (1997) *The Perpetrators of Racial Harassment and Racial Violence*, Home Office Research Study 176, London, Home Office and Statistics Directorate.

Smith D., Gray, J. (1985) *Police and People in London: The PSI Report*, PSI, London.

RACIAL SEGREGATION (It. *segregazione razziale*; Fr. *ségrégation raciale*; Ger. *rassische Absonderung*) The verb 'to segregate' comes from the Latin *segregare* (composed of *se(d)*, away, and *grex, gregis*, herd). It generally signifies the identification and then the exclusion and isolation of an individual or group from other individuals or groups. The crucial distinction here is between two kinds of segregation, namely, *de jure* segregation (legal separation) and *de facto* segregation (separation in practice, in the absence of any legal requirement).

There are numerous examples of *de jure* segregation. In recent times the two most widely discussed are post-slavery Southern USA and South Africa under the apartheid regime. The condition of ewish populations (JEW) under Nazi regimes can also be considered an extreme form of *de jure* segregation – ews were registered, forcibly confined o ghettos (GHETTO) and then removed o concentration camps (CONCENTRA-TION CAMPS AND DEATH CAMPS). 3lack people in the United States had, of course, been oppressed by SLAVERY, yet the transformation promised by the abolition of slavery under the 13th Amendment to the Constitution passed n 1865 was counteracted first by the unlawful violence and then by discrimiatory legislation that came to be known as JIM CROW laws. These two developments together effectively reversed the advances secured by blacks in the so-called period of 'Reconstruction', during which they were able to vote and hold political office, including securing election to Congressional seats. Indeed, the ederal government had countered the attempts of a number of Southern states o deny blacks access to certain better-paying forms of employment by intro-ducing provisions for EQUALITY before he law and equal voting rights. The consequence of these developments was hat many elements of the previous racial hierarchy were reconstituted, so forestalling the prospect of former slave-nasters having to encounter their former slaves on anything like terms of racial equality.

The first JIM CROW laws, imposing racial segregation on railway trains and rams, were enacted in Tennessee in 1875. Other Southern states quickly ollowed this precedent and soon racial segregation was legally enforced across he South in public facilities such as hospitals, prisons, cemeteries and, per-aps most significantly, in schools. Such segregation was endorsed by two rulngs of the US Supreme Court. The first, n 1883, was that the Civil Rights Bill passed by Congress in 1875, which had given all citizens equal access to public facilities, did not apply to what were termed personal acts of social discrimination. This was interpreted to mean that segregated facilities for blacks and whites were, after all, constitutional. The second landmark ruling of the Court, in 1896, was in the case of *Plessey* v. *Fergusen*. Here the Court decided that even though Plessey might be, as he claimed, seven-eighths white, he was categorized as a NEGRO and as such he was not entitled to travel in a railroad car designated for 'whites only'. With this ruling the Court established the principle of *separate but equal*, a principle it did not reverse until 1954.

De jure segregation can coexist with *de facto* segregation, but the latter is, by definition, more ambiguous and so harder to delineate. For example, although in the Southern USA much segregation was legally enforced, other segregation was the result of custom and practice. Alongside segregation in public facilities there existed myriad practices which reinforced or created segregation without the direct force of law. Such custom and practice was evident in various contexts: in the segregation of church congregations, for example, and, much later, in the barriers that were placed in the path of black people trying to register to vote. Black people wishing to register as voters would be required by white officials to satisfy a range of conditions that were never applied to white voters. These conditions usually involved demonstrating a certain standard of literacy, an understanding of the American Constitution and providing proof of 'good conduct', but their purpose was simple: to deny voting rights to black people. The full extent of *de facto* segregation faced by black people in the USA only really became evident as they migrated north – as they did in increasing numbers during the

First World War and in the following decades, to escape the restrictions of life in the South, as well as to take advantage of the greater economic opportunities available. Although there was no *de jure* segregation in the North, they nevertheless encountered there a substantial degree of *de facto* racial segregation, especially in the terms of residence. Such segregation – which led to the formation of what to all intents and purposes were black ghettos – was the product of several factors. While it is evident that black people might have settled in heavily black areas partly because they could then rely on a network of support from fellow-blacks, their decision on where to live was far from being a free choice. Newly arriving black migrants settled in areas that were impoverished – often areas that had formerly been occupied by the waves of foreign immigrants (FOREIGNER, MIGRANT) to Northern US cities, but black 'immigrants' were constrained not just by poverty. They also faced active racial discrimination in the housing market and the prospect of hostility and even violence if they sought to settle in a 'white area'. In this way the Northern ghettos did more than replicate the residential patterns of the South; they produced an even more insidious form of residential segregation.

In the UK the arrival of New Commonwealth immigrants from the late 1940s did not produce black ghettos (GHETTO) after the pattern of major cities in the USA. But their arrival in the centres of several British cities did give rise to what were described as lower-class ghettos composed of immigrants and the poorer and most deprived sections of the indigenous population (Castles and Kosack 1973: 313). In the housing market black immigrants then faced both direct discrimination from sellers, landlords and estate agents and indirect discrimination in the form of restrictive eligibility criteria in the allocation of public housing. There is strong evidence that local authority housing departments continue to follow practices that result in black people being disproportionately concentrated in the worst public housing on the least desirable estates (Ginsberg, 1992).

The struggle against racial segregation in the USA was pursued by both political and legal means by black activists and white activists alike. But it was a protracted and far from smooth fight and it encountered numerous setbacks. During the Second World War, whereas labour shortages had led to black people being recruited to work in jobs from which they had previously been excluded, their experiences in the armed forces were not without discrimination and humiliation. Many of them were routinely assigned to inferior duties and others served in segregated units led by white officers, in addition to which the American Red Cross insisted on distinguishing between black and white blood donors. Moreover, there were particular problems when black soldiers went on leave, especially in the Southern states, where they were treated as inferiors on the basis of colour (COLOURED), rather than simply as serving soldiers in the US armed forces and were thus prevented from using segregated facilities reserved for whites.

It was not until 1954 in *Brown* v. *The Board of Education* that the US Supreme Court reversed its earlier decision in favour of racial segregation. Yet this judgment did not resolve matters immediately, as was demonstrated by a succession of highly publicized and often violent events. For instance, the admission of the first black pupils to the formerly all-white local High School in Little Rock, Arkansas, in 1957 was achieved only after the sending of federal marshals in response to opposition not only from the local population, but also on the part of local law enforcers and the State Governor. Perhaps the most compelling protest against segregation was that of Rosa Parkes, who in 1955 refused to vacate a seat on a bus reserved for whites and was arrested. This led to a protracted and ultimately effective boycott of the bus company concerned and the eventual abolition of separate seating arrangements for blacks and whites.

Several organizations played major roles in this and similar struggles and in campaigns against racial segregation and in favour of civil rights: the National Association for the Advancement of Colored People (NAACP), the Urban League, the Congress for Racial Equality (CORE), and the Student Nonviolent Coordination Committee (SNCC), which was led by Martin Luther King. These struggles were pursued by various non-violent means – freedom rides, boycotts, sit-ins and occupations – but they invariably met not just with arrests and imprisonment, but also with violence, murder and assassination by white opponents of change. This process of confrontation between civil rights activists and defenders of segregation – epitomized by events in Little Rock and Birmingham, Alabama – may have begun in the South (KU KLUX KLAN), but eventually violent conflicts connected to racial inequality (RACE AND INEQUALITY) and racism erupted in other parts of the USA, notably in Harlem, New York (1964), Watts, Los Angeles (1965), and in 1968 in a number of US cities following the assassination of Martin Luther King.

The strength of popular protests against racial segregation and the denial of civil rights that it represented meant that civil rights became an important political issue in the USA in the 1950s and, more particularly, in the 1960s. In response, the first civil rights law since the days of Reconstruction was passed in 1957. In 1964 a more comprehensive Civil Rights Act was passed which outlawed racial discrimination in several spheres, for example by employers and in voting procedures. In 1965 further legislation was introduced to end racial malpractice in voter registration and the use of literacy and other voter-qualification tests that had served to exclude black voters for so many years.

In marked contrast to the aims and actions of the civil rights organizations cited above, the other response by black people in the USA to racial segregation and exclusion was to reject INTEGRATION and instead embrace black NATIONALISM and separatism (BLACK POWER). The most prominent early advocate of such a view was Marcus Garvey. Garvey's position was that the goal of equality between black people and white people was a white deception, that integration was impossible and that territorial separation was not merely preferable, but also a necessary prerequisite if black people were to prepare to return to Africa, as he advocated. Some of these views were evident in the programme of the BLACK MUSLIMS, an organization founded in the 1930s and revived by Elijah Muhammad after the Second World War. The idea of separating black people from white people also formed a central plank in the programme of the Nation of Islam, led by Louis Farrakhan, a former member of the Black Muslims. Though the notion of a separate black territory within the USA, or of a prohibition on interracial marriage (MIXED MARRIAGE) may have been rejected by many black people, in a sense they may be seen as a significant reaction to centuries of racial oppression of blacks by whites and, indeed, as a mirror-image response to racial segregation.

In South Africa separate development of white and black peoples was at the heart of the polity, indeed it gave the polity its *raison d'être* in the form of the apartheid, a doctrine which denoted 'apartness' or complete separation of races in which whites were in total ascendancy. This involved not only denial of political rights to non-whites, but also a stark degree of inequality based on the rigid and wide-ranging social and geographical segregation of whites and non-whites. Racial segregation had been central to the history of South Africa from the moment of the first white settlement and it came to play an important part in shaping the lives of the various racial groupings that made up the South African population. However, racial segregation did not become fully formed until the twentieth century, even though the conflict between Afrikaner nationalism and British imperialism, and between white workers and black workers for urban employment in a context where employment was already racially divided, provided fruitful soil for its advance.

The defeat of the Boers by the British in the war of 1899–1902 had led to the establishment of the Union of South Africa as a white dominion in which blacks were to be deprived of any political influence. There followed a series of political and legislative initiatives and judicial decisions that widened and deepened racial divisions. For example, in 1905 the Cape Parliament provided for the establishment of special schools that by law were to be restricted to children of 'European parentage or extraction or descent' (Sachs, 1973: 132). The first significant legislation was the Natives Land Act, which became law in 1913. This defined which rural areas could be owned and occupied by Europeans and which by non-Europeans. It thus anticipated some of the essential elements of the more draconian measures that were introduced after 1948 when the apartheid regime came into power. In essence, the Afrikaner electoral platform was that their survival depended on the elimination of non-whites from the electoral system and the promotion of race consciousness (DOUBLE CONSCIOUSNESS) – as opposed to class consciousness – in conditions in which, with urbanization and the growth of the mining sector, large numbers of white workers and black workers were brought together in conditions of relative proximity. In other words, as far as Afrikaners were concerned, they must dominate or else they would be dominated.

There were many significant milestones in the construction of apartheid, but among the most significant were the following: the Prohibition of Mixed Marriages Act (1949); the Population Registration Act (1950), which specifically classified each person according to race; the Immorality Amendment Act (1950), which referred to sexual relations between members of different racial groups; and the establishment of Bantu reserves (beginning with the Transkei in 1962), which were intended to create separate and eventually self-governing black homelands. The creation of such homelands was not, however, intended to remove all black workers from white areas as their presence to perform the tasks that whites were unwilling to perform was vital to the white economy. Instead, black workers employed in white zones in industry, commerce or domestic service were obliged to carry pass books which they had to show to police on demand; failure to do so was punishable at law. The consequence of these measures was that all social situations in South Africa came to be governed by racial criteria and were subject to racial restriction and separation: marriage and sexual relations; admission to an electoral role; residence and conditions attached to residence; admission to school and university education; access to specific occupations; contact between races in hospitals and places of entertainment; and so on. In addition, there were a plethora of sanctions and punishments to enforce these racial distinctions and barriers and these, not surprisingly, impacted most harshly on non-whites. [M. V., P. B.]

Beinhart, W., Dubow, S. (eds) (1995) *Segregation and Apartheid in Twentieth Century South Africa*, Westview Press, Boulder, CO.

Bonte, P., Izard, M. (eds) (1991) *Dictionnaire de l'ethnologie et de l'anthropologie*, PUF, Paris.

Castles, S., Kosack, G. (1973) *Immigrant Workers and the Class Structure in Western Europe*, Oxford University Press, London.

Ginsberg, N. (1992) 'Racism and housing', in Braham, P., Rattansi, A., Skellington, R. (eds), *Racism and Antiracism*, Sage, London.

Kuper, L. (1960) 'The heightening of racial tension', *Race*, 2(1) November.

Sachs, A. (1973) *Justice in South Africa*, Heinemann, London.

Silberman, C. E. (1965) *Crisis in Black and White*, Jonathan Cape, London.

Valeri, M., Bracalenti, R. (1996) 'La prostituzionalizzazione delle differenze', in Gindro, S., Bolaffi, G., (eds), *Il corpo straniero*, A. Guida, Napoli.

West, C. (1993) *Race Matters*, Beacon Press, Boston, MA.

RACIALIZATION (It. *razzializzazione*; Fr. *racialisation*; Ger. *Rassialisierung*) The recognition of the socially constructed nature of the term 'RACE' creates a problem for

authors who wish to write about 'RACE RELATIONS' without legitimizing the idea of race. Racialization is used therefore to refer to social relations to which 'racial' meanings are attached. The use of the term emphasizes the process of creating racial definitions and underlines the constructed rather than the given nature of race. So if an actor defines a relationship as a 'race' relation, he or she is racializing the relationship and *making* it a race relationship.

Actors may or may not believe that race is a given or real category. Nevertheless they may view aspects of society through a racial prism. Thus in the UK in the 1960s a shortage of housing accommodation was plain to see. There were immigrants (MIGRANTS) from the Caribbean and the Indian subcontinent in the areas of shortage. These two observations may have been of independent and unconnected facts. Nonetheless the public, and later the government, engaged in the racialization of the housing issue by attributing the shortage to the influx of immigrants. Housing in a number of large cities thus became a 'race' issue rather than a housing issue. In contemporary Europe social issues are often racialized; one result is to refocus attention on competition for scarce resources rather than on the problem of the inadequate supply. Thus the Front National leader Jean Marie Le Pen drew attention, in France, to the statistics of unemployment and immigration, seeking thereby to racialize the problem of unemployment.

In the UK the racialization of public debate is particularly apparent in discussion of law and order and, above all, in the politics of immigration (MIGRATION). As Solomos argues, for 'many on the Right [of British politics] race came to play an increasingly important role in public policy debates and official policy analysis. For many on the Right, immigration and race are important issues because of their supposed impact on the cultural and political values of British society' (Solomos, 1989: 2). In his view, what is said by politicians, and by others in authority and in the media (RACE AND THE MEDIA), helped to create the view that without firm action to control (black) immigration and to address local and national race-related issues, the entire fabric of British society was threatened. In this process, Solomos argues, the state played an active role, not just in policy formation, but also in shaping the wider political agenda. Nowhere is this better illustrated than in the way immigration came to be controlled in a racially specific way that both responded to and fed the idea that there was too much black immigration.

There were several contradictions in this approach: one was that firm immigration control was justified as an essential precursor to the establishment of 'good COMMUNITY relations'; but, by emphasizing the threat posed by further black immigration, the existing black population was depicted not merely as a threat, but implicitly at least, as the 'enemy within', and thus as a danger to social stability. And so, by racializing the public agenda, firm immigration control could be said to harm rather than improve community relations. This 'danger' was evident in unemployment queues, in the education system, as well as in terms of immigration control. It was particularly evident in matters of law and order, where the image of a disaffected black youth – alienated even from black communities themselves – infused public discussion of law and order issues. The controversy over 'mugging' (street robbery), which was at its height in the early 1970s, was highly racialized. Similarly racialized

was the prevailing discourse in later controversies about criminal statistics and 'stop and search'.

Racialization may also entail the deliberate construction of, for example, a division of labour based on 'race'. Clear examples are seen in former British colonies where Africans or Afro-Caribbean ex-slaves worked in unskilled manual occupations or as plantation hands; Asians as shopkeepers, traders and minor or middle officials in public services and administration; white settlers exercising economic and political power, or with high status or higher-paid jobs in management and administration. This division of labour may have been reinforced by legal job reservation or simply by custom and practice. The outcome was, nonetheless, a 'racialized' division of labour and labour market. Similar racialized divisions of labour may be found in contemporary Europe where they are closely paralleled by divisions based on nationality (CITIZENSHIP) (some Swiss hotels are staffed at the lowest levels by Cape Verde islanders, for example). Extreme forms of this phenomenon are found in Europe in the merchant fleets and on European offshore oil and gas installations. The 'racialized' stratification of these places of work makes steep differentials in wages and conditions of employment possible. [R. M.]

Banton, M. (1988) *Racial Consciousness*, Longmans, New York.
MacAll, C. (1990) *Class, Ethnicity and Social Inequality*, McGill-Queen's University Press, Montreal and Buffalo.
Miles, R. (1982) *Racism and Migrant Labour*, Routledge & Kegan Paul, London.
Smith, S. (1989) *The Politics of 'Race' and Residence*, Polity Press, Cambridge.
Solomos, J. (1989) *Race and Racism in Contemporary Britain*, Macmillan, London.

RACISM
(It. *razzismo*; Fr. *racisme*; Ger. *Rassismus*) From the Latin *ratio*, meaning 'nature' or 'quality', according to some sources; or from the ancient French *haraz*, meaning 'horse breeding', according to other sources. Though racism has been directed against both white and non-white groups, it is often assumed – especially in the UK – that racism applies exclusively to non-white groups. Indeed, in Britain in recent times the terms 'RACE', 'RACE RELATIONS' and 'racism' have all come to be equated with *colour* (COLOURED), reflecting the impact that post-Second World War black and Asian immigration (MIGRATION) to the UK has had on the way these matters are perceived. By contrast, in mainland Europe it is the practice to refer to 'racism, XENOPHOBIA and ANTI-SEMITISM' to indicate that a range of interconnected issues need to be addressed, as well as to emphasize that racism based on pigmentation does not represent racism in its entirety. It has often been argued that in recent years partly in response to the discrediting of biologically based 'scientific racism' (RACE), a 'new racism' (Barker, 1981) or 'neo-racism' (Balibar and Wallerstein, 1991) of cultural difference (DIVERSITY–SIMILARITY) has come to predominate in both the UK and mainland Europe. This focuses on such elements as national origin, linguistic differences, religion, dress and dietary customs as bases for justifying discrimination and disadvantage, while attempting to escape accusations of racism by avoiding reference to biology.

Conceptions of race have historically always included cultural (CULTURE) and biological dimensions (Miles, 1993: 87) and populations targeted by 'cultural racism' are usually those which were previously the objects of more biologically based discrimination (Rattansi, 1994: 54–56). Several examples help to illustrate this complex interweaving of the cultural and biological in racism: Turkish GASTARBEITER, for instance, who came to work in Germany from the 1960s onwards, encountered a degree of racism. Jews (JEW) arriving in Britain at the beginning of the twentieth century also encountered hostility and anxiety, as measured by popular and political reaction, which was also in many respects racist, and which prefigured the response to the later black and Asian immigration from the New Commonwealth. The 1905 Aliens Act was passed in the face of growing anti-Semitism. The Irish, who came to Britain in large numbers in the mid-nineteenth century, were also often described in racial terms, with reference made to their supposed innate, biologically determined capabilities and characteristics. On a visit to Ireland, the author Charles Kingsley described the Irish in terms replete with racial meaning as 'human chimpanzees', remarking that 'if they were black, one would not feel it so much, but their skins, except where tanned by exposure, are as white as ours' (cited in Husband, 1982: 12). This comment is significant for a number of reasons. First, it makes clear that, for Kingsley, the Irish were *racially* different, but in appearance they were *not different enough*. More generally, it suggests that WHITENESS is not an undifferentiated category. This point can be demonstrated by the contrasting attitudes to European immigrants to the USA: those of Slav and Mediterranean origin were widely regarded as a race apart from Northern Europeans, and Italian immigrants were described as the 'Chinese of Europe' (Warren and Twine, 1997: 205). It also draws attention to what Omi and Winant call *racial formation*. By this they refer to the process by which social, economic and political forces determine the content and importance of racial categories, and by which they are in turn shaped by racial meanings. Crucial to this formulation is the treatment of race as a *central axis* of social relations which cannot be subsumed under or reduced to some broader category or conception. (Omi and Winant, 1986: 61–62)

To explain how race becomes both meaningful and effective – that is to say, how the concept of 'race' has significant outcomes – they use the term RACIALIZATION to indicate 'the extension of racial meaning to a previously unclassified relationship, social practice or group' (ibid.: 64). This process has several elements. The first, and most important, is the determinist nature of views and perspectives on race. These take as given the idea that certain groups can be classified or identified as races which have inherent and unchangeable characteristics, and that these characteristics account for their capacities and behaviour. The second stage is the insistence that there is a racial hierarchy in which different races stand in relation to each other as superior and inferior – where the white races are invariably placed at the summit. What connects these two stages is the assumption that racial traits determine cultural traits and that a more advanced culture is a sure sign of racial superiority.

This analysis raises the question of whether, as some have argued, the term 'racism' should be used only with reference to the development of the concept of race in western culture, as exemplified in the writings of the French diplomat Gobineau (1853–55) and, especially, in the development of scientific racism. The question then arises as to whether these beliefs are sufficient in themselves to constitute racism. One view is that racism entails more than mere recognition of innate differences ascribed to membership of a specific racial grouping; it involves the *justification* of unequal or different treatment on this basis. This suggests that a distinction can usefully be made between racist *attitudes* and racist *practices*. On the one hand, a belief in the existence of distinct races may not lead to racist outcomes – perhaps because there is no opportunity for this to happen or perhaps because those holding such a belief lack the power to enforce it. On the other hand, racist views may underpin discrimination, disadvantage, exploitation and segregation – as in the case of the depiction and treatment of Africans in the colonial era (COLONIALISM) or in the case of *apartheid* (RACIAL SEGREGATION). In these circumstances, racism provides a vital rationale for inequality and exploitation. Even though the concept of the 'prejudiced non-discriminator' indicates that someone with racist views may be prevented from behaving in a racist way by legal prohibition or intervention, the difference between *outcomes* and *beliefs* is of pivotal importance in understanding the term 'racism' (PREJUDICE).

Conversely, it is quite conceivable for there to be a racist or racially discriminatory outcome without there being any racist motivation or any racist views being present, as is implied by the distinctions between unintentional and intentional discrimination and between indirect and direct discrimination, as well as by the focus on INSTITUTIONAL RACISM. The term 'indirect discrimination' refers to rules, regulations, procedures and criteria that have a discriminatory *effect*, irrespective of the motivations or intentions of the decision-makers or gatekeepers involved. Ginsberg's analysis of the nature and extent of racism in the UK housing market illustrates very well the operation and interplay of these *different* racisms, both intentional and otherwise. According to Ginsberg, first, there is direct racism (whether overt or hidden) of key individuals – such as vendors of property, estate agents and landlords – who may actively discriminate against black people who wish to buy or rent property. Secondly there is RACIAL HARASS-MENT of black people in and near their homes, which may act as a severe constraint on where they feel safe to live. Thirdly, there are policies and practices of local authority housing departments, building societies and estate agents which have served to disadvantage black people in various ways and at various times – as in the refusal by building societies to advance loans to buy property in specified areas (a practice known as 'red-lining') and in the application of restrictive residency requirements as a precondition for eligibility to be a council (public) house tenant. In practice, these different kinds of racism may combine: thus a local housing department may respond, perhaps unofficially, to the existence of hostility towards and harassment of black people by concentrating black tenants in specific (usually less desirable) estates (Ginsberg, 1992).

The term 'racism' can be applied in a restrictive and narrow way or in broader fashion. If its meaning is restricted, then it will be used only where human populations are divided into discrete races that are defined on the basis of biological criteria. In this context, reference might be made to successive UNESCO Declarations (in 1950, 1951, 1962 and 1976) that drew on genetic knowledge and anthropological analysis to refute the biological basis of race and contingent racial typologies. In this sense, racism can be said to be in retreat. But its retreat as a scientific concept has had a limited effect because as a social construct it remains a powerful force,

especially in the newer cultural racisms referred to earlier. Such formulations contain significant elements of racism partly because of the residue of older biological conceptions of 'racial stock' and partly because they stipulate that a particular cultural or ethnic or national group has 'essential' and inalienable characteristics or traits. The distinction between different forms of racism is useful in that it reminds us that expressions of racism – whether by individuals or in wider discourse – are prone to combine different combinations of biological racism, ETHNOCENTRISM and NATIONALISM. What is common to these different forms of racism is the notion that the variations among groups of humans are given, fixed and unalterable. The two elements combine in different degrees at different junctures to produce different manifestations of racism or, as is being increasingly argued, different racisms. [P. B., A. R.]

Balibar, E., Wallerstein, I. (1991) *Race, Nation and Class*, Verso, London.

Barker, M. (1981) *The New Racism*, Junction Books, London.

Cesarani, D. (1991) *Antisemitism in the 1990s: a Symposium, Patterns of Prejudice.*

Ginsberg, N. (1992) 'Racism in housing: concepts and reality', .in Braham, P., Rattansi, A., Skellington, R. (eds), *Racism and Antiracism*, Sage, London.

Gobineau, de J. A. (1967) *Essai sur l'inégalité des races humaines*, L'Harmattan, Paris.

Husband, C. (ed.) (1982) *'Race' in Britain*, Hutchinson, London.

Miles, R. (1993) *Racism after 'Race Relations'*, Routledge, London.

Omi, M., Winant, H. (1986) *Racial Formation in the United States from the 1960s to the 1980s*, Routledge, New York and London.

Parekh, B. et al. (2000) *The Future of Multi-Ethnic Britain* (The Parekh Report), Profile Books, London.

Rattansi, A. (1994) '"Western" racisms, ethnicities and identities in a "postmodern" frame', in Rattansi, A., West-wood, S. (eds), *Racism, Modernity and Identity*, Polity Press, Cambridge.

Warren, J., Twine, F. (1997) 'White Americans, the new minority', *Journal of Black Studies*, 28: 200–218.

RACISM AND MEDICINE (It. *razzismo e medicina*; Fr. *racisme et médecine*; Ger. *Rassismus und Medizin*)

In the Greek cities where they practised, Hippocratic doctors treated men and women, citizens and outsiders, freemen and slaves, Greeks or foreigners, whoever was in need. In the Hippocratic doctor's eyes, they were all human beings. Tangible proof of this humanity is offered by the vocabulary used – the Greek word *anthropos*, meaning human being, appears frequently in the writings of Hippocratic doctors, who used the word to refer to the patient. Everything referring to differences of sex, social status or racial origin was secondary; the sick person was paramount and had to be restored to health.

In contradistinction to this tradition, there is a deep and long-lasting connection between medicine and racism. This relationship has manifested itself in two distinct ways, which coincide in particular circumstances and with horrendous consequences. First, as a scientific discipline, medicine sought to establish a *scientific basis* for comprehending perceived racial differences. Secondly, doctors have used prisoners and concentration camp inmates for so-called 'scientific' experiments, notably, but not only, under the Nazi regime (CONCENTRATION CAMP AND DEATH CAMP). Humans have been reduced to the level of laboratory animals and subjected to experiments that frequently ended in death – and were often intended to do so.

Despite the Hippocratic oath, doctors have taken and continue to take part in crimes against humanity, sometimes on the pretext that this is in pursuit of 'scientific discovery' and thus somehow defensible. Notable in this context are the experiments carried out by the Nazis on those defined as 'subhuman' – principally, concentration camp inmates and prisoners of war of certain nationalities (CITIZENSHIP), though also those defined by the Nazis as 'feeble-minded'. Such experiments were not merely widespread, but routine. They encompassed skilled amputations and transplants which – given their purpose – were carried out in absurdly hygienic conditions: injections of pus into the legs and breasts to enable the 'study' of the effects of sulphanilamide; subjects were also forced to drink sea water to 'test' the effects of thirst, or left for hours in baths of ice so that the effects of cold on the body could be observed. The SS doctors involved (not more than 100, as against the 150,000 German 'civilian' doctors) believed in the importance this work would have for future medicine, but above all they believed in the need to create a new 'SS medical science'. It has been argued that if there had been at least some positive results, perhaps such experiments might be understood, if not justified – though few would accept such an argument and many would see it as a dangerous position to take. However, a careful evaluation of all the experiments conducted by doctors such as Fischer, Romberg, Gebhardt, Mengele and Schumann (all condemned to death at the Nuremberg Trials) found that not a single experiment added in the slightest to the progress of post-war medical science. Even today doctors and psychologists in many countries are used in the interrogation and torture of detainees. Their special responsibility is not to prevent torture, but to halt it before there is any 'visible' damage which might be seen in the event of a visit by an international commission.

Before the Second World War many doctors subscribed to the belief that (supposed) racial distinctions and differences had a significant part to play in diagnosing, treating, preventing and understanding various medical conditions. For example, it was thought that people suffering from sickle-cell anaemia must have 'African blood'. In 1927, J. S. Lawrence, an American doctor, finding a white person with this type of anaemia, wrote in the *Journal of Clinical Investigation* that he had paid close attention to the possibility that there had been some introduction of black blood into the family, and that as no evidence of black blood had been found some caution should be exercised in calling the malady sickle-cell anaemia (Goodman, 1997). In 1899 another American doctor, Thomas R. Brown, reported that he had often heard surgeons say that tumours found in black women had all the characteristics of ovarian cysts, but he asserted that because the patients were black, this could not be so, as cases of multilocular cysts were unknown in black women. The following year, Daniel H. Williams, an eminent African-American doctor, recalled that he had heard a doctor in Alabama putting forward the theory that perhaps the black race had not yet evolved to the stage where cysts manifested themselves. In response, Williams carried out a study that demonstrated that ovarian cysts were common in black women (including black women in Alabama).

It might be supposed that the idea of a distinct pathology for different races has now been replaced by approaches that are much more cautious about making assumptions about 'race' as a risk factor in certain diseases. This supposition is not necessarily accurate. For instance, in the journal *Seminars in Nuclear Medicine*, a study entitled 'Osteoporosis: the state of the art in 1987', cited race as one of the major risk factors in respect of the estimated 25 million Americans who suffered osteoporosis and the 1.5 million fractures recorded in the USA in connection with this condition each year. Until the nineteenth century it had been thought that blacks had denser bones than whites and that the mass of their bones shrunk more slowly with age. The article appeared to give renewed currency to this belief by stating (without equivocation) that blacks did not suffer from osteoporosis. The proof of this 'fact' lay in just one datum – preliminary research by a team led by the American physical anthropologist Mildred Trotter, entitled 'Densities of bones of white and negro skeletons'. Trotter and her colleagues had examined the density of bones in the skeletons of 40 black and 40 white adults. They rejected skeletons which showed signs of disease, but did not say how they had selected the skeletons, or if the samples had been chosen on the basis of cause of death, diet, or other risk factors for osteoporosis. Of the 10 bones from each skeleton subjected to examination, Trotter and her colleagues discovered that six tended to be denser in the blacks than in the whites; the other four showed no differences. The authors stated that the reduction in density took place 'at approximately the same speed' for each group, whether by sex or race.

Perhaps Trotter and her colleagues realized that their results were open to misinterpretation, because in a later article they included graphs which plotted age against bone density. These data confirmed the tendency towards reduction in density with ageing: the clusters of figures were more closely grouped towards the bottom of the graph. After a careful analysis of the study, it became obvious that it was impossible to find any difference in bone density between blacks and whites.

In each of the above-cited cases, it seems that the scientific creed was based on two presumptions. First, a serious disease or condition (sickle-cell anaemia, ovarian cysts or osteoporosis) was seen as congenital (that is, present in one 'race', but not in another), despite inadequacies of evidence and insufficient analysis of related factors. Secondly, a pan-racial concept was applied to every genetic phenomenon. Whatever seemed proven at a statistical level was applied to all the members of a so-called race. Thus it could be concluded that 'all blacks are immune to osteoporosis', 'all blacks are less prone to cardiac diseases', and so on. Also significant is the tendency to associate the appearance or spread of a disease or epidemic with the presence of a particular group. Following the return of the plague to Toulon in 1348, Jews (JEW) were accused of spreading the disease and were persecuted on this account. More generally, syphilis has typically been named after the people held responsible for its spread, so that in France it was known as 'the Neapolitan disease' and in Naples as 'the French disease'. Much more recently, when AIDS appeared in the early 1980s, it was immediately branded a 'gay' syndrome, since people were convinced that it was spread (only) by homosexuals. [A. M.]

Annas, G. J., Grodin, M. A. (1992) *The Nazi Doctors and the Nuremberg Code: Human Rights in Human Experimentation*, Oxford University Press, New York.
Bianchini, C., Marangi, M., Meledandri, G., Morrone, A. (eds) (2001) *Medicina internazionale*, SEU, Roma.
Cavalli Sforza, L., Cavalli Sforza, F. (1996) *The Great Human Diaspora: The History of Diversity and Evolution*, Addison-Wesley, Helix Books, New York.

Gobineau, de J. A. (1967) *Essai sur l'inégalité des races humaines*, L'Harmattan, Paris.
Goodman, A. H. (1997) 'Bred in the bone', in *Sciences*, 2: 20.
Katz, J. (1967) *Experimentation with Human Beings*, Russell Sage Foundation, New York.
Levinas, E. (1969) *Totality and Infinity* (trans. Alphonso Lingus), Duquesne University Press, Pittsburgh.
Mann, M. J., Gruskin, S., Grodin, M. A., Annas, G. J. (1999) *Health and Human Rights: A Reader*, Routledge, New York.
Marks, J. (1997) 'La Race, théorie populaire de l'hérédité', *La Recherche*, 10: 17–23.
Morrone, A. (ed.) (1995) *Salute e società multiculturale*, Raffaello Cortina, Milano.
Morrone, A. (1999) *L'altra faccia di Gaia*, Armando Editore, Roma.
Morrone, A., and Borgese, L. (2001) 'Popolazioni e ricostruzione delle origini dell'eterogeneità genetica umana' in C. Bianchini, M. Marangi, G. Meledandri and A. Morrone (eds) *Medicina internazionale*, SEU, Roma. pp. 77–131.
Mosse, G. L. (1991) *Nationalization of the Masses: Political Symbolism and Mass Movements in Germany from the Napoleonic Wars through the Third Reich*, Cornell University Press, Ithaca, NY.
Wieviorka, M. (1995) *The Arena of Racism*, Sage, London.

RECEPTION CENTRE (It. *centro di accoglienza*; Fr. *centre d'accueil*; Ger. *Aufnahmelager*) The expressions 'reception centre' and 'refugee camp' may generally be used interchangeably in a wide variety of situations to indicate any permanent or temporary structure used to shelter people in a condition of need. Reception centres usually include facilities provided for immigrants (MIGRANT) immediately after arrival in the country of destination, while refugee camps are more often shelters designed for refugees or asylum seekers (REFU-GEE, POLITICAL ASYLUM) awaiting assessment of their requests and camps accommodating displaced persons in areas near war zones. As a result of both the number of people seeking accommodation and the urgency of the situation, refugee camps are more widespread. Refugee camps are an instrument whose fundamental purpose is to guarantee protection to refugees according to the 1951 Convention of the United Nations.

Up until the beginning of the twentieth century, people fleeing their country of origin depended on aid from private groups for survival and lacked both legal rights and protection. However, since the end of the First World War, several international organizations have been set up to protect and assist refugees. Refugees are currently provided with legal protection and material assistance by the United Nations High Commission for Refugees (UNHCR), which was established in 1951 to resettle refugees still remaining in post-war displaced persons' camps, while the status of refugees is set forth in two United Nations documents: the 1951 *Convention* and the 1967 *Protocol Relating to the Status of Refugees*. Other national and international agencies involved in the setting up and running of reception centres are the International Rescue Committee, the International Committee of the Red Cross, the International Council of Voluntary Agencies, and the US Committee on Refugees.

Reception centres vary considerably depending on the kind of emergency, the number of people and the geographical area in which they are located. Most are able to guarantee basic living requirements such as food and shelter and hopefully special structures for children such as educational facilities (in Denmark, Sweden and the Netherlands

unaccompanied minors may be placed in reception centres which are specially designed for children falling within a certain age range). In many cases people are free to move in and out, although in other situations the freedom of guests is restricted due to lack of permission to stay in the host country.

Reception centres provided for migrants are often small – accommodating not more than 15–20 people – with guests being free to enter and exit at will once they have been identified, e.g. reception centres set up in Italy for BOAT PEOPLE fleeing from Albania and Turkey. Generally speaking, internal rules are established by each reception centre and guests are requested to moderate their behaviour accordingly. Some reception centres provide language training or assistance in seeking employment. Freedom of movement is restricted in reception centres for ILLEGAL ALIENS awaiting DEPORTATION and special refugee camps for asylum seekers awaiting identification and the completion of the relevant administrative actions necessary to define their refugee status, such as Iranian and Afghan migrants in the 800-bed refugee camp of Woomera in South Australia.

Not all reception centres and refugee camps are set up by the authorities of the state in which they are located. The refugee camps established in Macedonia during the crisis in the Balkans were administered by NATO troops as transit camps for the purpose of housing refugees pending humanitarian evacuation. These were closed camps with high wire fences and barbed wire patrolled by Macedonian police officers who guarded the gates and checked the identity documents of all who attempted to enter. [Gu. B., J. H.]

Amnesty International (1999) *Former Yugoslav Republic of Macedonia: The*

Protection of Kosovo Albanian Refugees, Amnesty International, www.webamnesty.org.

Hyndman, J. (2000) *Managing Displacement: Refugees and Politics of Humanitarianism*, University of Minnesota Press, Minneapolis.

International Organization for Migration (2000) *World Migration Report 2000*, IOM, Geneva.

REFUGEE

REFUGEE (It. *rifugiato*; Fr. *réfugié, personne déplacée*; Ger. *Flüchtling*) The term 'refugee', via Old French from the Latin *refugium* from *refugere* (to flee away), refers to people who have had to abandon or flee their country of origin as a result of serious threat to their lives or freedom such as natural catastrophe, war or military occupation, or fear of religious, racial or political persecution. As refugees are forced to abandon their country of origin and request admission to another country – not by choice or in order to improve their personal standing, but as a result of absolute necessity, being citizens of a state which cannot or will not guarantee the well-being of its citizens (CITIZENSHIP) – they are compelled to request international rather than national protection (UNHCR, 2000). Indeed, the very fact that refugees are fleeing their country of origin means they are no longer protected from persecution or killing by that state. The majority of countries have agreed to grant special protection on an international basis by setting up an international protection system in which a pivotal role is played by the United Nations High Commission for Refugees (UNHCR). The legal status of refugees is defined by two United Nations documents: the 1951 Convention and the 1967 Protocol Relating to the Status of Refugees. These documents – signed by 134 member states and thus among the most important legal instruments regarding refugees – specify the rights and duties of refugees. Refugees benefit from the right to *non refoulement*, which forbids a host country to send refugees back to a country in which their safety could be threatened. Furthermore, pursuant to international law, refugees must be guaranteed a series of economic, social and political rights as well as freedom of circulation (FREE MOVEMENT). The duties of the refugee are to respect the laws and regulations of the country in which they are granted EXILE and to maintain public order. Individuals guilty of serious crimes and crimes against humanity, as well as war criminals, may be refused refugee status. Refugee status may be granted to asylum seekers following a legal procedure in which the host country decides whether to grant refugee status or otherwise.

Citizens who are forced from their homes for refugee-like reasons, but who remain within the borders of their own country, are known as Internally Displaced Persons. Although such people do not qualify for refugee status, so large are their numbers that they are of growing concern to international aid organizations. In the past, refugees were expected to stay in the host country on a temporary basis and return to their country of origin as soon as the threatening conditions ceased. Nowadays the situation has changed and refugees often expect to settle in the host country.

The number of asylum seekers has grown considerably in recent years. Between 1985 and 1994, almost 5 million requests for asylum were registered in countries adhering to the Geneva Convention, with the refugee crisis reaching its peak in 1992 when member countries registered more than 80,000 applications for political asylum in just one month. The reasons for such an increase, especially in Europe, are as complicated and various as the number of conflicts – Iran–Iraq, ex-Yugoslavia, Africa – producing massive population flights, such as that of the Kurd population, one of the largest diasporas in Europe (DIASPORA). Another reason for the increase in the number of asylum seekers coming to Europe stems from the introduction of a new migrant evaluation policy (FORTRESS EUROPE) in the mid-1970s when it was impossible to enter Europe through the usual labour migration channels, so many economic migrants tried to enter as refugees. Previous national legislation, e.g. in Germany, had compelled many European host countries to grant refugee status to all who applied for asylum for humanitarian or political reasons, and as a consequence many countries had allowed a huge number of refugees to enter. The establishment of tougher legislation was a response to public opinion and to the call from national governments to try and stop this massive influx of 'false' refugees. Other responses included a reduction in the duration of legal procedures, the requesting of entry visas (VISA) – following the coming into force of the Schengen agreement (26 May 1995) – the placing of immigration officers in the countries of origin and transit, the reduction of freedom of movement in cases of 'ungrounded application for refugee status', the suspension of the need for a permit of stay, the awarding of temporary permits of stay, the withdrawal of refugee status and the right to work in the case of 'fundamental change' in the country of origin, fingerprinting and the implementing of exchanges of information between ministries in the countries involved. Implementation of tougher procedures to control the fraudulent

arrival of refugees has been a matter of great controversy in Europe as the strategies set up to control fraud often make the granting of visas to refugees an extremely difficult, lengthy and, on occasion, impossible task, even when asylum seekers are exposed to extremely high risks or come from inhuman or oppressive regimes. [J. H.]

Sassen, S. (1996) *Guests and Aliens*, New Press, New York.
Wihtol de Wenden, C. (1996) 'Les Réfugiés: droits de l'homme ou fait du prince?', *Esprit*, août–septembre.
UNHCR (2000) *The State of the World's Refugees. Biennial Report*, UNCHR: Oxford University Press, Oxford.

RELIGION AND ETHNIC CONFLICTS (It. *religione e conflitti etnici*; Fr. *religion et conflits ethniques*; Ger. *Religion und ethnische Konflikte*)

Religious and interethnic conflicts have been a constant and intertwined reality throughout the history of humankind. This entry offers (1) a general overview of the religious phenomenon in different cultural contexts; (2) a short discussion of diverse attitudes towards RACE and ETHNICITY in the main world religions; (3) an outline of history of ethnic-religious conflicts in Europe; and (4) a summary of the role played by religions in contemporary ethnic conflicts.

RELIGION

The term 'religion' derives from the Latin *religio*, through *relegere*, to collect again, in orderly fashion, or from *religare*, to tie. No precise corresponding term is found in ancient Greek, in which only similar concepts appear, such as *latreia*, religious service, *eusebeia*, piety, or even *threspeia*, relating to religious techniques. Religion is the belief in supernatural principles or entities whom humans can contact in their search for favours or salvation. The term does not necessarily imply the recognition of a personal divinity, as is the case with Buddhism, a philosophy which has come back into fashion. As a 'faith' it should be considered a personal relationship between humans and God.

There are three main kinds of religion: (a) positive religions, which arise following a revelation, and whose cults are administered by priests or ministers, and include rites (RITE), dogmas and mysteries; (b) natural religions, which are an aggregate of beliefs, more or less organically organized, in the existence and goodness of God; (c) personal religion, or faith, that is, the relationship of an individual with God, without intermediaries. Observation of social structures, both from a synchronic and a diachronic point of view, shows that some kind of religious organization is always apparent. The focus here is on an analysis of the positive religions. Individuals are conditioned, independently of their own will, by the religious beliefs of the society of which they are part. The social UNCONSCIOUS is also structured according to the values, rituals and traditions of religion. In some groups, religious belief is structured more uniformly, while in others it is composed of heterogeneous creeds. The history of a population often comprises several religious expressions which overlap and form the religious element of its social unconscious.

All human beings have their own fundamental conception of life, death and values, which also partly derives from the religious convictions of their group of belonging. A fine line is drawn between religion and two areas of psychological relevance: superstition and mental illness. Obsessive rituals, lucky gestures and amulets cannot simply be dismissed as expressions of childish naïvety or of 'primitivism' (PRIMITIVE), as all positive religions contain such elements as imposed rituals, gestures and words, or prescribed or forbidden foods. Even many widely accepted religious dogmas and beliefs can seem to be embedded with delusional ideas when approached from perspectives other than that of the believer. The transmission of religious values and ideas may follow unpredictable routes, overstepping generations and suddenly reappearing at different times and in different cultural areas, in a continuous process of transformation. The process can be detected through an analysis of MYTH and unconscious symbols. Some religious principles and beliefs can be transmitted unconsciously, overstepping whole generations and continents to find renewed vigour in unexpected eras and places, in a movement of continuous becoming.

The tribal religions of BLACK AFRICA, which are still practised by over 60 million people, are defined as prehistoric. However, on the African continent these religions are practised by only 12 per cent of the population, while 45 per cent are Christians and 40 per cent are Muslims.

The tribal religions of the Americas can be divided into 'Indian' – belonging to the people of North America and practised by populations of Mongol origins – and the religions of the Indio populations of South America. The former are characterized by faith in a cosmic power which is seen as the creator of life, the Great Spirit or Manitou, and are totemic cults. Among the South American religions, those of the Aztecs, the Mayans and the Incas have had great historical significance. These religions have disappeared today and Central and South America are mainly Catholic, although very distant traces of the ancient cults still exist in today's worship.

Of the ancient Asian tribal religions there remain traces in the perpetuation of the tradition of shamanism, which is an archaic set of rituals in which there are traces of Chinese Buddhism and Islamism. Shamans have the multiple role of priest, prophet and 'witch doctor'.

Among the historical religions, that is those teachings that claim that God has acted decisively in human history, Christianity appears in various forms, which refer back to their founder, Jesus Christ the Messiah, who came to the world to save mankind from the consequences of original sin. Christianity is divided into several confessions. The Catholic Church, which is highly centralized, is led by the Pope of Rome, the Vicar of Christ. The schismatic churches, such as the Orthodox churches which are mostly found in the East, have local leaders and many dogmas in common with Catholicism. The Reformed or Protestant Churches refer back to the origins of Christianity. For all of the above, the Holy Scriptures consist of the Old and New Testaments. Christianity was preceded by Judaism, whose history is documented and whose origins lie in Holy Scriptures. Written by the prophets, the Holy Scriptures are presumed to be of divine inspiration. Judaism is closely linked to the spiritual and historical-political vicissitudes of the Jewish people and is founded on Messianism, that is, the belief that a saviour is to come for the people of Israel.

The other main historical religions are Buddhism, Shintoism, Hinduism, Islam, Confucianism and Taoism. Buddhism derives from Indian Brahmanism and owes its name to Siddharta Gautama (563–483 BC) 'the Awakened one', its great preacher. In the fourth century BC the first divisions between the Theras, the old priests, and the lay members of the great community occurred. Modern Buddhism is divided into three great currents or 'vehicles'; *Mahayana* or the 'greater vehicle', *Hinayana* or the 'lesser vehicle' and *Vajrayana* or the 'diamond vehicle'. On the whole Buddhism does not propose belief in a God-person, but structures itself around daily practices, mainly aimed at meditation and ascesis.

Hinduism followed Veda and Brahmanism as the third stage of development in Indian religion. Hinduism does not have a founder and is characterized by a marked polytheism derived from the Vedic pantheon. One of its basic principles is the belief in reincarnation, which, through the rebirth cycle, brings humans back into living nature. This destiny, which is 'not conceived as an arcane and mysterious force, but as a complex series of situations which man creates himself through his actions' (Biardeau, 1995), has a key role and is known as *karma*.

Shintoism is the indigenous religion of Japan (where it is practised alongside Buddhism), according to which the Emperor descends directly from God. The term 'Shintoism' derives from the word *shinto* which, in Japanese, means 'unification'. More than a religion, Shintoism is the integration of religious creeds with the imperial deed of the deified sovereign. The 'Shinto' is the content of an imperial edict issued in 1868. This belief was formally revoked in the Constitution of 1947, in which the defeated Hirohito, in addition to renouncing many of his powers was also forced to repudiate his divine origin. The Shintoist Olympus contains a very high number of popular divinities who are worshipped in many local temples.

Islam (abandonment, submission) is the Muslim religion (from the Persian *muslim*, dedicated to God). It entails the belief in one God, Allah, which was revealed to humanity by the prophet Muhammad (AD 570–632) and originated in the Arab peninsula. Its development shows many Judaeo-Christian influences. Islam today is practised by over 17 per cent of the world population, of whom 27 per cent are Arabs. Throughout the centuries the religion has split into many schismatic currents such as the Sunnites, the Shi'ites, the Scythians and the Ishmaelites. All these currents refer to the Koran as their holy book, in which the faith in the only Supreme Being and in his prophet Muhammad is expressed. The Koran also contains theories regarding the Last Judgment, the survival of the soul, predestination, and Heaven and Hell.

Confucianism is a philosophic-religious current of thought, stressing moral order, the virtue of China's ancient rulers and gentlemanly education. Its founder was Confucius (551–479 BC). This movement almost always enjoyed the support of the emperors of the various dynasties, so much so that it has been identified as being China's official religious philosophy. Taoism is the other Chinese indigenous religious philosophy and derives its name from the *tao*, the way, or the rules to be followed to obtain the lengthening of life and immortality. It claims a mythical founder, Lao-Tzu (Old Master).

Any attempt to understand a society cannot fail to take into account its religious views. According to Mircea Eliade, one of the most influential scholars in the field, the sacred is an element of the structure of the conscience. At more ancient levels of CULTURE, living as a human being is *per se* a religious act, as feeding, sex and work have a sacred value. In other words to be – or to become – human means to be religious (Eliade, 1982). [S. G.]

Biardeau, M. (1995) *L'Hindouisme*, Flammarion, Paris.

Eliade, M. (1982) *A History of Religious Ideas*, University of Chicago Press, Chicago.

Grenier, J. (1973) *L'Esprit du Tao*, Flammarion, Paris.

Guillon, E. (1995) *Les Philosophes bouddhistes*, PUF, Paris.

Puech, H. C. (1999) *Histoire des religions*, Gallimard, Paris.

Roy, O. (1995) *Généalogie de l'islamisme*, Hachette, Paris.

Smith, J. Z. (1995) *The Harper Collins Dictionary of Religion*, Harper, San Francisco.

RELIGIONS AND ETHNICITY

All the most widely practised world religions accept the idea of 'brotherhood of all human beings'. While some of these religions see themselves as relevant to all ethnic communities, others are restricted to a particular COMMUNITY or group. In Hinduism, the idea of the basic unity of all created beings, including animals, is challenged by an acute awareness of the differences between human beings. Indeed, the *Bhagavadgita* (9.29) affirms the impartiality of the divine: 'I am the same in [alike to] all beings. None is hateful nor dear to Me. But those who worship Me with devotion they are in Me and I also them'. Yet the differences between people play a large role in both classical literature and the CASTE system. The term *mleccha* (barbarians) is used in the *Manusmriti* (2.23) with reference to the non-Aryans of Vedic India, and 10.45 distinguishes between those who emanated from the *purusha*, the primeval man, and the rest of the world's population, the *dasyus* (enemies of the gods).

In Judaism, the existence of different ETHNIC groups and cultures is explained by the story of the Tower of

Babel (Genesis 11: 6–9) and the idea that the three sons of Noah were the fathers of three different races (RACE). The rabbis of the Midrash teach that when God created Adam He selected the soil that He used from all four corners of the earth. Not only that, they say He used dark, light, red and yellow earth in order to make the first human being. Thus, no single person or race can claim to be more original or pure. The Talmud asks why God began with only one man and answers: 'So that no one of his descendants should be able to say: my father is better than your father' (Sanhedrin 37a). However, this basic unity of all human beings does not hinder the allocation of a special role to Jews: 'Ye shall be unto me a kingdom of priests, and an holy nation' Exodus 19: 6). Furthermore, Isaiah describes the role of the Jews as that of being 'a light to the gentiles'. From the Jewish point of view, the world is broadly divided into Jews and gentiles, ethnic and racial diversities (DIVER-SITY–SIMILARITY) having little importance as all non-Jewish people are considered equal.

In Islam the essential distinction which gives people their basic IDEN-TITY relates to religious communities (COMMUNITY). The unity of God (tawhid) also extends to the oneness of humanity. All are equally His creatures: 'O you men! surely We have created you of a male and a female, and made you tribes and families that you may know each other; surely the most honourable of you with Allah is the one among you most careful (of his duty); surely Allah is Knowing, Aware' (Koran 49: 13). According to the Muslim religion, the colours, races and languages of human beings are signs of God's wondrous creativity and play no role in the organization of the community. Indeed, the universalism of the tawhid demands that communities should be organized on the basis of religion or ideals. Islam holds that religion is the most important aspect of human life. Tribalism and ETHNOCENTRISM, whether based on racial, geographical, linguistic or cultural particularities, are refused as they emphasize differences which are merely marginal. According to Muslims, with the development of the nation state (NATION), the world shall be divided into Muslim and non-Muslim nations.

Christianity too should not be limited to any particular race or nation, as can be seen in the principles of Christian universalism set forth in the New Testament, and especially in the teaching and work of St Paul. According to Paul, 'There is neither Jew nor Greek, there is neither bond nor free, there is neither male nor female: for ye are all one in Christ Jesus' (Galatians 3: 28). For Christians, people of other races and nations are brothers and sisters in Christ under the one fatherhood of God: 'God so loved the world that He gave his only begotten Son, that whosoever believeth in him should not perish, but have everlasting life' (John 3: 16). Differences of race, sex, colour and physique are, or should be, seen by Christians as part of the richness of humanity. This view of the unity of humankind is held by almost all Christians, but there have been exceptions, notably in the Protestant world. Some members of the Dutch Reformed Church in South Africa, for instance, claimed that white races are superior to black or COLOURED races. The Roman Catholic Church and most Reformed Christian Churches vigorously oppose this view as totally unchristian.

Buddhism is a world faith and as such transcends ETHNIC and national identities in seeking to unite individual people and nations. This aim was made explicit in the Green Buddhist Declaration, prepared by members of the

International Buddhist Community for discussion at the World Fellowship of Buddhists in Colombo, 1984: 'Buddhism is not the possession of any race or nation but aspires to the unity of the human race on earth. Nationalism and racism are seen as forms of greed, hatred and delusion' (section 2.4). Buddhists believe all beings, not only humans, have within them the same Buddha Nature or nature of enlightenment and that the elements which seem to make people different, such as colour, race, nationality, social position, beauty or intelligence are impermanent (*anicca*) and illusory. The various ethnic groups, cultures and religions are viewed as different but equally valid human means of organization and expression. [Em. M]

Bowker, J. (1997) *Oxford Dictionary of World Religions*, Oxford University Press, Oxford.

ETHNIC-RELIGIOUS CONFLICTS IN EUROPE

One of the oldest expressions of religious conflict in the West is Christian–Islamic antagonism, which dates back to the Crusades led by the Western potentates. The aim of the Crusades was to free the Holy Sepulchre of Jerusalem from the new Islamic principality of the Seljukian Turks (even if Crusades were occasionally against other non-Christians or even against Christian heretics). Leading to a conflict of vast proportions, the Crusades recognized as Christian warriors the inhabitants of an area unified by a common faith (Christianity), which coincided with most of Europe. The aggressiveness of the Holy Wars constituted a paradoxical version of universalism: faith in the God of the Gospels required the evangelization of the infidels and the liberation of the holy places 'contaminated' by them (even if theoretically the Crusades did not aim to convert people but only to ensure the preservation of the sacred sites and access to them). All actions were performed in the name of a universal God and the mere fact that the Crusader was a 'soldier of Christ' meant he would be absolved of all his sins.

The Holy Christian war was opposed by the Islamic war, the *jihad*. The *jihad*, which originally started as the moral, internal, fight of the *Muslimuna* – 'he who faithfully abandons himself to God' – against himself, as a sinner, developed into a war against the *kafiruna* (the Christian infidels) which broke with the original universalistic inspiration of Islam.

Another contradiction led Christianity to produce particularism. The temporal power of the Bishop of Rome was probably the primary cause of this phenomenon. First and foremost, this led to the split of the Christian people, also under a cultural profile, into two churches: the Catholic Church of Rome and the Greek Orthodox Church of Byzantium. Secondly, it supported the ambitions of local princes and cities in plunging the Holy Roman Empire into crisis and provoking the transformation of the Empire into a Germanic nation or electoral principality. Furthermore, particularism led the clergy of various European countries to tend to see themselves as the only expression of the 'real Church of Christ'. As a consequence many antagonistic national churches were formed within the Catholic faith. The Reform, which for certain aspects can be defined as the revolt of the clergy and the peoples of Central and Northern Europe against the Church of Rome, gave rise to several conflicts such as the religious wars of France (second half of the sixteenth century) and the Thirty Years War (1618–1648). In many vays these wars can be considered similar to ethnic conflicts although they vere often internal wars fought within the same national community, such as the clash between the Huguenots and the Catholics in France.

The religious persecution of Jews in various times and places (JEW) may also be considered an interethnic conflict. The same holds true for other, sometimes deadly, conflicts in European history such as those between Poles and Russians (the Poles were Roman Catholic, while the Russians were Christian Orthodox), the expulsion of the Moors from Spain (so called Reconquista), and the expansion of the Germans eastward into Slavic-occupied lands. In nineteenth-century Europe the main cause of ethnic conflicts in Europe was the attempt to counter the expansion of Ottoman dominion in south-eastern Europe. The initiatives of the people of the area were inspired by the will to claim a distinct religious identity (Chrisian Greek Orthodox faith) in opposition to Turkish Islam. Contemporary ethnic conflicts in the Balkans and among the states founded following the dissolution of ex-Yugoslavia can – at least in part – be explained by the contradictions in the relationship between religion and poli- tics during the formation of national states in the nineteenth century. Other conflicts in Europe have had and still have important ethnic-religious compo- nents, e.g. the conflict between Catholics and Protestants in Northern Ireland and that between the Flemish and the Walloons in Belgium. [F. V.]

Johnson, J. T. (1997) *The Holy War Idea in Western and Islamic Traditions*, Penn- sylvania State University Press, Uni- versity Park, PA.
Ignatieff, M. (1998) *The Warrior's Honour: Ethnic War and the Modern Conscience*, Owl Books, London.

Wells, D. (1996) *An Encyclopedia of War and Ethics*, Greenwood, Westport, CT.

RELIGIONS AND ETHNIC CONFLICTS IN THE CONTEMPORARY WORLD

Religions have often been associated with 'holy war', despite the fact that the very concept of 'holy war' is a contra- diction in terms. Indeed, although almost all religions accept the concept of the just and righteous war (usually for defensive reasons), none of the major world reli- gions affirms that a war may be 'holy'. Even the *jihad* chiefly foresees warfare against evil or temptation, in no way requiring the conversion of others as there 'cannot be compulsion in religions' (Koran 2.256). Yet religions are undoubt- edly a potential source of discord.

GLOBALIZATION has been accused of helping to spark new religious wars by favouring conditions for the birth of quasi-religious political movements, and the rebirth of FUNDAMENTALISM. It is very difficult to distinguish between 'true' religious conflicts (if such conflicts really exist), ethnic conflicts in which religious elements play an important role, and conflicts in which religions are merely used as an excuse to mask other more fundamental factors of hostility. Indeed, most conflicts, at least in devel- oping regions, are stimulated by socio- economic and ecological causes (e.g. access to economic resources) rather than the alleged ethnic and religious motives, for example the Tutsi–Hutu war in post-colonial Africa. The 1995 World Summit on Social Development of the United Nations Research Institute for Social Development (UNRISD) made an attempt to classify the role played by religious factors in ethnic conflicts, and distinguished four different groups of conflicts.

Conflicts of the first group arise when a community sharing both religion and ethnicity sees itself as oppressed. Examples include Tibetan Buddhists in China; Sikhs in India; Muslim Palestinians in Israel's occupied territories; followers of Louis Farrakhan's organization, the Nation of Islam, in the United States (BLACK MUSLIMS); and Bosnian Muslims in ex-Yugoslavia. In each case, the religion practised by the community provides part of the ideological basis for their political opposition (which may reach the level of military action) against the dominant culture and its political institutions.

The second group's conflicts are rooted in the emergence of religious movements with strong political and social commitments, such as the 'theology of liberation' in Latin America. These groups are especially common among Roman Catholics in DEVELOPING COUNTRIES, and within urban Islamic communities in a number of countries.

Conflicts of the third-group type are linked to the founding of syncretistic (SYNCRETISM) religious movements among certain rural dwellers in the developing world. In northern and sub-Saharan Africa and South Asia, more or less syncretistic versions of Islam have evolved which mix traditional religious beliefs with Islamic norms. The struggle between those groups and those which uphold traditional versions of Islam has become particularly important in Pakistan and in many African countries. In Africa some conflicts are also stimulated by Christian syncretistic religions. The Lumpa Church of northern Zambia, the Holy Spirit Church of the Acholi of northern Uganda and the Napramas in north-east Mozambique are all examples of Christian syncretistic movements, diffused among ethnic minorities and strongly opposed by local governments.

The fourth source of religious-ethnic conflict is fundamentalism. Fundamentalists struggle against both co-religionists and against members of opposing religions. Examples are to be found among adherents of Christianity, Islam and Judaism, and also, some would argue, among Buddhists and Hindus. Very often, fundamentalists of any religion merge their religious goals with political and nationalist goals (NATIONALISM). Fundamentalist movements have played a pivotal role in many contemporary conflicts in Europe, the Middle East, Africa, India and Asia. [Em. M.]

Bangura, Y. (1995) *The Search for Identity: Ethnicity, Religion and Political Violence*, UNRISD, Geneva.

Haynes, J. (1994) *Religion, Fundamentalism and Ethnicity: A Global Perspective*, UNRISD, Geneva.

Horowitz, D. L. (1985) *Ethnic Groups in Conflict*, University of California Press, Berkeley.

Stavenhagen, R. (1990) *The Ethnic Question: Conflicts, Development, and Human Rights*, United Nations University Press, Tokyo.

RITE (It. *rito*; Fr. *rite*; Ger. *Ritus*) From the Latin *ritum*, of Indo-European origin, the term has a dual meaning and applies both to religious ceremony and to custom or habit.

A 'rite' comprises a more or less strictly codified series of actions involving objects, gestures and sounds having religious or social significance. In almost all cultures, MUSIC is a fundamental component of rites, with rhythm expressing the sexual connotations which are often part of these representations. This symbolic value of music has too often been neglected by anthropology, which has frequently limited itself to the analysis of the gestures and speech used in rites, which lose much of their meaning when considered separately from the sounds with which they are inextricably linked.

Whether rite derives from MYTH or the other way round remains an open question, although essentially a meaningless one. The human psyche – both of populations considered to be more evolved' and those wrongly viewed as PRIMITIVE – attributes symbolic value to certain gestures and objects, creating more or less rationally justified forms of ritual. Observing the many examples of ritual behaviour which could be identified in Western societies, Freud concluded that the obsessive rituals performed by Western man in order to ward off anxiety were the equivalent of the rites of exorcism practised by so-called savage (SAVAGE) populations:

> Obsessional prohibitions involve just as extensive renunciations and restrictions in the lives of those who are subject to them as do taboo prohibitions; but some of them can be lifted if certain actions are performed. Thereafter these actions *must* be performed: they become compulsive or obsessive acts. . . . The commonest of these obsessive acts is washing in water ('washing mania'). (1953 [1913–14]: 28)

The latter assumption – which compares the diseases of Western man to the rites of other civilizations – is, it could be argued, a flawed one. Every culture displays elements of ritual as well as pathological behaviour, and obsessive actions, although in some way a parody of ritualism, are emptied of the higher meanings with which rites are imbued, such as union with the divine, expiation, prayer, and expressions of sexuality and joy. Such rites can be individual or collective, and have a strong bonding and unifying quality which contributes greatly to the shaping of group identities

(IDENTITY). As such, different ritual expressions can be the cause of controversies, or even conflicts, in multicultural societies (MULTICULTURALISM), where the customs of certain groups are deemed unethical by other groups. Examples of such controversial rituals include practices of female genital MUTILATION, the ritual slaughter of animals, and even certain burial rituals, which can contravene local hygienic/sanitary measures. [S. G.]

Bell, C. M. (1999) *Ritual Theory, Ritual Practice*, Oxford University Press, New York.

Grimes, R. L. (1994) *Beginnings in Ritual Studies*, University of South Carolina Press, Columbia.

Freud, S. (1953 [1913–14]) *Totem and Taboo and Other Works*, in J. Strachey (ed.), *The Standard Edition of the Complete Psychological Works of Sigmund Freud*, XIII, The Hogarth Press and the Institute of Psycho-analysis, London.

ROMA (It. *rom*; Fr. *rom*; Ger. *Roma*)

The Roma people are often regarded as having a distinct ethnic IDENTITY, distinguished by their historically nomadic lifestyle, a concept of ethnic belonging, and the Romani, or Romanes, language. The Roma of Europe are, however, not a homogeneous people, but have great linguistic, cultural, social and historical differences.

The Roma people have been known by many derogatory and pejorative names, including *Gypsies*, *Tsigani*, *Tzigane*, *Cigano* and *Zigeuner*. Most Roma have always referred to themselves by their group names, or as *Rom* or *Roma*, meaning 'Man' or 'People'. (Rom, Roma, Romani, and Romaniya should not be confused with the country of Romania, or the city of Rome. These names have separate, distinct etymological origins and are not related.)

Nowadays there are more than 12 million Roma located in many countries around the world. An exact number is impossible to obtain, since they are not recorded on most official census counts.

The original Roma began their great migration from India to Europe, but they have dispersed worldwide. The Roma have been made up of many different groups of people from the very beginning, and have absorbed outsiders throughout their history. Because they arrived in Europe from the East, the first Europeans thought they were from Egypt, or some other vague non-European place, so they were called, among other things, Egyptians or Gyptians, which is where the word 'gypsy' comes from.

It was not until the second half of the eighteenth century that scholars in Europe began to realize that the Romani language is of Indo-Aryan origin, the root languages being ancient Punjabi, Hindi, and the Dardic languages. Up to today, basic words, such as some numerals and kinship terms, and names for body parts and actions, are of this origin. The Romani language has many spoken varieties, but all codes contain some words in use by all Roma. Certain groups have abandoned their language and adopted that of their sedentary neighbours (one example is that of the Rudari and Romanian).

Based on language, the Roma are commonly divided into three populations. These language communities are the Domari of the Middle East and Eastern Europe (the Dom), the Lomarvren of Central Europe (the Lom), and the Romani of Western Europe (the Rom). There is no universal written Romani language in use by all Roma. However, the codification of a constructed, standardized language – the Romani Chib – is currently in progress by members of the Linguistic Commission of the International Romani Union. There is an increasingly widespread tendency to write in Romanes, a language that has hitherto been oral. Not only are the words of Romani songs and fables being transcribed, but also 'private' documents and even literary works which have little to do with traditional FOLKLORE. Even though still confined to a handful of regional varieties, the publication of literary works in Romanes and the propagation of the language in written form may be a first step towards its unification.

There have been several great migrations or diasporas (DIASPORA), in Roma history. The first was the initial dispersal from India about a thousand years ago. Some scholars suggest there may have been several migrations from India. The second great migration, known as the Aresajipe, was from south-west Asia into Europe in the fourteenth century. The third migration was from Europe to the Americas in the nineteenth and early twentieth centuries after the abolition of Romani SLAVERY in Europe in 1856–64. Some scholars contend that a great migration is occurring today, since the fall of the Iron Curtain in Eastern Europe.

At the very beginning of the eleventh century, India came under attack by the Muslim general Mahmud of Ghazni, who was trying to push Islam eastwards into India, which was mainly Hindu territory. The troops that were assembled to fight the Muslim armies were all taken from non-Aryan populations that came from many different ethnic groups who spoke many different languages. This battle carried the composite army, the early Roma, further out of India and westwards into Europe, until they eventually crossed over into south-eastern Europe about the year

300. While this scenario is to an extent speculative, it is based upon sound linguistic and historical evidence.

As the ethnically and linguistically mixed occupational population moved further away from its land of origin, it began to construct its own ethnic identity, and with it the Romani language began to take shape. But the mixture of peoples and languages did not stop there, for as the group moved on, they took words and grammar from the areas they passed. In some instances outsiders were absorbed and, in the course of time, became one with the Romani group. In others, the mingling of small groups of Roma with other peoples has resulted in loss of the Romani identity. In Europe, Roma were either kept in slavery in the Balkans, or else moved on, reaching the northern and western countries by about 1500. In the course of time, as a result of having interacted with various European populations, and being fragmented into widely separated groups, Roma have emerged as a collection of distinct groups within the larger whole.

Only 80 years after their first appearance in Western Europe in the fifteenth century, the Roma fell under the penalty of banishment in almost all the nations of Western Europe. Despite their systematic EXILE, or transportation abroad, however, Romani people continued to reappear in the countries that they had left. There are several cultural elements that distinguish the many groups composing the Romani people from the majority population: Roma recognize and emphasize the distinction from the majority populations (gadze) and from other Roma groups. The language Romanes and its varieties also serve as a sign of social difference (DIVERSITY–SIMILARITY).

Roma culture accords central importance to the system of family organization: Bands are made up of vitsas, which are name groups of extended families with common descent either patrilineal or matrilineal, as many as 200 strong. A large vitsa may have its own chief and council. Loyalty and economic co-operation are expected at the household rather than the vitsa level. Marriages are of crucial importance for the forming of alliances between families, but there exists a strong demarcation of male and female spheres. Children are regarded as grown-ups and are integrated into the everyday lives of their parents. The professional structure gives high value to self-employment, so Romani groups are not integrated into the economies of the sedentary cultures. The Romani groups have a system of more or less institutionalized internal juridical and political self-governance. Further, there exists a social control system based on a conception of ritual PURITY/impurity. Their religions blend Christian (Catholic, Protestant, Orthodox), Muslim or free-church elements, with elements of a different origin.

While nomadism (NOMAD) was central to Roma life for several centuries, it remains doubtful if this pattern was inherent or if it was a reaction to exclusion and XENOPHOBIA from already settled communities. Historically, the labelling of all Romani people as nomadic 'wanderers' served to place them in an 'evolutionary opposition' to the 'civilized' people among whom they lived. Declaring the Roma nomads completed the tautological cycle. Nomadism was – and is – perceived as the pit of 'evolutionary achievement'. As the 'alien' ways of the Roma proved this point, they were easily excluded or persecuted. As a reaction to the lack of 'social integration', the Roma then were forced to leave the sedentary communities again. Nowadays, nomadism has ceased to be the dominant lifestyle of the

Romani people. Discourses on their nomadic character still continue, however, because they serve political goals. In declaring the Roma as not settled, states nowadays legitimize the withholding of CITIZENSHIP and other social rights from them

As a result of the attempts of nineteenth-century encyclopaedias to define the difference between the Romani and the European titular nations, the 'gypsy' stereotype changed from being a sign of social defiance to becoming a cultural difference (CULTURE). Behaviour that seemed socially unacceptable was simply related to an underlying drive that characterized the Romani 'race'. Thus the process of ETHNICIZATION of the Roma was well on its way.

As most unsettled PEOPLE who live among settled peoples seem to become convenient scapegoats, the Romani have regularly been accused by the local populace of many evils as a prelude to later official and legal persecution. Their relations with the authorities in the host country have been marked by consistent contradiction. Official decrees were often aimed at settling or assimilating them (ASSIMILATION), yet local authorities systematically attempted to keep them out of their towns. There have been many large-scale, state-sponsored persecutions and pogroms (POGROM) against the Roma throughout European history. The most infamous of these, the Holocaust (SHOAH) of the Second World War, is responsible for the deaths of up to 1.5 million Romani.

Long-established controls of and measures against SINTI and Roma were increased when in 1938 two official notes announced that Germany would now 'attack the problem in its root: the race'. Sinti and Roma first were forcefully settled, and then, in 1939–40, deported to Poland. In 1941 the German occupiers murdered Sinti and Roma living in Eastern Europe in great numbers. In 1942 Heinrich Himmler ordered the DEPORTATION of German 'Gypsy-half bloods' (*Zigeuner-Mischlinge*) and Sinti and Roma to Auschwitz-Birkenau, Dachau and Buchenwald. The same order was issued for the annexed territories of Austria, France and Poland, as well as the occupied Benelux countries. In the whole of Central Europe there is hardly a family that has not been affected by this attempt at GENOCIDE; most families lost members, and many were completely exterminated. Growing industrialization and especially persecution during the era of National Socialism destroyed the traditional life patterns and social structures of most families. Most old people, who could have handed on traditions and would have ensured that Roma social norms were observed, had been killed during the Holocaust.

Since the disintegration of the communist governments of Eastern Europe anti-Roma sentiments have rekindled in Eastern and Western Europe. Violent attacks against Romani immigrants and refugees (REFUGEE) have been permitted to occur with little or no restraint from government authorities. The Romani people remain the least integrated and the most persecuted people of Europe. Almost everywhere, their fundamental civil rights are threatened. Discrimination against Roma in employment, education, health care, administrative and other services is prevalent, and hate speech against them deepens the negative anti-Roma stereotypes which are typical of European public opinion. Anti-Roma attitudes also exist in the Americas to one extent or another. Misrepresentations in the popular press, books, films and television have contributed to negative stereotypes and characterizations. There still exists no significant international human rights

strategy initiative to monitor the human rights of the Roma and to provide legal defence in cases of human rights abuse.
[T. M., J. E.]

Encyclopedia Britannica (1999–2000) 'Gypsy', www.eb.com.

Fings, K., Heuss, H., Sparing, F. (1997) From 'Race Science' to the Camps. The Gypsies during the Second World War, Interface Collection 12, Hatfield.

Hancock, I. (1996) Origins of the Romani People, www.geocities.com.

Hund, W. D. (ed.) (1996) Zigeuner. Geschichte und Struktur einer rassistischen Konstruktion, DISS, Duisberg.

Kesler P., Kenrick D. (eds) (1999) In the Shadow of the Swastika. The Gypsies during the Second World War, Interface Collection 13, Hatfield.

Laughlin, J. M. (1999) 'European Gypsies and the historical geography of loathing', Review, Ferdinand Braudel Center, 22(1): 31–81.

Rossi, M. (1999) Gipsy Women Between Modernity and Tradition: Strategy of Integration, Dynamics and Social Change, Rom. Abstracts, EUROFOR-Conference 27.

Soravia, G. (1984) 'A wandering voice: the language of the Gypsies', UNESCO Courier, October.

UNESCO (1984) A Brief History of the Roma, www.geocities.com.

Van de Port, M. (1999) Gipsies, Wars and other Instances of the Wild. Civilization and its Discontents in a Serbian Town, Global Books, Amsterdam.

Wigger, I. (1996) 'Ein eigenartiges Volk. Die Ethnisierung des Zigeunerstereotyps im Spiegel von Enzyklopädien und Lexika', in Hund (ed.).

SABIR

SABIR (It. *sabir*; Fr. *sabir*; Ger. *Sabir*) Used in French language cultures to define a linguistic form almost identical to PIDGIN, the term 'Sabir' derives from the Portuguese word *sabir* (meaning 'to know', probably in the sense of 'to know how to speak' – *sabir parlar*). The term was coined in French in the seventeenth century when Molière used it in *Le Bourgeois Gentilhomme* (Act IV, scene v) to describe the ancient LINGUA FRANCA used on the coasts of the Maghreb and in the western Mediterranean ports. Unlike the lingua franca of the Eastern Mediterranean which used Arabic, Italian and Provençal words, the Sabir was composed of Arabic, Portuguese and Spanish terms. A cutting reference to Sabir can be found in Alphonse Daudet's rhyme: 'Le sabir . . . fait de mots bariolés amassés comme des coquillages tout le long des mers latines' (Sabir . . . formed from strangely variegated words, piled up like shells on the shores of the Latin seas'). [A. B., R. B.]

McArthur, T. (ed.) (1992) *The Oxford Companion to the English Language*, Oxford University Press, Oxford.
Mounin, G. (1993) *Dictionnaire de la linguistique*, PUF, Paris.

SADO-MASOCHISM

SADO-MASOCHISM (It. *sadomasochismo*; Fr. *sadomasochisme*; Ger. *Sadomasochismus*) Introduced by nineteenth-century sexology and taken up and redefined by psychoanalysis, where it is used to indicate a pathological relationship characterized by the exchange of suffering and reciprocal overpowering, the term 'sadomasochism' can be used to explain the UNCONSCIOUS dynamics which lead individuals or groups to inferiorize the other and thus to practise INTOLERANCE. First used by R. von Krafft-Ebing and Havelock Ellis, the term is formed from the surnames of two writers: *De Sade* and *von Masoch*. The sexual perversion of sadism, defined as the pleasure in making others suffer, is attributed to the former, and that of masochism, the taste for suffering and humiliation in a sexual context, to the latter. As Sigmund Freud maintains:

> Sadism and masochism occupy a special position among the perversions, since the contrast between activity and passivity which lies behind them is among the universal characteristics of sexual life. . . . But the most remarkable feature of this perversion is that its active and passive forms are habitually found to occur together in the same individual. A person who feels pleasure in producing pain in someone else in a sexual relationship is also capable of enjoying as pleasure any pain which he may himself derive from sexual relations. A sadist is always at the same time a masochist, although the active or the passive aspect of the perversion may be the more strongly developed in him and may represent his predominant sexual activity. (1905: 159)

Psychoanalysis also identifies sado-masochism outside the realm of sexual perversion, using the theory to describe an aspect of human psychology and behaviour. In this sense sado-masochism is part of both the dynamics of relationships with others (according to the idea of overpowering or submission) and the construction of the persona, through complex mechanisms of projection and dentification (with the victim or IDEN-TIFICATION WITH THE AGGRESSOR) as well as the determining of the psychological life of the person (e.g. the individual's relationship with his or her conscious and moral beliefs). Freud provided two concepts of sado-masochism. The first derives from his early formulation of the theory of instincts (Freud, 1915) and refers to an original sadism, not much different from AGGRESSION in general, from which masochism originates. The second derives from the introduction of the theory of the death instinct (Freud, 1920) and proposes the existence of a primary and indomitable masochism. Being a fundamental defence mechanism (Gindro, 1993), sado-masochism, as NARCISSISM, can be considered an attitude towards the world. It enters into play when the original desire for love is frustrated and – the individual not being able to avoid receiving or inflicting pain in the relationship with the other – suffering is transformed into pleasure: 'While narcissism prevents an understanding of the other, sado-masochism attacks it in an insane mechanism of projection and identification, negation and undeserved expropriation and appropriation' (Gindro, 1996: 256).

Sadism and masochism, married in a single theory expressing a single phenomenon, have thus been used by psychoanalysts to explain aggressive behaviour and self- and hetero-destructive tendencies. Originally described as a sexual perversion and thus generally understood as a libidinous transformation of inflicted or received pain, sadism and masochism have taken on a central role in the understanding of mechanisms such as those linked to guilt or moral complexes, behaviour involving a search for punishment and many unconscious dynamics which are often an intrinsic part of socialization and education processes. Interpreted in this manner sado-masochism has been central to the understanding of personalities characterized by profound moral rigidity, CONFORMISM, an extreme need for social 'order', servility and ambivalence towards authority (a tendency to identify the dominator and the dominated, which is summarized in the aphorism 'be weak with the strong and strong with the weak'). Of particular importance are the studies of Erich Fromm, who associated the features of the personality of sado-masochists with repressive ideology, and the description of the 'authoritarian personality' (PREJUDICE) proposed by Theodor W. Adorno and his team, who tried to combine the elements constituting a tendency towards RACISM and membership of totalitarian movements. Sado-masochism is thus partially distanced from sexual perversion to become a means of defending the relationship with the world: a means soaked in violence which, in a certain sense, allows tolerance of frustration and the checkmate which the relationship with the others implies. It is interesting to note how the sexual value (excitement caused by the pleasure of having sexual relationships with humiliated and overpowered objects, or being subjected to violence by objects held in a condition of inferiorization or submission) has been explicitly or latently highlighted by most of the institutions and social systems strongly marked by violence: slave societies (SLAVERY), prisons and totalitarian regimes.

Many artists have grasped and recounted this perverse weave of sexual fascination, violence and humiliation with great expressive skill. Regarding interethnic relations important examples include *Light in August* by William Faulkner (1932) and *A Place called Estherville* by Erskine Caldwell

(1949), both set in a context of black–white relations in the United States during the period of RACIAL SEGREGATION. Finally, as far as the connection between racial supremacy and sexual ambivalence towards members of a persecuted category or even a category destined for extermination in a Nazi camp is concerned, mentioned should be made of *The House of Dolls* by Karol Cetynski (1959) who preferred to sign this denunciation of the atrocities he had witnessed in a concentration camp (CONCENTRATION CAMP AND DEATH CAMP) with the pseudonym 'Ka-tzetnik 135633' (which signified his state as a deported person); or the film *Il portiere di notte* by Liliana Cavani (1974) who highlights the reciprocation between the protagonists of the massacre and the victim and the role of persecutor and persecuted. [S. G.]

Freud, S. (1905) *Three Essays on the Theory of Sexuality*, in *The Standard Edition of the Complete Psychological Works of Sigmund Freud* [*SE*], trans. J. Strachey, Hogarth Press and the Institute of Psycho-analysis, London, 1953 ff., Vii: 125–243.

Freud, S. (1915) *Instincts and their vicissitudes*, SE, XIV: 109–140.

Freud, S. (1920) *Beyond the Pleasure Principle*, SE, XVIII: 3–64.

Fromm, E. (1973) *The Anatomy of Human Destructiveness*, Holt Rinehart and Winston, New York.

Gindro, S. (1981) *Perversione e rivoluzione*, Edizioni Psicoanalisi Contro, Roma.

Gindro, S. (1993) *L'oro della psicoanalisi*, Alfredo Guida Editore, Napoli.

Gindro, S. (1996) 'Sesso e razzismo', in Bolaffi, G., Gindro, S. (eds), *Il corpo straniero*, Alfredo Guida Editore, Napoli.

SAVAGE (It. *selvaggio*; Fr. *sauvage*; Ger. *Wilder*) From the ancient French *salvage*, from the Latin *salvaticum* (from *silva*, 'forest') this term defines the inhabitants of forests who live far away from the cities of so-called civilized people, and has therefore also taken on the derogatory meaning of 'unsociable' or 'rough', or even of someone who rebels against conventions. The term 'savage' also includes unruly behaviour. Sociologists adapted the term from Montesquieu, who identified a pattern of social evolution divided into three periods or stages: savagery, barbarianism and CIVILIZATION. In recent times the word has ceased to be used by sociologists and anthropologists owing to the derogatory meaning it had acquired – as a result of its association with particular groups of people – and has been substituted by the apparently more neutral PRIMITIVE, which however has also taken on the same negative connotations.

The MYTH of the 'savage' conveyed a condition of human PURITY – combined with courage, goodness and simplicity similar to those of the first inhabitants of the earth during a hypothetical golden age – and was fuelled in the sixteenth century by the news from recently discovered lands. This conception was popular during the Enlightenment (*théorie du bon sauvage*: the concept of the Noble Savage) as an exhortation towards a return to nature, but it was abandoned at the end of the eighteenth century in favour of scientific positivism, which tended more towards the future than back to the origins of the human race. [S. G.]

Cocchiara, G. (1948) *Il mito del buon selvaggio. Introduzione alla storia delle teorie etnologiche*, Sellerio, Messina.

Montesquieu, de C. L. (1973) *Persian Letters* (1721), Penguin Books, London.

SCAPEGOAT: see AGGRESSION; PREJUDICE

SEASONAL MIGRANT WORKER (It. *lavoratore stagionale*; Fr. *travailleur saisonnier*; Ger. *Saisonarbeiter*) This

expression is used to describe a MIGRANT worker who leaves a less developed, neighbouring or close country for a few months in order to fulfil a periodical demand for employment, usually in the agricultural and tourism sectors. Mediterranean-style agriculture has always required seasonal workers to help during harvest times (with picking fruit and vegetables) and, in the past, the weakest local groups (women and young individuals) filled these posts. However, an increase in a population's standard of living means agricultural production dwindles and wages fall. The only solution is then to employ workforces from less-developed areas who expect lower wages and social status.

Seasonal workers, usually from North and Central African countries and Mexico, are now an essential element in the South European and the Southern United States agricultural production cycles. Working under international agreements, they are expected to return to their country of origin when the season terminates and both their permit of stay and their working conditions are regularized. However, a large number of factors lead agricultural employers to employ seasonal immigrant workers without residence permits or undocumented workers (ILLEGAL ALIENS) who are generally poorly qualified and supposedly transitory. Undocumented workers can be paid less than documented workers. In many regions, the use of immigrant workers has ensured the continuation of agricultural production, which otherwise would have disappeared due to its low productivity and profitability. This may lead to a long-term dynamic whereby employment conditions for immigrants carrying out tiring and badly paid jobs will worsen. Seasonal work in the tourism sector is more highly structured. A number of activities are slightly more prestigious and attract workers from poorer countries (e.g. with regard to Italy, from Eastern Europe) or even from developed countries (such as in Greece, where a large number of summer workers come from Central–Northern Europe). [E. R.]

Cadwaller, M. (1993) *Migration and Residential Mobility: Macro and Micro Approaches*, University of Wisconsin Press, Madison, WI.
Hoerder, D., Moch, L. P. (eds) (1995) *European Migrants: Global and Local Perspectives*, Northeastern University Press, Boston, MA.
Macioti, M. I., Pugliese E. (1992) *Gli immigrati in Italia*, Laterza, Roma and Bari.

SECOND GENERATION (It. *seconda generazione*; Fr. *seconde génération*; Ger. *zweite Generation*) The term

'second generation' refers to the children of first generation immigrants (MIGRANT). The conventional prognosis of position and prospects for the second generation is implicit in the range of problems that the first generation of immigrants encounters or is expected to encounter. Irrespective of the precise reasons for a given migration – which comprise some combination of so-called push and pull factors (PUSH FACTORS-PULL FACTORS) – immigrants will, it is assumed, experience general hostility and discrimination, as well as encountering difficulty in getting recognition for the skills and qualifications that they bring with them. They are likely to find it hard to understand and negotiate the norms of an unfamiliar society and many will have language problems. This initial social distance between immigrant and indigenous populations will impose serious limitations on the expected gains that may have precipitated the emigration and/or the choice of a particular country of immigration in the first place.

By contrast, the difficulties that serve to limit the prospects of the first generation of immigrants do not seem to apply to the second generation – at least at first sight – and if they do, presumably not to the same degree: the second generation will have been born or brought up in the country of immigration; hostility towards a given group of immigrants will have lessened with the passage of time – or so it is suggested; and, crucially, second generation youth will emerge from the schooling system with similar qualifications and similar expectations to those of their indigenous counterparts. In essence then, the hoped-for gains of migration are 'transferred' to the second generation precisely because the first generation will have encountered so many obstacles.

Several factors may interfere with this prognosis. For example, in the UK in the 1950s, 1960s and beyond, the label 'immigrant' was first employed invariably and specifically for what were then described as 'COLOURED immigrants', but this label was extended to apply to the second generation. The implication was that although many had been born in Britain and educated in British schools, they were nevertheless to be labelled as immigrants, and as such they supposedly lacked the attitudes, knowledge and skills required by employers. The label acted as a code word for

'colour' and as a signal to restrict opportunity, but it did so in a way that rationalized differential treatment without the STIGMA of colour differentiation (Allen, 1970: 164).

In some Western European labour-importing countries, notably Germany, there was a deep-rooted insistence that immigration was a temporary phenomenon, and thus there could be no second generation of immigrants. In Germany this attitude was well expressed by the chairman of the Committee on Foreign Labour of the Employers' Association who remarked that 'The great value of the employment of foreigners lies in the fact that we have here at our disposal a mobile labour potential. It would be dangerous to limit this mobility through a large-scale assimilation policy' (quoted in Ward, 1975: 24). In other words, the claim was that Germany had a *migrant* population, but not an *immigrant* population. The flaw in this viewpoint was that it ignored the ways in which a migrant worker became transformed into an immigrant. This process occurred for different reasons: because it took a foreign worker far longer to save money and because it ignored the process which Böhning (1972) described as a 'complete secondary socialization', whereby migrants absorbed the acquisitive norms of the society in which they now resided. The longer immigrants stayed, the more likely were they to seek means to bring over their families, including their children (FAMILY REUNIFICATION). For these and other reasons, by 1978 more than 25 per cent of immigrants in Germany were aged 17 or under. The consequence of the persistent refusal in Germany to accept that there could be a second generation of migrants was that policies on the education of GASTARBEITER children were developed in a hurried way, as an afterthought. In these circumstances and bearing in mind that many teachers regarded immigrant children as non-achievers, who lacked ability and were additionally handicapped by their failure to master the language and the customs and practices of the 'host' country, it is not surprising that a significant proportion of this second generation simply dropped out of German schools: it was estimated that in the 1970s the figure stood at 20 per cent (Blot, 1991). More significantly, these policies took an ambiguous stance on the future trajectory of Gastarbeiter children by adopting a dual strategy which seemed to place them between two worlds (DOUBLE CONSCIOUSNESS): foreign children were to be integrated into German society through achieving competence in the German language; yet they were to maintain contact with their country of origin through mother-tongue teaching (BILINGUALISM). Some observers saw this strategy as misconceived and even dangerous insofar as it seemed to promise different things to immigrants and indigenous Germans: the former were offered the prospect of a permanent presence and the latter could be reassured that the immigrant presence was, after all, temporary. Indeed, Castles (1980) saw this educational strategy as storing up potential disorder by creating a 'social time-bomb' fuelled by growing hostility towards foreign workers and by discontent among the second generation at their marginal position in society (MARGINALIZATION).

One way of comprehending the difficulties encountered by the second generation is to emphasize the social, psychological and cultural difficulties of their position (as opposed to the RACISM, XENOPHOBIA and discrimination that they encounter). The work of the American sociologist Bogardus (1971) is in this tradition. Drawing on the work of the Chicago School, he described the second generation of immigrants as a marginal generation (MARGINAL MAN). According to Bogardus, this generation exists between two realities – that of their family and that of the host society – which espouse clearly contradictory values. Where this produces a rebellion against parental authority it is to be seen not just as a conventional intergenerational conflict, but as a rejection of the core values and traditions to which their parents remain faithful and an acceptance of the mores of the new society. In this way the second generation becomes isolated from the preceding generation and its sense of a common ethnicity may be weakened, though in certain cases this is mitigated by an identification with grandparents – should the grandparents be present – who may offer a degree of continuity. A broadly similar analysis depicts the second generation as existing between two cultures. In this analysis the second generation – especially those born in the country of immigration – is regarded as being caught between the cultural expectations of their parents and the social demands of the society in which the first generation has settled. This may engender a feeling that they do not 'fit in' to either culture, but reactions to these circumstances vary. For example, various contributors to a study of migrants and minorities in Britain describe young Sikhs and Jamaicans responding to racism by initiating a process of ethnic redefinition or 'Creolization' which recreates a new cultural tradition that 'only has meaning in the British context'. By contrast, even though neither Italians nor Turks settled in Britain had encountered the same degree of racism or xenophobia experienced by black or Asian immigrants, a separate cultural tradition was discerned among each group, which was distinct from those of their respective countries of origin (Watson, 1977: 3).

An underlying problem in respect of the second generation is this: the first generation of (im)migrant workers who arrived in countries such as Germany and the UK in the post-Second World War period – whether or not they were directly recruited – came to remedy labour shortages. These were chiefly in industries and occupations in which sufficient indigenous labour was not forthcoming; pay and conditions were not attractive enough. Nevertheless, despite poor pay and conditions, and discrimination and disadvantage, immigrant workers could compare their situation with the poverty and unemployment that they had left behind in their country of birth. In addition, they could envisage a better future for their children in their new country. Whether this 'better future' would materialize was uncertain. It is possible that when the time came for second generation children to leave school and enter the labour market, the conditions that had attracted the first generation might have changed and the demand for labour that caused their parents to migrate might no longer prevail. Moreover, the aspirations that these children were likely to possess were often in sharp conflict with the discrimination that they faced. Finally, the education system might not necessarily equip the second generation with the skills and qualifications that their parents would have hoped for or anticipated.

As Modood et al.'s analysis of UK data shows, the educational outlook for the second generation (and, indeed, for subsequent generations) is not the same for all minority groups. Such differences are partly explained by differences in the level of qualifications possessed by different groups of migrants, that is the 'first generation'. Modood et al. concluded that in the UK

the ethnic minorities manifest a radical diversity, indeed extreme contrasts, in their educational attainment levels. . . . The situation today is a product of the different starting points of different groups, of different experiences in the educational system, but also of an ethnic minority educational drive . . . [which] can be seen by looking at the progress between the migrants' generation and young adults today. (Modood et al., 1997: 80–81)

Modood et al. found that in most groups the second generation (those aged 25–44) who were born in Britain or who had arrived as children had made significant progress. But they noted that many of those of Pakistani origin had no educational qualifications and that those of Bangladeshi origin had made no progress. On the other hand, Indian and African Asian men in this age group were more likely than whites to have university degrees (Modood et al., 1997: 81).

There is one other perspective on the 'second generation' that should be considered here and this is very well articulated by Stuart Hall in his exploration of the concept of *new ethnicities* (ETHNICITY). Hall's argument is that we are all *ethnically located* and that our ethnic identities (IDENTITY) are central to our sense of who we are. He stresses the extent to which the black experience (in Britain) is a *diaspora* experience (DIASPORA). This experience involves a process of 'unsettling, recombination, hybridization and "cut-and-mix"' (Hall, 1992: 258). In the case of young black British film-makers, for example, the diaspora experience may indeed reflect, *inter alia*, 'complex systems of representation and aesthetic traditions from Asian and African culture', but Hall argues that in spite of these rich cultural ' roots', the new cultural politics is operating on new and quite distinct ground – specifically on what it means to be 'British'. . . . There can, therefore, be no simple 'return' or 'recovery' of the ancestral past which is not re-experienced through the categories of the present. (Hall, 1992: 258)

P. B.]

Allen, S. (1970) 'Immigrants or workers', in Zubaida, S. (ed.), *Race and Racialism*, Tavistock, London.

Blot, D. (1991) 'Problemi posti dalla scolarizzazione dei figli di migranti, in Presidenza del Consiglio dei Ministri', *Atti della Conferenza sull'emigrazione*, Roma 13–16 August, Editalia, Roma.

Bogardus, E. S. (1971) *Immigration and Race Attitudes*, Ozer, Jerome S. Publishers.

Böhning, W. (1972) *The Migration of Workers in the United Kingdom and the European Community*, Oxford University Press, London and Oxford.

Castles, S. (1980) 'The social time-bomb: education of an underclass in West Germany', *Race and Class*, 21(4): 369–387.

Hall, S. (1992) 'New ethnicities', in Donald, J., Rattansi, A. (eds), *'Race', Culture and Difference*, Sage, London.

Modood, T. et al. (1997) *Ethnic Minorities in Britain: Diversity and Disadvantage*, Policy Studies Institute, London.

Ward, A. (1975) 'European capitalism's reserve army', *Monthly Review Press*, 27, Part 6.

Watson, J. (ed.) (1977) *Between Two Cultures: Migrants and Minorities in Britain*, Blackwell, Oxford.

SELF-FULFILLING PROPHECY (It. *profezia che si autoademnie*; Fr. *prophétie qui s'auto-réalise*; Ger. *selbsterfüllende Prophezeiung*) This expression was introduced by the American sociologist W.I. Thomas to describe the fundamental idea that if people define certain situations as real, then they are real in their consequences.

This proposal is sometimes known as 'Thomas's theorem'. According to Merton (1967), the self-fulfilling prophecy makes a considerable contribution towards explaining the dynamics of ethnic and racial conflict as it shows that many convictions – which seem to be the irrefutable evidence of factual observations – are actually the products of preconceptions or racial PREJUDICE. Merton offers as a clear example how many white workers in the United States were quite convinced that black people were totally against the principles of trade unionism. This conviction appeared to be borne out by the high number of black 'scab' labourers used during strikes. Applying the theory of self-fulfilling prophecy to this example, it can be argued that the convictions of the white workers were based on a chain of events which made it difficult for many blacks to escape the role of scab labour. Merton points out that the fact that black people became scab labourers because they were excluded from trade unions (and many types of employment) rather than being excluded from the unions because they were scab labourers can be demonstrated by the fact that the same workers have ceased to be scab labourers in industrial sectors in which, over the last few decades, they have been admitted to the trade unions.

The self-fulfilling prophecy can also be discerned in other spheres such as education, in terms of the expectations teachers have about certain groups of students, and in police attitudes to black criminality.

Self-fulfilling prophecy makes it possible to highlight the tragic vicious circle which victimizes people twice: first, because the victim is stigmatized (STIGMA) with an inherent negative quality; and secondly, because he or she is prevented from disproving this quality. Merton not only exposed this vicious circle, but also put forward possible ways of escaping from it. According to Merton (1967), by abandoning the initial definition of the situation – responsible for setting up the vicious circle – doubt can be cast on the initial presumption and a new definition of the situation introduced. The presumption is refuted by the successive course of events and thus opinion no longer produces reality. [M. V.]

McIver, R. M. (1948) *The More Perfect Union*, Macmillan, New York.
Merton, R. K. (1967) *On Theoretical Sociology: Five Essays*, Free Press, New York.
Myrdal, G. (1944) *An American Dilemma*, Harper & Brothers, New York.

SHOAH (It. *Shoah*; Fr. *Shoah*; Ger. *Shoah*) The Hebrew word *Shoah*, meaning catastrophe, describes the planned extermination or mass killing of Jews (JEW) during the Second World War, which is otherwise referred to as the Holocaust. Although both terms are used here, 'holocaust' – from the Greek *òlos* (all) and *kaustòs* (burnt) and late ecclesiastical Latin (twelfth century) *holocaustum* – is now considered by many to be an inappropriate word to describe the largest mass killings of the twentieth century because of its connotations of 'holiness' and 'sacrifice', which imply the sacrificial burning of a victim at an altar in atonement for sins to a divinity.

Persecution of the Jews in Germany followed immediately upon Adolf Hitler becoming Chancellor in 1933. In September 1935, the Nuremberg Decrees turned German Jews into people with no civic or legal political rights, whose existence was constantly being downgraded to the extent that in some towns all Jewish names were scratched off war memorials (RACISM). The Shoah *proper* can be seen as beginning on the night of 9–10 November 1938 when a nationwide POGROM known as *Kristallnacht (the* 'Night of Crystal') saw Nazi-inspired attacks cause widespread damage to Jewish property and institutions, the burning of 191 synagogues, as well as injury and death to many Jews. In the face of growing discrimination and persecution, thousands of Jews, including noted scholars, musicians, writers, lawyers and doctors, fled the country: out of a German Jewish population of 525,000 in 1933, 280,000 had emigrated or escaped Nazi Germany by 1939 (Gilbert, 1992: 95).

In Central and Eastern Europe, the sizeable Jewish population suffered many forms of economic, social and cultural discrimination in the years after the First World War, but by the mid-1930s discrimination had been transformed into persecution, systematic and otherwise. For example, there were a number of anti-Jewish pogroms in Poland between 1935 and 1937 – in Grodno (1935), Pryztyck and Minsk Mazowieck (1936) and Czestochowa (1937) (Eliach, 1998: 562). Such violence took place against a background of increasing ANTI-SEMITISM. Many Polish organizations began to include in their by-laws restrictions against Jews, making it clear that whereas 'Christians' and 'Aryans' were welcome, Jews were not. One of the leading Polish anti-Semites at this time was Cardinal Augustyn Hlond, Primate of the Catholic Church in Poland. Though he stressed that violence against Jews was 'un-Christian', his pastoral letter of February 1936 – read in every Catholic pulpit in Poland – attacked the Jews as 'freethinkers, Bolsheviks, usurers, and white slavers. Three and a half million Jews on Polish soil were three million too many,

ıe said; half a million would suffice'
Heller, 1977: 112–114, cited in Eliach,
1998: 562). The ideological connections
between the anti-Semitism of the Nazis
ınd that of the Poles in the later 1930s can
best be seen in the writings and activities
of leading members of the Polish intelli-
gentsia, who simultaneously justified the
actions of the Nazis in Germany and
vilified the Jews of Poland as the enemy
within (Eliach, 1998: 562).

With the German invasion of Poland
ın September 1939, which marked the
outbreak of war, Nazi-occupied Poland
immediately became what amounted to
the laboratory in which the *Final Solution*
was to be developed. The first step in this
process was taken when in October and
November 1939 the great majority of the
Polish Jewish population was confined
to ghettos (GHETTO). By June 1941,
when Nazi Germany invaded the USSR,
hunger, disease and forced labour had
already caused the deaths of an estimated 500,000 Polish Jews. Within days
of the attack on Russia, events took a
new turn: tens of thousands of Jews
living in territory controlled by the USSR
up to the moment of the Nazi invasion
are known to have been massacred.
Some of the worst of these massacres
occurred in Vilnius, Kaunas, Riga,
Bialystok and Minsk. With the active
complicity of the German army, the
Einsatzgruppen – 'special groups' of the
SS assembled and trained for this
specific task – routinely exterminated
huge numbers of Jews with machine-
guns and rifles. By the end of 1941, about
one million Jews had been killed using
what the Nazis and their accomplices
regarded as more or less 'conventional'
means: starvation, forced labour, mass
executions and the exhaust gases of
trucks. It was the opening of the
Chelmno extermination camp that can
be said to mark the beginning of a new
and much more systematic phase in the
destruction of European Jewry and a
new chapter in the history of humankind
(CONCENTRATION CAMP AND
DEATH CAMP).

The development of the Shoah is well
illustrated by a chronology of the events
that occurred between 1939 and 1945 in
Konin, a Polish *shtetl* – that is, a small
market town of between 1,000 and 20,000
having a sizeable Jewish population –
approximately 200 kilometres west of
Warsaw. When the Nazis entered Konin
in 1939 its population was about 12,100,
of whom 2,700 were Jews (Richmond,
1995: 10). This is what followed:

1939 Konin is annexed to the Third
Reich as part of the newly constituted Wartheland. On 22 September:
public execution of a Pole and a Jew
in the town square. Night of 30
November/1 December: first deportation of Jews to ghettos, most of
them going to Ostrwiec Swietokryski
and some to Jozefow.

1941 Last deportations signify the end
of the Jewish population of Konin.
During the Nazi occupation the
synagogue interior, the Jewish cem-
etery and sections of the Jewish
quarter are destroyed. Many thousands of Jews from the Konin region
die in massacres in the nearby
Kazimierz forest.

1942 Jews in Jozefow massacred. Jews
in Ostrwiec transported to Treblinka;
those remaining are transferred to a
local forced labour camp. Forced
labour camp established close to the
railway station in Konin.

1943 Jewish prisoners in Konin labour
camp revolt.

1944 Labour camp in Ostrwiec liqui-
dated – inmates transported to
Auschwitz. (Richmond, 1995: 471)

Historians of the Shoah can be divided
into two schools: the 'intentionalists',

who insist that ideology and planning played a central role in the destruction of European Jewry; and the 'functionalists', who view this process as a relatively chaotic approach and stress serious inefficiencies and incompatibilities in the way the extermination was managed. The difficulty for the 'functionalist' analysis, however, is to account for the huge efforts and powerful police and military organizations that were used for the systematic rounding up and transportation of Jews – employing resources that were sorely needed to move Nazi troops, supplies and equipment.

At a meeting of Nazi chiefs at Wannsee, a suburb of Berlin, on 20 January 1942, it was decided to abandon shooting and other 'traditional', yet relatively 'inefficient', means of murder and instead to begin gassing in the death camps of Chelmno (150,000 victims), Majdanek (60,000 victims), Belzec (600,000 victims), Sobibor (200,000 victims) and Treblinka (900,000 victims). Like Auschwitz, which was constructed later, these extermination plants all had their own railway stations, gas chambers and, because of the 'inefficiency' of mass burials, crematorium ovens. Together with the Nazi euthanasia programme, these facts render the 'functionalist' theory less than satisfactory.

The Nazi mass extermination programme reached its pinnacle with Auschwitz II (Birkenau), where more than 2 million deaths occurred (including many ROMA and Soviet prisoners of war). The total number of Jews killed in the Shoah is generally put at somewhere between 5.8 million and 6 million, though the precise figure will never be known with certainty.

Subsequently, there have been suggestions that the Jews killed in the Shoah invariably went passively to their deaths. The truth is that they resisted on numerous occasions not just in the ghettos, but even in the death camps. Moreover, if account is taken of the fact that the Jews involved in these revolts against overwhelming German military force were in a hungry, weakened and terrorized condition, these uprisings can be seen as 'among the most noble and courageous episodes not only of Jewish, but of world history' (Gilbert, 1992: 102). There were Jewish revolts in the following ghettos: Niewswiesz (July 1942); Mir (August 1942); Kremenetz (September 1942); Lashva (September 1942); Tuchin (September 1942); Krushin (December 1942); Minsk Mazowiecki (January 1943); Kuldischvo (March 1943); Stryj (April 1943); Warsaw – the most famous of the uprisings (April 1943); Lvov (June 1943); Kletsk (July 1943); Bialystok (August 1943); Bedzin (August 1943); Tarnow (September 1943); and Vilna (September 1943). There were Jewish revolts in the following Nazi death camps: Treblinka (August 1943); Sobibor (October 1943); Ponary (May 1944); Auschwitz (October 1944); Chelmno (January 1945) (Gilbert, 1992: 102).

There have also been persistent attempts to 'deny' the Shoah or Holocaust: by asserting that it did not take place at all; by insisting that the deaths that occurred in Auschwitz II and elsewhere were almost entirely the result of disease and hunger; and by claiming that the number of deaths – whether by deliberate extermination or through other causes – were no more than a tiny fraction of the generally accepted figure. Though such claims will offend survivors and their families (as they are, no doubt, intended to do) their main purposes are not only to attract converts to neo-Nazi organizations, but more widely, by influencing the uninformed and the credulous, to change assumptions about the Holocaust. Though denial of the Holocaust is a crime in the

Federal Republic of Germany, elsewhere the idea that the Shoah is a 'Jewish lie' is increasingly propounded: it is a claim expressed quite frequently in anti-Zionist circles.

In extreme right-wing circles to cast doubt on the Holocaust, or to deny it altogether – through the *appearance* of careful scholarship – has a special salience. For example, the prominent right-wing British historian, David Irving, launched a libel action in the High Court in London to dispute comments made about him by Deborah Lipstadt in her book *Denying the Holocaust*. Lipstadt had described him as having declared himself converted to the idea that the gas chambers were a myth and quoted him as describing himself as conducting 'a one-man INTIFADA' against the official history of the Holocaust (Lipstadt, 1994: 179). Irving not only lost the action, but in his judgment – delivered in April 2000 – the judge was unequivocal, labelling Irving as an active Holocaust denier, anti-Semitic and associated with right-wing extremists who promoted neo-Nazism, adding that Irving has, for his own reasons, persistently and deliberately manipulated historical evidence' (BBC News Online, 11 April 2001).

In France, much Holocaust denial writing has emanated from a former professor of literature at the University of Lyons 2, Robert Faurisson, and his associates. Thus in 1985 the University of Nantes awarded a doctoral degree to Henri Roques for a dissertation arguing that Kurt Gerstein, who had transmitted news of the gas chambers to the Allies, could not possibly have witnessed the gassings at Belzec, as he had asserted. Despite the fact that there existed a variety of documents attesting to Gerstein's presence at these gassings, Roques followed the usual practice of Holocaust deniers and simply ignored this material in his dissertation because it contradicted what he wished to demonstrate. After a public outcry, Roque's doctoral degree was withdrawn by the French Minister of Higher Education in 1986 (Vidal-Naquet, 1993: 115, cited in Lipstadt, 1994: 10).

In the USA especially, Holocaust deniers have not only been able to take advantage of 'freedom of speech', which is enshrined in the US Constitution, but have also exploited the idea that there *must be* 'two sides' to an argument. A recurring objection made by Holocaust deniers is that the Holocaust is treated as something that is not open to debate. This claim is ludicrous, for as Lipstadt remarks, 'There is little about the Holocaust that is *not* debated and discussed'. Conferences on the Holocaust continually debate a variety of questions – for instance: Is the Holocaust the same as other acts of persecution and GENOCIDE, such as 'ethnic cleansing' (ETHNIC CLEANSING) in ex-Yugoslavia? Might Jews have resisted the Nazis more forcefully? Were the *Judenrat* – Jewish councils installed by the Nazis in each ghetto – over-compliant in the face of various Nazi demands? (Lipstadt, 1994: xiii–xiv). Lipstadt explains that there is a vital distinction to be drawn between, on the one hand, evaluating evidence about the Holocaust – for example establishing that oral testimony is correlated with written documents, authenticating artefacts or re-evaluating previous conclusions on the basis of new evidence, and, on the other hand, debating the *fact* of the Holocaust. As she says, the latter is the equivalent of a scholar of Ancient Rome debating whether the Roman empire ever existed or a scholar of the French Revolution having to prove there was indeed a French revolution (Lipstadt, 1994: xiv). Whereas Holocaust deniers purport to be engaging in scholarly activity, the phenomenon of Holocaust denial is rooted in and explained by ANTI-SEMITISM. [P. B., A. Z.]

Amery, J. (1966) *Jenseits von Schuld und Sühne*, Szczesny Verlag, München.
Eliach, Y. (1998) *There Once Was a World: A 900 Year Chronicle of the Shtetl of Eishyshock*, Little Brown, Boston.
Gilbert, M. (1992) *Jewish History Atlas*, 4th edn, Weidenfeld, London.
Heller, C. (1977) *On the Edge of Destruction: Jews in Poland between the Two World Wars*, Columbia University Press, New York.
Levi, P. (1987) *If This Is a Man*, Sphere Books, London. (Originally published in Italian in 1958 as *Se questo è un uomo*, Einaudi, Torino.)
Lipstadt, D. (1994) *Denying the Holocaust: The Growing Assault on Truth and Memory*, Penguin Books, London.
Nirenstajn, A. (1958) *Ricorda cosa ti ha fatto Amalek*, Einaudi, Torino.
Picciotto Pargion, L. (1994) *Il libro della memoria*, Mursia, Milano.
Poliakov, L. (1966) *The History of Antisemitism*, Elek Books, London.
Richmond, T. (1995) *Konin: A Quest*, Jonathan Cape, London.
Shirer, W. (1960) *The Rise and Fall of the Third Reich*, Simon & Schuster, New York.
Vidal-Naquet, P. (1993) *Assassins of Memory, Essays on the Denial of the Holocaust*, New York.

SINTI (It. *Sinti*, Fr. *Sinti*; Ger. *Sinti*) - Sinti refers to the subgroup of Romani (ROMA) who have German CITIZENSHIP, though they live not only in Germany, but have settled or temporarily live in Austria, Switzerland, northern Italy, Belgium and the Netherlands. Before their persecution and DEPORTATION during the Holocaust (CONCENTRATION CAMP AND DEATH CAMP), many Sinti also lived in other Central European countries. Besides the Sinti, there are several other groups of Roma that have no German citizenship, like the Kalderash and the Xoraxane from Serbia, living in Germany. The German Sinti are culturally closely related to the Manush in Alsace (France), and the Sinti in Piedmont (northern Italy), the Netherlands and Belgium. Along with their settlement in Germany since the middle of the nineteenth century, they have developed an increased bonding with the regional sedentary cultures. They tend to maintain their cultural traditions and speak Romanes as well as the regional varieties. The majority of the Sinti is of Catholic belief, while a minority is Protestant. Some have joined other European free churches. [J. E., T. M.]

Encyclopedia Britannica (1999–2000) 'Gypsy', www.eb.com.
Fings, K., Heuss, H., Sparing, F. (1997) *From 'Race Science' to the Camps. The Gypsies during the Second World War*, Interface Collection 12, Hatfield.
Hancock, I. (1996) *Origins of the Romani People*, www.geocities.com.
Hund, W. D. (ed.) (1996) *Zigeuner. Geschichte und Struktur einer rassistischen Konstruktion*, DISS, Duisburg.
Kesler, P., Kenrick, D. (eds) (1999) *In the Shadow of the Swastika. The Gypsies during the Second World War*, Interface Collection 13, Hatfield.
Laughlin, J. M. (1999) 'European Gypsies and the historical geography of loathing', *Review*, Ferdinand Braudel Center, 22(1): 31–81.
Rossi, M. (1999) *Gipsy Women between Modernity and Tradition: Strategy of Integration, Dynamics and Social Change*, EUROFOR Conference 27.
Soravia, G. (1984) 'A wandering voice: the language of the Gypsies', *UNESCO Courier*, October.
UNESCO (1984) *A Brief History of the Roma*, www.geocities.com.
Van de Port, M. (1999) *Gipsies, Wars and other Instances of the Wild. Civilization and its Discontents in a Serbian Town*, Global Books, Amsterdam.

Wigger, I. (1996) 'Ein eigenartiges Volk. Die Ethnisierung des Zigeunerstereotyps im Spiegel von Enzyklopädien und Lexika', in Hund (ed.).

SLAVERY

(It. *schiavismo*; Fr. *esclavage*; Ger. *Sklaverei*) The term derives from the Latin *slavus* (to indicate an individual from Slav countries) and describes the social and economic doctrines and systems founded on slavery and in which slaves (*servus* in Latin) are considered merely objects at the total disposal of their owners. Slavery was practised in all ancient civilizations (CIVILIZATION), although in different ways depending on how the slaves came to be in this condition (capture, purchase, debt, etc.), whether they had any chance of liberation and what type of work they were expected to do (Meillassoux, 1992, identified slaves used for hard labour, domestic work, farming, maltreated slaves, etc.).

Slavery was sanctioned by Roman law and remained one of the more important legal concepts until the eighteenth century when it was challenged by followers of the Enlightenment. The slavery system underwent considerable change around the sixth century, when traditional slaves – one in 20 of the inhabitants of Imperial Rome – were flanked, throughout Europe, by 'serfs' (*servus casatus*). Unlike traditional slaves, serfs were no longer subject to the moods of their owners but were protected by legislation, although still forced to live on their owner's land. The increase in number of serfs was essentially based on the demographic growth of the lower classes, while the number of slaves was mainly fuelled by the subjugation (through capture or purchase) of individuals born and raised in other societies.

In the Middle Ages, the term *slavus* was first used to differentiate between slaves and serfs as most slaves in the Western world at that time came from Slav countries in Eastern Europe. Slaves always remained the property of their owners. The important geographical discoveries of the fifteenth century led to a new kind of slavery, later described as the slave 'trade' (from the Latin *trahere*, meaning to pull, extract), which involved all the European colonial powers (COLONIALISM), and saw Africans captured and sold or used as plantation slaves in Europe and, above all, the Americas.

Slavery undoubtedly existed in America before the slave trade, but the African slaves generated such huge economic and social benefits that the American market soon became by far the most important. African slave trading increased considerably in the eighteenth century when the so-called 'Great Trade' occurred. This developed through an exchange triangle created as a result of the difficulty found by white people in emigrating to certain areas in America and the need for low-cost human resources on plantations. European traders exchanged small quantities of goods for African slaves mainly from the western coast between Gorea and Mozambique, a stretch of land which included two important epicentres – the Gold Coast (now Ghana) and the Slave Coast. These slaves were usually prisoners of war sold by tribal chiefs; however, they were often also captured during raids. Slave-laden European ships reached the Americas (Antilles, Brazil, etc.) where those who had survived the atrocious conditions were branded and sold in exchange for money, bills of exchange and, above all, tropical produce (tobacco, sugar, coffee, cocoa and rice). As Marx and Engels observed, this led to a type of slavery which was no longer based on the owner directly exploiting slaves for labour purposes, but was based on slaves as barter material within a system of trade.

In the space of 400 years, between 12 and 15 million individuals were taken from Africa to the Americas as slaves and over 1.5 million died during the Atlantic crossing, which took several months. A unique phenomenon of Western history, the slave trade produced deep and irreversible effects on both the African economy – impoverishing the country by draining its workforce – and the relationship between white and black people. The humiliating conditions in which black slaves were forced to live had a strong effect on many aspects of everyday life. In many cases female slaves were considered no more than sexual playthings. The mixed-race children born of such encounters, whose skins were paler than those of unmixed parentage, were treated more favourably. The result of this preferential treatment was a skin-colour-based hierarchy (COLOURED) such as the systems adopted in Brazil and the United States for the classification of racial mixing (quadroons, octoroons).

With an increase in the intensity of slave trading, European traders (Portuguese and Spanish initially, followed by Dutch, English and French, as well as a smaller number of Swedish and Danish traders) involved in this type of exchange were called 'slave traders', nowadays a negative term but at the time used to describe upper-class traders with a good reputation. The trade was considered a mere commercial business by most of the Western world, justified by the fact that slavery had existed in Africa long before this particular trade. According to many others, the fact that it was run by Europeans meant that it was carried out more rationally and provided the few slaves capable of doing so

with the chance to experience a new civilization and convert to Christianity.

In his analysis of democracy in America Alexis de Tocqueville (1835–40) provided a pessimistic forecast regarding the possibility of ever overcoming the feelings of hostility produced by the slavery experience. According to Tocqueville, despite the fact that 'equality of conditions' was one of the bases of the democratic society, the condition of slavery in the United States was not only a matter of legal status, as in the ancient world, but also a matter of racial origin. Thus skin colour left no way open for either EMANCIPATION or the ability to forget. According to Davis (1966: 3) 'Americans have often been embarrassed when reminded that the Declaration of Independence was written by a slaveholder and that Negro slavery was a legal institution in all thirteen colonies at the beginning of the Revolution. "How is it", asked Samuel Johnson, "that we hear the loudest *yelps* for liberty among the drivers of Negroes?"' Tocqueville thought that no political solution could help overcome the social conflict provoked by the arrival of the black people in America as slaves. An interesting parallel of such pessimistic analysis can be seen in two later hypotheses – the existence of two separate nations or the return of black people to Africa – as the only means by which black people could really reach emancipation.

During the eighteenth and nineteenth centuries, following criticism from followers of the Enlightenment and a small number of other seventeenth-century intellectuals, abolitionist campaigns – above all in France and Great Britain – began to lead to the reconsideration of slavery and its interpretation from a political and social, and not only legal and economic, point of view. Revolts led by the slaves themselves (for instance in the United States, Antilles and Brazil) also played an important role. This resulted in growing opposition to the slave trade in countries such as Great Britain, France and Brazil officially opposing the trade. However, this did not result in an immediate decrease in slavery, due to both the high birth rate of slaves and the existence of clandestine traffic. Slavery was later officially abolished in Great Britain (1833), France (1848), the United States (1865) and Brazil (1888). Following an initiative by a number of philanthropists between 1822 and 1892, around 22,000 former slaves were returned to Liberia, from the Americas. A large number of businessmen objected to this as it was approved when the demand for human resources in the plantations was at a peak. (It was also one of the causes of the War of Secession between a number of American states, which had a total population of 9 million, around 3.5 million of which were slaves, and northern American states, with a total population of 22 million inhabitants comprising only 300,000 slaves). This new situation consequently led to a considerable increase in the cost of slaves and more attention being paid to the conditions in which they were forced to live. The fight against slavery continued in the twentieth century, initially supported by the International Convention of the Society of Nations (1926) and later by the approval of the fourth article of the *Declaration of Human Rights* by the United Nations, which prohibited any form of slavery.

Nevertheless, slavery continued to exist in a number of countries until quite recently (Saudi Arabia abolished slavery in 1963 and Mauritania in 1986) and there remain several types of labour that approximate to slavery. Apart from its concrete manifestations, slavery persists in more diffuse ways; as Rex and Tomlinson pointed out (1979: 12), Caribbean immigrants arriving in Britain came with 'the STIGMA of slavery', coming as they did from a culture, society and economy 'historically based upon the slave plantation'. [M. V.]

Bonte, P., Izard, M. (eds) (1991) *Dictionnaire de l'ethnologie et de l'anthropologie*, PUF, Paris.
Davis, D. B. (1966) *The Problem of Slavery in Western Culture*, Cornell University Press, Ithaca, New York.
Maestri Filho, M. J. (1984) *Terra do Brazil. A conquista luz*, Moderna, São Paulo.
Meilassoux, C. (1992) *The Anthropology of Slavery: The Womb of Iron and Gold*, University of Chicago Press, Chicago.
Rex, J. and Tomlinson, S. (1979) *Colonial Immigrants in a British City*, Routledge, London.
Steinberg, S. (1989) *The Ethnic Myth: Race, Ethnicity and Class in America*, Beacon Press, Boston, MA.

SOCIAL DISORGANIZATION (It. *disorganizzazione sociale*; Fr. *désorganisation sociale*; Ger. *soziale Desorganisation*) The situation which is created as a result of a crisis or collapse in the organization of a society. Some authors, including William I. Thomas and Florian Znaniecki, particularly addressed the state of social disorganization brought about by the migration phenomenon (MIGRATION). In these analyses, social organization is defined as the diminished influence of rules of social behaviour over the members of a group, and broadly coincides with what Durkheim defined as 'anomie'. However, even according to these authors, social disorganization never exactly corresponds to individual disorganization as it primarily concerns institutions, while individuals are only concerned secondarily. [U. M.]

Thomas, W. I., Znaniecki, F. (1918–20) *The Polish Peasant in Europe and America*, University of Chicago Press, Chicago and Boston.

SOCIAL UNCONSCIOUS: see UNCONSCIOUS

SOLIDARITY
(It. *solidarietà*; Fr. *solidarité*; Ger. *Solidarität*) The term 'solidarity', which derives from the Latin *in solidum* (meaning solid or obliged to be solid), describes the capacity of members of a group to act in agreement with regard to meeting or identifying interests and therefore be united with other persons. Common needs are the main reason for solidarity in a group.

During the nineteenth century, sociologists developed the concept of solidarity to define the individual's conscious agreement with the ideas and sentiments of the group, as well as its interests, and therefore conceived 'solidarity' to be a fundamental aspect of communal spirit. This type of solidarity, considered to be a typical aspect of pre-industrial societies, according to various authors was replaced by individualism and competitiveness following the industrial revolution and urbanization. Émile Durkheim (regarded as the founder of sociology) outlined the possibility of change in the forms of solidarity following social change. He identified 'mechanical solidarity' and 'organic solidarity' – the former arising among similar individuals and groups through social relationships with individuals who share common morals and being typical of PRIMITIVE societies; while the latter develops in complex societies due to the interdependence of dissimilar individuals and groups caused by the sharing of social tasks and is thus typical of modern societies. However, interdependence of individuals caused by the sharing of tasks is not enough to ensure social solidarity. This must be supported by a common faith in the fairness and morality of the rules of exchange and sharing of tasks within a social group itself.

Solidarity is currently treated as one of the main elements necessary for social consensus and, therefore, a stabilizing factor. It can be expanded through socialization among the new generations. Solidarity is not only an integrating factor for society as a whole, but also a value in individual groups or subgroups, including minorities and other social aggregations (e.g. class solidarity). From this point of view, solidarity may be directed towards values which encourage a group's INTEGRATION in society or opposing values which impede integration. Solidarity, intended as a moral value, may also be expressed as the responsibility of the strongest members to co-operate with or morally or physically support the weakest members (ALTRUISM). Solidarity in these cases may be either individual or collective.

Collective solidarity also occurs in a MIGRATION context; whereby ethnic groups settled in a foreign country, whose members are united by strong common interests, form a single, internally stable group (MIGRATION CHAIN). ETHNIC MINORITY groups often comprise subgroups formed according to different ethnicities or ideologies. Solidarity is often required of a host society in order to cope with the arrival of migrants and may take many different forms. The mass arrival of particularly needy people requires the host society to mobilize energy and esources to deal with the often extremely urgent needs of the newly arrived. A different kind of solidarity is required by the host society when rights are granted to foreigners and migrants whom it may consider to be competitors for social resources to whose development they have made no contribution. Solidarity thus polarizes the debate concerning immigration policies into a position which emphasizes the responsibility of the individual and a stance which highlights the social responsibility of the collective. Solidarity for immigrants should automatically imply their inclusion in the COMMUNITY of arrival (the right to be treated as a citizen). It should also imply the establishment of reciprocal relations (as solidarity cannot be considered as such if it is not reciprocal). Both these conditions, and above all the latter (the realization that help is also needed from immigrants), enforce treatment of foreigners as equals and thus create a relationship whereby all stand on equal footing.

Migration FLOWS – especially international migration flows – provide a major challenge both in political and ethical terms to the concept of solidarity and the constitution of fundamental community or national values. The extent to which migrants are allowed to enter and stay in a country and, thus, to share and access the country's wealth can be interpreted in terms of solidarity. The political and ethical dilemmas raised by migration flows are specifically connected to an understanding of the degree to which a newcomer can depend on solidarity links which existed prior to his or her arrival. The commitments and obligations of citizens to the state are a manifestation of the social dimension of solidarity which can even be considered egoistic in confirming the special status of those who belong to the community (CITIZENSHIP). [Le. Z.]

Alberoni, F. (1968) *Stati nascenti*, il Mulino, Bologna.
Alberoni, F. (1977) *Movimento e istituzione*, il Mulino, Bologna.

SPÄTAUSSIEDLER (It. *Spätaussiedler*; Fr. *Spätaussiedler*;

Ger. *Spätaussiedler*) 'Spätaussiedler' is a new term, created in 1993, to replace the word *Aussiedler*. Legally speaking, it is not clear how to separate the terms *Vertriebene* (expellee), *Aussiedler* (emigrant) and *Spätaussiedler* (late emigrant). The German federal law regarding Vertriebene defines expellee status (DEPORTATION) and carries it over to *Aussiedler*. In Section 4 of this law, Spätaussiedler status is defined. Unlike early MIGRANTS, Spätaussiedler must prove that in their country of origin they suffered disadvantages due to their ETHNIC affiliation, as in the case of the German DIASPORA population in Russia, which was subjected to a collective, war-induced fate. The special status of the German diaspora in Eastern Europe derives from the history of this group of inhabitants: first of all, due to past aggressive policies of the various German states with regard to Eastern Europe and the consequent expulsions and relocations; secondly, due to the resulting expulsionist policy of the Communist authorities. As immigrants, Spätaussiedler were always privileged in German politics. They automatically received German CITIZENSHIP and were supported by far-reaching, well-financed INTEGRATION programmes: language courses, equal opportunity initiatives, and so forth. However, since the beginning of the 1990s there have been cutbacks in these integration measures, resulting in an increasing crisis in the integration of

Spätaussiedler. Furthermore, due to the high number of migrants flowing into the country at the beginning of the 1990s, a series of obstacles were created to oppose immigration. Migrants now had to file applications at the embassy in their home countries, knowledge of the language had to be proved at the time of filing of applications, and admission quotas were set. The Social Democrat-Green (*rot-grün*) government is currently attempting to draw up a new integration policy. [J. B.]

Baaden, A. (1997) *Konzepte und Modelle zur Integration von Aussiedlern*, Berlin.
Baaden, A. (1997) *Aussiedler-Migration. Historische und aktuelle Entwicklungen*, Berlin.
Silagi, M. (2000) 'Der Status der Vertriebenen und Spätaussiedler nach § 7 StAG und § 40 a StAG', *ZAR. Zeitschrift für Ausländerrecht und Ausländerpolitik*, 20(1): 3–7.
Welt, J. (1999) 'Kontinuität und Wandel der neuen Spätaussiedlerpolitik', *Gesprächskreis Arbeit und Soziales. Perspektiven der neuen Aussiedlerpolitik*, 86: 11–18.

state. Stateless individuals can be considered foreigners as they are individuals extraneous to the national COMMUNITY. However, they also hold a particular position with respect to foreign FOREIGNER citizens, in that they cannot benefit from diplomatic protection by the state when it extends citizenship to citizens abroad, nor from any international obligations applied to states as regards the admission of foreign citizens into their territories. For example, stateless persons residing on Italian territory are subject to Italian law with regard to civil rights and national service and are considered Italian citizens for the purposes of penal law, while they are considered foreigners for other purposes. [S. P.]

Barel, B. (1998) 'Apolidia', in *Enciclopedia giuridica*, Treccani, Roma.

STEREOTYPE: see PREJUDICE

STATELESS (It. *apolide*; Fr. *apatride*; Ger. *Heimatlos, Staatenlos*) The internationally accepted definition of statelessness is set out in Section 15 of the *Universal Declaration of Human Rights* (1948) which affirms every individual's right to CITIZENSHIP. A stateless person is defined in the New York Convention of 28–09–54 on the Statute of Stateless Persons as an individual who does not have any kind of citizenship as no state considers him or her to be its citizen. The status of statelessness can originate from birth or derive from facts occurring after birth and which are not followed by the acquisition of citizenship in another

STIGMA (It. *stigma*; Fr. *stigmate*; Ger. *Stigma*) Deriving from the Greek *stizein* (meaning brand), the term is used to describe both an individual with any so-called physical 'difference' from what is considered normal and an individual held in disgrace for having transgressed so-called social norms (DIVERSITY–SIMILARITY). Both these cases lead to MARGINALIZATION in the social context. Stigmatized individuals' self-esteem may well be lowered if they accept this stigma, considering it 'objective'. At times, the stigma creates a downward spiral with devastating results, although sometimes such a feeling may be overcome on finding

scapegoat (PREJUDICE). However, it can also lead to a compensatory mechanism, whereby the individual exalts the stigma. In ancient Greece, the term was used to refer to the practice of human branding. In this sense certain practices of physical MUTILATION can be seen to have the purpose of branding and thus stigmatizing the individual. Until not so long ago, even a birthmark on the face or any other anatomical difference was considered to be a 'mark of God' and the unlucky individual in question was stigmatized. In more recent times, it is worth noting how certain forms of youth CULTURE have exalted stigma by encouraging members to pierce various parts of their body, wear tattoos, make scars more evident, etc. using codes from different ethnic traditions. This type of behaviour may be a sign that the meaning of any kind of stigma continually changes. [M. C.]

Goffman, E. (1963) *Stigma*, Prentice-Hall, Englewood Cliffs, NJ.
Said, E. (1978) *Orientalism*, Routledge and Kegan Paul, London.

STRANGER: see FOREIGNER

SYNCRETISM (It. *sincretismo*; Fr. *syncrétisme*; Ger. *Synkretismus*) The term derives from the Greek *syn* (together) and *krete* (Crete) and was first used by Plutarch to describe the fact that Cretans, who were often involved in internal conflicts, closed ranks when faced with INVASION by outside forces. It was originally a defensive concept meaning the overcoming of internal political differences in order to protect the freedom of a whole population and defeat an external enemy far worse than the internal friend-foe. The term 'syncretism' was, therefore, political since it concerned the determination to unite conflicting groups and create an alliance. Its meaning changed to a religious one as syncretic attempts were made to create a temporary alliance between the different interpretations of the Christian religion, without paying too much attention to dogmatic coherence.

The term assumed a pejorative meaning following the analyses of H. Usener (1898), who used it to refer to confused and mixed forms of religion. Religious and cultural syncretism have played an important role in the Americas, where a number of the most creative forms of syncretism were generated by the African DIASPORA. Slaves (SLAVERY) were forced to accept the moral laws and ethics of an alien religion and see their own beliefs reduced to the status of animism, superstition and magic (not only as a mark of defeat), while the conquering religion assumed the spiritual light of ecumenical redemption. Religious syncretism gradually became part of this scenario, a kind of implicit arrangement between winner and loser. The latter officially accepted conversion – inserting divinities and religious traditions into the religion of the winner – while the former unofficially acknowledged the continuance of the losers' religion on the outskirts of Christianity. Thus, religious syncretism emerged as a defensive compromise whereby alliance with the dominant religion was accepted in exchange for a certain amount of cultural TOLERANCE.

The term 'syncretism' has become a key word in helping to understand the transformation currently taking place with regard to the GLOBALIZATION and localization of traditional means of producing CULTURE and communication. Not only does the notion of syncretism lead to an understanding of a context created through rapid and confused mutations, but it can also help direct this growing communicative disorder along creative and open lines. Following the philosophical and religious use of 'syncretism' the derogatory meaning attributed to syncretism by philosophy and religion, generated by the superficiality that the term infers, has been reversed by anthropology which stressed that cultural syncretism implies innovative use of communication models. These models offer a much more appropriate answer to the cultural changes provoked by the need for a more xenophilic attitude. Syncretism is a concept which illuminates these possibilities: a mix of codes which recombines ETHNIC differences into a valued mix. The value of the syncretic approach lies in changes in the concept of culture – anthropologists no longer see culture as something that unites individuals, genders, groups, classes and ethnicities (ETHNICITY), but as a far more wide-reaching, decentralized, fragmented and conflictive element. Syncretism has now become more entrenched in a process which includes empirical research into new forms of culture and communication. Undisciplined and incoherent, cultural syncretisms emanate from every imperfection of contemporary life, challenging analysts to turn towards profoundly innovative, chromatic or even theoretical frameworks. [M. C.]

Canevacci, M. (1996) *Sincretismi, un esplorazione sulle ibridazioni culturali*, Costa & Nolan, Genova.

Stewart, C., Shaw, R. (eds) (1994) *Syncretism/Anti-Syncretism: The Politics of Religious Synthesis*, European Association of Social Anthropologists, Routledge, London.

Usener, H. (1899) 'Religionsgeschichtligen Untersuchungen', I, 69 sqq., Bonn, 1899).

THIRD WORLD

THIRD WORLD (It. *Terzo Mondo*; Fr. *tiers monde*; Ger. *dritte Welt*) The term 'Third World' was first used by Alfred Sauvy and Georges Balandier in the 1950s (Balandier, 1956). The concept is also associated with the Bandung Conference of 1955, during which 29 African and Asian nations formed a group of independent states that often opposed the two world blocs: the socialist countries and the industrially developed liberal economies. The concepts 'Third World' and 'developing world' were used to refer to a collective state of economic underdevelopment resulting from colonial exploitation.

Even though many of these nations had gained political independence, this did little to transform their dependence on wealthier nations as providers of raw materials and cheap labour – a situation conveyed by President Nasser's appellation 'proletarian nations'. In this sense it is a term which, at least at first, referred to a precise political theory: that once they had achieved independence, former colonial peoples (COLONIALISM) would have, as well as freedom, the opportunity to start an economic, social and political development different from those of the First and Second Worlds. The experience of the Algerian revolution, the spread of guerrilla groups in Central and South America, the Chinese cultural revolution, the Vietnamese resistance war and the liberation struggles in the Portuguese colonies in Africa, have all reinforced this political theory, at the same time expanding the area thought of as the Third World.

Following the failure of the 1973 Algiers summit, where the non-aligned nations stressed the need for a 'new international economic order', and after the crisis of the oil-producing countries, the term 'Third World' began to lose its political overtones. It began to be used, with some ambiguity, to embrace quite different geographical, social, economic, political and cultural realities, which had some factors in common. In this way, the term moved away from a definition based on historic and political variables (such as alignments, colonial past or the majority of the population being 'people of colour'). It now centres on one or more of the problems affecting these countries (low national income, economic underdevelopment, poor social organizations (SOCIAL DISORGAN-IZATION), instability of political structures or heavy indebtedness to the Western or Eastern powers). 'Third World' keeps its political dimension in a few limited contexts, but is more frequently used in a disparaging way (to refer to poverty, misery, desperation, etc.). This is even more apparent in studies of MIGRATION, where it is often applied not only geographically, but also to refer to the migrants themselves. For these reasons, it has become unpopular among many scholars. As a result, other expressions, such as DEVELOPING COUNTRIES, the south of the world or the majority (in relation to population) world, are widely used in preference to 'Third World'. [M. V.]

Balandier, G. (ed.) (1956) *Le 'Tiers Monde'*, PUF, Paris.

Grispo, R. (1970) *Mito e realtà del Terzo Mondo*, ERI, Roma.

Sebreli, J. J. (1975) *Tercer mundo, mito burgués*, Ediciones Siglo Veinte, Buenos Aires.

TOLERANCE (It. *tolleranza*; Fr. *tolérance*; Ger. *Toleranz*)

From the Latin *tolerare*, to endure, put up with. In everyday language the term 'tolerance' is used to signify the attitude of those who put up with ideas or behaviour of others which they do not agree with or of which they do not approve.

In the history of thought, the term has also acquired a more specific and somewhat different meaning, indicating a non-obstructive attitude on the part of a state towards the expression of ideas (philosophical, political and religious) which differ from dominant conceptions.

This type of tolerance was not unheard of in the ancient world, both in the East and in the West; for example, the decision of King Asoka of India (third century BC) to award equal rights to Hinduism and Buddhism and the edicts of the Roman empire (fourth century AD) which ended persecution of Christians. However, a comprehensive definition of tolerance was only formulated in the West in the modern era, as a reaction to the intolerance which had caused many religious wars in Europe and to the violence used against the indigenous people of America in the imposition of the Christian faith. The Reformation gave rise to a proliferation of religious faiths in Europe and the problem of tolerance became an urgent political question. Almost all European rulers found themselves having to deal with several communities which were not necessarily of the same religious persuasion as the sovereign. When the attempt to impose a single religion failed, European rulers had to accept that tolerance of different faiths in the same NATION was the sole way to ensure political stability. These issues were addressed in John Locke's liberal *A Letter concerning Toleration* (1689), in Baruch Spinoza's *Tractatus Theologico-Politicus* (1670) – in which tolerance is seen as being in the interest of religions and states themselves – and in Voltaire's *Treatist on Tolerance* (1763). The last of these, inspired by deist and Enlightenment ideas, is one of the strongest denunciations of INTOLERANCE, which Voltaire defines as the 'child of superstition'.

In the nineteenth century the concept of tolerance was extended to the political field by John Stuart Mill, and during the twentieth century it also came to include moral tolerance and the tolerance of 'different' and culturally related behaviour. Nowadays, the question of tolerance mainly concerns the coexistence of various ethnic groups within a single society. The UNESCO *Declaration of the Principles of Tolerance* signed by all member states (16 November 1995) extends the traditional conception of tolerance to 'the respecting, acceptance and appreciation of the infinite richness of our world's cultures, our manner of speech and the way in which we express our human qualities. It is encouraged by knowledge, openness of mind, communication and freedom of conscience. Tolerance is harmony within difference.'

The question as to whether tolerance should be unlimited or should exclude attitudes and behaviour considered to be 'intolerable' has often been a matter for discussion; for example, John Locke considered that tolerance should not be extended to atheists (on the basis of the tautological argument of their denying the existence of God). More recently it has been claimed that intolerant attitudes and behaviour, including RACISM, should not be granted the benefit of tolerance. Some serious questions arise when the principle of tolerance is applied to ethnic and religious minorities (ETHNIC MINORITY) who insist on defending traditional customs which restrict the freedom of their members. Should ethnic communities living in a free society have the right to refuse liberal principles and to govern themselves according to other mores and values? Should members of an ethnic minority have the right to govern themselves according to values based on racial or sexual discrimination? Could insistence on principles of autonomy and individual rights be a modern-day version of European ETHNOCENTRISM?

These difficult questions do not just divide liberals and non-liberals, but also pose problems among liberals themselves. Some scholars (Baker, 1994) have argued that the concept of individual freedom of conscience only applies to Western civilizations (CIVILIZATION). In non-Western societies the COMMUNITY as a whole must be considered. Many forms of tolerance are not based on individuals but rather on the community. For example the 'millet system' of the Ottoman empire was based on the right of each religious community (Christian, Jewish, Muslim) to impose its own religious rules on its members. Other scholars (Kymlicka, 1995) believe, on the other hand, that not all the rights of the various ethnic minorities can be given the same consideration. Thus, recognition of the right to autonomy of various ethnic groups cannot be an 'all or nothing' process, but should be a form of negotiation which promotes integration of minority groups with autochthon citizens. In this sense, a liberal society must tolerate all forms which promote CITIZENSHIP, and must be intolerant of cases which produce separatism. [U. M., Em. M.]

Aminrazavi, M., Ambuel, D. (1997) *Philosophy, Religion and the Question of Tolerance*, State University of New York Press, New York.

Baker, J. (ed.) (1994) *Group Rights*, University of Toronto Press, Toronto.

Bauman, Z. (1999) *In Search of Politics*, Stanford University Press, Stanford, CA.

Gress, D. (1998) *From Plato to NATO*, The Free Press, New York.

Hagendoorn, A., Nekuee, S., Hagendoorn, L. (eds) (1999) *Education and Racism: A Cross National Inventory of Positive Effects of Education on Ethnic Tolerance*, Ashgate, Aldershot.

Kymlicka, W. (ed.) (1995) *The Rights of Minority Cultures*, Oxford University Press, Oxford.

Locke, J. (1990 [1689]) *A Letter Concerning Toleration*, Prometheus Books, New York.

McIntyre, A. (1984) *After Virtue: A Study in Moral Theory*, University of Notre Dame Press, Notre Dame, IN.

Spinoza, B. (1983 [1670]) *Tractatus Theologico-politicus*, in Curley, E. (ed.), *Collected Works*, Princeton University Press, Princeton, NJ.

UNESCO (1995) *Déclaration de principes sur la tolérance*, UNESCO, Paris.

Voltaire, M. A. (2000) *Treatise on Tolerance and Other Writings* (1763), ed. Harvey, S., Cambridge University Press, Cambridge.

U

ÜBERFREMDUNG (PENETRATION OF A FOREIGN CULTURE)

(It. *inforestieramento*; Fr. *pénétration d'une culture étrangère*; Ger. *Überfremdung*) The German term *Überfremdung* has been used in technical language in Switzerland since the beginning of the twentieth century, to describe a condition in which the presence of foreign elements, whether in terms of people or culture, reaches such a level as to imply an alteration of the traditional and inherent features of the country in question. 'Überfremdung' can be seen as a more acceptable way of suggesting that 'foreignness' has adverse consequences that words such as 'bastardization' or degeneration – fairly common in racist language (RACISM). The specific situation which Überfremdung seeks to emphasize is not so much 'corruption' as the loss of cultural or numerical supremacy. According to Dominique Schnapper, in French-speaking Switzerland Überfremdung is described as 'surpopulation étrangère' (1992: 39, 68). Since the end of the Second World War the term 'Überfremdung' has been primarily used in a political context, although it also has economic connotations (the presence of foreign workers had slowed the rate of salary increases and reduced the power of autochthon workers).

Überfremdung has its roots in the widespread instinctive fear of seeing the NATIONAL CHARACTER threatened, possibly to the point of extinction. Latching on to this fear, a member of the Swiss Parliament, Schwarzenbach, succeeded in calling two referendums (in 1973 and 1974) aimed at approving the text of a law which, if the necessary majority were reached, would have meant the expulsion of at least half the foreign workers resident in Switzerland for less than three years. It would also have drastically reduced the number of naturalizations (CITIZENSHIP), SEASONAL MIGRANT WORKERS and cross-border workers. Today, the concept of Überfremdung seems to have been replaced by XENOPHOBIA directed at phenomena such as illegal aliens (ILLEGAL ALIEN), and drug trafficking connected to migratory activity. However, in several countries there is still considerable discussion of both the number of foreigners – considered to be so high that it could put an end to the national IDENTITY (NATIONAL PREFERENCE) – and the love of foreign cultures which could compromise national cultural identity (a good example being the recent debate in France over legal measures to prevent the use of non-French words). A certain fear of foreign presence can be detected in Italy, not because of its statistical importance, but in relation to the low birth rate, resulting in some alarmism, especially in the mass media, which paints a picture of a future in which the Italian 'race' is doomed to disappear. [M. V.]

Schmitz, W. (1994) *Modernisierung oder Überfremdung?*, Taschenbuch, Metzler.
Schnapper, D. (1992) *L'Europe des immigrés*, Éditions François Bourin, Paris.

UNCONSCIOUS (It. *inconscio*; Fr. *inconscient*; Ger. *unbewußtes, das Unbewußte*) The term

unconscious' derives from the Late Latin term *inconscium*, composed of the negative form *in*, and *conscium* meaning conscious. This dimension of unawareness accounts for behaviour, symptoms and other phenomena which manifest regardless of rational and conscious choice and, on occasion, actually appear to be in open contrast to the will and desire of the individual concerned. In this light the term has been used to explain the wealth, complexity and frequent ambivalence of human behaviour, and the fact that humans cannot be considered to be purely rational beings.

Feelings of RACISM and XENOPHOBIA, with the consequent forms of ethnic and racial PREJUDICE, have often been explained as being rooted in the unconscious. This is because: (a) racial and xenophobic intolerance are irrational social phenomena, which cannot be ascribed purely to factors of social competition of an institutional or economic type; (b) as the several expressions of INTOLERANCE (which on occasion have been characterized by profoundly destructive gestures and extreme violence) of categories of people who are perceived as being different in some way – during various historical periods and in widely differing contexts – are the expression of individual and collective pathological forms, such manifestations have also been analysed using the conceptual tools of psychopathology, including the theory of the unconscious; and (c) following the growing awareness of the role played by prejudice in determining ethnic and racial relations, studies on the matter have highlighted that the mechanism of formation of negative prejudices against certain categories of people can be interpreted as a form of rationalization, i.e. as the attempt on the part of individuals or entire social groups to provide plausible justification for those hostile sentiments whose origins lie in unconscious psychological processes.

The unconscious dimension of psychological life has been studied in the fields of philosophy and psychology, where the term is used both as an adjective (the attribution of contents and thoughts of which the individual is not aware) and as a noun (the metaphorical place, outside the sphere of consciousness, in which psychological events and mental processes, which operate according to their own laws, are placed). The view of the unconscious which has most influenced contemporary thinking is undoubtedly that of Sigmund Freud. However, interesting forerunners of the same notion can be found in ancient Greek culture. For example, strange incidents were often recorded during chariot races at the stadium in Olympia in Ancient Greece, where horses would suddenly appear to shy at some terrible apparition and run off the track, thus dashing their riders' hopes of victory. Such incidents, which were probably caused by the reckless movements or other mistakes made by the charioteers when excited by the prospect of winning, were attributed to *Taraxippos* ('Scarehorse' in Greek), a mythical spirit who would lie in wait ready to ruin the charioteers' race. This figure could almost be seen to be a metaphorical explanation of what was later to be described by Freudian psychoanalysis as a symptomatic act. Nevertheless, the Greeks had detected a mechanism the hidden meaning of which was only to be explained centuries later as an expression of the unconscious. Plato wrote in explanation of his theories on innate ideas in *Meno* (85, 32–74), that an innate awareness – possibly related to a past experience – exists within the unconscious of every person. This awareness remains dormant until the right technique to bring it to the fore is found.

Popular CULTURE and philosophy have always been aware that the human soul hides dynamic realities and drives unknown to people – realities and drives which, nevertheless, condition their behaviour. It is in the arts in particular (fine arts, MUSIC, literature, THEATRE), that the unconscious has most often been expressed, where conscious reality and unconscious perceptions blend. Here desires come to the fore and memories and experiences are forgotten in that dark area known as the unconscious. It may be said, therefore, that people have always been aware of the unconscious to some degree.

It was not until the end of the eighteenth century and the beginning of the nineteenth century that science began to use suggestive therapy techniques such as magnetism and hypnosis to influence the behaviour of certain individuals or encourage them to recall hidden or forgotten experiences. These newly emerging methods – especially when assessed in the light of the criteria of positivist science, which were becoming increasingly important in the mid-nineteenth century – were soon discredited, as their results were considered rather dubious and their practitioners were not known for a professional approach. Nevertheless, Auguste Ambroise Liébeault (1823–1904) – the French physician who founded the Nancy school of medicine supported by Hyppolite Bernheim (1840–1919) – did become famous and enjoyed an excellent reputation. Liébeault and Bernheim – in sharp contrast to Charcot, who put forward theories of hysterical pathology – both continued to support suggestive hypnosis as a suitable means of causing the re-emergence of details buried deep in the patient's unconscious. From this time onwards it was no longer considered scandalous to speak of an unconscious psychic reality. Pierre Janet (1859–1947) was another important forerunner of the psychodynamic theories of the unconscious. He carried out his studies on psychic automatism at the same time as Freud, addressing the aetiological significance in mental illness of the traumas which could be brought to consciousness through hypnosis. Sigmund Freud (1856–1939) systematically summarized all these theories by applying the hypothesis of the unconscious and its functions to his conception of the psyche in *The Interpretation of Dreams*, which he wrote in 1899 and subsequently amended in 1920. His early model of the psyche was a 'topic' and could be divided into the Unconscious (Ucs), the Preconscious (Pcs) and Consciousness (Cs):

We have described the relation of the two systems to each other and to consciousness by saying that the system Pcs stands like a screen between the system Ucs and consciousness. The system Pcs not only bars access to consciousness, but also controls the access to voluntary movement, and has control of the emission of a mobile cathectic energy, a part of which is familiar to us in the form of attention. (1899: 615)

From 1920 onwards, Freud theorized that the structure of the psyche was divided into three parts – the Id, the Ego and the Super-ego – each of which is partly unconscious, although only the Id is entirely composed of unconscious material (1923). The Freudian explanation of the unconscious has undoubtedly been the model of reference for the development of psychoanalytical thinking. However, it should also be mentioned that the idea of the unconscious is not limited to the experience of the individual. Although Freud had spoken of a heritage common to all human beings, composed of original unconscious elements transmitted phylogenetically – called *Urphantasien* (1915–17) – it is to Carl Gustav Jung (1875–1961) that we owe the postulation of the existence of a collective unconscious. In Jung's conception, the collective unconscious is inherited, transpersonal and consisting of the residue of the EVOLUTION of the human species (1934–54).

It is interesting to note how studies of the unconscious – from the psychoanalytical work of Freud and Jung to the ethnopsychiatric (ETHNOPSYCHIATRY) work of authors such as Géza Róhaim and Georges Devereux – have highlighted the substantially universal nature of unconscious contents and mechanisms, thus disclaiming, from a scientific and cultural point of view, the idea of any radical diversity between ethnic or racial groups (DIVERSITY–SIMILARITY). Obviously this takes on historical importance on consideration of the fact that the approach to differences between human beings (and their customs, traditions, languages and behaviour, as well as hypothetical levels of civil and cultural development) have often allowed the development, even in scientific work, of theories aimed at demonstrating that certain insuperable differences exist between the various human races (RACE). In the light of these findings, it is possible to state that unconscious contents and mechanisms are similar for all human beings, even though they may be susceptible to ongoing transformations as a result of the influence of interrelations with other cultures and societies. In particular, universal unconscious factors include: Eros, in the sense of the sum of life-preserving drives, including both heterosexual and homosexual love and sexual impulses; the fundamental impact on the psychological life of individuals of early relationships with parents or parental figures, according to

the mechanism which is known as the 'Oedipus complex' in Western culture; destructive and depressive tendencies; and certain basic psychological defence mechanisms (NARCISSISM, SADO-MASOCHISM). This universality of psychological processes might justify the assumption of the existence of a similar substantial uniformity of pathological manifestations. However, the influence of the environment is such that these basic universal elements are distributed in a different way each time to create specific dynamic structures. As a consequence, behaviour and thought contents which are not considered pathological in one cultural environment may be deemed to be so in another. Nevertheless, without entering into the ethnopsychiatric debate, certain pathological symptoms – especially those connected to phobic mechanisms, manifestations of obsessive rituals and depressive forms – seem to be recognized as such in all cultures. [S. G.]

Bolaffi, G., Gindro, S. (1996) *Il corpo straniero*, Alfredo Guida Editore, Napoli.

Ellenberger, H. F. (1970) *The Discovery of the Unconscious. The History and Evolution of Dynamic Psychiatry*, Basic Books, New York.

Freud, S. (1899) *The Interpretation of Dreams*, in Strachey, J. (ed.), *The Standard Edition of the Complete Psychological Works of Sigmund Freud [SE]*, vol. 4–5 Hogarth Press and the Institute of Psycho-analysis, London, 1953 ff.

Freud, S. (1915–17) *Introductory lectures on psychoanalysis*, SE, 15–16.

Freud, S. (1923) *The Ego and the Id* (1922), SE, 19, p. 462.

Gindro, S. (1981) *Perversione e rivoluzione*, Edizioni Psicoanalisi Contro, Roma.

Gindro, S. (1993) *L'oro della psicoanalisi*, Alfredo Guida Editore, Napoli.

Jung, C. G. (1934–54) *The Archetypes and the Collective Unconscious*, Routledge, London.

Vegetti Finzi, S. (1986) *Storia della psicoanalisi*, Mondadori, Milano.

Voltaggio, F. (1992) *L'arte della guarigione nelle culture umane*, Bollati Boringhieri, Torino.

UNDERCLASS (It. *sottoproletariato*; Fr. *classe sociale défavorisée*; Ger. *Lumpenklasse*)

The term 'the underclass' is derived from Marx's theory of 'a relative surplus population' or 'industrial reserve army' which provided a pool of disposable labour to be used in the service of capital accumulation – although Marx did not actually use the term 'underclass'. Weber saw this group in more cultural terms as people whose relative lack of economic power made them underprivileged 'outcasts', 'debtor classes' and the 'poor', some of whom would experience segregation because of ethnic processes (RACIAL SEGREGATION). More recently, the term 'underclass' has come to signify both Marxist labour market factors and Weberian cultural features of those who are persistently poor because they are usually or always unemployed and, hence, part of a 'cycle of deprivation' (Edgell, 1993). It tends to refer to a group who are not a 'reserve army' of labour, but a permanently marginalized section of the population (MARGINALIZATION). The term has been applied to different groups (Saunders, 1990). Some writers have used it to refer to women and what has been termed 'the feminization of poverty' as more women are lone parents who cannot afford full-time childcare and so are unemployed or in part-time employment. Others have used it to refer to ETHNIC MINORITY groups (Rex and Tomlinson, 1979) who, as a result of RACISM, are able to find menial, poorly paid jobs at times of full employment, but are amongst the first to be made redundant and the last to be hired (Modood et al., 1997).

The notion of the 'underclass' is used particularly in the USA, but has not been taken up to the same extent in Britain. William Julius Wilson (1987) argued that there exists a 'truly disadvantaged' underclass composed especially of young black men who reproduce cultures of poverty. The concept has been popularized in a much less sympathetic way in the writings of Charles Murray (1990), who argued that the underclass was established in the USA and emerging in Britain. According to Murray, the defining characteristics of the underclass are poor levels of education; high incidences of lone motherhood with men taking no responsibility for the children they father; voluntary unemployment and hence dependence on both welfare payments and violent crime – characteristics which are transmitted from generation to generation. In the USA, Murray argues, most of the underclass are black. He distinguished the underclass from the 'deserving poor' by arguing that they are responsible for their condition, having chosen to pursue what they see as their own best interests without moral or social considerations. In that context, he opposed the provision of state benefits for those living in poverty and argued for the re-moralization of the poor.

One reason that the concept of the underclass has not gained more ground in Britain, despite the enormous publicity given to Murray's ideas, has been the fact that it is both poorly defined and subject to unsympathetic analyses – including in Marx's original analysis (Mann, 1992). 'It obviously makes little sense to generalize to the point of arguing that women as a whole or blacks as a whole now represent the new underclass. Nor can we even claim that the unemployed per se are an underclass, for this is a category that is constantly shifting' (Saunders, 1990: 261). Murray's formulation also omits mention of RACISM, patriarchy, the causes of structural inequality or divisions between those living in poverty (Mann, 1992). In addition, some theorists have argued that the period referred to by some as 'late modernity' or as 'postmodernity' is characterized by rapid social changes. This means that the certainties associated with cultural and political collectivities of class, gender and ETHNICITY are being replaced by what Beck (1992) calls a democratization of risk where individual identities are more important to life trajectories than the collective biographies associated, for example, with social class (Giddens, 1991). In these circumstances, Murray's conception of the underclass is overly simplistic. For reasons such as these, the notion of social exclusion and policies to prevent it are attracting more support than notions of the 'underclass'. [A. P.]

Beck, U. (1992) *Risk Society*, Sage Publications, London.

Edgell, S. (1993) *Class*, Routledge, London.

Giddens, A. (1991) *Modernity and Self Identity*, Polity Press, Cambridge.

Mann, K. (1992) *The Making of an English 'Underclass'? The Social Divisions of Welfare and Labour*, Open University Press, Buckingham.

Modood, T., Berthoud, J., Lakey, J., Nazroo, P., Smith, S., Virdee, S., Beishon, S. (1997) *Ethnic Minorities in Britain: Diversity and Disadvantage*, Policy Studies Institute, London.

Murray, C. (1990) *The Emerging British Underclass*, Institute of Economic Affairs, London.

Rex, J., Tomlinson, S. (1979) *Colonial Immigrants in a British City*, Routledge, London.

Saunders, P. (1990) *Social Class and Stratification*, Routledge, London.

Weber, M. (1964) *The Theory of Social and Economic Organisation*, Collier-Macmillan, London.

Wilson, W. J. (1987) *The Truly Disadvantaged: The Inner City, The Underclass and Public Policy*, University of Chicago Press, Chicago.

V

VEHICULAR LANGUAGE (It. *lingua veicolare*; Fr. *langue d'appoint*; Ger. *Vehikel-Sprache*) A language may be defined as 'vehicular' when it is adopted for communication between members of different linguistic groups. An example could be a situation where an Italian speaker and a German speaker communicate in English. The definition of vehicular language can be said to be synonymous with LINGUA FRANCA. The prevalence of the use of certain vehicular languages over others at a given time or in a given field depends on linguistic, cultural and economic factors of predominance. English and French are currently the most widely used vehicular languages in the world, although the reasons for the prevalent use of French in the worlds of culture and of the arts, as well as in the official and informal contexts of international and intercontinental diplomacy, are by now purely historical. Nowadays, owing to its predominance in the fields of technology, business, scientific research and communication, English appears to be very close to achieving the status of vehicular language for the entire planet, and is spoken with varying degrees of fluency by about two billion people worldwide (Crystal, 1997). With regard to immigration (MIGRATION) in Europe, vehicular languages are often used to overcome the language barriers which hinder communication between immigrants and the structures of the host countries, especially in the initial stages. In countries of more recent immigration where immigrant FLOWS are comprised of people from extremely diverse linguistic backgrounds and who generally have little or no knowledge of the language of the host countries, first contacts are often negotiated using vehicular languages, although fluency in such languages is often inadequate on both sides.

The development and growth of a vehicular language into a universal language – as seems to be occurring in the case of English – brings distinct advantages in terms of communication between peoples and contributes to breaking down language barriers. However, this phenomenon of expansion could also imply the progressive impoverishment of other languages – and of the cultures of which such languages are bearers – and can have a homologating effect (HOMOLOGATION). Such expansion runs the risk of escalating into a kind of linguistic COLONIALISM, as hegemony of language could lead to actual cultural, social, political and economic hegemony. Certain authors, such as the North American linguist J. A. Fishman, have highlighted the fact that many processes of linguistic substitution (LANGUAGE SHIFT) are caused by the impoverishment of minority languages which results from the growing use and massive encouragement of the learning of the languages which have the greater use as vehicular languages. [A. B., R. B.]

Crystal, D. (1997) *The Cambridge Encyclopaedia of Language*, Cambridge University Press, Cambridge.

Fishman, J. A. (1989) *Language and Ethnicity in Minority Sociolinguistic Perspective*, Multilingual Matters, Philadelphia, PA.

VISA (It. *visto*; Fr. *visa*; Ger. *Visum*) A visa is a document issued by, or on behalf of, a traveller's country of destination, either to authorize entry, or to indicate to authorities that the holder has been assessed against that state's requirements for entry in a particular admission category. In this way a visa differs from a passport, which is normally issued by the holder's country of nationality or habitual residence (CITIZENSHIP). The precise effect of a visa in law depends upon the relevant provisions of the issuing state's entry control legislation. Visas are usually valid for a specific period of time although they may authorize entry for an indeterminate period or on a 'permanent' basis.

Visas are usually issued by officials of the issuing state's Ministry of Foreign Affairs, although in Canada's case this is done by Immigration Department officials. Most countries charge some sort of application or processing fee. Visas usually take the form of a stamped impression or counterfoil document that is placed in, or affixed to, a traveller's passport. However, other visa formats are in use: for example, the Canadian permanent resident visa is a multi-copy form. Electronic 'visas' may soon be in general use. Currently, most states require travellers to obtain a visa before seeking entry to the country in question. However, in a few cases, states do permit visa applications to be made upon arrival at a port of entry. Countries which impose legal obligations on transportation companies concerning the screening of travellers use visas as a signal to industry officials that passengers may be safely transported without offence. An additional interview or inspection upon entry may or may not be required. The validity period is often, though not always, renewable by Inter-

ior Ministry or other officials in the host country. Some countries, such as the United States, use visas as a means to confer on the holder the authority to work or engage in study. Other countries impose additional documentation requirements for students and temporary workers.

The conferral of 'status' is not a universal characteristic of visas. Under Canadian law, for example, the actual entry decision rests with the officer to whom the visa is presented upon arrival at a port of entry. In such cases the visa is mainly facilitative, indicating to the port-of-entry inspector that the holder has been 'pre-examined' and appears to meet all requirements for admission. Canadian visas must be presented within a specific period of time and, although they usually specify a period during which the holder may remain in Canada, that period is not mandatory for the port-of-entry inspector.

Where admission is not automatic, possession of a visa may grant certain process rights or appeal privileges to the holder. Visitor visa requirements are generally used either to generate revenue or as a MIGRATION control device. Used in this way their purpose is usually to restrict or manage the entry of nationals of countries whose presence is not welcome for foreign policy reasons or because of their propensity to cause various sorts of immigration control problems. Most countries have a general requirement for foreign visitors to obtain visas, but few states require visas of all aliens (FOREIGNER). Australia has one of the most nearly universal visitor visa policies, allowing the citizens of only a few countries to enter without a visitor visa. Canada has one of the least universal requirements, permitting the citizens of more than 50 countries and about 85 per cent of all foreign visitors to enter without a visa. Throughout the industrialized world, exceptions to visitor visa requirements are most commonly based on nationality and reciprocity. Most states have a 'transit without visa' period during which persons transiting through the country in question may enter and remain without a visa. Canada is one of the few exceptions to this rule. Canada does not permit citizens of countries whose nationals normally require a visa to transit through Canada without one. In other cases visa exemptions are based on the length of time for which entry is requested or the purpose for which entry is sought. For example, many countries permit airline safety inspectors and aircraft accident investigators to enter without visas in order to carry out their duties. [Me. B.]

Brush, M. (1978) *Explanatory Notes on Bill C–24: Immigration Act, 1978*, Canada Employment and Immigration Commission, Ottawa.

Canada Employment and Immigration Commission (1982) 'A study of current Canadian visitor visa policy' (unreleased confidential document), Ottawa.

Canada Employment and Immigration Commission (1988) 'Canada's visitor visa policy: the present CVV system, its strengths and weaknesses, options for change' (unreleased confidential document) Ottawa.

IATA Netherlands, *Travel Information Manual* (published monthly) Amsterdam Schipol Airport.

US Department of State, Bureau of Consular Affairs, Visa Services, Tips for U.S. Visas: Visitors – Business and Pleasure, www.travel_state.gov.

US Department of State, Foreign Affairs Manual, Visas, www.foia.state.gov.

W

WHITENESS (It. *essere bianchi*; Fr. *être blanc*; Ger. *Whiteness*) Whiteness may be seen simply as a lack of colour. Therefore some people are 'COLOURED' and the remainder, by default, white. For many centuries the words 'black' and 'white' have carried layers of additional meaning in Western European thought. White is associated with light, cleanliness and PURITY whilst black is associated with darkness, dirt and evil. Nineteenth-century references to Africa as 'the dark continent' carried multiple connotations (BLACK AFRICA), as a continent inhabited by dark-skinned people, living in a darkness unilluminated by Christianity, potentially evil, threatening (Joseph Conrad perfectly captures these sentiments at the end of the nineteenth century in his novel *The Heart of Darkness*). Ambiguous layers of meaning are never entirely absent from the use of the black/white contrast.

The notion of whiteness has also been institutionalized in a strong form. The most striking modern examples are the United States during segregation and South Africa under the apartheid regime (RACIAL SEGREGATION). In both these situations whiteness entailed the absence of blackness and conferred power and privileges institutionalized in law and custom. A white person was defined as one uncontaminated by black or coloured blood. In South Africa the discovery of inappropriate ancestors could lead to reclassification, forcing formerly 'white' people to relocate their homes, change their children's schools and, possibly, making long-established marriages illegal under the laws prohibiting sex between 'races' (MIXOPHOBIA, RACE). Although the discovery of a black or 'coloured' forebear could lead to such reclassification, a black or coloured person could not claim whiteness through a white forebear. The contamination of white by black was a one-way process.

The status of whiteness has, in part, provoked the counter-assertion that 'black is beautiful' and the demand that people of colour take pride in their blackness. The assertion that a black person shows signs of whiteness in his or her thinking or actions may be used as a criticism: 'black on the outside but white inside'. Such assertions may be used as a sanction by politically active members of 'black' minorities, especially against those who are believed to be collaborating with hostile white agencies (AFROCENTRISM, BLACK POWER, NEGRITUDE). Whiteness has also become a basis for ETHNIC POLITICS with extreme right-wing movements demanding 'white power' or 'white rights'. Such demands are most common amongst those who feel themselves marginalized (MARGINALIZATION) by the acquisition of civil, legal and political rights by groups previously subordinated on a 'racial' basis. All such usages further institutionalize the idea of distinct races which may be identified by colour. Whiteness is regarded as inherently unproblematic by 'white' people, but when threatened, their sense of whiteness becomes a basis for mobilization that may be referred to as 'RACIALIZATION' or 'ETHNICIZATION'. [R. M.]

Allen, T. W. (1994) *The Invention of the White Race*, Verso, London.

Conrad, J. (1996) *The Heart of Darkness and Other Tales*, Oxford University Press, Oxford.

Fanon, F. (1970) *Black Skin, White Masks*, Paladin, London.

Kohn, M. (1996) *The Race Gallery: The Return of Racial Science*, Jonathan Cape, London.

Malik, K. (1996) *The Meaning of Race*, Macmillan, New York.

XENOPHOBIA

(It. *xenofobia*; Fr. *xéno-phobie*; Ger. *Xenofo-bie*) From the Greek *xénos*, foreign, and *fóbos*, fear. The suffix 'phobia' means the term has a psychopathological meaning, for while fear can be an appropriate reaction to real danger, a phobia' is a disproportionate and unconscious reaction to a danger which is often imagined, and which leads to illogical and uncontrollable behaviour. Xenophobia has always been a part of the human psyche and lends itself to various levels of analysis.

In everyday language, as well as in official documents, xenophobia is often coupled with RACISM, and it is, in fact, difficult to clearly define the facets of meaning whereby the two terms diverge. We would like to focus here on the psychological factors which can lead to an uncontrollable fear of strangers (FOREIGNER), showing how the origins of such a fear are deeply rooted in the history of both individuals and societies. To do this we will concentrate on interpreting xenophobia as an archetypal reaction, rather than addressing its intimate correlation with racism.

Foreigners have been the object of fear since time immemorial. This is because they traditionally come from afar, bringing with them unknown languages and customs which can make them appear to be incomprehensible and fearsome even when their intentions are non-aggressive. Historically, foreigners have often arrived in another country in order to search for sustenance. At times they have come with decidedly hostile intentions, to pillage and plunder. As the latter has frequently been the case in the past – not only on the part of individuals but also of entire populations – the fear of foreigners is deeply rooted in the UNCONSCIOUS of both individuals and social groups. This fear has often been depicted in art and literature, as well as being handed down through popular beliefs (FOLKLORE). A particularly effective portrayal of a situation in which the fear of the unknown and the strange degenerates into uncontrollable fear is found in Alessandro Manzoni's masterpiece of Italian literature, *I promessi sposi*, where in the search for those who are spreading plague in Milan every strange or foreign mannerism becomes a cause for suspicion. That this phenomenon is a sadly persistent one can be seen nowadays in some of the phobic reactions arising following the terrorist attacks of 11 September 2001 in New York and Washington.

It is hard to say at which point the threshold from fear to phobia is crossed. Often, the fear of that which is foreign can be pervaded with a kind of fascination. The latter may be especially true for those whose lifestyles have limited horizons, for whom this fascination may be of an exotic or sexual nature, and have an almost magical, supernatural allure. As well as having a historical dimension, xenophobia can also be rooted in the personal history of the individual. At this level the unconscious origins of the fear of foreigners stem from the trauma experienced by a child at the birth of a younger brother or sister – the archetypal new arrivals. The entrenched middle-class FAMILY model found in Western societies seems to provide fertile ground for the development of this kind of mechanism, as the stronger the nuclear family, the greater the fear of expropriation by a younger brother or sister. This feeling is not only experienced by first-born children. All children perceive their brothers and sisters to be foreign entities who come to take away what belongs to them, chiefly the love of their parents, with all the ensuing Oedipal implications that such love, with its sexual connotations, entails. Paradoxically, this is felt even more strongly by only children, who may find themselves fighting imaginary demons in lieu of real-life siblings, which may sometimes lead to their developing certain paranoid pathologies. As children develop – and through education – this hatred of siblings usually turns to love. However, those who for various reasons are unable to operate this shift, often express this hatred through the social pathology known as xenophobia.

From a psychological point of view, therefore, the foreigner is initially perceived primarily as the 'Other', and is only viewed more objectively as someone coming from another country – whether as a guest or as an invader – once we move beyond this initial response. An understanding of the process of identity construction in psychological terms is essential to the analysis of xenophobic reactions; the Ego needs the Other in order to define itself and construct its IDENTITY, although in doing this it often fails to perceive that, to the other, it is we who are the 'Other'. The construction of identity requires a dialectic tension between these two poles, and involves a process of projection which can at times be felt as a danger of 'losing' oneself in the Other, leading to a loss of perception of one's identity and to a feeling of disorientation. This feeling can be compared to that which is experienced by all of us at some point during

our lifetime, when we happen to wake up in the night and not know where we are. We then try to locate familiar objects in the dark, anxiety rising until we find a point of reference which enables us to identify our surroundings, and only then are we able to relax and go back to sleep. What occurs then is that we experience a feeling of estrangement from ourselves. This is one of the most anxiety-ridden and unpleasant feelings we know, and is not necessarily connected with a displacement in place, such as foreign travel (Sartre, 1938; Camus, 1957).

The encounter with the Other – often perceived as an enemy or invader – can then indeed be a fearful experience. Overcoming such fear is difficult, and Western society seems to fare particularly badly in this respect, in that often the best alternative it has found to AGGRESSION towards other cultures is to assume an attitude of pity tinged with implications of inferiorization. Many authors (Kristeva, 1988; Gindro, 1993) have stressed how the fearful reactions elicited by the encounter with the other – both the other within and the stranger without – can set off unconscious defence mechanisms (NARCISSISM, SADO-MASOCHISM) which can trigger aggression. Xenophobia, both at an individual and at a group level, can be considered to be an expression of this defensive reaction, which can take on two, diametrically opposed, forms. The first of these is at the root of various kinds of NATIONALISM, and is an exaltation of one's own culture, coupled with an effort to banish or even destroy any diverse expressions – ranging from different languages to different ways of eating – in the name of a presumed cultural PURITY. Conversely, it may take the form of uncritical exaltation of another culture, which results, however, in emptying the culture in question of any depth of meaning, by ascribing to t an unreal, stereotyped and exotic quality. In both these cases what is lost is the possibility of establishing a peer relationship in which each individual, or each culture, is awarded equal dignity – the sole possible basis upon which to establish a non-xenophobic relationship with the other. [S. G.]

Camus, A. (1957) *L'Étranger*, Gallimard, Paris.
Commission Nationale Consultative des Droits de l'Homme (1997) *La Lutte contre le racisme et la xénophobie*, Documentation Française, Paris.

Freud, S. (1915–17) *Introductory Lectures on Psychoanalysis*, in *Standard Edition of the Complete Psychological Works of Sigmund Freud*, trans. J. Strachey, XV–XVI, Hogarth Press and the Institute for Psycho-analysis, London.
Freud, S. (1919) *The Uncanny, SE*, XVII: 217–252.
Gindro, S. (ed.) (1993) *La xenofobia*, A. Guida, Napoli.
Gindro, S. (1993) *L'oro della psicoanalisi*, A. Guida, Napoli.
Kristeva, J. (1988) *Étrangers à nous-mêmes*, Fayard, Paris.
Sartre, J. P. (1938) *La Nausée*, Gallimard, Paris.

Z

ZIONISM (It. *sionismo*; Fr. *sionisme*; Ger. *Zionismus*) Zionism, the idea of an autonomous Jewish homeland in Palestine, can be seen as an echo of the wider upsurge of NATIONALISM that occurred across Europe from the 1840s. Thus, in his book *Rome and Jerusalem* (1892), Moses Hess, an influential early Zionist who had been much influenced by Giuseppe Mazzini's ideas – which Hess saw as combining a vision of universalism with one of nationalism – compared the liberation of Rome, the eternal city of Christianity, with Jerusalem, the eternal city of the Jewish people (JEW). Yet Zionism was also, clearly, a response to circumstances that afflicted Jews specifically. The idea of Zionism was first formulated by Leo Pinsker, a graduate in medicine from the University of Moscow who had been decorated for service in the Crimean War. The pogroms (POGROM) of the early 1880s convinced Pinsker that ANTI-SEMITISM was ineradicable as long as Jews had no country of their own, though for Pinsker this did not have to be the Holy Land. In his pamphlet of 1882, *Autoemancipation*, Pinsker wrote

> the Jews are not a living nation; they are everywhere aliens, therefore they are despised. . . . The proper, the only remedy would be the creation of a Jewish nationality, of a people living upon its own soil, the auto-emancipation of the Jews; the emancipation as a nation among nations by acquisition of a home of their own. (Kochan, 1992: 123)

In Russia, in the late nineteenth and early twentieth centuries, anti-Semitism was a constant threat to Jews. At different junctures, it was tolerated (TOLERANCE), encouraged, provoked and/or organized by the state itself; it was ongoing as well as frequently violent and murderous. In the eyes of influential early Zionists, such as Theodor Herzl, what seems to have been of equal significance was the eruption of widespread anti-Jewish feeling in countries such as France, countries which were, they had supposed, more enlightened. Thus the Dreyfus trial in France (1894), and the subsequent Dreyfus Affair, converted Herzl to Zionism. In *Judenstaat* (The Jewish State), published in 1896, Herzl called for a World Council to discuss the idea of a homeland for the Jews. The First World Zionist Congress, which Herzl convened, was held in Basle in 1897. Herzl's argument focused on this one simple proposition: that only the creation of a Jewish homeland (and this alone) would solve the problem of anti-Semitism.

Though Herzl himself was severely criticized by other Zionist thinkers – for instance, Ahad Ha'am criticized him for his undue concentration on creating a political entity and lack of attention to the importance of creating a Jewish cultural renaissance – this was not the main source of criticism directed at Zionism from within Judaism. Early advocates of Zionism faced hostility to their ideas from several different sources within Jewish communities from Orthodox Jews who regarded Zionism as dangerously secular and as a usurpation of God's authority (insofar as they believed that only the Messiah could return the Land of Israel to the Jewish people); also from many secular Jews, who expressed either opposition or indifference to Zionist arguments. Indeed, many secular Jews saw the central idea of Zionism – a return to Jerusalem – as something that threatened their sense of belonging to the countries in which they had settled and in which they saw themselves as having been assimilated (ASSIMILATION). For example, the German Jewish community of the late nineteenth century was virtually unanimous in its opposition to Zionism. In Russia, there were different strands in Zionism: at first most of its adherents were middle-class Jews, but in 1906 a socialist-Zionist movement came into being. And although at first there was little support for Zionism among Jews in the USA or Britain, gradually this began to change. In America there were religious Zionists, or *Mizrachi* (who helped to soften Orthodox hostility towards Zionism) and labour Zionists. But neither group constituted a mass movement and most American Jews opposed Zionism at this time. This was readily understandable in that, by its nature, Zionism implied that Jews who had emigrated from Russia to the USA had travelled to the wrong country. Brandeis eventually provided a solution to this problem by assuring American Jews that support for Zionism did not necessarily require that they settled in Palestine.

There were similar divisions within the Jewish community in Britain. Zionism was opposed by religious Jews, by radical Jews and, especially, by prominent, more affluent Anglo-Jews whose families had lived in Britain before the influx of Jews from Eastern Europe in the late nineteenth century. Nonetheless, several prominent British Jews, for example Herbert Samuel, a member of the British Cabinet between 1914 and 1916, played a significant part in events leading to the issuing of the Balfour Declaration in 1917. This stated that Britain viewed 'with favour the establishment in Palestine of a national home for the Jewish people', and it marked a pivotal moment in Zionism. The Balfour Declaration bore witness to the efforts of, among others Chaim Weizmann (later to be the first President of the State of Israel), though it might still not have been issued had it not been for the fact that the British government thought that by encouraging Zionism at this time, Britain might bolster its own position in a region in which other powers, such as France and Germany, were or could be influential.

In the years between 1881 and 1914 millions of Jews emigrated from Russia to escape both anti-Semitism and poverty, and to seek a better and more secure future elsewhere. In this period about 60,000 Jews left Russia to settle in Palestine, most of them young socialist-minded pioneers, but the great majority settled in the USA, although significant numbers also went to Britain, South Africa and South America. With the rise of Nazism more Jews began to arrive in Palestine; this also reflected the fact that many countries chose at that time to close their doors to Jewish refugees (REFUGEE). What completely transformed the situation was the GENOCIDE of millions of Jews at the hands of the Nazis during the Holocaust (SHOAH). The experience of the Holocaust convinced many Jews, especially those who lived in countries which had fallen under direct Nazi control or Nazi influence, of the force of Zionist arguments which they once might have been inclined to resist, dismiss or ignore. Above all, it persuaded many Jews that without a Jewish state, not only might they not be able to practise their religion without interference but, worse, their lives might sooner or later be in danger.

In the years after the Second World War the authorities in the Soviet Union and various Soviet bloc countries (notably Poland, Hungary and Czechoslovakia) mounted attacks on Jews in the press (in which Jews were frequently referred to in thinly disguised code language as 'rootless cosmopolitans'), on Jewish institutions and on 'Zionists' at home and abroad. Of such attacks, amongst the most extreme were the so-called 'Doctors' Plot' (which accused prominent Jewish doctors of planning to murder Soviet officials) and the deliberately offensive accusation that before and even during the Second World War Zionists had co-operated with the Nazis. In the face of such officially sponsored anti-Semitism and anti-Zionism, many Jews wished to leave the USSR and other Eastern European countries. Until partial easing, with détente in the 1970s, Soviet bloc countries placed severe restrictions on Jewish emigration, especially emigration to Israel.

Since its creation in 1948, the existence, strength and legitimacy of the State of Israel has been central to Zionism in several ways: as the embodiment of a Jewish unity; as a country in which Jewish culture, IDENTITY and values could be preserved and developed; as a place of ingathering for Jews in the DIASPORA; as a refuge for Jews who may be persecuted (hence the Law of Return, which guarantees Israeli CITIZENSHIP to any Jew); and as protection for Jews who remain in other countries. However, for several reasons Zionism has also given rise to anti-Zionism. Notwithstanding Zionist aspirations for a Jewish state and spiritual arguments that Israel was the Promised Land, the State of Israel was created on territory that had for centuries been predominantly populated by Arabs. Israel's Arab neighbours did not accept Israel's legitimacy either before or after the War of Independence in 1948 or following subsequent wars in 1956, 1967 and 1973. In the 1970s anti-Zionism was fuelled by several factors: an anti-Zionist campaign in the USSR and several Soviet satellite states (notably in Poland) was given renewed life by Arab states in the aftermath of their defeat in the 1973 Arab–Israeli War. There followed an Arab campaign to compensate for this military defeat by other means: via an oil embargo and through a diplomatic offensive against Israel, a campaign which was supported by the Soviet bloc and which culminated in 1975 in the passing by the UN General Assembly of the now notorious Resolution which condemned Zionism as a 'form of racism and racial discrimination' and which thus effectively denied Israel's legitimacy.

The passing of this resolution was variously justified on the grounds that Israel's responses to attacks on its territory and its citizenry were disproportionate and sometimes contrary to international conventions; that Arab-Israelis were denied certain civil rights; and that Arabs living in Palestine prior to the establishment of the State of Israel had been forced to flee and were not permitted to return to their homes. In response to these charges it was argued that the equation of Zionism with RACISM (and apartheid) was anti-Semitic and thus itself racist; and that, taking advantage of the Cold War conflict, the Resolution attempted to cloak an attack on Israel in seemingly objective clothing and by giving it the authority of the international community. This argument is supported by the fact that in 1991 – in greatly changed political circumstances, given the collapse of the Soviet bloc – by a majority of 111 to 25 the UN voted to revoke the 'Zionism is Racism' resolution. This reversal is notable because it was only the second time that the UN has overturned one of its own resolutions. Nevertheless, the fact that the resolution

vas passed in the first place is, paradoxically, sufficient to have convinced
many Jews of the original Zionist case
that Jews cannot rely on others to protect
them; and thus for them it reinforces the
need for a Jewish State. [P. B.]

Eliach, Y. (1998) *There Once Was a World:
A 900-Year Chronicle of the Shtetl of
Eishyshok*, Little Brown, Boston, MA.

Englander, D. (ed.) (1992) *The Jewish
Enigma*, The Open University, Milton
Keynes (in association with Peter
Halban and the Spiro Institute).

Gilbert, M. (1992) *Jewish History Atlas*,
Weidenfeld & Nicolson, London.

Heller, J. (1992) 'Zionism and the Palestine
question', in Englander (ed.).

Howe, I. (1976) *World of Our Fathers: The
Journey of East European Jews to America
and the Life They Found There*, Touch-
stone, New York.

Kochan, L. (1992) *East European Jewry since
1770*, in Englander (ed.).

Appendix: Contributor Details

Contributor	Initials	Affiliations	Entries
1. Attilio Balestrieri	A. B.	Psychoanalytic Institute for Social Research, Rome	Bilingualism, Creole, Cross-cultural mediation, Cross-cultural medicine, Deportation, Developing countries, Ebonics, Genocide, Health and immigration, Health checks at frontiers, Healthy migrant effect, Identification with the aggressor, Illegal alien, International language, Language shift, Lingua Franca, Official language, Pidgin, Sabir, Vehicular language
2. Tahar Ben Jelloun	T. B. J	Writer	Intifada
3. Gianfranco Biondi	G. B.	University of L'Aquila	Evolution (theory of), Monogenism, Phenotype, Polygenism
4. Jochen Blaschke	J. B.	Berlin Institute for Comparative Social Research	Ausländer, Gastarbeiter, Spät Aussiedler
5. Guido Bolaffi	Gu. B.	Ministry of Welfare, Italy	Amnesty, Dual citizenship, Fortress Europe, Free movement, Reception centre
6. Massimo Bracalenti	M. B.	Psychoanalytic Institute for Social Research, Rome	Alienation, Intolerance, Mixophobia, Nation, National character
7. Raffaele Bracalenti	R. B.	Psychoanalytic Institute for Social Research, Rome	Bilingualism, Creole, Cross-cultural mediation, Cross-cultural medicine, Deportation, Developing countries, Ebonics, Ethnic enterprise, Extracomunitario, Genocide, Health and immigration, Health checks at frontiers, Healthy migrant effect, Identification with the aggressor, Illegal alien, International language, Language shift, Lingua Franca, Marginalization, Multiculturalism 2, Official language, Pidgin, Sabir, Vehicular language
8. Peter Braham	P. B.	Open University, UK	Anti-Semitism, Commission for Racial Equality, Diaspora, Eco-racism, Ghetto, Jew, Marginalization, Race and the media, Race relations, Racial discrimination, Racial harassment, Racial segregation, Racism, Second generation, Shoah, Zionism
9. Meyer Burstein	Me. B.	Department of Citizenship and Immigration of Canada	Visa

Contributor	Initials	Affiliations	Entries
10. Matilde Callari Galli	M. C. G.	University of Bologna	Adaptation, Conformism, Multiculturalism 1
11. Massimo Canevacci	M. C.	University of Rome 'La Sapienza'	Caste, Native, Participation, Stigma, Syncretism
12. Arturo Casoni	A. C.	Psychoanalytic Institute for Social Research, Rome	Complementarism, Cultural evolutionism, Genotype, Interculturalism
13. Alessandra Castellani	Al. C.	University of Rome 'La Sapienza'	Cultural areas
14. Angelomichele De Spirito	A. D. S.	University of Salerno	Fundamentalism, Primitive
15. Julia Eksner	J. E.	Berlin Institute for Comparative Social Research	Roma, Sinti, Nomad, Nomadic camp
16. Damon Freeman	D. W. F.	Indiana University	Jim Crow, Ku Klux Klan
17. Sandro Gindro	S. G.	Psychoanalytic Institute for Social Research, Rome	Aggression, Art and ethnicity, Circumcision, Cosmopolitism, Cultural determinism, Cultural relativism, Culture, Dance, Diversity-Similarity, Ethnic, Ethnic cleansing, Ethnicity, Exoticism, Folklore, Foreigner, Infibulation, Interculturalism, Music, Mutilation, Myth, Narcissism, People, Pluriculturalism, Race 1, Religion and ethnic conflicts, Rite, Sado-masochism, Savage, Theatre, Unconscious, Xenophobia
18. Gualtiero Harrison	G. H.	University of Bologna	Acculturation, Chauvinism, Enculturation, Eurocentrism
19. Jurgen Humburg	J. H.	UNHCR	Reception centre, Refugee
20. Carl Ipsen	C. I.	Indiana University	Family reunification, Nation, National preference
21. David R. James	D. R. J.	Indiana University	Ethnicity and race
22. Umberto Melotti	U. M.	University of Rome 'La Sapienza'	Alienation, Altruism, Citizenship, Colonialism, Differentialism, Ethnicization, Ethnocentrism, Ethnonationalism, Heterophobia, Homologation, Melting pot, Nationalism, Nostalgia, Push factors-pull factors, Race 2, Social disorganization, Tolerance
23. Schlomo Mendlovic	S. M.	Shalvata Mental Health Centre, Israel	Ethnopsychiatry

Contributor	Initials	Affiliations	Entries
24. Robert Moore	R. M.	University of Liverpool	Civilization, Ethnic politics, Ethnicity, Race and inequality, Racialization, Whiteness
25. Emilio Mordini	Em. M.	Psychoanalytic Institute for Social Research, Rome	Bioethics and ethnicity, Community, Intolerance, Religion and ethnic conflicts, Tolerance
26. Aldo Morrone	A. M.	San Gallicano Hospital, Rome	Racism and medicine
27. Tim Muecke	T. M.	Berlin Institute for Comparative Social Research	Roma, Sinti, Nomad, Nomadic camp
28. Karim Murji	K. M.	Open University, UK	Institutional racism, Prejudice
29. Matthew Oware	M. O.	Indiana University	Ethnicity and race
30. Francesca Pegazzano	F. P.	Psychoanalytic Institute for Social Research, Rome	Mixed race
31. Susanna Peltzel	S. P.	Lawyer	Equality, Exile, Flows, Frontier, Political asylum, Quota system, Stateless
32. Ann Phoenix	A. P.	Open University, UK	Black Muslims, Empowerment-disempowerment, Race and gender, Race and IQ, Underclass
33. Ali Rattansi	A. R.	City University, London	Cultural imperialism, Identity, Orientalism, Postcolonial studies, Push factors-pull factors, Race 3, Racism
34. Emilo Reyneri	E. R.	University of Milan 'Bicocca'	Invasion, Migration chain, Seasonal migrant worker
35. Olga Rickards	O. R.	University of Rome 'Tor Vergata'	Evolution (theory of), Monogenism, Phenotype, Polygenism
36. Renzo Rossi	R. R.	Psychoanalytic Institute for Social Research, Rome	Art and ethnicity, Dance, Music, Theatre
37. Renato Ruggiero	R. Ru.	Former Italian Foreign Minister	Globalization
38. Paola Schellenbaum	P. S.	Cariplo-ISMU Foundation, Milan	Multiethnic
39. Richard Skellington	R. S.	Open University, UK	Racial harassment
40. Mauro Valeri	M. V.	Ministry of Welfare, Italy	Acculturation group, Affirmative action, Afrocentrism, Anticipated socialization, Black Africa, Black Power, Boat people, Colour bar, Colour-blind society, Coloured,

Contributor	Initials	Affiliations	Entries
			Concentration camp and death camp, Cybernazis, Denizen, Double consciousness, Eco-racism, Emancipation, Ethnic minority, Ethnocide, Internal colonialism, Marginal man, Monoethnic state, Negritude, Negro, Neo-feudal adaptation, Racial harassment, Racial segregation, Self-fulfilling prophecy, Slavery, Third World, Überfremdung
41. Franco Voltaggio	F. V.	University of Macerata	Purity, Religion and ethnic conflicts
42. Charles Westin	C. W.	CEIFO, Stockholm	Migrant, Migration
43. Laura Zanfrini	L. Za.	Cariplo-ISMU Foundation, Milan	Assimilation, Mixed marriage
44. Zargani, A.	A. Z.	Writer	Anti-Semitism, Diaspora, Ghetto, Jew, Pogrom, Shoah
45. Ziglio, L.	Le. Z.	University of Trento	Family, Integration, Solidarity

Subject Index

Note: page numbers in **bold** refer to main entries (specific articles).

Name Index

Tocqueville, Alexis de 310
Trotter, Mildred 279
Ture, Kwame *see* Carmichael, Stokeley
Truman, Harry S. 170
Truth, Sojourner 245
Tylor, Edward 61

Vacher de la Pouge, Georges 94
Van den Berghe, Pierre 228
Van Djik, Teun xi, 254
Vanini, Giulio Cesare 221
Vecoli, Rudloph 32
Viswanath, Gauri 223
Voltaire (François Marie Arouet) 158, 318

Wallace, Alfred Russell 109
Waters, Mary 58
Weber, Max 38, 61, 94, 139
Weizmann, Chaim 335

West, Cornell 12
Westin, Charles, xiii, 73–4, 132
White, Leslie 55
White, Walter 41
Wieviorka, Michel 59
Wilkins, Roy 41
Williams, Robert L. 81
Wilson, James Q. 161
Wilson, William Julius 248, 324
Wilson, Thomas Woodrow 196
Winant, Howard 99, 100, 101, 275–6
Worth, Lewis 256

Yuval-Davis, Nina 86

Zangwill, Israel 175
Znaniecki, Florian 310
Zuchetti, Eugenio 91

Printed in the United Kingdom
by Lightning Source UK Ltd.
100557UKS00001B/1-33